Studies in Church History

20

THE CHURCH AND WAR

THE CHURCH AND WAR

PAPERS READ AT
THE TWENTY-FIRST SUMMER MEETING AND
THE TWENTY-SECOND WINTER MEETING
OF THE
ECCLESIASTICAL HISTORY SOCIETY

EDITED BY

W.J. SHEILS

PUBLISHED FOR
THE ECCLESIASTICAL HISTORY SOCIETY

BY

BASIL BLACKWELL

1983

© Ecclesiastical History Society 1983

All Rights Reserved. No part of this publication may be reproduced, stored in a retrieval system, or transmitted, in any form or by any means, electronic, mechanical, photocopying, recording or otherwise, without the prior permission of the Ecclesiastical History Society, which may be obtained from the editor.

Ecclesiastical History Society. *Summer Meeting (21st: 1982: University of Reading)*
The Church and war.—(Studies in church history; 20)
1. War and religion—Congresses
I. Title   II. Ecclesiastical History Society. *Winter Meeting (22nd: 198–: King's College, London)*
III. Sheils, W.J.
261.8'73   BT736.2

ISBN 0 631 13406 9

Printed in Great Britain

PREFACE

'The Church and War' was the theme of the two gatherings of the Ecclesiastical History Society which met under the presidency of Professor Christopher Holdsworth. The published papers comprise a selection of those offered at the summer conference held at the University of Reading in 1982 and at the following winter meeting at King's College, London. The theme proved to be unexpectedly topical in the light of the military actions in the South Atlantic and the debate about the precise form of the national service of thanksgiving and remembrance which subsequently took place. Many of the papers delivered at Reading recalled issues raised in the public discussion on the Falklands and those events also provoked much private discussion in less formal meetings at the conference. The contemporaneity of historical study was thus brought into sharper focus than usual.

Generous financial assistance has once again been received from the British Academy, for which the Society wishes to express its thanks.

W.J.Sheils

CONTENTS

Preface	v
List of Contributors	xi
Introduction	xv
Saint Augustine's views on the 'Just War' R. A. MARKUS	1
The Church's military service in the ninth century: a contemporary comparative view? JANET L. NELSON	15
The Church, warfare and military obligation in Norman Italy G. A. LOUD	31
Monasteries as war memorials: Battle Abbey and La Victoire ELIZABETH M. HALLAM	47
Ideas and Reality: some attempts to control and defuse war in the twelfth century (*Presidential Address*) CHRISTOPHER J. HOLDSWORTH	59
Propaganda for war: the dissemination of the crusading ideal in the twelfth century COLIN MORRIS	79
Missionaries and crusaders, 1095–1274; opponents or allies? ELIZABETH SIBERRY	103
Cities of God: the Italian communes at war DIANA M. WEBB	111
Medieval Waldensian abhorrence of killing pre-*c*.1400 PETER BILLER	129
Undesirable aliens in the diocese of York ROSALIND M. T. HILL	147
An English archbishop and the Cerberus of war ROY M. HAINES	153
The English clergy and the Hundred Years War A. K. McHARDY	171

CONTENTS

Omnino partialitate cessante: Clement VI and the Hundred Years War   179
DIANA WOOD

The way of action: Pierre d'Ailly and the military solution
to the great schism   191
R. N. SWANSON

Clerical violence in a Catholic society: the Hispanic
World 1450–1720   201
HENRY KAMEN

The 'weakness of conscience' in the Reformed movement in the
Netherlands: the attitude of the Dutch reformation to the use of
violence between 1562 and 1574   217
AUKE JELSMA

Clergymen and conflict 1660–1763   231
D. NAPTHINE and W. A. SPECK

The churches and the '45   253
FRANCOISE DECONINCK-BROSSARD

English evangelical dissent and the European conflict 1780–1815   263
DERYCK LOVEGROVE

Christian responses to the Indian mutiny of 1857   277
BRIAN STANLEY

The Instruments of Providence: slavery, civil war and the
American churches   291
PETER J. PARISH

'Ulster will fight and Ulster will be right': the protestant
churches and Ulster's resistance to home rule, 1912–14   321
R. F. G. HOLMES

War, the Nation and the Kingdom of God: the origins of the
National Mission of Repentance and Hope, 1915–16   337
DAVID M. THOMPSON

Et Virtutem et Musas: Mill Hill School and the Great War   351
CLYDE BINFIELD

The Cowley Fathers and the First World War   383
BRIAN TAYLOR

CONTENTS

Christian pacifism in the era of two world wars MARTIN CEADEL	391
The Sword of the Spirit: a Catholic cultural crusade of 1940 STUART MEWS	409
The fall of France GAVIN WHITE	431
Holy men and rural communities in Zimbabwe, 1970–1980 TERENCE RANGER	443
Abbreviations	463

CONTRIBUTORS

CHRISTOPHER J. HOLDSWORTH *(President)*
  Professor of Medieval History, Exeter University

PETER BILLER
  Lecturer in History, University of York

CLYDE BINFIELD
  Senior Lecturer in History, University of Sheffield

MARTIN CEADEL
  Fellow and Tutor in Politics, New College, Oxford

FRANCOISE DECONINCK-BROSSARD
  Université de Picardie, Amiens, France

ROY M. HAINES
  Professor of History, Dalhousie University, Nova Scotia, Canada

ELIZABETH M. HALLAM
  Assistant Keeper, Public Record Office

ROSALIND M. T. HILL
  Professor Emerita, Westfield College, University of London

R. F. G. HOLMES
  Professor of Christian History and Doctrine, Union Theological College, Belfast

AUKE JELSMA
  Professor, Theologische Hogeschool, Kampen

HENRY KAMEN
  Reader in History, University of Warwick

G. A. LOUD
  Lecturer in Medieval History, University of Leeds

CONTRIBUTORS

DERYCK LOVEGROVE
Lecturer in Ecclesiastical History, University of St Andrews

A. K. McHARDY
Lecturer in Medieval History, University of Aberdeen

R. A. MARKUS
Professor Emeritus of Medieval History, University of Nottingham

STUART MEWS
Lecturer in Religious Studies, University of Lancaster

COLIN MORRIS
Professor of Medieval History, University of Southampton

D. NAPTHINE
Lecturer in Drama, Newcastle College of Arts and Technology

JANET L. NELSON
Lecturer in History, King's College, University of London

PETER J. PARISH
Bonar Professor of Modern History, University of Dundee

TERENCE RANGER
Professor of Modern History, University of Manchester

ELIZABETH SIBERRY
Sidney Sussex College, University of Cambridge

W. A. SPECK
Professor of History, Hull University

BRIAN STANLEY
Registrar, Librarian and Tutor in Church History, Spurgeon's College, London

R. N. SWANSON
Lecturer in Medieval History, University of Birmingham

CONTRIBUTORS

BRIAN TAYLOR
    Rector of Guildford, St Nicholas

DAVID M. THOMPSON
    Lecturer in Modern Church History, University of Cambridge

DIANA M. WEBB
    Lecturer in History, King's College, University of London

GAVIN WHITE
    Lecturer in Ecclesiastical History, Glasgow University

DIANA WOOD
    Lecturer in History, University of East Anglia

INTRODUCTION

Future readers of the successive volumes of these *Studies* may well feel when they reach this one that its theme must have had peculiar relevance to actual events occurring in the spring and summer of 1982, but this concurrence was entirely accidental. The choice of theme for the meetings of the Ecclesiastical History Society in a particular year is made almost two years before they take place and could, therefore, not have arisen out of the peculiar interests and concerns which moved people in 1982. It is, however, scarcely surprising that many of the papers did draw on affairs in the southern Atlantic to give colour to their exploration of the past. An explanation for the choice of the theme must however look elsewhere.

From its very origin the Church has had to face a world in which wars and the rumours of wars have existed. War has been an enduring feature of human society to which individual Christians as well as the corporate institutions which they created, have had to respond. It is, therefore, very right that the Society should turn its attention to war, just as it has in the recent past examined the Church's approach to disease, or to the state.[1]

Yet besides this the theme demands attention since war presented the Church over the centuries with an anguishing question; to what extent did the ethic taught and demonstrated by the originator of the Christian faith have implications for the behaviour of men in society, was the command to love enemies and to turn the other cheek to be translated into relations between groups and states? In this sense the theme was part of a wider one which the Society had also studied, that of the relationship between the Church and the World.[2]

It is, of course, true that war has always been a theme dear to historians from Thucydides onwards, and that it has drawn the attention of many fine minds. Ever since the appearance of Nef's great book the role of warfare in changing society through the demands it makes for weapons and men has been increasingly appreciated, and this kind of approach is reflected in the well-known works of Contamine on the Hundred Years War, or Michael Howard on more recent conflicts.[3]

[1] W. J. Sheils, ed *The Church and Healing* SCH 19 (Oxford 1982);
Derek Baker, ed *Church, Society and Politics* SCH 12 (Oxford 1975).
[2] Derek Baker, ed *Sanctity and Secularity: the Church and the World* (Oxford 1973).
[3] John U. Nef, *War and Human Progress: an Essay on the Rise of Industry and Civilization* (New

INTRODUCTION

Since the Second World War war has also come on to the agenda of social scientists, particularly of people interested in applying communications and games theory to the avoidance of war or the management of conflict.[4] Such approaches are not overtly reflected in most of the papers here though it may be hoped that this book will be of interest to those for whom those approaches are natural and congenial. Henry Kamen's discussion of violent behaviour within the Hispanic World of the early modern period as well as Martin Ceadel's examination of 'Christian Pacifism in the Era of Two World Wars' should certainly attract the attention of such readers. Stuart Mews' treatment of the now curiously antique-sounding Catholic crusade of 1940, 'The Sword of the Spirit', should also attract them, providing as it does a link with many other crises. Mews writes of the episode's significance,

> More particularly it draws attention to the pressures and constraints involved in the mobilisation of religious commitments in the national interest and to the strategic considerations which impelled church leaders to opt for a particular course of action when confronted by a complex web of national needs, institutional inhibitions and popular sentiment.

Cardinal Hinsley's initiative does indeed throw 'light on several problems which arise when religion has to function in a modern society at a time of crisis', and armed, so to say, with Mews' words one may find a good deal of light in all the papers on those problems as they have appeared at far earlier periods than that of the very recent past. Many of the papers deal with the Church at a time of crisis, or faced with responsibilities as a result of its position in society, in such a way that the problems have a wide significance. Five themes seem to me to emerge.

The very first paper in the volume sounds one theme found elsewhere, the elucidation of whether and if so in what conditions, a Christian may take part in warfare. Robert Markus shows how Augustine's answer that the Christian could fight if the cause were just and the war carried on justly survived fundamentally unchanged through years when most of his ideas changed radically. Already too by his day there were few Christian

---

York 1950); Philippe Contamine, *Guerre, Etat et Société à la fin du moyen age: Etudes sur les Armées des rois de France, 1337–1494* (Paris 1972); Michael Howard, *The Franco-Prussian War* (London 1961); *Studies in War and Peace* (London 1970); *War in European History* (Oxford 1976); *War and the Liberal Conscience* (London 1978).

[4] See for example J. W. Burton, *Conflict and Communication* (London 1969); Michael Nicholson, *Conflict Analysis* (London 1970).

INTRODUCTION

pacifists left; Eusebius, Ambrose and Athanasius had pretty well won that argument. But Peter Biller's paper on the Waldensians and Ceadel's on this century shows the argument revived, in circumstances very different from those envisaged by Augustine. He, after all, was a citizen of an Empire which seemed to include, albeit by his time its power to include was weakening, most of the known world. Augustine scarcely envisaged wars of nation states, but rather wars of defence fought by the Empire against its mainly barbarous enemies. Yet Augustine certainly dominated the thinking of Christians about war for centuries and provides distinctions which are still widely used. Two papers, those by Colin Morris and Elizabeth Siberry, treat with ideas about Holy Wars, the Crusades, and the way they spread or related to the Church's more pacific approaches to those who occupied the Holy Land. Jelsma, discussing the attitude of the Reformed Church in the Netherlands towards the revolt against Spain, reveals the great hesitations felt in the early years, 1562–74, about the use of force which he attributes partly to theological ideas and partly to the aftermath of the Anabaptist movement.

Closely connected with ideas about taking part in war a group of papers approach the way that the Church was involved in actual wars, or the provision of resources for armies. Janet Nelson and G. A. Loud explore the military obligations which resulted from the vast lands with which the Church had been endowed, the first in ninth century Francia and England, and the second in Norman Italy. Many sides of the relations between the Church and a state in time of war appear in Alison McHardy's discussion of the English clergy and the Hundred Years War; not just the payment of taxes, but the treatment of alien priories, and the obligation on the clergy to be equipped with armour. Alien clergy as Rosalind still shows, could also find themselves caught between warring states at this time. The fact that so many 'clerks' served in government helped to blur the distinctions which might have arisen about what was proper for people in different callings. Similar blurrings, embodied in the language of ritual and spirituality, are revealed in Diana Webb's study of Italian communes at war and my own paper which concentrates on the way ideas about war interacted with practice in the time of Orderic Vitalis. One of the results of war, the establishment of institutions as thank-offerings for success in battle, is the subject of Elizabeth Hallam's paper. Battle Abbey and Nôtre Dame de la Victoire came into existence after the battles of Hastings and Bouvines.

But if the Church could, in a sense, gain from war, three papers show

INTRODUCTION

that war sometimes provided an opportunity for achieving the purposes of some of its members. Bishops in the Hispanic world expressed part of their sense of belonging to the local community by taking part in violent acts, whilst Pierre d'Ailly considered whether the Schism should be ended by military means, and most Ulster Protestants were prepared to defend what they saw as their religious liberties by violent means just before the First World War. Finlay Holmes touches there on a very contemporary theme, whilst Henry Kamen and R. N. Swanson treat problems less present, though not without their echoes in some recent pronouncements from Washington.

A fourth theme which can be distinguished is that of the interpretation of and varied reactions to war. The rich vein of sermon literature has been drawn upon by David Napthine and William Speck, and by Francoise Deconinck-Brossard in their explorations of English reactions to wars between 1660 and 1753. Sermons and minute books also give rise to Deryck Lovegrove's paper on the English dissenting reaction to the wars which followed the French Revolution. Newspapers, and journals, more especially those with an avowedly religious character, have been used by Brian Stanley and Gavin White looking for Christian responses to the Indian Mutiny of 1857 and the fall of France in 1940. Peter Parish draws upon all these types of evidence to build up an impression of the way the Churches in the northern states reacted to the American Civil War. The minute books of a religious order make the stuff from which Brian Taylor shows how the Cowley Fathers reacted to the First World War whilst Clyde Binfield creates from the evanescent pages of the school magazine a tapestry showing how Mill Hill responded to the same struggle. Cardinal Hinsley's papers lie at the centre of Stuart Mews' paper, whilst Terence Ranger has used interviews in his work on the experience of Christians in one district in Manicaland during the guerilla war in Zimbabwe between 1970 and 1980.

A final theme occurs in a number of papers, attempts by the Church to preserve peace and prevent the outbreak of war. It only forms the centre of two papers, those by R. M. Haines and Diana Wood, which both deal with the Hundred Years War. Haines reveals the problems facing an English archbishop acting as a negotiator for Edward III, whilst Clement VI emerges in Wood's contribution as almost hopelessly compromised in his desire to avert war by his partiality for the French case.

There are, therefore, some continuing themes in a group of papers which range over fifteen centuries in time and even though centred

INTRODUCTION

around mainland Europe and the British Isles, include pieces on wars in America, Latin America, Africa and India. But wide as is the scope of the whole volume one cannot pretend that it is comprehensive. It would have been good for the early Christian period to be represented, or for there to be more on the Reformation era. Many themes, like the spiritual care of combatants, or the attempt to prohibit the use of certain weapons, could do with far more discussion, and it would have been illuminating if particular conflicts had been discussed from the viewpoint of the churches on both sides. Yet some gaps are inevitable in a book which has two elements: papers invited by the president and committee of the Society form a small number, and further papers offered by members of the Society. The last gap mentioned, the lack of a two-sided discussion of a conflict, reflects two other things: the way that historical scholarship so often has confined itself to questions relating to one nation, and the way that the Church itself has splintered into national groupings. The medieval papers reveal that even when the institution had not split it was usually fairly ineffectual when competing interests were moving toward the arbitrament of war, partly perhaps because war itself was widely considered as the means through which God would make his intentions known. War indeed was held to be part of the mysterious workings out of providence, a judgement on the life of nations and individuals. That theme, too recurs again and again in the book as a whole, and most particularly in David Thompson's study of the proposed National Mission of Repentance and Hope of 1916. Now, perhaps, as recent events have shown Christians are not so certain that God's ways are expressed in these great clashes, whilst it is also clear that how the Church may react to a political crisis has not always been hot news. As White writes of 1940 'The Churches were talking to themselves, and no-one else heard them or felt they needed to hear them.' There are some signs of change now as the result of very present problems when groups with opposed interests can arm themselves with weapons far more deadly than any mentioned here. Hiroshima and Nagasaki, strangely perhaps, are unremarked in these pages, but it is the hope of the writer of this introduction, at least, that these papers as a whole may have a contribution to make not only to our knowledge of the past, but to the way we react to our dilemmas now.

Christopher Holdsworth   March 1983

SAINT AUGUSTINE'S VIEWS ON THE 'JUST WAR'

by R. A. MARKUS

A LONG AND very respectable tradition of thinking about the morality of warfare has accustomed us to looking at Augustine's views on the 'just war' through the wrong end of a telescope. By common consent, Augustine is the fountain-head of a tradition almost ubiquitous in medieval thought, and still to be discovered lurking, as recently as last April, in a leading article in *The Times*.[1] In reading Gratian, Thomas Aquinas, Vittoria or Cardinal Bellarmine, one is constantly reminded that, as the author of the most recent study of the just war in the Middle Ages put it, 'the influence of Augustine was all pervasive.'[2] The best of modern studies are, indeed, informed by a sense of the ambiguity of Augustine's legacy to medieval thought;[3] but even so, and unavoidably, they reinforce the tendency which leads us to think of Augustine as the father of this tradition of thinking. There is no need to question this consensus—indeed it seems to me to be very largely correct—to be conscious that there is nothing that can obscure the true nature of an original thought as radically as the tradition to which it gives rise. What, therefore, I am trying to do in this paper is, for once, to turn the telescope the right way round and to look at Augustine's thinking not in the long perspective of the tradition which his ideas inaugurated, but in the immediate context of his own intellectual biography.

The idea of the 'just war' is one of those which it is very easy to sever from its intellectual roots and its cultural setting. But ideas do not lead a disembodied existence; they encourage individuals

---

[1] *The Times*, 24 April 1982.
[2] [J.] Barnes, 'The just war' [in *Cambridge history of later medieval philosophy*, eds. N. Kretzmann, A Kenny, J. Pinborg (Cambridge 1982) pp 771–784,] at p 771 n 3.
[3] F.H. Russell, *The Just war in the Middle Ages* (Cambridge 1975) p 26 on Augustine's 'ambiguous legacy, worked out with great inner turmoil'; also p 10 n 1. On the neglect of 'genuine Augustinian opinions' p 27; on its crucial 'imprint' on medieval views pp 213, 292: on Aquinas and Augustine p 269.

and groups to take very definite attitudes towards their cultural and social environment. The assertion that under certain specifiable circumstances killing in war may be morally justifiable looks like a simple, unambiguous statement. It could, however, serve quite opposed ends: either to raise, or to lower, the barriers against violence in a society. But it will encourage one set of attitudes in a society in which war is unthinkable as a human activity, and quite different attitudes where it is readily accepted as normal, and sanctioned by the current norms of conduct. In the one case the assertion would tend to reconcile men to the possibility of envisaging warfare as occasionally justifiable in some specified circumstances: to make the unthinkable thinkable. In the other it would act as a restraining force: it would engender the reflection that what is generally accepted as allowable or virtuous is so only under the special conditions which are spelt out: it makes the unquestioned questionable. The force of the notion of the just war is determined by the antecedent assumptions current in the society. That a whole cluster of such antecedent assumptions in the minds of Western Christians concerning warfare underwent a long drawn-out revolution between the Apostolic age and the age of the Crusades it is hardly necessary to document since Adolf Harnack and Carl Erdmann; but it is still necessary to place Augustine somewhere on the map charting the course of this revolution.

The one thing which has emerged from almost all serious studies of Augustine in the last fifty years or so is that whatever can be said about almost any aspect of his thought is unlikely to be true of it over the whole span of his career as a writer and thinker. Of all writers Augustine is perhaps the most dangerous to approach without a constant awareness of the complexity of his mind, of the vitality which prevented his ever standing still, intellectually, and of the restlessness which was still capable of driving him on, in his seventies, to explore new vistas and to discard his habitual ways of looking at his world. Augustine changed his mind about many things, and has listed some of them in his *Retractationes*; but it would be a comparatively simple matter if one could be content with a catalogue of this sort. More crucially important than the explicit changes of view on particular matters, recorded or, for that matter, passed over in silence there, are the shifts of perspective which are not and cannot be recorded, which, sometimes, give a different twist even to statements which Augustine saw no reason to revise. I want to suggest that there is precisely such a change—or, to be more precise, two such changes—in his intellectual perspective, shifts in the things he was prepared to take for granted, that we need to reckon with in trying to understand his views on warfare.

The first time Augustine came to deal with the morality of warfare was in one of his early philosophical dialogues. He had freed himself from the grip of Manichaean teaching only recently; and having rejected the solution it offered to the problem of evil as far too easy, he had to find his own way of accounting for evil and wrong-doing. His explanation bears a strong imprint of his reading of the 'books of the Platonists' which had helped him to break with Manichaeism and prepared his conversion to Christianity. His purpose in the present work was to explore the possibilities of human freedom within the over-arching order he had come to see running through the *cosmos*. It was a world order in principle accessible to a well-educated and well-exercised intellect. Rationality and morality coincided: wickedness was to breach the divine order in the world, goodness lay in following it. Book I ends with a longish discussion of the philosophical commonplace that temporal law, if it is to be just, must in some way derive from an eternal law; the relatively brief discussion devoted to the morality of killing comes in this immediate context and is, in fact, the pivot on which Augustine's argument about the relationship between human and eternal law turns.[4] Like the public hangman in another of his early dialogues,[5] war, in the appropriate circumstances, is part of a well-ordered society's means of conforming to God's universal order and is thus rightly sanctioned by law.

For our purpose the context of the argument is far more important than what it actually asserts. Augustine's endorsement of warfare as (sometimes) right is part of the 'rational myth of the state' which underlay all his thinking about human society in the years immediately following his conversion to Christianity. In the words of a seminal study of Augustine's early ideas on society, 'Human society, as part of the universe, must be ordered in terms

---

[4] [De] Lib[ero] arb[itrio] I.5.11–13. Book 1 was written before Augustine's return to Africa in 388.
[5] *De ordine* II.8.25.

of the same hierarchies of sensible and intelligible, of bodies, souls and God. As sin cannot destroy or make incomprehensible the universal order, so the sins of society such as pride are reintegrated into the universe by their punishment and they image the proper order even in their sin.'⁶ Here Augustine's statements on war owe much to Roman writers, and, more fundamentally, they form part of what is essentially a Greco-Roman perspective on society.⁷

The cosmic vision of order as he had come across it in neo-Platonic writings had made a profound impression on Augustine; it dominated all his thought for ten years or so after his baptism, and, indeed, was never entirely effaced from his mind. But a tantalisingly different emphasis appears in a letter which, though it cannot be exactly dated, must have been written at least eight and perhaps as many as twenty-two years after this discussion between the young Augustine and his friend Evodius. In the letter Augustine takes a much more reserved view about killing in self-defence. It is a curious reversion to something very like the hesitancy attributed to Evodius in the earlier discussion, and overcome, at that time, by Augustine's argumentation. Replying in his letter to the questions of a correspondent, Augustine now counsels turning the other cheek, non-resistance in the face of attack, except by soldiers acting in a public function in defence of others.⁸ His views on war have interestingly, remained unchanged; but the instinctive attitudes behind them have undergone significant change. The very brief statement in the letter gives us no clue to the nature of or the reasons for Augustine's changed attitude; but as always with Augustine, it is related to profound shifts in the intellectual perspective in which his views took their shape. And, as always, these shifts are far more interesting than particular views he held on this or that subject, even the subject of war. To understand his views on war fully we need to place them firmly into their proper context in his intellectual development in each of their identifiable stages.

Apart from relatively brief allusions which give us little help,

---

⁶ F. E. Cranz, 'The development of Augustine's ideas on society before the Donatist controversy' *HTR* 47 (1954) pp 255–316, reprinted in *Augustine* [: *a collection of critical essays,*] ed. [R. A.] Markus [(New York 1972) pp 336–403] at p 346.
⁷ *Ibid.*
⁸ *Ep* 57:5. On its dating, A. Goldbacher in his edition of the letters *Pars* V (*CSEL* 58 Vienna 1952) pp 18–19.

Augustine on the 'just war'

Augustine was to return to a discussion of the morality of killing in war on two later occasions: once in his work *Against Faustus the Manichee* and, towards the end of his life, in the last books of the *City of God*. The work *Against Faustus* was written some ten years after the early discussion we have considered. It was completed probably in 398. Book XXII of this work contains what is in fact Augustine's fullest treatment of the theme of warfare. This is the book Augustine referred to when reviewing his work at the end of his life, he said that this book 'in which I vindicated the Old Testament patriarchs against his [Faustus's] calumnies, is of such length as scarcely any of my other books.'[9] It *is* a long book, and Augustine has given us the clue to his principal preoccupation in it: it is intended to refute the Manichaean attack on the Old Testament, its God and its patriarchs and their morals. In our section he is defending Moses, who waged war on God's command, avoiding the sins which would make war blameworthy: love of violence, vengeful cruelty, strife and implacable enmity, savagery, lust for power and so forth.[10] If God can command it, warfare cannot be inherently immoral under all circumstances; and Augustine could assemble enough evidence from the New Testament to cut the ground from beneath his Manichaean opponents' argument that the patriarchs of the Old Testament or their God, or both, stand condemned by actions which the morality of the New Testament and its God would force us to condemn. This is the structure of the argument of the five substantial chapters devoted here to the theme of the just war.

It has several things in common with Augustine's position as formulated some ten years before, including, most clearly, his adherence to the view that warfare can be morally justifiable. Moreover, now, as then, he was taking issue with Manichaean teaching and defending, as part of his polemic, the possibility of a war being just. There is, however, a significant difference at this point between the two arguments. In the earlier discussion Augustine had been preoccupied with questions about the nature and the origins of evil and wickedness. He was seeking an explanation for them alternative to the Manichaean. Now he is attacking the Manichees' rejection of the Old Testament and its

---

[9] *Retractationes* II. 33. 1.
[10] C[ontra] Faust[um] XXII.74. The discussion extends to cap 78.

God and upholding, against them, the unity of the New and the Old Testaments and of God's saving work which they attest. This, as he has himself told us,[11] was the burden of *Against Faustus*, the longest of his books. This difference in approach has some importance for our assessment of Augustine's attitude to war.

For in the intervening years Augustine's mind had undergone a profound upheaval. The argument he had deployed for seeing warfare in terms of a universal order, an order rooted in the eternal law and reflected in human societies, was impossible for him to deploy now. Ten years before, Augustine could believe in a rationally ordered universe, accessible to the rational faculties of properly educated men. He could be confident that this order could be realised in the rational control of mind over body and of rational will over action, and in human societies through the control of enlightened rulers and rationally devised law. Now this confidence had vanished. 'Whoever thinks', Augustine wrote about this time, 'that in this mortal life a man may so disperse the mists of bodily and carnal imaginings as to possess the unclouded light of changeless truth, and to cleave to it with the unswerving constancy of a spirit wholly estranged from common ways – he understands neither what he seeks, nor him who seeks it.'[12] Peter Brown comments, in an unforgettable chapter of his marvellous biography: 'Augustine, indeed, had decided that he would never reach the fulfilment that he first thought was promised to him by a Christian Platonism: he would never impose a victory of mind over body in himself, he would never achieve the wrapt contemplation of the ideal philosopher. It is the most drastic change that a man may have to accept. It involved nothing less than the surrender of the bright future he thought he had gained . . .'[13] That surrender involved the collapse of the whole 'rational myth of the state'. Order, to be sure, was still to be found in God's world; but it was not an order that could be taken so readily for granted that men could hope either to come to see or to realise it through their own intellectual and moral capabilities. 'Let us believe', Augustine wrote in 396, 'though we cannot grasp it, that He who made the whole creation, both spiritual and corporeal, disposed of all things

---

[11] See above n 9.
[12] [*De*] *Cons*[*ensu*] *ev*[*angelistarum*] IV. 10.20.
[13] *Augustine of Hippo* (London 1967) p 147.

in number weight and measure. But inscrutable are His judgements and His ways are past searching out.'[14] The closing allusion to Romans 9:33 provides the clue: the watershed in Augustine's mind was his re-reading of Saint Paul in the mid 390s. The power of sin in men's lives and of man's powerlessness to free himself unaided from it, and the hidden ways of God's grace may be Pauline commonplaces; but they had not, previously, produced fissures across the confident surface of Augustine's thought. Now his earlier confidence in human resources, intellectual and moral, is revealed to him as delusion. Salvation is no longer to be thought of as an ordered progression towards a distant goal; it involves sharp conflict between sin and grace. The germs of much of Augustine's later thought are to be found in his discovery of the power of sin over men, and much had to be re-thought in the new perspective thrust upon him by his re-reading of Saint Paul.

The just war, among other things, had been deeply embedded in the universal order, and Augustine's reflection on it was closely linked with his own theory of the eternal and the temporal law: the soldier in killing had been a *minister legis*,[15] executing a law which was itself distinct from but dependent upon a *lex aeterna*. This theory of law vanished, inevitably so, from Augustine's work from this time on. He now realised that he had to re-think his views on law, and he set out on the task, significantly, in the very work in which this extended discussion of warfare occurs: the *Contra Faustum*. This is the work in which we find his new theory of law elaborated for the first time. Augustine had to revise his legal theory, loosening the relationship between the eternal, the natural and the human law,[16] as a consequence of the collapse of his belief in a rationally ordered universe. The intellectual framework of his views on warfare had vanished in the ten years between the two discussions; but his views on warfare survived, on the whole unchanged.

Their survival would be tantalising had it been a case of an isolated fragment of thought surviving the collapse of the intellectual structure. But Augustine's views on war were now part of another closely integrated set of ideas. The central

---

[14] *Ad Simplicianum de diversis quaestionibus* I.2.22.
[15] *Lib. arb.* I.5.12; see above n 4.
[16] I have discussed this in my *Saeculum: [History and society in Saint Augustine's theology* (Cambridge 1970)] pp 87–91.

intention of the whole long book XXII of the *Contra Faustum* was, as we have seen, to vindicate the unity of God's saving work through the old and the new dispensations. The prophetic truth of the Old Testament was a central thread of Augustine's anti-Manichaean argument; but at this time, especially in the years from 398 to about 400, this idea became something of an obsession which overflowed into Augustine's interpretation of contemporary history. During these years Augustine was very ready to see the prophecies of the Old Testament being fulfilled all round him, and God's purposes being worked out only too visibly in the history of the Roman Empire in his own days. Like most educated Christians of his day, Augustine had succumbed to the spell of the collective illusion of the Theodosian epoch: the world, he said, had 'become a choir praising Christ'.[17] 'The few pagans that remain', Augustine is writing in 399–400, 'fail to realise the wonder of what is happening ... Now the God of Israel is himself destroying the idols of the heathen ... Through Christ the king he has subjugated the Roman Empire to the worship of his name; and he has converted it to the defence and service of the Christian faith, so that the idols, on account of whose cult his sacred mysteries had previously been rejected, should now be destroyed.'[18] All this happening now: *ecce nunc fit*,[19] *temporibus christianis*: in these heady years of the Theodosian régime's enforcement of Christian orthodoxy. These are the 'Christian times', and the history of his own days, during these few years around the turn of the century, seemed to Augustine to be unfolding in accordance with 'prophetic truth' (*secundum propheticam veritatem*). So in the *Contra Faustum* he is not content to answer the Manichaean rejection of the Old Testament by affirming the New as its fulfilment; the prophetic promises are always being fulfilled, even now, notably in the conversion of the rulers of the earth and the imposition of Christ's yoke on the nations through the agency of kings.[20]

This is the context in the late 390s in which Augustine's views on war must be read. It was not, by any means, unprecedented: Eusebius had seen the Constantinian Empire in much the same way, and found it easy to portray Constantine as God's warrior

[17] *Enarrationes in Psalmos* 149.7. For all this see my *Saeculum* cap 2.
[18] *Cons. Ev.* I.14.21.
[19] *Ibid* I.26.40.
[20] *C. Faust.* XIII.7, 9; XXII. 76.

Augustine on the 'just war'

and his wars as Christ's. Now, in the euphoria of the late 390s even Augustine came to share—for a time—the horrifying self-assurance of his contemporaries. We have been reminded how his prophetic view of contemporary history fuelled his endorsement of the régime's policies of religious coercion.[21] Non-violence (*mansuetudo*) had been appropriate to the age of the Apostles; now, in these 'Christian times', there is prophetic sanction for the use of force on Christ's behalf.

Although Augustine was more inclined to justify religious coercion than warfare in such terms, it can be no accident that his classic statement on warfare occurs in one of the works dominated by this way of thinking and written in the years while it held his mind in so firm a grip. Expressions of this sort reached a climax in Augustine's writings around 398–400, and began to die away soon afterwards, appearing only in fragments, to disappear completely in the course of the following decade. In the *City of God*, and especially in its last books, Augustine turned his back on the mirage of the 'Christian Empire' of the Theodosian dynasty, and on the assumptions about God's hand in human affairs which had sustained it.[22] But again, through this second upheaval in Augustine's intellectual perspective, his ideas on the just war survived intact, into the final phase of his thought.

War is a recurring theme in the *City of God*, as it is in the letters written during the fourteen years of its composition. It is discussed most fully in two chapters of the *City of God*, both regularly quoted by modern writers, XV.4 and XIX.7. In both Augustine is dealing with warfare in the course of expounding the fundamental ideas elaborated in that *magnum opus et arduum*: the distinction between the 'goods' of the heavenly and the earthly cities respectively, that is to say, between their respective values and ultimate purposes and the relativities between them. Having discarded the illusions, first, of a rationally ordered world and a socially attainable order, and later, of an assured historical destiny embodied in a particular political and social structure—that of the Christian Roman Empire—Augustine now offers us a vision of the

---

[21] See P. Brown, 'Religious coercion in the later Roman Empire: the case of North Africa' *History* 48 (1963) pp 283–305 repr. in *Religion [and society in the age of Saint Augustine* (London 1972) pp 301–331] and my *Saeculum* pp 36–37 and cap 6.

[22] See *Saeculum, passim* especially cap 2. I have noted the anomalous survival of the 'prophetic' notion in Augustine's correspondence with Boniface in 417 at p 33 n 2.

social order which springs from a vivid sense of conflicting purposes, of uncertainties of direction, of divergent loyalties and irresolvable tensions. Political power has become a means of securing some minimal barriers against the forces of disintegration. In this 'hell on earth'[23] all the institutions of political and judicial authority serve to keep conflict within check, to secure a breathing space. Now, in his old age, what impresses Augustine is the precariousness of human order, the threat of dissolution and the permanent presence of chaos just beneath the surface, into which the social order could be drawn at any moment, with the failure of human wills to hold the ring against disorder. And so, in its modest and drastically deflated role, politically organised society and its institutions have a more crucial place than ever before in Augustine's scheme of things. Read again the parable of the conscientious judge in the chapter which immediately precedes the longest discussion of war in the *City of God*: no political thinker, not even excepting Hobbes, has ever given a more powerful or more disturbing description of the contradictions inherent in human society than Augustine gives in this image of the conscientious judge, 'even in this most peaceful of states' which he asks us to imagine, who is compelled, despite himself, to dispense injustice. 'Will a wise man sit as judge in this darkness of social life (*in his tenebris vitae socialis*)', Augustine asks, 'or will he not dare? Of course he will sit', Augustine answers his question, 'for the solidarity of human society lays upon him this duty and draws him to its performance, and he would think it wrong to shirk it.'[24] The quest for justice and order is doomed; but dedication to the impossible task is demanded by the very precariousness of civilised order in the world.

This is now, at the end of his life, the framework of Augustine's statements on war. In the very next chapter he evokes the 'great evils, the horror and savagery' of war, only to reaffirm his view, stated in language startlingly similar to that used of the just judge in the preceding chapter, that a wise man will wage just wars and lament the necessity which lays this duty upon him. The language of 'necessity' is the language in which Augustine appealed to Roman officials and generals in Africa, just as it is the language in

---

[23] [*De*] *Civ*[*itate*] *Dei* XXII. 22. 4.
[24] *Ibid* XIX.6. See my discussion in *Saeculum* pp 99–100.

Augustine on the 'just war'

which he speaks of public duty 'compelling' or 'constraining' a man. These are the 'necessities' the just man may not avoid, but will pray to God to be delivered from.[25] War has become the limiting case of the fundamental relationships characteristic of human society: what it presents us with in the extreme and purest form are the inescapable tensions present in all social living. The moral demands made by war do not differ radically from other moral demands made on the just man by an immoral society.

I have not tried to trace even the outlines of Augustine's views on what makes wars justified or otherwise. What I have tried to do is to set his views into their context in his reflection on the order, or lack of it, in human affairs. The outlines of his views on the conditions which must be met for a war to be justifiable are tolerably well known. What I found surprising in trying to trace them in chronological sequence in Augustine's work is that, so far as I can see, they underwent no substantial change in the course of the transformations in Augustine's intellectual perspectives which I have been tracing. The core of his view was and remained that warfare, and especially killing in war, must be subject to the generally valid norms set for human conduct. This is what makes the 'theory of the just war' so easy to isolate from the web of concepts, assumptions and attitudes which go into the making of a man's mind: particularly a mind as complex, subtle and differentiated as Augustine's. An idea which can be so easily isolated from its living context is heaven's gift to the historian of ideas: he can define the idea with adequate precision, study its ramifications, origins, and—above all—its transmission and influence on future generations, and he can do all this whilst by-passing the intellectual biography in which its origins are embedded. Augustine's thought on the 'just war' has suffered more perhaps than any other idea from the uprooting to which it has been subjected by medieval lawyers and theologians in search of *auctoritates* and by modern historians in search of a homogeneous doctrinal tradition.

We are repeatedly told, for example, that Augustine checked the pacifist inclinations of early Christian thought.[26] Nothing could be further from the truth; the credit for that—if credit is what is due—must go to others. To Christians who had read Eusebius,

---

[25] *Epp* 189.6; 220.10; 229.2. cf. 138. 14–15.
[26] For the most recent example of this common view see Barnes, 'The just war' p 772.

Athanasius or Ambrose, the 'pacifism' of a Lactantius would have seemed something of an anachronism. By the time Augustine began to write, his views on the legitimacy of waging war—with or without the sophisticated intellectual structure in which they became incorporated in his exposition—would have been widely accepted among Christians. In the 390s, the frenzied tendency to equate Theodosius's empire with Christ's kingship led many Christians to think of Theodosius's battles in all the imagery of holy wars.[27] Even in the first part of the *City of God*, in one of the chapters rightly described as among the 'shoddiest passages' of that great work,[28] Augustine had distanced himself from this way of seeing the great Christian emperor. His own tormented intellectual career ended, by the time he was completing the *City of God*, in a decisive turning away from the readiness with which others were prepared to identify themselves with the values and institutions of their society. Although he never reverted to any version of an early Christian 'pacifism', war now became for him one of the tragic necessities to which Christians must at times resort in order to check the savagery which is liable to break out between, as well as within, political societies. He did not repudiate the possibility, even the necessity, of fighting a 'just war'; what he came to repudiate was a whole set of attitudes towards it induced by the euphoria which encouraged Christians to invest wars such as Theodosius's with a religious significance. He did not need to check his contemporaries' 'pacifist inclinations'—few of them can have had any. What he challenged was a more fundamental mood of Christian self-identification with a whole social structure, a system of institutions and functions, including that of war.

Before long a forger, impressed, no doubt, by Augustine's prestige, would hang on his name as notorious an expression of the notion of a holy war as is the letter *Gravi de pugna*. Our undergraduate students are far from being original when they insist on telling us that Augustine had prepared the ground for the crusades. What medieval canonists and theologians found in Augustine was a quarry of authoritative texts to quote according to need. If that quarry could supply materials for justifying a holy

---

[27] See Y.-M. Duval, 'L'éloge de Théodose dans la *Cité de Dieu* (V.26.1)', *Recherches augustiniennes* 4 (1966) pp 135–179.
[28] P. Brown, 'Saint Augustine', in *Trends in medieval political thought*, ed. Beryl Smalley (Oxford 1965) pp 1–21 repr. in *Augustine*, ed. Markus, pp 311–335, at p 319.

war, it also supplied, and did so in far greater quantity, means of restricting warfare and the practices involved in it, at a time when, as a recent scholar has said, 'war was the normal condition of society'.[29] In a world in which war and Christianity were both normal, they could coalesce readily. In Augustine's measured, if unsystematic, statements medieval moralists found some means of insisting, in however hesitant and often untidy fashion, that war is not a law unto himself which sweeps men along with its own momentum, but that like all human activity, if it is to remain thinkable, it must stand under the judgement.

University of Nottingham

[29] Barnes, 'The just war' p 771.

THE CHURCH'S MILITARY SERVICE IN THE NINTH CENTURY: A CONTEMPORARY COMPARATIVE VIEW?

by JANET L. NELSON

'COMPARISONS are odorous'. Modern historians, far from sharing Dogberry's repugnance, have found the scent of the comparative method irresistible. 'Perhaps even the future of our discipline' depended on its pursuit, wrote Marc Bloch in 1928.[1] Since then, comparison has become fashionable enough, and hardly remarkable in our contemporaries' work. Remarkable it certainly is, however, in the ninth century. I would like to begin by quoting a passage written in 857 or 858 by Archbishop Hincmar of Rheims:

> In the regions [of the English] the bishoprics and monasteries are not so endowed with ecclesiastical property as they are in these Gallic regions; and for this reason, military services are not rendered from the bishoprics of those [English] regions, but [instead] the costs of rewarding those who fight (*stipendia militiae*) are allocated from public resources (*ex roga publica*). Here, on the other hand, in our regions, our clergy, instead of being given a fourth part of the bishopric's income from renders and offerings, have an appropriate share (*pars congrua*) assigned them; then another share is assigned for lighting of churches, and another share goes to the hospices for the poor; but then a share goes to the fighting-men who are listed under the name of 'housed ones' (*casati*); and finally a share goes to the bishop and those who are under his direct command. Thus, at the dictate of necessity and the urging of reason, the rulers of provinces and churches have established

---

[1] 'A contribution towards a comparative history of European societies', in *Land and Work in Medieval Europe* (London 1967) pp 44–81. This paper originally appeared in the *Revue de Synthèse Historique* in 1928.

customary arrangements appropriate to the respective qualities of provinces and quantities of church property.[2] This passage, with its explicit cross-Channel comparison and modern-sounding relativist note, has received little comment from modern historians—partly, perhaps, because it occurs in one of the less well-known of Hincmar's works.[3] In fact that work, the *De Ecclesiis et Capellis*, is one of Hincmar's most interesting. As for the passage I have just quoted, I believe it is worth some attention in the context of the theme of 'the Church and war'.

I want to ask three questions of this ninth-century comparison. the first is: how far can we believe what Hincmar has to say of 'the regions of the English'? Hincmar alleges that warriors in ninth-century England were 'paid' at 'public expense'; that English bishoprics and monasteries did not owe any specific military service; and that the reason for this was the 'English' Church's relatively poor endowment with landed wealth. On the face of it, the first point hardly fits with recent accounts of Anglo-Saxon military institutions: that is, of a recruitment system in which service was owed by the 'whole people' and calculated on the basis

---

[2] *De Ecclesiis et Capellis*, ed W. Gundlach in Zeitschrift für Kirchengeschichte 10 (1889) pp 92–145 at p 135. (I cite this hereafter as *dEC*.) A new edition is being prepared by the MGH. Hincmar's covering letter sending the work to Charles the Bald is printed in *MGH* Epp 8 pp 52–5. The division of episcopal revenues into four (?equal) parts (for bishop, clergy, the poor, and church buildings) was laid down by Gelasius I: *Decretum Gelasii* in the Dionysio-Hadriana, Decreta Gelasii c 27, in *PL* 67, col 310. On the application of these arrangements in Gaul, see M. Rouche, 'La matricule des pauvres, évolution d'une institution de charité du Bas-Empire jusqu'à la fin du Haut Moyen Age', in M. Mollat ed, *Etudes sur l'Histoire de la Pauvreté*. 2 vols (Paris 1974) pp 83–110, esp 86–7, also J. Devisse, '"Pauperes" et "paupertas" dans le monde carolingien: ce qu'en dit Hincmar de Reims', in *Revue du Nord* 48 (1966) pp 273–87, esp 277 with n 15. Hincmar contrasts the Gelasian four-way division with the contemporary practice of a five-way division 'in these Gallic regions'.

[3] Until Gundlach's edition from Leyden Universitätsbibliothek MS 141, the work was known of only from Flodoard's mention, *Historia Remensis ecclesiae* III, 18 in *MGH SS* 13 p 508. It is therefore not printed with the bulk of Hincmar's works in *PL* 125 and 126. The work's interest was appreciated by P. Imbart de la Tour, *Les origines religieuses de la France: les paroisses rurales du IXe au XIe siècle* (Paris 1900), and by [E.] Lesne, *Histoire [de la propriété ecclésiastique en France*, 6 vols (Lille 1905–43)] 2 part ii (1926) who discussed part of the passage quoted above at pp 272–3 without, however, distinguishing between land and income from land. That Hincmar had both in mind is clear from his re-examination of the subject ten years later in the *Pro Ecclesiae Libertatum Defensione*, *PL* 125, cols 1050–1. See also the fine commentary on the *dEC* in [J.] Devisse, *Hincmar [Archevêque de Reims, 845–882*, 3 vols (Geneva 1975-6) 2 pp 829–45, noting the interest of the comparative passage (pp 839–40) but without any discussion of its relevance to the military service of the ninth-century church.

Military service in the ninth century

of one warrior for so many hides of inherited land.[4] In such a system the question of payment by the state did not arise: men came to the muster bringing their own provisions and, like the West Saxon levies of 893, 'having completed their period of service and come to the end of their food-supplies',[5] they expected to go home. Further, it is clear that church lands too were assessed for such contributions of warriors in the ninth century.[6] Hincmar then seems not to have been talking about the *fyrd*. Perhaps he had in mind the specialist warriors of the king's and ealdormen's retinues—men who certainly did expect a 'stipend', in the short run money and in the longer term land.[7] Asser in his *Life* of Alfred is explicit about the king's generosity with money to his fighting-men.[8] True, he mentions royal gifts of estates only in the context of Alfred's rewarding of his ecclesiastical helpers (including Asser himself),[9] but Alfred surely gave some lands to his *faselli*, and presumably his father King Æthelwulf had done so too.[10] Hincmar may be thought to imply that he believed that in England all such grants were made from the fisc and that the English kings who were his contemporaries did not try to exploit church lands or

---

[4] See [N.] Brooks, ['The] development [of military obligations in eighth- and ninth-century England', in P. Clemoes and K. Hughes edd, *England before the Conquest: Studies . . . presented to Dorothy Whitelock* (Cambridge 1971)] pp 69–84: a fine study that does justice to previous scholarship on this subject. Equally indispensable is E. John, *Orbis Britanniae* (Leicester 1966) pp 128–53, esp 139–42, placing military organisation firmly in social context.

[5] *Anglo-Saxon Chronicle* edd J. Earle and C. Plummer, *Two of the Saxon Chronicles Parallel* (Oxford 1892) s.a. 894 for 893 pp 85–6.

[6] Brooks, 'Development' p 70 and *passim*.

[7] See John, *Orbis Britanniae* pp 118–22. There is no direct evidence before the late tenth century, however, that the *fyrd* was organised on the lines of ealdormanic followings writ large.

[8] Asser, *Life [of King Alfred* ed W. Stevenson (Oxford 1904 repr 1959)] c 100, p 88.

[9] Asser, *Life* cc 77, 81, pp 62, 67–8. The monasteries given to Asser by Alfred were evidently royal proprietary churches.

[10] Asser, *Life* cc 53, 55, pp 41, 44, mentions Alfred's *faselli*. In c 76, p 60, listing the many peoples (including *pagani* – Danes!) from whom Alfred's following was recruited, Asser says the king 'endowed them all with money and estates'. (For the likely meaning of *potestas* here: 'power over lands', see D. Whitelock, *EHD* vol 1 (2nd edn London 1979) p 293, n 1.) Alfred's few surviving charters include two that perhaps represent grants to members of his following: *CS* 2 nos 581, 568. (For their likely genuineness see D. Whitelock, 'Some charters in the name of King Alfred', in [M.H.] King and [W.M.] Stevens edd *Saints, Scholars and Heroes*, [*Studies in Honor of C.W. Jones*] (Collegeville Minnesota 1978)] pp 77–98.) The argument of H.P.R. Finberg, *West Country Historical Studies* (Newton Abbot 1969) pp 11–28 (even allowing for the reservations noted by Whitelock, *EHD* p 522) suggests that some of the lands which Æthelwulf booked to himself in *CS* no 451 may have been intended for distribution to his following.

revenues, on the Carolingian model, to reward members of their *militia terrestris*. But given the pressing need of these kings, with Viking attacks increasingly serious from c850 onwards, to secure the service of their aristocracy, and given also the degree of control they exercised over the disposition of bishoprics and at least some rich minsters, it is difficult to believe that they never used episcopal or minster lands to make the equivalent of precarial grants. Mercian and Northumbrian kings had almost certainly done so a generation and more earlier.[11] It looks as if Egbert of Wessex did so too in the 820s and 830s.[12] I know of no evidence on the point from Æthelwulf's reign; but from Alfred's there is a hint in a letter of Pope John VIII to the archbishop of Canterbury that 'the king and others' have been 'wronging the house of the Lord' in a way the archbishop is urged to 'resist strenuously, making your service honourable'.[13] Vikings were not the only beneficiaries of Canterbury's material losses in the ninth century.

Hincmar says that military services were not rendered from English bishoprics as such. But was it just a coincidence that in 825, King Egbert 'sent Bishop Ealhstan and Ealdorman Wulfheard to Kent with a great force and they drove King Baldred over the Thames'; or that in 848 'Ealdorman Eanwulf with the men of Somerset and Bishop Ealhstan . . . fought against a Danish host . . . and made great slaughter . . . and won the victory'; or that in 871 Ealhstan's successor Heahmund was slain at the battle of Meretun?[14] As for the landed resources of the English church, charter evidence shows, *pace* Hincmar, that bishoprics and a very large number of minsters had been generously endowed with ecclesiastical property before the mid-ninth century.[15]

But if I hesitate to accept Hincmar's statements about ninth-century practice in England, that is not only because it jars with

---

[11] The evidence is ably discussed by P. Wormald in a forthcoming study, 'Bede, the *Bretwaldas* and the Origins of the *Gens Anglorum*' (1983).
[12] This is implied in *CS* no 421. For very interesting comments on the political context of this charter, see Wormald in J. Campbell ed *The Anglo-Saxons* (London 1982) p 140.
[13] I quote from Whitelock's translation of this letter in *EHD* p 882.
[14] *Anglo-Saxon Chronicle* s.a. 823 for 825, 845 for 848, 871, pp 60, 64, 72.
[15] For example, for the Canterbury evidence, see Brooks, *The Early History of Christ Church Canterbury* (forthcoming, Leicester 1983); for Winchester, see Finberg, *The Early Charters of Wessex* (Leicester 1964) pp 218–20; for Worcester, see Wormald in Campbell ed, *The Anglo-Saxons* pp 122–3 and the map *ibid* p 71 showing the large number of minster endowments up to c850.

Military service in the ninth century

what Anglo-Saxon evidence we have: it is also because, despite appearances to the contrary, Hincmar himself cannot be read as a contemporary witness here. What we might assume, given the intensification of contacts between Wessex and Francia precisely in the 850s,[16] to be hard data gained from a well-placed West Saxon informant, in fact comes from an authoritative text written over two and a half centuries before: Hincmar's source, as might have been guessed from the reference to the regions of 'the English', where a ninth-century insular informant would probably have distinguished between Mercians and West Saxons, is Gregory the Great's letter to Augustine, the famous 'Responses' recorded by Bede in the *Ecclesiastical History*.[17] Note that Hincmar cites what is to be 'found' there in the present tense: the churches '*are* not so endowed . . .'. The answer to my first question then is that the credibility of Hincmar's 'ninth-century' data for England must be rated low: which does not, however, make his comparison valueless from a historical standpoint, as we shall see in a moment.

The second question which I think worth asking is whether Hincmar in this passage throws any special light on the military service of the Frankish Church. For in this Hincmar was himself deeply implicated. True, we know a good deal about this from other sources.[18] On some aspects, capitularies are perfectly frank. Here is an example from Charlemagne's reign:

---

[16] See P. Stafford, 'Charles the Bald, Judith and England', in M. Gibson and J. Nelson edd, *Charles the Bald:* [*Court and Kingdom*, B.A.R. International Series 101 (Oxford 1981)] pp 137–51. Hincmar was closely involved personally in these contacts: he performed Judith's consecration in 856 for which he remodelled an English *ordo* (see Nelson, 'The earliest surviving royal *Ordo*', in B. Tierney and P. Linehan edd, *Authority and Power: Studies presented to Walter Ullmann* (Cambridge 1980) pp 29–48) and he had a hand in the Capitulary of 864 in which Charles the Bald's imposition of a new obligation to build fortifications was almost certainly influenced by recent West Saxon developments (see Brooks, 'Development' p 81; and for the capitulary see Nelson, 'Legislation and consensus in the reign of Charles the Bald', forthcoming).

[17] *Historia Ecclesiastica Gentis Anglorum* ed Plummer (Oxford 1896 repr 1975) 1, 27, p 48. The best discussion of this letter in its historical context is H. Mayr-Harting, *The Coming of Christianity to Anglo-Saxon England* (London 1972) pp 60–4, 269–71. Gregory's position and missionary concerns gave him in some ways a genuinely relativist outlook. Whether Hincmar cited Gregory's letter from Bede is uncertain: Devisse, *Hincmar* 2 p 822, n 696 shows there is no evidence for Hincmar's having a text of the *Ecclesiastical History* before the 870s. Hincmar could have cited from Pseudo-Isidore though again his use of this is late, and sparing, or from the Register of Gregory's letters (Devisse, *Hincmar* 3 p 1434, n 2): though Hincmar's own references to a *Regestum* are only from 870 onwards (*ibid*, p 1495, n 4), this seems his likeliest source in this passage in the *dEC* where he also refers to two other letters of Gregory.

[18] Lesne, *Histoire*, 2(ii) pp 456 *seq* remains indispensable. See also [F.] Prinz, *Klerus und Krieg*

19

No bishop or abbot or abbess...is to presume to give or sell a mail-shirt or a sword to an outsider (*extraneus*) without our permission, but only to their own vassals. If it should happen that a rector has in a church or holy place more mail-shirts than there are fighting-men of that church, he is to ask the king what should be done with them.[19]

Each rector then was responsible for the service owed by his—or her—own church: for equipping, and in the case of a bishop or an abbot personally leading, that church's warriors on campaign. This obligation was as far as I know never questioned by any Carolingian churchman: so firm was the *Einstaatung* of the Frankish Church.[20] The reforming Council of Ver in 844, for instance, was concerned that 'military affairs should suffer no disadvantage from the absence of bishops' who might be prevented by physical weakness or excused by royal indulgence from personal service with the army. The solution offered was that the bishops should place 'their men coming forward for the state (*res publica*)' under the command of a layman whom they considered suitably 'useful'.[21] We can guess both from ninth-century casualty-lists and from such private sources as letters that ecclesiastical contingents formed a very important component in Carolingian armies.[22] Charles the Bald's main complaint against Archbishop Wenilo of Sens in 859 was that he had not only failed to deliver to his king his due 'solace' (the euphemism is an old one but it is interesting to

---

[im *früheren Mittelalter* (Stuttgart 1971)] and *idem*, 'King, clergy and war at the time of the Carolingians', in King and Stevens edd, *Saints, Scholars and Heroes*, pp 301–329, though both the book and the article are patchy in their treatment of the ninth century.

[19] *MGH Capit* 1, no 74, c 10, p 167. The obligation of abbesses is rightly insisted on for the tenth century by L. Auer, 'Der Kriegsdienst des Klerus [unter den sächsischen Kaisern', in] *MIOG* 79 (1971) pp 316–407; 80 (1972) pp 48–70 at 63–4.

[20] The term is Prinz's, *Klerus und Krieg* pp 65, 91. See also Nelson, 'Charles the Bald and the Church [in town and countryside', in *SCH* 16 (1979)] pp 103–18.

[21] *MGH Capit* 2, no 291, c 8, p 385. In the same year, the Council of Thionville, *ibid* no 227, c 3, p 114, complained about lay-abbots, but acknowledged that monasteries served not only '*divina religio*' but also '*utilitas rei publicae*'.

[22] See e.g. *Annales Regni Francorum*, ed F. Kurze *MGH SSRG* (Hannover 1895) s.a. 753, p 11; *Annales Lauresshamenses*, s.a.791, *MGH SS* 1 pp 34–5; *Annals of St Bertin*, ed F. Grat et al (Paris 1964) s.a. 833, 834, 844, 876 pp 9 (with note g.), 13, 46–7, 209; Archbishop Hetti of Trier to Bishop Frothar of Toul, *MGH Epp* 5 pp 277–8; Lupus [of Ferrières,] *Correspondance*. [ed L. Levillain, 2 vols (Paris 1927-35)] 1. Epp 15, 17, 34, 35, 45, and 2. Epp 72, 83; Hincmar, *MGH Epp* 8 p 206, and a vivid passage in *dEC*, p 132, on the need for an efficient commissariat.

Military service in the ninth century

find it recurring in this Hincmarian text),[23] but had offered it instead to Charles' enemy. Charles was able to recover his position thanks not least to the loyalty of bishops whose 'solaces' evidently were forthcoming.[24] In 865 Charles issued particularly explicit orders about the service he demanded from the church in the Burgundian part of his realm:

> If men unfaithful to us join in rebellion, all our faithful men in each missaticum, bishops and abbots and counts and the abbesses' men, and the counts and our vassals and the other faithful men, are all to make arrangements to assemble. Our missi . . . are to be responsible for ensuring that each bishop, abbot and abbess should send his or her men there on time with the whole quota required, each contingent along with its banner-man (*guntfanonarius*) who, together with our missi, is responsible for his comrades.[25]

Nor was West Francia exceptional: in every Carolingian kingdom, the *militia ecclesiae* was vital to the king's successful prosecution of war—service regularly demanded and apparently for the most part assiduously performed.[26]

How did the system actually work? It is often argued that its basis was the precarial grant, which allowed royal vassals to be installed on church lands for what was effectively a rent (ninths and tenths).[27] But it looks as if such men, militarily important as they certainly were, remained in practice the king's men,[28] and

---

[23] *MGH Capit* 2, no 300, cc 6–7, 14 pp 452–3. The euphemism appears already in the reign of Childebert II: *MGH Capit* 1, no 7, p 16.

[24] Nelson, 'Charles the Bald and the Church' pp 115–6.

[25] *MGH Capit* 2, no 274, c 13, p 331. The mention of banners in relation to *ecclesiastical* contingents is noteworthy (and overlooked by C. Erdmann, *Die Entstehung des Kreuzzugsgedankens* (Stuttgart 1935) in his important chapter on holy banners). This seems to be the earliest recorded instance of the word *guntfanonarius*.

[26] East Francia: e.g. *Annals of Fulda*, ed Kurze, *MGH SSRG* (Hannover 1891) s.a. 872, 883, pp 76, 100; Notker, *Gesta Karoli*, ed H. Haefele, *MGH SSRG* (Berlin 1959) bk 2, c 17, p 83: a description, perhaps drawn from his own experience rather than from historical evidence, of Charlemagne's bishops, abbots and chaplains '*cum comitibus suis*' at the siege of Pavia in 774. (It is clear from the context that the reference is to military followings rather than 'attendants' as translated by L. Thorpe, *Two Lives of Charlemagne* (Harmondsworth 1969) p 163.) Italy: e.g. *MGH Capit* 2, no 221, c 13, p 103 ('*episcopi . . . in suis domibus cum suis vassallis*'); no 218, c 4, p 96: '. . . *abbates vel abbatissae si plenissime homines suos non direxerint, ipse suos honores perdant (!) et eorum bassalli et proprium et beneficium amittant*'.

[27] G. Constable, 'Nona et decima' *Speculum* 35 (1960) pp 224–50.

[28] Nelson, 'Charles the Bald and the Church' pp 107, 116, with further references. The exceptionally-rich evidence for the see of Laon is discussed by P. McKeon, *Hincmar of*

being perhaps of high status (counts, for example) and already powerful in their own right were more likely to answer a direct royal summons to the host than to form part of a church contingent. Who then were the *homines ecclesiae*? Part of the answer is that they were vassals picked by the bishop (or abbot or abbess), many of them probably his own kinsmen[29] and beneficed on episcopal lands. The rest of the answer is suggested by Hincmar in the passage I began by quoting: they were the *casati*, 'the housed ones', and those under the bishop's direct command.[30] For such warriors, whether endowed with a homestead (and thus enabled to marry) and a parcel of land, or resident still in their lord's establishment, a sizeable benefice might be a future hope: in the meantime they depended on distributions of moveable wealth, including money, and equipment to keep them 'prepared' for war. They formed the bishop's military household, and (assuming that Hincmar's 'shares' (*partes*) were equal) two-fifths of the bishop's income was spent largely on their support (though some non-military personnel will have been included among 'those under his direct command'). There is no doubting the importance of episcopal vassals in general, or of contingents of free tenants mobilised on occasion by ecclesiastical lords. But it may be suggested that perhaps the key element in the ninth-century system was composed of bodies of virtually full-time soldiers, maintained out of churches' moveable resources and available for service alongside the king's and his counts' and magnates' own household troops. In terms of sheer military experience, such men could make a unique contribution to the host. These were the professionals. Under able and committed leaders, they would fight fiercely and effectively against whatever enemy might threaten, not excluding the Vikings. Such a group, I think, were the men of the abbey of Corbie who acquitted themselves valiantly against a Viking attack in 859, and were led in person by their young abbot,

---

Laon and Carolingian Politics (Urbana-Chicago-London 1978) esp pp 179–85; but there is no reason to think the arrangements here unusual.

[29] As in the case of Hincmar of Laon: *PL* 124, col 981. Cp below p 27, n 47.

[30] The distinction between the bishop's military *familia* in this narrower sense, and the larger body of vassals whom he led to war is impossible to document directly from ninth-century sources. But Hincmar seems to refer to the former in *dEC* p 135; and there may be another reference in Lupus, *Correspondance*, 1, Ep 16, p 96: '*Homines nostri . . . censu rei familiaris in . . . servitio effuso, onere paupertatis gravantur*' (though Levillain translates: '. . . revenu de leur patrimoine').

Military service in the ninth century

Odo. Lupus of Ferrières wrote to him in mingled congratulation and distress:

> I'm particularly anxious . . . when I recall your way of pitching yourself unarmed right into the thick of battles. Your youthful energy gets drawn into them by your greediness for winning! I advise you, out of well-wishing affection, be content with only putting your troops in position—for that's as much as is suitable to your [monastic] vow—and leave it to the fighting-men (*armati*) to carry out their 'profession' with instruments of war.[31]

Lupus' reservations are about Odo's personal engagement in warfare, and the risks he runs, not about his church's military service against those whom the classically-inspired Lupus calls not 'pagans', but 'barbarians' or 'pirates'.

Hincmar's evidence is important, therefore, in helping to qualify the notion that the institutionalised military service of the Carolingian Church changed from a precarial base producing 'noble fief-holders' in the ninth century, to a ministerial base producing episcopal (or abbatial) retinues of warrior-dependants in the tenth century.[32] For Hincmar implies that the episcopal military household already in the 850s played an important role in the service of the Carolingian state, and indeed it probably had done so for the past century. Hincmar thought fifty a fair upper limit for a bishop's retinue when he toured his diocese.[33] In 870 the bishop of Laon came to an assembly contrary to royal orders 'with the whole company of his men' in 'an armed band' (*armata manu*). The bishop was told by royal officers that 'ten or twelve *casati homines*' plus clergy and servants would be considered an adequate entourage for this synodal appearance. The rest of his men should be 'prepared for the defence of the fatherland against the Vikings'.[34] Clearly the bishop's total following contained well upwards of a dozen men. This implies a scale of episcopal military

---

[31] Lupus, *Correspondance* vol 2, Ep 106 p 138. I have tried in my translation to bring out the play on words and ideas between Odo's monastic profession (*propositum*) and the profession of the *armati* ('*quod instrumentis bellicis profitentur*').

[32] Prinz, *Klerus und Krieg* p 166.

[33] *dEC* p 127, quoting VII Toledo, c 4 presumably via the Hispana, *PL* 84 col 407–8. (For the versions current in the ninth century, see Devisse, *Hincmar* vol 3 p 1409). But Hincmar asserted (*dEC* p 136) that his fellow bishops regularly violated this limit, travelling around their dioceses '*cum hoste collecta*'!

[34] Mansi 16, col 663.

retinue comparable with those documented for the East Frankish realm in the tenth century;[35] and I can see no reason for thinking the bishop of Laon unique, or even unusual, in the ninth, except in the sense of being unusually well-documented.

One or two further implications of general interest for the ninth century can be noted here. First, the ability of bishops and abbots to maintain followings on this scale indicates (if it does not presuppose) the growth of a money economy to facilitate the payment of renders and offerings, and the accumulation of episcopal incomes, in cash; for while some transfers to warriors were made in kind (weapons, for instance), it seems likely that the 'annual gifts' they received were in coin.[36] If this was already so in the ninth century, as it remained quite largely in the twelfth, then any monochrome picture of 'the feudal system' as one in which land was virtually the sole reward for military service, beneficed vassals the major and crucial component in armies summoned by kings, and liability neatly calculated on a standard ratio of land to men, is plainly in need of some retouching, as Prestwich and Gillingham have recently shown for England.[37] In Carolingian kingdoms too, the quotas of warriors due from churches in particular were apparently arranged bilaterally between king and bishop (or abbot or abbess): thus in 865, missus and banner-man together were to check that such an agreement had been carried out. In a given quota, the bishop's military household would form a key element. A useful periodisation of medieval military systems taking full account of the Church's part therein would therefore stress continuities through the early and central Middle Ages, say, from the seventh to the twelfth centuries, and contrast the later

---

[35] Lesne, *Histoire*, 2, ii, pp 481–2. Cp K. F. Werner, 'Heeres-organisation und Kriegführung im deutschen Königreich des 10 und 11 Jhdts.', in *SS Spoleto* 15 (1968) pp 791–843, esp pp 820–30 (repr in Werner, *Structures politiques du monde franc* (London 1979)), Auer, 'Kriegsdienst des Klerus' in *MIOG* 79 (1971) pp 376–7, and 80 (1972) p 68, nn 31–3. These figures will include members of episcopal *familiae* along with beneficial vassals.

[36] The implication of Hincmar's *De Ordine Palatii*, c 22 is that the West Frankish king's military following were paid annual gifts in cash. Asser c 100 explicitly mentions annual cash payments by Alfred to his *bellatores*, and Alfred in his will (Whitelock, p 536) left 200lb, to 'those who follow (*folgiad*) me'. For the abbot of Fleury's annual gifts to his *vassalli*, see G. Tessier, *Receuil des Actes de Charles II le Chauve*, 3 vols (Paris 1943–55) 1, no 177, p 468. See also below, p 25, n 39.

[37] J. O. Prestwich, 'The Military Household of the Norman Kings', in *EHR* 96 (1981) pp 1–35; J. B. Gillingham, 'The introduction of knight service into England', in R. A. Brown ed, *Proceedings of the Battle Conference* 4 (1982) pp 53–64.

Middle Ages when qualitative economic change permitted armies to be supported on tax revenue raised from ecclesiastical sources among others: a development which eased at least some of the most practical and embarrassing problems of the Church's involvement in war and in general made kings and princes less dependent on the Church's military service. A second aspect of the way in which the ninth-century Frankish Church organised its service may be significant. Through their recruitment of fighting-men, bishops and abbots and abbesses could provide a channel of social mobility to their *casati homines*, not differing in kind from the advancement of vassals by lay aristocrats[38] but perhaps operating on a larger scale and more continuously, in so far as money oiled the system (churchmen are conspicuous as lenders, and borrowers, in the ninth century).[39]

So much for what Hincmar's account of the allocation of episcopal revenues in West Francia has to tell us about the Frankish Church's *militia*, its 'solace' to the Carolingians. It is time to pose my third and last question: why did Hincmar affect the use of the comparative method? For in fact the difference he purported to explain did not exist. The English churches, I have argued, owed military service to their kings just as Frankish churches did; and so too did the Italian churches which Hincmar again alleged were unfamiliar with 'the heavy custom of our regions'.[40] The

---

[38] Cp Werner, 'Untersuchungen zur Frühzeit des französischen Fürstentums (8.–10. Jdts)', in *Die Welt als Geschichte* 18 (1958) pp 256–89; 19 (1959) pp 146–93; and the important contribution of C. B. Bouchard, 'The Origins of the French Nobility: a Reassessment', in *American Historical Review* 86 (1981) pp 501–32.

[39] Condemnations of the practice of usury by ecclesiastics are frequent in the ninth century. (There is a good example in *dEC* p 121). The taking of cash-payments by clergy of all ranks but especially bishops is also condemned. (Again, the *dEC* offers several examples: pp 107, 113, 123–4, 127). Both the bishops attacked by Hincmar (Rothad of Soissons, and Hincmar of Laon) were accused of simony, and one of pawning church plate. For the scale of the church's cash-contribution to successive Danegelds in Hincmar's time, see F. Lot, 'Les tributs aux Normands et l'Eglise de France au IXe siècle' in *BEC* 85 (1924) pp 58–78. All this should be set in the context of the relatively extensive monetisation of the economy of Charles the Bald's kingdom demonstrated by D. M. Metcalf, 'A sketch of the currency in the time of Charles the Bald' in Gibson and Nelson edd, *Charles the Bald* pp 53–84, and of the increasing tendency for the renders of peasants on ecclesiastical estates to be paid in cash.

[40] *MGH Epp* 8, no 198, p 206. In *dEC* p 135, Hincmar cites two letters of Gregory I to Italian bishops alongside the letter to Augustine: conditions in England and Italy are alleged to be the same and contrasted with the military service owed by the church in 'these Gallic regions'. But for the real situation in Italy, see above p 21, n 26, and C. Wickham, *Early Medieval Italy* (London 1981) pp 137, 140–2.

truth is that Hincmar—'incorrigible Hincmar', as M. Devisse was once moved to exclaim[41]—was not really concerned with the practice of contemporary English or Italian churches. He was no true forerunner of the Annales School. And yet his 'comparative method' was neither entirely bogus nor redundant. For Hincmar was trying to come to terms with a genuine contrast, not in space but in time: the contrast between the Church of the Apostles and the Fathers, not so richly endowed with worldly wealth and in which a bishop and his clergy might realistically hold their goods in common, and the Frankish Church of his own day with its vast estates and revenues, its bishops wielding power that had an unmistakeably economic and political, as well as legal and spiritual, basis.[42] It was Hincmar who imagined Frankish lay magnates jeering at him and his episcopal colleagues: 'those villains, those non-noble men . . . *Their* ancestors did not help [previous kings] to rule their kingdoms'. And instead of insisting as he easily could have done that Frankish bishops were noble to a man, Hincmar offered this hypothetical riposte:

> When God came in flesh . . . and disposed the government of His kingdom, he did not choose for this purpose rich men and noble men, but poor men and fishermen. And as it is written, 'He hath chosen the base things of the world and things which are despised to confound the things that are mighty'.[43]

Of course the debate is imaginary, the context polemical and the assertion unique in Hincmar's work (and indeed in early medieval writing, I think). But the very fact that Hincmar wrote this, even once, suggests that at least at this stage of his career he was conscious of the paradox that an 'established' Church, beneficiary over centuries of the gifts of the faithful, would be rich and its pastors aristocratic, where Christ and his followers had been poor and lowly. The apostles had had resources that were the mere

---

[41] Devisse, *Hincmar* 2 p 603.
[42] Hincmar shows his awareness of the contrast in a torrent of appeals to St. Paul and the age of the Apostles: *dEC* pp 125–36. He also attempts to rationalise the transition from apostolic arrangements to the acquisition of landed wealth by the Church: *ibid* pp 135–6. For similar concerns in Pseudo-Isidore and their specific ninth-century context, see the penetrating comments of W. Goffart, *The Le Mans Forgeries* (Cambridge, Mass. 1966) ch 1 esp p 20.
[43] *MGH* Capit 2, no 297, pp 440–1.

minimum required to enable them to preach the Gospel.[44] The situation of their ninth-century 'successors' was very different: they were accused of greed for worldly goods, not only by laymen but by their own parish clergy (prime victims of that cupidity) and by Hincmar himself.[45] The *De Ecclesiis et Capellis* is amongst other things a passionate appeal to the higher clergy to be content with modest personal consumption. But it is more than that. In it Hincmar offers one solution to the dilemma of the institutionalised Church. How could a church that was already so rich insist, as ninth-century churchmen so often did, on not just retaining lands but on gaining, or re-gaining, yet more? Because, answered Hincmar, their income was required to enable the Church to perform its military service to the kingdom that defended it. Hincmar was not justifying a system based on precarial grants that were, after all, still regarded in principle as mere temporary expedients.[46] He envisaged a more permanent solution in warriors maintained by and closely attached to ecclesiastical lords. Not the Church's warfare but the Church's wealth was the real problem. And the war, long since justified, would now justify the wealth.

For Hincmar this was a viable solution, first and foremost because the Church's military service could be conceived in ninth-century West Francia as a public service.[47] Hincmar saw in his own time as in the early Church a state which provided the benefits of peace and order to its subjects. He began the *De Ecclesiis et Capellis* by quoting St. Augustine: '"Honour the king." Don't say, "What does the king mean to me?" What then do possessions mean to you? Possessions are possessed through the laws of kings.'[48] For Hincmar as for Augustine, the ruler's *raison d'être* was his function in making and preserving law. To apply law within, to protect a law-ordered society from external attack, force would sometimes be necessary: the Church's offering of military 'solace'

---

[44] dEC pp 129–32.
[45] Such complaints were not new in the ninth century; nor was Hincmar then the only one to make them. But the depth of his concern in the *dEC* is very striking.
[46] Constable, 'Nona et decima'.
[47] Cp above p 20-1, nn 21, 26: and Hincmar of Laon's self-justification in *PL* 124, col 981, admitting that he had granted benefices on episcopal lands to his own kinsmen, but insisting that this benefitted both church and state.
[48] *dEC*, prefatory letter, *MGH Epp* 6, no 108, pp 53–4. For this theme in Hincmar's political thought, see Nelson, 'Kingship, law and liturgy [in the political thought of Hincmar of Rheims', in *EHR* 92 (1977)] pp 241–79.

to the ruler thus had automatic justification. Hincmar's view of the Carolingian state may have been rosy but it had a basis in political reality. Ninth-century churchmen did not only preach peace as the end of war but joined king and lay magnates in practical efforts to achieve it, as when the assembly of Soissons in 853 agreed that no public courts should be held in Lent except to deal with 'concord and making peace between disputants'—a curious foreshadowing of the Truce of God.[49]

Secondly, Hincmar could readily justify in patristic terms the Church's participation in warfare that was defensive, as it was increasingly often in the ninth century, and could also be presented as Christian (the Bretons though not pagans could be branded 'false Christians').[50] A saint seen by a monk in a vision defending his earthly *familia* and its property wore helmet and mail-shirt, and he felled his Viking enemy with blows none the less lethal for being invisible.[51] For centuries the Church had invoked God's power to 'destroy the enemies of your people'.[52] Now the Frankish bishops assured their king that he had been anointed (another symptom of the close entente between Church and state) like the victorious warrior-kings of the Old Testament, his role 'to defend from the wicked by royal strength the holy Church, that is, the Christian people committed to you by God'.[53] Because churchmen had to join in that defence, war had become a fact of ecclesiastical life. Pope Nicholas I in a moment of irritation at Frankish kings who used their bishops' military duties as an excuse for inaction on

---

[49] *MGH* Capit 2, no 259, c 8, p 269. The foreshadowing was noticed by Devisse, *Hincmar* 1 p 499 n 166. See also J. M. Wallace-Hadrill, 'War and Peace in the Early Middle Ages', in his collected essays, *Early Medieval History* (Oxford 1975) pp 19–38, esp 31–5, for a fairly optimistic assessment of the Carolingian Church's success in preaching peace (though I cannot share his view that 'Frankish bellicosity' had come to be in need of reactivating in the ninth century: there is too much evidence not only for inter-Frankish violence, but also – and contrary to a currently-fashionable view—for local and spontaneous resistance to the Vikings! Cp Lupus' letter, above p23).

[50] *PL* 125, col 966. For the Vikings as *pagani*, see Wallace-Hadrill, 'The Vikings in Francia', in *Early Medieval History* pp 222–7 (though in my view exaggerating the 'positive force' of Viking paganism in reality).

[51] *Translatio Sancti Germani Parisiensis*, cc 29, 30, ed C. de Smedt, *Analecta Bollandiana* 2 (1883) pp 90–1, 92.

[52] So, one of the prayers in time of war in the Gelasian Sacramentary ed L. C. Mohlberg, *Liber Sacramentorum Romanae Aeclesiae Ordinis Anni Circuli* (Rome 1960) p 215.

[53] Prayer at the handing over of the sceptre, *Ordo* of Louis the Stammerer (877), *MGH* Capit 2, no 304, p 461. For Hincmar's authorship, see Nelson, 'Kingship, law and liturgy', pp 246, 260.

other important business, might denounce such 'secular service' as reprehensible, quoting 2 Timothy 2:4: *Nemo militans Deo implicat se negotiis saecularibus*.⁵⁴ But how *un*typical a protest this was (both of Nicholas and his contemporaries) can be gauged from Hincmar's thinking this very same excuse appropriate in a carefully-worded letter to Nicholas written only months later.⁵⁵

We know more of Hincmar's thoughts than those of other ninth-century churchmen. But in finding a new application of Augustine's compromise with a violent world, he probably spoke for them all. The institutionalised warfare of the Church was not just permissible but necessary: in practical terms because it sustained the Carolingian state, in ideological terms because it transcended the opposition between apostolicity and landed wealth. The solution was *zeitbedingt* in both senses of that useful word: it was needed by churchmen at a particular time and it required the conditions of that time. In the tenth century, changed conditions—the collapse of the Carolingian state in West Francia and in Italy—left a mere warrior-clergy, so it is often claimed, without institutional support, at the mercy of the feudal laity. Yet even in those kingdoms (and the East Frankish case needs no further labouring since the solid demonstrations of Werner and Auer) something of the ninth-century system survived—and more perhaps than Erdmann allowed for—into the age of the Crusades. The liturgy of knighthood has ninth-century West Frankish roots (I am thinking of the benediction *super militantes* in the Leofric Missal),⁵⁶ and the earliest dubbing rituals should be linked with the warrior-households of particular bishops, that is, with the *familiae* of particular saints.⁵⁷ Can we believe that any wide gulf separates these *milites* from, on the one hand, those warriors of Carolingian bishops and abbots and abbesses who went to war behind their banners and kept their mail-shirts in holy places, and on the other, the *militia sancti Petri* and the soldiers of Christ?⁵⁸ At least, to end

---

⁵⁴ *MGH Epp* 6, no 38, pp 309–10.
⁵⁵ *MGH Epp* 8, no 198, p 206.
⁵⁶ Ed F. Warren (Oxford 1883) p 232. See Nelson, 'Earliest surviving royal *Ordo*', esp pp 36, n 37, and 38, n 41.
⁵⁷ G. Duby, *Les Trois Ordres* (Paris 1978) p 358. This point is missed by J. Flori, 'Chevalerie et liturgie' in *Le Moyen Age* 84 (1978) pp 245–78, 434–8.
⁵⁸ I. S. Robinson, 'Gregory VII and the Soldiers of Christ', in *History* 58 (1973) pp 169–92 esp 179.

where I began, there are comparisons that may repay some further sniffing out.

King's College London.

THE CHURCH, WARFARE AND MILITARY OBLIGATION IN NORMAN ITALY

by G. A. LOUD

ONE OF the most important intellectual problems which the Church faced in the Middle Ages was to reconcile warfare with the Christian message. But the presence of, and the necessity for, war affected not merely the intellectual attitudes and social message of medieval ecclesiastics. The institutional Church faced obvious practical problems when confronted with external warfare or civil disturbance. On the one hand the ruler might well, indeed usually did, require churches with extensive property and wealth to contribute to the burden of defending the community. On the other hand churches might well, especially if the ruler's authority was weak, face the need to defend themselves against the aggression of their neighbours. Churches therefore needed a military potential, whether or not the state laid this obligation upon them. Even the Church's attempts to control warfare, the Peace and Truce of God movements, tended to embroil it in military activity, since exhortation and spiritual sanction often needed the backing of force to convince a recalcitrant laity of the virtues of bridling its internal violence.[1]

The majority of secular rulers, as well as most churchmen, would probably have agreed that ideally the Church ought to be free of this most secular and undesirable of involvements. But in practice, given the institutional wealth and power of the Church, this was neither possible nor desirable. In return for their property and privileges churches had to contribute their share to the obligations of society, including those burdens connected with warfare. The complexities to which this issue could give rise can be well-illustrated by study of the Church in southern Italy in the eleventh and twelfth centuries.

When the Normans overran the area in the eleventh century,

I would like to thank Dr Chris Wickham for his advice on certain aspects of this paper.

[1] H. Hoffman, *Gottesfriede und Treuga Dei* (*MGH Schriften* 20, Stuttgart 1964) pp 104–129.

neither in the Lombard principalities of the west nor in the Byzantine theme of Langobardia were churches usually subject to formal military obligations, although they might not be wholly free form the indirect effects of such burdens. In the Lombard principalities ecclesiastical tenants might well be liable for service in their own right, and church lands were subject to corvées connected with the levying of the host.[2] Churches in the area of Byzantine rule had to pay the *strateia*, a contribution intended to finance military activities.[3]

The Norman invaders brought with them the alien concepts of fief and vassalage; the former unknown and the latter hitherto hardly-assimilated in the south, which had never fallen under the Carolingian yoke.[4] But they were generous to the Church, both with donations and with grants of immunity from all types of secular obligation. In most, and probably all, of southern Italy the rulers intended that the Church should be exempt from the provision of military contingents. Such was the case even on the island of Sicily immediately after its conquest from the Arabs, although there was still a very substantial Muslim population there, and as yet no large-scale Christian immigration.[5] Similarly, when lands held in fief were given to churches in the Norman principality of Capua they were freed from the obligation of service.[6] In a legal case of 1149 a layman claimed that his grandfather's performance of military service for a tenement showed that this could not have been owned by a church.[7]

---

[2] On the personal nature of military service in Lombard south Italy, [C.] Cahen, [*Le*] *Régime Féodal [de l'Italie Normande* (Paris 1940)] pp 28–30. The Lombard princes were reluctant to grant exemptions to individuals, even when giving them immunity from other public burdens, e.g. A. Gallo, 'I Diplomi dei principi langobardi di Benevento, di Capua e di Salerno nella traduzione Cassinese' *BISIMEAM* 52 (1937) pp 71–2 no 3. Pandulf I exempted the oxen and carts of Montecassino from carrying services with the host in 961, [E.] Gattula, *Accessiones [ad Historiam Abbatiae Casinensis* (Venice 1734)] pp 58–9.

[3] S. Borsari, 'Istituzioni feudali e parafeudali nella puglia bizantina' *A[rchivio] s[torico per le provincie] nap [oletane]* 77 (Naples 1959) pp 131–4.

[4] Cahen, *Régime Féodal* pp 41–51.

[5] [L. T.] White, *Latin Monasticism [in Norman Sicily* (Cambridge, Mass. 1938)] pp 62–3.

[6] *Reg[esto di] S. Angelo [in Formis*, ed. M. Inguanez (Montecassino 1925)] pp 100–2 no 34 (1099), a charter of prince Richard II, cf. *Cod[ice] Dipl[omatico Normanno di] Aversa*, [ed. A. Gallo (Naples 1927)] pp 399–401 no 53 (1073).

[7] *Reg. S. Angelo* pp. 207–212 no. 73. An English summary is given by [E. M.] Jamison, ['The] Norman Administration [of Apulia and Capua, most especially under Roger II and William I 1127–1166', *Papers of the British School at Rome* vi (London 1913)] pp 426–7 no 29.

Military obligation in Norman Italy

This is not to say that churches did not possess a military capability. The tenth-century evidence is often indirect, but nonetheless convincing. A series of grants from the Princes of Capua and Benevento in the years after 960 allowed churches to build or to possess fortifications.[8] A spate of modern work, most notably that of Pierre Toubert, has stressed that the primary purpose of the *incastellamento* of central and southern Italy at this period was the economic development of hitherto under-utilized territory.[9] But it is very difficult to separate the development of fortified centres from considerations of defence and military activity, and in a recent article Toubert himself has admitted that perhaps he has underestimated the military aspect of the *incastellamento*.[10] In the charter of Pandulf I of Capua to the abbey of Montecassino of 967 conceding the regalian right of fortification three sites are specifically named. Two, S. Angelo in Theodice and S. Giorgio a Liri were *castra* proper, that is fortified villages. The third, Rocca Janula, was a fortress pure and simple, designed to protect the approach to the abbey itself.[11] A similar fortress was built for strategic purposes by Abbot Manso of Cassino at Roccasecca in 995, a site the name of which shows that it was hardly the most suitable for habitation.[12] The abbey chronicle described Manso as habitually accompanied by a retinue of cavalry (*equites*). His successor, Abbot John II, personally led the attack which in 997 ravaged and burnt the township (*municipium*) of Pignatero, which had rebelled against the monks' rule. Abbot Atenulf, c1019, sent soldiers to drive the Counts of Venafro from the *castra* of Vitecuso and Aquafundata.[13]

---

[8] R. Poupardin, *Etude sur les Institutions politiques et administratives des Princepautés Lombardes de l'Italie meridionale (IX–XI siècles)* (Paris 1907) pp 108–10, 113, 115 nos 120, 121, 124, 131, 136. The best text of no 121 (967) is now *Chron[icon] Vult[ernense]*, ed. V. Federici (3 vols, Fonti per la storia d'Italia 58–60, Rome 1924–38)] 2 pp 162–4.

[9] P. Toubert, *Les Structures du Latium médiéval. Le Latium méridional et la sabine du IXe siècle a la fin du XIIe siècle* (2 vols, Rome 1973) 1 pp 303–368.

[10] [P.] Toubert, 'Pour une histoire [de l'environnement économique et social du Mont-Cassin (IXe–XIIe siècles)' *Comptes Rendus de l'Académie des Inscriptions et Belles-Lettres* (Paris 1976)] p 701.

[11] L. Tosti, *Storia della Badia di Montecassino* (3 vols, Naples 1842) 1 pp 226–8. For Rocca Janula see the pre-1944 photograph [L.] Fabiani, [*La*] *Terra [di S. Benedetto* (2 vols, Miscellanea Cassinese 33–4, Montecassino 1968)] 1 facing p 64.

[12] *Chron[ica Monasterii] Cas[inensis*, ed. H. Hoffmann, *MGH SS* 34 (1980)] bk 2 cap 14, pp 194–5. See F. Scandone, 'Roccasecca. Patria di S. Tommaso d'Aquino' *Archivio storico di Terra di Lavoro* i (Caserta 1956) 33 seq.

[13] *Chron Cas* bk 2 caps 16, 20, 37, pp 196, 204, 240.

Two factors led to a growth in military involvement by the churches of southern Italy in the years after 950. First, the Lombard princes deliberately conceded land and regalian rights, above all that of fortification, to the great abbeys in an attempt to provide a counterweight to a restive lay nobility.[14] Secondly, there was the arrival of the Normans. Churches with extensive landed holdings had to defend them during the turbulent generation (c1020–1050) in which the newcomers established themselves in the Campania, Samnium and northern Apulia. Montecassino succeeded in doing this, but the other great abbey of the principality of Capua, St. Vincent on Volturno, was less successful, and many of its lands and *castra* were permanently lost.[15] When in the second half of the century the Normans moved into the Abruzzi, the abbey of St. Clement of Casauria similarly developed and utilised a very considerable military capacity. Vigorous fortification of the abbey itself and of its lands was undertaken, the abbots personally led the defence, and indeed c1124 Abbot Gizo was alleged to have mustered as many as 4000 armed men to recover some of the monastery lands.[16] That the great abbeys which possessed extensive franchises should have, in this disturbed period, troops of their own to defend themselves is hardly surprising. Evidence for a wider clerical involvement in military affairs is more difficult to discover. Nonetheless, whatever the immunities conceded to churches by lay rulers, it seems probable that many of them in fact had troops of their own. For example, the bishops of Troia and Acherenza were killed fighting on the side of the Byzantines against the Norman invaders of Apulia at Montemaggiore in 1041.[17] They were hardly likely to have been unaccompanied. The bishop of Cassano led Calabrian attempts to resist the Normans in 1059.[18] Similarly the bishop of S. Agata dei Goti was part of the army with which Prince Robert II of Capua and Count Rainulf of

---

[14] J-M. Martin, 'Elements préféodaux dans les Princepautés de Bénévent et de Capoue (fin du VIIIe siècle—debut du XIe siècle): modalités de privatisation du pouvoir' *Structures féodales et féodalisme dans l'Occident méditerranean (X^e–XIII^{e}siècles)* (Rome 1980) pp 574–5.

[15] Fabiani, *Terra* 1 pp 63–83. Toubert, 'Pour une histoire' pp 697–700. *Chron Vult* 1 p 231, 3 pp 78–9, 84. M. del Treppo, 'La vita economica e sociale in una grande abbazia del Mezzogiorno. S. Vincenzo al Volturno nell'alto medioevo' *ASNap* 74 (1956) 101–11.

[16] *Chron[icon] Casauriense*, [Muratori 2(2)] cols 865–6, 880–1, 882 (Abbot Gizo), 885–6.

[17] *Annales Barenses*, *MGH SS* 5 p 54.

[18] Geoffrey Malaterra, *De Rebus Gestis Rogerii Calabriae et Siciliae Comitis*, ed. E. Pontieri, Muratori new edn. (1925–8) bk 1 cap 32, p 22.

Military obligation in Norman Italy

Alife defeated Roger II of Sicily at Nocera in 1132.[19] Very few charters of enfeoffment survive from Norman Italy, but one which does was given by the abbey of St. Lawrence, Aversa, in that same year of 1132.[20] The early twelfth century was a period in which the government of the princes of Capua and the dukes of Apulia was becoming less and less effective, and the 1130s saw a civil war in southern Italy as Roger II strove to unify the whole area under his rule. There was thus a real need for churches to be able to defend themselves.

Of course the Church could employ moral and spiritual as well as temporal weapons. One device which the great monasteries used was to secure oaths from lay rulers and nobles to defend and protect their property. Montecassino in particular adopted this practice, but in the early twelfth century so too did Casauria and La Cava, near Salerno.[21] The Peace and Truce of God came late to southern Italy, under papal auspices at the Councils of Melfi in 1089 and Troia in 1093.[22] But in the years after this some local bishops attempted to promote them. In 1105, when the duchy of Gaeta was riven by internal dispute, Bishop Albert secured an agreement from all the contending parties, including the duke, Richard de l'Aigle, to protect the property and personnel of the Church.[23] At about the same time four Abruzzi bishops combined together to excommunicate a local count who had, among other sins, attacked church lands. The biographer of one of these prelates, Bishop Bernard of Marsia, particularly praised his hero's attempts to bring concord to those quarrelling.[24] But there can be little doubt that when the lay ruler was unwilling or unable to help, churches had to be prepared to defend themselves by physical as well as spiritual means.

---

[19] *Monumenta Bambergensia*, ed. P. Jaffe (Bibliotheca Rerum Germanicarum 5, Berlin 1868) pp 442–4 no 259.

[20] *Cod Dipl Aversa* pp 51–2 no 31.

[21] G. A. Loud, 'Five unpublished charters of the Norman Princes of Capua', *Benedictina* 27 (Rome 1980) pp 173–4 no 3 (1099). Gattula. *Accessiones* pp 222 (1105), 225 (1106-7), 229 (1112), 239 (1123). G. Tescione, *Roberto, Conte normanno di Alife, Caiazzo e S. Agata dei Goti* (Caserta 1975) pp 46–7 no 3 (1094–1105), 49 no 5 (1105). A. de Francesco, 'Origini e sviluppo del feudalismo in Molise' *ASNap* 34 (1909) pp 669 n 1, 670 n 1. *Cod[ex] Dipl[omaticus] Caiet [anus]* (4 vols, Montecassino 1887–1960) 2 pp 178–80 no 282 (1107). All of these were to Montecassino. *Chron Casauriense* col 1006. [Archivio della badia di S. Trinita di] Cava [dei Tirreni,] Arm. Mag. E. 21 (1111).

[22] Lupus Protospatharius, *Annales* ad. an. 1089, MGH SS 5 p 62. Mansi 20 col 790.

[23] *Cod Dipl Caiet* 2 pp 174–6 no 280.

[24] *Vita Sancti Berardi*, *ASB* Nov 2 (1894) pp 133–4.

The position changed with the successful incorporation of the whole of southern Italy into a unified kingdom by Roger II. The state was both willing and able to defend its churches. The question was rather what contribution the Church was to make to the defence of the state.

The king of Sicily faced both the problem of maintaining his internal control over the disparate parts of his dominions, and that of defending the *regno* against his external enemies. With relations with the papacy uncertain, both the Eastern and Western Empires hostile, and political exiles including the former prince of Capua ready to exploit any internal difficulties to regain their position, this latter consideration was naturally of major importance. Hence in the early 1140s, perhaps during his long stay at Silva Marca in Apulia in the summer of 1142, king Roger began a major reorganization of military obligations on the mainland, creating a special and extensive category of fiefs owing service directly to the monarch.[25] Almost certainly connected with this was a law, the details of which are known from a later revival by Frederick II, which forbade alienations to the Church which would lead to a diminution in such service.[26]

These measures were part of a much wider, and very determined, royal campaign to prevent the alienation of regalian rights as a whole. In 1144 a full-scale investigation into the validity of existing privileges was undertaken.[27] At about the same time a general decree was promulgated against the alienation of regalia, which was incorporated in both of the surviving manuscripts which purport to contain king Roger's legislation.[28] Ecclesiastical franchises were particularly affected by the king's determination to reserve criminal jurisdiction, at least, even in the case of the most

---

[25] [E. M.] Jamison, 'Additional work [on the Catalogus Baronum' *BISIMEAM* 83 (1971)] pp 15–17.

[26] *Liber Augustalis* bk 3 cap 29, 'De rebus stabilibus non alienandis', *Die Konstitution Friedrichs II von Hohenstaufen für sein Königreich Sizilien*, edd. H. Conrad, T. von der Lieck Buyken & W. Wagner (Cologne 1973) pp 284–6. White, *Latin Monasticism* p 62 dates this simply 'before 1148'.

[27] [K. A.] Kehr, [*Die*] *Urkunden* [*der normannisch-sizilischen Könige* (Innsbruck 1902)] pp 348, 424–7 nos 10–11.

[28] Clause 4 of the Vatican MS (Cod. Vat. Lat. 8782), and clause 3 of the Cassinese (Cod. Cas.468), F. Brandileone, *Il Diretto romano nelle legge normanni e sueve del regno di Sicilia* (Turin 1884) pp 97, 120. The Cassinese, the later of these two sets of assizes, must be dated before 1153, [E. M.] Jamison, ['The administration of the County of] Molise [in the twelfth and thirteenth centuries] I', [*EHR* 44 (1929)] pp 548–552, 556–7.

privileged churches, over really serious crimes, a resolve equally strongly maintained by Roger's successors.[29] The regalian right over fortifications was also revived and strengthened, and in some cases, notably the abbey of Montecassino, churches were deprived of some of their strongholds.[30]

Henceforth property which was part of a fief owing military service could only be given to a church on one of three conditions. Either the former lay owner remained responsible for the service, or the church was exempted by the king from the service owed, or the church was henceforth itself responsible for the service. Exemptions were occasionally given. For example, in December 1156 king William I gave the archbishop and cathedral of Palermo the fief of Broccato, and exempted both the demesne and the tenants from knight service.[31] But from the king's point of view such generosity was much less serious on the island of Sicily than in the mainland provinces, especially in those near to his vulnerable northern frontier. Hence, as part of the organization of the defence of the realm in the 1140s churches which had hitherto been free of the burden of military obligations to the lay ruler found themselves subject to them. As one of the royal constables, Count Bohemond of Manopello, said to an Abruzzi abbot dissatisfied with this new state of affairs, 'the lord king . . . has many who pray for him in his kingdom, but few who fight'.[32]

The defensive resources of the kingdom at the end of king Roger's reign were recorded in a text, now universally known as the *Catalogus Baronum*, drawn up *c*1150, and revised *c*1167.[33] This recorded the fiefs both of churchmen and of laymen in all the mainland provinces except Calabria. But the role of the Church in the *Catalogus* raises certain problems which have not been fully elucidated.

---

[29] E.g. [R.] Pirro, [*Sicula Sacra* (2 vols, Palermo 1733)] 2 pp 1021-2 (1144) for the monastery of S. Angelo di Brolo; *ibid* 2 pp 1046-7 (1145) for S. Maria Annunziata of Mandanici; *ibid* 1 p 109 (1177), William II to the archbishop of Palermo; *ibid* 2 p 935 (1209), Frederick II to the Hospitaller priory of Messina. Cf. Fabiani, *Terra* 2 pp 19–20, 39–41.
[30] *Annales Casinenses* ad. an. 1140, *MGH SS* 19 p 309.
[31] Pirro 1 pp 97–8.
[32] *Chron Casauriense* col 892.
[33] *Cat[alogus] Bar[onum]*, ed. E. M. Jamison (Fonti per la storia d'Italia 101, Rome 1972).] Its editor is very insistent, 'Additional work' pp 3–7, that it was not 'a mere register of normal military service', but a record of the *magna expeditio*, the extraordinary defensive military levy.

To begin with, only twenty-two churches are in fact recorded.[34] Quite a few of these are, as one might expect, in the Abruzzi, since this was the most vulnerable area threatened by an imperial invasion. E. M. Jamison has shown that in some cases property which was ultimately held by churches was recorded in the *Catalogus* under the names of lay tenants, responsible for the service not to the churches but to lay tenants-in-chief. The examples which she cites are the bishop of Aprutium and the abbeys of Casauria and St. John in Venere. Ultimate proprietorship, and part of the revenues and other services remained with the church.[35] This practice was quite widespread in the Abruzzi region. To the cases advanced by Jamison one can add others. Thus three fiefs listed in a royal charter of 1185 as the property of the bishop of Valva were shown in the *Catalogus* as being held by laymen, one in chief and two by a sub-tenant.[36] What is also very interesting here is that while the bishop of Aprutium and the abbeys of Casauria and St. John in Venere were all listed as holding fiefs in their own right,[37] the bishop of Valva was not. There may be the slight possibility that these particular territories were acquired by the see after the compilation of the *Catalogus*. We know for example that the bishopric was given another fief, for which knight service was owed, by Henry VI in 1195.[38] But if that was the case, what contribution did the bishop of Valva make to the defence of the realm in the time of Roger II? One suspects that in the Abruzzi lay tenants-in-chief and their vassals were very commonly responsible for the service from church lands, but to confirm the ubiquity of this practice systematic investigation of the property of all the major churches would be needed. One factor which should certainly be stressed is that the presence of these laymen with fiefs on church land, and apparently very little connection with the churches in question, was not solely the result of pressure from the royal government to ensure that military service was performed. Sometimes this was the product of the forcible alienation by

---

[34] Cahen, *Régime Féodal* p 131.
[35] Jamison, 'Additional work' pp 18–21.
[36] Orsa, Prezza and Raiano, Kehr, *Urkunden* p 439 no 20 (there wrongly dated to 1170). For the correct date, N. Kamp, *Kirche und Monarchie im Staufischen Königreich Sizilien* (3 vols, Munich 1973–5) 1 p 61 n 6. Cf. *Cat Bar* pp 243, 245 arts 1188, 1195 (henceforth cited by article no only).
[37] *Cat Bar* arts 1204–8, 1217, 1221.
[38] [F.] Ughelli, [*Italia Sacra* (2nd ed, 10 vols, Venice 1717–22)] 1 cols 1129–30.

Military obligation in Norman Italy

laymen of church property, as for example the *castrum* of S. Velentino, seized by a certain Richard Turgisius from the monastery of Casauria in 1140, and recorded under his name in the *Catalogus Baronum*.[39] Another factor which might lead a church to have no apparent connection with military service rendered for land, which sources other than the Catalogue suggest was the property of that church, was genuine divided ownership. The complications of Lombard inheritance law meant that many *castra* in the Abruzzi were held in common. Hence a layman who held part of a property while a church had the rest might render service for the whole fief.[40]

The church with the heaviest military obligation in its own right listed in the Catalogue was the abbey of Montecassino, recorded as providing 60 knights and 200 sergeants for the extraordinary levy.[41] In this case the obligation was one for the whole extensive franchise held by the abbey, and not for any specific fiefs. The peculiar position of Montecassino was signified by the fact that whereas, normally, two sets of obligations were recorded, one a 'normal' quota, and the other with the *augmentum* showing the full total of knights actually available (a distinction also present in eleventh and twelfth century Normandy),[42] only one figure is given in this case. The peculiar juridical position of Montecassino, maintained despite some interference with its franchise by Roger II, and its key strategic position on the Via Latina between Rome and Capua, help to explain this anomaly. When other churches were recorded in the Catalogue their obligation was usually for particular fiefs, and not for their land as a whole.[43] But within the huge Cassinese franchise, with its (by the mid-twelfth century) thirty three *castra* there was clearly a very substantial military class, and indeed quite an elaborate social structure within that class.[44]

---

[39] *Chron Casauriense* cols 1008–9. *Cat Bar* art 1014.

[40] Hence the Abbot of St. Bartholomew, Carpineto, obtained Vicalvi by an exchange with the Bishop of Penne in 1123, Ughelli 1 col 1118, but later ⅓ of this was held by a vassal of a lay tenant-in-chief, *Cat Bar* art 1196. For another example of a church holding ⅔ of a *castrum* see *Chron Casauriense* col 1007 (1136).

[41] *Cat Bar* art 823.

[42] On the *augmentum*, Cahen, *Régime Féodal* pp 69–71. Cf. C. W. Hollister, *The Military Organization of Norman England* (Oxford 1965) pp 75–81.

[43] An exception is the monastery of St. John in Lamis, near Foggia, though here an *augmentum* is recorded, *Cat Bar* art 376.

[44] For the *castra* see the bull of Alexander III of 1159, PL 200 col 77. For the abbey knights

On what basis was it decided which church lands should be held in fief, and which in free tenure? As we have seen, even in the Abruzzi there is no great consistency in the obligations recorded in the *Catalogus Baronum*. Why did the bishops of Aprutium, Forcone and Penne owe service for fiefs, either held in demesne or by vassals, but not those of Chieti, Marsia and Valva? With regard to Valva it has been suggested that the answer may lie in fiefs for which the service was actually done by lay tenants, who, though performing the service for eclesiastical land, were vassals of lay barons rather than of the church. But even if this element of 'hidden' service was widespread in the *Catalogus*, problems still remain. We know that lay fiefs existed on the land of the bishop of Aprutium, but the latter also held in chief a series of fiefs for which he himself owed, with the *augmentum*, 24 knights and 40 sergeants.[45]

The problem becomes more complicated when one turns from the frontiers to Apulia. Here some prelates, the bishops of Tricarico, Civitate and Melfi, and the abbot of the Holy Trinity, Venosa, for example, held fiefs,[46] but the total represented only a small minority of the Apulian bishops and abbots. In the principality of Capua there are, with the exception of Montecassino, no ecclesiastical contingents listed at all. Was this because churches had always been firmly exempt from service in Capua, whereas in Apulia before 1140 this principle was less firmly applied? But I know of no pre-1140 instance of an Apulian church actually doing service to the duke for a fief. An obvious explanation might be that the fiefs for which Apulian churches owed service had been recently acquired, after the imposition of the new royal obligations in the early 1140s. In one case at least this seems to be correct. The abbot of St. Mary at Banzi is recorded as holding Banzi itself for three knights, or seven with the *augmentum*.[47] In 1153 Abbot Roger of Banzi was selling property, including a church, to the abbey of La Cava in return for a substantial sum in cash and precious goods which he proposed to

see the *Lex Municipalis* of Pontecorvo (1190), ed Fabiani, *Terra* 1 pp 427–30. There are elaborate thirteenth-century regulations for service, *ibid* 2 pp 176–9. In some of these, e.g. those for the *castrum* of S. Pietro in Fine, there are references to nobles; Montecassino, Archivio dell'abbazia, Registrum II Bernardi (Reg no 6) fol 13^V.

[45] *Cat Bar* art 1221.
[46] *ibid* arts 107, 386, 402, 408.
[47] *ibid* art 87.

use to liquidate the debt owed to the king *'de castello Bancie'*.[48] That the abbey had recently purchased Banzi and its territory is also suggested by its omission in two bulls of Paschal II listing the monastery's possessions, whereas it is recorded in a later bull of 1172.[49]

But this was clearly not the case for every ecclesiastical fief recorded in the *Catalogus Baronum*. The bishop of Melfi owed, with the *augmentum*, 8 knights and 100 sergeants for the fief of Gaudiano, which had been given to his see as far back as 1097 by Duke Roger of Apulia. There was furthermore no mention of military service in the latter's donation charter, rather the duke exempted the property from all service and dues to the state.[50] Similarly, the abbot of Venosa owed his contingent for a series of fiefs, most of which had been given to his house by Counts Robert and William of the Principate between 1096 and 1105.[51]

It seems certain therefore that fiefs already owing military service which had been newly acquired by churches would still owe that service, unless specifically exempted by the king. But it is by no means clear what criteria were used to decide which property already owned by churches c1140 should henceforth be classed as royal fiefs for which service, and the accompanying financial obligations, were owed. Some churches may have been penalized for the indiscretion of their prelates during periodic moments of political crisis. Montecassino was distrusted by the Norman kings after it had thrown in its lot with the imperial invasion of 1137.[52] But it is difficult to make any coherent connection—the abbots of Venosa were by no means out of favour at the royal court, and their church held the tombs of Robert Guiscard and other famous ancestors of the king.[53]

---

[48] Cava, Arm. Mag. H. 15.

[49] P. F. Kehr, 'Papsturkunden in Salerno, La Cava und Neapel', *Nachrichten der K. Gesellschaft der Wissenschaften zu Gottingen. Phil-hist. Klasse* (1900) pp 221–7 nos 2–3 (1102 & 1106). P. F. Kehr, 'Papsturkunden in Rom. Die romische Bibliotheken III', *ibid* (1903) pp 149–150 no 4 (1172).

[50] *Cat Bar* art 402; Ughelli 1 cols 923–4.

[51] Corneto (1096 & 1105), half of Asoli Satriano (1098), Orta (1101) and S. Giovanni in Fronte (1105), L. R. Ménager, 'Les fondations monastiques de Robert Guiscard', *QFIAB* 39 (1959) pp 95–101 nos 21, 23–4, 27–8; *Cat Bar* art 408.

[52] White, *Latin Monasticism* p 57. Most of the supposed royal diplomas for Montecassino are thirteenth-century forgeries, C-R. Brühl, *Urkunden und Kanzlei König Rogers II von Sizilien* (Cologne 1978) pp 164–172.

[53] For Abbot Egidius of Venosa's influence, *La Historia o Liber de Regno Sicilie di Ugo Falcando*,

One criterion which might have been used was whether or not the church held regalian rights such as that of levying the *plateaticum* toll, which were normally conceded to holders of royal fiefs (*feuda in baronia* as they were later known) as a recompense for the service owed.[54] But the abbey of La Cava, which all but rivalled Montecassino as the richest and most extensive property holder among mainland monasteries, held both regalian fiscal rights as the *plateaticum* and also *castra* which it had been given the right to fortify by the dukes of Apulia,[55] and yet was not recorded in the *Catalogus Baronum*.

Therefore, either the clerical contingents listed there were simply the result of arbitrary arrangements made by the Norman rulers with some churches, but not others, on no very rational basis, or the *Catalogus* is, at least insofar as clerical fiefs are concerned, incomplete. Perhaps both of these statements are true. Although extremely detailed and where ownership can be checked very accurate, the Catalogue has survived only at third-hand, as a late thirteenth-century copy of an early thirteenth-century copy of the original manuscript. It lacks neither omissions or alterations in the proper order of fiefs, and the likelihood is that some privileged churches have been deliberately ignored.[56] But on quite what basis the choice was made is by no means clear. There is evidence to suggest that churches other than those listed made enfeoffments themselves, and had a military potential. A charter of William I to La Cava of 1154 gave the abbot and his successors the right to promote vassals of the monastery to knighthood, but unfortunately the document's authenticity, in its present form at any rate, is

---

ed. G. B. Siragusa (Fonti per la storia d'Italia 22, Rome 1897) p 138. For the tomb of Guiscard, William of Malmesbury, *Gesta Regum*, ed. W. Stubbs (2 vols, RS 1887-9) 2 p 322.

[54] Jamison, 'Molise II', *EHR* 45 (1930) pp 22-4, 'Additional work' p 14.

[55] [P.] Guillaume, *Essai [Historique sur l'Abbaye de Cava* (Cava dei Tirreni 1877)] pp xvii-xviii appendix E (1100), xxvii-xxviii appendix H (1123). L. von Heinemann, *Normannische Herzogs- und Königsurkunden aus Unteritalien und Sizilien* (Tübingen 1899) pp 19-20 no 10 (1111).

[56] Jamison, 'Additional work' pp 23-56, especially 29, 46-7, & 58. This may be the case with La Cava, which was much favoured by the Norman kings, not least in that it supplied the monks for William II's cherished foundation of Monreale; White, *Latin Monasticism* pp 134-6. Certainly the royal justiciar William of S. Severino, in a charter of 1187, was very careful to distinguish between land of the monastery within his barony of Cilento and the fiefs of that barony; Cava, Arm. Mag. L. 21.

Military obligation in Norman Italy

questionable.[57] Many of its details may however be accurate. The monastery of St. Lawrence, Aversa, which we have already seen making an enfeoffment in return for knight service in 1132, granted fiefs on its lands around Foggia in Apulia to men of knightly status in the 1180s.[58] A sergeant of the bishop of Aversa witnessed a charter in 1151.[59] One also wonders whether knights who acted as advocates of churches in legal cases had any formal links with those institutions.[60] On the other hand we must be careful not to assume that all references to *servitio* and *feuda* in ecclesiastical documents imply *military* obligations. The fiefs of St. Lawrence, Aversa, at Foggia were granted for rent, not service, presumably because the monastery itself lacked obligations to the king. But such terminology was used in a very vague sense in southern Italy. Both in the Campania and in the Abruzzi, even as late as 1200, one can find 'fiefs' which were held by sharecropping arrangements, or in return for food-renders, small money-payments or corvées.[61] Even within the military context *feudum* might have different meanings.[62]

The strongest evidence to suggest that the *Catalogus Baronum* is at best a very incomplete guide to the military potential of the south Italian Church comes in a similar, but much briefer, text which was copied as an appendix by the scribe of the manuscript through which the Catalogue itself has been preserved—a list of the prelates holding fiefs in the Capitanata c1243.[63] Most of those named were not included in the *Catalogus*. Many of the fiefs listed were held by laymen in the mid-twelfth century.[64] In some of these cases one may well be dealing with the phenomenon familiar from the Abruzzi—laymen performing the service owed from

---

[57] Guillaume, *Essai* pp xxxv–xxxvi appendix L. Jamison, 'Molise II' pp 10–11.
[58] *Cod Dipl Aversa* pp 210–211 no 113 (1181), 233–4 no 125 (1184).
[59] *ibid* pp 102–3 no 59.
[60] E.g. *Regesto di S. Leonardo di Siponto*, [ed. F. Camobreco (Rome 1913)] p 5 no 4 (1129), 14 no 21 (1144), 15–6 nos 23–4 (1146).
[61] *Reg S. Angelo* pp 137–40 no 49 (1157). *Codice Diplomatico Sulmonese*, ed. N. F. Faraglia (Lanciano 1888) pp 51–2 no 40 (1178), 60–1 no 45 (1201). Ughelli 1 cols 1125–7 (1195).
[62] Jamison, 'Additional work' pp 9–10.
[63] *Cat Bar* arts 1428–42.
[64] E.g. Montecalvo, held in 1243 by the abbot of S.Elena, in the Catalogue by a layman, *Cat Bar* arts 1428, 385; Casale S. Trifone, held 1243 by the abbot of St. John in Plano, in the mid-twelfth century by Count Godfrey of Lesina, *ibid* arts 1430, 387; Ururi and Ilice, held 1243 by the bishop of Larino, earlier by tenants of the Count of Civitate, *ibid* arts 1437, 307, 309.

lands actually owned by a church. We know, for example, from a legal case roughly contemporary with the compilation of the Catalogue, that a man listed in the latter as owing one knight for property at Castiglione near Foggia was in fact a vassal of Montecassino, and according to the court, the abbot was responsible for ensuring that the service was performed, though the Catalogue makes no mention of this.[65] But in other instances churchmen were said in 1243 to hold fiefs which were not listed in the *Catalogus Baronum*, and which were very clearly in the possession of those churches in the 1150s. Thus the thirteenth-century fief of S. Lorenzo, held by the Bishop of Troia, was one of the properties of that see included in a confirmation of its possessions by William I of 1156, and then held free of regalian obligations, including the *collecta* (financial aids, including those from fiefs).[66] St. Stephen in Juncarico, a fief held by La Cava in 1243, was in the twelfth century a subordinate cell of the abbey.[67] The *casale* of Torremaggiore, held by the abbey of that name, was another fief in the 1243 list, although it had been confirmed as being free from all service by Robert Guiscard, and by king Tancred in 1192.[68]

Our conclusions must be two-fold. The *Catalogus Baronum* was as its modern editor has made clear, not an immutable register of obligations, but a document designed to meet a specific situation at a specific time. Military obligations were revised and altered, and the Catalogue was only one of the documents generated by this problem. Other registers of fiefs and service, now lost, were made.[69] One cannot simply say that assessments were revised under Frederick II, and that heavier military obligations were imposed on the Church during his reign. This was almost certainly true, but new obligations were laid on churches under the Norman kings

---

[65] *ibid* art 400. *Le Colonie cassinesi in Capitanata* IV *Troia*, ed. T. Leccisotti (Miscellanea Cassinese 29, Montecassino 1958) pp 93–5 no 28. English summary by Jamison, 'Norman Administration' pp 432–3 no 37.

[66] *Cat Bar* art 1433. *Les Chartes de Troia (1024–1266)*, ed. J. M. Martin (Codice Dioplomatico Pugliese 21, Bari 1976) pp 239–41 no 75. *Collecta* is a rather ambiguous term in a twelfth-century context, but it certainly includes the feudal aid, Jamison, 'Molise II' pp 8–9, 28–9 doc 5 (1226).

[67] *Cat Bar* art 1440; Cava, Arm. Mag. H.10 (1152), I. 11 (1174).

[68] Guiscard's diploma of 1067 is known only from that of Tancred, ed. in T. Leccisotti, *Il Monasterium Terrae Maioris* (Montecassino 1942) pp 79–82.

[69] Note the reference to quaternions of fiefs in the Molise document of 1226 cited above n 66.

too, and not only in the years immediately after the unification of the *regno* by Roger II. In many cases these were for fiefs owing service to the king obtained by churches. But service might also be required from newly-consolidated blocks of ecclesiastical demesne, perhaps built up from small beginnings. This was probably the case for the service of 20 sailors for the royal fleet from the tenement of S. Lucia from which William II exempted the bishopric of Lipari-Patti in Sicily in 1177.[70] Another, and clearer, example was S. Severo in Apulia, developed in the twelfth century by the monks of Torremaggiore from an open village into a substantial walled settlement, some of whose inhabitants were of knightly status, with, by the early thirteenth century, its own constable.[71] By the time of Frederick II it was, perhaps hardly surprisingly, no longer treated as the allodial property of the abbot, but as a royal fief.[72]

All this suggests that churches on which these new obligations were placed were able to fulfil them, and indeed it was because they had the military capacity to fulfil them that they were given such burdens. Not only did the *Catalogus Baronum* conceal ecclesiastical proprietorship of many lands behind a screen of laymen actually performing the military service for such lands, but behind the quotas laid down for the *magna expeditio* of the mid-twelfth century, the south Italian Church was much better able to involve itself in the defence of the kingdom than might at first be supposed. Up to 1140 the Church in Norman Italy was largely absolved from military obligations to lay rulers. But it was not, and never had been, defenceless, and after 1140, albeit in a very unsystematic fashion, the state recognized this and took steps accordingly.

University of Leeds

---

[70] Kehr, *Urkunden* pp 444–5 no 24, cf. White, *Latin Monasticism* pp 63, 98.
[71] M. Fuiano, *Città e Borghi in Publia nel medioevo* (Naples 1972) pp 137–47, 170–2 doc no 11. For the constable, *Regesto di S.Leonardo di Siponto* pp 86–7 no 138 (1203).
[72] Matthew Paris, *Chronica Majora*, ed. H. R. Luard (7 vols, RS 1872–84) 3 p 555.

MONASTERIES AS 'WAR MEMORIALS':
BATTLE ABBEY AND LA VICTOIRE

by ELIZABETH M. HALLAM

CHARTERS, CHRONICLES and letters which record the foundation of religious houses in the period 1050–1250 abound in the images of both war and peace. Whereas king Henry I of England, a military leader of renown, founded an abbey at Cirencester for the repose of his soul and the stability of his realm,[1] Bernard of Clairvaux, that celebrated man of religion, wrote of the new Cistercian abbey of Rievaulx as an outpost of his lord which he proposed to occupy.[2] The juxtaposition of such conflicting ideas is epitomised by the military orders, formed to fight holy wars against the infidel; and a logical symbol of the triumph of Christianity is the foundation of a monastery such as Louis IX's Franciscan friary at Jaffa, created in 1252 after the capture of this Moslem stronghold,[3] or the building of Alcobaça by Alphonso I of Portugal (c1153) after his great victory over the Moors at Santaren.[4]

Far more startling is the monastery intended to glorify the triumph of one Christian ruler over another in battle. Such an institution might *a priori* appear a product of the period after c1250, when political crusades were quite frequently mounted by one sacral king against another; and indeed, Charles of Anjou founded the Cistercian abbey of Vittoria in c1273–4 to commemorate his defeat of the Hohenstaufen at Tagliacozzo.[5] Much later, too, in 1438, archbishop Henry Chichele was to create All Souls' College

---

[1] *The Cartulary of Cirencester Abbey, Gloucestershire*, ed C. D. Ross 1 (London 1964) pp 21–3.
[2] *St Bernard of Clairvaux seen through his Selected Letters*, ed and trans B. Scott-James (Chicago 1953) pp 130–1.
[3] William of Saint-Pathus, *La vie et les miracles de Monseigneur Saint Louis, roi de France*, ed M. C. d'Espagne (Paris 1971) p 40.
[4] P. L. Janauschek, *Originum Cisterciensium Tomus I* (Vindobonae 1877) p 110.
[5] *Ibid* p 261 (he also founded Realvalle to celebrate the battle of Benevento); Muratori 16 p 670; F. Ughelli, *Italia Sacra sive de episcopis Italie et insularum adjacentium* 7 (Rome 1659) p 810.

Oxford in memory of Henry V and the many others who had lost their lives in the wars with France.[6] In the eleventh and twelfth centuries the Church had manifested a particularly strong disapproval of internecine strife between lay rulers, and the peace of god, which could however involve a holy war against peacebreakers, was an attempt to curb the warfare endemic in western society.[7] Likewise, penances were on occasions laid by the Church on victorious armies.[8] Yet two crucially important military engagements in this period, Hastings in 1066 and Bouvines in 1214, were commemorated and celebrated by major religious foundations: Battle abbey and Notre Dame de la Victoire.

The creation of these monasteries and their role as 'war memorials' are a telling illustration of the ability of two powerful rulers, William the Conqueror and Philip Augustus, to stamp the imagery of secular authority and bellicose concerns upon institutions which represented the reforming church at its most withdrawn from lay preoccupations. Explanations for how they were able to do this must be sought in the general context of lay patronage of monasteries in this period, and in royal patronage in particular.

In setting these royal foundations in their context, several considerations must be borne in mind. One is that monasteries were built for a great diversity of reasons, both sacred and secular, during this period.[9] The creation of an ecclesiastical community

---

[6] *Statutes of the Colleges of Oxford* 1 (London 1853): *Statutes of All Souls College* pp 4–8, 10–12.

[7] H. E. J. Cowdrey, 'The peace and truce of God in the eleventh century', *PP* 43 (1970) pp 42–62; [C.] Erdmann, [*The Origin of the Idea of Crusade*, trans M. W. Baldwin and W. Goffart (Princeton 1977)] pp 62–4: 'the many provisions of the peace of God's resolutions against breakers of the peace amount to no less than a new form of war, one provided for this time by the church itself' (p 63).

[8] [R. H.] Bainton, [*Christian attitudes towards war and peace, a Historical Survey and critical re-evaluation* (New York 1960)] pp 109–116.

[9] S. Wood, *English Monasteries and their patrons in the Thirteenth Century* (Oxford 1955); [C. N. L.] Brooke, ['Princes and kings as patrons of monasteries, Normandy and England', *Mendola* 4 (1971) pp 125–44]; [E. M. Hallam, 'Aspects of the] monastic patronage [of the English and French royal houses, c1130–1270', unpublished Ph D thesis, University of London, 1976]; [E. M. Hallam,] 'Henry II [as a founder of monasteries', *JEH* 28 (1977) pp 113–132]; E. Mason, '*Timeo barones et donas ferentes*', *SCH* 15 (1978) pp 61–75; R. Mortimer, 'Religious and secular motives for some English monastic foundations', *SCH* 15 (1978) pp 77–85; C. Holdsworth, 'A Cistercian monastery and its neighbours', *History Today* 30 (August 1980) pp 32–7; J. C. Ward, 'Fashions in monastic endowment: the foundations of the Clare family, 1066–1314', *JEH* 32 (1981) pp 427–51.

might be at once an expression of piety, a means of securing eternal salvation, a fulfillment of a vow or penance, and a statement of the wealth, power and pretensions of the founder. The more secular the approach of the patron, the greater the problems for the religious, and particularly for those strict orders such as the Cistercians, whose customs were designed to isolate them from the snares of worldliness.

The potential problems and tensions were at their most acute where royal founders and patrons were involved; for to a monarch, an imposing religious foundation could be an important statement of royal power and God-given authority. A new and splendid church was a durable manifestation of holy kingship. The symbolic value of the magnificent dynastic church was to be exploited consciously and consistently by both the French and English ruling houses after the middle of the thirteenth century.[10] Yet much earlier than that, royal patronage of monasteries frequently had a significant, if less explicit, political dimension.[11] For this and other reasons, the new, strict orders at times found their royal patrons the source of major difficulties in the eleventh and twelfth centuries.

Henry II of England, for example, by making relatively small grants to the exceedingly austere order of Grandmont, probably helped to precipitate a major crisis in its organisation; while Louis IX of France, that most pious of monarchs, had the Cistercian abbey of Royaumont, founded (though not used) as his burial church, ornamented far too lavishly for the rules of the order to allow, and in 1253 the general chapter ordered much of the decoration to be torn down.[12] The power of the king in both the secular and ecclesiastical spheres, his spiritual attributes and temporal wealth, could make it difficult for the most determinedly austere of monks to resist his gifts. A graphic illustration of this is given by the biographer of Hugh of Lincoln, the remarkable

---

[10] [E. M. Hallam,] *Capetian France* [*987–1328* (London 1980)] pp 260–3; E. M. Hallam, 'Royal burial [and the cult of kingship in England and France, 1060–1330', *J Med H* 8 (1982) pp 359–80. The role of Westminster and other English houses in upholding the 'status of the dynasty' in the period 1066–1154 is somewhat exaggerated in E Mason, 'Pro statu et incolumitate regni mei . . .', *SCH* 18 (1982) pp 99–117.

[11] 'Henry II', *passim*. This theme is treated more fully in my forthcoming study of the monastic patronage of the English and French royal houses.

[12] 'Monastic patronage' pp 241; 368–71; E. M. Hallam, 'Henry II, Richard I and order of Grandmont', *J Med H* 1 (1975) pp 165–86; *Capetian France* p 232.

Carthusian monk elected as third prior of Henry II's monastic foundation at Witham in Somerset. The king was tardy in providing funds for the building of the church and instead looked for a lavish book of scriptures to present to the community. He discovered the celebrated Winchester bible, recently completed by the black monks of St Swithuns, took it away from its owners and gave it to the Carthusians at Witham. At first, they were delighted with the gift, but it was not long before one of the St Swithuns monks visited Witham and described the king's abduction of their valued book. Prior Hugh, greatly shocked, immediately offered to return the volume to its rightful owners; but the monk was horrified, and reminded Hugh that 'it would be fatal to his own church that Hugh should on any pretext decline a royal gift which had so fortunately won the king's favour.' Such were the problems of royal patronage that the bible had to be returned in secret.[13]

What were William the Conqueror's intentions when he founded Battle abbey in about 1070? In this period, great caution must be used in drawing evidence from even near-contemporary accounts of the progress of monastic foundations. The monks themselves frequently composed both their foundation charters and chronicles from common material.[14] In Battle's case, however there are no such early documents extant. During the twelfth century its community developed a stirring and dramatic account of its foundation and early history. The twin aims were to extricate it from the jurisdiction of the bishops of Chichester, and to emphasise the special connections of Battle with the conquering Norman race. To that end, William the Conqueror was portrayed as making a vow before the battle of Hastings that if God granted him victory he would found a monastery on the battlefield as an atonement and for the salvation of all, and that he would give it special and unusual privileges and liberties worthy of its elevated status.[15]

---

[13] *Magna Vita Sancti Hugonis*, ed D. L. Douie and H. Farmer, 1 (London 1961) pp 85–7; 'Henry II' pp 118–19.

[14] M. Chibnall, 'Charter and chronicle: the use of archive sources by Norman historians', *Church and Government in the Middle Ages*, ed C. N. L. Brooke, D. E. Luscombe, G. H. Martin and D. M. Owen (Cambridge 1976) pp 1–17.

[15] [*The*] *Chronicle of Battle* [*Abbey*, ed and transa E. Searle, OMT (Oxford 1980)] pp 13–23; [A.] Gransden, *Historical Writing in England c550–c1307* (London 1974)] pp 272–9.

Monasteries as 'war memorials'

The story was drawn together from local tradition and from accounts of the Conquest in Norman sources such as, perhaps, Wace's *Roman de Rou*.[16] Its first written appearance seems to have been in the charters forged for the Battle monks by the Westminster atelier[17] in 1154–5, and used to pursue the jurisdictional dispute with Hilary bishop of Chichester.[18] In one of these, purporting to be Battle's foundation charter, the Conqueror declares:

> *quod cum in angliam venissem et in finibus Hasting' cum exercitu applicuissem contra hostes meos qui mihi regnum anglie iniuste conabantur auferre, in procinctu belli iam armatus coram Baronibus et militibus meis cum favore omnium ad eorum corda roboranda votum feci ECCLESIAM quandam ad honorem dei construere pro communi salute si per dei gratiam obtinere possemus victoriam. Quam cum essemus adepti votum deo solvens in honore SANCTI TRINITATIS ET BEATI MARTINI confessoris Christi ecclesiam construxi pro salute anime mee et antecessoris mei regis EADWARDI et uxoris mee MATHILDIS Regine et successorum meorum in regno et pro salute omnium quorum labore et auxilio Regnum obtinui et illorum maxime qui in ipso bello occubuerunt. Et quia in hoc loco sic constructa est ecclesia deus mihi victoriam prestitit in bello, ob victorie memoriam ipsum locum Bellum appellari volui.*

The house is to be given liberties and exemptions modelled upon those of Christ Church Canterbury.[19] The Battle chronicler, writing in the 1180s, brings the same scene vividly to life. He makes William declare that, confident in God's aid,

> I make a vow that on this very battlefield I shall found a monastery for the salvation of all, and especially for those who fall here, to the honour of God and his saints, where servants of God may be supported: a fitting monastery, with a worthy liberty. Let it be an atonement: a haven for all as free as the one I conquer for myself.

---

[16] *Chronicle of Battle* pp 15–23.
[17] *Facsimiles of English Royal Writs to AD 1100 . . .*, ed T. A. M. Bishop and P. Chaplais (Oxford 1957) pp xxii–xxiv.
[18] [E. Searle,] 'Battle abbey and exemption [: the forged charters', *EHR* 83 (1968) pp 449–80].
[19] Quoted from *ibid* p 469; see also *RR* 1 (1913) pp 16–17 no 62.

A monk of Marmoutier, in those days renowed for the quality of its monastic life, suggested that the house should be founded in veneration of the blessed Martin (of Marmoutier) and the duke agreed.[20]

The story is inflated and grandiose, and is a product of twelfth-century hindsight, but because of the dearth of earlier material, it has to be scrutinised carefully for any light it can throw on William's motives when he founded the abbey. Here it is more promising than might at first sight appear. Professor Searle suggests, for example, that while certain elements in it, such as William's vow on the battlefield, and the remarkably wide grants of liberties to the new house, must be discounted as exaggeration,[21] a reliable tradition probably underlies Battle's claims to exemption, in that the Conqueror and his sons allowed the community to enjoy genuine and important, if unrecorded privileges.[22] The Battle legend may similarly provide certain clues about William's intentions for his new foundation.

At first sight, the notion that the Conqueror created Battle abbey as an atonement for Hastings is a beguiling one; and it is given emphasis in both the chronicles and charters of the house. If the house's foundation dated from 1070, then it more or less coincided with the penance laid upon William's army by Pope Alexander II, with the recrowning of William by the papal legates, and with the replacement of Stigand by Lanfranc as archbishop of Canterbury. All these events have recently been seen as gestures of reconciliation between the duke and a reforming pontiff who had not initially supported William's English campaign.[23] Such an interpretation has much to recommend it, but in view of William's cordial and co-operative relationship with the papacy in the years before 1066, ably demonstrated by David Bates, it is more probable that the Conqueror invaded England with at least tacit papal support.[24] Moreover penances laid on victorious armies were by no means infrequent during this period; and the fulfillment of the 1070 penance may be seen not as a

---

[20] *Chronicle of Battle* pp 23, 36–7.

[21] *ibid* pp 15–23.

[22] 'Battle abbey and exemption' pp 15–23; see also J. H. Denton, *English Royal Free Chapels, 1100–1300, A Constitutional Study* (Manchester 1970) pp 82–5.

[23] C. Morton, 'Pope Alexander II and the Norman conquest', *Latomus* 34 (Brussels 1975) pp 362–82, with an edition of the penance on pp 381–2.

[24] [D. Bates,] *Normandy [before 1066* (London 1982)] pp 198–202; Erdmann pp 188–9.

special conciliatory gesture towards a hostile pope, but more as a ritual recognition by a lay ruler of the church's disapproval of strife between Christian leaders.[25] Likewise Battle abbey could be seen to have a votive significance but it is improbable, and uncharacteristic of the king, that this was his only purpose in founding it.

In comparison, it has often been suggested that William and his wife Matilda had founded the twin abbeys of La Sainte Trinité and St Etienne at Caen (c1059–66) in expiation for their marriage, which was deemed incestuous by reforming elements in the church.[26] Yet the earliest royal—and significantly—papal documents of these abbeys refer only to the glory of God and the salvation of the souls of William and Matilda as motives for the foundation, and the story of the penance comes in a later interpolation by Orderic Vitalis into William of Junnèges's history of the Conqueror.[27] While the abbeys may have marked a general reconciliation with the church over the marriage, they were, equally, a 'grand gesture', an imposing symbol of William's authority in an economically and politically important area of the duchy. In all his dealings with the church, William revealed himself as perhaps conventionally pious, but also as an authoritative and dominating ruler who would not brook opposition or interference. While his foundations at Caen and at Battle were undoubtedly an expression of piety, the likelihood is that the king himself viewed them as symbols of power rather more than as gestures of contrition.[28]

Battle's site and the name chosen for it seem to support that emphasis, and the Battle legends supply some interesting evidence in this context. The Battle chronicler makes much of William's insistence that Battle abbey should be sited on the exact spot

---

[25] Bainton pp 109–112; A. Vanderpol, *La Doctrine scholastique du droit de guerre* (Paris 1919) p 117.

[26] *Normandy* pp 199–201; for a recent discussion of the problem see C. Bouchard, 'Consanguinity and noble marriages in the tenth and eleventh centuries', *Speculum* 56 (1981) pp 268–87.

[27] *Les actes de Guillaume le Conquérant et de la reine Mathilde pour les abbayes Caennaises*, ed M. Fauroux, *Mémoires de la société des antiquaires de Normandie* 37 (Caen 1967) p 13; William of Jumièges, *Gesta Normannorum Ducum* ed J. Marx (Paris/Rouen 1914) pp 141–2. I am grateful to Dr Bates for discussion of these matters.

[28] Brooke pp 128–33; M. de Bouard, *Guillaume le Conquérant* (Paris 1966) p 60; D. C. Douglas, *William the Conqueror* (London 1964) pp 336–42; 'Monastic patronage' pp 49–51.

where Harold fell. That was despite the problems presented by the high, waterless hill, so fully and graphically described in the text. The forged foundation charter also stresses that the abbey was constructed in the place where God gave William his victory,[29] and it is significant that a similar line was taken by the Anglo-Saxon chronicler who compiled his work at Peterborough c1121, using earlier sources.[30] Battle abbey was, he said, built 'in the same spot where God permitted [William] to conquer England'.[31] Even more striking was the name given by William to his foundation, the *monasterius de bello*. It was an unusual and audacious gesture aimed at the conquered Anglo-Saxons, the church, and the king's rivals,[32] and one which marked the house out in perpetuity as a memorial of William's martial victory.

The foundation of Nôtre Dame de la Victoire by Philip Augustus was even more blatantly a celebration of military triumph than was the building of Battle abbey. The battle of Bouvines, fought on 27 July 1214, resulted in the resounding defeat by the French king's army of the numerically superior forces of Ferrand count of Flanders, Renaud of Boulogne and Otto of Brunswick; and taken with the rout of their ally king John of England a few weeks earlier, was a major and outstanding triumph of the Capetian ruler over his powerful adversaries. Philip and his court immediately made much of this momentous event.[33] William the Breton, in his vast work, the *Philippidos*, written c1214–24, portrayed Bouvines as the triumph of good over evil in a holy crusade against God's enemies, and as a 'national' victory obtained with miraculous intervention. Later, c1229, Louis IX under the guidance of his mother Blanche of Castile was involved with the foundation of the Victorine abbey of Sainte Catherine du Val-des-Ecoliers in Paris. It was intended to be made in memory of his father and his grandfather and for the great victory at Bouvines bridge.[34] The abbey of La Victoire near Senlis was, however, the most striking

---

[29] *Chronicle of Battle* pp 43–5; above note 19.
[30] Gransden pp 92–4.
[31] *EHD* 2 (1953) p 163.
[32] *Chronicle of Battle* p 20; Brooke pp 134–5.
[33] *Capetian France* pp 132–3, 178–9.
[34] Blanche and Louis were probably major benefactors rather than founders of the house; *Gal C* 7. p 851; 'Monastic patronage' pp 231–2.

Monasteries as 'war memorials'

memorial of all. Georges Duby suggests that '*ce fut de la bataille le vrai monument commemoratif, le conservatoire de son souvenir*'.[35]

Such a statement can be made with confidence because it is amply demonstrated in the abbey's earliest documents. The original cartulary is lost, but two copies, dating from the eighteenth and nineteenth centuries respectively, have been preserved, and the better of the two was edited and published by M. Vattier in 1887–90.[36] Vattier also traces the early history of the house in his introduction to the cartulary. He shows that the foundation stone of the abbey was laid on Ash Wednesday 1221 by Warin, bishop of Senlis, the king's chancellor, who had deployed Philip's army at Bouvines, and who was made responsible for creating the house.[37] In his testament of 1222, Philip Augustus made substantial endowments to the abbey '*quam jussimus edificari juxta pontem de Charentone pro salute anime nostre*',[38] but he died before work was completed and the foundation charter was to be given by his son and successor Louis VIII in 1223.[39] Pope Honorius III granted full spiritual protection to the community in October 1223,[40] and in the Spring of 1224 the abbey was taken over by the monks of St Victor in Paris.[41] That was the mother house of an important Augustinian congregation renowned for its learning and much favoured by the French kings.[42] Warin was to keep a close watch on the progress of La Victoire, which was situated close to his cathedral city. The church was consecrated in his presence in May 1225; he was to give the community substantial endowments; and the anniversary of his death in 1227 was to be remembered each year by the monks.[43]

---

[35] G. Duby, *Le dimanche de Bouvines, 27 Juillet 1214* (Paris 1973) pp 183–4.
[36] H. Stein, *Bibliographie générale des cartulaires Français* (Paris 1907) p 266; Archives départementales Oise H 742, published in [A. Vattier,] 'Cartulaire [de l'abbaye de la Victoire', *Comité archéologique de Senlis: comptes-rendus et mémoires*, 3rd ser, 2 (Senlis 1887) pp 33–60; *ibid* 4–5 (Senlis 1889–90) pp 129–33]; A[rchives] N[ationales] LL 1469.
[37] [A. Vattier, 'L'abbaye de la Victoire:] notice historique', [*Comité archeologique de Senlis, comptes-rendus et mémoires*, 3rd ser, 2 (Senlis 1887) pp 3–32] at p 6.
[38] *Recueil des actes de Philippe Auguste, roi de France*, 4 ed M. Nortier (Paris 1979) pp 468–72 no 1796.
[39] below note 47.
[40] 'Cartulaire' p 35; AN LL 1469 p 4.
[41] 'Notice historique' p 10.
[42] 'Monastic patronage' pp 173–4, 193–4, 203–4, 231–3.
[43] 'Notice historique' pp 10, 20.

Despite the generosity of the bishop to La Victoire, it was the Capetian royal house which was to gain full credit for its establishment. In a later charter, Louis VIII stressed that he had created the abbey at his own expense,[44] and in his first donation to the house, made in June 1224, Warin himself, as a good royal servant, emphasised the rôle of Philip Augustus as the founder.[45]

The earliest charters to the house lay great stress on the abbey as a memorial of the battle of Bouvines. In his grant of June 1224 Warin declared that Philip

> *ob remedium anime sue et ob eam devotionem quam ut vir prudens qui edificavit domum suam supra petram, non immemor beneficii ab eo qui Dominus est fortis et potens in prelio in Boviniarum bello recepti grata mente conceperat . . .*

founded La Victoire in honour of Our Lady, the mother of God and of Victories, and called it Our Lady of Victories.[46] Equally unambiguous was Louis VIII's foundation charter of 1223, attested by Warin as chancellor. The preamble declared that Philip,

> *habita consideratione ad eam quam Dominus exercituum illi dedit in Bovinarum bello victoriam, abbatiam ab ipso nominatam Victoriam prope Silvanectum fundasset in honore et nomine beate et gloriose semper virginis Mariae, matris illius domini qui fortis est in prelio, et fundatam dotasset bonorum suorum partibus inferius annotatis . . .*

The king confirmed the foundation in his father's memory.[47]

The motives of the founder, Philip Augustus and of his ecclesiastical servant and chancellor Warin are thus spelt out unambiguously in the early documents of the abbey of La Victoire. There is no hint of penance or of contrition, but an emphasis on the God-given victory of French arms. The name of the house, like that of Battle, was intended to serve as a perpetual reminder of its origins. It is perhaps fitting that Philip Augustus's only major religious foundation should commemorate one of the most politically significant events in a reign which itself marked a major turning-point in the fortunes of his dynasty.[48]

---

[44] *Gal C* 10, inst pp 233–4, noted in 'Cartulaire' pp 42–3.
[45] 'Cartulaire' pp 38–9; AN LL 1469 pp 5–6.
[46] *ibid.*
[47] 'Cartulaire' pp 33–5; AN LL 1469 pp 1–3; *Gal C* 10 inst p 232.
[48] 'Monastic patronage' pp 195–207; Capetian France pp 126–35; 198–9.

Monasteries as 'war memorials'

The contradiction of ideas which emerges so clearly in the creation of Battle abbey and of La Victoire as 'war memorials' takes on an extra interest at a time when the English churches have refused to glorify the successful British campaign in the South Atlantic, their leaders insisting, despite strong political pressure, on holding a service of memorial rather than one of triumph. The medieval church was equally overt in its condemnation of war, but there is no evidence to suggest the either William the Conqueror or Philip Augustus experienced any opposition in establishing far more durable monuments of their military achievements. The special powers of the king in the church and as a patron of monasteries ensured that even at the time when ecclesiastical castigation of war was at its most emphatic, powerful lay rulers could still use religious houses, the symbols of peace and prayer, to commemorate martial victories.

Public Record Office.

IDEAS AND REALITY: SOME ATTEMPTS TO CONTROL AND DEFUSE WAR IN THE TWELFTH CENTURY

by CHRISTOPHER J. HOLDSWORTH

THE TRACK to be explored in this paper was laid down when I realised how relatively unexamined the actual working out of Christian ideas about war within the medieval period is. Recent years have seen appear a notable book about the development of ideas on the Just War, and a great deal of work on the role of the military aristocracy and on its ideals, but upon the coming together of Christianity and actual events there seemed to me very little, at least in the period which interests me most.[1] The one series of events which has attracted attention within what one can call loosely the twelfth century is, of course, the Crusades, but I decided to put them rather at the edge of my focus since they raised special questions, and to invite a scholar who has devoted much time to their elucidation to give a paper upon a crusading theme later in the conference. Yet when one turns for guidance for the history of western Europe there is only one book which stands out, *La Guerre au Moyen Age* by Philippe Contamine which appeared in the Nouvelle Clio series as recently as 1980, and it, as one would expect from its author's earlier achievement, is strongest when it deals with the period of the Hundred Years War.[2] Nonetheless it is a remarkable achievement, and one to which I am deeply indebted. But given the fact that the subject is still so unmapped, only two approaches seemed feasible to me, one where I would try to look at a series of specific wars and see what the Church did about them, or one where I would look at a source or group of sources, and see what it, or they, had to say about war and the Church. I quickly decided

---

[1] [Frederick H.] Russell, *The Just War* [*in the Middle Ages* (Cambridge 1975)]. For full bibliography see Contamine as in note 2. Many books exist for the period after 1200, relatively few before.
[2] *Nouvelle Clio*, 24 (Paris 1980), cited below as *La Guerre*.

that to attempt an overview of the whole twelfth century, a third possibility, would be beyond my powers, whereas a narrower focus could perhaps produce something very concrete which could be used later by others to create the wider picture. Finally I plumped for an approach through a source, largely because this seemed to me more manageable within the time I had at my disposal, both in the sense of time for preparation and time for delivering a paper. I hope this will not seem to you a retreat from responsibility, and that you will find this approach legitimate and will find that it does also provide some very specific wars, at least as seen through one pair of eyes. But whose did I choose? Well, out of the many whom one could have used one pair presented themselves very urgently, those of the Anglo-Norman chronicler Orderic Vitalis.

To specialists in the period Orderic needs no excuse, no introduction, but before a wider audience I should defend my choice.[3] Orderic spent all but the first ten years of his life in the monastery of St Évroul, in the diocese of Lisieux, where he had been taken by his father from Shrewsbury, the region of his birth and early education, in 1085. There he followed the orderly and restricting life of a Benedictine monk until his death some time in the 1140s, but his society was not so enclosed and protected that he did not know what was going on beyond its walls. Through patrons and benefactors, other visitors both secular and religious, and the exchange of letters and books, the cloister reverberated with the echoes of a wide world stretching north as far as Scotland, south west to Spain and south east to the Holy Land, but with its centre in the duchy of Normandy and in what St Bernard, a contemporary of Orderic, once called 'that unhappy kingdom beyond the seas'.[4] What went on beyond the Rhine, or north of Flanders, created little noise at St Évroul, its ears caught predominantly what the Normans were doing, whether north of the waters which divided England from Europe, or well to the

---

[3] This paragraph is based on Marjorie Chibnall, *The Ecclesiastical History of Orderic Vitalis* I (Oxford 1980) pp 1–44, 113 (and note 1), and cited subsequently as *EH*, followed by book (and where they exist chapters) with volume and page in brackets. Her article 'Feudal Society [in Orderic Vitalis', *Proceedings of the Battle Conference 1978* ed R. Allen Brown (Ipswich 1979)] pp 35–48 discusses many of the problems dealt with below.

[4] '. . . miseram illam ecclesiam transmarinam', Saint Bernard, epistola 240.2 in *S. Bernardi Opera* edd J. Leclercq and H. Rochais VIII (Rome 1977) p 124. For a translation see B. Scott James, *The Letters of St. Bernard of Clairvaux* (London 1953) p 282.

Ideas and Reality

south in Southern Italy and Sicily, or still further across the eastern Mediterranean, literally Outre Mer, in Palestine. All this we know because Orderic had the interest and ability to record what he could discover about the Norman world in his great Ecclesiastical History upon which he laboured for over a quarter of a century from at least as early as 1114 to as late as 1141.[5] So Orderic commends himself because he enables us to catch the flavour of events over a long period—his interests in fact stretched well back into time, but he was peculiarly well placed to comment upon affairs from the time of William the Bastard to the reign of Stephen, a stretch of nearly a century. But he also leaps off the shelf now because Dr Marjorie Chibnall has provided Orderic with a more than adequate setting in her masterly edition, of which the first volume appeared in 1969 and the sixth and final in 1980.[6] It is this edition, the result (like Orderic's own history) of twenty-five years' work, which enables one to really read Orderic for the first time as he deserves, and my duty and pleasure is to salute that achievement, without which I would not have dared to embark on my small exploration. My intention is to show what he can tell us about the attempts of the Church to control and defuse warfare particularly within what he himself called 'our part of the world', by which *he* meant, Italy, Gaul, Spain, England and Flanders, but which in this paper will mean principally Normandy, France and England.[7] What he has to say about affairs in the Holy Land will not lie within my focus, although he declared that never had the historians of warfare been offered a 'more glorious subject' than in the Crusades.[8]

That remark, however, provides a direct way into the world of Orderic, for it at once suggests that in itself he saw nothing peculiarly immoral or wrong in warfare, those who engaged in it were not for him indulging in unChristian behaviour which needed regret. One does not find in Orderic any commendation of Christian pacifism, indeed it is hard to find such within orthodox circles in the twelfth century, though some of the groups who

---

[5] *EH* I pp 29–34, VI, p xviii.
[6] The first volume to appear, number II, contains books III and IV, the last to appear, number I, contains books I and II in summary form with introduction and *index verborum*.
[7] *EH* XI, 29 (VI p 136).
[8] *Ibid* IX 1 (V p 4). This phrase seems his own: it does not occur in Baudri of Dol upon whom he based his account.

came to be regarded as heretical did believe that the command to turn the other cheek had application to behaviour in society.⁹ But it is worthwhile underlining that not long before Orderic's lifetime, in 1054 to be exact, a council meeting at Narbonne had declared that 'no Christian should kill another Christian, for whoever kills a Christian undoubtedly sheds the blood of Christ'.¹⁰ That pious hope belonged in fact to one attempt to control warfare, that expressed in the so-called Peace and Truce of God, to which we shall return in a moment. It also fitted into the tradition expressed in the penitential literature that the killing of another person, even at the command of a king, was something which needed atoning for by fasting, prayer and alms-giving.¹¹ Even so it comes as something of a surprise to find the so-called Penitential of Theodore laying down the same penance for killing a man in a public war as for masturbation.¹² Orderic, however, scarcely reflects that world which was already passing by his day—the last known penances imposed on a whole army were those imposed on William's army sometime before 1070, and it is interesting that Orderic does not refer to this.¹³ It is only where he talks about various individuals expressing regret for the excessive shedding of blood that we sense the old view had not entirely gone, and he also, as we shall see, condemned certain other kinds of behaviour in war.¹⁴ Peace, on the other hand, was to be hoped for and it is worth reminding ourselves, particularly in view of some of Orderic's attitudes, that he belonged to a Church where prayers for peace formed a regular part of the liturgy.¹⁵ Such prayers normally followed the canon of the Mass and so the desire for peace in society at large was placed close to the most sacred moment in the formal rites of the Church, just as the giving of the

---

⁹ *La Guerre* pp 462-65.
¹⁰ [H. E. J.] Cowdrey, 'The Peace and Truce [of God in the Eleventh Century]' *PP* 46 (1970)] p 54.
¹¹ For the penitential tradition see *La Guerre* pp 427-30, and [G. I. A.] Draper ['Penitential discipline and public wars in the Middle Ages' *The International Review of the Red Cross* (1961)] pp 4-18, 63-78.
¹² [A. W.] Haddan and [W.] Stubbs, [*Councils and Ecclesiastical Documents Relating to Great Britain and Ireland,*] book I cap II. 9, and cap IV. 6; vol III pp 178, 180.
¹³ For the text see D. Whitelock, M. Brett and C. N. L. Brooke, *Councils and Synods with other Documents relating to the English Church* I part II, 1066-1204 (Oxford 1981) pp 581-84, and the discussion by H. E. J. Cowdrey, 'Bishop Ermenfried of Sion and the Penitential Ordinance following the battle of Hastings' *JEH* 20 (1969) pp 225-42.
¹⁴ See below pp 68-73.
¹⁵ Cowdrey, 'The Peace and Truce' p 50 note 27.

Ideas and Reality

peace, the *pax*, symbolising the unity and concord between the people of God met to celebrate the liturgy, came at an earlier moment in the rite. Since peace was desirable Orderic approved the making of peace, and so recorded from time to time the fact that peace-makers, sometimes specified as clergy, had been active in a particular dispute.[16] But although when recounting battles he often thought it right to say a good deal about their to and fro, when it came to peace negotiations he was, on the whole, reticent and one gets little impression of how such things were managed.

Yet there was one group of Christians for whom it had been accepted by Orderic's time that warfare was inadmissible, the clergy. The tradition that the work of a clerk, or a monk, did not sit well with the work of a soldier went back to at least the council of Toledo in 400, and had been reasserted in the Carolingian period and much nearer to Orderic's own day.[17] At the council at Rheims presided over by pope Leo IX in 1046 it was laid down that the clergy should not carry arms and Orderic refers to this decision quite unambiguously, but in a manner which is itself revealing.[18] At Rheims he wrote the pope 'prohibited priests from bearing arms or taking wives. From that time', he continued 'the fatal custom began to wither away little by little. The priests were ready enough to give up bearing arms but even they are loath to part with their mistresses or to live chaste lives.' It is only when one lets his words sink in that one realises his 'fatal custom' was not the bearing of arms by priests but their proclivity to marry. Orderic, indeed, belonged to a world which held that offences against sexual *mores* should be far more seriously dealt with than killing in war, and it is therefore not surprising that what he says about the two fighting bishops who do occur in his pages, Odo of Bayeux and Geoffrey of Coutances, should hardly register much surprise at their behaviour.[19] Odo, it is true, is

---

[16] *EH* IV (II p 219),—bishop of Durham mediates with king of Scots; IV (II p 310), Cardinal priest and monks make peace count of Anjou and king William; VIII (p 234), bishop of Seez fails at seige of Courcy; X, 3 (V p 206), pope Urban in S. Italy; XII, 21 (VI pp 260–64), homily on peace by Calixtus at Rheims; XIII, 37 (VI pp 522–24), truce made by papal legate between England and Scotland. Other peace-makers are mentioned in VII, 53; X, 5; XI, 45 (IV p 52; V p 218; VI p 180).

[17] *La Guerre* pp 431–32. F. Poggiaspella, 'La chiese e la partecipazione dei chierici alla guerra nella legislazione conciliare fino alle Decretali di Grigorio IX' *Ephemerides iuris canonici* 15 (1959) pp 140–53 is entirely theoretical.

[18] *EH* V, 12 (III pp 120–22).

[19] Cf. Draper p 18.

stigmatised when he rebels against his half brother William the Conqueror, or his nephew Rufus, because rebelling was wrong, not bearing arms in itself, but Geoffrey is described in a very cool, neutral, manner.[20] He is called 'a man of noble birth, devoted more to knightly than clerical activities, and so better able to instruct knights in hauberks to fight than clerks in vestments to sing psalms'. The fact that he fought against the Danes and the English is recorded without further comment, save that through his activities he amassed much land which he handed on to his nephew Robert of Mowbray.[21] But this attitude, surprising as it may seem nowadays, was not so strange in an age when great churchmen held their estates from rulers in return for military service (among other responsibilities) and often travelled with an armed retinue.[22] Even a saintly man like Anselm was expected to concern himself with the provision of a well-equipped troop of knights for the king's use.[23] Fighting bishops were not common in Orderic's time, but to him they did not seem so very blameworthy. But if even warring clerics could be excused, is there then no sign of the existence of attempts to limit the occasions and manner of war in Orderic? The answer clearly must be in the negative or I would be about to conclude my paper now, so let us look at Orderic again. I propose to divide my discussion according to what became the classical distinction between the two kinds of necessary conditions under which a war could be said to be just, *jus ad bellum*, and *jus in bello*.

It is not my purpose to discuss the origins and development of the theory of the Just War, Professor Markus has discussed some sides of this problem in his paper, but it is I think reasonable to apply this distinction to Orderic even though the whole theory had some way to develop when he wrote.[24] An important stage in that development, Gratian's *Decretum*, was not completed until Orderic had nearly finished writing, but the main author upon whom Gratian relied, Augustine, although long dead, lived on through his

---

[20] For Odo *see EH* VII, 8 (IV pp 40–44); VIII, 2 (IV pp 124–134). For Geoffrey, *EH* VIII, 23 (IV p 278).
[21] *EH*, IV (II p 266).
[22] *La Guerre* pp 431–33.
[23] R. W. Southern, *Saint Anselm and his biographer* (Cambridge 1963) pp 155–60.
[24] Cf. Russell, *The Just War* pp 16–85.

Ideas and Reality

works which were in the library at St Évroul.[25] What evidence, then, does Orderic provide about the conditions under which war could be justified?

In the first place there are clear statements here and there that the justice of the cause was significant to him and to his contemporaries. This comes out in his discussion of the invasion of England, the wars between Normandy and France over control of the Vexin, the wars of two of the sons of William the Bastard against the third for control of Normandy, and of successive rulers of Normandy against the Counts of Maine. Orderic was at pains, for example, to state the elder William's claim to Maine, but elsewhere made it clear that there were two sides to the question, and that there was some justification on the other side too.[26] Of all the cases mentioned perhaps the most interesting is that of Henry I's movement against his elder brother Robert, duke of Normandy which led ultimately to his defeat and capture at the battle of Tinchebrai in 1106. Here when presenting his account of the campaign which began the year before in 1105 Orderic has the aged bishop of Séez urging the king on to action on the ground that the Church in Normandy was suffering under the misrule of an incompetent ruler. The occasion for his harangue, seeing the actual church at Carentan near Barfleur packed with 'peasants' chests and various tools and gear of all kinds sounds genuine enough, though the actual words ascribed to the prelate are more likely to be an invention.[27] They do however represent what Orderic thought likely to have been said, and so when he has the bishop declaiming 'Rise up boldly in the name of God, win the heritage of your fathers with the sword of justice, and rescue your ancestral land and the people of God from the hands of reprobates', he was saying something which attempted to justify a war which certainly was hard to justify by the accepted standards. It is I think peculiarly significant that Orderic has Henry himself explicitly claim a year later before the great battle that he had not come 'out of greed for any worldly lordship' (*pro cupiditate terreni honoris*), but rather 'in response to the tearful petitions of the poor

---

[25] *EH* I p 16; G. Nortier, *Les Bibliothèques Médiévales des Abbayes Bénédictines de Normandie* (Paris 1971) pp 98–108, and table following p 191.
[26] *EH* III (II p 117) and X, 7 (V p 227).
[27] *Ibid* XI, 11 (VI pp 60–64 esp 63).

... to help the Church of God'.[28] Here it seems to me Orderic was specifically trying to clear Henry from the charge that he was going to war for a cause which Augustine had condemned: to the bishop of Hippo war for gain or domination of others was unjust.[29] But if this 'more than civil war' as Orderic called it, where families were often divided against each other, required a careful justification it is clear too how difficult it was to establish the justice of a particular case to the satisfaction of all parties.[30]

A peculiarly testing case for Orderic, of course, was the Norman invasion of England in 1066, since he had been born in England of a Norman priest father and, almost certainly, an English mother, yet had been exiled at the will of his father to Normandy for the whole of his adult life, save for a single visit to England.[31] He has the pope declare the duke's claim to England as the heir of Edward to be just, whereas Harold is a perjurer (and later a tyrant), but elsewhere he reports the rebels' of 1075 claim that William had presumptuously invaded England and unjustly slain its true heirs.[32] Certainly also he shows at least two Normans, one a cleric, the other a layman, declining to accept office and lands in England because they declined to have any part of the plunder.[33] Here again there seems an awareness of Augustine's caution against wars for temporal gain, found also in the penitentials of an earlier period which lay down that if money had been taken in a foreign province from a conquered enemy a third of it should be given to the Church and the poor and that penance should be done for 40 days.[34] There are hints at these points in Orderic that Norman propaganda did not entirely convince even Normans, even though the case had been, they claimed, adjudicated in some sense by the supreme authority in the Church.[35] The case of 1066 was *sui generis*, but two other cases reveal other aspects of the problem of establishing the justice of a cause.

[28] *Ibid* XI, 20 (VI p 86).
[29] *La Guerre* p 425; and Russell, *The Just War* p 21, on wars of conquest.
[30] *EH* XII, 5 (VI p 200). The phrase itself may be a reminiscence of Lucan, *Pharsalia*, i.1.
[31] *EH* I, pp 2, 5, 25.
[32] *Ibid* III (II pp 142 and 170), IV (II p 312).
[33] *Ibid* IV (II p 272) and VI, 8 (III p 256).
[34] Draper pp 12–13; Penitential of Theodore in Haddan and Stubbs, book 1, cap VII. 2 p 182.
[35] *EH* III (II p 142).

Ideas and Reality

The count of Maine was willing that his case should be considered by what he vaguely described as a meeting of 'kings, counts and bishops', but no such body had any regular existence, and those of us who live in an age which has an international tribunal know how rarely both parties to a dispute are willing to submit themselves to its arbitration. William Rufus was, in some senses, therefore, much more practical when he said he was willing to trust his case to swords, lances and missiles, to the justification of battle that is to say.[36] After the battle he is made to claim that he was given victory by the will of God, whilst the loser, count Helias says that he has lost by a 'change of fortune', a more neutral explanation which was perhaps more acceptable to those on the losing side.[37]

The case of the king of France against the king of England who was also duke of Normandy over his treatment of his brother Robert and Robert's son William, raises another difficulty entirely: where a case was submitted to a higher tribunal, that tribunal appears to have been hampered from obtaining all the information it needed and to have been influenced by partiality for one of the parties. The analysis of the dispute would take me far beyond the bounds of this paper, it is sufficient to know that the case came firmly into the papal court when the king of France raised it at the council of Rheims presided over by Calixtus II in 1119.[38] The pope then agreed to take up the matter with Henry, who was not present at Rheims, but when he did so, Calixtus was, according to Orderic, entirely won over by his arguments.[39] William of Malmesbury, whom we should expect to take the Anglo-Norman side, went so far as to have the pope say that he had never found a juster cause than Henry's.[40] But how could Calixtus have judged adequately on very partial information not tested in any public manner, and how could he have retained impartiality when as the king rose from prostrating himself at his feet, he reminded his visitor that they were kinsmen?[41] It is also surely relevant to remind ourselves that the establishment of right, whether in claims

---

[36] *EH* X, 8 (V p 230).
[37] *Ibid* X, 8 (V pp 238 and 248–50).
[38] *Ibid* XII, 21 (VI pp 256–60 and 264).
[39] *Ibid* XII, 24 (VI pp 282–290).
[40] *De gestis regum Anglorum*, ed W. Stubbs (*RS* 1887–9) ii 482.
[41] The pope's grandmother was Henry's great aunt (*EH* VI, p 283 note).

to estates or to lordship over others, was by no means a simple matter then, when inheritance customs were by no means settled.⁴² All armed struggles, whether those we should call international or those we should call civil, were more like family quarrels where one party ultimately pushed its claims to the test of arms. So the practicalities of establishing *jus ad bellum* were by no means simple, but Orderic's testimony suggests that it was considered important to try to claim that right was on one's side. To that extent some attention was paid to the theory in practice, though it remains a very open question whether the attention was paid because the theory had the prestige of a Father of the Church behind it, or because the theory in fact accorded with more widely diffused and less attributable views about justice.

Besides, however, *jus ad bellum* there were ideas about *jus in bello*, rectitude in the conduct of war; to what extent does Orderic portray a society concerned about this? Three aspects of behaviour in war-time emerge in his chronicle which seem to be relevant, the avoidance of attacking certain people and their property, the avoidance of fighting at certain seasons, and the avoidance of certain manners of fighting. The first and second of these bring us to what are generally known as the Peace of God and the Truce of God, although by Orderic's time the two were not always distinguished, which had been developed by churchmen from 975 and 1027 respectively as a means of 'self-defence as far as any was possible' in an age when central authority was weak.⁴³ They were part of an attempt to reform society at a time of crumbling lay authority which began in the turbulent land south of the Loire and rapidly spread across southern and south-eastern France. The Peace of God was probably first proclaimed in Normandy at a council in Caen in 1047 after William had won the battle of Val ès Dunes, but Orderic's first clear reference to it comes in his account of a council at Rouen, held nearly 50 years later in 1096.⁴⁴ There it was decreed that 'all churches and their churchyards, all monks, clerks, nuns, women, pilgrims and merchants and their households, and

⁴² *EH* VI, p 188 note 5, and Marjorie Chibnall, 'Feudal Society' pp 37–40.
⁴³ The extensive literature is well discussed by Cowdrey 'The Peace and Truce' (the phrase cited is on p 46), and *La Guerre* pp 433–38. The ambiguity is well indicated by the statutes of the Council of Lillebonne in 1080 which begin '*Pax Dei quae vulgo treuia dicitur . . .*' *EH* V, 5 (III p 26).
⁴⁴ *EH* IX, 3 (V p 20: where the clause to be quoted comes in the middle of clauses about the Truce, showing how by then the two were merging).

Ideas and Reality

oxen and horses at the plough and men leading the plough, and men harrowing and the horses with which they harrow, and men who fly to the ploughs, and all lands of religious houses and money of the clergy shall be in peace at all times, so that no one shall ever presume to attack or seize them, or rob or molest them in any way'. Some of the categories mentioned here were peculiar to this Council but some of them, like the protection of property of the church, go back beyond the Peace movement of the late tenth century to legislation made in church councils in the sixth century. And Augustine had argued that profaning churches, among other things, was to be avoided if a just war was not to degenerate into a war moved by an unworthy intention, which was *ipso facto* unjust.[45] But whereas the Peace movement tried to protect those who could not protect themselves the Truce of God attempted to declare certain times and seasons closed. Orderic first mentions it in his account of the Council held at Lillebonne in 1080 which had been called by king William, though it, too, may first have been imposed on Normandy by the council at Caen in 1047.[46] Details of what it actually involved are first given when Orderic describes the council held by pope Urban at Clermont in 1095, and the already mentioned council of Rouen, held the following year.[47] Although the details are slightly different the essential points were the same: long stretches of time at the holiest periods of the year, before and after Easter, and before and after Christmas, and a large slice of every week ('from sunset on Wednesday until dawn on Monday'), and certain feast days and their vigils were declared to be times when 'no man shall attack or wound, or kill another, and no one shall take a distraint, or plunder'. The provisions of both Truce and Peace were protected by the threat of anathema and excommunication, and at the council of 1096 an oath was formulated which was to be taken by all men of over twelve years old. This bound the swearer to protect the decisions of the council, and to go to the aid with arms of any bishop or archdeacon who was trying to enforce the decisions of the council against those who refused to take the oath or uphold the decisions.[48] So Orderic's day had a formidable battery of intentions to limit war

---

[45] *La Guerre* p 426.
[46] *EH* V, 5 (III p 26, and see note 43 above).
[47] *Ibid* IX, 2 (V p 13) and IX, 3 (V p 20).
[48] *Ibid* IX, 3 (V p 20).

by declaring certain people, places and times 'out of bounds', but the question imposes itself 'How far were these Queensberry rules followed?'

Orderic himself commented that the provisions of the Council of Rouen 'remained almost without effect' and put the blame for this on the duke of Normandy, the king's brother Robert, who was unable 'to enforce justice', that is to say keep order.[49] But even if this were true at that time, whilst Robert remained nominally in control, elsewhere Orderic has cases where the limitations were observed. A young knight, for example, returns the horses which he had taken from a monk because his mother tells him he will be damned eternally if he doesn't, or a bishop succeeds in rescuing his young clerk by threatening interdict on an army which had carried him off.[50] But the persons of the clergy were not always held in such high respect: even a pope was seized at the altar by the emperor in 1111.[51] The precariousness of the situation may well be indicated in the fact that Orderic included in his Chronicle a long vision seen by a priest, Walchelin, in 1091 part of whose message is that those who attack clerics merit unbearable torments after death if they do not repent and do penance.[52] Supernatural threats that is to say were needed to reinforce laws made on earth. Attempts to protect the property of the Church seem equally to go off at half-cock. The bishop of Le Mans excommunicates rebels and finds himself in prison for his pains, whilst of the bishop of Séez it is said that he often tried to excommunicate his enemies 'but he could rarely or never bring his rebel subjects to make a firm peace or keep it'.[53] As for the property and persons of peasants given some protection by the Peace, it is surely symptomatic that Orderic records that a certain Richer of Laigle should be 'remembered for ever' when, moved by the sight of a wayside crucifix at whose foot a group of peasants huddled, he forbade his men to attack them. Days and seasons supposed to be out of bounds were, if anything, even less respected.[54] The peace of Advent and Lent, for example, was broken, whereas king Stephen

---

[49] *Ibid* IX,3 (V p 24).
[50] *Ibid* VI, 6 (III pp 242–44); VIII, 16 (IV pp 234–36).
[51] *Ibid* X, 1 (V p 196).
[52] *Ibid* VIII, 17 (IV pp 236–50, esp p 238).
[53] *Ibid* VIII, 11 (IV p 194) and VIII, 18 (IV p 252).
[54] *Ibid* XII, 20 (VI p 250).

Ideas and Reality

fought the battle of Lincoln on the feast of the Purification.[55] Henry I, on the other hand, is said not to have wanted to attack a fortress because it was the feast of the Invention of Holy Cross, although the attack took place because some of the knights had not heard his order.[56] Curiously enough the king with the least pious reputation, Rufus, is the only one recorded to have postponed an attack when he allowed a besieged garrison a truce over Saturday and Sunday 'out of reverence for the Lord's burial and resurrection'.[57] Some stories are told to make the point that violators of restricted days will get their deserts: for example a siege tower 'unrighteously' (Orderic's word) made on the orders of Robert of Bellême at Christmas time is destroyed by fire 'by God's just decree', but such incidents suggest that the Truce was at least as often broken as observed, not unlike some truces very close to us.[58] Nonetheless the standard was there, just as it was for protected people and property, reminding those who fought that some limits to their ferocity should be observed. And this leads me to the third aspect of Orderic's picture of the achievement of right behaviour in war, the avoidance of certain manners of fighting.

In the first place it is worth observing in passing that Orderic does not appear to have believed that the use of any particular weapon or machine of war was unChristian. Although Urban II had pronounced against the use of the crossbow at the Council of Clermont, a prohibition repeated at the second Lateran Council of 1139, Orderic records its use without any special comment.[59] His attitude was in fact to become the predominant one, and the first known effort to stamp out the use of a particular means of making war failed completely.

Indiscriminate slaughter, on the other hand, certainly seemed bad to Orderic: on these grounds he condemned William for his harrying of the north and believed that God would punish him.[60]

---

[55] Ibid XII, 8 (VI p 208): XII, 13 (VI p 218): XIII, 43 (VI pp 540-542).
[56] Ibid XI,45 (VI p 182).
[57] Ibid X, 10 (V p 258).
[58] Ibid VIII, 16 (IV p 235): cf. XIII, 23 (VI p 460: death to violators of Pentecost).
[59] Ibid XII, 10 (VI p 212-14: this event is peculiarly striking since it is the attempt by Juliana wife of Eustace of Breteuil, to kill her father Henry I). See also *balista* and *balistarius* in *Index Verborum* (I p 256). For the attempt to outlaw see *La Guerre* pp 165–66. The discussion by [James T.] Johnson, [*Just War Tradition and the Restraint of War* (Princeton, New Jersey 1981)] pp 128–29 does not seem so well based.
[60] EH IV (II p 232).

Robert of Rhuddlan, too, was stigmatised for the way he pursued the Welsh, slaughtering some, imprisoning others and selling some into slavery. In his case God's disapproval came when he was caught and outnumbered by Welsh raiders on the Great Orme and decapitated.[61] Various groups were thought by Orderic to fight in a peculiarly 'dirty' way: he singles out the Welsh, Scots and Angevins, not surprising choices, one may think, for an Anglo-Norman.[62] Attacking a man without due warning as did Robert of Mowbray, king Malcolm of Scotland in 1093, was also reprehensible.[63] Those who 'hit below the belt', so to say, sometimes receive a merited rebuke. The man who plunged his sword into the entrails of the defenders of a castle which he stormed later fell into the hands of his brother with whom he was estranged 'by the just judgement of God' and was imprisoned by him.[64] Retribution in the other world, not this, was expressed in that vision of Walchelin already mentioned when the clerical visionary sees a knight with a great clot of blood adhering to his heels near his spurs. This, he is told, feels like heavy fire to the knight and afflicts him because he used to use 'sharp spurs in my eager haste to shed blood'.[65]

In contrast to such reprehensible behaviour Orderic, occasionally, praises behaviour of soldiers. Noteworthy is his often quoted account of the battle of Brémule where he says that only three of the nine hundred knights who fought were killed. The reasons he gives for this, to us, strange result (though it can be paralleled elsewhere) mix the practical with the idealistic. 'They were', he wrote, 'all clad in mail and spared each other on both sides, out of fear of God and fellowship in arms; they were more concerned to capture than to kill the fugitives. As Christian soldiers they did not thirst for the blood of their brothers, but rejoiced in a just victory given by God, for the good of holy Church and the peace of the faithful'.[66] Mail may well be the most significant factor, for once a man clad in it were unhorsed he might be easily knocked over but not so easily killed, and this degree of protection enabled men who

---

[61] *Ibid* VIII, 3 (IV pp 138–40).
[62] *Ibid* XIII, 41, 37, 26 (VI pp 536, 518, 472).
[63] *Ibid* VIII, 22 (IV p 270).
[64] *Ibid* XI, 6 (VI p 44).
[65] *Ibid* VIII, 17 (IV p 248).
[66] *Ibid* XII, 18 (VI p 240). There is a good discussion of parallel battles in *La Guerre* pp 413–18.

Ideas and Reality

usually knew each, or at least recognised one another's badges, to concentrate on taking prisoners who could provide rich ransoms. Some years earlier at the siege of Chaumont in the autumn of 1098 the French defenders of the castle win Orderic's praise for aiming their arrows at the mounts of their attackers rather than their riders, thus showing that they 'never forgot their duty to God or respect for humanity', but it is surely more likely they aimed to achieve two ends by these means, to hit the larger target, so disabling the assault, and to leave the smaller, but more valuable, target unharmed.[67] With such considerations we find how seemingly moral behaviour may, in fact, have had a more material explanation, but it is not easy to disentangle the meaning of acts susceptible to a number of interpretations.

A similar difficulty of interpretation faces us with Orderic's pictures of the archetypal bad knight, Robert of Bellême and of the good knight, Geoffrey of Mortagne, or his bad and good countesses, Helwise, countess of Évreux and Isabel countess of Conches, wife of Ralph Tosny.[68] In them we see obviously good or bad traits from a religious point of view—being God-fearing and devoted to the Church, or shaming and oppressing it, along-side more secular traits—boldness in battle, strength and size of body, gentleness, good manners and so on. Such a combination of worldly and other-worldly standards may tempt one to try and ascribe different standards as being due to what could be called a secular chivalric tradition or to religious teaching.[69] This seems to me by Orderic's time an impossible exercise, because the links between soldiers of the world and the Church were so long-standing and, so to say, multi-directional; the Church had sanctified arms and arms had entered into the Church producing a mixture well ravelled together (if such a positive version of unravel is permissible). Let us look at certain aspects of this mixture which help, I believe, to explain why the Church's efforts to limit warfare were in some senses not pursued with enormous enthusiasm or crowned with much success.

For a long time before Orderic's day the Church had come to accept that the profession of soldier was one which could be pursued by a Christian. A theory of society where each of the

---

[67] *EH* X, 5 (V 216–18).
[68] *Ibid* VIII, 5 (IV pp 158, 160); VIII 14 (IV pp 212–14).
[69] Cf. Johnson pp 122, 133–38.

three orders, priests, knights and peasants had their proper work had emerged by the Carolingian period and by that time too services of blessing for the principal weapons of the mounted soldier, his sword, armour, helmet and banner had developed.[70] Although the earliest *ordo* where the soldier himself is blessed comes from 1093, there is little to show in Orderic what went on when he says that someone was made a knight.[71] But it is interesting to find that those military saints, Maurice, Sebastian and George who are invoked in that *ordo*, the *Ordo of Cambrai*, appear in his pages along with Demetrius, Theodore, Eustace and the southern French soldier Saint William of Gellone.[72] Orderic himself, it is worth remarking, tells us that he was called Vitalis after one of the companions of St Maurice.[73] The soldier saints are mentioned by Orderic when he writes about a chaplain of Hugh earl of Chester who collected stories 'of the combats of holy knights' which he amassed from the Old Testament and more recent, Christian history. Such tales Gerold of Avranches told to the 'great lords, simple knights and noble boys' of the earl's household and so we see a fairly new form of Christian exhortation being spread.[74] No less than five of the earl's knights were so moved that they became monks in Orderic's own community at St Évroul, and he tells of many other knights who finally found what he called 'a safe harbour of life under the Rule'.[75] Yet it is significant that Orderic was prepared to admit that laymen could live a life in the world which God would find acceptable provided that they redeemed their sins by plentiful alms giving.[76] Orderic, albeit a monk, could see salvation being found beyond the cloister and although his vision was halting, in this respect he was moving

---

[70] Georges Duby (translated by Arthur Goldhammer), *The Three Orders* (London 1980); *La Guerre* pp 420–33, 441–43; J. Flori, 'Chevalerie et liturgie. Remise des armes et vocabulaire "chevaleresque" dans les sources liturgiques du IXe and XIVe siècle' *Moyen Âge,* 84 (1978) pp 247–78, 409–42, a most valuable discussion with texts.
[71] *Ibid* p 275. *EH* VIII, 1 (IV p 120): for other examples see *Index Verborum* at *militaria, arma* and *militia, arma* etc.
[72] *EH* VI, 2–3 (III pp 216, 218–26). For chivalric saints, banners and war cries see *La Guerre* pp 470–74.
[73] *Ibid* XIII,45 (VI p 554).
[74] *Ibid* VI, 2 (III p 216).
[75] *Ibid* VI, 4 and 2 (III pp 226, 216).
[76] *Ibid* VI, 8 (III pp 260–62). This passage is well discussed by C. Harper-Bill, 'The Piety of the Anglo-Norman Knightly Class', *Proceedings of the Battle Conference, 1979* ed. R. Allen Brown (Woodbridge 1980) p 65. The whole article is very rewarding.

Ideas and Reality

towards that crossroads signalled many years ago by Chenu, where the life of the Gospel began to be lived in the world.[77]

Yet Orderic lived too in a world where the inheritance from the past was treasured and clung to. Men expected God to make known his pleasure concerning their affairs by signs which could be read by those with eyes to see. So the swarm of flies which plagued Odo and the rebels stuck in Rochester signified divine displeasure, whilst as the Conqueror lay on his death bed he was encouraged to feel that God had granted him his successes because his cause was just.[78] It was therefore natural for men to ride into battle invoking his aid whether directly as with the Norman's cry of '*Dieux aide*', or indirectly by calling upon their favourite saint, as did the count of Mantes when he called to St Julian.[79] In France the practice of priests accompanying their parishioners to battle with their banners was encouraged by Louis VI and his bishops under pain of excommunication, and there is at least one battle in the west where Orderic says that the king heard Mass before going to fight: Stephen at the battle of Lincoln.[80] The forcing ground for such practices seems to have been the Holy Land, but everywhere they served to reassure combattants that God was concerned with their fate.[81] After the battle an observer like Orderic could claim that those who died at Hastings deserved to do so for sins they committed, though here he seems to have believed something very like corporate guilt for things done in the past by one's compatriots.[82] Yet he was able to believe too that men who had God on their side would not be defeated however strong their enemies, as with the emperor Alexius, or contrariwise, as with William Clito, a man could do nothing however many allies he

---

[77] M. D. Chenu, 'Moines, clercs, laïcs au carrefour de la vie évangélique' *RHE* 69 (1954) 59–89 and reprinted in his *La théologie au douzième siècle* (Paris 1957) which was translated by Jerome Taylor and Lester K. Little as *Nature, Man and Society in the Twelfth Century* (Chicago and London 1968) pp 225–51.

[78] *EH* VIII, 2; VII, 15 (IV pp 128, 90).

[79] *Ibid* X, 24; X, 7 (V pp 362, 226). Cf. French cry 'Montjoie', XII, 12 (VI p 216).

[80] *Ibid* VIII, 24 (IV p 288); XI, 34, XII, 19 (VI pp 156, 244); XIII, 43 (VI p 544).

[81] Fasting before battle, *EH* IX, 10, XIII, 4, the second in Spain, (V p 108; VI p 400); prayers and preaching, IX, 10 (with sacrament), IX, 13, IX, 15 (with sacrament) (V pp 108, 110, 138, 164); battle cry to Jesus, IX, 9 (V p 76).

[82] *Ibid* III (II pp 176–178); the crimes were the murder of the Atheling Alfred and to have 'slaughtered' King Harold Hardrada and earl Tostig. This last self-defence one would have thought.

had, if God was against him.[83] But besides the use of God as an explainer of otherwise inexplicable happenings, Orderic often appealed to 'fortune' in battles, as in other situations, which may suggest that he was finding the older tradition of explanation less satisfying.[84] But his traditional stance emerged clearly when he tells of various dramatic gestures which could redeem a life-time marred by evil-doing, whether they be entries into the monastic life on the point of death, or merely a heartfelt prayer as a man died. Robert of Rhuddlan for instance as he sinks down 'riddled with darts' (spears of some sort) commends his soul to God and St. Mary. And so Orderic's epitaph for his tomb at St Évroul ends with the invocation

'Spare him, I beg, who called on blessed Mary
Even as he fell transfixed with many weapons;
Forgive his guilt; grant him abiding treasures
That he may chant with the eternal chorus. Amen'.[85]

At the end, indeed, the Church was prepared to bury in specially sacred spots these fearful warriors and to permit their warlike deeds to be hinted at in their epitaphs. The knightly tomb, indeed, was to have a rich and complex future, but here in Orderic we certainly find the achievements of war being allowed in churches. Archbishop Agobard of Lyons, a Carolingian prelate, who had insisted that all warlike pictures in churches should be removed, would probably have been surpised at these epitaphs, but not long after Orderic's time the shield of even a humbler knight was hung up in the church in his memory.[86] This we know from that extraordinary book of counsel for recluses, the *Ancrene Riwle*, where this practice is mentioned in the course of a discussion of Jesus' deed of knighthood on the Cross. And that brings me to a final point with which I gauge we may leave Orderic and his world.

The work of a knight, the work of Christ, the work of a monk,

---

[83] *Ibid* VII, 5, and XII, 45 (IV p 16; VI p 368).
[84] Cf. *EH Index Verborum* at *fortuna* (I, p 295).
[85] *EH* VIII, 3 (IV pp 140 and 147). Other epitaphs stressing military prowess are in IV, 350 (II p 350, for Waltheof); V, 9 (III pp 90, 90–92, for Rollo and William Longsword); VIII, 1 and 36 (IV pp 110, 336 for William the Bastard and Hugh of Grandmesnil); XI, 4 and XII, 45 (VI pp 36, 378 for Walter Giffard and William Clito). The whole topic of warrior epitaphs would repay study.
[86] *La Guerre* p 471; *The Ancrene Riwle*, part 7 as modernised by M. B. Salu (London 1955) p 174.

were all inextricably linked because they seemed varieties of battle.[87] The hermit in his cell, the monk in his cloister, the knight in his lord's household all served, *militare*, they belonged to their distinct *militia* but for each the struggle could be hard and long.[88] The fight of the religious against the devil was not so different from the knight striving against an enemy (assuming God was on his side), and so monasteries where monks fought could not incongruously be described as 'the fortresses by which Normandy is guarded' where men learnt to fight against devils and the sins of the flesh.[89] The tradition which saw the religious life as an extended military metaphor was old by Orderic's time, stretching back as it did throughout the Rule of Benedict to St Paul.[90] This Christian tradition could find much in the Old Testament too to feed it—the Book of Psalms for example was packed with battle prayers and not surprisingly monks not too far from Orderic's St Evroul drew lively battle scenes in their Psalter.[91] Benedict may have thought the Book of Kings and the Heptateuch a little too lively for monks, at least late in the day, but there were plenty of stirring military exploits elsewhere in the story of the children of Israel which could be interpreted in terms of spiritual things.[92] So one world merged into another at a profound level—once, at least, more superficially, in a scene reminiscent of the *Comte d'Ory*, when Louis VI and his knights entered a monastery disguised as monks and then took it over and made it a fortified place.[93] Castles and monasteries were the most obvious things in what has been called 'a stone civilisation' and the way of life in one deeply affected the

---

[87] *La Guerre* pp 468–70: Duby, *The Three Orders* pp 33, 78, 103, 115.
[88] *EH, Index Verborum* provides numerous examples (I pp 324, 325), to which may be added for *militia* (II p 7) and *milito* (II p 12). Uses of the verb *dimicare* are also significant (and here the splendid *Index* fails) (II pp 12, 244; III p 144).
[89] *Ibid* VII, 15 (IV p 92: the phrase is attributed to king William). For the fight of the monk one may cite as an example Bernard, *In Cantica Canticorum*, I. 9 (edd Leclercq and Rochais, I, p 7) 'Sed et in quotidianis exercitiis et bellis, quae nulla hora pie in Christo viventibus desunt a carne, a mundo, a diabolo, sicut militiam esse vitam hominis super terram experimini in vobismetipsis . . .'.
[90] Eg. *Rule* [*of St Benedict*, trans J. McCann (London 1952)] p 7 Prologue: 'To thee are my words now addressed . . . that renouncing thine own will to fight for the true King, Christ, dost take up the strong and glorious weapons of obedience'; Eph 6: 11–17.
[91] For example at Canterbury in the Eadwine Psalter: C. M. Kaufmann, *Romanesque Manuscripts 1066–1190 (A Survey of Manuscripts Illuminated in the British Isles*, ed J. J. Alexander, Oxford 1975) 3 pp 96–7 and figure 183.
[92] *Rule*, cap 42 p 100.
[93] *EH* XII, 1 (VI p 184).

other.[94] So it is perhaps not so surprising that the Church, in which monasteries were still the most significant institutions in Orderic's time, did not succeed to any very great extent in limiting war. Standards were held up, but at the last one lot of soldiers would take the others in, provided they received an adequate payment.

University of Exeter

---

[94] 'Civilisation de la pierre', a phrase of Boutruche cited by Contamine; *La Guerre* p 128.

PROPAGANDA FOR WAR
THE DISSEMINATION OF THE CRUSADING
IDEAL IN THE TWELFTH CENTURY

by COLIN MORRIS

IT WAS accepted in western Europe, in the twelfth and thirteenth centuries, that there was an obligation upon the military classes, and indeed on Christians generally, to take up arms in defence of the Holy Sepulchre, or to participate in other expeditions authorised by the ecclesiastical hierarchy. War ceased to be, for Christians, a regrettable necessity, and became a virtue, and armies were summoned by the trumpet-blasts of the Prince of Peace. There has been a great deal of work by historians in recent decades on the transformation of earlier Christian ideology, and we now understand much more about the origins of crusading ideas, the discussion of warfare by theologians and canon lawyers, and the profound changes in spirituality which accompanied the rise of militarism. There is however a technical aspect of the subject which is less often considered: the actual methods by which the new ideals were communicated to western society generally. By any standards, it was a remarkably successful exercise in publicity. It was also, in the first instance, very rapid. Urban II announced the expedition to Jerusalem at the Council of Clermont in November 1095, and he fixed the date of departure as 15 August 1096. The summons was heard by groups far wider than the princes and their households, and by Easter 1096 an army led by Peter the Hermit had already arrived in Cologne on its way from northern France. Within a few months, therefore, and well in advance of the papal deadline, the message had spread to all levels of society over a wide geographical area. A system of communication as effective as this deserves our respect and study. It would be a mistake to conclude from the total absence of modern technology that the control of opinion was unimportant in the twelfth and thirteenth centuries. It was, on the contrary, vitally important, because there were no adequate means of governmental coercion and control, and the stability of society depended on the acceptance of common, or at least complementary, standards of belief and behaviour. Of these norms, the commitment of the upper classes to the maintenance of holy war was one of the most persistent. Its acceptance was general and long-lasting. Beginning with Louis VII, all the French kings for well over a century participated in a papally authorised crusade, and the kings of England (perfidious Albion!) at least promised to go. All of this is testimony to the power of the persuaders in these centuries, and it may be interesting to see how they operated to disseminate the ideal of holy war.[1]

Observers of the first crusade were well aware of the spectacular speed with which the movement spread, and regarded it as one of the signs of God's blessing upon it. 'It is certain', wrote Baudri of Bourgueil, 'that the Holy Spirit, who *blows where he wills*, both animated them to undertake such great travails and inspired in them an undivided concord.'[2] Robert the Monk has a remarkable story which expresses the thought much more emphatically:

> In order that it might be made clear to all the faithful that this journey was decreed by God and not by man, it happened—as we learned afterwards from many people—that on the very day on which these things were said and done, the reverberating report of that great decree shook the whole world. Even in the maritime islands in the Ocean it was spread abroad that the Jerusalem journey had been thus established at the Council... It is clear therefore that this was the work of no human voice, but of *the Spirit of the Lord* who *fills the whole earth*.[3]

This miracle is both unspecific and unsubstantiated, but it draws our attention to both the historical and the theological ideas of the time. Theologically, it was accepted that the dissemination of information was one of the functions of the Christian revelation,

---

[1] The best survey of the communication of ideas at the time is J. Benzinger, 'Zum Wesen und zu den Formen von Kommunikationen und Publizistik im Mittelalter'. *Publizistik* 15 (1970) pp 295–318. There are brief discussions of particular aspects by C. H. Haskins, 'The spread of ideas in the Middle Ages', *Speculum* 1 (1926) pp 19–30; G. Duby, 'The diffusion of cultural patterns in feudal society', *Past and Present* 39 (1968) pp 3–10; and C. Morris, *Medieval Media. Mass Communication in the Making of Europe* (Southampton 1972).

[2] Baudri, [Historia Jerosolimitana] prol. (*RHC, Occ* IV p 9, citing John iii. 8).

[3] Robert [Historia Iherosolimitana] i.3 (*RHC, Occ* III p 730, citing Wisdom of Sol i.7).

Crusading propaganda

indeed was the proper work of the Holy Spirit. The feast of *divisio apostolorum* was observed in more and more churches, to celebrate the time when, empowered by the Holy Spirit, the apostles had separated to take the Gospel to all the outlying regions of the world. This became an important theme of religious art, especially at the abbey church of Vézelay, where the tympanum on the west front depicted, not the Last Judgement, which was a more usual theme, but the descent of the Holy Spirit upon the apostles and, in the outer ranges, the distant peoples awaiting the word of faith.[4] The dissemination of the announcement at Clermont was therefore a direct manifestation of the power of the Spirit. This could be asserted all the more confidently because there existed no system of formal communication which could be expected to achieve it. The official structure was to charge the bishops with the circulation of information through preaching and the holding of synods. The possibility of doing this had certainly been improved during the period of the Gregorian reform, and there are some signs of an attempt to use it. We are told that Urban instructed the bishops, assembled at Clermont, to 'announce this throughout the churches committed to you, and preach the way to Jerusalem manfully and with zeal'.[5] Nevertheless, it was not an efficient procedure. The bishops did not have an adequate preaching organisation at their disposal; indeed it was only in the eleventh century that the idea began to emerge that preaching was a duty of the priests as a whole, as distinct from the personal prerogative of the bishop. It is not surprising that we hear little about the preaching of the first crusade by the bishops.[6] The narratives stress, as against this, the way the news travelled like

---

[4] Similar themes appear on an altar-piece commissioned about 1150 by abbot Wibald of Stavelot, now in the Musée de Cluny at Paris; and in the mosaics of one of the great domes at S. Mark's, Venice.

[5] Baudri i. 4 (*BHC, Occ* IV p 15). So also the Fleury narrative (*RHC, Occ* V p 356).

[6] Modern historians have discerned some signs of it in operation, which on investigation are not completely convincing. Thus Ordericus Vitalis, in the account which he gives of the origins of the first crusade, reported the return of bishops from Clermont to Normandy, and the holding of a synod at Rouen to promulgate the decrees. His account of the synod, however, contains no mention of the crusade; *Ecclesiastical History* ix 3, ed M. Chibnall V (Oxford 1975) pp 18–25. Ekkehard of Aura commented that the eastern Franks, because of the schism, were slow to hear of the expedition, but that is not necessarily a specific comment about the absence of episcopal preaching; Hierosolymita 9 (*RHC, Occ* V pp 17–18).

wildfire without the operation of the official system. Guibert of Nogent was particularly impressed by this:

> It was not necessary for any ecclesiastical person to make orations in churches to stir up the peoples, since one man told another, both by word and example, at home and elsewhere, about the plan to set out ... A great rumour spread into every part of France, and everyone to whom the advancing report first brought the pope's command then approached all his neighbours and family about undertaking the way of God (for so, metaphorically, it was called).[7]

As the French Revolution was marked by the Great Fear, so the first crusade was nourished by the Great Rumour. The astonishment of contemporaries was understandable, for the news had travelled at a speed which seemed unbelievable by routes which they barely knew to exist. They identified three of these. The first was the mission of Peter the Hermit, who was immensely the most successful of the popular preachers, and far more so than any episcopal preachers. Robert the Monk specifically commented that his followers esteemed him above bishops and abbots.[8] The ten-nineties saw the rapid development in northern France of the so-called 'poverty and preaching' movement, and it is interesting to find that the description given by Guibert of Nogent, who apparently saw Peter himself, is strongly reminiscent of the work of other travelling preachers at the time. Like Robert of Arbrissel, Peter attempted to resettle prostitutes in respectable society, and like Tanchelm of Antwerp he was venerated as semi-divine, and hairs plucked from the tail of his mule were kept as relics.[9] So successful was Peter's preaching that it came to be believed that he had initiated the crusade as a result of a vision which he had seen on a previous pilgrimage to Jerusalem, and it is probable that versions of this story were already circulating among his followers in 1096.[10]

---

[7] Guibert [of Nogent, Gesta Dei per Francos] i.1,ii, 6 (*RHC, Occ* IV pp 124, 140). So Baudri i 6 (*ibid* p 16): '*Praedicabant episcopi, et voce liberiori jam illud idem vociferabantur laici . . .; alii alios cohortabantur et in angulis et in compitis, inde singuli sermocinabantur*'.

[8] Robert i 5 (*RHC, Occ* III p 731).

[9] Guibert ii 8 (*RHC, Occ* IV p 142).

[10] Anna Comnena attributed the origin of the movement to Peter, and it is reasonable to suggest that this was what she heard from the crusaders themselves. The story that Peter was in possession of a heavenly letter was in circulation in Germany shortly after 1100;

Crusading propaganda

Another force which was immensely effective was the use of the cross as a badge. Whereas few writers mentioned the existence of a preaching programme by the bishops, almost every one who described the crusade mentioned the impact of the cross symbol. It was, we are told, an 'example and incitement' and was received with such enthusiasm that some recruits claimed that it had been miraculously implanted upon them, and others branded themselves with crosses.[11] Yet others asked their bishops or priests to bestow the cross on them.[12] The Great Rumour, we are told, roused the magnates as well as the populace,[13] and it was still a relatively unfamiliar sight to find laymen taking an active initiative in a religious movement. Robert the Monk described the process in his account of Bohemond prevailing on his followers to join him. He was said to have torn up two lengths of rich cloth and made crosses in preparation, and then to have addressed them: 'If any man is the Lord's, let him join himself with me. You knights, who now are mine, be God's instead, and undertake with me the way of the Holy Sepulchre.'[14] We have, then, the picture of a movement which was spread, not by the rather clumsy machinery of communication offered by the diocese, but by report and rumour, by popular preaching to mass audiences, by the infectious enthusiasm generated by the badge of the cross, and by the initiative of princes who had friendly relations with Urban and the Gregorian papacy. The signs are that Urban himself encouraged the use of the new methods of propaganda, although it can hardly

---

there are grounds for believing that the vision of Peter at Jerusalem was recorded in a 'Lorraine chronicle' composed shortly after 1099; and the earlier section of the chronicle of Albert of Aachen, which preserves the story, may have been written soon after the First Crusade. See the discussions by [H.] Hagenmeyer, *Peter [der Eremite]* (Leipzig 1879) and P. Knoch, *Studien zu Albert von Aachen* (Stuttgart 1966).

[11] Baudri i 5, 8 (*RHC, Occ* IV pp 16–7).

[12] Guibert ii 7 (*RHC, Occ* IV p 142), where the control by the authorities is stressed more than in Baudri. We hear of the gift of cross-badge and ring by the abbot of Cluny in a charter of 15 June 1100; A. Bernard and A. Bruel, *Recueil des chartes...de Cluny* (Paris 1876–)v p 89. It has been suggested that the issue o crosses was a mechanism to prevent unwanted elements from enrolling: H. E. Mayer, *The Crusades* (Oxford 1972) p 42, but contemporary descriptions emphasise its spontaneous character. For the whole subject, see F. de Mély, 'La croix des premiers croisés,' supplement to P. Riant, *Exuviae Sacrae Constantinopolitanae* (Geneva 1904).

[13] Baudri i. 8 (*RHC, Occ* IV p 17): '*Nec tantummodo populares citramontanos homines is rumor excivit, sed palatinos consules et regios tyrannos civit.*'

[14] Robert ii. 4 (*RHC, Occ* III p 741).

be supposed that he envisaged their full consequences. He toured France after Clermont, consecrating great ecclesiastical buildings and preaching to the crowds who assembled for the occasion. Although we only know specifically that he preached the Crusade at Angers and Limoges, it is a reasonable assumption that it was his regular theme, and indeed that the papal tour was one of the main sources of the rumour which spread across France. It is also likely that Urban inspired, and perhaps authorised, the preaching of Peter the Hermit, who began his campaign in Berry when the pope was in the neighbouring districts.[15] Contemporaries ascribed the use of the cross as a badge to an instruction from Urban at Clermont; in that case, he must be credited with the invention of one of the most successful instances of the 'logo' in history. He also approached directly a number of secular princes, and we can find some trace of negotiations with Raymond of Saint-Gilles, Robert of Flanders, and Robert of Normandy and with the city of Genoa.

This image of Urban II as a master of the media becomes less surprising if we remember that the new opportunities were the result of recent changes in the organisation of society. One of the most obvious instances is the emergence of the princely courts as a major influence in politics and patronage, so that they formed a natural centre for the dissemination of crusading propaganda. At the same time, the growing cities provided places where the surrounding population could be reached, and they were the basis for the preaching campaign of Peter the Hermit.[16] The rise of the city schools was helping to facilitate the flow of ideas and information. Several of the leading popular preachers and hermits had taught in the schools, and it is possible that Peter the Hermit himself came from the same background.[17] Although the preaching of the first crusade was much the most spectacular instance so far of successful mass communication, the

[15] We are also told that at Angers the pope authorised the preaching mission of Robert of Arbrissel, but it is not clear whether he was commissioned to preach the crusade. Conversely, it is unlikely that German preachers such as Gottschalk and Volkmar received any papal authorisation.

[16] Guibert ii. 8 (*RHC, Occ* IV p 142): '*urbes et municipia praedicationis obtentu circumire vidimus.*' Peter's concern for prostitutes is further evidence of a city-based ministry. That is not to say that his recruits were mainly from the urban poor. There is some divergence in the sources about the social origins of his followers. Cf Hagenmeyer, *Peter* pp 108–28.

[17] Contemporaries agreed on his sharp intelligence; Hagenmeyer, *loc. cit.*. It is another matter whether he had ever studied or taught in a cathedral school, but it is interesting that the crowd was said to obey him '*ac si magistro*': Guibert, *loc. cit.*

Crusading propaganda

potentialities of the new structures had already been shown. The anxiety of officialdom to silence the teaching of Berengar of Tours about the eucharist, as much as thirty years before, was the result of concern that the question 'has so filled the land that not only clerks and monks, whose office it is to concern themselves with such matters, but also the very laity discuss it in the streets.'[18] The Investiture Contest, moreover, had brought propaganda on a large scale into the market-places, and the appeal of Gregory VII to public opinion had been based in large part on his contacts with lay courts, such as those of countess Matilda and of Robert of Flanders.[19] Urban II, the disciple and successor of Gregory, followed his methods and used them to propagate the crusade.

The successful capture of Jerusalem in 1099 made necessary a new and sustained propaganda campaign in defence of the holy city. It included immediate military support, the encouragement of pilgrimage and, eventually, the preaching of new crusades. It had already been evident in 1095-6 that an expedition to the eastern Mediterranean could not be recruited through the use of diocesan machinery (just as, subsequently, the bishops proved unable to overcome the threat of the Catharist heresy). The structures which would maintain the Christian presence in Jerusalem had to be established on a different basis, and in practice this meant papal supervision of appeals to popular sentiment and to the sympathy of princes, such as had already been apparent in the first crusade. The steady development of better administration in the course of the twelfth century strengthened this papal supervision, and the point had been taken that there must be no repetition of the disorderly features of the first crusade. Bernard of Clairvaux warned his hearers in 1146 against setting out prematurely as Peter the Hermit had done.[20] A great variety of structures was devised to regulate the provision of aid to the defence of Jerusalem. The orders of the Hospitallers and Templars were created for charitable and military purposes, and Paschal II's bull for the Hospital in 1113 may reasonably be regarded as the first papal recognition of an international religious order. Eugenius III issued the first crusading

---

[18] M. R. James, *Catalogue of Manuscripts of Aberdeen* (Cambridge 1932) p 36.
[19] See I. S. Robinson, 'The Friendship Network of Gregory VII,' *History* 63 (1978) pp 1–22, and, more generally, his excellent book *Authority and Resistance in the Investiture Contest* (Manchester 1978).
[20] Text in J. Leclercq, ['L'encyclique de S. Bernard en faveur de la croisade'] *RB* 81 (1971) pp 299–300.

encyclical, *Quantum Predecessores*, at the time of the second crusade, and thereafter it became standard practice to issue such letters to initiate a crusade.

Whatever new methods were devised of directing the efforts of the faithful towards Jerusalem, preaching remained of basic importance. Its significance was appreciated by contemporaries from the beginning. Urban's speech at Clermont was several times described as a sermon, and he himself as a 'sower of the word'.[21] Even when writers were emphasising the way in which the message was passed on hand-to-hand by the laity, the words they used were those appropriate to preaching: *monere, sollicitare, sermocinari*. On the crusade itself, sermons remained important. In his brief obituary notice about bishop Adhemar of Le Puy, the author of the *Gesta Francorum* reported:

> He used to keep the clergy in order and preach to the knights, warning them and saying, 'None of you can be saved if he does not respect the poor and succour them. You cannot be saved without them, and they cannot survive without you.[22]

At the crucial moment when the crusaders were outside Jerusalem, their flagging spirits were roused by a march round the city, followed by a series of sermons.[23] It is fascinating to observe the continuity in some techniques of crowd control: this is essentially what would more recently be called a 'demo' followed by a teach-in. Throughout the twelfth century, preaching campaigns were planned with increasing efficiency, and remained crucial to the crusading movement. The writer of a satirical poem, preserved in a manuscript of the thirteenth century, warned his hearers against the danger of going to a sermon and being bounced into a rash decision:

Ire si vis ad sermonem,	If you go to hear the preachers,
Cave, precor, Ciceronem	Do beware of clever teachers,
ne per verbi rationem	Who can (with their style and gloss)
Reddat crucis te prisonem.	Make you captive to the Cross.

---

[21] Baudri i. 3 (*RHC, Occ* IV p 12): '*Publicae praedicationis causa papa Romanus, Urbanus nomine, venit in Gallias, et prout erat disertus seminiverbius, verbum Dei passim seminabat*'.

[22] R. Hill, *Gesta Francorum* (Oxford 1979) p 74. A very different view was expressed by Saint Andrew in a vision: '*cur negligit episcopus predicare et commonere et cum cruce quam prefert cotidie signare populum?*'. [J. H. and L. L. Hill, *Le <Liber> de*] *Raymond [d'Aguilers* (Paris 1969)] p 69.

[23] Raymond pp 144–5.

Crusading propaganda

Si me modo vis audire	Would you give me your attention?
Unam rem te volo scire;	There is something I should mention.
Si tu crucem vis subire	If you want a cross to carry
Atque crucis iter ire,	And are not inclined to tarry,
Precor, prius hoc inquire	You must check the real position:
Quam sunt ille vie dire	Are the roads in good condition?
Modo potens es exire,	Or you'll start with courage burning—
Forsan ipsas cras redire.	And next day you'll be returning.
Tam per rupes quam per rura	Country roads have rocks and cracks;
Sunt impedimenta dura.[24]	They are really cul-de-sacs.

Unfortunately, our knowledge of the presentation of crusading propaganda by its preachers is limited. There are some descriptions, but very few texts. It amounts, in the twelfth century, to one recruiting sermon for each crusade—a modest enough allowance. For the first crusade, we have the reports of Urban's address at Clermont in November 1095.[25] In one sense, this is magnificent evidence, because Urban's speech was perhaps the most abundantly reported in human history up to that date, but it is much less clear what sort of material we have here. I think myself that there is only a small element of genuine reporting, but that (along with other influences) the composition has been shaped by the experience of crusading preaching in the years between 1095 and the date of composition, in most cases shortly before 1110. The texts are therefore of interest in illustrating the early history of crusading preaching, even if they are not really reminiscences of Clermont. For the second crusade we have the so-called encyclical of Bernard of Clairvaux, which is an address to audiences to whom he could not preach personally, and which is probably quite close to his sermon material.[26] For the third crusade, there is an address to the German nobility by bishop Henry of

---

[24] The text, which appears incomplete, is printed in H. Pflaum, 'A strange crusader's song' *Speculum* 10 (1935) pp 337–9.

[25] The earliest four of these may conveniently be consulted in translation in L. and J. Riley-Smith, [*The Crusades, Idea and Reality* (London 1981)] pp 40–53. The surviving sermons are surveyed in R. Röhricht, 'Kreuzpredigten gegen den Islam', *ZKG* 6 (1884) pp 550–72, an old article which is still of value.

[26] The case for treating this composition as '*un modèle de style oral*' is stated by J. Leclercq, ['Pour l'histoire de l'encyclique de saint Bernard sur la croisade', *Études de Civilisation médiéval. Mélanges offerts à E-R*] *Labande* (Poitiers n.d.) pp 479–90. The versions of the text are discussed by J. Leclercq, *RB* 81 (1971) pp 282–308.

Strasburg in 1188, and for the fourth a sermon by abbot Martin of Pairis at Basle in 1200 or 1201.[27] It is a scanty list, and one is aware of how many of the greatest preachers are not represented at all: nothing for instance from Peter the Hermit, and nothing from Fulk of Neuilly. Even if we extend the list to include sermons preached actually on crusade, that provides only the two in Portugal when the Anglo-Flemish expedition visited it in 1147.[28] If we look forward into the thirteenth century, we are somewhat better informed, in part because of the concern of Innocent III and Honorius III to regulate crusading preaching. This, however, produced a new approach, and in trying to represent the situation in the twelfth century, it is perhaps safe to use only one later source: a collection of materials designed for preaching in England about 1216, which incorporates some traditional material and gives a glimpse into the workshop of the speaker.[29] Even with these supplements, it is a rather thin ration of evidence, and there is the additional question whether the chroniclers have provided a faithful record of what was said. For our purposes, it does not greatly matter whether these precise words were spoken, but the fact is that a chronicler may require a rhetorical composition different from the original: it would, for instance, be natural to drop any immediate references or detailed instructions, which would have been important for the audience who actually heard the address.

At this point we must cast our eyes along a tempting short-cut. Although we have so few sermons, we have a regular sequence of papal crusading encyclicals from Eugenius III's *Quantum Predecessores* (1145/6) onwards, and it has been suggested that we can use these to reconstitute the character of the preaching. G.

---

[27] For the texts, see [A.] Chroust [ed, *Quellen zur Geschichte des Kreuzzuges Kaiser Friedrichs I*, MGH SRG ns 5 (Berlin 1928)] pp 123–4; and Gunther of Pairis [in P. Riant, *Exuviae Sacrae Constantinopolitanae* I (Geneva 1877)] pp 61–4, of which there is a translation in L. and J. Riley-Smith, pp 69–71.

[28] 'De Expugnatione Lyxbonensi' [in W. Stubbs, *Itinerarium Peregrinorum*, RS 38 (London 1864)] pp cxlii–clxxxii; tr. by C. W. David (New York 1933). See the discussion in E.-D. Hehl, *Kirche und Krieg im 12 Jahrhundert* (Stuttgart 1980) pp 137–40, 259–61. In addition, there is a sermon preached at Jerusalem in the early twelfth century printed by C. Kohler, 'Un sermon commémoratif de la prise de Jérusalem par les croisés, attribué à Foucher de Chartres', *Revue de l'Orient Latin* 8 (1900/1) pp 158–64.

[29] [R.] Röhricht, 'Ordinatio [de Predicatione S. Crucis in Anglia', in his *Quinti Belli Sacri Scriptores Minores* (Société de l'Orient Latin 1879)]. I am grateful to Dr E. O. Blake for drawing my attention to the particular interest of the so-called 'Ordinatio'.

Wolfram, who exercised a strong influence on later German studies of crusading propaganda, went so far as to say that the disappearance of the sermons was no particular loss, because their content was the same as that of the encyclicals.[30] There is some substance in this. The popes saw themselves as addressing the faithful at large, and expected their letters to be read and expounded in church, and in 1147 abbot Adam of Ebrach is said to have already followed this procedure: 'he went up into the pulpit and after the reading of the letters of the apostolic see and of the abbot of Clairvaux, he made a brief exhortation and prevailed on all who were present to enter this service'.[31] At the same time, it cannot be assumed that the sermons were the same in content and style as the encyclicals which they expounded. The preachers were intended to present papal policy in the vernacular tongue and in a way which brought it home to the day-by-day concerns of the audience, and the essential question is how far the pope's original intentions were being faithfully represented. Several scholars have emphasised that, although Eugenius III was a protégé of Bernard of Clairvaux, their attitudes to the preaching of the second crusade were by no means identical.[32] It is gratuitous to assume the identity of encyclical and sermon, of the authoritative text and its interpretation.

This is not the time to survey the doctrine of holy war in the surviving sermons, but it is relevant to our theme to observe by what means the preachers strove to grasp the attention and sway the emotions of their audience. They presented their appeal on public occasions which had been carefully planned. Thus Louis VII, having resolved to depart on the crusade, summoned a large assembly (including some who had taken the cross and many who

---

[30] G. Wolfram, ['Kreuzpredigt und Kreuzlied', *Zeitschrift für deutsches Altertum n.f.* 18 (1886)] pp 89-132. The standard work on the encyclicals is U. Schwerin, *Die Aufrufe der Päpste zur Befreiung des Heiligen Landes* (Berlin 1937).

[31] Thus Alexander III in 1181: '*litteras ... universis faciatis ecclesiis publice legi, et exponatis earum tenorem*', *PL* 200, 1297 A; [G. Waitz ed, *Ottonis et Rahewini*] *Gesta Friderici* [*I Imperatoris*, *MGH SRG* (Hanover 1912)] i.42 p 60.

[32] The differences are examined by J. Leclerq, *Labande* pp 479-90, and G. Constable, 'The second crusade as seen by contemporaries', *Traditio* 9 (1953) pp 247 *seq*. There is no way in the twelfth century of validating the statement that '*ein vergleich der überlieferten stücke mit den kreuzzugsbullen ergibt dass die prediger im wesentlichen mit denselben argumenten und in derselber form zu wirken suchen.*' (Wolfram pp 89-90). The comparison might arguably be more valid for the thirteenth century, when the control of preachers was tighter, and their briefing more thorough.

had not) to hear Saint Bernard at Vézelay on Passion Sunday 1146. In the same way Adam of Ebrach preached in Bavaria at a *generalis curia*.[33] When the sermon was in a city, a large turn-out might be guaranteed by reports circulating in advance. When Martin of Pairis preached in Basle cathedral in 1200 or 1201, the crowd 'had already heard that other provinces around had been stirred by famous preachers to this service of Christ'.[34] The audience might be so large that the sermon had to be delivered in the open air, like Urban's at Clermont or Bernard's at Vézelay, where a wooden platform was specially built for him.[35] The sermon took place within a setting of liturgy and ceremonial. It was frequently, perhaps normally, part of a mass, and it may well be significant that the English sermon materials of 1216 contained a meditation on the presence of Christ in the eucharist; the implication is that the hearers are invited to decide for Christ in the Lord's own presence.[36] Sometimes, the sermon received an even more dramatic setting. When the Lisbon crusaders were about to assault the city, they heard a sermon by a priest carrying a fragment of the true cross, and at its end they prostrated themselves in adoration and, at his instruction, made the sign of the cross all together.[37] The most dramatic preaching of all was probably that of Saint Bernard, for several contemporaries reported the miracles which accompanied it. We have to see these sermons in an emotional, a revivalistic, context.

When we turn from the setting to the words of the preacher, it is clear that serious trouble was taken to bring their meaning home. Sermons to lay audiences would normally be in the vernacular, and although the sermon materials prepared for use in England in 1216 were in Latin, the language of record, it is significant that the stories provided for illustration often have their punch-lines recorded in French. When the preacher had no

---

[33] V. G. Berry ed and tr, *Odo of Deuil: De profectione Ludovici VII in Orientem* (Columbia 1948) pp 6–7; *Gesta Friderici* i. 42 p 60.

[34] Gunther p 61, cf *Gesta Friderici, loc, cit.: 'cunctis qui aderant, ex priori rumore excitatis'*.

[35] Similarly at the sermon of the bishop of Oporto the Lisbon crusaders, being too numerous to get into the cathedral, assembled in the *coemiterium episcopii*. Robert i. 1 (*RHC, Occ* III p 727); Odo pp 8–9; De Expugnatione Lyxbonensi p cxlvii. The open-air sermon at Clermont, in late November, should be regarded with some suspicion, since it is doubtful whether there really was a large lay attendance there.

[36] *Gesta Friderici, loc. cit.: 'missarum ex more sollempnia celebrans'*; De Expugnatione Lyxbonensi, p. clii: *'completo sermone, post expletionem missae'*; Röhricht, 'Ordinatio' p 10.

[37] De Expugnatione Lyxbonensi p clxxv.

language in common with the audience (a situation which arose not infrequently in such an international undertaking) an interpreter would be in attendance, as when archdeacon Alexander of Bangor translated into Welsh the sermons of archbishop Baldwin in 1188.[38] Sermons could be expressed in direct language designed to appeal to the hearers, and went further in this direction than papal encyclicals would do. Naturally enough, this type of plain speaking was directed mainly to the military classes. The English preaching materials included, in the fashionable mode, a series of stories or *exempla* 'both to keep the attention of the hearers and to avoid boredom'. They are simple stories of Christian courage, sometimes told of a famous man, and always having a snappy ending. Thus a knight who had been wounded four times insisted, in spite of the doctors, on returning to fight the Saracens again: 'My Lord Jesus Christ suffered five wounds for me, and I will suffer for him a fifth wound to add to the four I have suffered'. Sometimes a pun is included to enliven the story further. Usually these defy translation, as in the famous last words of Hugh de Beauchamp in battle: 'My name is Beauchamp, but never was I in a *beau champ* until now.'[39] The preachers often referred sharply to everyday experience. When an assembly of German nobles paid no attention to recruiting appeals, bishop Henry of Strasburg complained that 'any minstrel or play can capture your attention if it entertains you.'[40] The undertaking of the crusade was expressed in terms which would readily appeal to knights and barons: they were urged to display their courage, to be faithful to the brave example of their fathers, to redress the wrongs of their Lord, who had been deprived of his inheritance. The aim of the recruiting sermons was enlistment, there and then: 'So now, brave warriors, give your help to Christ, add your names to the Christian army.'[41] The texts are studded with urgent appeals: '*Viam sancti Sepulchri incipite.*'[42] The fixing of the sign of the cross on the garments was

---

[38] Gerald of Wales, *Itinerarium Cambriae* i. 5, ed J. F. Dimock, *Giraldi Cambrensis Opera* VI, RS 21 (London 1868) p 55. Sometimes a team of interpreters might be needed, as when the bishop of Oporto preached to the Anglo-Flemish crusade: '*episcopus sermonem coram omnibus lingua Latina habuit, ut per interpretes cujusque linguae sermo ejus omnibus manifestaretur*' De Expugnatione Lyxbonensi, p cxlvii.
[39] Röhricht, 'Ordinatio' pp 24–5.
[40] Chroust p 123.
[41] Gunther p 63.
[42] Robert i. 1 (*RHC, Occ* III p 728).

the mark that an individual had been recruited. The English sermon notes contain a selection of phrases suitable for appealing for a commitment, usually beginning '*Surge ergo*', 'Arise therefore'. The preacher was even content with the laconic reminder '*Surge ergo, etc.*', and presumably knew by heart the standard ways of continuing it. The scatter of sermons which we possess contain only a limited range of ideas, but they are very much rooted in the outlook of the military classes. They offered a clear and simple way of service, a *devotio*[43] to use a word which occurred at the time, through which the warrior could place his sword at Christ's service.

This development of a military spirituality was even more evident in the other method of propaganda I would like to consider: the song. Joan Littlewood was able to present a pageant of the first world war in its songs in 'Oh! What a Lovely War!' and one could almost do the same for the crusades.[44] We are told that, as the knights went into battle at Antioch on 9 February 1098, they sang war-songs (*cantus militares*) so joyously that it seemed they regarded the battle as a game.[45] When archbishop Anselm of Milan began recruiting for an expedition in 1101 he admonished the cream of the Milanese youth to

> take the cross and to sing the song of *Ultreia Ultreia*. And at the word of this wise man many men of all classes throughout the cities of Lombardy and their villages and townships took the cross and sang the same song of *Ultreya Ultreia*.[46]

---

[43] See the short but stimulating essay by F.-W. Wentzlaff-Eggebert, '*Devotio* in der Kreuzzugspredigt des Mittelalters', *Festgabe für Kurt Wagner* (Giessen 1960) 26–33.

[44] The best collections are those by J. Bédier and P. Aubry, *Les chansons de croisade avec leurs mélodies* (Paris 1909) and [U.] Müller, [*Kreuzzugsdichtung* (Tübingen 1969)], which consists mainly, but not exclusively, of German materials. Overwhelmingly the greatest part of the modern discussion of crusading lyrics is by German scholars, especially F. W. Wentzlaff-Eggebert, *Kreuzzugsdichtung des Mittelalters* (Berlin 1960); [G.] Spreckelmeyer, [*Das Kreuzzugslied des lateinischen Mittelalters* (Munich 1974)]; [S.] Schöber, [*Die altfranzösische Kreuzzugslyrik des 12 Jahrhunderts*, Dissertationen der Universität Saltzburg 7 (Vienna 1976)] and [P.] Hölzle, [*Die Kreuzzüge in der okzitanischen und deutschen Lyrik des 12 Jahrhunderts* (Göppingen 1980)]. The brief discussion in the text of this paper is indebted to all these works, and most notably to Schöber. In English there is a recent article by R. L. Crocker, 'Early Crusade Songs', in T. P. Murphy, *Holy War* (Ohio 1976) pp 78–98. A. Hughes, 'La musique populaire médiévale, une question de tout ou rien', *La Culture populaire au Moyen-Âge* (Montreal 1979) pp 103–20, does not deal with crusading songs, but has some important comments on the extent to which music was popularised.

[45] Raymond p 57.

[46] Landulf, *Historia Mediolanensis* c.4. (*MGH SS* XX) p 22.

Crusading propaganda

Ultreia or *outrée* appears to have been a pilgrim shout ('onward!') which later was used as a battle-cry. It was said about 1133 that the events of the first crusade were well-known from *cantica* which were widely known, and certain *carmina*.[47] About the middle of the century, Gerhoh of Reichersberg, commenting on the text 'He put a new song in my mouth', remarked on the new hymnology which was evident in monasteries, and continued:

> The praise of God is also spreading in the mouth of laymen who fight for Christ, because there is nobody in the whole Christian realm who dares to sing dirty songs in public; but, as I have said, the whole earth rejoices in the praises of Christ, in songs in the vernacular as well, especially among the Germans, whose language is specially suitable for good songs.[48]

Gerhoh adds that women whose husbands and sons had gone to the wars against the pagans joined in the worship in nunneries. Gerhoh, incidentally, was proud of German singing, and described elsewhere how, on returning from the battle of Ascalon, 'the Germans were singing as usual, and as usual the Frenchmen were shouting'.[49]

All of this establishes that, as we might expect, music was an important vehicle for the transmission of crusading ideas, but it is more difficult to know precisely what sort of songs are involved in each case. There were epics which were based on the crusades or were influenced by the crusades. These were very important in shaping opinion but, precisely because a great deal has been written about them, I do not want to discuss them now. If we therefore limit ourselves to the shorter lyrics, to songs in the modern usage of the word, we must first ask what their function was. Gerhoh was clearly talking about songs for pilgrims to sing together, and we know of German pilgrim songs which probably

---

[47] *Chronicon S. Andreae* iii 21 (*MGH SS* VII p 545). The precise meaning is not clear. It is fair to assume that the *cantica* are *chansons de geste* of the type of the *Song of Antioch*, but what were the *carmina*? The most likely explanation is that they were hymns and canticles for liturgical use, of which one or two, designed to celebrate the festival at the capture of the city of Jerusalem, survive. There is not much indication that any crusade produced lyrics, whether in the vernacular or Latin, which briefly recounted the past events; but for a different view see Schöber p 55.

[48] Müller no. 7. The reference is to Ps.xl.3 (English style).

[49] *MGH Lib* III p 431.

originated in the eleventh century, and were still in use on the crusades:

In gotes namen fara wir,	In God's name we make our way,
seyner genaden gara wir,	And we journey in His grace.
Nu helff uns die gotes kraft	Power of God help us today,
und das heylig grab,	And the Holy Place
da got selber ynne lag	Where Himself God lay
Kyrieleis.[50]	Kyrie Eleison.

Such songs do not survive in other vernacular languages; perhaps Gerhoh was right about German community singing.[51] In French and Provençal, the songs are addressed to the audience. This would not preclude group singing, but they were not designed for it. They are essentially recruiting addresses, and were so regarded by contemporaries. In Provençal they were sometimes described as sermons or appeals: *sermo, prec, conseil, prezicansa*. When in 1189 Huon d'Oisi wrote a scathing attack on his fellow trouvere, Conon de Béthune, for returning quickly from the third crusade, he complained:

Mout fu Quenes preus, quant il s'en ala,	Conon was bold, before he went away,
De sermouner et de gent preechier.[52]	To preach to people and give sermons there.

This aspect is strengthened if we accept a modern view that the performance of these songs was essentially declamatory, with the music acting as a background to the words. The earliest French recruiting-song to survive was composed for the second crusade, and it displays these 'preaching' characteristics vividly. It is addressed to knights (and is thus a very early example of the *sermo ad status*) and interprets the crusade in the light of concepts which would be familiar to them. This is an approach which can be observed in encyclicals and sermons, but it is taken further in the songs. God has made his plea to them, He has been dishonoured, His enemies have seized His fiefs, in which He had been recognised

---

[50] Müller no.8.
[51] It is however probable that songs such as the one in the text were sung by a clerk or cantor, with the pilgrims joining in the *Kyrie* at the end. On this see W. Mettin, 'Die ältesten deutschen Pilgerlieder', *Philologische Studien. Festgabe E. Sievers* (Halle 1896) pp 277–86.
[52] Huon d'Oisi, *Maugré tous sainz*, Müller no 21, stanza III; discussed in Schöber pp 148–68.

Crusading propaganda

as lord. It is a religion which makes large demands, but they are explained in terms readily accessible to knights:

Chevalier, mult estes guariz,	Knights, now is this a time of grace,
Quant Deu a vos fait sa clamur	For God has brought to you a plea
Des Turs e des Amoraviz	Against the Turks and Moorish race
Ki li unt fait tels deshenors;	Who treated him dishonourably.
Cher a tort unt cez fieuz saisiz,	They wronged Him and they seized His fief,
Bien en devums aveir dolur,	And we must feel the deepest grief,
Cher là fud Deu primes servi	For there God first was served by men,
E reconuu pur segnuur.	Who recognised His lordship then.
Ki ore irat ad Loovis	Whoever goes with Louis now,
Ja mar d'enfern avrat pouur,	Need never fear the devil's horde;
Char s'alme en iert en pareïs	His soul will go to Paradise
Od les angles nostre segnor.	With the angels of the Lord.
Pris est Rohais, ben le savez,	You heard about Edessa's fall;
Dunt Christïens sunt esmaiez,	The Christians are sore oppressed.
Les mustiers ars e desertez,	No churches are in use at all;
Deus n'i est mais sacrifiez,	God's sacrifice is nowhere blessed.
Chivalers, cher vus purpensez,	Knights, please reflect upon this word,
Vus ki d'armes estes preisez,	You who in arms are most esteemed
A celui voz cors presentez	Present your bodies to your Lord,
Ki pur vus fut en cruiz drecez.	Who on the cross your life redeemed.
Ki ore irat ...	Whoever goes...
Alum conquere Moïses	Let's go to rescue Moses then–
Ki gist el munt de Sinaï	His body is in Sinai.
A Saragins nel laisum mais	Let's take him from the Saracen,
Ne la verge dunt il partid	And get his staff that, raised on high
La roge mer tut ad un fais,	Opened a road across the sea,
Quant le grant pople le seguit,	And Israel went across dry-shod
E Pharaon revint aproef,	While Pharoah followed furiously.
Il e li suon furent perit.	He and his men were slain by God.
Ki ore irat...[53]	Whoever goes...

A Latin song, also composed in France for the second crusade, is much longer and more complex, but it displays the same

---

[53] The full text is in Schöber pp 72-5, and is discussed in detail there and by H. Gelzer, 'Zum altfranzösischen Kreuzzugslied *Chevalier, mult estes guariz*', *Zeitschrift für Romanische Philologie* 48 (1928) pp 438-48. There is a recording of this song, and those quoted subsequently (although not with precisely the same text and interpretation as I have adopted) by David Munrow and the Early Music Consort of London, *Music of the Crusades*, Argo Stereo ZRG 673.

characteristics of an address, and at one point provides some rather heartening instructions to the departing crusaders:

Nam tamen ita properet,	But people mustn't rush off there
quin coniugi provideat	until they've taken special care
de rebus necessariis	to leave their children and their wife
una cum parvis liberis;	all the necessities of life.
quod quidem nisi faciat,	Unless this is attended to,
ignoro quid proficiat.[54]	I can't see what good it will do.

Recruiting songs are rare until the third crusade, and then there is a great outcrop of them: about forty in the vernacular, not to mention the many Latin laments on the loss of Jerusalem. They also show some changes, a fact which has led scholars to separate them from crusading songs proper, and to categorise them (in one form or another) as love songs which mention the crusades. A crusading song proper (*Kreuzzugslied, Kreuzlied*) would on this view only apply to a song which reflects the official teaching, as expressed in the encyclical which introduced the crusade. This assertion is no mere question of literary genres, but raises wider issues about the propaganda of the period, and I must therefore close this paper by looking at the new features of these songs. The first is the appearance of personal reflection as part of the poem. The composer writes in the first person, of his own experience. On examination, however, it proves that this element does not supersede the 'preaching' aspect of the song, for most of the stanzas still speak of the need to respond to God's appeal; it is simply that the *sermo* or *prezicansa* has come to include, as one of its component parts, an element of personal testimony. Since the composers of the songs were usually laymen, nobles themselves or clients of the nobility, they shared a common experience with their audience which was not accessible to any clerical preacher, and this influenced the whole character of the recruiting-song, and above all one element which now became very prominent: the theme of love. It would be best to examine this with reference to one of the best loved of the crusading songs: the *Ahi, amors!* of Conon of Béthune, written before his departure on the third crusade:

---

[54] *Fides cum Ydolatria*, Müller no 9, stanza XII; discussed in Spreckelmeyer pp 119–31, and A. Hilka and O. Schumann, *Carmina Burana* (Heidelberg 1930) ii pp 93–9.

Crusading propaganda

Ahi, Amors, com dure departie
me convenra faire de la millor
ki onques fust amee ne servie!
Dieus me remaint a li par sa douçour
si voirement ke m'en part a dolor.
Las, k'ai je dit? Ja ne m'en part je mie;
se li cors va servir Nostre Signor,
li cuers remaint del tot en sa baillie.

* *

Por li m'en vois sospirant en Surie,
car je ne doi faillir mon Creator:
ki li faura a cest besoing d'aïe,
saciés ke Il li faura a grignor.
E saicent bien li grant e li menor
ke la doit on faire chevallerie
ou on conquiert paradis et honor
et pris et los, et l'amor de s'amie.

* *

Dieus est assis en son saint iretaige:
ore i parra se cil le secorront
cui il jeta de la prison ombraige
quant il fu mors ens la Crois ke Turc ont.
Saichiés, chil sont trop honi ki n'iront
s'il n'ont poverté ou viellece ou malaige,
et cil ki saint et jone et riche sont
ne poevent pas demorer sans hontaige.

* *

Tous li clergiés et li home d'eaige
qui ens ausmogne et ens biens fais morront,
partiront tot a cest pelerinage
et les dames ki chastement vivront
et loiauté feront ceaus ki iront.
E s'eles font, par mal consel, folaige,
as lasques gens et mauvais le feront,
car tot li boin iront en cest voiage.[55]

Alas, O Love, it is most hard to part—
As part I must—from her who is of all
The best who ever has been loved or served.
God, in His goodness, bring me back to her
As surely as I part from her in grief.
What do I say? Yet I shall never part;
Although my body goes to serve my Lord,
My heart remains behind at her command.

* *

For her, I go with sighs to Syria,
For I must not neglect my Lord's command.
Whoever in His need will fail Him now
Knows that, in Judgement, he in turn will fail.
So let the great and little all take note
That they should take the field in chivalry
Where paradise and honour can be won,
And reputation, and their lady's love.

* *

God is besieged in His inheritance
And we shall see how people will respond
Whom He redeemed from darkness and the grave
By dying on the cross the Turks now hold.
You know, they are dishonoured who refuse,
Unless they are too poor or old or sick,
Those who are healthy, and are young and rich
Cannot without disgrace remain behind.

* *

All clergy and all senior citizens
Who do good works and freely give their alms
Will count as going on this pilgrimage,
And so do ladies faithful to their men
By living chastely while they are away.
If they are led astray and are seduced,
It must be with the cowardly and bad—
For all good men will go upon crusade.

[55] Müller no.20; discussed in Schöber pp 106–26.

This particular song spoke to contemporaries. It was known not only in its native France, but in Italy and Germany, and it must have represented the aspirations of its audience. Its opening words declare it as a love song, and it begins with a skilful expression of the *topoi* of love and parting, the division (as Conon expresses it) of his body and his heart. It is, however, not a straightforward love lyric. It uses this theme in order to engage the attention of the hearers—a 'soft sell' approach which was a common device in the poems of the time—and proceeds to make a direct recruiting appeal. This was one of Conon's two songs which were satirised by Huon d'Oisi when he complained that Conon preached too much, and it makes a direct plea for God's threatened inheritance, and for the cross which the Turks had captured. This crusading appeal is expressed in terms appropriate to aristocratic ideals. It will be a dishonour not to go: '*ne poevent pas demorer sans hontaige*'. Both heavenly and earthly honour are involved in answering the call: it is a matter of acquiring

'*paradis et honor
et pris et los, et l'amor de s'amie.*'

In an unusually positive assertion, Conon stresses that those who are unable to go will also share in the enterprise: the clergy, the aged, and the ladies (whose contribution, significantly, is to be faithful and chaste). There is no reason to dismiss the concern with love as a mere artifice. It was, rather, an acute social problem as, for the first time since the growth of the fashion of so-called 'courtly love', great numbers of the nobility were confronted by the demand that they should leave their ladies for the sake of God. It was an authentic expression of the crusading ideal from the point of view of its lay leadership—of '*chevallerie*', to use Conon's still relatively new expression. There had been some attempt in the papal encyclicals, and more in the sermons, to bring together lay aspirations and crusading ideals, but in these recruiting songs the two are combined much more fully into one pattern of belief and action.

There is perhaps one point which should be added, although it is in truth rather an obvious one. Medieval songs operated a great deal by *topoi*, commonplace situations and standard phrases, and

Crusading propaganda

they are a ceaseless obstacle in our attempt to understand them, because of the modern cult to achieve self-expression through the avoidance of set forms. In medieval verse, such forms do not hinder self-expression, but facilitate it. Thus, the dramatic demand for conversion and the mixture of heavenly and worldly aims in another song can be seen, not as conventional but as sincere; or rather, to be precise, as sincere because they have come to form a new convention:

Parti de mal e a bien aturné,	Giving up evil and turning to right,
Voil ma chançun a la gent fere oïr,	This is my song, which I ask you to hear.
K'a sun besuing nus ad Deus apelé,	Now God has called us to join in his fight,
Si ne li deit nul prosdome faillir,	Let no true gentleman hold back in fear.
Kar en la cruiz deignat pur nus murir:	Since on the cross he was humbled and slain
Mult li doit bien estre gueredoné,	We should be glad to give recompense here.
Kar par sa mort sumes tuz rachaté.	We were redeemed by his dying in pain.

* *

Mult ad le quoer de bien enluminé	He is enlightened with good in his heart
Ki la cruiz prent pur aler Deu servir,	Who takes the cross and who serves on God's side;
K'al jugement ki tant iert reduté,	And at the Judgement, where all must take part,
U Deus vendrat les bons des mals partir,	When God the good men from bad will divide,
Dunt tut le mund deit trembler e fremir,	And all humanity is terrified,
Mult iert huni ki serat rebuté	He is disgraced who is left on his own
K'il ne verad Deu en sa maesté.	And not allowed to see God on His throne.

* *

Mult iert celui en cest siecle honuré	He will be greatly esteemed in these parts
Ki Deus donrat k'il puisse revenir.	Whom God allows to return safely home.
Ki bien avrad en sun païs amé	He who has loved well before he departs
Par tut l'en deit menbrer e suvenir;	Must keep the memory where'er he roam.
E Deus me doinst de la meillur joïr,	May God allow me enjoyment of her
Que jo la truisse en vie e en santé,	Best of all ladies, loving and fair,
Quant Deus avrad sun afaire achevé!	After the Lord ends His own great affair!
E il otroit a sa merci venir	And may He show His mercy to those lords
Mes bon seignurs que jo tant ai amé	With whom I once was bound in such close love
K'a bien petit n'en oi Deu oblié![56]	That almost I forgot the Lord above!

[56] Full text and discussion in Schöber pp 173–84.

Only a fraction remains of the vast amount of twelfth-century crusading propaganda which must have existed, and of that fraction we have examined only a few survivals. They do, however, point us in the direction of certain conclusions. Crusading propaganda was one aspect of the new social forms and means of communication which were characteristic of the period. It existed outside the old diocesan system, which could not have sustained such an enterprise, and belongs to the many institutions which in the twelfth century assumed an international character transcending old boundaries: the Cistercians, the regular canons and appeals to Rome are other instances which, different in kind, are similar in being essentially common to Christendom as a whole. As in the other cases, papal initiative was important in creating this propaganda, but it was by no means under papal control. The propaganda showed a remarkable capacity to spread outside the official programme of preaching, and was welcomed by new social groups and transmuted into a form which embodied their own aspirations. We shall never know what the poor, who followed Peter the Hermit, made of the crusading message, although some historians have not been reticent in speculating what it might have been. We are rather better informed about the aristocracy of the later twelfth century, and there we find in the crusading songs, the announcement of a programme which offered the rewards of salvation, honour and love, while demanding in return conversion and commitment. It was not a specially elevated message, in the form in which the aristocracy received it; perhaps for that very reason, it proved satisfying, and endured for a long time as an ideal. The preaching of the crusades was a spectacularly successful example of propaganda, and one of the major reasons for its success was the fact that it was not completely controlled and regulated by a central authority. The propagandists included popular preachers and aristocratic song-writers, as well as representatives who had been carefully briefed by papal encyclicals; the conduct and content of their campaign was in part centrally directed and in part an indigenous expression of the ideals of various social groups. Crusading propaganda was in one sense a dramatic expression of the international standing of the papacy. Viewed from another angle, it was a demonstration of that spirit of initiative and 'do-it-yourself' which is characteristic of twelfth-century lay society.

University of Southampton

MISSIONARIES AND CRUSADERS, 1095–1274: OPPONENTS OR ALLIES?

by ELIZABETH SIBERRY

The Christian missions to the Muslims in the Near East during the Central Middle Ages have already attracted much attention from historians,[1] but as yet no real attempt has been made to analyse the relationship between those who advocated peaceful conversion by means of preaching and teaching, in other words a programme of missionary work, and the crusaders, who sought to defeat the enemies of the faith in battle. In the past, historians have tended to portray advocates of missions as opponents of the crusades and it has been suggested that by the late thirteenth century, as a result of a series of Christian defeats in the Near East, the missionary ideal had won a great deal of support and that this was one of the factors which contributed towards the decline of the crusading movement.[2] The aim of this paper is to challenge this thesis. The first step towards this reappraisal will be to examine the attitude of certain prominent supporters of a policy of peaceful conversion towards the crusades.

The exact details of Peter the Venerable's journey to Spain in 1142–3 are still a matter for debate,[3] but it is clear that this experience prompted him to commission translations of the *'Qur'ān* and several other Islamic treatises and to write his own summary and refutation of Muslim doctrine.[4] In the first book of the *'Liber contra sectam sive haeresim Saracenorum'*, Peter contrasted his own

---

[1] Examples of the extensive literature on this subject are E. R. Daniel, *The Franciscan concept of mission* (Kentucky 1975) and [J.] Richard, [*La papauté et les missions d'Orient au moyen âge XIIIe–XVe siecles* (Rome 1977)].

[2] [P. A.] Throop, [*Criticism of the crusade. A study of public opinion and crusade propaganda* (Amsterdam 1940)] p 288; S. Runciman, 'The decline of the crusading idea', *Relazioni del X congresso internazionale di scienze storiche. Storia dei medievo*, vol 3. *Bibliotheca storica sansoni*, nuova serie vol 24 pp 650, 652; [J.] Prawer, [*Histoire du royaume Latin de Jérusalem*, 2 vols (Paris 1970) 1]pp 389–90: [E.] Stickel, [*Der Fall von Akkon* (Frankfurt 1975)] pp 224–40.

[3] See C. J. Bishko, 'Peter the Venerable's journey to Spain' *Studia Anselmiana* 40 (1956) pp 163–75.

[4] J. Kirtzeck, *Peter the Venerable and Islam* (Princeton 1964) pp 14, 27–30.

attitude towards the Muslims with that adopted by many of his fellow Christians: 'I do not attack you as our people often do by arms, but by words; not by force but by reason; not in hatred but in love.'[5] This oft quoted statement has prompted some historians to suggest that the Abbot of Cluny was at least dissatisfied with the goals of the crusading movement and lukewarm in his support for the Second Crusade.[6] In fact, as Virginia Berry has shown, this was far from the truth.[7] Peter the Venerable's main aim in commissioning the translations was to strengthen the faithful against Muslim propaganda and to provide Christians with a weapon for future ideological conflicts. He did not reject the use of force as a means of maintaining and defending the Holy Land. On the contrary, he praised those who had taken part in earlier expeditions to the East[8] and he exhorted men to join Louis VII's army.[9] Indeed Peter played an important part in the preparations for the Second Crusade and, although he was disillusioned by the reversal of Christian fortunes at the siege of Damascus in 1148, he was closely involved in Abbot Suger's attempts to launch another crusade in the early 1150s.[10] Peter's only reservation was that monks should not take the cross. Like Bernard of Clairvaux, Peter stressed the importance of the monastic vow of stability and he exhorted the religious to remain in the cloister and to pray for the success of the expedition.[11]

Far from their being an obstacle to conversion, contemporaries seem to have regarded the crusades as a means to that end: they believed that military conquest of the Near East would create the right political conditions for the Muslims to enter the Christian fold of their own volition. Hence in the early thirteenth century James of Vitry, Bishop of Acre and Oliver, later Bishop of Paderborn, discussed the likelihood of the peaceful conversion of the Muslims and pointed out the similarities between Islam and

---

[5] *Ibid* p 231.
[6] See *ibid* pp 20–3, 161; J. Leclercq, *Pierre le Vénérable* (Abbaye Saint Wandrille 1946) pp 248–9.
[7] [V. G.] Berry, ['Peter the Venerable and the crusades' *Studia Anselmiana* 40 (1956) pp 141–62.
[8] Peter the Venerable, *Letters*, [ed G. Constable 2 vols (Cambridge, Massachussetts 1967)] I p 141.
[9] Peter the Venerable, 'Sermones tres' ed G. Constable, *Revue Bénédictine* 44 (1954) pp 232–54.
[10] Berry pp 147–50, 154–62.
[11] Peter the Venerable, *Letters* I p 220. See also Constable, 'Opposition to pilgrimage in the Middle Ages', *Studies in religious life and thought—eleventh and twelfth centuries* (London 1979) pp 136–7.

Missionaries and crusaders

Christianity. But they also preached the cross and played a prominent part in the Fifth Crusade.[12] Oliver's attitude was summed up in a letter which he wrote to Sultan al-Kamil in 1221. In this he used the threat of another crusade as a means of persuading the Egyptian leader to allow Christian missionaries to preach publicly.[13] At the time of Louis IX's Egyptian crusade, an anonymous trouvère predicted that the king would conquer and convert the Sultan[14] and one of the main purposes of Louis' North African campaign seems to have been to persuade the Sultan of Tunis to accept Christianity.[15] The Provençal troubadour Daspols lamented that, if the king had lived, he would have defeated the Muslims and brought them into the Christian fold.[16]

In this period much of the missionary work in the Near East was carried out by the new orders of friars, the Franciscans and Dominicans, and it has been suggested that they formed a large body of opinion which was hostile to the use of force against the Muslims.[17] Proponents of this thesis cite the example of Saint Francis' behaviour during the Fifth Crusade. They point out that during his stay in the camp he visited Sultan al-Kāmil and sought to convert him to Christianity. Moreover Francis predicted the disastrous defeat of the Christian army in August 1219[18] and after the capture of Damietta he denounced the immorality and licentiousness of the crusading host.[19] But there is no indication that he objected to the actual use of the crusade against the Muslims.[20] On the contrary Francis supported the crusaders'

---

[12] See Richard pp 34–7; R. C. Schwinges, *Kreuzzugsideologie und Toleranz* (Stuttgart 1977) p 273.
[13] Oliver of Paderborn, *Die Schriften* ed H. Hoogeweg (Tübingen 1894) p 299.
[14] 'Un serventois, plait de deduit de joie' *Chansons de croisade*, edd J. Bédier and P. Aubry (Paris 1909) pp 252–3.
[15] See J. Longnon, 'Les vues de Charles d'Anjou pour la deuxième croisade de Saint Louis: Tunis ou Constantinople' *Septième centenaire de la mort de Saint Louis* (Paris 1976) pp 191–2, 195.
[16] 'Fortz tristors es e salvaj'a retraire', 'Les derniers troubadours de la Provence' ed P. Meyer, *Bibliothèque de l'école de chartes* 30 (1869) p 286.
[17] See Stickel p 233; Prawer p 389.
[18] S Bonaventure, 'Vita Sancti Francisci' Golubovich, series 1, *Annali* vol 1 pp 33–5; Thomas of Celano, 'Vita Sancti Francisci' *ibid* p 17.
[19] 'L'estoire de Eracles' *RHC Occ* II, pp 348–9.
[20] For this thesis see L. Bréhier, 'Les missions franciscaines au moyen âge' *Saint François d'Assise: son oeuvre-son influence 1226–1926*, edd H. Lemaître and A. Masseron (Paris 1927) pp 288–9; H. Daniel-Rops, *Cathedral and crusade: studies of the Medieval church, 1050–1300* trans. J. Warrington (London 1957) p 501; G. Basetti-Sani, 'Francis of Assisi', *Concilium* 7 (1968) pp 9–10.

endeavours against the Egyptians and he won much respect for his ministrations to the army.[21]

In the following decades the Franciscans and Dominicans launched a series of missions to the East,[22] but at the same time they became the papacy's main agents for preaching the cross:[23] receiving financial contributions, issuing indulgences and redeeming the vows of those unfit to go to the Holy Land.[24] And chroniclers throughout Europe praised the friars' skill as preachers and recorded the number who took the cross.[25] When Henry III of England announced his intention of going on crusade in 1250, the English Franciscan Adam Marsh praised his devotion and, far from questioning the value of the king's proposed expedition, as one historian has suggested,[26] he prayed for its success and exhorted clerks to take this opportunity to emulate the apostles and spread the Christian faith.[27] Significantly, at the time of the Second Council of Lyons in 1274, two of the main apologists of the crusade were friars: Gilbert of Tournai belonged to the Franciscan Order and Humbert of Romans was a Dominican. At Pope Gregory X's request they composed memoirs in which they offered suggestions about possible means of recovering the Holy Land and they also gave some information about the attitude of the faithful towards the crusading movement as a whole.[28] Humbert's enthusiastic support for the crusades is particularly interesting because as Minister-General of the Dominican Order from 1254 to 1263 he had been responsible for sending friars to the Near East and North Eastern Europe and he had received reports about the success of their missions.[29] He was optimistic about the peaceful

---

[21] See James of Vitry, *Lettres* ed R. B. C. Huygens (Leiden 1960) pp 132–3.

[22] Richard pp 41–7.

[23] See 'Bulle d'Innocent IV pour la croisade' ed P. F. Delorme, *Archivum Franciscanum Historicum* 6(1913) pp 386–9; Urban IV, *Régistres* ed J. Guiraud (Paris 1901) I no 326.

[24] Matthew Paris accused the friars of greed and complained that they gave the cross indiscriminately to the poor, the old and the sick; *Chronica maiora* ed H. R. Luard (London 1872–80) IV pp 9, 133–4, 635; V pp 188–9, 400–1, 405.

[25] Paulinus of Venice, 'Chronologia magna' ed Golubovich (Florence 1913) II p 87; Vincent of Beauvais, 'Memoriale omnium temporum' *MGH SS* XXIV p 161; Salimbene, ['Cronica', *MGH SS* XXXII] p 218.

[26] Moorman, *History* p 301.

[27] Adam Marsh, 'Epistolae' ed J. S. Brewer, *Monumenta Franciscana* 2 vols (London 1955) I pp 416, 431, 434–7.

[28] See Throop pp 11–23, 69–104, 115–213.

[29] See R. P. Mortier, *Histoire des maîtres généraux de l'ordre des frères precheurs* 2 vols (Paris 1903) I pp 521–3, 527–32.

conversion of the Prussians, but he stressed that only force would succeed against the Muslims.[30]

In this period missionaries and crusaders could work in partnership because, although in certain circumstances the crusade might act as a stimulus to conversion, there was never any suggestion that actual force should be used to compel the Muslims to abjure their faith. In the twelfth century the theologian Peter Lombard maintained that men should be converted of their own free will[31] and the canonist Gratian stessed that God was not pleased with forced service.[32] The Church's position was reaffirmed by other writers[33] and it was stated clearly by Thomas Aquinas. In his *Summa Theologica* he argued that the Christians were justified in waging war upon the Muslims in order to prevent them from hindering the faith of Christ by their blasphemies. But at the same time he emphasised that the heathen 'are by no means to be compelled to the faith in order that they may believe, because to believe depends on the will.'[34]

Notwithstanding this, from the 1260s there is some evidence of opposition to the crusades on the grounds that they hindered the conversion of the Muslims and it is important to assess its significance. In his treatise *Opus maius*, dated c1266, the English Franciscan Roger Bacon exhorted Christians to follow the example of the early church which had converted the Gentiles by preaching alone. Writing in the aftermath of Louis IX's defeat at Mansurah, Roger questioned the value of further crusades:

> if the Christians are victorious, no one stays behind to defend the occupied lands. Nor are unbelievers converted in this way, but killed and sent to hell. Those who survive the wars together with their children are more and more embittered against the Christian faith because of this violence and are

---

[30] Humbert of Romans, 'Opus tripartitum' [ed E. Brown, *Fasciculus rerum expetandarum et fugiendarum* 2 vols (London 1690) II] p 195.

[31] Peter Lombard, 'Sententia' *PL* 192, col 711. See also J. S. C. and L. Riley-Smith, *The Crusades: Idea and reality 1095–1274* (London 1981) pp 9, 29, 54.

[32] Gratian, 'Decretum' *Corpus iuris canonici* ed A. Friedberg 2 vols (Leipzig 1879–81) Causa 23 quaestio 6 canon 4: 1. See also *Summa 'Elegantius in iure divino' seu Coloniensis*, edd G. Fransen and S. Kuttner (New York 1969) p 74.

[33] See Walter Map, *De nugis curialium* ed M. R. James (Oxford 1914) p 47; Ralph Niger, *De re militari et triplici peregrinationis Ierosolimitane* ed L Schmugge (Berlin 1977) pp 65–6, 168, 196.

[34] Thomas Aquinas, *Summa Theologica* ed P. Caramello (Rome 1962) II ii quaestio 10 art 8.

indefinitely alienated from Christ and inflamed to do all the harm possible to Christians.³⁵

But if one examines Roger's other works, it is not always clear that he advocated preaching and teaching rather than the use of force. For example, in the '*Opus tertium*' and '*Compendium studii philosophiae*', while he looked forward to the adoption of the Christian faith by the Tartars and the union of the world in one sheepfold, he expected the Muslims to be destroyed.³⁶

In what seems to have been a direct reply to Roger Bacon's argument, Humbert of Romans recorded that some people:

> are asking what is the purpose of this attack upon the Saracens? For by this they are not aroused to conversion, but rather are provoked against the Christian faith. When we are victorious and have killed them moreover we send them to hell, which seems to be against the law of charity. Also when we gain their lands we do not occupy them as colonists . . . because our countrymen do not want to stay in those regions and so there seem to be no spiritual, corporeal or temporal benefits from this sort of attack.³⁷

It should be remembered, however, that the purpose of Humbert's treatise was to warn Pope Gregory X of any possible source of opposition to his proposed crusade and he gave no indication that these critics reflected a large body of opinion.

At the same time, in the penultimate sentence of his memoir submitted to the Second Council of Lyons, the Dominican William of Tripoli dismissed the need to use force against the Muslims:

> solely by the word of God, without philosophical argument, without military weapons, they will seek like simple sheep the baptism of Christ and will enter into the flock of God.³⁸

William also quoted prophecies which showed that the time was right for the conversion of the Muslims and his statements have prompted some historians to suggest that he represented an ever-increasing body of opinion which condemned the use of the crusade in the Near East.³⁹ But there is no evidence to support this

---

³⁵ Roger Bacon, *Opus maius* ed J. H. Bridges 3 vols (London 1897–1900) III pp 120–2.
³⁶ *Idem*, 'Opus tertium' and 'Compendium studii philosophiae' ed J. S. Brewer, *Opera quaedam hactenus inedita* (London 1859) pp 86, 402–3.
³⁷ Humbert of Romans, 'Opus tripartitum' p 196.
³⁸ William of Tripoli, 'De statu Saracenorum' ed H. Prutz, *Kulturgeschichte der Kreuzzuge* (Berlin 1883) pp 517–18.
³⁹ See Throop pp 120, 122; Prawer pp 389–90.

conclusion. The main purpose of William's work was to point out the similarities between Islam and Christianity.

The only other criticism of the use of force against the Muslims came from the Joachites, the followers of the twelfth-century Abbot Joachim of Fiore.[40] Joachim saw history as a series of complex patterns and his grand design was the doctrine of the three *status*: the ages of the Father, Son and Holy Spirit. He drew parallels between the Old and New Testaments and predicted the glories of the forthcoming third age.[41] According to Joachim's plan of history, the third *status* would begin between 1200 and 1260 and he prophesied that a race of *viri spirituales* would emerge and convert the Jews and Gentiles to Christianity. Joachim never attacked the actual concept of the crusade, but towards the end of his life he had come to believe that further expeditions would achieve nothing and that the Christians would triumph over the Muslims by preaching not fighting.[42] After his death in 1202, his ideas were taken up and developed by his followers. For our purposes their most important work was the commentary on Jeremiah, *Super Hieremiam*, composed between 1243 and 1248.[43] There is some dispute as to whether its author was a member of a Joachite circle in Calabria or a Spiritual Franciscan,[44] but it seems to have been a popular work and was quoted by a number of chroniclers, in particular the Italian writer Salimbene. According to his account, the author prophesied that Louis IX's Egyptian crusade would come to nothing[45] and he condemned further attempts to launch a crusade. He pointed out that another crusade could actually be harmful to the church, for, by sending Christians to the barbarous nations 'under the appearance of salvation and the cross', the prelates altered the balance of power and consequently they weakened the barrier which protected Christendom from the

---

[40] For further details, see M. W. Bloomfield, 'Joachim of Flora: a critical survey of his canon, teachings, sources, biography and influence' *Traditio* 13 (1957) pp 249–313.
[41] See M. Reeves, *Joachim of Fiore and the prophetic future* (London 1976) pp 2–22.
[42] Joachim of Fiore, *Expositio super Apocalypsim* (Venice 1527) fol 133^v–134^v and *Liber Figurarum* edd L. Tondelli, M. Reeves and B. Hirsch-Reich, 2 vols (Turin 1953) II Pl.14. See also E. R. Daniel, 'Apocalyptic conversion: The Joachite alternative to the crusades' *Traditio* 25 (1969) pp 137–9; J. E. Siberry, 'Criticism of Crusading, 1095–1274' (unpub. Cambridge Ph.D. thesis, 1982) pp 240–3.
[43] See M. Reeves, [*The*] *influence of prophecy* [*in the later Middle Ages: A study in Joachimism*] (Oxford 1969)] p 518.
[44] *Idem* 'Abbot Joachim's disciples in the Cistercian Order' *Sophia* 19 (1951) p 367.
[45] Salimbene pp 236–7.

heathen. The author of *Super Hieremiam* also clearly referred to a third age in which a race of *viri spirituales* would emerge and convert the *gentes incredulas*[46] and the same argument was to be found in another Joachite treatise, *Super Esaiam*, and a collection of figures known as *Praemissiones*.[47] In addition Salimbene claimed to have been shown a verse prophecy which had been sent to various cardinals and to a Dominican provincial chapter before the election of Pope Gregory X in 1271, and he included one version of this, together with his own commentary, in his chronicle. According to Salimbene's interpretation Gregory's early death was the result of his repeated efforts to launch another expedition against the Muslims, and he also pointed out that the crusade was now against God's plan since the year 1260 had passed. Henceforward those outside the church would be converted by peaceful means.[48] There is no evidence, however, that the Joachites represented a large body of opinion and the extent to which they had developed the concept of apocalyptic conversion by the mid thirteenth century has recently been challenged by the foremost scholar in this field.[49]

To sum up, in the period before 1274 there is little evidence to show that those who supported a programme of missionary work were opposed to the crusading movement. On the contrary, they seem to have regarded it as a stimulus to conversion and the new orders of friars became the foremost apologists of the crusades. Admittedly from the 1260s there is some evidence of criticism of the use of force against the Muslims, but its extent and significance have been exaggerated. There is no indication that Roger Bacon reflected a large body of opinion, and the importance of the Joachite idea of apocalyptic conversion has also been overstated. Such views were confined to a very small circle. At the time of the Second Council of Lyons the traditional idea of the crusade still enjoyed considerable support from the faithful.

Sidney Sussex College, Cambridge.

---

[46] Pseudo Joachim, *Super Hieremiam Prophetam* (Venice 1525) fols 2^v, 50^v, 57^r–58^r. For a similar prophecy see Reeves, *Influence of Prophecy* p 312.
[47] Pseudo Joachim, *Super Esaiam Prophetam* fol 56^v and *Praemissiones* (Venice 1517); Reeves, *Influence of Prophecy* p 521.
[48] Salimbene pp 492–5.
[49] See M. Reeves, 'History and Prophecy in medieval thought' *Medievalia et Humanistica* new series 5 (1974) pp 63–4.

CITIES OF GOD: THE ITALIAN COMMUNES AT WAR

by DIANA M. WEBB

TO BELIEVE that a political community might justly go to war in defence of its legitimate interests was a necessity of daily life to the city states of northern and central Italy from the twelfth century onwards. This belief as such was of course hardly confined to them among medieval European societies, but there are certain features of the Italian experience of war which, taken with the character of the cities themselves, contributed significantly to the emergence and formulation of those secular attitudes to political life which are so often regarded as typical of renaissance culture. The Italian cities lived close to the papacy, which claimed the authority to identify the enemies of the Church and to declare on them wars which were not merely just but holy.[1] Insofar as the enemies of the Church proved to be Italians, or to be operating on Italian soil, those cities which allied themselves with the papacy could acquire the tincture of holiness for wars that were essentially fought in pursuance of local interests. There could be little doubt, for example, that the immediate cause of the great battle of Montaperti, fought on 4 September 1260 between the guelfs of Tuscany, headed by the Florentines, and the Sienese, aided by Florentine ghibelline exiles and by German troops of Manfred of Sicily, was the territorial rivalry of Florence and Siena in southern Tuscany, and most immediately of all the struggle for control of the little town of Montalcino.[2] Manfred and his allies, like Lewis of Bavaria and his ally the Lucchese tyrant Castruccio Castracani, another local enemy of Florence, two generations later, were however the enemies of the Church, and thus Florence's war-effort was sanctified.

It was unlikely that the Church would be regarded as the sole

[1] On different aspects of this whole subject see F. H. Russell, *The Just War in the Middle Ages* (Cambridge 1975); [C.] Erdmann, [*The Origin of the Idea of Crusade* tr M. W. Baldwin and W. Goffart (Princeton 1977)]; [N.] Housley, [*The Italian Crusades: the Papal-Angevin Alliance and the Crusades against Christian Lay Powers* (Oxford 1982)].

[2] For an outline of Sienese-Florentine rivalry in the thirteenth century, F. Schevill, *Siena: the History of a Medieval Commune* (New York edn 1964) pp 149–91, may conveniently be cited.

arbiter of the justice (or even the holiness) of wars which arose fundamentally from pressures within the cities and on the hotly-contested boundaries between their territories. On the one hand, the cities regarded themselves not only as political but as innately spiritual communities; on the other, their governments were as busy as their monarchic counterparts in France, Spain or England, in attempting to 'nationalise' their clergy. If Philip the Fair could demand the fiscal and moral support of the French clergy for a war undertaken rather inconsequentially against the duke of Gascony in 1294, similar situations might arise with humdrum frequency in the crowded political space of Italy.

The Florentine chronicler Giovanni Villani described an incident which took place at Florence in 1328-9:

> An impost of 12,000 gold florins was made on the clergy on the authority of an old papal letter (although it had been ordered before by the priorate which existed at the time that [Lewis] the Bavarian was advancing on Florence by way of Arezzo and Castruccio was alive and was approaching from the direction of Pistoia), so that they might contribute through their benefices to the defence of the city and its *contado* against the rebels and persecutors of holy church. The said clergy, ungrateful and unthinking, did not want to pay this impost, and it was necessary to force them to pay . . .

The clergy appealed to the pope and slapped an interdict on the city which was finally lifted by the bishop in February 1329.[3] The enemies of guelf Florence were obviously the enemies of the Church, and this belief became an integral part of Florentine mythology. It reached a climax at once logical and paradoxical when in 1375-8 Florence went to war with the papacy itself. In October 1376 Salvestro de' Medici thought that it must be possible to argue against observance of the interdict the pope had laid upon the city 'Since the pope is not following the will of God', and by the end of the same year the chancellor Coluccio Salutati had designated the city's anti-papal alliance 'sacred'.[4]

The experience of war with the papacy nevertheless imposed a strain on the more conservative guelf patricians as well as on the

---

[3] [G.] Villani, [*Cronica* ed F. G. Dragomanni 4 vols (Florence 1845)] 3 pp 105-6 (bk 10 cap 109).
[4] R. C. Trexler, *The Spiritual Power: Republican Florence under Interdict*, (Leiden 1974) pp 124, 159.

Cities of God

common people, insofar as the interdict withdrew from them the exhibition of the sacrament.[5] It was also a decisive experience for those sections of the governing elite whose ideas came to be expressed by the early humanists. In the preamble to the redrafted statute of the Florentine *parte guelfa* in 1420 it was explained that guelfdom implied the defence of the Church in the spiritual sphere, the defence of liberty in the secular sphere.[6] In his account of the outbreak of the war with the papacy, written in the 1430s, Leonardo Bruni described how the Florentine ambassador Donato Barbadori expounded Florence's immaculate guelf record to the pope at Avignon in 1375. Retiring from the papal presence with a dusty answer Barbadori addressed himself to an image of the deity, to whom he appealed from the sentence of his vicar; God loved not servitude, but liberty, in the defence of which he would assist the Florentines.[7] In the complex of ideas current at Florence in the early fifteenth century we can see at one and the same time the attempt to distinguish between the sacred and the secular and the continuing belief in the spiritual character of the political community and its direct access to God for the defence of liberty, which is held to be sacred. In the fourteenth century, certainly, it is not a matter of denying divine involvement in earthly affairs nor even of challenging the power of the Church to mediate between the secular community and the divine. On the contrary, the local church should at all times loyally undertake this mediation and not seek to withdraw its labour or to hedge its membership of the community with qualifications and exceptions. The belief that God looked with disfavour on infringements of Florentine liberty and would condone armed action in its defence is vividly expressed in Villani's account of the expulsion of Walter de Brienne, duke of Athens, after his brief tyranny over the city in 1342–3. The duke had seized power on the feast of the Nativity of the Virgin, 8

---

[5] *Ibid* pp 126–7, 159–60. See further the whole chapter 'Religion and the Interdict', pp 109–62.

[6] '*Universitatem Guelforum, si ad divinum respicias, cum Romana Ecclesia, si ad humanum, cum Libertate coniunctam reperies . . .*' Quoted by H. Baron, *The Crisis of the Early Italian Renaissance*, 2 ed (Princeton 1966) p 468 n 8.

[7] '. . . *ad effigiem Dei conversus, Barbadorius (is enim maiori spiritu nitebatur), magna voce, ita ut pontifex exaudiret, "Deus!, inquit, nos legati, florentini populi nomine, ab hac sententia vicarii tui inique lata, ad te tuamque aequitatem appellamus. Tu, qui falli non potes, nec ira inflecteris, nec servitutem populorum sed libertatem amas, et tyrannos libidinesque odisti, florentino populo libertatem suam defendent subvenies, ac propitius protectorque aderis!*'" Muratori 19 pt 3 pp 215–16.

September 1342, thus disregarding the reverence due to her; God therefore permitted the citizens to use force to regain their liberty on the feast-day of her mother, Saint Anne, 26 July 1343. Anne's day was thereafter kept 'like Easter' at Florence, by communal decree.[8] We shall have occasion later to discuss the custom of commemorating saints whose feast-days had seen notable civic victories.

On the intellectual level, the conception of the city as a spiritual community could draw on a rich fund of biblical and Augustinian imagery. In the statutes of a Marian confraternity at Arezzo, approved in 1262, heaven itself was described as a *congregatio celestium civium*.[9] Historically, it was of considerable significance that at a crucial stage in the development of urban autonomy the Church had lent its authority to the promotion of civic liberty, a word that for post-Gregorian churchmen had powerful associations. In cardinal Boso's biography of Alexander III the association of the liberty of the Church with the liberty of the cities in face of Frederick Barbarossa is a recurrent theme. In 1165 the Lombards 'remained steadfast against the enemies of the church and those who were attacking their liberty'; in 1175 the Lombards submitted their quarrels with Barbarossa to arbitration, 'Saving the freedom of the Church of Rome and of ourselves for which we are fighting'.[10] From his curialist standpoint Boso could not but contemplate with pleasure the spectacle of the 'chosen company of the warriors of Milan' at Legnano in 1176, who 'offered prayer to God and his apostle Peter and to blessed Ambrose', particularly as in time past the Milanese had challenged the claims of the successor of Peter in the name of the tradition of blessed Ambrose.[11] The people of Alessandria in 1175 defended themselves against Barbarossa 'with the aid of St. Peter, whom they saw at their head mounted on a white charger and clad in flashing armour.'[12] The apostle perhaps had in mind a future appearance as pope Julius II.

An anonymous Milanese annalist however puts the matter

---

[8] Villani 4 p 37 (bk 12 cap 17).
[9] G. Meersseman, 'Études sur les anciennes confréries dominicains: Les Congrégations de la Vierge'. *AFP* 22 (1952) p 110.
[10] L[iber] P[ontificalis] ed L. Duchesne 3 vols (Paris 1955–7) 2] pp 413, 429. The translations are from *Boso's Life [of Alexander III* trans G. M. Ellis (Oxford 1973)] pp 67, 92.
[11] *LP* p 433; *Boso's Life* p 97.
[12] *LP* p 428; *Boso's Life* p 90.

Cities of God

differently. At Alessandria in 1175 'God fought for the citizens.'[13] There is no intrusion of the prince of the apostles, the emblematic saint of Rome, in this Milanese rendering of events. In August 1160, as the Milanese prepared to do battle with Barbarossa,

> Archbishop Oberto and the archpriest Milo and the deacon Galdino and Alghisio the treasurer exhorted the people and in the name of almighty God and the blessed Ambrose informed them that they should go forth to war confidently, knowing that God was with them . . . When therefore they had celebrated the divine office and made confession and received penance, they went forth to war with the *carrozzo*, which they had made during the night.[14]

Oberto and his clerks were to go into exile as adherents of Alexander III in 1162, after Barbarossa's destruction of Milan. The deacon Galdino, succeeding Oberto as archbishop in 1168, returned to the city, now rebuilt, as Alexander's legate and a powerful figure in Lombardy. Alexander may have seen such men as his agents, and perhaps that was how they saw themselves; but the Milanese annalist clearly saw them on the morning of battle with Barbarossa in 1160 as the pillars of the Milanese church, the men who spoke encouraging words in the name of God and the blessed Ambrose. In 1160, of course, the papal alliance with the Lombard cities was not yet cemented, but the annalist regarded Alexander as betraying his Lombard allies when he made peace with Barbarossa in 1176.[15]

Boso mentions the presence of the Milanese *carrozzo* at Legnano in 1176.[16] The first known appearance of this ceremonial civic war-chariot was at Milan in 1039, when archbishop Aribert devised a chariot bearing standards and a crucifix in order to encourage the local population, whom he had mobilised against the Italian supporters of the emperor Conrad.[17] The sense of the holiness of the urban community and the sanctity of its warfare was embodied in the *carrozzo* and in the images and banners that it

---

[13] *Annales Mediolanenses, MGH SS* 18p 377.
[14] *Ibid* p 369.
[15] *Ibid* p 378: '*Sed Longobardos deseruit et episcopos depositos restituit, et quos ipse creaverat desposuit.*' Galdino's biographer strongly emphasises both his pro-papal and his civic role: B. Mombritius, *Sanctuarium seu Vitae Sanctorum*, n ed 2 vols (Paris 1910) 1 pp 561–3.
[16] *LP* pp 432–3; *Boso's Life* p 97.
[17] Erdmann pp 53–6; H. E. J. Cowdrey, 'Archibishop Aribert of Milan' *History* 51 (1966) pp 12–13.

bore. Becker has recently drawn attention to the sculptured tympanum of the main portal of the church of San Zeno at Verona, where the saint confers a banner on the *milites* and *pedites* of the commune, arrayed either side of him.[18] In 1213, the *carrozzo* of Milan fell into the hands of the Cremonese, and the officials of the commune entrusted to the safekeeping of the archdeacon and archpriest of Cremona the gilded cross from the *carrozzo* and the iron cross-shaft on which it had stood.[19] A certain code of conduct clearly governed the treatment of a captured *carrozzo* insofar as it was a religious object, even if that code was not always observed to the letter. In 1248 Frederick II's siege of Parma ended in ignominious defeat at his nearby foundation of Vittoria, and the *carrozzo* of Cremona was taken and placed *honorifice*, as Salimbene carefully observes, in the baptistery at Parma. Unfortunately, those who did not love the Cremonese, such as the Milanese and Mantuans and others, when they came to see the baptistery and saw the *carrozzo* of their enemies there, took the ornaments from Berta (the *carrozzo* was called Berta, Salimbene adds helpfully), so that they could have them as relics (perhaps we should translate 'souvenirs'). The wheels were left, and the wagon, on the floor of the baptistery, and the shaft of the standard stood upright against the wall.[20]

In 1213 Cremona rather than Milan had enjoyed papal approval, because the citizens were supporting the pope's new candidate for the empire, Frederick of Hohenstaufen. In 1248 they were still supporting Frederick, who had in the meantime turned out to be antichrist, and Parma therefore was now in the right, as the friar Salimbene clearly believed: 'Parma went to war on behalf of the church, and fought valiantly, in the expectation of aid from heaven and victory.'[21] It is hard, nonetheless, to believe that such considerations prevented the Milanese in 1213 or the Cremonese in 1248 from believing in the sanctity of their cause and their *carrozzo*. Right, as officially defined, did not always triumph, after all. In 1250 the Cremonese got their own back and captured the *carrozzo*

---

[18] M. B. Becker, *Medieval Italy: constraints and creativity* (Bloomington, Ind. 1981) p 40; G. H. Crichton, *Romanesque Sculpture in Italy* (London 1954) p 31. For banners in the service of the church, Erdmann pp 35–56.
[19] J. F. Böhmer, *Acta Imperii Selecta* (Innsbruck 1870) pp 637–8 n 927.
[20] Salimbene, [*Cronica MGH SS* 32] p 203.
[21] *Ibid* p 384.

of Parma on a day which was afterwards known at Parma as black Thursday.²² In 1281 the two communes decided on an exchange of *carrozzi*. The account given of this remarkable event by an anonymous chronicler of Parma vividly evokes the involvement of the local clergy. The Cremonese had brought the restored *carrozzo* into Parmese territory:

> Early in the morning, the lord bishop of Parma, with all the clergy with the banners of the localities with great joy approached the *carrozzo* of Parma, which was called Regolium of Parma, and led it into the major church of Saint Mary of Parma... On the following Tuesday the lord bishop, the lord *podestà* and the lord captain, with the knights and the whole people, with trumpets and the standards of all the localities and the bells of the whole city rung, took the said *carrozzo* from the cathedral into the piazza with great joy and much speech-making, so as to go and lead it to Cremona to assist the Cremonese and the Lodese as had been agreed; and then, as it was all white, there were painted upon it the blessed Virgin Mary and other figures.

The *Chronicon Estense* adds that the Parmese had repainted the *carrozzo* of Cremona and given it a new standard and generally made it better than it had ever been, which in view of Salimbene's account of the dilapidation it had undergone was just as well.²³

'By the thirteenth century', according to Erdmann, 'the *carroccio* was widespread and often had no religious meaning whatever.'²⁴ This impression can certainly be given by the numerous mentions of the *currus* in north Italian chronicles of the early thirteenth century which exhibit an unadorned and relentlessly secular narrative character. Much, however, as so often, depends on what we mean by 'religious'. The late thirteenth-century eulogist of Milan, Bonvesin della Riva, who gives a detailed description of the Opicino de Canistris of Pavia who wrote a eulogy of his city in go with it '*ut iuxta currum quotidie divinum celebretur ab eo ministerium*'.²⁵ The anonymous cleric of Pavia who wrote a eulogy of his city in 1330 seems to imply that mass was celebrated in or on the

---

²² *Chronicon Parmense*, Muratori 9 pt 9 p 19.
²³ *Ibid* p 38; *Chronicon Estense*, Muratori 15 pt 3 p 45.
²⁴ Erdmann p 56.
²⁵ *De magnalibus urbis Mediolani* ed F. Novati *BISIMEAM* 20 (1898) p 153.

carrozzo.²⁶ Giovanni Villani records that the *carrozzo* of Florence was kept in the baptistery, the church of the city's patron John the Baptist, but looking back at the year 1260 from the distance of a generation or so he seems to see the *carrozzo* as emblematic of the pride and pomp of the *popolo vecchio*, which met defeat at Montaperti.²⁷

The mid-thirteenth century, the period of the final struggle with the Hohenstaufen and the establishment for a while of Angevin ascendancy in Italy, witnessed the foundation in several cities of quasi-military societies of zealous laymen dedicated to the defence of the church and the extirpation of heresy.²⁸ The members of the short-lived *Militia Jesu Christi*, instituted at Parma in 1233, were exempted by Gregory IX from the exaction of oaths, from military service for other than just causes, and from the payment of excessive taxes or imposts which the municipality might try to impose on them. As Meersseman puts it, the urban government was forbidden 'to mobilise the knights of the *militia*, as they might mobilise other citizens, for purely political military expeditions'.²⁹ It is easy to see how circumstances might induce communal governments to identify the Church's battles as their own and thus to favour such societies and endorse their privileges. It is equally easy to see how in the century of the rise of the *popolo*, of acute tension in many cities between *milites* and *pedites*, and the steady growth of civic governmental autonomy under the leadership of the *popolo*, many features of these societies might come to seem objectionable. Villani was one of many who were sardonic at the expense of the tax-exempt members of the Militia of the Virgin, popularly known as the *cavalieri gaudenti*.³⁰

If guelfdom was compatible with, indeed dependent on, a certain orientation of political and social self-interest, ghibellin-

---

[26] *Liber de laudibus civitatis ticinensis*, Muratori 11 pt 1 p 25: '*Cum ad solempnem et generalem procedant exercitum secum aliquando ducunt plaustrum trahentibus pluribus paribus boum panno rubeo coopertorum, quod plaustrum vulgo carocium dicitur. In quo tabernaculum est ligneum, capiens aliquam hominum quantitatem; in cuius medio sublimis est pertica, sursum erecta cum pomo erea deaurato, in qua inter alia insignia rubeum tentorium ponitur et vexillum longissimum rubeum cum cruce alba et desuper ramus olive, et ita, celebratis in illo missarum solempniis. ordinate procedunt.*'

[27] Villani 1 pp 294–5 (bk 6, cap 76).

[28] See the recent brief summary by Housley pp 56–7.

[29] G. Meersseman, 'Études sur les anciennes confréries dominicaines: Les Milices de Jésus-Christ' *AFP* 23 (1953) pp 275–308; the quotation is on p 301.

[30] Villani 1 p 338; Housley p 56 n 94.

ism was certainly not simply identical with heresy. Alliance with king Manfred and the ghibelline exiles of Florence did not prevent the Sienese in 1260 from seeing the defence of the city against the massed guelfs of Tuscany as a cause in which they could, indeed must, invoke the protection of their patron the Virgin. In the collection of statutes issued by the victorious Sienese government in the autumn of 1262 we find numerous provisions for benefactions to churches and religious orders and for the persecution of heretics and their sympathisers, as well as for the doing of honour to Saint George, the patron of Manfred's German soldiers. It was George's leadership and intercession above all, the government declared, that had stirred the son of the highest to rescue the Sienese from the enemy 'who like a raging bear sought brutally to destroy the city of Siena and its whole people'.[31] The invocation of the sacred right of self-defence lies not far below the surface.

Our descriptions of the processions which took place at Siena on the eve of Montaperti and of the ceremony in which a representative of the commune, supported by the bishop, laid the keys of Siena on the altar of the Virgin while a notary drew up the city's deed of gift of itself to the queen of heaven, are all, unfortunately, late in date, none of them earlier than the later fourteenth century.[32] It is hard to believe that the citizens did not have solemn recourse to their patron at such a moment; for a comparison we need think only of Salimbene's description of the supplications made to the Virgin by the citizens of Parma in 1247, when they presented her with a model of the city made all in silver.[33] An unimpeachably contemporary source however

---

[31] *Il Constituto* [*del comune di Siena dell'anno 1262* ed L. Zdekauer (Milan 1897)] Caps 119–122, pp 53–4 concern the punishment of heresy and are immediately followed by the provisions for civic honours to George (caps 123–6, pp 54–6). Civic protection of the Cistercian house of San Galgano, which was closely associated with the life of the commune, was to be proclaimed annually on the feast of the Assumption (cap. 103, pp 49–50) and there are numerous grants of money and building materials to other churches and orders.

[32] Two of these accounts are accessible in [*Cronaca Senese di Autore*] *Anonimo*, Muratori 15 pt 6, pp 57–61, and [*Cronaca Senese conosciuta sotto il nome di Paolo di Tommaso*] *Montauri*, ibid pp 194–222. These and the other extant accounts are subjected to exhaustive criticism from an art-historical viewpoint by E. B. Garrison, *Studies in the History of Medieval Italian Painting*, 4 vols (Florence 1954–62) 4, pp 5–58, who is sceptical of the value of the traditions supposedly embodied in them. The present writer hopes to publish a study of some aspects of the Virgin's rulership of Siena, which traditionally derives from 1260.

[33] Salimbene p 196.

survives which illuminates the war of Montaperti and the mundane involvements of the clergy in it from quite a different angle. This is the *Libro di Montaperti*, a collection of documents connected with the raising of the Florentine army in 1260, which was actually captured on the battlefield and kept at Siena until the sixteenth century.[34]

On 8 April and again on 10 August 1260 the Florentines gave thought to the problem of how many of the rectors of rural communes, rural watchmen and *cappellani* of both urban and rural churches should be required to go with the army and how many should be permitted to remain at home.[35] Among the citizens of the Porta San Pancrazio sector of the city which had been elected to serve as foot-soldiers with the *carrozzo*, several, including the barber Volontario and the smith Tornanbene, claimed to be *cappellani*, perhaps reckoning that they stood at least a chance of staying home.[36] The rectors and *cappellani* of the countryside had the responsibility of keeping a register of the names of extra-urban citizens liable for military service;[37] it was they too who answered to the officials of the commune as they went about the *contado* during the summer extracting promises of quantities of grain for the supply of Montalcino, the little town in southern Tuscany which was the current bone of contention between Florence and Siena. The supplies exacted from the rural churches are listed separately, with the names of the priests who spoke for them and who, like their secular counterparts, took an oath of obedience to the Florentine officials. In the *plebatus* of San Pancrazio, for example, the priest Gualterotti, *custos* of the church of San Pietro *ad Salvivolpi*, claimed to be *procurator cappellanorum dicti plebatus*, and promised three *modii* of grain on their behalf.[38] On 11 August the notary of the *podestà* enjoined three named clerics, '*ut sint in communi concordia*', to see that the quotas of grain imposed on them were in fact transported to Montalcino.[39] The local churches in their capacity as meeting-places and broadcasting-stations were to be used to track down absentees from the host. The names of those

[34] *Il Libro di Montaperti* ed C. Paoli (Florence 1889).
[35] *Ibid* p 53.
[36] *Ibid* p 13. Volontario and Tornanbene are listed as *cappellani* elsewhere, in a partial list of the male inhabitants of the San Pancrazio sector p 323.
[37] *Ibid* p 373.
[38] *Ibid* p 116.
[39] *Ibid* p 117.

who had not turned up were to be published throughout the churches of the city and *contado* on the next Sunday, when mass was sung.[40]

The Florentine army claimed John the Baptist as their *vexillifer, precursor et dux* or alternatively their *patronus et defensor*.[41] By 1260 he had performed this role for over a century. The judge and chronicler Sanzanome, who died some time after 1230, believed that in 1145 the Florentines dedicated to the Baptist the prisoners they had taken in a skirmish with the Sienese and sent them home. A generation later they were still congratulating themselves on this act of piety as they prepared for another clash with the Sienese, calling upon *sanctum Iohannem caput nostrum*. When a Florentine victory over Pistoia in 1228 seemed to have resulted in a lasting peace, Sanzanome dwelt fondly on the friendly co-operation between the Baptist and Pistoia's patron Saint James.[42] Military demonstrations on enemy territory were regarded as a suitable way of celebrating the Baptist's feast-day, 24 June.[43] While we cannot be sure in what terms the Virgin was invoked at Siena on the eve of Montaperti we do know that in the official redaction of the terms of Montalcino's submission to Siena, drawn up only a few days later, she was *defensatrix et gubernatrix* of the city, and that the victorious *carrozzo* had been made in her honour and that of Saint George.[44] She too received the dedication of prisoners of war at her altar before their release.[45]

In his massive catalogue of the images of the saints in Tuscan painting, Kaftal remarks that a saint may appear in the painting of a certain city bearing an olive-branch which is absent from his iconography elsewhere. This signifies the fact that the city in question won a notable victory on his feast-day.[46] This form of

[40] *Ibid* p 371.
[41] *Ibid* p 369.
[42] *Sanzanome Iudicis Gesta Florentinorum ab anno 1125 ad annum 1231*, ed G. Milanesi (Florence 1876) pp 133, 134, 148.
[43] In 1288 '*il di di san Giovanni Battista vennero i Fiorentini schierati in sul prato d'Arezzo, e in quello dinnanzi alla porta della città feciono correre il palio, siccome per loro costuma si facea per la detta festa in Firenze, e fecionvisi dodici cavalieri di corredo*': Villani I p 448 (bk 7 cap 120). Villani records other such expeditions against Arezzo after the victory of Campaldino in 1289 (p 462), again against Arezzo in 1290 (p 468) and against Pisa in 1292 (p 478).
[44] *Il Caleffo Vecchio del Comune di Siena* ed. G. Cecchini, 3 vols (Siena 1932–40) 2 p 846.
[45] The *Anonimo* p 51 cites an instance in 1234; and on 16 September 1313 the prisoners taken when Monteguidi surrendered to Siena '*furno offerti a la Vergine Maria al Duomo per onore della Vergine Maria*' (*Montauri* p 246).
[46] [G.] Kaftal, [*Iconography of the Saints in Tuscan Painting*] (Florence 1952) p xx.

commemoration in fact seems to be very much a Tuscan, and above all a Florentine habit; all but one of Kaftal's examples are Florentine. The feast-day of Saint Barnabas, 11 June, witnessed not only the battle of Colle Val d'Elsa in 1269, which represented revenge on the Sienese for Montaperti, but the defeat of the Aretines at Campaldino in 1289. 28 July, the feast of pope Victor I, saw a victory over the Pisans in 1364, and the feast of Saint Denis (9 October) was remembered for the final conquest of Pisa in 1406. It must have been very gratifying when in 1439 Florence's friend Eugenius IV beatified Andrea Corsini, the bishop of Fiesole who had died in 1373, and only the next year his feast-day, 4 February 1440, saw the great victory of Anghiari.[47] In the later years of the thirteenth century the early Egyptian martyr Victor appeared among the patrons of Siena, in remembrance of the fact that on his day, 15 May 1229, the Sienese had acquired control of Sarteano. The fourteenth-century chronicler ranked this campaign together with the war of Montaperti as the *due sconfitte* the Sienese had inflicted upon the Florentines. Perhaps this association of ideas accounted for the promotion of Victor late in the thirteenth century. The cathedral had possessed relics of him at the beginning of the century, but his position among Siena's official patrons does not seem to have been assured much before 1300.[48] A few years later, however, he would appear with the other patrons around the Virgin's throne in the *Maestà* of both Duccio and Simone Martini.

One of the Sienese statutes promulgated in the autumn of 1262 stated that the officials of the commune were to be prepared to provide a site for the erection of a chapel in honour of God and the blessed Virgin 'and of those saints on whose feast-day the Lord gave the Sienese victory over their enemies'.[49] The fourth of September, the day of Montaperti, was the feast of pope Boniface

[47] Kaftal, cols 129-36 (Barnabas), 1012 (Victor), 307-8 (Denis), 51-3 (Corsini).
[48] Kaftal, cols 1011-16: G. Gigli, *Diario Sanese* (Siena 1722) p 109; *Anomino* p 61. Ordericus, a canon of the cathedral, speaks of relics of Victor in about the year 1215: *Ordo [Officiorum Ecclesiae Senensis* ed J. C. Trombelli (Bologna 1766)] p 325. In 1274 the bishop invokes Victor among the other patrons while in 1284 his successor does not: G. A. Pecci, *Storia del Vesconado della Città di Siena* (Lucca 1748) pp 233-4, 240. In 1287, however, he appears when the bishop grants an indulgence to assist the building of a chapel for the blessed Ambrogio Sansedoni: *ASB* Martii 3 p 242.
[49] *Il Constituto* p 29; G. Tommasi, *Dell'Istorie di Siena* 2 vols (Venice 1625-6) 2 p 14. By the time the chapel was approaching completion, in 1277, it seems to have been regarded as dedicated to Saint James: G. Milanesi, *Documenti per la Storia dell'Arte Senese* 3 vols (Siena 1854-6) I pp 155-6. The *Anonimo* p 90, refers to an *altar* of Saint Boniface.

I, to whom, as it happened, it was believed that the cathedral of Siena had originally been dedicated. Was it then at least in part in reminiscence of Montaperti that it was later decreed that offerings of candles made in the cathedral on Saint Boniface's day, as well as the money tribute payable to the commune by Montacino, should belong to the *Opera di Santa Maria*, the cathedral office of works?[50] However this may be, the statute of 1262 makes quite clear the principle on which the Sienese and the Florentines alike proceeded.

It is not perhaps entirely easy to grasp the contemporary psychological significance of such enactments. Villani records that it was on Saint Barnabas' day in 1269 and 1289 that the Florentines won their two great victories, but it is without any apparent implication that the saint was in any way responsible.[51] Yet more was involved than simply a way of marking the date on the calendar. In honouring a saint whose day had given them victory, the Florentines and the Sienese were implicitly affirming that there was a harmony between the political community, with the secular ends that it pursued through warfare, and the Church whose co-operation, after all, it demanded in war and in all the incidents of civic life. In April 1311, Villani records, 'there arrived at Florence relics of the blessed apostle Saint Barnabas, which cardinal Pellegrue sent from the papal court to the commune of Florence, because he knew that the Florentines held him in great devotion'.[52] This was a gesture of thanks from the cardinal, Clement V's nephew and legate, for help received two years previously in Lombardy. Whether or not he was aware of the cause, he clearly knew that Barnabas, a saint more usually associated with Milan as that city's first archbishop, had entered the Florentine pantheon.

[50] This regulation is accessible in the vernacular recension made in 1309–10: *Il Costituto del Comune di Siena volgarizzato nel MCCIX–MCCCX* ed A. Lisini 2 vols (Siena 1905) 1 p 67. It seems to have been first made in 1274: Siena, Archivio di Stato, Statuti 3 fol 1^V, and then appears in the 1287–97 collection in the form in which it was to be translated in 1309–10: *ibid*, Statuti 5 fol 18^V. I am indebted to Dr Peter Denley for help in tracing these references. There was however another element in the complex relationship between Boniface, as an ancient patron of Siena, and the Virgin and her church: the belief at this period that it was he who had saved the Pantheon from destruction and caused it to be dedicated to Mary. For this see *Ordo* p 324; A. Middeldorf-Kosegarten, 'Zur Bedeutung der Sieneser Domkuppel' *Münchener Jahrbuch der Bildenden Kunst* 21 (1970) p 85.
[51] Villani 1 pp 361 (bk 7 cap 31), 459 (bk 7 cap 131).
[52] *Ibid* 2 p 154 (bk 9 cap 13).

There were of course difficulties in the way of ascribing military success too complacently to the divine intervention or to the intercession of a saint. How was one to account for defeat and failure? Sienese chroniclers, looking back at Montaperti from the distance of the fifteenth century, were too tactful to represent the battle as a victory for the Virgin over the Baptist, but they did permit themselves the jibe that it did the Florentines no good to call upon Zenobius and Reparata, the older patrons of Florence who had only yielded ground to the Baptist in relatively recent times.[53] In the fifteenth century certainly, in the full knowledge that the results of Montaperti had been rapidly and permanently undone by later defeats, some Sienese seem to have felt the incongruity of making a war-leader out of Mary and tried to stress rather Sienese obedience to her dictates, Sienese humility and penitence, as having merited the display of the divine mercy in 1260. As Agostino Dati, the chancellor of the republic, observed in his *Historia Senensis*, written in 1456-7, the Sienese were not claiming that 'she had fought against the enemy with white horses or drawn sword as the Romans boast the sons of Tindaris did for them'.[54] One cannot but think of cardinal Boso's picture of Saint Peter at Alessandria in 1175. In fact, as we have already seen, the Sienese statutes promulgated in the aftermath of victory in 1262 attributed the victory of Montaperti as such to George, a true military saint, rather than to the Virgin, and did so in suitably trenchant language.[55] When a thirteenth-century chronicler of Piacenza thinks he will apportion responsibility for a victory, a pleasingly human mixture of explanations is the result. In 1215 the Cremonese were frustrated in an attack on Piacenza by a combination of 'the divine power, the protection of the citizens of Piacenza who stayed at home for the defence of their city and the

---

[53] Montauri p 212; H. Peyer, *Stadt und Stadtpatron in mittelalterlichen Italien* (Zurich 1955) pp 46-52.

[54] A. Dati, *Opera* (Siena 1503) p 231: '*Proinde arbitror Reginam coelorum atque eius civitatis principem...domi militiaeque acrem se prebuisse, tuendam libertatis auctorem, nunquam saluti nunquam principatus sui dignitati defuisse, non autem vel albis equis vel districto gladio adversum hostes pugnavisse, id quod Tindaridas Romani pro se fecisse gloriantur, sed invicta illa dextera virtute, quae totius mundi Redemptorem genuit.*' The theme of Sienese humility and repentance is emphasised to excess by L. Politi, *La Sconficta di Monte Aperto* (Siena 1502).

[55] *Il Constituto* p 54: '*Cum beatissimum Georgium, militem militum, quem in nostrum et communis Senarum vexilliferum et potissimum defensorem eligimus, in cunctis negotiis civitatis Senarum invocantes ipsius nomen, plenum potentia ac virtute, in prelio noviter habito...ipse verus omnipotens, ipsius beatissimu Georgii precibus et meritis, nobis et comuni et populo Senensi contra hostes ipsos victoriam tribuerit triumphalem...*'

assistance of Fiorenzuola and Castel Arquato and of the archers of the Val di Taro who came to the city'.[56] It may be the chronicler's intended implication that earthly arms are the visible instruments of the divine power, but his actual mode of expression is not so sophisticated.

When it came to accounting for military and political failure, on the other hand, few chroniclers were better capable of moralistic gloom and a rich ambiguity of response than Giovanni Villani. The immediate explanation for the defeat of Montaperti was of course treason in the Florentine ranks. The standard-bearer was treacherously struck down and *cavalleria e popolo* alike lost heart when they saw the standard fall. In a wider perspective, however, 'thus was the madness of the ungrateful and arrogant people of Florence abased'. Villani was even prepared to see the defeat as a punishment for the Florentines's execution, in 1258, of the abbot of Vallombrosa, ostensibly for plotting against the city, but in reality because he was of the ghibelline Beccaria family of Pavia.[57] A subtler formulation of the same basic idea occurs much later in the chronicle. In 1340 Villani himself was a hostage at Ferrara for the fulfilment of an agreement between Florence and Mastino della Scala of Verona. The Florentines had paid Mastino a large sum for the city of Lucca. On taking possession of Lucca, they were immediately besieged in it by the Pisans. The Florentines made a sally against the besieging forces and were defeated; Lucca was lost. When the news reached Ferrara, one of Villani's fellow-hostages asked him why God had permitted this to happen. The Pisans were greater sinners than the Florentines; they were, after all, ghibelline. Villani replied that the Florentines lacked charity, to be met with the indignant response that more works of charity were done at Florence in a week than at Pisa in a month. Villani now pointed out the difference between the kind of charity that is more properly called alms-giving, and *la vera carità* in which the Florentines had failed towards God and man. Instead of resting content with the extensive boundaries God had permitted them, they had restlessly sought to expand at the expense of their neighbours; and they had also failed in charity within the city and towards one another.[58]

---

[56] *Annales Plancentini Guelfi, MGH SS* 18 p 429.
[57] Villani 1 pp 301–2 (bk 6 cap 79); pp 286–7 (bk 6 cap 65).
[58] *Ibid* 3 pp 369–70 (bk 11 cap 135).

In the eyes of its citizens the city never ceased to have a spiritual character which was only partly dependent on its standing in relation to the official Church. The effective pastor, the effective preacher, the effective papal diplomat, was he who could convince the people that their best interests would in fact be served by hearkening to the voice of the Church. That rectitude did not guarantee success was (and is), however, the most commonplace of lessons taught by human experience. Military failure taught the lesson in a particularly bitter, humiliating and memorable form. The commune might go to war fortified by the intercessions (as it believed) of its patron saints, by the co-operation and support of the local clergy, even by political alliance with the papacy and the comforts of guelf respectability, but it still might not be enough. If on the one hand Italians would not consent that they should go to war or refrain from war at the behest of the Church, on the other it was all too clear that the mechanism which awarded success or failure in war was beyond the institutional control of the Church.[59] Villani saw that an explanation, if one could be had, must lie deeper in the sinful nature of man. Humanists of a later generation would abandon the attempt to find explanations anywhere but in the play of secular forces, seeking to rationalise the more impalpable and mysterious elements in human success or failure by means of a developing concept of *virtù*. In this guise the continuing belief in the moral and spiritual dimension of the unique city was transmuted and modernised.

Two ways in which the political experience of the Italian cities differed from that of other medieval European societies may perhaps be singled out by way of conclusion. The first was the relative ease with which the city could be apprehended as a unity and a community. Whatever factional or social conflicts in reality impaired its unity, its identity did not have to be painfully built up over geographical distance by the governmental and propagandistic efforts of a royal entourage. Defined by its girding walls, its cathedral church, its public buildings, the city could be and was represented visually, offered as it were on a plate to the divine power as the pious women of Parma offered their silver model to the Virgin in 1247 or as San Gimignano offered the Tuscan city of

---

[59] Cf. Housley's remarks (pp 170–2) on the mental repercussions of failure in wars designated crusades by the papacy.

Cities of God

that name or the Dominican Ambrogio Sansedoni offered Siena in early fifteenth-century images by Taddeo di Bartolo.[60] The second point was that the Italian cities lived cheek by jowl with the papacy, the Roman Church in its guise as a political power. Where else did one have the opportunity to go to war with the papacy? The apprehensible, imaginable political community maintained its sense of a spiritual identity even as it laid claim to secular autonomy, and both might at a given moment have to be defended against papal policy and papal allies. At another moment it might be happily possible for a city to pique itself on its fidelity to Rome, on the identity of its liberty with the interests of the Church. The ambivalence of the 1420 statute of the Florentine *parte guelfa*, with its attempted distinction between the secular and the spiritual spheres, was rooted in the medieval experience of the Italian cities, and in the shaping of that experience warfare had played a major part.

University of London
King's College

[60] Kaftal, cols 3, 437–8.

MEDIEVAL WALDENSIAN ABHORRENCE OF KILLING PRE-c1400[1]

by PETER BILLER

WALDENSIANS figure high among the protagonists in accounts of medieval pacifism.[2] The two areas on which these accounts usually concentrate correspond to two broad areas in the sect's history—the genesis of abhorrence of killing during the formative early years, and the perseverance (or decline) of this position during the later centuries of an underground and only slowly changing movement—and they are also the two themes of this paper. The first theme poses a question. Is the received account of the genesis of this position satisfactory?

A man may be killed *in nullo casu et nulla occasione, nulla causae ratione*: thus the first appearance of the Waldensian doctrine in a polemic by Alain de Lille (before 1202, probably 1190s).[3] Selge's is the received account of its development: combatting the Cathars (from the 1180s) the Waldensians, while extending their *Schriftprinzip*, encountered Cathar rejection of killing and became convinced of the new testament arguments. The Cathars were the historical catalyst.[4]

One problem with this is the difficulty of finding evidence that Cathars were making this attitude manifest before the Waldensians. Alain is one of several early authors explicit on the doctrine when describing Waldensians and silent on it when describing Cathars.[5]

---

[1] Acknowledgement is due to Dr R. I. Moore for discussion of the first theme in this paper.
[2] Most recently [P.] Contamine, [*La guerre au moyen âge*] (Paris 1980) pp 465–8. For a recent Waldensian account see [G. Gonnet and A.] Molnar, [*Les Vaudois au moyen âge*] (Turin 1974) pp 179–80.
[3] *PL* 210 col 394. On Alain's treatise see M.-T. d'Alverny, *Alain de Lille. Textes inédits* (Paris 1965) pp 156 and n 1, 160–1; [C.] Thouzellier, [*Catharisme et Valdéisme en Languedoc*] (Paris 1966) pp 81–3, 94–106. The date late 1180s/early 1190s is suggested by [K.-V.] Selge, [*Die ersten Waldenser*, Arbeiten zur Kirchengeschichte 37], 2 vols (Berlin 1967) I p 132 n 10.
[4] *Ibid* pp 156–7.
[5] For example, the anonymous *Manifestatio* (c1200–9) ed A. Dondaine, *AFP* 29 (1959) p 271; from c1213–8 the [*Hystoria Albigensis* by Peter of] Vaux-Cernay [edd P. Guébin and E. Lyon. 3 vols (Paris 1926–39)] I pp 18–19, III p 7. The earliest attribution to the cathars is Ebrard of Béthune, *Liber Antiheresis, M[axima] B[ibliotheca] V[eterum] P[atrum]* ed M. de La

Alain's text also hints at a less narrow context, a *prise de conscience* of contemporary warfare, massacres, judicial executions and opinion on these areas. Consider his themes.[6] Jews may not be killed: reverberations of massacres in northern France (1171, 1192)? Heretics may not be killed: the move in opinion, law and deed to the death-penalty and the excommunication of the Waldensians in 1184 are immediately evoked. Capital punishment of thieves: this recalls Valdes' early concern with the relief of famine, and the hanging of large numbers driven by starvation to theft (explicit in the famine year of 1197).[7] Warfare (implied by Alain's defence)—the southern French canvas is crowded: holy warriors, on the little crusade to the south in 1181, or coming into Lyons in 1191 on their way to the Holy Land; Aragonese attacks on the count of Toulouse; mercenaries—who were stamping their new name, *ruttae*, into vernaculars by the 1170s.[8] Later evidence of Waldensian use of military disguises,[9] a sighting of a Waldensian on a road near the Saône in the 1230s dressed as a crossbowman,[10] and earlier mention of men of war on the road in the company of heretics (Cathars?)[11] combine to suggest a possible manner of direct contact with these allegedly godless and murdering men.

One may suggest the spectrum of contemporary reactions and opinion as the context into which to set the forming of

---

Bigne 28 vols (Lyons, Geneva 1677, 1707)] 24 cols 1556–8; date probably pre–1212, M.-H. Vicaire, '"Contra Judaeos" méridionaux au début du xiiie siècle. Alain de Lille, Evrard de Béthune, Guillaume de Bourges', *CaF* 12 (1977) pp 274–8. The chapter on killing in the Waldensian anti-Cathar treatise, *Liber antiheresis* (ed Selge 2 pp 252–7) relates to God's alleged contradictoriness in ordering and not ordering killing, not to Cathar rejection of killing, and is a later addition (Thouzellier p 271), and is thus not evidence for early Cathar holding of the doctrine.

[6] *PL* 210 cols 394–8.

[7] F. Curschmann, *Hungersnöte im Mittelalter*, Leipziger Studien aus dem Gebiet der Geschichte 5, I (Leipzig 1900) p 158.

[8] H. Grundmann, 'Rotten und Brabanzonen—Söldner-Heere im 12. Jahrhundert', *DA* 5 (1942) pp 428–34.

[9] [Pseudo-] David [of Augsburg, *De inquisitione hereticorum* ed W. Preger, *ABAW* PhK 14, 2 (1876)] p 217. See also the *Pseudo-Reinerius treatise*, ed. [J.] Gretser, [*MBVP* 25 (1677)] col 273. The first recension of this treatise is studied in [A.] Patschovsky, [*Der Passauer Anonymus. Ein Sammelwerk über Ketzer, Juden, Antichrist aus der Mitte des 13. Jahrhunderts, MGH Schriften* 22] (Stuttgart 1968) and the second in [M. A. E.] Nickson, ['The "Pseudo-Reinerius" treatise, the final stage of a thirteenth-century work on heresy from the diocese of Passau', *Archives d'histoire doctrinale et litteraire du moyen âge* 42 (1967)] pp 285–314; the two recensions are not distinguished in the present paper.

[10] [*Anecdotes historiques d'*]Étienne de Bourbon [ed A. Lecoy de la Marche (Paris 1887)] p 280.

[11] William of Puylaurens, *Chronica* ed J. Beyssier, *Mélanges d'histoire du moyen âge* 18 (1904) p 120.

Waldensians and killing

Waldensian doctrine: in the case of the *ruttae* a spectrum from the popular reaction of the *capucionati* to the Lateran Council (1179) whose high concern (and debate?) about mercenaries may have come to the notice of one group present, Valdes and some Brothers. Opinion on such issues developing in learned circles provides parallels (Huguccio's notion of the innocence of the starving man who steals was spreading by the 1190s,[12] and Peter the Chanter was opposing the death-penalty for heresy[13]), and there was probably some common area of basic sources, the *glossa ordinaria* on key biblical passages and the collection of anti- as well as pro- texts in *Causa* 23 of the *Decretum*. Alain's presentation of Waldensian abhorrence of killing includes extensive quotation from *Causa* 23, one use of the *glossa ordinaria* parallelled by Peter the Chanter (on heretics), and one use later parallelled by a member of Peter's circle (on Jews).[14] Was this academic simply dressing up Waldensian views in learned terms? Perhaps not: reference by a Waldensian converted in 1210 to a text which appears in *Causa* 23,[15] and free use both of the *glossa* and the *Decretum* in much later Waldensian literature make it not implausible that Alain was representing Waldensians accurately.[16]

The suggestion here, then, is of a broader context: the climate of opinion and impressions about contemporary bloodshed, in

---

[12] G. Courvreur, *Les pauvres ont-ils des droits? Recherches sur le vol en cas d'extrême nécessité depuis la 'Concordia' de Gratian (1140) jusqu'à Guillaume d'Auxerre (1231)*, Analecta Gregoriana 3 (Rome, Paris 1961) pp 148 ff; another example of impact on contemporaries, the story of a starving man stealing in order to be hanged in a letter of Peter of Blois c1196–8, ibid pp 9–10.

[13] [J.] Baldwin, [*Masters Princes and Merchants. The social views of Peter the Chanter and his circle* 2 vols (Princeton 1970)] I pp 321–2.

[14] These notes are given in the absence of a modern edition.

  a. Gratian's *Decretum*. PL 210 col 394 : *Deum . . . peribit* (see C 23 q 5 pars I); *Item . . . voluntatem* (ibid c I). Cols 394–5: *Poena . . . commendandam* (c 2); Col 395: *Quod . . . apparebit* (ibid); *Ex . . . necari* (c 3); *Gregorius . . . fiat* (c 7); *similiter . . . unitatem* (see q 4 c 38 and q 5 c 7 pars 2). Alain's counter-polemic col 398: *miles . . . jussus* (c 5 c 13); *unde . . . consilium* (c 8); cols 398–9: *Hieronymus . . . agere* (c 28–9, c 31, c 41 bis, c 40).

  b. *Glossa ordinaria*. Col 395: *Augustinus . . . veritatem* (see the *glossa* on 2 Kings 17:22, and Peter the Chanter in Baldwin 2 pp 215–6); *De Judaeis . . . nostrae* (see the *glossa* on Psalms 40:14, and Thomas of Chobham, *Summa Confessorum* ed F. Broomfield, Analecta Mediaevalia Namurcensia 25 (Louvain, Paris 1968) p 434).

  c. Roman law. Col 396: *licet . . . tutelae* (on this Roman law tag see F. H. Russell, *The Just War in the Middle Ages* (Cambridge 1975) p 42).

[15] Selge I p 158 n 85.

[16] See quotations in fourteenth-century Waldensian texts edited in [P. P. A.] Biller, ['Aspects of the Waldenses in the Fourteenth Century' (Oxford D.Phil thesis, 1974)] pp 268–9, 279–81, 287, 291, 294–5.

various areas, bearing upon the Waldensian Brothers when, in the last (two?) decade(s) of the twelfth century, they were extending their new testament literalism and arriving at absolute rejection of killing in all circumstances.

What role did this doctrine play in the sect—very soon an underground movement, more fixed in doctrine and organisation—in the following centuries? Here is the second theme of this paper, a suggestion: that there is a need to precede discussion of the later persistence or decline of this doctrine, usually based on a handful of out-of-context quotations of later Waldensian affirmations of it, with closer description of the modes of its presence in the later middle ages, based on examination of the ways in which it was embodied and articulated, the conditions affecting its dissemination, and conjecture about the darknesses bequeathed by the nature of the surviving evidence. How was the doctrine perceived by the Brothers? How was it formulated in relation to specific areas—and which areas?— of bloodshed? How did it come through to the *credentes*? How did it affect action? How did knowledge of it trickle through to the outside world? A schematic view of the doctrine's embodiment is reflected in the tripartite division of the following sketch: Brothers; *credentes*; knowledge in the outside world. Though some later evidence is used the study is primarily directed to the period before 1400.[17]

How did the Brothers perceive the doctrine? Details of a novice's instruction in scripture by a senior Brother do not survive. Extended treatment of the doctrine is not found in the Brothers' epistles and little pocketbooks, though these do contain some simple but powerful views underpinning the doctrine. The Brothers' images of themselves as the humble and the persecuted form the first points in two antitheses. An epistle written by Italian Brothers (*c*1367) puts the first succinctly, in a commentary on I Corinthians I: 25–31: preachers (the apostles, the Brothers) are the weak of this world, the ignoble (by birth), and the contemptible (in terms of fortune of temporal goods), and are set against the powerful (by rule) and the noble (by birth).[18] The second is especially pointed in the alpine dialect poems of the pocketbooks:

---

[17] Developments during and after the Hussite period in general lie outside the range of this paper; see n 28.
[18] Biller pp 278–80.

Waldensians and killing

on the one hand the Waldensian, the man *mot pacific . . . ben suffrent* (who) *non se volon defendre* (*Evangeli de li quatre semencz*),[19] the man who will not kill (*Nobla Leiçon*);[20] on the other hand the persecutor, and the man who will kill. The two antitheses—humble/powerful, peaceful/violent—come together and lend force to what might otherwise be a conventional banality in another poem, *Novel sermon*, where in a numerical arrangement of moral groups the first among six companies of servants of the world are *regidor que governan lo mont*, who, coveting castles, estates, delight and honour, *fan guerras e batalhas* whereby many are killed.[21]

The extended theology of the doctrine only survives from Brothers' conversations with inquisitors or, rather, treatises based on such conversations. The apparently promising discussions between Brother Raymond of Sainte-Foy and Fournier (1319-20)—used by Contamine, misguidedly[22]—are not used here: Raymond was giving ground under pressure and demonstrably misrepresenting his Brothers' views, and these prevarications were totally undermined by his final choice to die on a set of doctrines which included the utter illicitness of all killing, of criminals or in any war, stated simply and without discussion.[23]

More useful is the treatise (*c*1291) of the inquisitor Moneta of Cremona, who states that the *argumenta* and *responsiones* come not only from heretics' writings but *ex ore eorum*.[24] This, its length, and Moneta's accuracy make it the most useful of inquisitorial sources. Moneta's presentation of Cathars and Waldensians together is a drawback more apparent than real, for he does this where he thinks their views overlap, and carefully distinguishes where they, or their bases, do not.

Fitfully then, through Moneta's text, the Brothers' statement of their position may be discerned.[25] The Roman Church's

---

[19] [H. J.] Chayter, [*Six Vaudois Poems* (Cambridge 1930)] p 68.
[20] [*Les*] *Troubadours* [ed R. Nelli and R. Lavaud 2 vols (Brussels 1960–6)] 2 p 1070.
[21] Chaytor pp 20, 93.
[22] Contamine pp 467–8.
[23] [*Le registre d'inquisition de Jacques*] *Fournier* [*évêque de Pamiers (1318–1325)*, Bibliothèque Méridionale, Third series 41 3 vols (Toulouse 1965)] I p 120. In numerous hearings (Aug 9 1319–Jan 16 1320) Raymond gave ground. On the latter date he presented his (by then modified) view on capital punishment as that also of fellow Brothers (p 76). However, the Brother who taught Raymond, John of Lorraine (pp 99–100), also taught the *credens* Uguette, who described his teaching as absolute prohibition of killing (p 522).
[24] Moneta [of Cremona, *Adversus Catharos et Valdenses* ed T. Ricchini (Rome 1743)] p 2.
[25] *Ibid* pp 508–46.

persecution is illicit, the true church being distinguished by the suffering not the infliction of persecution. All killing in war and in punishment was illicit before the law, some was licit after the law, but again with Christ it became illicit again, with the cessation of the *lex occisionis* and *lex vindictae*. Texts, especially from Matthew, apply as unglossed precepts (not counsels) to all, clerical or lay, private or public. Threats should produce flight; resistance by the sword to injury to person or property is illicit. Precepts of mercy, the natural law and God's reservation of vengeance all exclude judicial execution, as does also the good of the individual, who may yet be converted. In particular there should be no judgements in the Church; the apostles did not wield the sword; the Church's preaching of crusade is condemned.

Finally, in the last part of his exposition Moneta makes a defence in which the use of the material sword is made to depend on the broader question of the derivation of temporal lordship from God. Waldensian rejection of temporal lordship may be implied, but perhaps more a position of reservation and withdrawal, indicated by a not clearly stated exposition of Romans 13:1, where subjection to higher temporal authority is admitted, but described as praised according to worldly and not divine praise, good according to the world, not according to God.[26]

Ironically Moneta's presentation—prolix, with a certain repetitiousness and lack of order and formality, a catena of simply and literally interpreted texts—reflects the theological style of the Brothers' books, but it has two potentially misleading emphases. An apparent emphasis in the discussion of texts on judicial execution: in the context of contemporary judicial notions of war, the conflation of war and justice in, for example, *Causa* 23, and the relative paucity of references to war in the new testament one must assume the implicit inclusion of military killing. This is confirmed by Moneta's insertion of a brief exposé of 'just war' doctrine.[27] Another apparent emphasis, on act rather than inner disposition, reflects the exigences of particular arguments— Brothers opposing Roman restrictions of texts to motive. The

---

[26] *Ibid* pp 537, 544. This is paralleled in [Salvo] Burci, [*Liber supra Stella*], ed [I. von] Döllinger, [*Beiträge zur Sektengeschichte des Mittelalters* 2 vols (Munich 1890)] I p 69. See A. Molnar, 'Romani 13 nella interpretazione della prima Riforma' *Protestantesimo* 24 (1969) pp 65–76.

[27] Moneta p 530.

Waldensians and killing

Brothers' penitential literature contains ample concern with inner disposition.

Broad continuity in this theology may be *suggested*: much is already found in Alain (1190s), much still present in the *Nobla Leiçon* (c1400); much perhaps still implied with Oecolampadius pressing the last medieval Brothers in 1530 to accept the licitness of rulers wielding the sword in judicial execution and defensive warfare?[28]

The Brothers' varied articulations of this doctrine in relation to particular forms or occasions of bloodshed do not, in general, survive; what little filters through owes its emphases, in part, to the direction of clerical and inquisitorial interest. Objections to executions of particular heretics survive, not of particular criminals. Opinion about more exclusively secular warfare hardly appears, but inquisitors do sometimes allow the filtration of opinion about wars of greater clerical concern. First place is taken by prelates' responsibility in general—*papa et omnes episcopi sunt homicide propter bella*[29]—and in particular the rejection of the crusade *ultra mare*[30] (where Waldensian rejection of indulgences and the holiness of the lord's sepulchre buttressed rejection of killing). Western crusades also appear: the Albigensian crusade—its preachers are murderers;[31] the giving of the cross against those fighting against rebels;[32] the 'Northern crusade', in a reference to conversion by sword and slavery in a German source (c1266).[33]

Only occasionally is the historical setting of the articulation of the Brothers' abhorrence of killing made both specific and dense in texture. The words deployed in one treatise—commune, *signoria*, people—transport one into the Italian urban landscape of its author, a nobleman, possibly an assistant of the Inquisition, writing

---

[28] [V.] Vinay, [*Le confessione di fede dei Valdesi riformati* Collana della facoltà Valdese di teologia 12 (Turin 1975)] pp 56, 58. See however the comment of [Claude de] Seysell, [*Adversus errores et sectam Valdensium* (Paris 1520)]f 87^v: (concerning killing) *Neque ipsi tam late defendant*. See also R. Cegna, 'Per uno studio della genesi ideologica della violenza nel Valdismo Ussita in Piemonte', *Bollettino della società di Studi Valdesi* 138 (1975) pp 15–54.

[29] Nickson p 296.

[30] For example, Étienne de Bourbon, p 296; (c1241) Moneta p 531; (c1260–70) Anselm of Alexandria, *Tractatus de haereticis* ed A. Dondaine, *AFP* 20 (1950) p 319; (late fourteenth century) Gretser p 309; (1395) [W.] Preger, ['Beiträge zur Geschichte der Waldesier im Mittelalter', *ABAW* PhK 13/1 (1877)] p 73.

[31] Étienne de Bourbon p 296.

[32] Gretser p 309.

[33] Preger p 245; see also Nickson p 297.

in Piacenza (1235). During a discussion about killing the Brothers are envisaged addressing the people, a picture possibly part literary flourish part observed reality: *O populi, notate bene* ... (how prelates force communes to kill heretics, but are unconcerned about those) *qui habent gladium ad latus et faciunt adulteria et homicidia.*[34] The vocabulary hints at the contrasts of class of the Italian city: the Brothers are the *Pauperes*; they address the people—should one say *popolo*?; the sword-bearers, said by the Brothers to have the conventionally ascribed vices of their class, adultery and murder, are presumably the nobility of Piacenza. Heretical opposition (it is not clear whether Waldensian or Cathar, though probably both) in Moneta's treatise momentarily illuminates other parts of the mid-thirteenth century Italian landscape: the period after Frederick II's second excommunication (1239), with heretics attacking the pope for declaring war on him and seeking the help of many belligerents;[35] inter-city warfare and prelates' blessing of an urban *carroccio* to be borne into battle for what must sometimes be an unjust cause—*cum diversae civitates ad invicem pugnent*, heretics argue, *constat alteram injustam habere causam; quare ergo Praelati illius partis benedicunt carroccium ejus?*[36]

How did the doctrine come through to the *credentes*? Some early evidence bears on conversion. A model conversion described by a German inquisitor (*c*1266) accords the doctrine a distinct role. Brothers addressing potential converts (whose nobility is noteworthy, in view of the social simplicities of the Brothers' literature) describe the clergy—*ipsi pugnant & bella inducunt, & mandant occidi & incendi pauperes, quibus dicitur 'Omnis qui acceperit gladium* ...'—and contrast themselves—*nos vero persecutionem patimur*.[37] The meeting-point of such propaganda and pre-existing opinion among potential converts is hinted at in another part of this source, where abhorrence at the use of the sword is listed as one of the causes of lapsing into heresy,[38] and also in a trial of a Toulouse citizen who had gone to hear a Brother's sermon (*c*1224), but who also talked with others about religion, possessed, borrowed and read books (including the new testament), and *pluries*

[34] Burci ed Döllinger 2 p 72.
[35] Moneta p 513.
[36] *Ibid* p 397.
[37] Gretser p 273.
[38] See above and n 33.

Waldensians and killing

recitavit in publico et coram pluribus a poem attacking the church, particularly for its wars.[39] What is present here, conjecturally—experience of bloodshed, independent formation and exchange of opinion—remains elsewhere hidden.

The larger phenomenon was very soon not conversion but the tradition of Waldensian faith passing from generation to generation in families of *credentes*, and it is on such *credentes* that more evidence bears—the presentation of the doctrine by travelling Brothers to existing *credentes*, and in two areas: the Brothers' attempts to communicate the doctrine, principally in sermons; the Brothers' attempts to shape consciences and action, principally in confession.

An initial impression of *credentes*' reproduction of the doctrine of abhorrence of killing in trial records is its scarcity relative to the doctrine on oaths, its emphasis on judicial execution, and its relative scarcity after 1400. The grille imposed between us and *credentes* by the records explains some of this. Oaths were contentious at the very start of the trial, and thus convenient to concentrate on.[40] Could there have been present earlier an opinion expressed in 1520—that the doctrine *non magnopere ad fidem pertinet*?[41] More clear is the influence of the question-list on areas discussed. A German inquisitor working in Stettin (1392–4) early on asked about killing in general, but then switched to judicial execution[42]—as the doctrinally more difficult case? In this case at least the inquisitor, equipped with a list which included a question on killing,[43] sometimes put the question and was answered; *credentes* tried in Strasbourg (1400), not asked about killing, said nothing about it.[44] These distant communities were linked—both taught, for example, by Brother Nicholas of Solothurn[45]—and thus

---

[39] [Paris Bibliothèque Nationale Collection] Doat 25 f 199ʳ. The poem, by Guilhem Figueira, is in *Troubadours* 2 pp 804–14; note especially verses 2, 7–10.

[40] See, for example, the difficulty over oaths at the beginning of Agnes Franco's trial (1319), and the predominance of oaths in the subsequent doctrinal discussion, Fournier I pp 123-7.

[41] Seysell f 87ᵛ.

[42] [*Quellen zur Ketzergeschichte Brandenburgs und Pommerns* ed D.] Kurze, [Veröffentlichungen der historischen Kommission zu Berlin 45, Quellenwerke 6 (Berlin, New York 1975)] p 83 (general); pp 117, 120, 124, 150, 173, 202, 203, 210, 231, 259 (judicial).

[43] *Ibid* p 74.

[44] The trial is in [T. W.] Röhrich, [*Mittheilungen aus der Geschichte der evangelischen Kirche des Elsasses* 3 vols (Strasbourg 1855)] I pp 43–4. It should be noted that the local community had killed a defecting Brother; see n 80.

[45] *Ibid* pp 46, 74, and Kurze pp 81, 89.

contrasting question-lists may be producing a contrast in belief more apparent than real.

Relative scarcity is further explained by an obvious point, best illustrated in a vignette of a *credens* and his hearing the doctrine. Peter Marti of Montespieu (near Castres, diocese of Toulouse) was a *credens* (*c*1233–40) heavily committed to the Brothers: he made his ploughman give them corn annually; as persecution began to bite he was acting as their *nuncius* in dangerous circumstances—meeting Brothers in a cabin in the woods, trying to lead Sisters to safety from Castres. In 1236 he received Brothers, William Montanher and another, and put them up for 2 or 3 nights, during which time on one occasion he, his wife, and his ploughman ate at the table with them, after they had blessed bread, and then heard them preach, *inter cetera quod non erat jurandum neque occidendum, etiam pro justicia*. The kiss of peace followed.[46]

Six other *credentes* in the area did not report the doctrine. Was the ploughman's silence the lack of memory, real or pretended, so often alleged in trials? Or should one invoke in his case the comment of an inquisitor (1395) about *credentes* holding beliefs *pro suis capacitatibus* (mental? moral?) *plus et minus*?[47] More concrete is the simple fact that the *credens*, Marti, who did report the doctrine, had so much more contact with the Brothers than the six who did not. This is the largest point, encountered in other trials: revealing a spectrum ranging from the extensive and precise comprehension of Waldensian doctrine of a *credens* who received and heard the Brothers every year to the slightness of understanding of a *credens* who had only the blurred memory of one furtive nocturnal sermon over several decades.

Marti's case reminds us that in the 1230s the Sisters, *mulieres Valdenses*, were still pastorally active.[48] A second vignette, from

[46] Toulouse [Bibliothèque Municipale Ms] 609 f 249^v.
[47] Preger p 249. See the same inquisitor's observations of stupidity in particular *credentes* he questioned, Kurze pp 232, 245.
[48] Early literary references to the Sisters preaching are supplemented by their appearances in early French trials. *a*. Probably Castelnaudary, probably early, when *Valdenses stabant publice in terra* (Toulouse 609 f 96^r): a *credens* staying with Sisters *c*4 years; they taught (f 96^v). *b*. Castelnaudary *c*1205, ibid f 252^v. *c*. Narbonne *c*1225, visiting house, *ibid* f 251^r. *d*. Pradellas *c*1226, a Sister induced her brother *verbis suis et monitionibus* to become a Waldensian Brother, Doat 23 f 139^r. *e*. Lautrec *c*1227, preaching in a smith's house, Doat 22 f 77^r. *f*. Castres *c*1237-9, Toulouse 609 f 248^v, 249^{r-v}, 250^r. *g*. Gourdon pre-1241, lodged, Doat 21 f 204^r; f 207^v. *h*. Montcuq pre-1241, Doat 21 f 215^r; renting a house for 2 years, f 219^r; f 221^{r-v}. *i*. Montauban pre-1241, Doat 21 f 222^v; preaching, f 222^v-3^r; renting house

Waldensians and killing

Quercy (pre-1241) reveals them preaching to a woman: Guillelma heard *praedicationem earum et credebat quod essent bonae mulieres et audivit ab eis quod non debebat homo iurare nec occidere*, and believed this was good.[49] This raises a further question about varying reaction to Waldensian preaching. The meagre figures of trial records show more female than male *credentes* remembering and repeating the doctrine under interrogation—six out of seven in Quercy (pre-1241) were women,[50] seven out of eleven in Stettin (1392-4).[51] Meagre: but there is the background of general comment on the appeal of the Waldensians—to women and the womanly (c1190-2),[52] to workmen, women, and idiots (c1266)[53]—and though this may derive in part from the *topos* of the moral characteristics of the heretic it may also derive in part from reality observed and reported through the lens of this *topos*, and for this reason it lends force to the question. Did Waldensian abhorrence of killing find a special resonance among the (theoretical) class of non-combattants, women?

Inquisitorial literature provides only a wisp of a possible reference to distinct female experience of war: for example, being scandalised at priests forcing the weak and girls to travel far to church *tempore gewerre* (in a list of causes for lapsing into Waldensian heresy, c1266).[54] Interrogations may provide further support with, perhaps, nuances of tone—male *credentes* tending more to repeat affirmatively the terms of a set question on killing,

---

for a year, and when visiting a *credens'* house *docebant quod non iuraret nec mentiretur*, f 228^{r-v}; giving *pacem*, f 239^v; giving *monitiones* in a *credens'* house, f 248^v; 253^v-4^r; one *exponebat passionem Domini*, f 281^r-2^v. References do not appear in those later trials up to the early sixteenth century which I have examined. Against the statement that women were no longer received into the Order by the early fourteenth century, M Schneider, *Europäisches Waldensertum im 13. und 14. Jahrhundert*, Arbeiten zur Kirchengeschichte 51 (Berlin, New York 1981) p 47, one may cite the formulae for reception of women into the Order mentioned in Strasbourg c1400 (Rohrich I pp 42-51) and a reference to them by two of the last medieval Brothers in 1530: *ad quendam locum, ubi nonnullae nostrae mulierculae, quas dicimus sorores, agunt vitam in virginitate* (Vinay p 38, see also p 46). Most probably the *Verkirchlichung* of the sect and growing conservatism made the Sisters become more like conventional female religious, in general excluded from pastoral activity. It is worth noting that the majority of references to the Sisters in trials come from female *credentes*.

[49] Doat 21 f 222^v.
[50] *Ibid* f 214^v, 217^v, 218^r, 222^v, 223^v, 224^v(women); 216^v(man).
[51] Kurze pp 120, 124, 150, 202, 203, 210, 259(women); 83, 117, 173 231(men).
[52] Bernard of Fontcaude, *Adversus Waldensium Sectam*, PL 204 col 821.
[53] Gretser p 263.
[54] Preger p 245.

without addition or colour, female *credentes* sometimes not only affirming but also adding distinctive touches. Uguette, *interrogata* on capital punishment, produced standard Waldensian doctrine, but then volunteered (*dixit eciam*) that killing *christianum in bello quocunque est peccatum* (1320);[55] Grete, asked if criminals could be killed without sin, said 'No', and added that she had heard that one should *orare pro raptoribus* (1393).[56] However evidence is too scanty for a firm answer.

Trial records, then, show the doctrine filtering through in simple form to the *credentes*, receiving comprehension, assent, and committal to memory: principally among those who heard sermons or instruction in confession often and had regular contact with the Brothers (and, at an early stage, Sisters?); varying according to the capacity of the *credens*; sometimes encountering already developed opinion, and perhaps evoking a sharper response from women. Trial records are less revealing on the Brothers' attempts to shape consciences and affect action in confession. There is material on confession in the Brothers' pocketbooks. One may look at a late alpine dialect tract on the seven deadly sins, *Che cosa sia pecca*, which devotes more space to wrath than any other sin, concentrating in particular on desire for vengeance,[57] and then look at a trial from this area (1495) with its vignette of a probable reader of the tract, a Brother, exhorting a *credens* who has just confessed to beating a man,[58] and link the two to indicate and exemplify this area: Brothers' pressures on the consciences of their *credentes*. It is difficult, however, to find further examples—only one general description (c1266) of Brothers dissuading *credentes* (probably) from fighting on crusade;[59] the only instance to survive of pressure on a particular *credens* to avoid military service—leading a contingent in the service of a nobleman—was of pressure from another *credens*.[60] 'Only instance to survive'—one may suspect

---

[55] Fournier p 527.
[56] Kurze p 124; see also pp 202, 259.
[57] [*Il Vergier de Cunsollacion e altri scritti* ed A. D.] Checchini, [Antichi Testi Valdesi I (Turin 1979)] pp 34–41.
[58] Paris Bibliothèque Nationale, Ms Lat 3375(I) f 245ʳ.
[59] *peregrinari* (as soldiers?) . . . *ultra mare dissuadent*, Nickson p 302.
[60] Kurze p 204. The equivocations of the *credens* (*ibid* pp 203–5) and conflicting testimony from other witnesses about whether he had ever confessed to a Brother (pp 178, 234) cast doubt on his faith, and suggests a question: was it partly the self-evidence of the fact that a genuine *credens* would not engage in military service that usually keeps this fact out of trial records?

that inquisitors were less interested in, and therefore have not preserved for us in trial records, the Brothers' efforts in confession over these centuries to coax their *credentes* towards some degree of withdrawal from private, judicial[61] and military violence.

There is at least fitful illumination of this foreground, the Brothers' use of preaching and confession to press this doctrine on to the consciences of the *credentes*; almost unlit is the wider setting, the implications of Waldensian rejection of much in the Church which bore on peace, violence and war. This area is implied by an inquisitor (1395), in his affirmations of orthodoxy. Against rejection of all in the Mass beyond the *Pater Noster* and the words of consecration he lists prayers in the Mass and their rationale, *inter alia* prayers for temporal benefits (including special prayers in time of war?) and the *Dona nobis pacem*.[62] Against rejection by the Brothers of the notion that a church is holier through consecration he restates one function, among others—there, in a church, one should pray *pro pace*.[63] Against the Brothers' rejection of ecclesiastical chant and music he affirms that in churches and processions one should sing and pray *tempore belli* (among other ills).[64] Perforce *credentes* participated in local parish churches—in external act: that they did this *ne notentur* and *propter homines* (for most, though not all, acts of worship) is a cliché of treatises and trial records. Is one to suppose that in their quiet inner withdrawal there was especially strong mental reservation about those manifold areas in which, in the local church, liturgy and the holy were interlaced with peace and war? No evidence bears directly on this.

What was the impact of Waldensian abhorrence of killing on the outside world? How far should one think in terms of an arena of public opinion on war and capital punishment in which the 'left-wing' position of opposition was ascribed to this evangelical heresy and heresy in general? To ask this question is to presuppose the enquiry how and in what ways was the Waldensian position known to the outside world, to laymen and—leaving aside inquisitors, with their (varying) specialist knowledge—to church-

---

[61] An exhortation in a Waldensian epistle not to take disputes *a li juge seglar* (Checchini p 6) refers to withdrawal from secular jurisdiction; see also Vinay p 42.
[62] (Pseudo)-Peter of Pilichdorf, *Tractatus contra Waldenses* '*Cum dormirent homines*' ed J. Gretser *MBVP* 25 cols 293–4. See n 90 below.
[63] *Ibid* cols 289–90.
[64] *Ibid* cols 292–3.

men? What follows is a sketch of some approaches to this first question.

The suggestion here is of two periods, the earlier one being one of openness and considerable public knowledge. Early on there was on the one hand pre-occupation at a high level in the Church, where the hesitations about war and judicial killing of those 'right-wing' Brothers who returned to the Church drew the attention of southern French bishops and Innocent III (1208, 1210),[65] and on the other hand, at a lower and humbler level, parallel public openness exemplified in a vignette from a trial record in which a *credens* (before, probably long before, 1241) recalls Brothers visiting his *operatorium*, their sermons, and his own disputing with Franciscans *utrum homo deberet occidere*.[66]

One may suggest that in the second period, as the sect went underground, there was a slow decline in local public knowledge except in those areas where *credentes* lived in great numbers. For example, the casualness of a conversation reported in 1335, in which a *credens* walking along a road to Pinerolo told a non-Waldensian that if he were of their law (Waldensian) he would not take up a spear,[67] suggests the confidence of the massive Waldensian presence in the valleys, unconcerned about such seepage of information to non-Waldensians.

Elsewhere one may suggest considerable ignorance, fitfully illuminated by the occasional publicity of executions, and sermons relating to Waldensians. The list of articles in a sentence read out before an execution might include abhorrence of killing: the execution of a Brother produced talk in pubs in Foix and Pamiers (1320), at one point allegedly including reference to his abhorrence of killing.[68] Two widely separated examples of sermons noting Waldensian abhorrence of killing—one delivered in Laon (1235),[69] the other in Prague (1384)[70]—indicate another possible oral source

[65] Thouzellier pp 216, 219, 225, 229–30, 234.
[66] Doat 21 f 216^v.
[67] [G. G.] Merlo, [*Eretici e inquisitori nella società piemontese del trecento* (Turin 1977)] p 171.
[68] Fournier pp 170–1, 175. An execution could also present an unpacific picture in the bitterly violent last words of a condemned Waldensian—for example, *si status noster non esset minoratus potestatem mortis quam exercetis contra nos modo exercuissemus contra vos omnes*, and *si quiete nostra fides . . . in suo robore perstitisset . . . eam . . . constitueramus manu valida defensare* (Nickson pp 293, 308). Another ms of the latter; Michaelbeuern, Man Cart 85 f 125^v–6^v.
[69] C. H. Haskins, *Studies in medieval Culture* (Oxford 1929) p 250.
[70] *Quellen zur Böhmischen Inquisition im 14. Jahrhundert* ed A. Patschovsky, *MGH Quellen* II (Weimar 1979) p 320.

Waldensians and killing

of knowledge. Stephen of Bourbon's mid-thirteenth century compilation for preachers had material including the doctrine:[71] did knowledge spread through its use?

When turning to knowledge in the literate world the dispersion of written sources containing the doctrine and, sometimes, evidence about their reading constitute the main tangible theme. In France one may cite historical literature: the *Hystoria Albigensis* (*c*1213–18), which specified the doctrine, was much dispersed, and already translated in the thirteenth century.[72] One may also cite theological literature: William of Auvergne's *De Fide et Legibus* (*c*1230), part of which attacked opposition to military and judicial killing by contemporary heretics,[73] was also much dispersed.[74] So long as such works were read one may conjecture some knowledge of the doctrine (ascribed to Waldensians or, less specifically, heretics) in learned circles. Humbert of Romans is a later thirteenth century example: he wrote of (unspecified) heretical opposition to crusades, and is known to have read the *Hystoria Albigensis*.[75] From the schism period one may cite Pierre d'Ailly, who read the section on killing in the *De Fide et Legibus*.[76]

However the main sources were, obviously, treatises specially devoted to the Waldensians. The example taken here is the particular case of the German-speaking area, where the two main accounts (*c*1266[77] and 1395)[78] present an interesting parallel and contrast. The parallel is wide dispersion. The first still survives in 54 manuscripts.[79] Notes of ownership and provenance suggest,

---

[71] Étienne de Bourbon p 296.
[72] Vaux-Cernay 3 pp xl–lxx.
[73] William of Auvergne, *De Fide et Legibus* (Paris 1469?) 5 v f 33^v–7^v. I take the one specification of Cathars (f 36^v), implicitly one among several groups of opponents, to indicate that William thought of several heretical groups or heretics in general opposing killing.
[74] N. Valois, *Guillaume d'Auvergne. Évêque de Paris (1228–1249). Sa vie et ses ouvrages* (Paris 1880) p 326.
[75] Vaux-Cernay 3 p xciii n 5.
[76] In a tract *Utrum indoctus* in J. Gerson, *Opera Omnia* ed L. E. Dupin, 5 vols (Antwerp 1706) I col 658. I owe this reference to Dr Robert Swanson.
[77] See Patschovsky and Nickson.
[78] Ed J. Gretser *MBVP* 25 cols 277–99.
[79] To add to mss listed in Patschovsky are: Karlsruhe 364² f 6^r–8^v (Döllinger I pp 702–3); and Harburg II 1 4° 4 f 129ra–34vb. And to those listed in Nickson: Würzburg Univ Lib, M ch f 51 f 10^r–17^r, Salzburg St Peter's, B 1 37 f 372^r–5^r; St Pölten, 83 f 53^v–84^r; Olomouc Statni Archiv, 224 f 225ra–9vb; Krakow Univ Lib, 1309 f 257rb–71rb; it also exists in Brno Archiv, Mesta N 62 S 90 (text virtually irrecoverable through fire damage), and once existed in another ms whose contents are known via Brno City Archives, 7254 f 65^v.

143

before c1400, concentration in religious houses in upper and lower Austria and Bavaria; one manuscript, however, came into the hands of a master at Prague, later professor at Krakow (ob1407),[80] another, in German, into the hands of a knight of a Bavarian/Austrian family.[81] The second survives in 45 manuscripts.[82] It was also dispersed among religious houses in south-east Germany and Austria, but also to the north (Church of St Mary, Gdansk[83]—which also, by the 15th century, had a copy of the earlier treatise),[84] Poland (Dominican convent at Wroctaw),[85] Moravia (Metropolitan Chapter of Olomouc),[86] and Bohemia (by 1404);[87] a parish priest in north-western Bohemia (Plana) was one owner.[88] The main contrast, however, is in content: the latter manuscripts suggest, for the period after 1395, a schematic map of something surprising, a literary source for knowledge about the Waldensians in which Waldensian abhorrence of killing—present in the earlier source—is conspicuous by its absence.[89]

This omission was probably a deliberate decision by the author, an experienced inquisitor who had talked to converted Brothers and had at his disposal when writing both Moneta and some Waldensian literature.[90] It may relate to a dark area not yet mentioned: Waldensian use of violence, self-defensively, against the inquisition—threats, arson, sometimes killing, with the knowledge and counsel of the Brothers.[91] However the fact that

[80] Krakow Univ Lib, ms 1309 f 257rb–71rb; marginalia throughout by Bartholonaeus of Jaslo, M. A. (Prague)—information of Dr J. Baumgart, Dir. Krakow Univ. Lib.
[81] Vienna Nat Lib, 2846, inside front cover. *Thomas de Trenwach miles*; on the family, Patschovsky p 13 n 54.
[82] Biller pp 355–6.
[83] Gdansk, Mar F 294 f 203^v–26^v.
[84] Nickson p 264.
[85] Wroclaw, I Q 43 f 42^r–77^v.
[86] Olomouc State Archive, MC 57 f 157ra–74vb.
[87] Gdansk, Mar F 295 f 191^r–218^r.
[88] Prague Univ Lib, XIII E 5 f 152^v–82^v.
[89] Its dispersion must be set on a map which contains shades—the continuing dispersion of earlier literature, and the dispersion of near contemporary literature, both of which contained both the doctrine and notes on Waldensian violence (see below and n 91). Among later literature, however, the 1395 treatise stands out for its accuracy and popularity.
[90] Sources and authorship were examined in Biller pp 354–62; a study is being prepared for publication. The last topic tackled in the treatise is the taking of oaths, usually in such treatises adjacent to the topic of killing. One might suggest the possibility that the treatise was never finished—broken off just before the treatment of killing.
[91] See Merlo pp 150–2. Most references are given in Molnar pp 183–4; the attempt there to import some elements of *revendications sociales* is unconvincing, and the incidence of

thirteenth-century treatises had been able to combine reference to such use of violence with description of the doctrine still makes this decision curious. Had the violence intensified?[92]

There is another possibility. An elusive but intriguing reference in a letter (c1368) to a doubt about *justicia* preceding the conversion of a Brother to the Church[93]—in trials questions about *justicia* usually refer to one part of the doctrine's application, opposition to judicial execution—suggests that this may have meant a crisis of conscience about contradictions between Waldensian doctrine and practice. Was the author of 1395 aware, perhaps, of a controversy about killing among these later fourteenth-century German-speaking Brothers, and therefore remained silent?

* * * * * * *

The firmer ground is written: on the one hand the doctrine itself, still found in the later middle ages, written in the pocketbooks carried around in secret by the Brothers; on the other hand the treatises which dispersed a certain picture of the Waldensians in the (literate) outside world among whom the period after 1395 witnessed, in the German-speaking area, a decline in the attribution to the Waldensians of abhorrence of killing. Between the two lies murky and boggy ground. The drawbacks in the attempt made earlier in this paper to sketch the modes of embodiment of the doctrine, in particular its transmission and implementation among *credentes* are only too evident; the extreme scarcity of evidence; more specifically, the way in which what evidence does survive almost determines a picture of passive reception of doctrine by *credentes* — because so little survives of their independent experience of and opinion about bloodshed; more generally, the chasm lying between the schematicism of such an approach by a modern historian and the delicacies of the thing itself, the meeting-point of doctrine and countless individual consciences and occasions of moral choice. In such a nebulous area, may one hypothesise further? The final suggestion here is that the

---

violence and the Brothers' involvement are unduly minimised—see the planning of a killing of a renegade Brother in Strasbourg pre-1400 (Röhrich pp 43-4), and the norm implied by Brothers' question to Oecolampadius in 1530, *an liceat nobis, plebeculae nostrae consulere, ut interficiant falsos fratres proditores* (Vinay p 44).

[92] See, for example, the description of recent violence in a letter by the inquisitor Zwicker (1395), Preger p 246.

[93] Biller p 324.

waning in the picture of Waldensian abhorrence of violence held in the outside world may have been preceded by a waning in the embodiment of the thing itself, a long slow ebbing of the spirit and energy with which the doctrine was taught and implemented, under several possible pressures: (perhaps) the early decline in influence of the sisters;[94] (more clearly) over centuries, the self-defensive needs of settled and secret comunities; finally, growing conservatism under the slow process of *Verkirchlichung*.

University of York

[94] The suggestion here, and earlier in the paper, is that there is a case that marked abhorrence of violence may have been found among those women attracted to the Waldensian faith; no broader thesis is implied.

UNDESIRABLE ALIENS IN THE DIOCESE OF YORK

by ROSALIND M. T. HILL

PLACED as they are at the extreme outpost of Western Europe, the British Isles have been, over the centuries of their recorded history and probably for millennia before the Roman invasion, a melting-pot of peoples. R. G. Collingwood described them, correctly if unflatteringly, as an ethnic scrap-heap. As each new set of immigrants arrived they were scrutinised, assessed and usually heavily criticised by the resident population before being allowed to settle down. Matthew Paris may have been a little uncertain as to what, in the thirteenth century, constituted a foreigner, but nevertheless he was quite clear in his own mind that all those whom he considered to be foreigners were bad, unless they stayed in their own countries. Foreign laymen, he suspected, would do anything, even to poisoning their fathers-in-law with blue venom, in order to lay hands on English estates. Foreign clergy were nearly as bad—of one set of Poitevins he remarks that they had faces like play-actors, and were moreover given to wearing indecent boots. Matthew was a particularly intolerant critic, but some two hundred and fifty years later Andrea Trefisano noted that 'the English have an antipathy to foreigners, and imagine that they never come into the island but to make themselves masters of it, and to usurp English goods,' although he admits that the natives, when they see a handsome foreigner, are apt to remark that 'he looks like an Englishman'.

Still, we in England have always lived by trade, and the foreign merchant was no stranger by the time his rights were defined in Magna Carta. The foreign cleric who held an English benefice was no stranger either, although in the thirteenth and fourteenth centuries his numbers were grossly exaggerated. In time of war the existence of such clergy could present problems, which sometimes caused odd repercussions.

The short war in the south-west of France which is usually known as the War of St Sardos is curiously reflected in the records of the diocese of York. The war itself was not of great importance. There was always a certain amount of local friction on the marches of the Duchy of Aquitaine, where a canny local vassal could usually gain some advantages by discreetly playing off his immediate lord, the King of England, against his overlord the King of France. In September 1323 one such squabble prompted Charles IV of France to require Edward II of England to do homage for Gascony, but he agreed, very reasonably, to postpone the ceremony until July 1324 on account of Edward's difficulties at home. July came and went, with no sign of the coming of the English king but plenty of unrest along the border. In August 1324 Charles led an invading army into Gascony, and although the English commander there, the earl of Kent, soon negotiated a truce, Edward did not at first acknowledge it. It was not until May 1325 that the two kings came to an agreement which was intended to be as permanent as any settlement in the troubled waters of Anglo-French relations could be at the time.

What, you may ask, had this remote and inconclusive quarrel to do with the diocese of York? The government in England clearly felt that it raised in an acute form the whole question of beneficed aliens, a question which had been exercising the minds of the King's Council for the past thirty years. On 13 October 1324 a royal writ was sent out, apparently to all dioceses though few copies have been preserved, in the following terms:—

> Since war has broken out between us and the King of France, it has been ordained by us and by our Council that aliens, whether secular canons or beneficed clergy, in any churches, cathedrals or collegiate establishments, who are subjects or adherents of the said King of France, or bound to him by friendship or affinity or in any way whatsoever, Flemings only being excepted (the Flemish trading connection was far too valuable to be put at risk) who . . . dwell near the seacoast or navigable rivers, shall be removed to rather remote places, in which they can dwell without suspicion . . . Provided that such persons shall have provision made for them from the goods of their benefices at the rate of eighteen pence a week, and forty shillings annually for clothes and shoes, which provision is to be conveyed to them by their proctors, who shall be Englishmen.[1]

[1] B[orthwick] I[nstitute, York], Reg. 9, f 649 (new foliation given).

Undesirable aliens

The rest of their income is to be paid into the Exchequer. The archbishop himself is required to give a complete list of all the persons who are to be subjected to this kind of internal exile.

The allowances proposed, coming to something more than nine-and-a-half marks a year, were not lavish, but they did not represent starvation wages. Still, a man who had been used to the revenues of the archdeacon of Richmond would have found them meagre enough. But before we contemplate the spectacle of numbers of sad, uprooted Frenchmen condemned to settle in comparative poverty in such places as Bainbridge or Kirkby Lonsdale it would be wise to press the inquiry a little further.

Archbishop Melton knew Edward II better than did most of that unfortunate king's subjects, and his first reaction seems to have been that the whole affair was rather foolish. He did not hurry to reply until a second writ, couched in terms similar to those of the first, was despatched to him from Langley on 26 January 1325.[2] Attached to this writ in the addenda to Melton's register, but undated, is the following terse note:

> Since we have not known, and still do not know, whether any of the foreign canons or rectors or other beneficed persons in our diocese are subjects or allies of the King of France, or are bound to him by friendship or affinity or in any other way, we have not been able to obey the mandate contained in your writ, and still cannot do so without danger of grave error, wherefore we beg your Highness to hold us favourably excused.[3]

This letter is not dated, and does not appear in the main text of the register. It is not certain that it was ever formally issued. Perhaps it was superseded by the arrival of another mandate, for on 10 November 1324 a writ of *Venire Facias* was sent to all English bishops, ordering them to cite all beneficed clergy who were subjects of the King of France to appear before the treasurer and take an oath that they would do nothing to harm the King of England. To this writ Melton replied by sending a list of those of his clergy who were liable to appear.[4] The list is not a long one, but it is interesting. It excludes the archdeacon of York, Peter de Pres, and five prebendaries whose names suggest a French origin

---

[2] *Ibid* f 649^v.
[3] *Ibid*.
[4] *Ibid* f 650.

though they presumably came from parts of France which did not owe direct allegiance to Charles IV, namely Bertrand de Fargis, Hugh d'Angouleme, Aymo of Savoy, Robert de Valognes and Gaillard de Durfort. It does, however, start with the name of Elias de Talleyrand, archdeacon of Richmond and scion of a great house in Perigord, and includes Hugh de St Loup, proctor of the abbot of Cîteaux in respect of the church of Scarborough, the proctor of the abbot of Aumale in respect of the churches of Paull, Skeffling, Owthorne, Skeckling, Aldborough and two others, the priors of four alien priories, Pontefract, Holy Trinity York, Ecclesfield and Lewes in respect of their appropriated churches, and the rectors of Stokesley in Cleveland, and, Linby and Weston in Nottinghamshire.

Of these, Talleyrand presented no problem. He had been provided by the pope in November 1324[5] and held in plurality the bishopric of Limoges. I can find no evidence to suggest that he ever visited England, and his work in the archdeaconry was done successively by two officials, both of them Englishmen. His proctor, later appointed vicar-general, was Geoffrey de Normandi, and he certainly appeared at Bishopthorpe on November 2, when he took the oath to Archbishop Melton.[6] Within three weeks he had disappeared, presumably to France, taking with him his seal of office, which was not recovered, and no more was heard of him in the archdeaconry.[7] The prior of Lewes was primarily the responsibility of the bishop of Chichester. Of the three alien priories Pontefract and York subsequently obtained letters of denization. Ecclesfield was still a reasonably prosperous house in 1337. Nothing is known of the fate of the three rectors, except that in 1321 Peter de Vernon of Stokesley had already been in trouble with the archbishop for farming out his church without permission 'at the request of our lady the Queen'.[8] She of course had been a French princess and was Charles IV's sister.

All in all, this attempt to round up potentially undesirable aliens in the diocese of York seems to have had curiously little result. The archbishop himself was less than enthusiastic, and the Council seems to have decided that the results did not justify the trouble

---

[5] [*The Register of William*] Melton, [*Archdeacon of York 1317-40*]i ed R. M. T. Hill, CYS 70 (1977) p 20.
[6] *Ibid.*
[7] *Ibid* p 21.
[8] *Melton* ii, ed D. Robinson, CYS 71 (1978) p 74.

Undesirable aliens

and expense of issuing further writs. At all events, when the Hundred Years' War broke out in 1336, the King, though he demanded a list of alien benefice-holders,[9] seems to have taken no steps towards removing them to remote places.

University of London
Westfield College

---

[9] BI, Reg. 9, f 688^v.

AN ENGLISH ARCHBISHOP AND THE CERBERUS OF WAR

by ROY M. HAINES

FOR MUCH of his political life John Stratford was to be actively engaged either in unleashing or in muzzling the dogs of war. On occasion he seemed to be endeavouring to combine these disparate functions. Here I propose briefly to examine his involvement in and his attitude to the three-headed monster represented by the perennial Anglo-Scottish conflict, civil strife within England, and the initial phase of the Hundred Years' War. I am, of course, appreciative of the fact that in the fourteenth century it is difficult to determine the originators of particular policies and equally hard to discern the attitude of prominent men to such policies when formed. Much is known about the course and outcome of diplomatic negotiations; remarkably little about the thinking of those at the heart of policy making.

The theme of the present conference, 'Church and War', should not be allowed to beguile us by its apparent simplicity. Fourteenth-century man was well aware of the Church in its all-embracing sense—Western Christendom—but more intimately involved in its local manifestations. It is a commonplace that the interests of the *Ecclesia Anglicana* by no means always coincided with what were considered to be the interests of the Church as a whole. For instance, with respect to war we find that the papal policy of peace[1]—or more accurately of peace in the west to enable war to be waged against the 'infidel' in the east— was one to which English churchmen on occasion could pay no more than lip service. It made way perforce for bellicose policies nearer home; policies which, among other things, served to safeguard the liberties of the English church, or so the argument ran. Churchmen indeed knew two masters: the papacy at arm's length and the king at close quarters. Such considerations will assist our

---

[1] For which see in particular, H. Jenkins, *Papal Efforts for Peace under Benedict XII, 1334–42* (London/Philadelphia 1933); E. Déprez, 'La conférence d'Avignon (1344)' in *Essays in Medieval History presented to T. F. Tout*, eds A. G. Little and F. M. Powicke (Manchester 1925) pp 301–20.

understanding of Stratford's attitude, particularly when the demands of war made inroads on ecclesiastical liberty. The clergy as *possessionati* had to pay; the manner in which payment was demanded, not to mention the nature of individual demands, often went beyond the law's allowance.

There was a variety of ways in which war was either countenanced or positively assisted by clerics. At the highest level they were officers of state and royal councillors; they attended parliament, where it was their duty to give counsel concerning hostilities or to assent to them; in their dioceses bishops were the willing or unwilling agents of justificatory propaganda;[2] as holders of extensive estates they were subject to taxation to provide the sinews of war; and, moreover, they were expected to defend threatened areas of the countryside with their retinues.[3]

Stratford's political career was launched in 1317 with a summons to his first royal council. Subsequently he was to serve a diplomatic apprenticeship as resident envoy to the curia, then at Avignon. His elevation in 1323 to the see of Winchester, unpopular though it was with his political master, Edward II, ensured that his status of diplomatic envoy skilled in the minutiae of negotiation was enhanced to that of a leader of future embassies.

The immediate aftermath of Stratford's promotion to Winchester was a close and critical examination of his diplomatic activity, primarily with respect to the Scottish question. Stratford was under orders to secure an aggravation of ecclesiastical sentences against the Scots, whose imperviousness to the Church's censures was alleged conventionally by the English to smack of heresy. At this point national or nationalistic interests were intertwined with religious ones. The view of the king and his

---

[2] W. R. Jones, 'The English Church and Royal Propaganda during the Hundred Years War' *JBS* 19 (1979), pp 18–30; J. R. Wright, *The Church and the English Crown 1305–1334* (Toronto 1980) app 11 'Prayers for the Crown'.

[3] H. M. Chew, *The English Ecclesiastical Tenants-in-Chief and Knight Service, especially in the thirteenth and fourteenth centuries* (Oxford 1932). Only later than Stratford's time was there an attempt to array both secular and regular clergy. In 1418, in response to a writ for that purpose, Bishop Lacy of Hereford returned that he had found 43 men-at-arms and 200 archers in Hereford archdeaconry, 36 and 233 respectively in that of Shropshire. *The Register of Edmund Lacy, bishop of Hereford a.d. 1417–1420* ed A. T. Bannister (Hereford 1917) pp 32–4. In general, B. McNab, 'Obligations of the Church in English Society; Military Arrays of the Clergy, 1369-1418' in *Order and Innovation in the Middle Ages; Essays in Honor of Joseph R. Strayer* edd W. C. Jordan, B. McNab and T. R. Ruiz (Princeton 1976) pp 293–314.

An English archbishop and war

council was that if Scotsmen were to be appointed bishops, unrest would be fostered in the northern region. Stratford, of course, was merely an agent of the government, his room for manoeuvre circumscribed by a detailed indenture. He demonstrated skill in rebutting the charge that he had failed to prosecute the king's interests with sufficient vigour. Stratford's defence emphasised the irenic nature of his mission. Pressure from the papal curia and ecclesiastical processes had brought about the truce of 1323. Thereafter, declared Stratford, his primary object had been to preserve peace rather than to insist on an aggravation of sentences. All that he could do following papal absolution of the errant Scots was to maintain royal rights and to mitigate damage to the English church. He was obliged to convey the papal argument that as Englishmen were unable to enter Scotland in safety, Edward II's claim that only such ought to be appointed to Scottish sees was calculated to leave souls destitute of pastoral care.[4] Reading between the lines, it would seem that in Stratford's opinion there was a dichotomy between the path of peace, entailing papal recognition of Robert Bruce's title, and the devious diplomatic expedients being forced upon himself.

After the fall of Edward II a new Scottish policy was adopted under the aegis of Roger Mortimer and Queen Isabella. This led to the notoriously unpopular treaty of Northampton (1328) whereby claim to suzerainty over Scotland was relinquished, Robert Bruce was recognised as king, and arrangements were made for the marriage of his son David to Edward III's infant sister, Joan of the Tower. Various rumours were current. The allegedly nefarious Bishop Orleton was implicated as prime mover in the derided policy, though in fact he was *persona non grata* with the ruling clique and, since he was abroad, could not have taken part in the preliminary discussions.[5] Another contemporary suggestion was

---

[4] *Foedera* (3 edn, The Hague 1739–45) 2, ii pp 90 *seq*. Politically speaking Edward's contention was not unreasonable, since the Scottish clergy tended to oppose English pretensions. See [P. A.] Linehan, 'A Fourteenth Century History [of Anglo-Scottish Relations in a Spanish manuscript]' *BIHR* 48 (1975) p 110 n 5.

[5] [R. M.] Haines, [*The*] *Church and Politics* [*in Fourteenth-Century England*] (Cambridge 1978) pp 109–10. Stratford was at the parliament which met at York in Feburary 1328. There the young Edward acknowledged Scotland to be a separate kingdom. The arrangements were concluded at Edinburgh and ratified at Northampton: G. W. S. Barrow, *Robert Bruce and the Community of the Realm of Scotland* (London 1965) pp 360–9; E. L. G. Stones, 'The Treaty of Northampton, 1328' *History* ns 38 (1953) pp 54–61; Linehan, 'A Fourteenth Century History' pp 106–22.

that Mortimer had devised the peace to leave his hands free to deal with Henry of Lancaster.[Stratford has been labelled too emphatically a Lancastrian and, on the basis of a misreading of an entry in the Vatican registers, has ever been accounted a kinsman of Earl Henry.] At present, however, his view of the Scottish settlement can only be surmised. In any case, the new policy was of brief duration. Robert Bruce's death, David II's youth, the determination of Edward Balkliol, and the ambition of Edward III combined to subvert the new arrangements. Inevitably a return to the traditional policy was popular; equally inevitably it opened up a fresh round of hostilities between the Scots and the English. There is no reason to suppose that Stratford, by then chancellor and shortly to become archbishop, was other than in sympathy with the turn of events. Serious divergence from royal wishes would have entailed friction; what we know of him at this time points in the opposite direction. It so happens that in a collection of sermons in Hereford cathedral library, at least some of which can be attributed with confidence to Stratford when archbishop, there is one which is pertinent to the matter in hand. It was preached on the theme *Domine salvum fac regem* and the expositor makes much of the wise king who safeguards his people, in contrast to the *Rex insipiens*—an epithet used in the political sermons of 1327 at the time of Edward II's deposition.[8] Emphasis is laid on the frightful weather conditions and other hardships of the Scottish campaign. But, argues the preacher, God has given the English a king worthy to fight their battles—God is on his side.[9] Such a king pours out not only money and temporal possessions, but in the manner of

---

[6] This statement is said to have been made by Stratford at the time of the Salisbury parliament (1328): *Calendar of Plea and Memoranda Rolls . . . of the City of London 1323-1364* ed A. H. Thomas (Cambridge 1926) p 80.

[7] *CalPL 1305-42* p 313. Cf Vat[ican] Arch[ives], Reg Aven 36, fols 393^v-4^r; Reg Vat 94, fol 154^r. This is a licence for Stratford, as bishop of Winchester, to appoint two notaries, issued at the petition of the earl of Lancaster and dated 13 June 1330.

[8] H[ereford] C[athedral] L[ibrary] MS P.5 XII. The '*Sermo pro salute regis*' begins at fol 79^v. For background to the sermons: W. D. Macray, 'Sermons for the Festivals of St. Thomas Becket' *EHR* 8 (1893) pp 85-91; E. W. Kemp, 'History and Action in the Sermons of a Medieval Archbishop' in *The Writing of History in the Middle Ages* edd R. H. C. Davis and J. M. Wallace-Hadrill (Oxford 1981) pp 349-65. For the 1327 sermon see Haines, *Church and Politics* p 169. The text (Eccles 10.3) was said to have been Bishop Orleton's.

[9] HCL MS P.5 XII, fol 80^v: '*Certe credimus quod hodie dedit nobis Deus regem qui pugnat bella nostra pro nobis et Deus pro eo*'. The tone of this sermon may be compared to that in Bodleian Library, Bodley MS 649. See Haines, '"Our Master Mariner, Our Sovereign Lord": a Contemporary Preacher's view of King Henry V' *Mediaeval Studies* 38 (1976) pp 85-96.

An English archbishop and war

Christ exposes his body to death and to every danger, as well as his brother and his friends. A just war, declared the preacher, was one fought for faith (*pro fide*), for right (*pro iure*), and for country (*pro patria*). All three elements, if one considered the matter, were to be found in the Scottish war.[10] We cannot be certain, it has to be admitted, that this apologia for Edward III's Scottish campaign was delivered by Stratford, but it could well have been. Mention of the king's brother, John of Eltham, may be significant, since the archbishop is known to have celebrated a requiem mass in Westminster Abbey at the time of Eltham's burial there in January 1337.[11]

Whereas Stratford's cooperation in Edward III's Scottish policy was eminently defensible, not only in the eyes of English laymen, but also in those of the English clergy, his involvement in the civil strife which led to Edward II's overthrow and which momentarily re-emerged in the early years of his son's reign was more controversial.

Despite the tyrannous nature of Edward II's last years following his success against Thomas of Lancaster and his allies at the battle of Boroughbridge (1322), few have been found to defend those who, at a risk of civil war, joined the insurgent force of Mortimer and Queen Isabella in 1326. The reasons for this are understandable, but not in my view entirely satisfactory. It has been assumed that Stratford was one of the major organisers of the coup, remaining in France for the purpose.[12] The assumption is groundless. We know Stratford was in England for some months prior to Isabella's coming, and though it is agreed that he advocated the queen's role as peacemaker in France,[13] evidence is lacking for his being a party to some long-term plot against Edward II. The government, however, took no chances; the bishop's loyalty was assured by the imposition of heavy recognisances. Initially Stratford made no move to join the insurgents. Eventually he did so and was rewarded with the deputy-treasurership.[14]

---

[10] *Ibid.* For background to and discussion of such theories; J. D. Tooke, *The Just War in Aquinas and Grotius* (London 1965); F. H. Russell, *The Just War in the Middle Ages* (Cambridge 1975).

[11] BL Cotton MS Faustina B. V (Historia Roffensis), fol 79ᵛ.

[12] E.g. M. McKisack, *The Fourteenth Century* (Oxford 1959) p 82.

[13] Haines, *Church and Politics* pp 157-8.

[14] For the financial pressure on Stratford and a list of the recognisances see N. M. Fryde,

The point is that Stratford, though bound by an oath of fealty to the monarch, was willing to side with an invading army, albeit after a period of sitting on the fence. In the event the manifest unpopularity of Edward II and of the Despensers meant that military operations were minimised and that the bulk of those in authority joined Isabella. Thus it was that Stratford became one of the architects of the political revolution which displaced Edward II. When the dust had settled involvement in the affair became somewhat of an embarrassment; so much so that it was an attack on another episcopal leader of the revolution, Adam Orleton, that revealed for posterity the so-called articles of deposition—attributed to Stratford—which were intended to justify Edward II's replacement by his son.[15] The content of these articles need not detain us here, but in a sense they provide justification for Stratford's own conduct. One criticism of the king is particularly apposite; that by misgovernment he had lost Scotland, Ireland and Gascony. It was inadmissible for a monarch to lose territory; Edward II, despite his personal athleticism, had proved singularly ineffective in war.

The regime of Mortimer and Isabella did not mark the end of the civil strife engendered by Edward II's rule. Stratford soon felt that his hopes for the new reign had been traduced; Mortimer's greed and misgovernment[16] merely replaced those of the younger Despenser and of Robert Baldock. In consequence Stratford was prepared once again to associate himself with a potential rebel, this time Henry of Lancaster. Of his thoughts on the matter we know little, but in mid-September the bishop was with the earl's forces at Higham Ferrers,[17] while in October at the Salisbury parliament he was alleged by some to have been the earl's spokesman. According to what may be a contemporary account, Stratford left parliament early and was forced to flee from would-be assassins—Mortimer's agents—eventually taking shelter in

---

'John Stratford, Bishop of Winchester, and the Crown, 1323-30' *BIHR* 44 (1971) pp 153-9. Stratford was appointed as deputy treasurer 6 November 1326.

[15] *Responsiones*, cols 2765-6 in R. Twysden, *Historiae Anglicanae Scriptores Decem* (London 1652). Lambeth MS 1213 pp 300-6, is the source used by Twysden.

[16] This seems to have been the contemporary opinion, if this is correctly reflected in the chronicles. Some modern writers, e.g. N. M. Fryde, *The Tyranny and Fall of Edward II 1321-1326* (Cambridge/New York 1979) cap 15, give a more favourable view of the Mortimer/Isabella regime.

[17] Hampshire Record Office, Winchester Reg Stratford, fol 110^r (entry dated 11 Sept. 1328).

An English archbishop and war

Waltham chase. This story prompted Dean Hook in the nineteenth century to evoke an imaginative picture of Stratford as a Robin Hood figure with a partiality for venison shared by another much later Stratford man.[18] Nothing daunted by his experiences the bishop proceeded to attend a hastily summoned meeting of 'Lancastrian' sympathisers in London. His heart was not in the matter; he withdrew to his diocese of Winchester. The reason for this is obscure, but it could be that he was unhappy with the politically inept conduct of Reynolds' successor at Canterbury, Simon Mepham.[19] The insurrection ended in fiasco; Lancaster's force submitted to Mortimer and the young Edward, the leaders prostrating themselves knee-deep in mud.[20] As it turned out, Stratford's purpose was achieved by other means; Mortimer was taken prisoner in Nottingham castle and subsequently put to death. Edward III was then free to rule in person. At once he turned to Stratford, who assumed the great seal as chancellor and shortly thereafter succeeded Mepham as metropolitan.[21]

Whereas, both with respect to Scotland and to the internal situation in England it is difficult to deduce Stratford's personal justification of his actions, there is somewhat less of a problem with respect to the war with France, the early stages of which are well documented, as to some extent is Stratford's reaction to it. There can be little doubt that at the outset of the French negotiations with which he was concerned in the 1320s Stratford was anxious to arrive at a peaceful settlement. Indeed, this was ostensibly the chief aim of English diplomacy. But the question of Gascony and Ponthieu, which King Charles IV had confiscated following the destruction of the bastide at Saint Sardos, proved intractable. The papal envoys initiated a dialogue and Stratford, who with others had been instructed to review the diplomatic processes since Edward I's time, was an excellent choice for one of

---

[18] W. F. Hook, *Lives of the Archbishops of Canterbury* 4 (London 1865) p 16. The circumstantial account of Stratford's flight (with some inaccuracies) is in *Vitae Arch[iepiscoporum] Cant[uariensium]*, Wharton 1. p 19. Wharton ascribed the authorship to Birchington, a Canterbury monk, but this is no longer accepted. Lambeth MS 99, fols 136^r–46^v provides Wharton's source. See also n 6 above.

[19] BL Cotton MS Faustina B.V, fol 52^{r-v}. This particular chronicler, William Dene, is clearly prejudiced against Mepham.

[20] *Ibid.*

[21] Stratford received the seal 28 November 1330. He was elected archbishop by the Canterbury monks 3 November 1333 and translated by Pope John XXII 26 November.

the leaders of a delegation to treat with Charles.[22] This was to be the first of four such embassies on which Stratford served. Negotiations hung fire; the English envoy complained of French prevarication. Eventually it was decided that Queen Isabella's personal intervention would alone be effective. It has already been suggested that this expedient, warmly supported by the papal envoys and by Stratford, has been misconstrued. The papal interpretation was that the English were seeking an irenic outcome and that Isabella herself was an 'angel of peace'.[23] It so happened that despite his extended diplomatic involvement, Stratford was not one of those who subscribed on the king's behalf to the treaty of Paris of 31 May 1325.[24] This was as well in view of the outcome, the French monarch's failure to return the Agenais.

An immediate consequence of the treaty was the necessity for Edward II to perform homage for his continental fiefs. Fearful of leaving England, and pleading illness, the king was persuaded to allow his young son Edward to act in his stead. Stratford was appointed one of the prince's guardians. On the basis of Archbishop Reynolds' mandate offering an indulgence for the safe return of the queen and her son, this disastrous move may be imputed in part to Stratford's influence.[25] To infer that he acted from sinister motives would nonetheless be unwarranted. To summarise his position at this stage we might suggest that throughout the French negotiations Stratford was scrupulously loyal to his master, Edward II. No blame fell upon him as a consequence of royal irritation in the wake of the Paris treaty. Above all, there is no evidence of a treasonable understanding with the self-exiled queen. He seems to have been genuinely striving after peace.

The successful invasion of Isabella and Mortimer and the substitution of Edward III as king brought a new but temporary entente with the French at the end of March 1327.[26] Stratford was again one of the principal negotiators. As in the case of Scotland,

---

[22] [*The*] *War of Saint Sardos* ed P. Chaplais, Camden Soc 3rd ser 87 (1954) pp 68-9 (from) PRO C47/27/12/50), 192; *Foedera* 2, ii pp 118-19: 15 November 1324.

[23] *Lettres secrètes Jean XXII*, nos 2407-9; *CalPL 1305-42* p 468: 5 March 1325.

[24] *Foedera* 2, ii pp 137-8; *English Medieval Diplomatic Practice* ed P. Chaplais (London 1975) 2, pl 15-16.

[25] E.g. *Registrum Hamonis Hethe, diocesis Roffensis a.d. 1319-1352*, ed C. Johnson (*CYS* 48-49 1948) pp 356-8.

[26] *Foedera* 2, ii pp 185-6..

an unlooked-for factor was to disturb the precarious truce; this time it was the death of Charles IV within a year of its conclusion. Charles' widow having given birth to a daughter, Philip count of Valois was proclaimed king. This elicited a formal protest by the English government, pointing out Edward III's claim through Isabella, which was conveyed to Paris by Bishops Orleton and Northburgh.[27] It was this mission that Stratford was later to single out as the precipitating factor in the French war.[28] And so the dynastic issue brought an element which, though not entirely new, was to prove a crucial factor. For the moment, however, it was necessary to dissemble, or at any rate to bow to pressure. Under pain of forfeiture the youthful Edward was forced to perform homage in 1329 at Amiens. Two years afterwards a formula was devised for its recognition as liege homage.[29] Such accommodation subsequently became the focus of criticism, since it ran counter to Edward III's claim to the French crown. It was Stratford who, in 1341, was to be castigated as the prime mover in so deleterious an arrangement.[30] For the time being such policy served to relieve presure, though at the price of Edward's humiliation. Stratford, who had accompanied the king in 1331 on his surreptitious journey to France, was given the task of securing parliamentary endorsement. He posed the question: was there to be a treaty with France, or war? The way of peace was adopted and Stratford himself was named to a further embassy destined for Paris.[31]

Diplomatic exchanges continued and in the following year, 1332, Stratford informed parliament of King Philip's intention to go on crusade and of his wish that Edward accompany him. One of

---

[27] *Vitae Arch Cant* p 29 (Lambeth MS 99, fol 140^v). Cf. *Foedera* 2, iii p. 13. For some modern discussion of the situation in 1328: John le Patourel, 'Edward III and the Kingdom of France' *History* 43 (1958), especially pp 174–6; [E.]Perroy [trans D. C. Douglas *The*] *Hundred Years War* (London 1951) pp 80–2; [E.] Déprez, *Les préliminaires [de la guerre de cent ans]* Bibliothèque des Écoles Françaises d'Athènes et de Rome 96 (Paris 1902) pp 34–7 (on p 36 'Chichester' should read 'Chester').

[28] *Vitae Arch Cant* p. 29. '*Qui* [Bishops Orleton and Northburgh] *juxta ordinationem hujusmodi eis legationem injunctam tunc assumentes, gressus suos versus Franciam direxerunt: quae quidem legatio maximam guerrae praesentis materiam ministravit*'. Cf. BL Cotton MS Faustina B. V, fol 79^v.

[29] *Foedera* 2, iii p 27. Déprez, *Les préliminaires* pp 42–6, 72–3, 227–9 discusses the implications. Cf Perroy, *Hundred Years War*, pp 83–4, 93.

[30] *Vitae Arch Cant* p 40 (Lambeth MS 99, fol 146^r); W[inchester] C[athedral] L[ibrary], Winch[ester] Cart[ulary], no 518, printed (with a number of significant errors) in [G.L.] Harriss, *King, Parliament, and Public Finance [in Medieval England to 1369]* (Oxford 1975) app A pp 521–2.

[31] *Rot Parl* 2 pp 60–1.

the chroniclers states that it was decided to commend the idea, with the proviso that once affairs in England, Scotland and Ireland were settled the English king would mount a crusading army of his own. The clergy were allegedly more circumspect, fearing the inevitable subsidy.[32] In both English and French camps the crusade was more a diplomatic counter than practical politics. Stratford's immediate concern was the position of Edward Balliol in Scotland and Philip's support for King David. Rumour had it that the French king intended to invade the southern counties of England.[33] Regardless of such developments Stratford seemingly remained hopeful of securing accommodation with Philip. In the spring of 1334 he made another journey to France; the sole prelate in a delegation appointed to continue the interminable legal processes of Périgueux, Agen and Montreuil.[34] Summarising the results of this mission in a letter to Bishop Grandisson of Exeter, Stratford sounded what was intended to be a note of optimism; he now knew more about the French king's intentions than ever before.[35] However, many who awaited the outcome of the protracted negotiations were unimpressed. The Rochester chronicler declared that already some twelve thousand pounds had been expended on embassies to little or no purpose.[36]

Even Stratford's elevation to Canterbury did not bring immediate relief from diplomatic duties abroad. On 9 October — interestingly enough the feast of St. Denys—he was enthroned in his cathedral church. Scarcely more than a fortnight later he was in France.[37] This time, wrote Geoffrey le Baker, Philip, 'the tyrant calling himself king of France', was unbending in his attitude to Scotland, to Gascony, and to the payment of his father's expenses for military operations in the latter. Philip is supposed to have prophesied that there would never be perfect peace among Christians until the king of France exercised justice over the combined realms of France, England and Scotland—and from

---

[32] BL Cotton MS Faustina B.V. fol 60^v.

[33] Concern was expressed at the prospect by Bishop Hethe of Rochester: BL Cotton MS Faustina B. V, fol 65^{r-v}.

[34] *Foedera* 2, iii pp 108–11.

[35] [*The*] *Reg[ister of John de] Grandisson*, [*Bishop of Exeter a.d. 1327–1369*] ed F. C. Hingeston-Randolph (London/Exeter 1894-9) p 274.

[36] BL Cotton MS Faustina B.V, fol 75^v. This must have been a conservative estimate. In 1334 Stratford himself accounted for more than £1000. PRO E101/311/6; E372/179/34.

[37] BL Cotton MS B.V, fol 75^v; Vitae Arch Cant p 20.

England![38] Stratford could only have returned home with the apprehension that a firm settlement was as distant as ever. But while coastal defence and Scottish campaigns preoccupied the English authorities, they did not abandon diplomacy. Further embassies to France were coupled with an extension of continental alliances; a plan seemingly pressed by councillors other than Stratford.[39] It had become clear that Philip had no intention of abandoning the Scots and that an outbreak of hostilities with France was only a matter of time. Edward, too, was guilty of provocation, for he gave asylum to Robert of Artois, indicted as forger, poisoner, abettor of assassins and traitor to his overlord, Philip.[40] Matters came to a head early in 1337 when Edward's council was engaged in discussing whether the king, now in his twenty-fifth year, should claim or abandon his 'inheritance'. Other issues on the agenda were the detention of Gascony and the ways and means so far adopted for the resolution of mutual grievances.[41]

According to Stratford's later defence of his actions it was the Westminster parliament (of March 1337) which gave assent to war against Philip for the recovery of France and also to the policy of German and other continental alliances.[42] At that stage Stratford was forced to accept the imminence of war,[43] made inevitable by Philip's confiscation of Gascony and Ponthieu in May 1337.[44]

Approaches to the emperor posed a special problem for Stratford, since Louis of Bavaria was under papal sentence of

---

[38] *Chronicon [Galfridi le] Baker [de Swynebroke]* ed E. Maunde Thompson (Oxford 1889) pp 55–6. Cf the supposed (undated) dictum ascribed to Philip in letters of William of Norwich (*alias* Bateman) of late 1340. Vat Arch, Reg Vat 135, fols 112^v–14^r, printed in Déprez, *Les préliminaires* pp 423–6; *Registres de Benoît XII, Lettres Closes et Patentes* no 2981.

[39] Bishop Burghersh, who was frequently employed on embassies in the Low Countries, seems to have been particularly concerned, and also perhaps William Kilsby. It is true, however, that Stratford was alleged in 1341 (*Libellus famosus*) to have urged the German and other alliances '*importuna instantia*': *Vitae Arch Cant* p 24 (Lambeth MS 99, fol 138^r).

[40] For Artois see H.S. Lucas, *The Low Countries and the Hundred Years War, 1326–1347* (Ann Arbor 1929) pp 113–14, 176–81; Déprez, *Les préliminaires* pp 224–6; B. J. Whiting, 'The Vows of the Heron' *Speculum* 20 (1945) pp 261–78; G. T. Diller, 'Robert d'Artois et l'historicité des chroniques de Froissart' *Le Moyen Âge* 86 (1980) pp 217–31.

[41] *Foedera* 2, iii pp 155–6. Cf the varying date and account of proceedings in BL Cotton MS Faustina B.V, fol 79^r.

[42] *Vitae Arch Cant* p 30 (Lambeth MS 99, fol 141^r). Cf Harriss, *King, Parliament, and Public Finance* p 234.

[43] *Vitae Arch Cant* p 30. '*Et demum dicto pacis negotio tanquam desperato totaliter derelicto*' (Stratford's *Excusaciones*).

[44] Déprez, *Les préliminaires* p 154 n 1.

excommunication. Tentative efforts to secure Avignon's acquiescence in the English policy brought a resounding denunciation of the emperor and all his works: the mainstay of that 'hypocrite of devilish presumption' the anti-pope Pietro de Corbara. Pope Benedict urged Stratford to lend his voice to the curial arguments.[45]

As was to be expected, Stratford, cooperated with the king in disseminating the government's justification of hostilities. The conflict was none of Edward's making; he had always sought peace. It was Philip who had detained lands in Aquitaine and spurned offers of a dynastic alliance. Regardless of a truce the Scots had killed the earl of Atholl, while Philip, under cover of preparation for a crusade, had mobilised a fleet, captured English ships, killed those on board, and plundered the Channel Islands and the south coast towns.[46]

In December 1337, some two months after Edward had appointed proctors to claim his 'lawful inheritance' of France, Benedict XII sent cardinals to England for a last-ditch effort to stave off war. Stratford received the envoys, whom he escorted to Westminster, where they made determined efforts to win over the bishops to the papal viewpoint. Each bishop was approached individually and urged to respond to the arguments put forward.[47] These tactics failed and the cardinals' reasoning cut equally little ice in parliament, though Edward conceded an extension of the truce, supposedly at their urging.[48]

From Berwick on 28 March 1338 Edward wrote to Stratford, announcing his warlike intentions. The archbishop, like a latter-day Moses, was to pray continually for his master's triumph.[49] The cardinals still nursed hopes of peace and Stratford and Bishop Bury of Durham accompanied them to the continent. Baker, intent on branding Philip as an obstinate tyrant, suggested that the cardinals took ship with a light heart, thinking the war as good as over. Officially archbishop and bishop were still pressing for a peaceful

---

[45] Vat Arch, Reg Vat 132, fol 52^{r-v}. A letter of the same tenor to the king is at fols 51^{r}-2^{r}. See *Registres de Benoît XII, Lettres Closes et Patentes* nos 1418-22; Déprez, *Les préliminaires* pp 415-7.
[46] *Foedera* 2, iii pp 183-4, 187, Cf BL Cotton MS Faustina B.V. fols 80^{v}-1^{r}.
[47] [*Adae*] *Murimuth* [*Continuatio Chronicarum*] ed E. Maunde Thompson (*RS* 1889) p 81; BL Cotton MS Faustina B.V, fol 81^{v}; *Chronicon Baker* p 60.
[48] *Foedera* 2, iii pp 198, 200; iv pp 3-4.
[49] *Foedera* 2, iv p 10. A similar instruction to the archbishop of York follows, *ibid* pp 10-11.

An English archbishop and war

solution,[50] but Stratford must have committed himself to support the war. Indeed he was to play an active part. Between July 1338 and mid-October of the following year he spent 456 days on the continent in royal service. His doings during that period were remarkably unclerical. Openly he continued to act as a diplomat, secretly he directed an espionage network. His agents reconnoitred Dieppe and the coast of Normandy, observing the shipping and pumping the sailors for information; they tried to determine the size of the French army assembling at Amiens, as well as the plans for its deployment; and they smuggled intelligence of ships on the coast of Flanders and in the ports of Wissant and Calais. Other agents visited the major cities of Flanders and Brabant to test the political leanings of those in authority, while in Arras and parts of Picardy attempts were made to foster support for Robert of Artois.[51]

Stratford's proceedings must have been anathema at Avignon. Benedict XII wrote to scold Edward for accepting the vicariate of the Empire and exercising his authority to the detriment of ecclesiastics. The pope's representations resulted in Edward's agreement to Stratford's resumption of talks with the cardinals.[52] An undated letter suggests that Stratford and his colleague Bury stayed close to the king, urging that only by means of the cardinals' mediation could an honourable and profitable peace be secured. At the same time they are said to have advocated a tactical sortie, lest Edward's apparent inaction should bring dishonour.[53] The ensuing campaign of Thiérache did something for Edward's self-esteem. For the rest, shortage of money and supplies continued to plague the English king and his councillors. Already in England murmurings were heard about exactions made on the king's behalf.[54]

Stratford's absence abroad had left others responsible for the taxation and purveyance which war entailed. He returned to

---

[50] *Chronicon Baker* p 61; PRO C49/46/8: undated letters [1338–9] of credence explaining continental developments to the duke of Cornwall and the 'home council'.
[51] These details are from Stratford's expense account, PRO E101/311/35; E372/184/42.
[52] Vat Arch, Reg Vat 133, fols 120ʳ–3ʳ; *CalPL 1305–42* pp 569–70; *Foedera* 2, iv pp 37–9 *seq*; *CalPatR 1338–40* pp 194, 196.
[53] PRO C49/file 46/8. '*Primerement ils deivent dire coment . . . lercevesque et levesque de Duresme sont venue au roi et ont bien dit qe par mediacion des cardinaux non autre manere ils ne trouent pees.*'
[54] BL Cotton MS Faustina B.V, fol 83ʳ. '*Insolita et inaudita onera, exacciones per partem regis sunt petita.*'

England as principal councillor charged with the task of supplying Edward's army and subsidising his continental allies. Already there was a debt of £300,000 and Stratford's attempts to raise additional taxation in parliament met with a disconcerting show of resistance.[55] If adequate concessions were to be made to the commons the king's presence was necessary. When Edward arrived from Ghent, where he had laid formal claim to the French throne, lords and commons granted a ninth of grain, fleeces and lambs, but only on conditions contained in a series of petitions. These Stratford and others were instructed to draw up in statute form. The fourth of these statutes sought to eradicate long-standing clerical *gravamina*: abuses of purveyance, of royal presentation to benefices by reason of the vacancy of sees, and of the custodianship of bishoprics.[56] We know that Stratford was vitally concerned about such matters and on 30 May 1340 he sent a private letter to his provincial bishops to accompany a 'charter of liberties' for the Church—in fact the fourth statute of the recent parliament. Thus Stratford was in two minds: on the one hand he wished to support the war effort, on the other what he conceived to be the liberties of the Church. Even before his return to England in 1339 Stratford had felt it his duty to react against irregular means adopted by the chancery for levying taxes from ecclesiastics and had urged his fellow prelates to defend the Church's interest in parliament. Moreover, he had urged the denunciation of those who took grain or other goods from clerical property—a direct attack on purveyance and other forms of financial coercion.[57]

There is consistency in Stratford's attitude. While not questioning the 'justice' of his royal master's claim to France, he was unable to condone infringements of ecclesiastical liberty even on that account. As a lawyer he felt an obligation to safeguard the Church's future position, war notwithstanding. In other respects

---

[55] As Stubbs remarked in *Constitutional History of England* (Oxford 1874–8) 2 p 381, 'It was at the parliament of October 1339 that the first symptoms appeared of a disposition to make conditions before consenting to a grant.'

[56] *Ibid* p 383; *Statutes* 1 pp 281–94. The (later) commons' petitions, of March 1340, are in Harriss, *King, Parliament, and Public Finance* pp 518–20 (from WCL Winch Cart no 297).

[57] Haines, *A Calendar of the Register of Wolstan de Bransford, Bishop of Worcester 1339–49* (Worc Hist Soc 1966) pp 67–8, 511–12. There is a very carefully written copy of the 'charter' (omitted from Bransford's register) in Lincoln Record Office A/2/12 (portion of a Norwich register from Bishop Bek's time). For Stratford's mandates from the continent: *Reg Grandisson* pp 914–5; *The Register of Ralph of Shrewsbury, Bishop of Bath and Wells 1329–1363* ed T. S. Holmes (Som Rec Soc 1896) pp 357–8.

his behaviour was ambivalent. His spiritual superior, Benedict XII, could not admit Edward's claim to be the 'rightful king of France'. Inevitably there was friction. Edward had to counteract rumours current at Avignon that he was an oppressor of ecclesiastics.[58] At this difficult juncture Stratford was reappointed chancellor (28 April 1340). His task was unenviable: to reduce the burden of royal debt and to counsel economies, for which Edward showed no inclination. Regardless of the situation the king was determined to return to the continent. In Orwell haven Stratford sought out the impetuous monarch, desperately but unsuccessfully tried to postpone his departure until a more propitious time, and ended by surrendering the great seal.[59] His position had become untenable. The king determined to throw caution to the winds and set sail. On 24 June 1340 he won a naval battle at Sluys, thus confounding his over-cautious mentor.

Although Stratford himself no longer held the chancellorship, his brother did. The elder statesman retained his preeminent position and his hand can be descried most notably in arrangements at the parliament of July 1340 for the avoidance of double taxation under the terms of the grants of the clerical tenth and of the ninth.[60] Edward, however, remained critically short of funds and the Stratford government was unable to supply his needs from the grant of wool. Reluctantly the king was forced to conclude the truce of Espléchin on 25 September 1340. Recriminations against the royal councillors at home were rife among the coterie around the king in Flanders, notably Bishop Burghersh, Geoffrey le Scrope and William Kilsby; men who were accounted Stratford's enemies. The landing of Edward and a few companions at Tower Steps on the night of 30 November is a well-known story. Stratford was the primary target of royal wrath, but he judiciously sought refuge at Canterbury with his monks. There he defended himself with vigour and skill from a spate of accusations. Details of this conflict need not be recounted here[61] but the pamphlet

---

[58] Déprez, *Les préliminaires* p 420 (from PRO C70/743 m3).

[59] *Foedera* 2, iv p 78. The elaborate story of Stratford's caution is in [*Robertus de*] *Avesbury*, [*De Gestis Mirabilibus Regis Edwardi Tertii*] ed E. Maunde Thompson (*RS* 1889) pp 310-12. Cf BL Cotton MS Faustina B.V, fol 84ᵛ.

[60] *Rot Parl* 2 p 119 no 17.

[61] See, for instance, D. Hughes, *A Study of Constitutional Tendencies in the Early Years of Edward III* (London 1915) caps 7-9; G. T. Lapsley, 'Archbishop Stratford and the Parliamentary Crisis of 1341' *EHR* 30 (1915) pp 6-18, 193-215; [B.] Wilkinson, '[The] Protest of the

warfare between the parties has some bearing on Stratford's attitude to the French war. The so-called *Libellus famosus* drawn up on the king's behalf, alleged that Stratford following the de facto assumption of the French kingdom by Philip of Valois pressed Edward to ally with the German princes against Philip and so exposed the king to the expenses of war. Stratford, it was alleged, proved a broken reed when it came to raising the essential subsidies. Thus Edward, frustrated of his hope of capturing Tournai, was compelled to accept a humiliating truce.[62]

According to Stratford's step-by-step rebuttal of the *libellus*, the claim that the French crown had devolved on the English monarch by hereditary right was made at the Northampton parliament of 1328; a claim vindicated by Bishops Burghersh and Orleton, who were sent to impede Philip's coronation. This was the principal occasion of war, Stratford declared, and none of his responsibility, for he had been excluded from affairs. Subsequently he laboured long in the field of diplomacy in the interest of peace, crossing the sea thirty-two times and making various other journeys to Scotland. Despite diplomacy, peace could not be secured nor war delayed. It was Philip's fault that hostilities began. Furthermore, it was not his, Stratford's, doing that the policy of alliance with the Germans was adopted; it followed from deliberation in parliament.[63] As for the royal lack of resources, Stratford argued that it stemmed from no remissness on his part; the merchants entrusted with the disposal of wool had not honoured their engagements. With no further hope of peace both he and the other prelates had undertaken heavy obligations for loans contracted on Edward's behalf. As for any delay in the payment of the subsidy, the arrangements had all been approved in full parliament.[64]

Earls [of Arundel and Surrey in the Crisis of 1341]' *EHR* 46 (1931) pp 181–93; Harriss, *King, Parliament, and Public Finance* caps 12–13. The principal chronicle source is *Vitae Arch Cant*.

[62] For the terms of the truce of Esplechin: *Foedera* 2, iv pp 83–4; *Avesbury* pp 317–23; BL Cotton MS Faustina B.V, fols 86ᵛ–7ʳ.

[63] For the *Libellus famosus* (as Stratford dubbed it), and for his *Excusaciones*, see *Vitae Arch Cant* pp 23–7, 27–36 (Lambeth MS 99, fols 138ʳ–9ᵛ, 139ᵛ–44ʳ).

[64] The financial problems of the period 1339–43 are fully considered by Harriss, *King, Parliament, and Public Finance* caps 11–13. For Edward III's attempts to raise money from wool: T. H. Lloyd, *The English Wool Trade in the Middle Ages* (Cambridge 1977) cap 5. To the pope Edward suggested: '*Vere credo quod archiepiscopus voluit quod propter defectum pecunie perditus fuissem et interfectus*'. Vat Arch, Reg Vat 135, fol 114ʳ.

An English archbishop and war

Following his reconciliation with the king in 1341[65] Stratford continued to act as principal councillor, though neither he nor his relatives, the bishops of London and Chichester, held specific office. His stance was much as before; he resisted infringements of ecclesiastical liberty but actively assisted the war effort. The papacy had not abandoned hope and kept the cardinals hovering expectantly in the Low Countries. Edward's measures to apply the income of all benefices held by aliens to defray the country's urgent needs brought a stern remonstrance from Benedict's successor, Clement VI. To Stratford he pointedly stressed the danger to Edward's salvation; occupiers of ecclesiastical goods were guilty of sacrilege.[66] Stratford, prior to his episcopal council of 1346, responded by writing privately to his suffragans, deprecating 'certain novelties' introduced against God, His Church and His ministers.[67] Nonetheless the archbishop, realising the propoganda value of an invasion plan of 1339 discovered at Caen, published it at St. Paul's cross.[68]

Following Edward's return to the continent in 1346 English successes were considerable. The Crécy victory was followed by the taking of Calais, while in the north of England the Scots were defeated at Neville's Cross. These and other successes in Gascony and Brittany may well have confirmed that God was indeed on the side of the English. Even the financial situation appeared less crucial, though Stratford had to stomach the government's efforts to bludgeon the bishops for loans,[69] while urging the anticipation of the dates of payment of tenths.[70]

---

[65] *Vitae Arch Cant* p 41 (Lambeth MS 99, fol 146^v) gives 3 May 1341; *Rot Parl* 2 p 127 no 8 seemingly implies 7 May, but Wilkinson, 'Protest of the Earls' p 184 n 2, argues that '*Meisme cesti jour*' in fact means 3 May. A further reconciliation took place on 23 October in Westminster Hall: see n 30 above.

[66] Vat Arch, Reg Vat 139, fols 273^v–4^r; *CalPL 1342–62* p 25: 24 April 1346.

[67] E.g. *Reg[istrum Johannis de] Trillek, [episcopi Herefordensis a.d. 1344–1361* ed J. H. Parry (Hereford 1910)] pp 272–3. Various papal letters exhorted Stratford to resist novelties and to emulate St. Thomas, his predecessor, e.g. Vat Arch, Reg Vat 137, fol 172^v; 138, fol 100^r.

[68] *Murimuth* pp 205–12; *Avesbury* pp 363–7.

[69] Wiltshire County Record Office, Salisbury Reg Wyville 1, has an original writ bound between fols 164 and 165. See also *Reg Trillek* pp 308–9.

[70] The biennial tenth of 1342 was followed by the triennial tenth of 1344 and another biennial tenth in 1346. For the last Stratford sent letters urging his suffragans to anticipate the dates of payment and to persuade their clergy to do likewise. See *Reg. Trillek* p 277; CUL Ely Reg Lisle, fol 72^r.

How then is Stratford's attitude to war to be assessed? Clearly he was a patriot, hence his angry reaction in 1341 to the stigma of treachery.[71] In the eyes of English patriots the war with France was of Philip of Valois' making and that with the Scots essentially just. Stratford was no pacifist, whether it was a question of civil strife or of external war. Despite a lifetime spent in attempts to avoid conflict, once it materialised he felt that his duty as a leading churchman and statesman was to play a full part in securing the success of English arms. For much of his diplomatic career Stratford was at one with papal endeavours for peace; only at certain points, where to English eyes the papacy appeared partial, did a conflict of loyalties force him to play a double game. Edward's needs necessitated exceptional measures, hence the 'novelties' enforced against the English church. Surely, wrote Clement in 1344, Stratford had not relinquished his former role as its defender?[72] He need not have worried unduly; irregular attempts to mulct the Church remained repugnant to Stratford.[73] At the national level he was prepared to accept a policy, whether involving peace or war, provided that it had been properly ventilated and approved in parliament. Invariably he stressed lawful authority and its appropriate exercise. But the Church's liberties lay beyond the scope of secular control. For Stratford peace and the concomitant relief from taxation and other burdens were preferable to war, however just or excusable. And not merely from the standpoint of the English church, but from that of the people as a whole. In 1348 as the archbishop lay dying, if we are to credit his biographer in the odour of near-sanctity,[74] it almost seemed that Edward's victories would at last muzzle the Cerberus of war. Alas! this was not to be. Only the mouth of civil war remained effectively stopped.

Dalhousie University

---

[71] *Vitae Arch Cant* pp 34–5 (Lambeth MS 99, fol 143^r).
[72] Vat Arch, Reg Vat 137, fol 172^v. '*Nosque a multis stimulati fuerimus ut propterea contra te procedere deberemus.*'
[73] Stratford is by some considered to have weakly acquiesced in Edward's repudiation of the 1341 statutes. However, some of his provincial legislation is a robust defence of church rights. The king continued to be wary of his minister where ecclesiastical liberties were concerned, but neither party wished to risk a further rupture like that of 1341.
[74] *Vitae Arch Cant* p 41 (Lambeth MS 99, fol 146^v).

THE ENGLISH CLERGY AND THE HUNDRED YEARS WAR

by A. K. McHARDY

THE CONTRIBUTION made by the Church to the English war effort during the Hundred Years War was immense. It is the purpose of this paper to describe the forms which this contribution took, and then to offer some reflections on it.

The most important clerical contribution to the war was financial: the taxes voted by the clergy in their two convocations and collected by themselves for the benefit of the crown. These corresponded to the lay subsidies voted in parliament. Normally such taxes were tenths of clerical income as it had been assessed, about 1291, for the benefit of the papacy.[1] No new assessment of clerical wealth was made in the fourteenth or fifteenth centuries, but during the decade 1371 to 1381 a series of experimental taxes was levied from clergy and laity alike.[2] These experiments, culminating in the notorious poll tax of 1380–1 which provoked open rebellion, were not repeated. But in the fifteenth century successive governments tried to tap the wealth of the chantry and stipendiary chaplains through a series of taxes of the poll tax type. Unlike the fourteenth-century poll taxes these measures were imposed at infrequent intervals (in 1406, 1419, 1430, 1436, 1449), but, like them, were abandoned because they failed to bring in the hoped-for revenue.

To attempt to put a figure on the value of clerical taxes to the English crown throughout the Hundred Years War would be so hazardous as to serve little purpose.[3] Two comments may, however, be made. One is that the value of a clerical tenth from Canterbury, by far the wealthier of the two provinces, has been

---

[1] *Taxatio Ecclesiastica Angliae et Walliae Auctoritate P. Nicholai IV circa A.D. 1291* (London 1802).
[2] For the clergy these experimental taxes were: 1371, grant of £50,000; 1377, poll tax; 1379, subsidy proportionate to wealth; 1380–1, poll tax.
[3] For lists of grants made by the two convocations during the fourteenth century see D. B. Weske, *The Convocation of the Clergy* (London 1937) Appendices A and B. For the fifteenth century recourse must be had to the *Calendars of Fine Rolls*.

calculated at £16,000.[4] On a very rough estimation the taxes levied on the basis of the 1291 assessment should have resulted in the crown realising about £432,000 from the southern province during the fourteenth-century phase of the war, and about £466,000 in the fifteenth-century phase. The other is that most collectors were eventually able to satisfy the exchequer for the sums they owed.[5] To have satisfied the crown did not necessarily mean that a collector had gathered in all the sums due from his area; sometimes it meant that he had himself paid the contributions of others and then had to seek the help of the lay power in obtaining reimbursement.[6]

In fact, the lot of a collector was not a happy one, and those deputed to perform this task were among the unsung heroes of the English war effort. Most were heads of religious houses,[7] and they and their subordinates expended very large amounts of time, travel, ink, wax, and parchment in furthering this business for the crown.[8] They met much opposition, as a stream of writs of aid, issued on their behalf, testifies;[9] sometimes they even had to face danger.[10] It is small wonder that exemption from this chore was an eagerly-sought privilege.[11]

The clerical subsidies 'freely' voted in meetings of convocation provided the bulk of the crown's clerical income, but a list of benefits to the war effort must also include a reference to the alien priories.[12] Seized whenever there was war with France, these

[4] M. McKisack, *The Fourteenth Century* (Oxford 1959) p 287.
[5] London, PRO, E359/15, Enrolled Accounts (Clerical Subsidies), which covers the period 1370-98.
[6] E.g., *CPR 1401-5* pp 223, 250, 318.
[7] PRO, E359 gives information about all collectors of tenths and their attorneys.
[8] The process of collection is described by W. E. Lunt, 'The Collectors of clerical subsidies granted to the king by the English Clergy', in *The English Government at Work*, ed W. A. Morris and J. R. Strayer (Cambridge, Mass. 1947) II 227-80. The collectors were allowed to claim their expenses at the exchequer and these sums, which varied widely on different occasions, are recorded on the Enrolled Accounts.
[9] See, e.g. *CPR 1385-9* pp 281, 423; *CPR 1391-6* pp 304, 603.
[10] In the spring of 1381 a collector of the clerical poll tax was beaten up in the deanery of Bicester, Oxon., L[incolnshire] A[rchives] O[ffice], Reg[ister] 12 [(Register of John Buckingham, Memoranda)] fol 226.
[11] Life exemption from being made a tax collector was granted to the abbot of Croxton Kerrial (Leics.), at the instance of the earl of Nottingham, on 7 Nov. 1385, to the abbot and convent of Garendon (Leics.) for sixty years on 31 March 1386, and to John Thorpe abbot of Wellow (Lincs.) for life on 12 Sept. 1388, *CPR 1385-9* pp 45, 123, 506.
[12] See Marjorie Morgan, *The English Lands of the Abbey of Bec* (Oxford 1946), and Donald Matthew, *The Norman Monasteries and their English Possessions* (Oxford 1962).

dependencies of foreign houses were farmed out—usually either to the priors themselves, or to king's clerks or to members of the royal family—to the ultimate benefit of the exchequer.[13] Again, the cash value cannot be computed, though, in this case, it might not have been substantial, for all the priories were small, most were poor, and their numbers, due to denization, disintegration or dissolution were declining throughout the war.[14] Probably the vast amount of ecclesiastical patronage which the seizure of these priories brought to the crown was indirectly more profitable than the farms themselves.[15]

Thus the clergy contributed their share, and sometimes more than their fair share,[16] towards the war finances. They also played their part in defending the realm against attack. This was true both in the north, where the bishops of Durham and archbishops of York traditionally took the lead in organising resistance to invasions from Scotland,[17] and in the south, where heads of religious houses, as well as bishops, were commissioned to help to provide defence against French raids.[18] Less well-known, perhaps, was the continuing duty of the clergy to provide themselves with arms and to act as a 'home guard'.[19]

This can be seen as a parallel to the obligation of the laity to be armed for civil defence. As far as the laity of the late middle ages

[13] Commissions to farm the alien priories are to be found in the *Calendars of Fine Rolls*.
[14] Marjorie Morgan, 'The Suppression of the Alien Priories' *History* 26 (1941) pp 204–12, and A. K. McHardy, 'The Alien Priories and the Expulsion of Aliens from England in 1378' *SCH* 12 pp 133–41.
[15] It has been calculated that 1,600 presentations were made by the Crown to benefices in the gift of alien priories in England and Wales, when in the king's hand, between 1349 and 1378, J. R. L. Highfield, 'The Relations between the Church and the English Crown from the death of Archbishop Stratford to the Opening of the Great Schism' (D.Phil. thesis, Oxford 1951) p 190.
[16] In the parliament which sat from 24 Feb. to 29 March 1371 the council asked for a grant of £100,000 making it clear that half was to come from the clergy, *The Anonimalle Chronicle* ed V. H. Galbraith (Manchester 1927) p 67.
[17] The value of clerical organisation and leadership was shown in a most spectacular way at the battle of Neville's Cross, near Durham in 1346.
[18] For bishops as organisers of local defence see H. J. Hewitt, *The Organisation of War Under Edward III, 1338–62* (Manchester 1966) pp 11, 13. Examples of commissions to heads of religious houses to organise defence even in a period of nominal peace can be found in *CPR 1405–8* pp 303, 306.
[19] This subject has been discussed by [Bruce] McNab, ['Obligations of the Church in English Society:] Military Arrays [of the Clergy, 1369–1418', in *Order and Innovation in the Middle Ages: Essays in Honor of Joseph R. Strayer* ed W. C. Jordan, B.McNab and T. R. Ruiz (Princeton N.J. 1976) pp 293–314.] The three paragraphs which follow are based on this article except where otherwise stated..

were concerned, their obligations to be armed can be traced to the Statute of Winchester of 1285.[20] When the clergy's obligation to bear arms—an obligation at variance with canon law[21]—was imposed is not so easy to discover. Most of the evidence dates from 1369 and later, but Bishop Buckingham of Lincoln referred twice to the work of his predecessor John Gynewell (1347-62) in connection with arming the clergy.[22] Indeed, the ordinance setting out details of the armour and weapons required by the clergy for the defence of the kingdom had become, by the late fourteenth century, so much a part of diocesan life that Thomas Rippeley, official of the archdeacon of Leicester, included it in his formulary of documents on diocesan administration.[23]

The resumption of hostilities in 1369 gave rise to a national effort to compel the clergy to arm themselves, and the death of Edward III, with consequent French raids on the south coast, produced a similar flurry of activity. General arrays of the clergy were ordered in 1400, 1415, and in 1418. Thereafter this practice of arraying the clergy appears to have ceased.

It must be admitted that not all attempts to make the clergy into a home defence force were successful. Individual bishops, especially of coastal dioceses,[24] were active in holding parades. In large dioceses such gatherings were supervised by commissaries, usually on an archidiaconal basis.[25] It is almost certain, however, that there were many defaulters, especially in inland areas. Neither in Bedfordshire nor in Lincolnshire were there good responses to the clerical call to arms, and not all the enthusiasm of so loyal a crown servant as Bishop Buckingham of Lincoln could make soldiers out of the chaplains in the deanery of Rutland.[26]

Though instances of direct military action by clerics are rare (a spectacular exception being the 'Norwich Crusade'[27]) the clergy more than made up for this by their non-violent contributions. The

---

[20] William Stubbs, *Select Charters and other Illustrations of English Constitutional History* 9th ed, rev H. W. C. Davis (Oxford 1870) pp 464-6.
[21] McNab, 'Military Arrays' p 293.
[22] LAO Reg. 12 fols 70^v, 77^v.
[23] Cambridge, Gonville and Caius MS. 588/737 fols 85^v-86.
[24] E.G., Rochester and Llandaff in 1415, McNab, 'Military Arrays' p 303.
[25] *Ibid* pp 300, 302; LAO Reg. 12 fol 153^v.
[26] *Ibid* fols 77^v-78^v.
[27] M. E. Aston, 'The Impeachment of Bishop Despenser' *BIHR* 38 (1965) pp 127-48 for a full account with references.

most basic of these was the part they played in the organisation of warfare. It is well known, though perhaps insufficiently remembered, that it was clergymen, the king's clerks, who, especially in the fourteenth-century phase of the war, organised the financing of expeditions, who ordered the equipment and saw to its safekeeping, and who hired and paid skilled craftsmen such as armourers and tentmakers, without whose services no expedition could be mounted.[28] Once in the field it was clerics who organised such essential activities as the day-to-day receipt and disbursement of money as well as undertaking the more conventionally ecclesiastical role of army chaplains.[29]

Back at home, clerical influence on public opinion and morale was all-pervasive, for it was through the machinery of the Church that ordinary people—those, that is, who would not hear of proceedings in parliament—were informed of the course of the war and urged to pray for its success. If this chain of command was effective the war effort was prayed for not only in every parish church in the land but also in every chapel and religious house.[30]

Thus clergymen can be seen to have been active in every aspect of the Anglo-French war, even in those areas which might be regarded as typically lay, even military. No characteristically clerical attitude to war is immediately obvious, though it is clear that there were some critics of the general policy. Thomas Hoccleve disapproved of the Anglo-French war because he thought both sides should be allies in a war against the infidel.[31] While William Langland shows signs of pure pacifism.[32] Both, however, were men who had been unsuccessful in their quest for ecclesias-

---

[28] A. E. Prince, 'The Payment of Army Wages in Edward III's Reign' *Speculum* 19 (1944) pp 137–60; T. F. Tout, *Chapters in the Administrative History of Mediaeval England* (Manchester 1920–33) esp. Vol. IV chap. XIV.

[29] H. J. Hewitt, *The Black Prince's Expedition of 1355–1357* (Manchester 1958) pp 17, 84. Richard Courtenay (bishop of Norwich from 1413) accompanied Prince Henry on his expedition against the Welsh in 1407, and later joined Henry, then king, on his invasion of Normandy, and died of dysentery during the siege of Harfleur, Emden (O) 1 p50b.

[30] H. J. Hewitt, *The Organisation of War Under Edward III, 1338–62* (Manchester 1966) pp 160–4; W. R. Jones, 'The English Church and Royal Propaganda During the Hundred Years War' *Journal of British Studies* 19 (1979) pp 18–30; A. K. McHardy in *SCH* 18 (1982) pp 215–27.

[31] V. J. Scattergood, *Politics and Poetry in the Fifteenth Century* (London 1971) pp 222–3 quoting from Hoccleve's *Regement of Princes*.

[32] *The Vision of Piers Plowman*, passus X 11 364–71 (The version used here is the translation by Terence Tiller, London 1981, which in general follows the B text).

tical promotion, and their anti-establishment, and hence anti-war, attitude could be attributed to disappointed ambition.[33] Some lollards too, were critical of the endemic warfare in which their country was engaged,[34] but such a view was, of course, only a small part of their anti-establishment stance, and it could be argued that pacifist sentiments expressed by heretics served merely to discredit peace in the eyes of the general public.

At the same time as members of the clergy were acting like laymen in the prosecution of the war, and becoming, in a sense, indistinguishable from them, the laity were acquiring skills and positions once the exclusive preserve of the clergy. This process is most obvious in the area of education. The number of schools cannot be given with any accuracy nor can the extent of literacy be precisely measured. Nevertheless, there is evidence that education was becoming more widely available in the period 1350 to 1450 and that some at least of the beneficiaries were laymen. The evidence is of two kinds. First, the foundation of schools whose permanence was guaranteed by endowments, schools like Winchester College (1373) and like Wotton-under-Edge, the earliest endowed grammer school (1384). In the first half of the fifteenth century the founding of new endowed schools took place at a steady, if modest rate.[35]

Second, the proceedings of courts, both ecclesiastical and lay, in which defendants and witnesses were often described as to status, occupation and literacy. From the late fourteenth century, Miss Gabel tells us, the privilege of benefit of clergy was claimed by increasing numbers of laymen. Their claims were based on the fact that they were literate, and that 'literacy' was traditionally equated with 'clergy'. The standard of learning, in this context, was not necessarily high. 'Literate' is an inexact term, and it has been suggested that some men acquired the minimum skill needed to pass the clerical reading test while they were in prison awaiting trial. Even with these cautions in mind the evidence of increasing lay literacy produced by Miss Gabel is impressive: men in a wide variety of trades and occupations were learning to read. By the

---

[33] Both, though in orders, were married; Hoccleve after a long wait for promotion which never materialised.
[34] *Heresy Trials [in the Diocese of Norwich, 1428–31]* ed [Norman P.] Tanner [(Camden Society, Fourth Series 20, 1977)] pp 71, 142; A. K. McHardy in *SCH* 9 pp 132–3.
[35] Nicholas Orme, *English Schools in the Middle Ages* (London 1973) pp 320–1, 197.

mid-fifteenth century literate craftsmen were common, at least in some areas, and even literate labourers could be found.[36]

At the same time as the clergy were losing their monopoly of literary skills they were being ousted from their preeminent position in the royal administration. In the fourteenth century, setbacks in the progress of the war provoked the dismissal of clerical chancellors and treasurers, as in 1340 and 1371.[37] But in the fifteenth century the lower ranks of the royal administration underwent a change of personnel from clergy to laity which was unrelated to political vicissitudes and which was to prove irreversible. Professor Storey, who has recently described this important process, suggests that the crucial years in which lay administrators (whom he calls 'gentleman-bureaucrats') ousted king's clerks from their majority position in royal service were from 1425 to 1450, the very time when the Hundred Years War was dragging to its close.[38] These years saw another blurring of the distinction between clerics and laity: the apparently increasingly common practice of marriage by men who had remained for many years in minor orders. This is a point which, for lack of statistical evidence, cannot be proved conclusively, but the examples to be found of married clerks seem to rise in number during the fifteenth century. They now included not only disgruntled failures like Langland and Hoccleve, but also successful administrators, some of whom married in prosperous middle age,[39] and, almost certainly, parish clerks.[40]

More fundamental even than these developments were the attacks of the lollards, who belittled the Mass, which was the central plank of the clerical monopoly, and called for more emphasis on clean living, preaching, and superior Biblical knowledge among the clergy.[41]

---

[36] Leona C. Gabel, *Benefit of Clergy in England in the Later Middle Ages* (Smith College Studies in History XIV no. 1–4, 1928–9) pp 76–84.

[37] *Handbook of British Chronology* edd F. M. Powicke and E. B. Fryde (2 edn London 1961) pp 84, 101.

[38] R. L. Storey, 'Gentleman-bureaucrats', in *Profession, Vocation, and Culture in Later Medieval England: Essays dedicated to the memory of A. R. Myers* ed Cecil H. Clough (Liverpool 1982) pp 90–109.

[39] *Ibid* pp 98–102.

[40] Eton College Register 1, fols 56ᵛ, 57ᵛ for an example of a parish clerk who was married and had a daughter.

[41] *SCH* 9 pp 131–45; *Heresy Trials* ed Tanner, *passim* and J. A. F. Thomson, *The Later Lollards 1414–1520* (2 edn Oxford 1967) *passim*.

Thus in the course of the Hundred Years War the clergy can be seen merging into the laity through their contributions to the war effort, so that they had no distinctive attitude and played no exclusive roles; further, there were no roles, not even that of military commander, which men in holy orders did not play. At the same time the laity were acquiring skills and occupying positions which had formerly been clerical preserves, and in some quarters the spiritual basis of the clerical estate was even being called in question.

Yet the whole position of the clergy in the fourteenth and fifteenth centuries was based on the fact that they were distinguished from the laity: in appearance, by the tonsure; in social custom, by their celibacy; in law, by such things as benefit of clergy; and even the humblest of them in subtle social status.[42] It was this fact of difference which had won for the clergy their privileges (mainly judicial) and, above all, their property.

It is, perhaps, unreasonable to criticise the English church for entering so whole-heartedly into the conduct of the Hundred Years War, yet by doing so it contributed to that blurring of the line between the clergy and the laity which we have seen taking place in other areas of life. Once clerical distinctiveness and exclusiveness were gone, men would, and did, begin to call in question the clergy's right to those advantages which had been the rewards of their difference.

University of Aberdeen

---

[42] In the surviving poll tax assessment of 1377–81 even unbeneficed chaplains are described as 'dominus': PRO, E179 (and sub-numbers) *passim*.

OMNINO PARTIALITATE CESSANTE: CLEMENT VI AND THE HUNDRED YEARS WAR

by DIANA WOOD

THE ATTITUDE of the Limousin pope Clement VI to the early stages of the Hundred Years War between France and England occasioned conflicting verdicts. These varied predictably according to the nationality of their authors. One of the pope's biographers, the Frenchman Jean la Porte, hailed him as a creator of concord, a lover of peace[1]. By contrast the Englishman William of Ockham accused Clement of being 'schismatic', in the sense that he deliberately provoked hostilities between the two countries and favoured one side against the other.[2] The German Conrad of Megenberg tried to adopt a *via media*. Replying to Ockham he claimed that he had himself seen Clement sending out cardinals to conduct peace negotiations between the kings of France and England. On the other hand, he was driven to admit Clement's partiality, excusing it somewhat feebly on the grounds that the Holy See had always adhered more to France than to other nations, so one read.[3] Some impression of the truth of these differing judgements can be gleaned from the registers of Clement's correspondence, from the political *collationes* he delivered both as pope and earlier as Pierre Roger, the trusted counsellor and official of Philip VI, Valois, and from contemporary accounts of a peace conference over which the pope presided at Avignon in 1344.

As the servant of the French crown Pierre Roger had watched the deterioration of Anglo-French relations from 1328 onwards. In this year the primary causes of the Hundred Years War were

---
[1] *Tertia Vita Clementis VI* in S. Baluzius, *Vitae Paparum Avenionesium* ed G. Mollat (Paris 1914–27) 1 p 288. On its authorship see Mollat, *Étude critique sur les 'Vitae Paparum Avenionensium'* (Paris 1917) pp 34–40.
[2] [William of Ockham, *De Electione Karoli IV* in] Conrad of Megenberg, *Tractatus [contra Wilhelmum Occam* ed R. Scholz *Unbekannte Kirchenpolitische Streitschriften aus der Zeit Ludwigs des Bayern, 1327–54* (Rome 1911–14) 2] p 352.
[3] Conrad of Megenberg, *Tractatus* p 381.

brought into focus.⁴ On the death of the last Capetian without male issue Edward III advanced his unsuccessful claim to the throne of France. The accession of his rival, Philip VI, automatically raised the other issue, the anomalous status of the sovereign ruler of England as the feudal vassal, and by implication the inferior, of the sovereign ruler of France for the duchy of Aquitaine. The position was emphasised because liege homage had to be performed at the beginning of each reign. Pierre Roger was immediately dispatched to England to demand the homage, and on his return to France was sent to Aquitaine to supervise confiscation of its revenues, pending performance of the ceremony. In fact, it was performed the next year. Thereafter Pierre was heavily involved in Anglo-French diplomacy, among other things trying to negotiate treaties, leading embassies to Avignon on matters connected with the war, and preaching rousing sermons in support of the French cause.⁵ As cardinal, from December 1338 onwards, he had a special responsibility for Anglo-French affairs.⁶ Benedict XII died on 25 April 1342, at a time when an English invasion of Brittany threatened. It seems probable that in such emergency circumstances the predominantly French college of cardinals took into account Pierre Roger's previous diplomatic experience when they elected him as Benedict's successor.

Clement expressed his longing for peace the moment he was elected: indeed, the letter sent to the rulers of Christendom announcing his appointment stressed his zeal for peace.⁷ As he later boasted to two of his cardinals, so determined had he been that he should not be reputed lukewarm in this vital cause that he had written to the belligerent kings of France and England even before his papal coronation.⁸ The chance preservation of a series of letters

---

⁴ On the causes of the war see J. le Patourel, 'Edward III and the kingdom of France' *History* 43 (1958) pp 173-89 and 'The origins of the war' in *The Hundred Years War* ed K. Fowler (London 1971) pp 28-50; J. Palmer, 'The war aims of the protagonists and the negotiations for peace' *ibid* pp 51-74.

⁵ For these events see [J. E.] Wrigley, 'Clement VI [before his pontificate; the early life of Pierre Roger, 1290/91-1342]' *Catholic Historical Review* 56 (1970)] pp 456-7, 461-6; [E.] Déprez, *Les préliminaires [de la guerre de cent ans. La papauté, la France, et l'Angleterre* (Paris 1902)] pp 39-41, 148, 171; [E.] Perroy, [*The*] *Hundred Years War* [trans by W. B. Wells (London 1951)] pp 33-123.

⁶ Wrigley, 'Clement VI' pp 467, 472.

⁷ [Clément VI, *Lettres closes, patentes et curiales se rapportant à la France* edd E.] Déprez [, J. Glennison and G. Mollat, 3 vols (Paris 1901-61)] 1 no 4.

⁸ Déprez, 2 no 2726, letter of 14 August 1346.

Clement VI and the Hundred Years War

Clement wrote as pope-elect evidence the truth of his boast. In these he emphasised his determination to labour for peace as his office demanded, and added that his natural desire for Anglo-French harmony had been increased with his elevation to the Holy See.[9]

The letters Clement wrote as pope also reverberate with his concern for peace.[10] Writing to the two cardinal-legates empowered to negotiate a settlement between England and France within a fortnight of his coronation he enlarged on this concern. Christ had committed his special gift of peace to his vicar in the Church Militant so that it could be perpetuated. The pope bore the office of *speculator*, or overseer, which enabled him to watch over his flock as a pastor, promoting those things which were conducive to peace and checking all those scandals by which the salvation of souls was so grievously impaired.[11] It was almost as if the pope had a monopoly of peace as he had of power and authority.

The concept of peace was in fact closely linked with the pope's special responsibility for the salvation of souls. By peace Clement seems to have meant the good order and harmony of the Christian society, without which it could not achieve its aim of salvation. Preaching in consistory on the return of two cardinal-legates from a later peace mission he elaborated on the Augustinian antithesis of the two cities, that of Jerusalem, signifying heaven, and that of Babylon, denoting hell. These two he applied to the opposing conditions of peace and war. Amid a cluster of contrasting statements he declared that Babylon, that is, war, meant confusion, Jerusalem order; in Babylon was spoliation, in Jerusalem faithful possession; in Babylon was the bitter hatred caused by fighting, in Jerusalem mutual love; Babylon was ruled by diabolical tyranny, while Jerusalem was ruled by divine dominion, and so on. Finally, in Babylon was damnation, and in Jerusalem salvation,[12] by which

---

[9] See his letters of 10 May 1342 to Philip VI of France and to queen Joan, ed E. Déprez, 'La guerre de cent ans à la mort de Benoît XII: l'intervention des cardinaux avant le conclave et du pape Clément VI avant son couronnement' *RH* 87 (1903) pp 58–76 at pp 73 and 75 respectively.

[10] See for example, Déprez, 1 nos 94, 178, 292, 326, 1155, 1326, 1462, 1590.

[11] *Ibid* no 94.

[12] [Paris, Bibliothèque] S[ain]t[e] G[eneviève MS] 240, fol 449ᵛ: '*De ista etiam contrarietate loquitur Augustinus xvii° De Civitate Dei cap° xvi°. Dicit enim quod civitas Dei, que per Iherusalem significatur, inimica est civitas dyaboli Babilon que confusio interpretatur . . . Et videtur michi . . . quod iste due civitates habent x contrarias condiciones . . . . Primo in Babilonia est confusio, sed in Iherusalem ordinatio . . . Quinto in Babilonia est spoliato, sed in Iherusalem fida possessio . . . Septimo*

he meant that only through the good order and harmony of the Church could salvation be achieved. War, he emphasised, was instigated by the devil, the ruler of Babylon.[13] As the vicar of him who 'wished that all should be saved and that none might perish',[14] so he described himself, he was bound in his official capacity to seek peace by all possible means.

Did Clement VI do this? Before the question can be answered his early ideas on the just war and its application to France, which so clearly influenced his later attitude, need to be examined. These emerge mainly from a *collatio* preached on Ash Wednesday 1338 on the text of 1 Maccabees, 3, 58: 'Arm yourselves and be valiant, men, and be prepared for the morning, so that you may fight against the nations which are gathered together to destroy us and our holy place'.[15] In his role as military propagandist Pierre Roger reminded intending soldiers that what mattered was the defence of the state rather than the weapons and accoutrements of war: these were granted them merely to arouse their aggressive instincts.[16] By this stage war was a certainty. Philip had confiscated Aquitaine, in reply to which Edward had presented his defiance to 'Philip of Valois who calls himself king of France', and had formed an alliance with the excommunicate imperial usurper Louis of Bavaria.[17]

Pierre's criteria for waging war were based on Augustine. He concentrated especially on the need for justice and truth in the cause, and for malice and evil in the enemy, which necessitated invasion or resistance.[18] It was a simple enough matter to prove the total injustice of Edward's and Louis of Bavaria's cause. Louis had trumped up a cause by pretending that Philip held possessions

---

in Babilonia est contumnacia inpugnacio, sed in Iherusalem mutuo dilectio, Octavo in Babilonia est dyabolica tirannizatio, sed in Iherusalem divina dominatio . . . Decimo in Babilonia est dampnatio, sed in Iherusalem salvatio . . . . Modo videtur michi quod per istas duas civitates . . . recte significantur due forme valde contrarie, videlicet bellica conmotio et pacis adeptio'. Compare Augustine, *De Civitate Dei,* bk 17 cap 16, *CC* 48 p 581.

[13] St G 240 fol 450^r: '*Rex enim Babilonis dyabolus est et instigator bellice conmotionis dyabolus est*'. Compare *MGH Const* viii no 90, p 115.

[14] *Ibid* no 23, p 44. Compare I Timothy, 2, 4.

[15] St G 240, fols 308^r–14^r. The dating given by Wrigley, 'Clement VI' p 464, n 1, seems preferable to that given by G. Mollat, 'L'oeuvre oratoire de Clément VI' *Archives d'histoire doctrinale et littéraire du Moyen Age* 3 (1928) p 252 no 49.

[16] St G 240, fols 310^v–11^r: '*Nec enim sunt milites propter hastiludia nec propter orneamenta* [sic] *sed illa eis permittuntur ut sint magis exercitati ad defensionem reipublice, pro qua debent militare*'.

[17] Perroy, *Hundred Years War* p 93.

[18] St G 240, fol 309^r. Compare Augustine, *Contra Faustum* bk 22, cap 74 in *CSEL,* 25 p 672.

which pertained by right to the empire. But of course this was demonstrably false, since Philip held only what had belonged to his predecessors, predictably hailed as *principes christianissimi, devotissimi et iustissimi*.[19] In any event, because of his manifold crimes, which were listed, Louis had been deprived of all imperial, royal, and ducal status.[20] This neatly invalidated the argument about imperial possessions: they were no concern of Louis if he did not hold the imperial office. The only real cause Louis embraced, as Pierre knew, was the money promised him by Edward III.[21]

The Limousin considered that war should be waged only against the disobedient and rebellious.[22] Turning his attention to Edward he therefore cast him in the role of the disobedient and rebellious vassal. This line of argument enabled him to concentrate on the feudal issue involved in the war and to ignore Edward's claim to the French throne, for French interests dictated that the conflict should be seen purely in feudal terms. Edward's many disobedient and rebellious acts meant that Philip had every right in feudal terms to lay hands on the duchy of Aquitaine.[23] In fact, Edward's harbouring of the recalcitrant French vassal Robert of Artois, who was *inter alia* suspected of poisoning his aunt Matilda, had provoked the confiscation. Not, of course, that Philip wished to appropriate Edward's *dominium* of Aquitaine, so Pierre enlarged, but simply to impose justice in the way any lord might lay hands on his own feudal domain. The lordship of Aquitaine in any case belonged to Philip *de iure*: Edward, as a vassal, had only the use of it. Even if the French king had intervened without a just cause, his vassal would have had no grounds for action: the most that he could have done would have been to request that justice should be done to him; and Philip was prepared to deal justly with anyone. It was blatantly obvious that the French king had a just cause and his adversaries an unjust one.[24] And ultimately, as Pierre could not

---

[19] St G 240, fol 311ᵛ.
[20] *Ibid* fol 313ʳ⁻ᵛ.
[21] *Ibid* fol 311ᵛ.
[22] *Ibid* fol 309ʳ.
[23] *Ibid* fol 311ᵛ.
[24] *Ibid* fol 311ᵛ: '. . . ordinavit ducatum Aquitanie ad manum suam realiter poni, non ad finem ipsum suo dominio appropriandi, sed sibi ad finem iustitiam faciendi, sicut domini consueverunt ponere manum in feudis suis. Quorum eciam habent de iure dominium directum, licet eciam vasalli habeant dominium utile . . . . Et certe, domini, bene scitis, quod eciam si dominus ponat manum in feudo minus iuste, vasallus non debet propter hoc contra dominum rebellare, sed requirere quod iustitia sibi fiat, quam dominus rex paratus est facere cuicumque. Patet ergo quomodo dominus rex habet iustam causam et ipsi iniustam'.

resist pointing out, no king with a just cause could fail. When a king knows that he is waging an unjust war he must expect his sin to be visited on his own head, but when justice is on his side he is fired by the thought of victory, and says with David, 'The lord will help me, and I shall destroy my enemies'.[25] Such were the views of the future Clement VI. Unless they were to alter with the change in nature which elevation to the Holy See brought, he would surely find it difficult to fulfil his promise to work for peace.

Some disquiet seems to have been felt about Clement's impartiality right from the start. In announcing his election to the Plantagenet the Sacred College found it necessary to reassure him that at such a critical time there could be no one less inclined to acts of partiality.[26] By contrast the Valois, on hearing of Benedict XII's death, had sent his son John, duke of Normandy, to Avignon to press for Pierre's election. The fact that he and his companion, the duke of Burgundy, arrived too late to influence the proceedings did not matter as things turned out. But they were in time for the papal coronation, at which they performed the service of *strator*, a privilege usually reserved for the emperor.[27] A little later Philip wrote confidently to Peter of Aragon about the terms of the treaty of Malestroit (1343) by which envoys were to be sent to the pope *'lequel est ben nostre ami'*.[28]

At the subsequent meeting of envoys, held at Avignon in 1344, Clement was supposed to be acting as the *'ben ami'* both of Philip and of Edward III.[29] Writing to Philip in May 1344 he had stressed his intention to proceed *'non auctoritate nostra, sed ex potestate attributa nobis a partibus'*.[30] In other words he was to act as a private person rather than as the embodiment of the papal office. This practice of arbitration, by which sovereign rulers submitted their disputes to a strictly impartial 'common friend' for adjudication, had become

---

[25] *Ibid* fols 311[r-v]. Compare Psalm 117, 7.
[26] Letter of 8 May 1342, *Foedera*, 5 (London 1708) p 311; '. . . *credimus vestram serenitatem non potuisse pro nunc meliorem habere et minus intendentem ad actus partiales faciendum*'.
[27] Déprez, *Les préliminaires* pp 389–92.
[28] J. Miret y Sans, 'Lettres closes des premiers Valois' *Moyen Age* 29 (1917–18) p 69.
[29] For a full account see [E.] Déprez, 'La conférence [d'Avignon (1344): l'arbitrage pontifical entre la France et l'Angleterre' in *Essays presented to T. F. Tout* (Manchester 1925)] pp 301–20.
[30] Déprez, 1 no 812.

established by the late-medieval period.[31] The 'friend'—usually the pope or a neighbouring prince—acted in his private capacity to show that he was not a superior judge: that way there could be no threat to the sovereignty of either of the belligerents. Why Clement VI should have chosen this course is something of a mystery. By acting as a private person he let slip a golden opportunity to judge between two of the most powerful rulers in Christendom and to demonstrate his papal superiority over them. It is possible that it was a ploy to persuade Edward III, with whom relations had become soured over the issue of papal provisions, to send his representatives to the curia. Edward, for his part, when he empowered his envoys, made great play of the fact that Clement would be acting '*non ut judice, set ut privata persona*', and that he would preside '*extrajudicialiter et amicabiliter*'.[32] It was as if the king were savouring it as a calculated attempt to deny papal supremacy.

Once the conference started some doubt was cast on the sincerity of Clement's intentions to act unofficially by the fact that he conducted only one session alone.[33] The rest were presided over by the pope and six cardinals or just by two cardinals.[34] The cardinals' normal role was to represent the pope in his official rather than his private capacity. In any case it was virtually impossible to separate the peace discussions from the other affair being thrashed out officially by the pope and the English envoys, that of papal provisions.

English anger about papal provisions and taxation had exploded in commons' petitions to parliament in both 1343 and 1344. Xenophobia apart, the English thought that money extorted from them by the curia was being used to finance their enemies. Edward III had therefore issued writs preventing the execution of papal mandates in England, and had blocked all appeals to the papacy.[35]

---

[31] For its use during the fourteenth century see P. Chaplais, 'Règlement des conflits internationaux au XIVe siècle (1293–1377)' *Moyen Age* 57 (1951) pp 269–302 esp 286–8.

[32] See his letters of 20 May 1343 and 29 August 1343, *Foedera* 5 pp 366 and 382 respectively.

[33] [John Offord [?]], *Journal des conférences [d'Avignon (22 octobre–29 novembre 1344)* ed K. de Lettenhove, *Oeuvres de Froissart* 18 (Brussels 1874)] p 251: '. . . *venimus coram domino nostro papa solo sine aliquo cardinali sibi assistente*'.

[34] *Ibid* pp 235, 237, 238, 240, 241, 245, 248, 250, 254.

[35] See the letter of one of the English envoys (probably John Offord, dean of Lincoln) to the archbishop of Canterbury, in which he reports Clement's accusations against Edward, ed [K.] de Lettenhove, *Lettres [des ambassadeurs anglais envoyés à Avignon (septembre–novembre 1344)* in *Oeuvres de Froissart* 18 (Brussels 1874)] p 216. In general see [G.] Mollat, *Les papes [d'Avignon, 1305–78* 10 ed (Paris 1964)] pp 431–4; W Pantin. *The English Church in the Fourteenth Century* (Cambridge 1955) pp 81–7.

Papal nuncios and collectors were more than likely to be arrested and imprisoned on arrival.³⁶ The discussions Clement was holding with the English on such matters formed an acrimonious sub-plot to the main drama of the peace conference. Often the sub-plot and its issues predominated.

The week the conference opened an offensive letter from Edward to one of the cardinals about procurations, in which he was denied the normal courteous forms of address, was read out in consistory.³⁷ Early in November anti-papal edicts were stuck to the doors of Westminster Abbey and St Paul's: these were read out three times in consistory.³⁸ At this, pope and cardinals determined to send ambassadors to England, with the threat that if they were molested, reprisals would be taken against the English envoys at Avignon.³⁹ A few days later Clement created one of the French envoys to the peace conference, Louis de la Cerda, prince of the Fortune Islands, and authorised a crusade to enable him to conquer his still-pagan domain.⁴⁰ So bad were Anglo-papal relations that the English believed that the expedition would be turned against them. Louis, assisted by Philip VI and Clement, would invade the 'island of Great Britain', pretending that it was another of the Fortune Islands in rebellion against the Holy See.⁴¹ The English were well aware of the papacy's claim to possess all islands.⁴² Understandably the discussions about papal provisions were angry. One of the envoys, probably John Offord, dean of Lincoln, described a heated session which took place in October 1344. Examining Edward's infringements of ecclesiastical liberties, the pope warned that excommunication processes had already been prepared against him. Only the papal longing for peace had

---

³⁶ Mollat, *Les papes* p 432.
³⁷ De Lettenhove, *Lettres* p 226: '... en taunt que est dist en meysme le brief: "A toy Gaillard de La Mote", sauns plus cortoysement parler, et hier fust leu ledit brief en consistoire ...'.
³⁸ *Ibid* p 227.
³⁹ *Ibid* p 228.
⁴⁰ For Clement's authorisation see J. Zunzunegui, 'Los orígines de las misiones en las islas Canarias' *Revista española de teología* 1 (Madrid 1940–41) no 16 p 393. On Louis see G. Daumet, 'Louis de la Cerda ou d'Espagne' *Bulletin Hispanique* 15 (1913) pp 38–63.
⁴¹ Adam Murimuth, *Continuatio Chronicarum* ed E. M. Thompson (*RS* 93) p 163. For England's attitude to the papacy see J. Barnie, *War in Medieval Society. Social Values and the Hundred Years War, 1337–99* (London 1974) pp 52–3.
⁴² L. Weckmann, *Las bulas alejandrinas de 1493 y la teoria politica del papado medieval* (Mexico 1949) p 61 n 2.

prevented their publication. Indeed, asserted Clement insincerely, if Philip had committed such atrocities he would have been excommunicated a long time ago. He then moved on to a diatribe on the theme *nos sumus superior suus non ipse noster*, during which he touched on the argument that England was a papal fief. He insisted on reading aloud all the correspondence between Innocent III and King John which contained the terms on which John had submitted England to the Holy See. When the dean commented a little unwisely that King John had had no right to prejudice his successors in this way Clement lost his temper. '*Et incoepit aspere loqui*'—and he began to speak roughly—wrote Offord.[43]

Against this inauspicious background it must have been difficult for the English to see Clement as a private and impartial mediator. But whatever his role, private or official, he was incapable of seeing things from any but the French viewpoint. The English began with a clear statement of intent:[44]

> ... *petitio nostra est de regno et corona Ffranciae, et quod nichil aliud petere vellemus, sed audire vias pacis aperiendas nobis et super illis tractare.*

Since Clement's views had not altered since 1338, he intended to concern himself only with feudal matters, and had already agreed to the French request that the claim to the throne should not be discussed.[45] So much for the impartiality of the arbiter. Surprisingly, when negotiations broke down, after about three months talking, it was not with the expected bang, but with a whimper.[46] In writing to the English king the following year to try to induce him to send his ambassadors back Clement gave the significant promise that he would not be disposed more to one side than the other.[47] By the year 1348, still vainly trying to get the envoys back, the pope wrote in the astonishing terms of *omnino partialitate cessante*—ceasing entirely from partiality.[48] It is extraordinary that an 'impartial' judge should have published such an overt admission of his former bias.

---

[43] De Lettenhove, *Lettres* pp 216–7.
[44] *Journal des conférences* p 236. This statement was repeated at intervals throughout the conference: see *ibid* pp 237 and 238.
[45] *Ibid* p 237.
[46] Déprez, 'La conférence' pp 318–20.
[47] Déprez, 2 no 1844.
[48] *Ibid* no 3742. See also no 3812.

Some of the practical ways in which this bias worked have long been recognised. The marriage alliances he tried to arrange for France were a means of securing allies for her, or at least of neutralising enemies.[49] It was Clement who so skilfully detached the Flemings from their English alliance.[50] Then there were the considerable sums of money lent by both pope and cardinals to Philip.[51] The pope's loans invariably coincided with a fresh burst of hostilities in the war.[52] There were, in addition, various grants of tenths made to Philip for the defence of the realm, while such favours were denied to Edward.[53]

Traditionally the only war in which the papacy was involved was the crusade, the holy war waged in defence of the universality of the faith, which could be initiated by the pope alone.[54] Clement was determined to start a crusade, primarily to halt the Turkish advance in the Eastern Mediterranean, where Christian territories were threatened with annihilation.[55] Holy war should have taken precedence over all other conflicts. The pope accordingly pointed out to Edward III that holy wars were the only fitting ones for Christian kings and princes to pursue,[56] and he repeatedly urged him to make peace with Philip so that he might be free to go on the crusade.[57] His attitude to Philip was different. While he would doubtless have liked the Valois to crusade, this was not to be at the expense of France's safety. He therefore granted the king *pro defensione regni* the use of the tenths which had been collected for

---

[49] K. Fowler, *The King's Lieutenant: Henry of Grosmont, First Duke of Lancaster, 1310–1361* (London 1969) p 92.
[50] H. S. Lucas, *The Low Countries and the Hundred Years War* (Michigan 1929) pp 474–80.
[51] Between 26 November 1345 and the end of February 1350 Clement and his family lent Philip VI 592,000 gold florins and 5,000 écus: see M. Faucon, 'Prêts faits aux rois de France par Clément VI, Innocent VI et le comte de Beaufort (1345–60)' *BEC* 40 (1879) p 571.
[52] *Ibid*.
[53] See Clement's grant to Philip of 16 November 1344, for example; Déprez, 1 no 1250. See also Déprez, 2 no 3812, where Edward's request is refused.
[54] See Pierre Roger's sermon on the crusade preached before John XXII in 1333, St G 240, fol 299ᵛ: '*Est enim negotium istud specialiter ex duobus: prima ex potestatis plenitudine, quia nullus alius potest passagium generalis indicere. . .*'. For the similar views of the canonists see M. Villey, 'L'idée de la croisade chez les juristes du moyen âge' *Relazioni del X congresso internazionale di scienze storiche* 3 (Florence 1955) pp 569–80, and in general see F. H. Russell, *The Just War in the Middle Ages* (Cambridge 1975) pp 115–16, 123–5, 200–01.
[55] For the situation at the start of Clement's pontificate see J. Gay, *Le pape Clément VI et les affaires d'Orient* (Paris 1904) pp 15–31.
[56] Déprez, 1 no 1582.
[57] *Ibid* nos 1326, 1462, 1590; 2 no 1844.

the crusade under John XXII.[58] As Pierre Roger, Philip's representative, he had himself solemnly sworn that the money would not be used for any purpose other than the crusade,[59] and he had later failed to persuade Benedict XII to disregard that vow.[60] Clement VI also ordered that the crusading indulgences granted to other areas of Christendom should not run in France, by which he ensured that the best soldiers would remain to defend their fatherland.[61] The defence of France seemed to supersede that of the universal church. Clement never seems to have wavered in his conviction that France was engaged in a purely defensive and therefore just war. His most unrestrained expression of this as pope occurred in the letter of sympathy he wrote to the duchess of Normandy on the death of her father, John of Bohemia, at Crécy in 1346. John's last hours had been spent *in iusto bello regnum Francie defendendo*.[62]

Clement's views had altered not a whit since he delivered his *collatio* in 1338. Pinpointing the problem, he admitted that there could be no injuries to France, the country of his origin, which did not injure the pope himself.[63] He could not separate the private person from the office of pope, and so he could not cease altogether from partiality. To that extent Ockham was correct. But on the basis that it is quite possible to favour one side and, simultaneously, to desire peace Clement's reputation as a lover of peace can also be sustained. Conrad of Megenberg's *via media* was ultimately the right one: Clement was both peaceloving and partial.

University of East Anglia

---

[58] Déprez, 1 no 914.
[59] See Pierre Roger's sermon before John XXII of 1333, St G 240, fols 307^{r-v}.
[60] Wrigley, 'Clement VI' p 463.
[61] Déprez, 1 no 1704.
[62] Ed L. Klicman, *Acta Clementis VI, Monumenta Vaticana Res Gestas Bohemiae Illustrantia* 1 (Prague 1903) no 721, p 431.
[63] Déprez, 2 no 2760.

THE WAY OF ACTION: PIERRE D'AILLY AND THE MILITARY SOLUTION TO THE GREAT SCHISM

by R. N. SWANSON

THE TRADITIONAL role of the medieval latin church in legitimising warfare tends to fall into two main categories. On the one hand, there are the secular political wars, in which the church can perhaps be seen as a third force: while called on to legitimise and support partisan conflict between supposedly Christian antagonists, it could also work as a force for peace. On the other hand, there are the religious wars, to which the church was itself a party, either in warfare against infidels, or against those who, in their obstinacy, refused to recognise and accept the authority of the Roman church.

Against these two generic types, there is a third model which also requires consideration; one rarely encountered, and in which the church had to act not as an outsider or onlooker, nor as one of the parties, but as both. This was conflict in which the potential struggle was neither against enemies of the church, nor merely between members of it, but actually within the church. It was a problem of this sort which arose in 1378, in the unique circumstances of the rival elections to the papacy of Urban VI and Clement VII, initiating a schism which was to last for forty years and more.

The immediate response to this double election was the division of Europe into two separate obediences, as Urban VI established himself (not without difficulty) at Rome, while Clement VII settled at Avignon. While there were some countries which took their time about coming to a decision on the problem of allegiance—either because of internal political difficulties, as in Portugal, or because of the proclamation of a state of neutrality, as in the other Iberian realms—by 1382 the essential division of Europe had been effected. England, Germany, and most of Italy remained loyal to Urban VI, the claimant first elected. France was the principal supporter of Clement VII, along with parts of

Germany (most of which later defected), Scotland, and (when they made their final decision) the Iberian kingdoms with the exception of Portugal.[1]

The initial tragedy of the schism was precisely this taking of sides, for whatever reason. Having declared their support for a claimant, it was virtually impossible (except by revolution) to change that standpoint: to accept someone as supreme pontiff necessarily involved acceptance of his claims to be the unique possessor of the Petrine inheritance and all that that entailed. Having made a partisan declaration, it was therefore unlikely that it would be overturned with ease. Yet the double election itself was a unique event, unprecedented not because it was a schism, but in its nature in that the college of cardinals, having first elected Urban VI, later denounced his election as invalid and elected Clement VII in his stead. The issue was therefore one which required an essentially legalistic resolution of the problem of the validity of one or other (or neither) of the elections, rather than (as in so many earlier schisms) having been a virtually clear-cut case of partisan divisions which could not be justified at law. But, when the considerations of a possible solution to this unique problem were effectively pre-empted by partisan declarations of allegiance, the difficulties of finding a means of reunifying the church were merely compounded. Small wonder, therefore that it took so long for the schism to be extinguished, and that the church in the meantime had to suffer the traumas of having at first two, and later three, contenders for the papal throne, as well as experiencing the birth-pangs of the conciliar movement.

Despite the difficulties inherent in the search for an end to the schism, human ingenuity did not fail. From the early 1380s, three main strands of discussion are discernible: the ways of conciliarism, negotiation, and abdication. The first would require a decision on the legal and other issues raised by the schism at an assembly claiming to represent and act on behalf of the whole church; the second would produce a decision on the validity of the elections of 1378, and take things from there; the third would avoid the legal issues by requiring both contenders to resign their claims

[1] For the divisions of Europe, see E. Delaruelle, E.-R. Labande, and P. Ourliac, *L'église au temps du grand schisme et de la crise conciliare*, FM 14 (2 vols, Paris 1962–4) 1 pp 19–42; [R.N.] Swanson, *Universities, [academics, and the great schism* (Cambridge 1979)] ch 2 and map 1 at p xiii.

The military solution to the great schism

and permit a third election of an undisputable pontiff. The first real summary of these three main options was contained in the tract, *Utrum indoctus in iure divino posset iuste praeesse in ecclesiae regno*, produced at Paris *c*1381 by Pierre d'Ailly. He was later to be one of the leading prelates of the French church, and a major figure in the debates of the council of Constance; but at this point was still continuing his theological studies at the university of Paris, and only just beginning his public career. In this tract, the three solutions are grouped together as features of a general means of resolving the problem of the schism which he described as the *via amoris*. But they were by no means the only possible solutions under consideration at that time. D'Ailly specifically contrasts them with—and, indeed, in his ordering, makes them secondary to—another possible method, the *via rigoris*. This scheme involved a forceful response to the claims of the schismatics (for d'Ailly, the supporters of Urban VI) in order to bring about their physical defeat by the use of excommunication and the onslaughts of war: *per excommunicationes et bellorum impugnationes*.[2]

Appeals to the *via rigoris* (or *via facti*, as it is more usually known) occur spasmodically throughout the schism, although in chronological terms they are perhaps concentrated towards the start of the period. They also seem to be particularly associated with the supporters of Clement VII and his successor, Benedict XIII.[3] Appeals for the use of force intermingled with French dynastic ambitions on the continent, in particular the Angevin

---

[2] The whole tract appears in [*Johannis Gersonii . . . opera omnia*, ed L.E.] Dupin [(5 vols. Antwerp 1706)] 1 cols 646–62; the definition of the solutions is at col 657. The surviving version of the tract is incomplete, having been re-edited by d'Ailly after 1409: see G. Ouy, *Le receuil épistolaire autographe de Pierre d'Ailly, et les notes d'Italie de Jean de Montreuil*, Umbrae codicum occidentalium 9 (Amsterdam 1966) pp xii–xiii. On d'Ailly, see L. Salembier, *Le cardinal Pierre d'Ailly* (Tourcoing 1932) and for the most recent statement of his early career and status within the university of Paris in the 1380s, A.E. Bernstein, *Pierre d'Ailly and the Blanchard affair: university and chancellor of Paris at the beginning of the great schism* (Leiden 1978) pp 60–9. For a general survey of his political and ecclesiological thought see F. Oakley, *The political thought of Pierre d'Ailly: the voluntarist tradition* (New Haven and London 1964).

[3] H. S. Denifle and E. Chatelain, *Chartularium universitatis Parisiensis* (4 vols, Paris 1891–9) no 1667; [N.] Valois, *La France [et le grand schisme d'occident* (4 vols, Paris 1896–1902)] 2 pp 419–20; Oxford, Balliol college, MS 165B, pp 222–4: advocacy of the *via facti* by Jean Goulain and Raoul d'Oulmont. See also the support for the use of force contained in a poem circulating at Paris in 1381; its arguments are summarised (with references to the text) in N. Valois, 'Un poème de circonstance composé par un clerc de l'université de Paris (1381)' *Annuaire-bulletin de la société de l'histoire de France* 31 (1894) p 215.

pretensions to the throne of Naples,[4] and were also a factor in the aspirations of the duke of Orleans to acquire a kingdom in Italy, the 'kingdom of Adria'.[5] But in this latter instance dynastic priorities within France were perhaps more influential in Valois politics than papal hopes: Clement VII certainly seems to have been more interested in converting the papal states into the kingdom of Adria as part of the process of establishing himself at Rome than the duke of Orleans was in actually conquering the territory.[6] However, the supporters of Clement VII were not the only ones to advocate the *via facti*: on the Romanist side it is apparent in Urban VI's intervention in the Neapolitan succession to secure the throne for Charles III;[7] while in English foreign policy it is manifest in the 'crusades' launched by John of Gaunt to secure the Castilian throne for himself, and by the bishop of Norwich in the Low Countries in the early 1380s.[8]

Yet although so invoked, the *via facti* failed to gain any really consistent support. While there are instances of effective conquests—that of Avignon and the Comtat for the Pisan popes with the help of French forces in 1410–11 springs immediately to mind[9]—they were few and far between. To be successful, the *via facti* was dependent on princely power, and, with the divisions within Europe, additionally required a unanimity of purpose on the part of the princes and a sufficient imbalance of forces between the rival obediences to permit one or other to achieve a military success which would prove unequivocally that God was on the victor's side. Neither precondition prevailed, and as the schism became entrenched, the possibilities for the implementation of the *via facti* declined. Moreover, serious doubts might be raised about the validity of the whole process or of the result of any such 'ordeal by battle'. The outcome might be more reflective of human than divine factors and, crucially, its ability to *prove* that the vanquished

---

[4] For the background to this, and its opening stages, see M. de Bouard, *Les origines des guerres d'Italie: la France et l'Italie au temps du grand schisme* (Paris 1936) pp 45–73.
[5] *Ibid* pp 144–54; P. Durrieu, 'Le royaume d'Adria' *Revue des questions historiques* 28 (1880) pp 43–78.
[6] M. Nordberg, *Les ducs et le royauté: études sur la rivalité des ducs d'Orléans et de Bourgogne, 1392–1407* (Uppsala 1964) pp 84–5.
[7] M. Rothbarth, *Urban VI und Neapel* (Berlin and Leipzig 1913).
[8] E. Perroy, *L'Angleterre et le grand schisme d'occident* (Paris 1933) pp 175–209, 223, 227–8, 235–6, 243, 259.
[9] Valois, *La France* 4 pp 159–72.

The military solution to the great schism

claimant had been legitimately defeated and had therefore never been validly pope might be questioned. Two of the major writers on the schism in the 1380s, Conrad of Gelnhausen and Henry of Langenstein, seem to have accepted this point even before d'Ailly got round to listing his solutions. Gelnhausen particularly emphasised that the legal problems would remain unresolved, in that there would have been no juridical decision on the issues raised in 1378. Even after the military decision, these legal issues might be glossed over only to be raised again later.[10]

The practicality or otherwise of the *via facti* produced one line of opposition to its implementation; its morality might lead to another. Here it is necessary to return to d'Ailly, for he is one of what appears to be a very small number of writers to consider this point in his discussion of the various solutions which he propounded in 1381.[11] His discussion is less emotional than Wycliffe's virtually contemporaneous denunciations of the Flanders crusade, and certainly less motivated by personal considerations. Whereas Wycliffe seems to have viewed that crusade as an opportunity for continuing his attacks on the papacy and the friars, and for reinforcing the pacifistic tendencies of the doctrines which were to become lollardy,[12] d'Ailly's concern is rather more theoretical, moralistic, and certainly much calmer. It is certainly much more specifically concerned with the problems confronting the Church in having to deal with the schism and its threatened internecine war. D'Ailly's consideration of the *via rigoris* thus presents a real discussion of the validity of the use of force in response to the schism, in essentially moral terms. In the end, he clearly decides against its use although, as he said elsewhere in the tract, his purpose was not to determine but to suggest—modestly he claimed—that the actual decision on the solutions had to be taken by those better and wiser than himself.[13]

---

[10] The tracts in which their comments appear were both produced in 1379. For Gelnhausen's *Epistola brevis*, see H. Kaiser, 'Der "kurze Brief" des Konrad von Gelnhausen' *Historische Vierteljahrschrift* 3 (1900) p 385; for Langenstein's statement in his *Epistola pacis*, see BN MS lat. 14644, fol 160ᵛ. Langenstein repeated his rejection of the *via facti* in his *Epistola de cathedra Petri* in 1394: A Kneer, *Die Entstehung der konziliaren Theorie: zur Geschichte des Schismas und der Kirchenpolitischen Schriftsteller Konrad von Gelnhausen (†1390) und Heinrich von Langenstein (†1397)* (Rome 1893) p 142.

[11] Dupin 1 cols 657–60.

[12] See in particular his tract *Cruciata*, printed in *John Wiclif's polemical works in latin* ed R. Buddensieg (2 vols, London 1883) 2 pp 588–632.

[13] Dupin 1 col 657.

The presentation of the arguments for and against the use of force is fairly schematic: firstly, those supporting the military solution are presented; then follow the contradictory arguments. In favour of warfare and excommunication, he appeals principally to the authority of canon law and the bible. The citations from the latter are perhaps those which might be expected. He thus cites Matthew 18:9—'If thine eye offend thee, cast it from thee'—and also refers to the fate of Dathan and Abiron in their schism against Moses (Numbers 16).[14] The references to canon law are surprisingly few: only one specific citation is given, of the electoral decree of Nicholas II of 1059 (D.23, c.1); although he does also mention in passing possible support from other similar canons and the later glosses.[15] However, there is no canonistic discussion of either holy or just warfare, or mention of the main canonistic justification for hostilities which derived from causa 23 of the *Decretum*.[16]

Only two other authorities are mentioned by d'Ailly in support of the *via rigoris*. One is the early thirteenth century Parisian theologian, William of Auvergne, to whose tract *De fide et legibus* there is a brief but telling reference.[17] The other author mentioned is Ovid, introduced in tag form at the end of two agricultural analogies (both probably commonplaces): one required the separation of the sick sheep from the rest of the flock in order to prevent the spread of infection; the other required the separation of rotten grain from the good to the same end.[18]

This brief listing was all that d'Ailly seems to have considered necessary in order to summarise the arguments for the *via rigoris*. He noticeably ignores a number of the problems which might have been raised by actual use of the military solution for the schism. In particular, he makes no reference to the actual leadership of the struggle, nor to its formal authorisation. Presumably he had in mind something like the papal proclamation of an anti-

---

[14] *Ibid* cols 657–8.
[15] *Ibid* col 657. An erudite legalistic justification for the use of force is given by Raoul d'Oulmont in his tract of 1397: Oxford, Balliol college, MS 165B, pp 222–4.
[16] On this see F. H. Russell, *The just war in the middle ages* (Cambridge 1975) ch 3; S. Chodorow, *Christian political theory and church politics in the mid-twelfth century: the ecclesiology of Gratian's Decretum* (Berkeley and Los Angeles 1972) pp 228–46.
[17] Dupin 1 col 658. The reference is to *De legibus*, c.1: see Guillielmus Parisiensis, *Opera omnia* (2 vols, Paris 1674) 1 pp 28–9.
[18] Dupin 1 col 658. The tag is derived from Ovid, *Metamorphoses* 1 line 191.

The military solution to the great schism

heretical crusade, in which the secular princes would assume much of the responsibility for its conduct. Other writers were not so taciturn: Wycliffe's tracts at least deal with the problem of authorisation in their anti-papal attacks;[19] and other contributions to the debates implicitly tackle the difficulty of leadership when considering the issue of princely intervention in the schism, even if they often fail to make any direct statement for or against the *via facti*.[20] But d'Ailly appears to be totally unconcerned with these issues, and moves straight on to consider the arguments opposing the *via rigoris* and favouring the *via amoris*. Here he argues, as he says, *multipliciter*, but there is certainly much more sign of real argument, and of a real concern for the issues.[21]

Not surprisingly, the bible reappears among the authorities cited. 'They who live by the sword shall perish by the sword' (Matthew 26:52); but that is not his real concern. It is clear that, for d'Ailly, the vagueness of the divisions within the Church, and the ease with which the warfare could degenerate from a struggle between supporters of the rival papacies into straightforward international conflict, justified solely by the superficial claim to be fighting on behalf of one of the claimants, is also important. Hence, perhaps, his frequent references to the parable of the intermixed tares and wheat in Matthew 13.[22] D'Ailly is also concerned with the scandals which warfare would introduce into the Church, and with the deaths which would result when there is insufficient evidence that the people concerned are being wilfully schismatic, but are instead confused and misled. He is concerned with the precise nature of their stands: are those against whom this crusade is to be thrown positively rejecting Clement VII and his claims, or merely unsure, and awaiting a proper determination of the issues? And, if the latter, are they then actually schismatics who should be treated in this manner? Towards the end of the

---

[19] See n 12.
[20] Despite his opposition to the *via facti* (above, n 10), Langenstein seems frequently to have fallen into the trap of invoking force to be exercised by secular authorities when considering their role in terminating the schism. See the considerations of his *Epistola exhortatoria imperatoris et aliorum regum et principum ad pacem ecclesie universalis*, and of his later letter to Rupert of the Palatinate urging action based on the precedent of the 1130s, in Swanson, *Universities* pp 54–5, 88–9. Similar difficulties arise with another tract of the 1380s, the so-called *Tetragonus Aristotelis* (ibid pp 55–6).
[21] The arguments favouring peace are at Dupin 1 cols 658–60.
[22] Matthew 13:24–30.

discussion, d'Ailly gets very close to a precise definition of his view of the whole schism, with the argument that warfare cannot be justified in terms of anti-heretical action because neither side has yet committed heresy: neither side is actually disputing the role of the papcy within the Church, merely the personality of the occupant of the papal throne.[23] The dispute is therefore not doctrinal, but organisational. It does not affect the state of salvation of the individual soul, because the dispute is not over a matter of faith and orthodoxy, but is merely a problem of a disputed succession.[24] In this one insight, d'Ailly summarises both the simplicity and the extreme complexity of the whole difficulty of the schism.

The bible was not the only authority cited by d'Ailly in countering the arguments favouring the *via rigoris*. Again, however, what references there are are brief, and for the most part allusions rather than actual quotations. His main authority is Duns Scotus' commentary on the *Sentences*, in the version known as *Opus Oxoniense*.[25] Augustine and Lactantius are also brought in—the first in consideration of an Augustinian contribution to the *glossa ordinaria* to the bible, the second as little more than a tag—to assist in building up the arguments against too hasty a decision for and implementation of the *via facti*.[26]

D'Ailly's consideration of the morality of the use of force to settle the issues raised by the elections of 1378, and his seemingly clear decision against it, represents almost the only real discussion of the military solution contained in the early tracts on the schism. Elsewhere, and at other times, it is simply mentioned *en passant*—sometimes simply to be rejected—and with no real development of the ideas (although Raoul d'Oulmont's lengthy legalistic consideration in the mid-1390s is a major exception to this rule).[27]

[23] Dupin 1 cols 658, 660.
[24] For other considerations along these lines see Swanson, *Universities* pp 52-3.
[25] Dupin 1 col 659. The references are to the commentary at 3, dist 39; 4, dist 15, q.3; 4, dist 25. The closest parallels seem to be at Johannes Duns Scotus, *Opera omnia* (12 vols, Lyons 1639) 8 pp 994-5; 9 pp 220-1, 563.
[26] Both citations are at Dupin 1 col 659. The Augustine is a reference to the gloss *Multitudo non est excommunicanda, nec princeps populi*, to Matthew 13:29, *Ne forte* (not, as d'Ailly has it, Matthew 13:28, *Vis imus*). The Lactantius citation is *Divinarum institutionum* 5,1,2.
[27] The generally dismissive attitude is apparent in the manner in which the *via facti* is referred to among attempts to stimulate discussion of possible solutions to the schism at the university of Paris in the early 1390s: *Chartularium*, 3 pp 614, 625. There is a brief discussion of the use of force in Jean Gerson's *De jurisdictione spirituali* of 1391, which

The military solution to the great schism

Usually some hints of an appeal to the *via facti* can also be read between the lines of appeals for secular intervention to secure a resolution of the schism.

Part of the reason for the decline in interest in the *via facti* as time passed may well have been a recognition of its futility: that the time for the military solution had passed with the entrenchment of the dispute and (particularly after 1389 and 1394) with the establishment of definitely separate papal successions in the two obediences. The use of force had to be an immediate response to the problem; by the 1390s both sides were perhaps becoming accustomed to a state of peaceful (if hostile) co-existence. Moreover, as time passed, the exact meaning of the term *via facti* seems to have altered. Initially it had been seen as a determinative method which would have provided clear evidence of the divine disposition with regard to the merits and claims of the contenders. By 1395 it had become a means by which the rivals could be pressurised into accepting that they would have to work together towards a solution. The use of force was thus seen as part of the process of implementing a different solution—usually at that point as the preliminary stage in forcing the contenders towards acceptance of the *via cessionis*, the way of abdication, by forcibly preventing them from enjoying the pecuniary and other benefits of their headship of the Church.[28] The distinction between the two definitions of the *via facti* was to some extent a matter of degree, and the use of force as a form of blackmail might in itself merit condemnation. Thus, a somewhat paradoxical situation developed. One of the principal advocates of the *via cessionis* was Simon de Cramaud, who in his major work, *De subtractione obediencie* (completed in its final form in 1398), was bluntly to dismiss the *via facti* as originally defined as *omnino dampnabilis*.[29] But the idea of the subtraction of obedience was itself condemned in debates held in France in 1398 as no better than the *via facti*; and when a Cologne author came to gloss parts of the *De subtractione obediencie* in 1401 he was to arrive at precisely the same conclusion.[30]

---

perhaps reflects the influence of d'Ailly's earlier ideas (*Jean Gerson, oeuvres completes, 3: l'oeuvre magistrale*, ed P. Glorieux (Tournai 1962) pp 6–7). For Oulmont see above n 15.

[28] See, for example, the *Conclusio universitatis juribus*, produced at Paris c1394, discussed in Swanson, *Universities* pp 91–2.

[29] Oxford, Balliol college, MS 165B, p 85.

[30] H. Bourgeois du Chastenet, *Nouvelle histoire du concile de Constance* (Paris 1718) preuves, p 13; R. Swanson, 'The university of Cologne and the great schism' *JEH* 28 (1977) p 8 n 1.

Yet even if attention was concentrated on the ways of council, resignation, and negotiation, there was bound to be some element of force or coercion involved in any solution which had to be implemented after forty years and more. But the basically military option for settling the schism, the scheme which would have involved the total conquest of one obedience by the other, had been rejected. Pierre d'Ailly's consideration of the arguments for and against that solution in his tract of 1381 shows that the rejection was inspired not merely by logistics, but by a serious concern about the morality of using force in such extraordinary circumstances.

University of Birmingham

CLERICAL VIOLENCE IN A CATHOLIC SOCIETY: THE HISPANIC WORLD 1450–1720

by HENRY KAMEN

FEW COUNTRIES have been more notorious for having a militant clergy than Spain: the experience of the Carlist wars and Franco's war gives sufficient evidence of this. Unfortunately, these are examples of state conflicts in which the Church happened to participate, and the present paper is concerned less with the institutional violence of the state than with the inherent violence of the Church itself. War as such does not enter into the discussion, since war can be declared only by the state, not by the Church. Interestingly, however, though much ink has been spent discussing whether Christians and the Christian state may go to war, there has been less debate over whether the clergy may legitimately resort to force. In what follows I propose to suggest that the participation of the Hispanic Church in violence arose not simply from identification with the institutional violence of the state but from the peculiar development of the Church itself. Violence in this context will be seen to be not dysfunctional but normal, a logical relationship between the Church and society.[1] Participation in violence became a recognisable feature of the Hispanic Church: the problem is to understand how and why this occurred and seemed acceptable.

The militancy of the bishops has never been in doubt. The most obvious example is Antonio de Acuña, the embattled bishop of Zamora, who in 1520 at the age of sixty set out to fight for the Comuneros at the head of three hundred of his diocesan clergy, all armed to the teeth at his specific orders. When captured and confined in the castle of Simancas, he used his authority to persuade a servant girl to smuggle a knife to him; with this he murdered his gaoler and tried to escape but was recaptured and

---

[1] See Lewis A. Coser, 'Some functions of deviant behavior and normative flexibility' *American Journal of Sociology* 68, ii (Sept 1962). For a broad discussion of violence, see Randall Collins, *Conflict Sociology* (New York 1975).

garrotted on the direct orders of Charles V.[2] Acuña was a relic of the late fifteenth century, when great clergy such as archbishop Carrillo of Toledo used their spiritual and temporal authority to wage war against the crown, both against Henry IV, whom they dethroned in one of the more spectacular deposition ceremonies (1465) of the later Middle Ages, and against queen Isabella. There is no doubt that the extraordinary power of the upper clergy impressed Ferdinand and Isabella enough to make them take over the Military Orders and assert their political authority over the Church; but no move was made to interfere with the internal ordering of the great bishoprics. Thus the see of Toledo, whose holder was judged by a contemporary to be 'not a prelate but a pope',[3] remained in undisturbed control (in 1519) of over 1,900 benefices, several military fortresses, an army of a thousand men, and exercised secular jurisdiction over 19,000 vassals.[4]

Without venturing further into an examination of the resources of the Spanish Church,[5] it would appear that the position of the see of Toledo provides a self-evident answer to any enquiry about clerical violence. Indeed, the phenomenon appears to have continued uninterruptedly into the modern age. Two hundred years later, around 1700, we find exactly the same situation recurring. When the war of the Spanish Succession broke out, in the sane and liberal age of the early rationalists, the following report from the French ambassador in Madrid seems to take us back to the Middle Ages: 'The bishop of Calahorra has mounted a horse at the head of 1,500 clergy of his diocese, all well armed and mounted, to defend the frontier of Navarre'.[6] It was by no means an isolated example. In that very same year, 1706, the bishop of Murcia, Luis de Belluga, subsequently a cardinal and founder of the university of Murcia,

---

[2] Joseph Pérez, *La Révolution des 'Comunidades' de Castille (1520-1521)* (Bordeaux 1970) pp 242, 634-8. During his campaigns, Acuña punished any of his clergy caught reading the breviary instead of attending to the tasks of war.

[3] [Tarsicio de] Azcona, *La Elección y Reforma [del Episcopado español en tiempo de los Reyes Católicos* (Madrid 1960)] p 42.

[4] Tarsicio de Azcona, in Ricardo García-Villoslada, ed *Historia de la Iglesia en España* 5 vols (Madrid 1980) vol IV, i p 132.

[5] These, oddly, have never been adequately studied. The most informative source, both on revenue and organisation, is [Antonio] Domínguez Ortiz, *La Sociedad española [en el siglo XVII. Vol II: El Estamento eclesiástico* (Madrid 1970)].

[6] Ambassador Amelot to Louis XIV in 1706, cited in [Henry] Kamen, *The War of Succession [in Spain, 1700-1715* (London and Bloomington 1969)] p 249.

marched to relieve the port of Alicante at the head of 1,300 troops.[7] There were also parallels in the colonies. In approximately the same generation, in far-off Paraguay, the mainly Spanish members of the Society of Jesus had trained and armed the biggest fighting army in the entire New World, to protect the settlements against outside attack.[8]

Can we affirm, on the basis of this evidence, that the Hispanic Church was still essentially the band of warriors familiar to medievalists, that it had not like other churches evolved into the modern age and was still living in the past? Was the Church still a medieval institution, warming its hands round the fires of the Inquisition, virtually a law unto itself, appealing to crusading principles that were now merely a memory in the rest of the Christian and indeed the Catholic world?

The truth is that between my two terminal dates, 1450 and 1720, chosen because they embrace an apparently unaltered pattern from archbishop Carrillo through to cardinal Belluga, the peninsular Church went through at least two significant processes of change—Humanism and the Counter Reformation—whose impact has only recently begun to be measured. Despite the very exceptional case of cardinal Cisneros, to whom in his own words 'the smell of gunpowder was sweeter than all the perfumes of Arabia',[9] the Spanish episcopate underwent some changes in the generation after Carrillo. From the late fifteenth century the concept of the ideal bishop was present in the mind of many reformers (if the example and writings of bishop Alonso Tostado of Avila may be taken as representative), and helped to set new standards of behaviour. The crown actively pursued a policy of appointing honest, reliable and peaceable prelates.[10] It is arguable how far the new attitudes penetrated the Church, but there seems little doubt that by the early sixteenth century, and a whole generation before Trent, the higher clergy and religious orders were beginning to see their role in somewhat different terms.

[7] *Ibid* p 288. On Belluga see also R. Serra Ruiz, *El pensamiento del cardenal Belluga* (Murcia 1963).
[8] [Philip] Caraman, *The lost Paradise*. [*An account of the Jesuits in Paraguay 1607–1768* (London 1975)].
[9] Cited in W. H. Prescott, *History of the Reign of Ferdinand and Isabella* (London 1841) p 708.
[10] On all this, see Azcona, *Elección y Reforma*, especially chap IX. On the broader question of reform in the orders, see José García Oro, *Cisneros y la reforma del clero español en tiempo de los Reyes Católicos* (Madrid 1971).

Their most notable representative was Hernando de Talavera, royal confessor, first archbishop of Christian Granada and epitome of the reformed, nonmilitarist clergy of this epoch.

We can trace to this same period the development of new humanist and neo-Erasmian attitudes to war. War as such was of course legitimate: Francisco de Vitoria, the great master of early sixteenth-century thought in Spain, put it precisely: 'Christians may serve in war and make war'.[11] Though the conclusion would seem to be in direct opposition to Erasmus' pacifism, in fact the school of Salamanca went much further than he, and in far more convincing detail, towards limiting the occasions when war might be used. Looking both at the arguments used, and at the intention of the arguments, it appears that the theologians went a long way towards trying to define war out of existence. 'War', Sepúlveda insisted, 'must never be anything else but a means to achieve peace'.[12] The attitude was consistent both with the mood and the reality of Spain, for all these writings came out at a time when Spain was totally at peace. From about 1512, when Navarre was incorporated into Spain, to about 1567, when the first levies were made for the duke of Alba's invasion of the Netherlands, continental Spain remained free of any serious war commitments: it was an astonishing half century of peace during which some thinkers even felt it right to reject the legitimacy of Spain's conquest of the American Indians.[13] There is no good reason, therefore, to imagine that the Salamanca definitions of a just war were simply a shoddy exercise in justifying Spanish imperialism.

Dedication to peace and opposition to militarism was more deeply-rooted in Spanish attitudes of this time than is commonly recognised, though it is not a simple matter to disentangle the various motives involved. Las Casas was certainly not alone in believing that the faith must be spread by peaceful methods, and the strong support for his cause from the Cortes and in the royal council was continuing testimony to the influence of the liberal

---

[11] Quoted in [J. A.] Fernández-Santamaría, *The State, War and Peace.* [*Spanish Political Thought in the Renaissance 1516–1559* (Cambridge 1977)] esp pp 130–44.

[12] *Ibid* pp 220–1.

[13] Lewis Hanke, *The Spanish Struggle for Justice in the Conquest of America* (Philadelphia 1949) is a useful guide to the extensive literature. Mario Góngora, *Studies in the Colonial History of Spanish America* (Cambridge 1975) p 57, notes that 'the "military mission"/i.e. the idea that Spain had a duty to subjugate barbarians/began to lose ground as early as 1526'.

Clerical Violence and the Hispanic World

Dominicans and Franciscans.[14] At the same time there was considerable pressure on Charles V to persist in a policy of so-called 'peace among Christians', which at first sight would appear to be a demand for reconciliation with Catholic France, but which in reality was a far more profound expression of opposition to any military commitment in Germany and northern Europe. The 'peace lobby' must never be underestimated when we consider the making of Spain's foreign policy. It is too easily forgotten that it was a junta of Spanish theologians who advised Philip II in 1566 that 'in view of the evils to the Church that a rebellion might cause, Your Majesty can without offence to God or sinning against your conscience grant freedom of worship' to the people of the Netherlands; and that it was a Spanish government official who in 1624 maintained that 'Christ never ordered conversions by force of gun, pike or musket'.[15]

These apparently pacific attitudes, however, and the search for an acceptable doctrine of war and peace, were quickly overtaken not so much by the direct rejection of non-violence (Sepúlveda had, after all, observed that 'even though neither Christ nor the apostles waged war, Christians are not necessarily prohibited from engaging in violence'[16]), as by two broad developments that were to be of consummate importance in the history of the Spanish Church.

In the first place, the gradual growth of royal patronage (*Patronato Real*) over the Church soon brought it completely under state control. Ferdinand and Isabella managed to coax out of the papacy (for reasons connected more with the need for Spanish help against the French invasions than with the fact that the pontiff was a Spaniard, Alexander VI) bulls confirming their absolute control over the Church in Sicily and America, and extensive control over the Church in Spain (where by now the Inquisition was largely a government body).[17] Charles V, helped by the fact that his former

---

[14] It is interesting that the debate was carried on as far afield as London, by Las Casas' fellow Dominican and friend, the ill-fated Carranza: see J. I. Tellechea Idigoras, *Tiempos Recios. Inquisición y Heterodoxías* (Salamanca 1977).

[15] These and other references to the wars in Flanders are set in their context in Henry Kamen, *Spain 1469–1714: a Society of Conflict* (London 1983) ch 3.

[16] Fernández-Santamaría, *The State, War and Peace* p 215.

[17] Royal supremacy over the American Church rested on papal bulls of Nov 1501 and July 1508; these gave the crown the right to control all finance, nominate all clergy from bishops down to parish priests, licence all ecclesiastical buildings, and exclude all papal

tutor, Adrian of Utrecht, was now pope—the first and last Dutchman to hold the post—completed the process of royal control.[18] By the early sixteenth century, precisely when northern European monarchs were using religion to take over their national churches, the crown in Spain enjoyed almost unlimited control over ecclesiastical administration, appointment of clergy, church land and revenue, and all without the slightest change in religion.[19]

The direct links of Church with state, amounting to a virtual integration of the two, made it inevitable that churchmen should enter the service of the state, not indeed in the old medieval way illustrated by the careers of Wolsey or Cisneros, but simply as civil servants. Recent research has shown how changes in the system of higher education at Salamanca, Alcalá and Valladolid, through the elitist university colleges (*colegios mayores*), created a single bureaucracy that went on to serve both state and Church. Clergy became identified with the state, not as clergy but because they had received the requisite administrative training in public universities, qualifying as graduates (*letrados*) in law.[20] *Letrados* from the *colegios mayores* made up the cream of the state bureaucracy. The way in which the *colegios* trained both clergy and laity without distinction for government service, may be seen from the careers of a small sample (338 men) of their graduates in the early sixteenth century: about one-third went into civil administration, one-third into the Church, one-tenth into the Inquisition.[21] The elite in both Church and state thus rose through the selfsame educational system. Not surprisingly, *letrado* laity were therefore qualified to enter the bureaucracy of the

jurisdiction: see C. H. Haring, *The Spanish Empire in America* (New York 1947) ch X. In Sicily the king himself exercised papal jurisdiction, following a medieval privilege (the *Monarchia Sicula*) by which he could act as papal legate.

[18] Charles V was granted absolute control over all clerical appointments in Spain in 1523, and appeals to Rome against the Inquisition became impossible because the Inquisitor General exercised appellate jurisdiction in place of the pope. There is a useful discussion of the integration of Church with state in José Antonio Maravall, *Estado Moderno y Mentalidad Social, siglos XV a XVII*, 2 vols (Madrid 1972) vol I, part 2, ch IV.

[19] For the sale of Church lands under Philip II, see Isabel López Díaz, 'Las desmembraciones eclesiásticas de 1574 a 1579' *Moneda y Crédito* (June 1974).

[20] The boost to a clerical bureaucracy was given by Ferdinand and Isabella, who made university degrees essential for employment in higher administration. Recent studies of the bureaucracy include [Richard L.] Kagan, *Students and Society [in Early Modern Spain* (Baltimore 1974)] and J. M. Pelorson, *Les letrados: juristes castillans sous Philippe III* (Poitiers 1980).

[21] Kagan, *Students and Society* p 132.

Clerical Violence and the Hispanic World

Inquisition (inquisitors were required to be trained in law, and did not have to be clergy); it followed that clergy could also enter the service of the state. The *colegio* of San Ildefonso at Cisneros' university of Alcalá was created in 1508 expressly to train churchmen for the ecclesiastical bureaucracy; but by the late seventeenth century one-fifth of its clergy graduates were in fact entering careers in civil administration.[22] Priests served at all levels of the ladder, up to the topmost level of viceroy: a prominent early example was Pedro de la Gasca, a simple priest appointed in 1545 to subdue the Pizarro rebellion in Peru, a task he accomplished with astonishing efficiency.[23] The result was that whereas in other west European states the administration was becoming laicised, with clergy appearing only rarely in the upper bureaucracy, in Spain the clergy shared administration and therefore the exercise of secular power equally with the laity. Foreign travellers not surprisingly obtained the impression that it was a priest-ridden society; a seventeenth-century archbishop commented that 'in no country do clergy enjoy more privileges than in Spain'; and modern Spanish historians have talked of a 'Tibetisation' of Spain.[24] It would take us too far afield to discuss these views; the evidence remains clear enough that many Spanish clergy had full access to the coercive apparatus of the state, and that their use of violence was fully legitimised by prevailing Church-state relations.

The second major development was the process of overseas colonisation. This brought clergy actively into a position of authority, both secular and moral, over non-Christians, and provoked extensive debate over the precise responsibilities involved. Under the pioneering circumstances in which Spanish missionaries worked—they were the first missionaries in Christian history to be also the agents of a colonial power—immense authority over the life, limb and livelihood of natives was granted to them, since in the early days there was no adequate structure of state government in the Indies. Not only, then, did

---

[22] *Ibid* p 131 n 49.
[23] W. H. Prescott, *History of the Conquest of Peru* (London 1901) pp 360 ff. Clergy also staffed the councils of state, acted as governors, diplomats and at virtually all levels of the bureaucracy: see Dominguez Ortiz, *La sociedad española*, vol 2 ch X.
[24] The archbishop is cited in *ibid* p 196. The concept of 'Tibetisation' apparently originated with Américo Castro but has been repeated by others.

clergy supervise Indians in all aspects of secular life; they extended their authority so far as to turn many of the missionary-guided Indian communities, known variously as *doctrinas* and 'civil congregations',[25] into virtually independent republics in which the missionaries *were* the state, taking over direction of finance and defence, and encouraging the natives to take up arms even against the Church's bishops. Not surprisingly, violence and war became part of the evangelical enterprise. The most astonishing scenes were registered in the missions of Mexico, where on one occasion two Franciscans armed a troop of Indians and under cover of night destroyed and burnt down two churches which were felt to be in competition with their own monastery. In 1550, when the clergy of Michoacán and New Galicia were quarrelling over the limits of each diocese, clergy of the former invaded the latter diocese, pillaged and sacked a church and kidnapped the priest; in 1559 other clergy sacked a Dominican friary in Puebla, robbed it and knocked the prior's teeth out.[26] If these incidents can be written off as the high life of a colonial clergy, the military power of the Jesuits must be taken more seriously. In their Guaraní 'reductions' in South America, from a total population in 1647 of 21,000 they managed to create an army of 7,000 men, a force large enough to act in defence of the Spanish presence in the area: between 1657 and 1697 the Guaraní troops came seven times down the river Paraná to defend Buenos Aires against foreign attack.[27]

A less obvious dimension of colonial rule than this institutional violence, was the personal violence involved in the exercise of clerical authority. A recent article in English has returned to the theme of Franciscan maltreatment of the Indians.[28] Certainly the early friars felt that the gospel could not be spoon fed. The famous defender of the Indians, the Franciscan Motolinía, believed (to Las Casas' horror) that the faith must be preached quickly, 'if necessary by force'. The great scholar of Mexican culture, friar

---

[25] On *doctrinas* and congregations see for example A. Tibesar, *Franciscan Beginnings in Colonial Peru* (Washington 1953), and L. B. Simpson, *Studies in the Administration of the Indians in New Spain* 4 vols (Berkeley 1934–40).

[26] Robert Ricard, *La Conquista Espiritual de Mexico. Ensayo sobre el apostolado y los métodos misioneros de las órdenes mendicantes en la Nueva España de 1523-4 a 1572* (Mexico 1947) pp 440–1.

[27] Caraman, *The Lost Paradise* pp 102–4.

[28] Inga Clendinnen, 'Disciplining the Indians: Franciscan Ideology and Missionary Violence in Sixteenth-Century Yucatán' *Past and Present* 94 (1982) pp 27–48.

Clerical Violence and the Hispanic World

Bernardino de Sahagún, would rouse his Indians at night in order to beat them, and described how he 'lovingly propelled them towards heaven by blows'.[29] The Franciscans and their spokesmen were dedicated to the natives, and some gave up their lives as martyrs in the process, but their paternalistic use of force helped eventually to feed the racial discrimination that Spaniards constructed into their colonial regime.[30] For many missionaries the natives were beings without the capacity to become fully rational: this was inevitably used to excuse the arrogance and violence of the clergy to their flocks.

It has been suggested with good reason that the missionary resort to violence consisted of little more than the adoption of disciplinary norms traditional among the Indians themselves This is undoubtedly true in the American context, but ignores the fact that there was ample precedent within the peninsula itself for the exercise of force in converting a subject population of differing race. Spain had its own internal 'natives', the despised Moriscos. Here is a report from the Spanish ambassador in Paris, Francés de Alava, informing Philip II's secretary Zayas in 1569 that on one of his many visits to Morisco Granada,

> I was utterly shocked to see that the priests did not treat those people in the gentle way they should have done; I frequently witnessed the clergy turning around in the very middle of the consecration, between the host and the chalice, to see if the Moriscos and their women were on their knees, and from that position subjecting them to such horrifying and arrogant abuse, a thing so contrary to the worship of God, that my blood ran cold; and after mass the priests would walk through the town with an attitude of menacing contempt towards the Moriscos . . .[31]

---

[29] Lewis Hanke, *Aristotle and the American Indians* (London 1959) pp 21, 88.

[30] The friar Gerónimo de Mendieta was typical of those whose care for the Indian demanded in return an attitude of deference: see John L. Phelan, *The Millennial Kingdom of the Franciscans in the New World* (Berkeley 1956). On the use of force, Charles Gibson, *The Aztecs under Spanish Rule. A History of the Indians of the Valley of Mexico 1519–1810* (Stanford 1964) p 117, says that 'punishment and force played a larger role in Mexican conversion than is customarily recognised', and refers to 'routine beatings and imprisonments in the doctrinas'.

[31] Citied in part in Fernand Braudel, *The Mediterranean and the Mediterranean World in the Age of Philip II* 2 vols (London 1973) 2 p 788. For Christian-Morisco tensions, see Louis Cardaillac, *Morisques et Chrétiens: un affrontement polémique (1492–1640)* (Paris 1977).

It was a radical change from the early days of conquered Granada, when the city's first archbishop Hernando de Talavera had respected the persons and culture of the Moors. There can be little doubt that the deterioration in race relations could be attributed not simply to the internal conflict of civilisations but also to the aggressive aspects of the colonial experience and the rise of what has been termed 'racial conceit',[32] though surprisingly no historian of the Moriscos has sought to make any connection between the two developments. Yet it seems obvious that if many clergy in greater or lesser degree shared the colonial arrogance instilled by two generations of contact with coloured people in America, it might influence or be influenced by their attitude to their own minorities. In much the same way the new Spanish practice of using blacks as servants and thus relegating coloured people to an inferior role, had arisen out of the extension of black slavery from America.[33] Within this context clerical violence seems to have arisen out of a colonial mentality rather than out of ecclesiastical elitism.

The humanist attempt to place war and violence on a rational footing, an enterprise that toned in well with Spain's half century of peace under Charles V, was thus superseded from mid-century by the closer identification of Church with state, and by the speedy triumph of a colonial-type arrogance.[34] The Hispanic Church was now the Church militant. In emphasising this point I am concerned less with the Church's participation in the institutional violence of the state—as instanced by the campaigns of the bishops of Calahorra and Murcia during the war of the Spanish Succession, or even the spectacular and anachronistic picture of a cardinal, the

---

[32] Michael Banton, *Race Relations* (London 1967) pp 45–50, section on 'Imperialism and racial conceit'. There are some comments on racialism in the Spanish empire in Philip Mason, *Patterns of Dominance* (London 1970) ch XI. The theme of Spanish racialism in the sense of 'blood purity' is developed in Henri Méchoulan, *Le Sang de l'autre ou l'Honneur de Dieu* (Paris 1979).

[33] 'Le commerce des Indes a restably en ce pays le droit de servitude, tellement qu'en Andalousie l'on ne voit presque point d'autres valets que des serfs. Ils sont la plupart maures, ou tout a fait noirs', testified Antoine de Brunel in 1655: cited in Antonio Domínguez Ortiz, 'La esclavitud en Castilla durante la edad moderna' *Estudios de Historia Social de España* vol II (1952) p 380.

[34] The arrogance was of course not only clerical but also lay. In the Netherlands, for example, Benito Arias Montano in 1573 commented to Philip II that 'the arrogance of our Spanish nation is intolerable': Luis Morales Oliver, *Arias Montano y la política de Felipe II en Flandes* (Madrid 1927).

Clerical Violence and the Hispanic World

infante of Spain, commanding the victorious army at Nördlingen in 1634—than with its acceptance of violence as a structural everyday part of its social functions.

Towards the end of the sixteenth century the clergy in Spain numbered 40,600 secular priests, 25,400 male religious and 25,000 nuns, or close to 100,000 personnel in a population of just over eight millions; the proportion has been estimated at some 1.2% of the population.[35] This was arguably a fairly low proportion, though in practice clergy tended to be concentrated in the cities, where their impact was more noticeable. Prior to the early sixteenth century there is no record during this period of any adequate reform of the secular clergy. By the 1540s the complaints made by bishops of the standards of their parish priests, could be compared with those of reformers in England or in Germany: ignorance, illiteracy, crime and immorality were among the more common accusations. Apart from education, which was obviously a major concern, a fundamental problem was the social status of the clergy. One of the drawbacks of the medieval 'sacral society' idealised for us by some modern Catholic scholars,[36] was that the clergy partook fully in the life of society and therefore shared all the vices of their flocks. Spanish reformers, however, both before and after Trent, were convinced that the position of the clergy in society must be changed; they felt that the Don Camillo type of priest—human, earthy, drinking with his parishioners—was at the root of the decline in standards and must be eliminated. Bishops began a vigorous campaign to separate the clergy from some compromising social functions, in effect to break up the integrated 'sacral society' and reclaim for the Church a distinct sacred role that had long been blurred. From 1565, for example, the reforming bishop of Burgos, cardinal Mendoza, banned his clergy from carrying arms.[37] How effective such decrees were may be judged from another issued by the archbishop of Seville in 1645 forbidding his priests 'under any pretext whatsoever, by day or by night, in towns or in the countryside or anywhere else, from carrying, or

---

[35] Rounded off from data by Felipe Ruiz Martín, as summarised in García-Villoslada, ed *Historia de la Iglesia* vol 4 pp 18–19.
[36] By, for example, Charles Journet, *L'Eglise du Verbe Incarné* (Paris 1941) and Jacques Maritain, *Man and the State* (London 1954) pp 143–5.
[37] Nicolas López Martínez, 'El cardenal Mendoza y la reforma tridentina en Burgos' *Hispania Sacra* XVI (1963) p 88.

keeping in their houses or anywhere else, any firearms such as pistols, carbines or any other sort of firearm'.[38] In the early seventeenth century the Madrid chroniclers Barrionuevo and Pellicer give abundant details of the criminal violence of members of the clergy and religious orders.[39] The criminal records for Madrid in the late seventeenth century suggest that priests continued to be caught up in violence: more often, it is true, on the receiving end, with clergy being murdered, shot at and beaten up; but frequently also there were cases of clergy as originators of violence.[40]

Narrowing our focus from a broad social to a narrow religious context, here is the case in 1574 of the parish priest of St Dominic's in Toledo, prosecuted by the Inquisition. He apparently came down from the altar in full dress when the entire community was at mass, went up to a parishioner, abused him, hit him several times then ordered him thrown out of the church:[41] a prime example of clerical violence in a Catholic society. The Inquisition's concern, of course, was not with the violence but with the apparent sacrilege. Contrast the case to the very clear instructions of the Spanish bishops that clergy should behave with decorum: 'the priest', says an episcopal directive to the churches of the see of Mondoñedo in 1614, 'when he is at the altar dressed to say mass, must be reverent and silent as befits so high a ministry, and not disturb his parishioners';[42] an injunction that seems to have been tailor-made for the incident of 1574 in Toledo, and suggests that such cases were not unusual. Emphasis on the sacramental character of the priest, then, was intended to set him apart so that his sins should not be social ones; directives banning clergy from going to wedding feasts, for example, always cite past histories of the scandal caused by drunken priests. The move to make the clergy into a separate caste was not elitist in the derogatory sense, but part of an attempt to pacify the clergy, abstract them from lay

---

[38] Quoted in Pedro Herrera Puga, *Sociedad y Delincuencia en el Siglo de Oro* (Granada 1971) p 387.
[39] Jose Deleito y Piñuela, *La vida religiosa española bajo el cuarto Felipe* (Madrid 1963) pp 101–5.
[40] Records of the Sala de Alcaldes for the years 1665 to 1700, in A[rchivo] H[istórico] N[acional], Madrid, section Sala de Alcaldes, Inventarios de causas criminales, vols 2786–8.
[41] AHN, section Inquisition, bundle 123, document 16.
[42] AHN, section Clero, vol 6374, fol 15.

Clerical Violence and the Hispanic World

society and integrate them more fully into the body of the teaching Church. Measures to this effect can be found in church synods in Spain way back into the 1470s,[43] but it seems certain that no effective action was taken before the 1560s.

The attempt to separate the clergy was probably bound to fail in a nation where priests at all levels acted as functionaries of the state. Even if the strengthening of episcopal control managed to reduce violence and establish order in some dioceses, in others there is ample evidence of failure. In 1638 the bishop of Córdoba, friar Domingo Pimentel, made a secret visit to his diocese and drew up a report in his own hand on clergy such as the following: Luis de Castillejo, 'who goes out at night armed and improperly dressed, and very seldom says mass'; Melchor de Contreras, 'who spends all his money on women, and goes out at night armed'; the deacon Francisco de Estrada, 'who goes out at night like a lay person, armed with sword and buckler'.[44]

It is sometimes argued that the outrages committed by clergy took place because of clerical immunity, so that immunity in itself might be considered the greatest single fomentor of clerical violence. The point was often made by contemporaries when, for example, they complained of the privileges of familiars of the Inquisition.[45] It is true that notorious cases appear to confirm the special treatment accorded to clergy: when the viceroy of Valencia exercised rough justice on a friar-bandit in 1680 by hanging him without trial, he was made to do public penance barefoot and was summarily recalled to Madrid.[46] If, however, we consider such cases in detail the question of immunity becomes clearly tangential: clergy no more resorted to violence because of immunity than criminals now resort to crime because the death penalty has been abolished. Indeed, the very identification of Church with state, and the frequent role of clergy as state administrators, meant that in such a system delinquent clergy were more rather than less likely to have their alleged privileges

---

[43] José Sánchez Herrero, *Concilios Provinciales y Sínodos Toledanos de los siglos XIV y XV* (La Laguna 1976).

[44] José Cobos Ruiz de Adana, *El Clero en el Siglo XVII. Estudio de una visita secreta a la ciudad de Córdoba* (Cordoba 1976) pp 164, 167–8.

[45] For disputes involving immunity and familiars, see for instance H. C. Lea, *A History of the Inquisition of Spain* 4 vols (New York 1906–8) I p 447.

[46] [Henry] Kamen, [*Spain in the*] *Later Seventeenth Century* [*1665–1700* (London 1980)] p 210.

ignored. In these circumstances the Inquisition tended to supplant the Church as a zealous defender of clerical privilege, which helps to explain the continuous and bitter quarrels between the Holy Office on one hand and the Church and secular authorities on the other.[47] Ecclesiastical crime, like lay crime, was fostered less by privilege than by the social environment: this brings us to what, after the 'administrative' and 'colonial' roles, constituted the third great instigator of violence, the 'communal' tradition.

The Counter Reformation, to judge from the very little that we know about its impact in Spain, probably did little to blunt the intense community spirit which bound villages to their priests. As in all primitive societies, where the religious functionary is allotted a secular role normally alien to his ritualistic activities, in Spain the communal tradition of Mediterranean societies assigned a crucial function to the priest and local clergy. It is perhaps unnecessary to emphasise that this role did not imply piety or even trust on the part of parishioners.[48] There is reason to argue that the community often exploited its clergy by forcing them into the role, that no other sector could adequately fulfil, of being a channel for social protest: protest against taxes, involving the clergy in a broad range of tax frauds; protest against authority, involving them in certain types of violence, most specifically banditry; and protest against injustice, involving them in every significant popular revolt of both medieval and modern times. In each of these roles, the clergy emerge as the harbingers of violence; we may suspect that the behavioural standards of the Counter Reformation often had little impact on their conduct. Clerical immunity became an issue only perhaps in the case of tax fraud, where the lower clergy persistently claimed that they were exempt in all respects from the taxes on food, the *millones*, while their superiors as vigorously argued that the exemption was limited. The vital point to emphasise, in tax fraud as in all the other cases of illegality, protest and violence, is that the clergy never acted as a separate elite, but always in concert with and enjoying

---

[47] Typical of such confrontations were those in Granada in 1623 and 1682, and in Barcelona in 1696: Henry Kamen, *La España de Carlos II* (Barcelona 1981) pp 364–7.

[48] Recent studies that touch on the relationship between priest and parishioner include William A. Christian Jr, *Person and God in a Spanish Valley* (New York 1972), and Julian Pitt-Rivers, *The People of the Sierra* (Chicago 1971); but in general the religious sociology of the western Mediterranean remains curiously unexplored.

the active support of a section of the local community. Clerical violence in this sense was not intrinsically clerical, but rather the front line of community violence.

Evidence from the late seventeenth century confirms this presentation amply. When clergy committed tax fraud they did so on a grand scale, not to benefit themselves so much as to cater to the general public. In 1684 in Seville we have the case of the monastery of St Basil, from which 'five religious went out with guns to smuggle in a herd of pigs'; and in the same year in Guadix we have the local priest 'who attacked Antonio Gutiérrez (of this tax administration) with a carving knife, . . . and when I went to his house I found two dead cows, ten calves, and fourteen live goats, all of which he had as though it were a public butcher's shop'.[49] Banditry likewise was notorious for being condoned and connived in by local clergy. Most famous bandits of the period were pious Catholics, fugitives were invariably sheltered by local clergy on the principle of sanctuary, and occasional clergy—like the friar Francisco Sánchez in 1693 in Valencia, personally responsible for several robberies and murders—were themselves bandit leaders.[50] The issue of involvement in popular revolt is so well documented that it needs little elaboration. It is sufficient to cite the parish priest in Valencia in 1693, a year of peasant uprisings, who was accused of 'preaching publicly that the peasants had no obligation to pay taxes to their lords, that the burdens were unjust and that they should not hesitate to steal from the lords'; and the circumstances of the war of the Succession in Aragon in 1705, when the archbishop of Saragossa claimed that 'the origin and cause of the rebellion in this kingdom have been friars and clergy, and particularly village priests, who are the only directors of their flocks'.[51]

This outline discussion leads to a few tentative conclusions. Firstly, it appears that clerical violence in the Hispanic environment was not intrinsic to the nature or ideology of the Church.

---

[49] Both cases documented in reports of Aug and Nov 1684 to the council of Finance in Madrid, Archivo General de Simancas, section Consejo y Juntas de Hacienda, bundle 1075.
[50] The theme of banditry is covered in J. Reglá, *El bandolerisme català del Bárroc* (Barcelona 1962); José Deleito y Piñuela, *La mala vida en la España de Felipe IV* (Madrid 1967) pp 98–105; and Kamen, *Later Seventeenth Century* pp 207–12.
[51] Kamen, *Later Seventeenth Century* p 221, and *The War of Succession* pp 264–5.

Spanish theologians were more usually concerned to argue against the desirability of force. The humanist period of the early sixteenth century was notably one when war was restricted by theorists to fairly narrow limits; but even the Counter Reformation was more concerned to secure the elimination of violence among Christians, as a step towards restoring respect for the sacred, than many commentators would lead us to believe.[52] Secondly, however, despite these observations it is true that the Spanish Church and its clergy were more associated with violence than churches in other countries at the time. I have offered three broad categories of explanation for this. At a fundamental social level, the 'community' role of clergy was highly important; but it was of course not peculiar to Spain, and the phenomenon can be analysed in any other nation, Catholic or Protestant. It should be added that the Tridentine emphasis on parish organisation may have helped to bind priest and parish together in a way that the reformers did not necessarily intend. More uniquely, the 'administrative' and 'colonial' functions of the clergy set them apart not only from Protestant but even from all other Catholic countries, creating a situation to which there were only vague approximations in other parts of western Europe. It will not go unnoticed that in all this little has been said about the notorious violence of the Spanish Inquisition, but a little reflection should make it clear that by its close identification with the state and by its primary obsession with ethnic groups in Spain as also in America and Asia, the Inquisition is merely another example of the process that has been outlined. The extraordinary participation of the Spanish clergy in violence did not therefore necessarily arise from any peculiar fanaticism, but can in some measure be attributed to accidents of political and imperial history and, at the community level, to an active sharing of pastors in the everyday travails of the life of the people of God.

University of Warwick

---

[52] The active stand of the Spanish clergy against witchcraft persecution, and the very low execution rate of the Inquisition in the sixteenth and seventeenth centuries (some two a year), are matters often forgotten when the record of the Hispanic Church is discussed.

THE 'WEAKNESS OF CONSCIENCE' IN THE REFORMED MOVEMENT IN THE NETHERLANDS: THE ATTITUDE OF THE DUTCH REFORMATION TO THE USE OF VIOLENCE BETWEEN 1562 AND 1574

by AUKE JELSMA

THE MOST important cause of the French civil war, starting in 1562, was religion. Of course, there were other motives too, especially the resistance of nobles to the centralization of power in Paris, but it was the struggle for freedom of religion which gave this war such a destructive character. The young Calvinist churches provided their warriors with all the mental and spiritual support they needed. In their opinion it was a struggle for the sake of God; it was a just war. As *magistratus inferiores* the nobles had the right, even the duty, to control and eventually to oppose the higher authority of the king. With arguments borrowed from the old testament and natural law they even defended the right of violent resistance to the government. Theological support came also from Geneva, especially from Theodore Beza. Without the Calvinist reformation there would not have been such a violent civil war, such a revolt, at that moment in the history of France.[1]

The same judgment can be made about the insurrection in Scotland: a holy war in the opinion of John Knox and his Calvinist followers. They saw it as their duty to overthrow the false government of queen Mary Stuart and her devilish advisers. In 1554/5 John Knox had received a theological training in Geneva.

---

[1] A. A. van Schelven, *Het 'heilige Recht van Opstand'* (Kampen 1920) gives a summary of the most important French authors defending violent resistance to the government. Beza is supposed to be the author of *Du droit des magistrats sur leurs sujets* (1574). He was *moderateur* of the synod of La Rochelle in 1571, which gave open support to the struggle of the Huguenots. See for the text of this synod: J. Aymon, *Tous les synodes nationaux des Églises Réformées de France* (The Hague 1710) 1 part 2 pp 98-111.

There he had found the theocratic model which he hoped to imitate in his own country. We can repeat what we concluded about the civil war in France: without Calvinism no revolt, not at that moment in the history of Scotland.[2]

About the relation between the Reformed movement in the Netherlands and the eighty-years-war, the Dutch revolt, the same opinion has been expressed. Of course, nobody doubts that there were other than religious factors in this war.[3] The situation in the Netherlands was totally different than in Scotland and France. In the first stage of the war catholics and protestants were fighting side by side. It was not only a religious war. The supposition has even been made, that it was not in the first place a religious war. When in 1574 the town of Leiden had been rescued from the siege of the Spanish troops, the government of the town decided to bring out a medal. There arose discussion about the inscription on the medal. Some wanted the words *'haec ergo libertatis'*, 'this happened for the sake of freedom'. But the ministers gave preference to the words: *'haec ergo religionis'* or 'this happened for the sake of religion'.[4] Certainly, it was not only a religious war.

There was another difference from the situation in France and in Scotland. It was not a civil war in the real sense of that word. The protestants in the Netherlands did not fight against catholic countrymen as happened in France. At least, that was in principle not the intention. Resistance was aimed at a government far away in Spain.[5] It was a struggle against Spanish hired troops, sometimes

---

[2] The most important author on this subject next to J. Knox was George Buchanan: *De iure regni apud Scotos* (1579). See for the cooperation between Calvinism and nobility the text of the Covenant in 1557: *A Source Book of Scottish History II (1424–1567)*, edd W. C. Dickinson and G. Donaldson (Edinburgh 1958) pp 148–150. The successor of J. Knox, Andrew Melville, had also studied in Geneva and held the same theocratic ideal as Knox himself, as we see in his 'Second Book of Discipline' printed in *A Source book of Scottish History III (1567–1707)* pp 22–30.

[3] One of the best writers on the revolt of the Netherlands, Geoffrey Parker, quotes with approval that 'we have considered the religious side of the struggle too much'; *Spain and the Netherlands, 1559–1659, ten studies* (Glasgow 1979) pp 19, 20.

[4] Quoted by L. J. Rogier, 'De tolerantie in de Statenbond der Verenigde Nederlanden' *Terugblik en Uitzicht* 1 (Hilversum/Antwerp 1964) pp 85, 86.

[5] In 1559 king Philip II left the Netherlands. He never came back, but he held the most important decisions in his own hand. The general feeling against being ruled by a (hated) foreign government grew extremely when, in 1567, the duke of Alva came with a strong army to punish the Netherlands for the iconoclasm of 1566. Of course, there were elements of civil war in this conflict too, for example when the army of William of Orange tried to conquer towns wanting to stay faithful to the king.

The attitude of the Dutch reformation to the use of violence

of German origin. But it was also a struggle for freedom of conscience, for freedom of religion and most historians assume that the war could not have been so successful for the Dutch without the convinced support of the Reformed movement, without the religious force of Calvinism.[6] The most frequent arguments for this view are:

1) From France Calvinist ministers penetrated into the Netherlands. They hoped to achieve there the same success as they had found in their own country.[7]

2) When the civil war broke out in France, there was also amongst the Reformed groups in the southern parts of the Netherlands an increase in resistance. In a synod in Antwerp in 1562 the ministers decided that it was permitted to use a restricted form of violence against the government. When members of the Reformed movement were arrested, it was permissible to break down the doors of the prison.[8]

3) However complicated the phenomenon of the iconoclastic fury in the Netherlands may have been in 1566, nobody can deny that there was a connection between Calvinist preaching and iconoclasm.[9]

4) During this period—between 1562 and 1568—there had been contact between members of the nobility and delegates of the Reformed consistories. They deliberated about the possibility of starting a united resistance to the government as had happened in France. The consistories organised fund-raising for this goal.[10]

5) In 1573 William of Orange, the leader of the resistance, openly joined the Reformed movement. He was not the man to take such a decision solely for religious motives. He changed in religion only

---

[6] This is even the opinion of Geoffrey Parker, however much attention he has given to other influences. His study *The Dutch Revolt* (London 1977) gives the best survey about this war in recent times.

[7] This does not mean, that all the preachers coming from France or Geneva hoped to unchain a religious war.

[8] See A. A. van Schelven, 'Het begin van het gewapend verzet tegen Spanje in de 16e-eeuwsche Nederlanden' *Handelingen en Mededeelingen van de Maatschappij der Nederlandsche Letterkunde te Leiden over het jaar 1914–1915* (Leiden 1915) pp 126–156.

[9] Phyllis Mack Crew wrote a very interesting study about this subject [*Calvinist Preaching and Iconoclasm in the Netherlands 1544–1569* (Cambridge 1978)]. J. Scheerder, [*De beeldenstorm* (Bussum 1978)] made an investigation in all the places where iconoclasm had been. His conclusion was, that generally speaking the iconoclastic fury was a religious, not a political movement.

[10] A short overall picture has been given by D. Nauta, *Aard van de opstand in de Nederlanden des zestiende eeuw* (The Hague 1976), for the fund-raising (three million guilders) see pp 40, 41.

when political reasons made such a step necessary or at least desirable. He had such a reason now; he needed the support of this movement for his war.[11]

Because of these and other arguments it is possible to reach the same conclusion about the war in the Netherlands as about the situation in France and Scotland: without Calvinism no revolt, not at that moment in the history of the Netherlands. It is not difficult to defend this point of view. But it is not the whole truth. I think it is necessary to fill out the picture. Therefore I want to support in this article the thesis that, especially in the Netherlands, the Reformed movement hesitated to defend the right of revolt, to justify this war. Of course, the warriors themselves tried to vindicate their own conduct, but the majority of the leaders of the Reformed movement withdrew from the warriors the support which generally was given in France and in Scotland.

In 1574 the synod of the Reformed churches in the provinces of Holland and Zealand, assembled in Dordrecht, accepted a regulation about the task of ecclesiastical meetings consideration of which proves illuminating. This synod was the first meeting of delegates of these churches in liberated territory. During the previous two years, 1572 and 1573, both provinces had for the greatest part accepted the authority of prince William of Orange. The situation should not be idealised. More than once towns had been forced to this choice by the hard-handed gangs of the prince. They had to choose between robbery by the hired troops of Spain or by the *geuzen*, the beggars of the prince.[12] The robbery by the Spanish troops usually came first. And because people are always hoping for improvement, always supposing that the future can't be worse than to-day, there was support for the prince.

In 1573 the new rulers of these provinces decided that the Reformed church should have a monopoly in this part of the Netherlands.[13] In other words, the old church had to be reformed

---

[11] About the religious feelings of William of Orange, H. A. Enno van Gelder has written an article 'The godsdienst van Prins Willem van Oranje' *Van Beeldenstorm tot Pacificatie* (Amsterdam/Brussel 1964) pp 80–115.

[12] See for the course of events during this "second revolt", as he called it, G. Parker, *The Dutch Revolt*, or S. Groenveld, H. L. Ph. Leeuwenberg, N. Mount, W. M. Zappey, *De kogel door de kerk?* (Utrecht 1979) pp 80–95.

[13] Fugitives, often from the southern parts of the Netherlands, having left their country after the coming of Alva in 1567, came back, following the trail of the *geuzen*, the pirates of the prince. Together with them they imposed on the original population of the

The attitude of the Dutch reformation to the use of violence

with or without the consent of the people. All church-buildings became the property of the Reformed church. Roman Catholic worship was forbidden. The preachers of the Reformed movement applauded. They enjoyed the new situation. But this is not the same as a theological justification of the revolt. Precisely in these parts of the Netherlands preachers were not prepared to do that. The result was accepted, not the violence. When in 1574 the delegates of the still small protestant groups (at the most comprising ten per cent of the population) came together in Dordrecht for a further development of the organisation of the church, they took a remarkable decision. They pronounced that in ecclesiastical meetings, like a synod, only discussion about ecclesiastical affairs would be permitted. In subjects with ecclesiastical and political aspects the churches would comply with the decisions of the government.[14] No politics in the church. How meek were these leaders of the Reformed movement! They did not want to become involved in wordly matters.

This was a strange agreement especially in that situation! Nobody could be sure if the revolt would have lasting success. Spanish troops wandered about plundering. In this period Leiden was besieged. The prince desperately needed all the support he could get. Nobody knew at that moment what would be the result of the dramatic events in Holland and Zealand for the other provinces of the Netherlands. The recent changes in government would surely have very important consequences not only for religious but also for social, political and economic life. There were many problems asking for a solution. In that critical moment the delegates of the Reformed churches took the decision that they did not want to give their opinion about wordly matters.

We do not know the motives behind this pronouncement, but it seems to me a reasonable explanation, that the Reformed churches did not want to become involved in political questions,

---

conquered towns a 'Calvinist minority-dictatorship', as L. J. Rogier called it in *Eenheid en Scheiding* (Utrecht/Antwerp 1968) p 82. After some time the original Reformed groups in these parts of the Netherlands accepted the new possibilities.

[14] The text of the synod of 1574 is edited by F. L. Rutgers, [*Acta van de Nederlandsche Synoden der zestiende eeuw* (The Hague 1889)] pp 120-220. The text is as follows '*De dienaren ende ouderlinghen sullen wel voor hen sien datze niet en handelen inden Consistorien, Classen ende Sijnoden, dan t'ghene dat kerckelick is. Maer die dinghen die ten deel kerckelick ten deel politisch sijn, alsoo daer veel dinghen in huwelixen saecken voorvallen, soo daer eenighe swaricheijt in voor valt, soo sullen sij aen het oordeel ende autoriteijt der Overheijt aensoecken*' p 149. See on this synod R. H. Bremmer, *Uit de geboortegeschiedenis van de Gereformeerde Kerken in Nederland* (The Hague 1977).

did not want to be held responsible for the war, for the use of violence, for the revolt against the king. But can we then still speak of a revolt, supported, stimulated, motivated by the Reformed movement?

This regulation of the synod of Dordrecht is rather unique for a Calvinist church. We don't find the rule in the ecclesiastical law of the churches of Geneva or France. And that is really remarkable, for it is known that the Reformed church in the Netherlands affiliated itself as far as possible with the order in these churches. But this special rule was more typical for Lutheran or even Anabaptist attitudes than for a Calvinist church. And that is the reason, why this regulation became for me, thinking of the opinion of the Dutch churches about the revolt, an eye-opener. But it can not function as decisive proof. We must look further. What had happened previously?

A very important synod of the Reformed churches in the Netherlands had been held in 1571, in Emden, East-Friesland, just outside the territory of the Netherlands, for reasons of security. There the foundation of ecclesiastical organisation had been laid. And it is again remarkable to read the results, the *acta*, of this synod. The synod confines itself strictly to typical ecclesiastical problems.[15] We get the impression that these ecclesiastical leaders did not even see the political issues of their time.

This aloofness from the political questions had not been the intention of William of Orange. From other sources it is known, that he himself had pleaded for an organisation of all the different and scattered protestant groups in and outside the Netherlands. He needed such a solid structure for the sake of the revolt. His most important spokesman in that time was Marnix of Sint Aldegonde, a member of the lower nobility, who had studied in Geneva. In 1566 he took the risk of writing a defence of the iconoclastic fury of that year. During the following years he became the right hand man of the prince. In his name he wrote a letter to all those hidden groups in the Netherlands but also to the Dutch fugitives in London and in Germany, pleading for a synod to create an organisation comparable with the Calvinist church in France.[16] To

---

[15] The text of the synod of 1571 F. L. Rutgers pp 42–119. See on this synod: *De synode van Emden 1571–1971* [(Kampen 1971) edd D. Nauta, J. P. van Dooren, Otto J. de Jong].

[16] See W. F. Dankbaar, [*Hoogtepunten uit het Nederlandsche Calvinisme in de zestiende eeuw* (Haarlem 1946)] pp 41–85.

The attitude of the Dutch reformation to the use of violence

prepare such a synod he organised a consultation of churches in Bedburg, again just beyond the border of the Netherlands, in the duchy of Jülich and Cleve, in the summer of 1571. The influence of Marnix in Bedburg was very important. It was he who asked the synod of Bedburg to give support openly to the revolt of the prince. At his request the synod summoned all the Reformed churches in the Netherlands to cooperate with the prince. At his request the synod pronounced that the prince had a direct vocation from God himself to lead the struggle for the recovery of freedom in the Netherlands. At his request the synod pronounced that the Christians in the Netherlands had the right to use violence in this just war. These pronouncements were necessary to help people who got into trouble with their conscience. This 'weakness of conscience', as it was called, proved to be an important hindrance for the war of the prince. Therefore Marnix asked the synod in the name of the prince for these clear statements.[17] And so, thanks to the endeavours of Marnix, the prince got the support of the church for his war. Finally, he got the recognition that he was involved in a just war. But this consultation was only a preparation for the real synod in Emden. There the conclusions of Bedburg had to be affirmed.

Against this background it becomes understandable that the prince was so deeply disappointed by the results of the synod of Emden. No word about the right to revolt, no word about his vocation in this regard, no word of support for the struggle for freedom, no help to push people over the threshold of their 'weak consciences'. In 1572 the consistory of the Reformed church in Keulen even decided to change some words in the pronouncements of Bedburg. There had been mention of 'the recovery of the Netherlands'. But that was a political judgment. The consistory

---

[17] '. . . *voorghedraghen van Philippus van Marnix, genaemt van Mont St. Aldegonde, uut name ende van wege mijnes Genadigen Heere den prince van Oranien etc. (. . . .) dese naest volghende articulen: (. . .) Item dat daer een goede overeenkominge ende onderlinge verstandt opgericht wordden mach in politicke saeken, belangende de wederoprichtinge der Nederlanden. Ende dat tot dien eynde alle gemeynten verstandt ende overdracht hebben mit sijner Excellentie, overschrijvende wat daer sekerlijcx omgaet. -Sy hebben beloefft, een yegelijck sijn beste hierin te doene voor so vele, als een yeder gemeynte vernemen kan. Item datse eendrachtelijck besluyten willen over de beroepinge sijner F(urstliche) G(nade) ende de gerechticheyt der were ende waepens etc., om de swacke gewissen deste beter daerdoor te stillen etc. -De vergaderinge en twijfelt daer niet aen en sullen arbeyden tselvige in te belden.*' The text of the synod in Bedburg is edited by J. F. G. Goeters, *400 Jahre Bedburger Synode* (Jülich 1971); quotation pp 18, 19 (with a german translation).

wanted to speak only of 'the recovery of the church in the Netherlands'[18] and that is not the same thing!

What the synod of Dordrecht also decided in 1574 had already been reality in Emden: an ecclesiastical organisation should only make pronouncements about ecclesiastical affairs. Unmistakeably a rejection of the request of the prince! A letter of the prince has survived, in which he openly voiced his disappointment about the results of the synod of Emden.[19] The Dutch churches did not give him the support he wanted. There were too many members hindered by this 'weakness of their consciences'. They could not easily agree with the revolt. They could not easily believe in the divine vocation of William of Orange. The people did not even give money for the hiring of troops, (at least) not as much as he had hoped. He had to use his own capital for this war against the duke of Alva.

It is true, there were Dutch warriors too involved in this war. Some nobles, having lost all their property through the measures of Alva, used their own gangs. For them there was no retreat. They could only go on with their desperate revolt. These small groups were enlarged by unemployed seamen. They directed their actions against the central government and the hired troops of Spain. Their activities also had a religious element. They robbed the rich monasteries unscrupulously. They hated the rich catholic church. Calvinism gave these gangs an excuse for violence. When they conquered a town for the prince, they forced the local church to a Calvinist reformation, even without the agreement of the already existing reformed groups.[20] But there is no reason to conclude on the grounds of their often cruel activities that, generally speaking, the Reformed movement in the Netherlands supported the use of violence against the government. Many of the Dutch fugitives in London and elsewhere and I suppose the

---

[18] W. F. Dankbaar p 63.

[19] W van 't Spijker, 'Stromingen onder de reformatorisch gezinden te Emden' *De synode van Emden 1571-1971* pp 72-74.

[20] A striking example can be found in the archives of Kampen in Overijssel. In 1578 118 family-heads asked the local government's permission for protestant services in one of the churches. Before the government could take a decision the army of the prince took possession of the town. The *geuzen* pillaged churches and cloisters. Calvinism had won. But there is a great difference between the list of the 118 family-heads and the list of members of the Calvinist church in 1579. Only a few names appear on both lists. The majority of protestants must have wanted another reformation. See A. J. Jelsma, 'De calvinisering van Kampen' *Theologische Hogeschool Kampen 1982* vol 18 (1982) pp 3-8.

The attitude of the Dutch reformation to the use of violence

majority of the secret gatherings of believers in the Netherlands, still had the conviction that violence against the magistrates was a sin. Even when the revolt proved to be a success, these believers were not prepared to give a theological justification of this deluge of violence. They accepted the result, they enjoyed their freedom, but they did not want to justify the war. No worldly matters in ecclesiastical meetings. No discussion about these ugly affairs. Reformed ministers had another task, the preaching of the gospel in often empty church-buildings. No official acknowledgment of the revolt.

'Weakness of conscience', so the reluctance to accept the use of violence against the government had been called in the synod of Bedburg. This 'weakness' became visible in different places. In 1562 there had already been a conflict about the use of violence between the Reformed churches in the southern parts of the Netherlands and the Dutch church in London. The question had been aroused by the civil war in France. How far can you go in your resistance to the magistrate? that was the question. Is it permitted to carry weapons for defence while attending a hedge preaching? Is it permissible to free prisoners? Or is it really necessary to accept humbly the killing, the burning of protestant prisoners? How far can you go? The consistory of Antwerp, and later the synod in this important port also, decided that a limited use of violence could not be condemned. The answer of the Dutch church in London was a vehement rejection of this point of view. This was Anabaptist behaviour, according to the Dutch fugitives in London, and absolutely reprehensible. Two members of the pro-violence faction in Antwerp proceeded to a meeting in London to discuss the matter. But London held the conviction that the use of violence was forbidden. New fugitives from the Netherlands were asked for their opinion in this affair. When they did not reject every use of violence they were excommunicated. That could be very dangerous, as we know from the example of Adriaan of Haemstede who, after his excommunication, was sent back to the Netherlands with his wife and his children.[21]

---

[21] See a letter of members of the Dutch church in London in which they complained about the use of violence in the Netherlands: J. H. Hessels, *Epistulae et Tractatus cum reformationis tum ecclesiae Londino-Batavae Historiam Illustrantes (1544–1622)* (London/ Amsterdam 1889) 2 no 104 p 357. For the conflict between the consistories of Antwerp and London A. A. van Schelven, *Kerkeraads-Protocollen [der Nederduitsche Vluchtelingenkerk te London 1560–1568*

Looking at the whole period between 1562 and 1574 we must conclude that there was, during these years, a strong current amongst Dutch reformers condemning every use of violence against the magistrate, in spite of the opinion of the Calvinist church in France and Geneva. The influence of French ministers, preaching in the southern parts of the Netherlands, was demonstrable but not great enough to overrule the 'weakness of conscience' in this respect.[22]

It is true, there was a wave of violence in 1566, but it is also clear that this iconoclastic fury was not really the beginning of a violent revolt against the government. It was for the most part nothing more and nothing less than a cleansing of the churches, to make these buildings better suited for reformed preaching. The movement did not really endanger political relations. The reaction of the Spanish government has been extremely overdone and one of the most important reasons for the revolt. Even this cleansing was condemned by the majority of the Dutch reformers within and outside the Netherlands.[23]

It is true, there was contact between delegates of the consistories and members of the nobility during these years. They considered the possibilities of joint action. There is no reason to exaggerate the distaste for violence. What happened in France did make a great impact on the Reformed movement in the Netherlands, but this impact could not remove the religious distaste for the use of violence against the magistrate.

It is true, there was fundraising organised by the consistories with the possibility that this money could be used for the hiring of troops. But this was not the purpose of the fundraising. The consistories originally intended to offer king Philip II this money in exchange for a free exercise of their religion.[24] It is possible to regard the collection as an effort to prevent a real revolt.

(Amsterdam 1921)] pp 308–323. About Adriaan van Haemstede, Patrick Collinson, *Archbishop Grindal 1519–1583; the struggle for a Reformed Church* (London 1979) pp 134–146; A. J. Jelsma, *Adriaan van Haemstede en zijn martelaarsboek* (The Hague 1970).

[22] About the differences between the Reformed groups in the Netherlands, W. van 't Spijker in *De synode van Emden 1571–1971* pp 50–75.

[23] About the relations between the Reformed ministers and the troubles of 1566, Phyllis Mack Crew pp 140–182.

[24] I don't agree with the suggestion of J. Scheerder p 115, that the offering of the money was only a pretext and not a serious appeal. It was well known in the Netherlands how badly the Spanish king needed money. More careful about the fund-raising is Phyllis Mack Crew p 17.

The attitude of the Dutch reformation to the use of violence

It is true that William of Orange became a member of the Reformed church, hoping for more support and impressed by the activities of the Calvinist church in France. He must have hoped to overcome by this step the 'weakness of conscience' of so many members of the Reformed movement in the Netherlands. We can only conclude that he had less success than he had expected. The official attitude of the church remained disappointing for him.

During the whole period between 1562 and 1574 we can distinguish resistance against a theological justification of the revolt. The Reformed movement in the Netherlands exhibited a hesitation concerning this problem in a way we do not find in France or Scotland.

What was the background of the 'weakness of conscience', of this fear of violence? There are three important reasons.
1) The Dutch Reformed movement was not as fully Calvinist as the Reformed churches in France and Scotland. Indeed, the southern parts of the Netherlands were strongly orientated towards France and Geneva. It was in these parts that the revolt began.[25] But elsewhere the situation was totally different. There the Reformed movement had more connection with the reformation in Germany and was more open to Lutheran influence. For Lutheran believers it was unthinkable to start a revolt against the government for the cause of religion. In these northern parts of the Netherlands the urge for a revolt was less strong than in the southern parts. The persecution was usually confined to Anabaptist radicals.[26] In the course of these years most Reformed groups were indeed prepared to accept a more Calvinist organisation, comparable with the protestant church of France, but this did not mean that they lost their almost Lutheran, sometimes even Anabaptist fear of violence.
2) Still more important must have been the impact the radical reformation had left behind. Just as in Germany, there had already been a religious revolt in the Netherlands thirty years before. In that situation many people had sold all their possessions and bought weapons to join the struggle of John of Leiden and his followers for the Kingdom of God, which was coming in Münster. There had

---

[25] Especially the towns of Valenciennes and Tournai.
[26] See I. M. J. Hoog, *De Martelaren der Hervorming in Nederland tot 1566* (Schiedam 1885). As far as I could discover in the archives of Kampen only rebaptised people were killed there.

already been a justification of the use of violence in the service of God during those years. The pamphlets of the reformer of Münster, Bernt Rothmann, were scattered all over the Netherlands. He had tried to prove, and he did so with success, that there sometimes can be a shift in the will of God. In earlier times Christians had only to suffer for the sake of God, he agreed. But now the time had come to rise up, to fight with the weapons in the hand for the kingdom.[27] That was the reason why it was indeed so important for John of Leiden to become accepted as the second David, the new king, the last king before the coming of Christ. This was not only pride, and self-importance in him. He had to be the highest authority in the eyes of his believers, higher than the bishop of Münster, higher even than the Emperor. He had to convince his followers, that he really had a vocation from God to become the leader in this last war.[28] That was the only way to liberate the believers from the 'weakness of their conscience'. In fact William of Orange did the same thing as John of Leiden when he tried to convince the Reformed movement of his divine vocation.

After the failure in Münster in 1535 there had been great confusion. Gangs of robbers wandered about the country, hated by the inhabitants of the Netherlands. A strong distaste developed for the conviction of founding the kingdom of God by violence.[29]

3) The third arguement is connected with the second. The new leader of the Anabaptist movement, Menno Simons, taught his followers to distance themselves completely from the world. The Mennonites did not want to become involved in worldly matters. Some of them, we don't know how many, later joined the Reformed movement.[30] It was not so easy for the children of these

---

[27] B. Rothmann, 'Bericht von der Wrake' *Die Schriften Bernhard Rothmanns*, ed by R. Stupperich (Münster 1970) pp 284–297.

[28] J. M. Stayer, *Anabaptists and the sword* (Lawrence, Kansas 1973) pp 227–280; A. J. Jelsma, 'De koning en de vrouwen; Münster 1534–1535' *Gereformeerd Theologisch Tijdschrift* vol 75 (1975) no 2 pp 82–107.

[29] See the excuse of the Dutch consistory because they had called the church of Antwerp Anabaptist: '*Oeck zo bekenden wij dat wij wel behoirden onsen brief minnelicker gescreven te hebben (. . .) also oft wij hen den oproerischen Wederdoperen ende den ghespuys des Thomae Munzeri waren ghelijck achtende*' A. A. van Schelven, *Kerkeraads-protocollen* pp 320–322.

[30] This process began soon after the fall of Münster in 1535. A famous example was Wouter Delen, teacher in Amsterdam, who was involved in an Anabaptist revolt in this city in 1535 and took refuge in London. There he became one of the most important leaders of the Dutch Reformed fugitives. See A. F. Mellink, 'Prereformatie en vroege reformatie

The attitude of the Dutch reformation to the use of violence

Mennonites to justify a violent revolt against the government. They only wanted to pronounce that ecclesiastical meetings should discuss nothing but ecclesiastical affairs.

In short, through the influence of the Lutheran reformation in some parts of the Netherlands, through the extremely unpleasant memories of the agressive Anabaptist movement, through the pacifist influence of the Mennonites, the Reformed movement in the Netherlands could not give the warriors in the revolt against Spain the same theological support as the warriors in France and Scotland received from their religious leaders.

This judgment applies only at the beginning, the first stage of the eighty-years-war, and not for the whole period. During the war the catholic element disappeared from the revolt.[31] In the northern parts of the Netherlands something like national feeling developed. The struggle for freedom became in that situation no longer resistance to a God-given government but only obedience to their own government against foreign occupation. But also in that period the rule stayed in force, that ecclesiastical meetings would only deal with ecclesiastical problems.[32] No politics in the church. Don't be too quick to describe the Reformed movement in the Netherlands as the soul of the revolt. In the Dutch reformation there was too much of this 'weakness of conscience' for that to have been the case.[33]

Theologische Hogeschool
Kampen
The Netherlands

1517–1568' *Algemene Geschiedenis der Nederlanden* VI (Haarlem 1979) p 159. His son Petrus Delen was one of the ministers in London accusing the Reformed Church of Antwerp because of the use of violence against the government.

[31] Important reasons for this process 1) the violence of the *geuzen* in 1578 in Ghent and its environs; 2) the decree of pope Gregory XIII in 1578, in which he threatened to excommunicate every catholic who gave his support to the Dutch revolt; 3) the defection of the stadholder of the northern part of the Netherlands, count Rennenberg, to the Spanish side. see L. J. Rogier, *Eenheid en Scheiding* pp 88–96.

[32] The rule was repeated at all the following synods and is still in use today in some Reformed Churches in the Netherlands, with the consequence that these churches have always to defend their discussions about political issues.

[33] I should like to thank Mrs. K. Harris for her help in checking my use of English.

CLERGYMEN AND CONFLICT 1660–1763

by D. NAPTHINE AND W. A. SPECK

THE VIEWS of clergymen towards virtually any activity under the sun, and many over it, are preserved in an inexhaustible seam of sermons published between the Restoration of Charles II and the end of the Seven Years' War. Thousands were listed by Sampson Letsome in his *The Preacher's Assistant*, which appeared in 1753, and in an updated sequel by J. Cooke in 1783. Nor were these all-inclusive.[1]

Faced with this mass of evidence, historians are forced to be selective. They can concentrate on the works of certain preachers, on precise dates or on particular genres of sermon, such as those preached at Assizes or funerals.[2] The authors of this paper have studied three types. One of them is working on the Jeremiad in the years 1660–1720, Jeremiads being sermons preached during, immediately after, or on the anniversary of such national disasters as the plague in 1665, the fire of London in 1666 and the hurricane of 1703. War featured in them as one of the many visitations of Providence held to be afflicting the nation. The other addressed himself specifically to fast and thanksgiving-day sermons published during the wars of 1739 to 1748 and 1756 to 1763. These were delivered expressly to comment on military setbacks and failures, and to celebrate victories.

Jeremiads were often preached upon days of fast and humiliation ordained by the State, and in many cases before civil authorities. On such occasions they were delivered by clergymen firmly established in the Anglican hierarchy, as well as those of lesser stature, and their preaching gave expression to concepts also upheld by nonconforming Protestant preachers. They assumed the

---

[1] The B. L. copy of the 1753 edition (1025 R 8) has manuscript notes at the end listing 'sermons in the Museum not taken notice of in this book.' These can now be supplemented with titles recorded in the Eighteenth-century short-title catalogue, which are accessible on BLAISE. The authors wish to thank the ECSTC and BLAISE for producing a print out of fast and thanksgiving day sermons published between 1756 and 1763 currently held by the B.L.
[2] Thus Dr. Barbara White used *Assize sermons 1660–1720* for her Ph.D thesis (Newcastle upon Tyne Polytechnic, 1980).

existence of a moral universe in which God intervened by particular acts of Providence to punish the vice and immorality of a nation when human sanctions had proved insufficient. Occurences such as plague, famine, storm and war were deemed to be examples of divine justice which could only be averted by a speedy and sincere national repentence. They saw a nation guilty of such provoking sins as blasphemy and drunkenness, luxury and pride, ingratitude and insubordination, to list the more commonly mentioned ones. To stave off the wrath of God they urged the abandonment of such vices, and the adoption of virtuous behaviour which accorded with His will. Otherwise He might abandon or even destroy England altogether, as He had done Sodom and Gomorrah.

These preachers tended to dwell on the uncertainties and miseries that daily confronted their congregations. As Jeremiah Dodson observed in 1665 'health and sickness, peace and war, prosperity and adversity, interchangeably succeed each other in this our earthly pilgrimage'.[3] These vicissitudes were the direct result of the sin of Adam, and a settled state of affairs could only be achieved if that sin were permanently renounced. While individuals could expect to be rewarded or punished in accordance with their transgression or repentance in the life to come, communities and nations could only be dealt with in this existence, which was the reason for these visitations. When afflictions such as war occurred, it was the duty of individuals to acknowledge the justice of the punishment and their contributions to it.

As a nation England was held to be especially blessed, being singled out by Providence for particular care and concern. John Prince was airing a commonly held view when he said in 1722 that 'we of this church and nation, by the disposition of Almighty God, have some Guardian Angel, that watches over us, I do no more question, than I do the truth of some of those miraculous deliverances, which from time to time have been vouchsafed unto both.'[4] In the long catalogue of 'miraculous deliverances' which he might have mentioned, one of the more significant was the Restoration, which had rescued Englishmen from the oppression of anarchy and civil war. The calamities of the Interregnum had

---

[3] J. Dodson, *The preachers precept of consideration* (London 1665) p 2.
[4] J. Prince, *An anti-pestilential pill* (London 1722) p 7.

Clergymen and conflict 1660–1763

occurred when God left men to their own evil devices. As John Edwards explained in 1665, God 'often leaves a nation and persons to themselves and their own sinful wills and ways. But alas! there is no greater punishment than this, and no plainer sign of God's displeasure.'[5] The roots of conflict lay firmly planted in human nature, and only divine intervention prevented them from growing. What happened when God ceased to inhibit their growth in the 1640s was described by Henry Hesketh:[6]

> We had pulled down the best Government, and torn in pieces the best church upon earth, and murthered the best governours that perhaps ruled either. The anarchy and confusions that succeeded the one, and the oppressors and mountebanks that step'd into the room of the other, were punishments alone big enough; and when those had tyranniz'd and lorded it over us, harassed and worn us even unto death, by their cruelties and vain experiments of relief, for some years divine justice seemed satisfied, and his goodness was wearied in beholding our sufferings and hearing our cries.

The cessation of internal conflict, and the return of the monarchy, were not the result of man's actions, but the consequences of divine mercy.

Because God had taken a merciful path, it meant that He had attempted to reform the nation by blessings rather than afflictions. Yet the nation was still as sinful as ever, and because of this the recurrence of civil strife was to be feared. God's act of mercy on behalf of the nation required an equivalent effort by the people to ensure the continuance of peace. The judgements of plague and fire so soon after the Restoration gave rise to anxieties that the effort was not forthcoming. Thus Jeremiads preached in commemoration of both the plague and the fire voiced apprehensions about the ultimate political stability of the nation. The fears articulated by Sancroft were echoed throughout the period:[7]

> The Devil of rebellion and disobedience, which not long since possest the nation, rent and tore it till it form's again, and pin'd away in lingring consumptions, that cast it oft times

---

[5] J. Edwards, *The plague of the heart* (London 1665) p 29.
[6] H. Hesketh, *A sermon preached before the right honourable Lord Mayor and aldermen of the city of London* (London 1682) p 19.
[7] W. Sancroft, *Lex ignea, or the school of righteousness* (London 1665) p 50.

into the fire, and oft times into the water . . . to destroy it; is now through God's mercies cast out, and we seem to sit quiet, and sober at the feet of our Deliverer, cloth'd and in our right minds again. But yet this ill spirit, this restless fury . . . walks about day and night seeking rest, and finds none; and he saith in his heart, I will return some time or other to my house, from whence I came out. Oh let us take heed of preaching that God, who alone chains up the fury, least for our sins to permit him to return once more . . . and so our last estate prove worse than the former.

They were very conscious that internal peace was on a slippery footing, for schisms and factions persisted, people complained about the authorities, and the monarch and laws established to uphold the work of God were abused by all sections of society. Each judgement of whatever complexion was held to be a sure indication that God was about to desert the nation once again. The fact that He did not do so reflected upon His goodness in withholding the fatal punishments. But for how long could the nation try His patience?

To fulfill the promise of the Restoration it was necessary for each individual to practise Christian virtues, which to Sancroft included[8]

all the offices and instances of duty between man and man . . . reverence and obedience to our superiors; courtesie and humanity to our equals; kindness and condescension to our inferiors; gratitude and thankfulness to our benefactors; justice and upright dealing towards all; truth in our words and faithfulness in our trusts, and constancy and honesty in all our actions.

The exercise of these positive virtues was consistent with a rigid and hierarchical political and social order. God had allotted every individual a place, given them due rights and responsibilities, the abuse of which would incur His wrath. Any ideas that things could be otherwise, and tendency towards 'levelling', were the product of man's sinful pride. Such had caused the Civil War, and threatened it again. If moderation replaced enthusiasm, then schism and faction would disappear; if humility replaced pride then England could once again be a God fearing nation, its people

---

[8] *Ibid* pp 31–2.

happy and contented rather than miserable and factious; if obedience to superiors were forthcoming, practised in the knowledge that those superiors would not act oppressively, then unity would replace division and peace would replace conflict. The way to prevent civil war was to practise religious duties with humility and sincerity. As Benjamin Calamy argued 'most of the duties of religion are so absolutely necessary to the good order, quiet, and peace of societies, that men have found it highly expedient to oblige one another to the observance of them.'[9] Calamy, one of Charles II's chaplains, was referring to the religious duties prescribed by the established church; yet his sentiments were echoed in Jeremiads preached by dissenting clergy, who would also have agreed with Henry Hesketh's observation that 'divided societies last not long.'[10] Yet they failed to agree upon religious duties in practice. On the contrary the established clergy held the dissenters responsible for creating the conditions which brought about civil war. They therefore supported the legal suppression of dissent, thus ensuring the persistence of the very conditions which in their sermons they abhorred.

Where the notion that civil war was a national judgement of the utmost severity could easily be understood, when it came to foreign wars the visitation took on a more complex character. As with civil war the underlying cause was still held to be the sinfulness of the people. Thus John Edwards urged his congregation in 1698 to 'remove the cause of all your fears and dangers, that is, renounce your sins, which either in themselves or through the judgement of God do not only procure the wars, but make them unsuccessful and fatal to us.'[11] Yet a successful foreign war could also be construed as a blessing, and even as a moral imperative. Jonathan Owen stressed this in 1694, when he asserted that 'the Great God rules and upholds both kingdoms and commonwealths by second causes and subordinate means, such as merchandising abroad, trading at home; and sometimes by just, necessary and defensive wars.'[12] Here war was not a judgement

---

[9] B. Calamy, *A sermon preached before the right honourable the Lord Mayor, the aldermen and citizens of London* (London 1684) p 5.
[10] H. Hesketh, *A sermon* (London 1682) p 25.
[11] J. Edwards, *Sermons on several occasions and subjects* (London 1698) p 208.
[12] J. Owen, *England's warning by late frowning providences* (London 1694) p 16.

upon England. Quite the reverse; this particular war was necessary because of the despotic nature of the enemy, France; it was just because it was being conducted against the standard bearer of the Catholic faith committed to the defeat of Protestantism and the supremacy of the anti-Christ; and England was not the aggressor but had a duty to align herself with God's forces. Even in such circumstances, however, the sinfulness of the nation could well provoke God to allow England to be defeated as a just punishment.

Wars against foreign powers, therefore, were not necessarily to be seen as judgements upon the nation, even though the logic of the Jeremiad philosophy, with its view that sin was the true cause of all war, should have led to the conclusion that they were punishments for sinfulness. This ambiguity can be resolved by recognising the political function of the sermons, which were sponsored by the State to implore the blessing of God upon the nation's military endeavours. Even the great storm of 1703 was pressed into service for this purpose. Thus John Griffith, preaching on the phenomenon, took the occasion to warn that 'our dissentions, our unnatural animosities, and uncharitable behaviour one towards another . . . lay us open, an easie prey to an enemy.'[13] John Edwards called for the positive exercise of virtuous behaviour in time of war, noting that 'some sins do directly obstruct the good success of the war; as, on the contrary, some vertues, as temperance and sobriety, continence and chastity, self-denial and contentment, mutual peace and concord, do in their own nature promote it.'[14] Paradoxically the same virtues necessary to prevent civil wars were required to ensure the nation's military success in foreign conflicts.

If the nation were at war, however, for whatever reason, a satisfactory conclusion could only be obtained by enlisting God's help. Richard Chapman emphasised this by urging his congregation to pray 'that God would . . . bless and prosper all our undertakings, particularly those we now stand at present engag'd in for his honour and for the good of Europe, against the most barbarous and insulting of adversaries.'[15] The storm which occasioned the 1704 sermons was to severe that it aroused concern

---

[13] J. Griffith, *A sermon preached Jan 19th 1703/4* (London 1704) pp 14–15.
[14] J. Edwards, *Sermons* (London 1698) p 201.
[15] R. Chapman, *The necessity of repentance asserted* (London 1703) p 10.

Clergymen and conflict 1660–1763

about God's intentions. It was seen as a very real warning that God was about to inflict defeat upon the nation, or even subjugate it to a foreign power. Since that power was Catholic it seemed like another indication that God had deserted the nation. When events like this occurred, and two visitations appeared as if in tandem, then the only thing that mattered was for the nation to implore God's mercy and that the war should be successfully waged. When this occurred, then it gave rise to rejoicing. Josiah Woodward, noting the successes of 1706, observed that[16]

> it hath . . . pleased the Lord of Hosts, to whom be all honour and praise for ever, to crown our late campaigns with astonishing success, with the most compleat and honourable victories that many ages can produce, attended with the conquest of great towns, wealthy provinces, and even of several kingdoms. Our royal fleets also ride in triumph both at home and abroad, without any dispute about the empire of the sea by the late pretending rival.

Because the victories were the result of God's mercy they reaffirmed His special relationship with the nation, even though the people were still sinful and continued to leave themselves open to divine punishment.

War was one of a number of God's punishments, along with fire, plague and storm. All could have severe consequences for a nation, but whereas fire was a judgement pure and simple, war was not. Civil strife could be little but a judgement; but a war against France could be seen as just and necessary. Although this view suited the authorities, the Jeremiad was not just the mouthpiece of the State. Those who preached them were convinced that they were giving expression to the will of God and not just to that of their rulers. To those who suggested otherwise, or as Calamy put it 'would represent religion as a meer engine of state, and mystery of government, to possess the minds of the vulgar with the belief of a God, and a life to come, thereby to render them more tame and gentle, submissive and obedient', he replied 'I have not time now to confute or expose this wild supposition, for which there is not the least ground of evidence.'[17]

---

[16] J. Woodward, *A sermon preached before the right honourable the Lord Mayor and aldermen of the City of London* (London 1706) pp 18–19.

[17] Calamy, *A sermon* (London 1684) pp 7, 8.

Jeremiads paraded before their congregations an ideal that their preachers believed could be achieved. That ideal was a Protestant society, united under the law of God, peaceful because those laws were obeyed, and prosperous as a result of that obedience. Conflict was the result of sin and vice, which divided the nation and weakened it in the face of its enemies, both internal and external. If the nation, blessed with God's covenant, failed to reform its manners, then it would be punished by severe visitations. Ultimately, if the transgressions persisted, then God would desert England, leaving her to be torn apart by civil war, or overrun by a foreign, and what was worse, a Roman Catholic power.

The fact that France continued to represent the major threat to Britain in the War of the Austrian Succession and the Seven Years' War ensured that these messages were hammered home again later in the eighteenth century, in the fast and thanksgiving sermons preached during those conflicts. The Jacobite rebellion of 1745 even gave preachers a last opportunity to animadvert on civil as well as foreign war.

Fast sermons rang changes on three persistent themes. First, preachers argued that Britain enjoyed a special relationship with God, just as the Jews had done in Biblical times. 'Do not we succeed the Jews "to whom were committed the oracles of God?"' asked Isaac Smithson in 1756. 'Are not we, a chosen generation, a peculiar people as were they?'[18] Secondly, despite the providential blessings which this had entailed, like the Israelites of old the British were guilty of ingratitude, disobedience to God and a disposition towards sin. Thirdly, just as God had chastened Israel with afflictions, and finally had cast her off, so He punished Britain for backsliding, and, unless there was a sincere repentance and reformation of manners, He would ultimately forsake her too.

When illustrating the special dispensations of Providence towards the British, since most sermons were delivered by Anglican ministers, their preachers betrayed a conviction that God was particularly well disposed towards the English. They might include Scotland geographically, by pointing out that Britain was an island, remote from continental embroilments and placed in a particularly favourable latitude, giving her the benefits of a bounteous nature. But historically their examples tended to be

---

[18] I. Smithson, *A sermon occasioned by the declaration of war against France* (London 1756) p 9.

Clergymen and conflict 1660–1763

overwhelmingly from English history. God had given England the finest Constitution and the most perfectly reformed Church in the world. Mixed monarchy protected the liberty and property of Englishmen from tyranny. The Church of England had purged the Christian religion of the impurities which had corrupted it since the fifth century, thereby restoring the primitive Church rather than establishing a new one, as more radical Protestants had done. Providence had preserved these manifold blessings by intervening constantly in English history, for instance by scattering the Armada in a storm, revealing the Gunpowder plot, restoring Charles II, changing the wind in 1688 so that William could arrive safely at his destination, and bringing about the peaceful accession of the House of Hanover.

When demonstrating how the English had been guilty of black ingratitude for these blessings, preachers drew examples from all seven of the deadly sins. In the central decades of the eighteenth century, however, they particularly stressed two phenomena; the decline of religious zeal and the growth of luxury. 'Have we not chang'd the primitive piety, the honest frugality and strict virtue of our ancestors into prophaneness, luxury and extravagance?' charged George Conen at the time of the Forty-five.[19] 'Surely the Gospel of Jesus Christ was never treated with greater malice and contempt by Jews or Heathens, than it has been in this Christian country?' expostulated the bishop of Salisbury on the same occasion.[20] 'Luxury has indeed, too long, set up her inchanting standard amongst us' lamented William Drake, 'and too many, God knows, have listed volunteers under her fatal banners.'[21] By the time the Seven Years' War broke out the catalogue had been extended, as John Brown's influential *Estimate of the Manners and Principles of the Times* bears witness. Thomas Scott noted 'the numerous, repeated well-supported complaints of the vast increase, within a few years, of infidelity, of popery, of enthusiasm, of luxury, of all sorts of vices, in the higher, in the middle, and in the lowest class of our people.'[22] In *A National Fast a national mockery of*

---

[19] G. Conen, *A sermon preached at the parish church of St. George the martyr in Southwark* (London 1745) p 20.
[20] Thomas Sherlock, bishop of Salisbury, *A sermon preached at the cathedral church of Salisbury* (London 1745) p 14.
[21] W. Drake, *A sermon preached at Hatfield* (York 1745) p 17.
[22] T. Scott, *Great Britain's danger and remedy* (London 1757) p 15.

God, without real amendment both in principle and practice M. M. Merrick blamed 'the several sorts of infidelity among us' for 'the reigning vices and immoralities', which he proceeded to elaborate:[23]

> Hence arise those numerous heresies and schisms, that swarm so thick among us, at this day; which, together with the formidable increase of Popery, on the one hand, and Enthusiasm and Fanaticism on the other, seem to threaten the speedy and total destruction of our Sion, both within and without.
>
> Hence it is likewise that so many among us, so thoughtlessly riot in luxury and intemperance, in chambering and wantoness, some living equally unconcern'd, in a constant state of undissembled fornication; others, equally unconcern'd, in downright secret, if not open, adultery; as tho' they believed there were neither God nor Devil, neither Heaven or Hell to come . . . Some moreover living in a total dissipation of mind, in a perpetual giddy round of intoxicating amusements and diversions; and, as a natural consequence of all this, in a general neglect perhaps of all religious worship . . . Deplorable numbers more still, in a profligate abandon'd course of drunkenness and debauchery of all kinds; of cursing and swearing, lying and slandering, cozening and defrauding one another. . .

It is interesting that both Scott and Merrick deplore the rise of Enthusiasm, a reference to Methodism, which they regarded as another sign of the general fall from Grace in recent years. John Dupont was more explicit in identifying them as 'those who by professing too much pretended zeal, manifestly and very sensibly injure them both' [God and religion] :[24]

> The persons I would denote are a set of either real or feigned enthusiasts, who have endeavour'd of late years to make an unwarrantable schism in the Church, and one might conjecture, without any breach of charity, that they would not be less backward in fomenting divisions also in the State, if a proper opportunity should offer, since some of their favourite tenets avowedly tally with the exploded errors of the Church of Rome. The appearance of those men who

[23] M. M. Merrick, *A national fast a national mockery* (London 1761) pp 9, 11.
[24] J. Dupont, *National corruption and depravity the principal cause of national disappointments* (York 1757) pp 12–13.

make themselves priests from the lowest of the people, and are not of the tribe of Levi, cannot but remind those who are a little read in History, of those sectaries which abounded about a century ago, and which contributed not a little to increase the broils and confusions of that unhappy period.

Because the English were unmindful of God's concern for them, He periodically chastised them for their sins, as warnings to repent. Thus in history He had visited upon them Mary Tudor, Charles I, Oliver Cromwell and James II, and now threatened them with the Pretender. To these human agencies were added the scriptural afflictions of pestilence, famine and war. 'Various are the methods which the God of Nations has recourse to, when he wou'd make them sensible of his displeasure' asserted John Chafy. 'Sometimes from the phials of his wrath he pours forth a pestilence upon them, that he might make them sick of their iniquity: sometimes a famine, in order to starve them out of it: but more frequently he unkennels the blood-hounds of war, to worry them into their duty, or else to hunt them to their destruction.'[25] Unfortunately for the prophets of doom, there was no visitation of the plague in the middle of the eighteenth century, so a murrain amongst the cattle had to be pressed into service. 'Nor is it unlikely' warned Edward Lewis 'that our guiltless cattle suffer first, to prepare us for what may follow, and to give us timely warning and space for repentance.'[26] Nor was there much in the way of famine. On the contrary, most of these years saw bumper harvests. But there were food shortages at the start of the War of Jenkins' Ear, and again at the outset of the Seven Years' War, which were exploited by the fast day preachers. Laurence Holden noted the irony of holding a general fast at a time of dearth in 1757.[27] 'We have had a grievous murrain long raging amongst our cattle' commented James Snowden,

> and this last year the earth has been so sparing and unpropitious in its grand production that we have from thence received some forebodings of a famine of bread. Hence then these three great evils, war, pestilence and famine, seem, after a sort to have united their forces against us; any one of which, if long continued in any degree, is

---

[25] J. Chafy, *A sermon preached at Broad-Chalk in Wiltshire* (London 1757) p 9.
[26] E. Lewis, *Mercy and judgement* (London 1747) p 12.
[27] L. Holden, *The vanity of crying to God* (London 1757) p 21.

sufficient to break the heart of the stoutest nation upon earth.[28]

Although two of the four horsemen of the Apocalypse were virtually unknown in eighteenth-century Britain, their companions, War and Death, were almost as familiar as ever. While it is true that there was nothing on the scale of the civil war in the previous century, an armed rebellion also broke out which led to the last battles to take place on British soil.

The Forty-five was therefore the last occasion in which preachers could animadvert on the affliction of civil conflict within their own community. Thomas Wilson emphasised that this was a special affliction, more grievous than an international conflict,[29] being

> not blood and rapine between nation and nation, who are unfortunately engaged in war with each other; (and who having no particular ties of nature, friendship and civil intercourse, may feel a kind of savage joy in their mutual miseries and distresses, which will seem to lessen them) but blood and rapine among members of the same body politick:—a war in our own bowels;—a civil war: which of all earthly evils is most big with misery. Words are too feeble to express, or imagination to conceive, its horrors.

If it were to succeed, it would be a manifest sign that God had weighed Britain in the balance and found her wanting. As the archbishop of York put it[30]

> if this rebellion, rising from a cloud no bigger than a man's hand, should grow up into a frightful storm and scatter desolation round us, it will owe its progress to the countenance and support of France and Spain, our old and inveterate enemies . . . God forbid their wicked machinations should take effect! Providence has often confounded them, and we humbly hope will find out a way to save us once again: But if they are ordained to be the scourges of a sinful people, the punishment will sit the heavier upon us, for coming from the hands of those whom we despise and hate.

The French and Spaniards had a fifth column working for them,

---

[28] J. Snowden, *The duty of fasting* (Oxford 1757) p 23.
[29] T. Wilson, *A sermon preached at the parish church of the Holy Trinity in . . . Bungay in Suffolk* (London 1745) p 9.
[30] Thomas Herring, archbishop of York, *A sermon preached at the cathedral church of York September the 22nd 1745* (York 1745) pp 24–5.

Clergymen and conflict 1660–1763

the Jacobites, whom the dissenter Samuel Chandler contrived to identify as the most sinful elements in the country:[31]

> possibly the shaking of these kingdoms, throughout the whole frame of them, may be necessary to the thorough settlement of it for the future, and the permitting all the corrupt and rotten members of the constitution, the men of desperate principles, morals and fortunes, those curses of a nation, to declare openly the inward rancour of their hearts, and unite under the banner of the invader, may be the only possible natural expedient to discover and extirpate them, and the only method resolved on by Providence to purge the dregs of atheism, impiety and iniquity from the midst of us, to establish more firmly the foundation of the national peace for the future, and more closely to unite the remaining, the yet recoverable, uncorrupted and virtuous part of the nation.

The notion that Butcher Cumberland and 'Hangman' Hawley were in the vanguard of virtue against sinners suggests that Providence did indeed work in a mysterious way its wonders to perform.

Although they saw the rebellion as a judgment upon the nation for its sins, no preacher really thought that it would succeed, even in its early days when the rebels seemed to be conquering Scotland. John Dupont preached a sermon at Aysgarth on 10 November 1745, in which he observed[32]

> 'Twould be presumptuous to pretend to dive into the secrets of Providence, or unravel its mysteries; but if we may judge from the manifest infatuation and divisions which already appear amongst our rebellious and apostate brethren, and that unanimity and spirit which, to the honour of Englishmen so universally prevails amongst our selves . . . We may be bold to say that God has already espoused our cause, and declar'd himself in our favour.

He was a bit previous, as his Yorkshire congregation might have put it, for two days earlier the Young Pretender had crossed the border with his army, and in the ensuing four weeks was to take the rebellion into the heart of England. But his text was prophetic enough.

---

[31] S. Chandler, *The danger and duty of good men under the present unnatural rebellion* (London 1745) p 38.

[32] J. Dupont, *The insolent invasion of Sanacherib against Jerusalem repelled and defeated by God* (York 1745) p 10.

It was somehow inconceivable, despite the crying sins of the nation, that God would overturn the finest Constitution and Church in the world with the agency of France, the most absolute monarchy, and Popery, the most superstitious religion, 'which retains little of Christianity but the name; and under the denomination of Christian, has in many instances restor'd the heathen idolatry.'[33] As the archbishop of York's chaplain admonished his hearers in the parish churches of Pickering and Thornton[34]

> Will you tamely resign our excellent constitution in Church and State, the work of ages—the masterpiece of human wisdom—the wonder and envy of the whole earth—to a band of mountaineers, headed by a Papist? Will you give up your country, the happiest country under Heaven, the land of Knowledge and Liberty, to an unciviliz'd and barbarous multitude?—Will you deliver up your children to be slaves, the most wretched of all slaves, the slaves of Popish Pride and Cruelty for evermore?

The answer was surely 'No'; an affirmative was unthinkable. 'I hope the mighty are not so sadly fallen, nor the use of the weapons of war so perished' commented William Drake in a sermon preached on 6 October 1745, 'as to be obliged to wear the iron yoke of slavery and arbitrary power, beat out for us on the anvils of France and Spain, and to be fitted to our necks by the unpolished hands of our uncultivated neighbours in the North.'[35]

Clearly war, even a civil war, was justified if one had right on one's side. The clergy had to balance the view that warfare was evil, an afflicting Providence, with the conviction that to fight could be a moral imperative. 'Our sins are the real cause of our misfortunes; our enemies are only the ministers of vengeance in the hands of Providence' Philip Barton admonished the House of Commons in January 1740. 'We have evidently lost the sobriety and seriousness of our forefathers, and are sunk into a delicate effeminacy and love of pleasure.'[36] On the same day the bishop of

---

[33] Samuel, bishop of Chester, *A sermon preached before the House of Lords . . . December 18, 1745* (London 1745) p 19.
[34] J. S. Hill, *False zeal and Christian zeal distinguished, or the essentials of Popery described* (London 1745) pp 25–6.
[35] W. Drake, *A sermon preached at Hatfield* (York 1745) pp 17–18.
[36] P. Barton, *The nature and advantages of a religious fast* (London 1740) pp 11–12.

Norwich assured the House of Lords that the war with Spain was justified:[37]

> If then the Almighty, the God of order, and Fountain of Power, has given the sword into his vicegerent's hands, to preserve his subjects quiet at home; to guard them from injuries abroad: If in one, as well as t'other, he is not to bear the sword in vain, it remains to be enquir'd when it may justly be unsheath'd in war, and how far we may, without presumption, depend on the Almighty for assistance in it . . . His Majesty justly asserts in his Declaration, his being obliged to make use of the power which God has given him: His people with one voice join in the same Declaration with him. Both of them, by the most glaring proofs, convinc'd of insults and indignities, of depredations and cruelties, that our countrymen have met with; such as must raise the resentment of a nation, as much distinguish'd by their courage in war, as by their skill in trade.

The bishop of London resolved the dilemma in a sermon preached in 4 February 1741:[38]

> It is a melancholy consideration that creatures endued with reason and humanity should ever come to employ force against one another, and make the dreadful addition of the miseries of war to the many unavoidable sufferings of life . . . yet when injuries of pernicious consequence are done to a nation, and persisted in, and no competent redress can be obtained, it becomes then, both necessary for particular societies and beneficial to humane society in general, that invaded rights be vigorously asserted by the only way left. When the sword is drawn for justice alone, and ever ready to be sheathed as soon as that is granted; then Heaven may be appealed to . . . But if the assertors of a righteous cause be in other respects a sinful people, it is evidently just for God, who hath the cognisance of both these things, to regard whichsoever of them infinite wisdom shall direct; and make even the injurious party the rod of his anger, and the staff in the day of his indignation, to correct or destroy, if their wickedness deserve it, such nations as, though right in their

---

[37] Thomas Gooch, bishop of Norwich, *A sermon preached before the House of Lords . . . January 9th 1739* [40] (London 1740) pp 10–11.
[38] Thomas Secker, bishop of London, *A sermon preached . . . Feb 4, 1740/1* (London 1741) pp 4–5.

disputes with their enemies, are wrong at the same time in matters more serious.

Lack of success in war, therefore, was not to be imputed to the injustice of waging it, but to continued indulgence in vice, as George Fothergill explained in *The unsuccessfulness of repeated fasts consider'd and apply'd*, a sermon preached on 9 January 1745, the sixth fast day to be proclaimed since the outbeak of the War of Jenkins' Ear. He had no doubt that fighting first Spain and then France was justified and necessary. The naval and military setbacks experienced by British forces were therefore due to the nation's ungodliness and immorality.

Conversely thanksgiving sermons were careful to stress that military success, while it might indicate God's approval of the justice of a war, did not also imply that He was pleased with the moral disposition of the nation. Samuel Lavington disabused his audience of any such conceit when he preached at Bideford on 29 November 1759:[39]

> It is not impossible that we may be so vain and arrogant as to . . . imagine that our extraordinary success is the reward of our extraordinary piety, and that it is because we have more religion and virtue than the rest of the world, that we have been so greatly and signally prospered. If indeed we sink into a forgetfulness what manner of people we are, we may thus imagine; but if we examine into the moral and religious state of the nation, if we enquire where any considerable numbers (in proportion to the bulk of the people) who are eminent for true godliness, for piety and purity, and for the profession and practice of pure and uncorrupted Christianity, reside, whether in the city or country, we have reason to blush at our hasty and mistaken computation, and to confess that we are preserved from general desolation as Sodom and Gomorrah might have been, by some few righteous persons found among us. For did ever iniquity abound more?

Thanksgiving sermons also followed a basically similar pattern. Victory in battle was not to be ascribed to the actions of men alone, but to God. Consequently, in order to continue to deserve the blessing of Providence on the armed forces, it was necessary

---

[39] S. Lavington, *God the giver of victory* (London 1760) pp 23–5.

Clergymen and conflict 1660–1763

for the nation to repent of its wicked ways, and to show gratitude for divine assistance by obeying God's will.

In order to demonstrate that success was providential some preachers went into details about the circumstances in which victory had been achieved. Thus Joseph Stennett explained the outcome of the battle of Dettingen:[40]

> if it be consider'd, that nothing appears to have been wanting either of skill or resolution on the part of the enemy, that they had greatly the advantage in their numbers, in the choice of the ground, of the manner of the attack, and to which I will add, the confidence they always have in the experience and ardour of their Gens d'armes, who are justly esteemed some of the finest and bravest troops in the whole world, while at the same time they were not ignorant that the far greater part of our British soldiers labour'd under the disadvantage of having never yet had an opportunity to see an enemy in the field, let all these things, I say, be consider'd, and then we shall not much wonder, that a nation, so void of the knowledge of God, should make themselves almost sure of victory; and since under all these disadvantages it has issued in our favour, surely every rational observer must own the extraordinary interposition of divine providence in our behalf.

The suppression of the Jacobite rebellion furnished preachers with numerous illustrations of providential intervention. Why did the rebels stay in Edinburgh so long after their initial success at Prestonpans, which they could have followed up with advantage? Why were British troops able to get across from the continent to oppose them in record time? Why did the storm of rain and hail on the morning of the battle of Culloden stop before the fighting began? The answer to all these questions was, Providence. It infatuated the Young Pretender and his adherents to stay in Scotland until England had been secured. It caused the wind to blow unusually favourably for the transport of troops from the continent. It created the weather conditions conducive to victory at Culloden.

Some preachers even suggested that Providence approved of the

---

[40] J. Stennett, *A sermon preached in Little Wild street the 17th of July 1743* (London 1743) pp 26–7.

slaughter of the rebels on the battlefield. 'In the plains (sic) of Culloden' asserted Thomas Gibbons 'the rebel army, after a prodigious, but righteous, slaughter, was totally routed by the British forces.'[41] 'Tho' their numbers, by all accounts, exceeded ours, how inconsiderable was the loss on our side?' queried John Allen. 'I believe History can hardly produce a victory and slaughter so great, with so little loss on the side of the conquerors. 'Tis true, one life of a free Briton is worth a thousand of theirs, but in a mere military computation our loss was as nothing.'[42] 'And now it remains that we rejoice' John Barker exhorted his hearers,[43]

> not that so many carcases were spread over the field of battle; not that Drummossy moor became an Aceldama, a field of blood; not that men tore one another to pieces by multitudes, and that Culloden was hardly able to bury or even to number her slain: We rejoice not that swords and bayonets, and the garments men wore, and the ground they stood on, were dyed and drenched in blood, and that their lives were destroyed by hundreds and thousands, and souls in equal numbers sent into Eternity . . .
>
> Over these things we lament, as the sad effects of war, and the reproach as well as calamity of human nature; But we rejoyce when our enemies made it necessary to oppose them, that it pleased God to preserve us from their outrage, to deliver them into our hands, and to cause them that hate us to flee or fall before us.

Few preachers were able to rise above such sentiments, one of them being Thomas Ashton, who urged his hearers, and readers,[44]

> to distinguish, as much as we can, between our own preservation and the destruction of our enemies, and though we cannot ever be sufficiently thankful for one, let us not shew an unmanly triumph in rejoicing over the other. Revenge is a sign of a little mind, and as unacceptable to God, as unbecoming in man. Let no spirit of that sort be mix'd with our Thanksgiving. The slaughter of so many of our fellow creatures is only to be justify'd on the foot of

---

[41] T. Gibbons, *The deliverance and triumph of Great Britain* (London 1746) p 23.
[42] J. Allen, *Rejoice with trembling* (London 1746) p 16.
[43] J. Barker, *A sermon occasioned by the victory obtained over the rebels* (London 1746) pp 27–8.
[44] T. Ashton, *A sermon preached in the collegiate chapel at Eton* (London 1746) p 18.

necessity. They were slain, as enemies; let them be remember'd, as men.

Jeremiah Gill, a dissenter, could even find it in his heart to pray for the Pretender, 'who was the principal author of our domestick troubles and confusions.'[45]

In the Seven Years' War the victories of the year 1759 seemed to be especially providential. 'We should count it our duty to take a delight in ascribing our success to Divine Providence' concluded Samuel Lavington, 'because it endears and sweetens our victories to consider them as proceeding from God, and as being an eminent and signal display of Divine Favour'[46]. He then proceeded to argue that the victory of Minden, and the taking of Guadeloupe, Louisbourg and Quebec, could not have been achieved against natural disadvantages without the assistance of supernatural powers.

There were some incidents, however, which did not fit immediately into a pattern of providential concern for British military efforts. Two in particular taxed the clergy, who had their work cut out to explain them; the deaths of Colonel James Gardiner at Prestonpans and General James Wolfe at Quebec. Gardiner's death especially concerned Philip Doddridge, the distinguished dissenting minister, since they had been personal friends. How a Christian hero could meet such a grim fate clearly worried him.[47]

> To have poured out his soul in blood; to have fallen by the savage and rebellious hands of his own countrymen at the wall of his own house; deserted by those who were under the heaviest obligations that can be imagined to have defended his life with their own; and above all to have seen with his dying eyes the enemies of our religion and liberties triumphant, and to have heard in his latest moments the horrid noise of their insulting shouts:—is a scene, in the view of which we are almost tempted to say, where were the shields of angels? Where the Eye of Providence? Where the remembrance of those numberless prayers which had been offered to God for the preservation of such a man, at such a time as this?

---

[45] J. Gill, *The importance and improvement of our late national deliverance* (London 1746) p 23.
[46] S. Lavington, *God the giver of victory* (London 1760) p 13.
[47] P. Doddridge, *The Christian warrior animated and crowned* (London 1745) pp 27–8.

Doddridge solved the problem to his own satisfaction by claiming that Gardiner died a martyr. Wolfe's death in the moment of victory was also problematic. Again it was explained, if not explained away, by making it a glorious death. To the archbishop of Armagh he set an example of the supreme sacrifice.[48]

Perhaps even more controversial was the implication that God not only blessed British arms but also approved of the actions of those who directed them, the king and his ministers. This made Providence an agent in political as well as in military matters. Signs that preachers differed in their politics can be detected even in wartime fast and thanksgiving sermons. For instance, those staunch for the government would include faction and a disposition to criticise authority among the sins allegedly bringing the nation close to destruction, while those opposed to the government would castigate corruption in high places amongst their catalogue of prevalent immoralities. When thanksgiving sermons were preached for peace in 1748 and 1763, however, the political aspects became more explicit. Neither peace was held to be completely satisfactory, both being regarded as sacrificing gains made in the wars. While all preachers had to present peace as a blessing, those who upheld the administration went out of their way to rebuke critics of the treaties of Aix la Chapelle and Paris. Joseph Stennett accused those who condemned the first as being 'the same set of men who justified and applauded the scandalous treaty of Utrecht' i.e. the tories.[49] John Richardson detected the machinations of the Jesuits behind the complaints of those who opposed the second.[50]

Such differences might have delighted those whom all preachers united to condemn, the sceptics who scoffed at the very notion of Providence intervening in mundane affairs. Judging by references to these in sermons they seem to have been regarded as an increasing menace. Significantly more preachers took the occasion to attack such scepticism in the Seven Years' War than in the War of the Austrian Succession. Why this should have been the case is not clear. Perhaps the concept of Providence received a setback from the controversies over the London earthquakes of 1750 and the Lisbon earthquake of 1756, which occurred between the two

---

[48] *A sermon preached in Christ Church, Dublin . . . Nov 29, 1759* (Dublin 1759) pp 17–18.
[49] J. Stennett, *A sermon preached at Little Wild Street . . . April 25, 1749* (London 1749) p 14.
[50] J. Richardson, *The sovereign goodness of the most high in putting an end to destructive wars* (London 1763) p 10.

wars. At all events those who believed in the constant interference of God in the affairs of men were clearly on the defensive against those who attributed such phenomena to natural causes. They clung fiercely to the notion of providential intervention in wars, since an attack on that would undermine their basic cosmology, which believed in metaphysical sanctions for morality. 'If there be such a thing in the world as Divine Providence' argued Nathaniel Ball, '(and that there is the course of nature shows through all her works) it cannot but operate in the momentous concerns of empires and kingdoms.'[51] 'Never can Providence be seen more conspicuously' agreed Richard Dayrell, 'never can man appear more weak than in times of dangers, difficulties and distresses;—and—can there be times more dangerous, more difficult and distressful, than when nation riseth up against nation?'[52]

It would be interesting to trace when and how this notion ceased to be accepted as a prime explanation of the cause and consequences of wars.[53] In all the furore over the thanksgiving service for the Falklands conflict nobody seriously rebuked the clergy for not asserting that God was on our side in it. Yet between 1660 and 1763 clergymen would have had a field day on such an occasion. A Protestant country renowned for its love of liberty was fighting a just war against a Popish nation infamous for its tyrannical regime. At the time of the amphibious operations the weather in the South Atlantic was unusually mild. The Argentinian bombs miraculously failed to detonate. The discrepancy in the numbers slain on each side was almost as remarkable as the casualty figures at Culloden. Yet only in praying for those slain on the enemy side were a few wartime sermons of the eighteenth century comparable to that delivered in St Paul's in July 1982. Otherwise the differences were so marked as to record a major shift in the thinking of clergymen on conflict in the last three hundred years.

University of Hull
Newcastle College of Arts & Technology

[51] N. Ball, *True religion, loyalty and union recommended to all orders of men* (London 1757) p 2.
[52] R. Dayrell, *A sermon preached before the . . . Commons . . . November 29, 1759* (London 1759) p 8.
[53] Roland Bartel traces the demise of the public fast days, which first came under serious criticism in the War of American Independence and finally petered out in Victoria's reign, in 'The story of public fast days in England' *Anglican Theological Review* (1955) 37 pp 190–200.

THE CHURCHES AND THE '45

by FRANÇOISE DECONINCK-BROSSARD

THE LIMITS of this short paper will not allow me to give a full account of the question, but only to consider some aspects of the sermons preached on the occasion of the 1745 Jacobite rebellion. There was a spate of sermons published at the time, not only by famous whig bishops, understandably eager to prove their zeal for the house of Hanover, but also by unknown members of the inferior clergy who felt the need to express their loyalty to the establishment. In many cases, the sermons they preached were the only ones they ever published. It is worth noting, in this respect, that the names of only five antijacobite preachers are to be found in the *DNB*. This phenomenon, namely the crucial part played by humble preachers, is all the more remarkable as it is in marked contrast with other fields of eighteenth-century pulpit oratory. (Charity sermons, for instance, could only be delivered by bishops or archdeacons or by well-known speakers with a good preaching reputation). Besides, non-conformist ministers were as anxious as their Church of England counterparts to be regarded as pillars of the Hanoverian cause, so that they too had many sermons printed for the occasion. From the available evidence, it is reasonable to assume that they sold well. On the flyleaf of any one of these pamphlets, John Hildyard, the York printer, with his usual advertising techniques, set out a list of other sermons published on the same theme, as an incentive to buy further books on the subject.

The most striking feature of these sermons is their mutual resemblance. They all use the same words, the same examples, and even the same quotations, so much so that it is often difficult to know a preacher's denomination, unless the title page specifically mentions it. It looks as though the preachers were guided by the same political and religious blueprints.

One of the most popular biblical references, for instance, is the story of Sennacherib's invasion of Judah, which was alluded to as early as September 1745. The preacher chose to elaborate on the episode as related in the second book of the Chronicles (2

clergy of their diocese, and reminded them of their duty to preach the doctrine of civil obedience. Thus, John Daville, master of a grammar-school at York, dedicated to the archbishop the sermon he had preached at the end of September 'in Obedience to his Grace's Instructions to his Clergy'.[6] Silence in these circumstances would have meant nothing short of treason.

Indeed, the rebellion had to be fought precisely because it questioned Britain's political institutions, as one writer noticed from the start:

> Should We give up our present King, the King of our Choice, we may give up the Choice of our King, and so give up our Constitution, for ever.[7]

The threats of civil war loomed large on the horizon. The preachers reminded their congregations of all the horrors of internecine struggles:

> And, to give you a full and compleat Notion of the Mischiefs of publick Perjury and Rebellion, I must pass before your Eyes a melancholy Scene of a fruitful and happy Country made a Place of Desolation and a Field of Blood; I must represent to you Friends, Neighbours, Brethren, all at fatal Variance, and sheathing their Swords in one anothers Bowels; I must represent to you all Property confounded, and our Goods and Possessions made the Prey of the next Invader; I must fill up the frightful Scene with Houses torn down and rifled; Temples, which now appear in their just Beauty and Magnificence, defaced, and levelled with the Ground; Villages burnt up; Cities laid in Ashes: In one Word, I must represent to your Eyes (what I hope you will never see but in Imagination) our excellent King, possessed of as much Justice and Mercy and Good-nature as ever Prince was endowed with, falling by the Hands of blood-thirsty Rebellion; our Country ruined; our Religion, Laws and Liberties wrested and torn from us.[8]

Such unusual devices in eighteenth-century pulpit rhetoric as the

---

[6] John Daville, *A Sermon Preached at York, On Sunday the 29th of September, 1745. On Occasion of the Present Rebellion* (York n.d.).

[7] Robert Hargreaves, *Unanimity, Recommended* [stc] *in a Sermon, Preached September the 22nd. 1745. The Sunday before the Association at York* (York 1746) p 19.

[8] Thomas Herring, *A Sermon Preach'd At the Cathedral Church of York, September the 22nd, 1745; On the Occasion of the Present Rebellion in Scotland* (York 1745) pp 15–16.

repetition of 'I must', the accumulation of gloomy scenes, and the acceleration of sentence rhythm appealed to the imagination of the hearers to convey the reality of the horrors of civil war. It is also worth noting the close interconnection of politics, religion, and economics, which was a recurrent theme in the sermons of the time. The preachers felt that free trade could only develop in a country that provided the appropriate background, that is to say political freedom and religious tolerance, because a totalitarian regime could not allow the necessary competition:

> And as it is certain that nothing but Liberty can make Commerce flourish, so nothing but the Success of Commerce can give Life and Vigour to our respective Crafts.[9]

In short, the orators had a clear-cut view of the world. There was, on the one hand, a constitutional monarchy that could guarantee the individual's inalienable rights to think and trade as he pleased. On the other hand, Catholic countries whined under the threefold burden of arbitrary power, religious persecution and economic oppression. The constant interference of theology, politics and economy enabled the bishop of Chester to draw an unexpected parallel between taxation and transubstantiation:

> The chief Agents in this Rebellion may make fair Promises, but no one will believe them, but they who have Faith to believe Transubstantiation. Do they tell us they will ease us for our Taxes? But will they not rather impose much heavier upon us?. . .
>
> Instead of those tolerable Burthens we now bear (and which the Papists and their Fellow-labourers have brought upon us, by defending our selves against their Plots to destroy us) all we have will be too little to satisfy their Cravings. The Demands of *France* for the Support of an abdicating Monarch and his Family; the Demands of the Court of *Rome* for it's [sic] Expence on that Account; the Reimbursing the *English* Papists and others of this Nation for their Contributions to that Purpose; the Satisfaction to be made for the dispossessing of the right Heir to the Crown, as he is called, for 40 or 50

---

[9] John Brown, *The Mutual Connexion between Religious Truth and Civil Freedom; Between Superstition, Tyranny, Irreligion, and Licentiousness: Considered in Two Sermons Preached in Septemb. 1746, At the Cathedral Church of Carlisle, During the Assizes Held there for the Trial of the Rebels* (London n.d.) p 21.

Years; the Restitution of Religious Houses, Church Lands, and Tythes to the regular *Romish* Clergy, with a long, very long & *caetera*, will amount to an immense Tax indeed.[10]

Whether or not he was right in assuming that taxes would necessarily increase if the Stuarts were restored to the throne is irrelevant here. What is important is the relationship between religious controversy and economic theory. It sounds obvious to the bishop that it would be naïve to believe that a Catholic could keep his promises, whether financial, religious or political.

Now, these preachers were convinced that Britain had not only the best taxation system, but also the best constitution in the world:

> The temporal Prosperity and Happiness of a People depends in a great measure on the Form of its Government, and the Laws it is governed by; and in both these necessary Requisites we are singularly happy, and excel. For our Constitution or Civil Government is admirably calculated for the Good of the whole Community; nay, I may add, of almost every Individual; since every Order of Men in it has its proper Share and Influence in the Management of its publick Concerns, and has its distinct Province to act in. The Prince has a Prerogative essential and peculiar to himself, the Peer has his Privilege, whilst the Commoner's Vote gives him an equal Influence in Publick Determinations and Counsels. Of these three Orders the State is happily compos'd, who (tho' they have been mostly unanimous under the prudent and mild Administration of his present Majesty, and some other good Princes) have sometimes been a mutual Check upon each other's Incroachments, have nobly curb'd a Tyranny and Tyrants in opposition to that very absurd and untenable Doctrine of indefeasible and hereditary Right. This wise Polity, this just Equilibrium of Power is the Bulwark and Support of our Independency and Freedom; to this we owe our Affluence at Home, our lucrative and extensive Commerce Abroad. 'Tis this happy Mixture and Disposition

---

[10] Samuel Peploe, *Popish Idolatry a strong Reason why all Protestants Should Zealously Oppose the Present Rebellion. A Sermon Preached in the Cathedral Church of Chester, On Sunday, the 13th of October, 1745, The Mayor and Corporation Being Present* (London 1745) p 14.

of Government, which makes us the Admiration and Envy of our Neighbours.'[11]

It was therefore logical that they should have felt that they were fighting for a good cause:

> The Cause for which we strive is the Cause of God.—We fight for Light and Truth against Error and Darkness—We fight for Reason and Freedom against the most wicked Tyranny that ever was known in the World—We fight for the Authority of *Christ* our Lord, against the impious Damnation of *Rome*—We fight for Christianity as it appears in the Discourses of *Christ* Himself, and the Writings of his Apostles; against Popery, the most execrable Corruption and Perversion of Christianity that can enter into Human Imagination.[12]

The idea that God was on the side of the Hanoverian cause had already been conveyed by the reference to Sennacherib's invasion of Judah. Indeed Hezekiah, whom the preachers identified with George II, had told his people that they need not be afraid of the impending war because God was with them to help them and fight their battles (2 Chronicles 32: 7–8). So it should be no surprise to find our preachers repeating time and again after Culloden that God had granted them victory in a just war:

> This is that blessed Establishment, which we have all imaginable Reason to conclude is highly acceptable to our God; since he has so often before, and now very recently done such great Things for its Continuance and Preservation, when *the Princes of this World and the Powers of Darkness* were so strongly united against us, as to make the Success of their execrable Attempt even more than probable, had not the Almighty most seasonably interpos'd, and *saved us with the Shield of his Strength and the Sword of his Excellency*.[13]

---

[11] John Du Pont, *The Peculiar Happiness [and Excellency of the British Nation consider'd and explain'd: A Sermon Preach'd at Aysgarth, October 9, 1746. Being the Day appointed by Authority for the Celebration of a General Thanksgiving to Almighty God, for the Success of His Majesty's Arms, under His Royal Highness the Duke of Cumberland; and for the entire Suppression of the late wicked and most unnatural Rebellion in Scotland* (London 1747)] pp 11–13..

[12] J. S. Hill, *False Zeal and Christian Zeal distinguish'd, or The Essentials of Popery describ'd. A Sermon Preach'd in The Parish Churches of Thornton and Pickering, in Yorkshire. On Occasion of the Present Rebellion* (York 1745) pp 29–30.

[13] John Du Pont, *The Peculiar Happiness* pp 18–19.

So convinced were these preachers that British people were 'the Darlings of God's Providence'[14] and that they were waging a just war, that even in the darkest hours of 1745 they never lost hope. When the dissenting minister Thomas Bradbury preached on Guy Fawkes's night that year, the text of his sermon was 'God is with us' (Isaiah 8: 9–10), which he proceeded to explain:

> These Words agree to the Situation that the People of God are oftentimes brought into. Here's,
> 1. Their Danger by confederate Enemies, where Fear is on every side. They are vexed with all manner of Adversity.
> 2. Their great and only Security, the Hope that is set before them, the Lord is with us. Or you may give the Distribution another Turn; that here's a Prospect of Deliverance to the Church under all their Affrightments and Dangers.[15]

Although he acknowledges that 'our Distress at this Day is like theirs, who are mentioned in this Text',[16] his confidence will not be shaken.

If God is on the side of the establishment, then conversely the rebels deserve their punishment, whether it be death on the battlefield, imprisonment, hard labour or hanging. The theme is developed in a sermon with a significant title, *The False Claims to Martyrdom Considered*:

> These false Cries of Persecution have been the Ground of false Claims to Martyrdom; for it is not Suffering alone that constitutes the Character of a Martyr, but the Cause for which a Man suffers . . . . Whoever has deservedly drawn on himself the Resentment of publick Justice, thro' any Instance of wrong Conduct, by engaging in a Sedition or Rebellion, suffers not as a Martyr, but is punish'd as a malefactor, and a criminal Opposer of just Authority.[17]

Besides, the sermon is not devoid of pity for these young men's untimely deaths. However sympathetic the preacher may have felt towards the individuals—for he was more tolerant and open-minded than many of his contemporaries, he could not help

---

[14] *Ibid* p 6.
[15] Thomas Bradbury, *God is with Us: A Sermon on the Fourth of November, 1745* (London 1745) p 1.
[16] *Ibid* p 15.
[17] Benjamin Nicholls, *The False Claims to Martyrdom Considered. A Sermon Preached at St Anne's Church, Manchester, Nov. 2, 1746. Being the Sunday after All-Saints Day* (London 1746) pp 22–23.

The churches and the '45

thinking they had received a fair reward for the principles they had acted upon:

> But let us not suffer ourselves to be so imposed upon; sorry we may be for the untimely End of our Fellow-Creatures, but to honour them with the Title of Martyrdom for publick Offences is to disgrace the Character, and to blaspheme our Religion.[18]

Other preachers even went as far as emphasising the clemency shown by the government in the necessary suppression of what they regarded as 'unnatural', that is to say unjustified, subversion:

> Was the ancient Law of Retaliation. . . to take place. . . The Life of every individual Rebel, who drops by the Hand of the Executioner, would be a very inadequate Satisfaction for the great Numbers of Loyalists, who perished in their Country's Cause, bravely contending for Religion and Liberty. Let then this Theme of Mercy. . . be considered in every Light possible, and we shall not be able to find, strictly speaking, the least Claim these Men can pretend, to expect the Benefit of it at present. Instead thereof, all honest Men. . . have Cause to rejoice in their Fall.[19]

Strange as they may seem to our modern ears, these words were written by one of the most moderate antijacobite preachers, Thomas Maddock. Actually, one may say that, in so far as only one hundred and twenty people were executed altogether in London, York and Carlisle in the aftermath of the rebellion, the suppression of the rising was not cruel by eighteenth-century standards, which proves the preacher right. The civil war he and his colleagues so dreaded had to a large extent been avoided, though, of course, the conflict had taken its toll of human lives on both sides, as unfortunately military contests will do. Hard as the preachers tried to explain that their enemies had deserved their fate, they could not conceal the bloodshed that had taken place:

> [the rebels at Culloden] aton'd in Part for their past Barbarities and not to be extenuated Perfidiousness, with a large Effusion of their Blood. Thus it pleas'd the Almighty to

---

[18] Ibid p 27.
[19] Thomas Maddock, *A Sermon Preached at St. George's Church, in Liverpool, Before the Worshipful The Mayor and Corporation, On the Ninth of October, 1746. Being The Day of Publick Thanksgiving, Appointed by Authority, For the Suppression of the late Unnatural Rebellion* (London 1746) p 15.

deliver us, by this one important and decisive Blow, from our domestick Enemies and Troubles. How much he was graciously pleased to intefere in that critical Moment, when every Thing that is dear to a free and Protestant People was at Stake, the little Blood that was spilt on our Side undeniably evinces; whilst Thousands of our Adversaries lay weltring and expiring at our victorious Feet.[20]

However, it is reasonable to assume that the preachers, using all their powers of persuasion to paint vivid pictures of the horrors of civil war and to rekindle the fear of Popery and France, had been instrumental in preventing the rebellion from swelling to uncontrollable proportions. The king was aware of this. That is why he promoted Thomas Herring to the see of Canterbury as a reward for following the advice he had been given by Lord Hardwicke:

> One thing I have always observed is:—that representing the Pretender as coming (as the truth is) under a dependence upon French support; I say, stating this point, together with Popery, in a strong light, has always the most popular effect.[21]

Université de Picardie,
Amiens (France).

---

[20] John Du Pont, *The Peculiar Happiness* pp 26–27.
[21] R. Garnett, *EHR* vol 19 p 535.

ENGLISH EVANGELICAL DISSENT AND THE EUROPEAN CONFLICT 1789-1815

by DERYCK LOVEGROVE

IN NOVEMBER 1789 a notable address was delivered at the meeting-house in Old Jewry in the city of London to the society formed to commemorate the glorious revolution.[1] The overtly political tone of Richard Price's words to that audience of dissenters and fellow-sympathisers appeared to Edmund Burke to epitomise the democratic and levelling spirit already operating with such devastating results across the Channel.[2] Eight years later the fear of dissenting ambition was if anything enhanced. In a rising tide of clerical polemic dissenters were accused of a variety of evils including anti-establishment activity, schism, covert Jacobinism, regicide and the encouragement of fanaticism and ignorance among the lower classes. At a time when England was embroiled in a long and costly struggle with revolutionary France the real charge was that of siding with the enemy; of implicit disloyalty. The principal difference from 1789, a distinction not always apparent to the accusers, was that those now engaging their attention were evangelicals, men of an entirely different stamp from the provocative rationalists surrounding Priestley and Price.

This shift of clerical attention to orthodox dissenters was a significant development. Viewed from the national perspective they represented an ecclesiastical and social force of greater potential than the handful of highly articulate rationalists entertaining avant garde religious, political and intellectual views in urban centres such as London and Birmingham. Their importance lay particularly in the high level of active social contact achieved, and it is no coincidence that establishment polemic entered its most strident phase precisely when that social impact was at its most potent and dynamic, in the years immediately after 1797.

The mid 1790s witnessed not only the rise of the overseas missionary effort spearheaded by dissenters, but also the launching

[1] Richard Price, *A Discourse on the Love of Our Country* (London 1790).
[2] Edmund Burke, *Reflections on the Revolution in France and on the Proceedings in Certain Societies in London relative to that Event* (London 1790) p 12.

of a highly effective nationwide programme of home evangelism penetrating the most remote rural communities, using both ordained and lay itinerant preachers, organised and financed through an impressive network of itinerant associations and seminaries, and informed by a comprehensive, new periodical publication, *The Evangelical Magazine*. At the moment when the establishment principle had been overthrown in France by overt means, a rapid erosion appeared to be taking place in England through more subtle, less tangible, yet equally subversive channels.

The foundations for the suspicion of disloyalty had been laid somewhat earlier. Orthodox dissenters of a traditional stamp like John Clayton, minister of the King's Weigh-House chapel in London, remained conspicuously loyal and quietist,[3] but a new generation of evangelical leaders had emerged in the early 1790s; men like David Bogue the Independent minister at Gosport, James Hinton the Baptist pastor of a mixed congregation of dissenters in Oxford, Mark Wilks of Norwich and Robert Hall of Cambridge, representing a new individualist and voluntarist view of society at large. In striking contrast to the pessimistic Calvinism with which their predecessors had been associated, their own meliorist version of the doctrine espoused the general spirit of progress of the age and in doing so linked them somewhat anomalously with the rationalist inheritance of the eighteenth century. As the revolution in France moved in an increasingly ugly direction, so their initial approbation changed to an embarrassed silence and even denunciation.[4] But the damage had been done: if any assistance was necessary those who supported the establishment now found it easy to associate the increasingly active evangelicals with the agencies of subversion, destruction and violence and to represent them from the most extreme point of view as fifth-columnists.

[3] In *The Duty of Christians to Magistrates: a Sermon, occasioned by the late Riots at Birmingham* (London nd [1791]). Clayton argued that dissenters were not as a body disaffected towards the government.

[4] Their broad approval for the principles and the spirit behind the French revolution had been expressed in a number of publications, including: *Reasons for Seeking a Repeal of the Corporation and Test Acts, Submitted to the Consideration of the Candid and Impartial*. By a Dissenter [David Bogue] (1790); Mark Wilks, *The Origin and Stability of the French Revolution; A Sermon, preached at St Paul's Chapel, Norwich . . . July 14, 1791* (Norwich 1791); Robert Hall, *Christianity Consistent with a Love of Freedom* (London 1791). The change in attitude was not universal, however, for James Bicheno, Baptist minister at Newbury, continued to show a distinct sympathy for the young French republic and a corresponding opposition to British militarism. Mark Wilks also retained outspokenly radical views.

English dissent and the European conflict

In spite of the democratic sympathies expressed and the imprisonment of at least one orthodox dissenter for the public statement of such ideas,[5] and notwithstanding the crescendo of accusation concerning the political provenance and sinister atavism to be detected in the wave of evangelical activity, the surviving records of dissenting associations concerned with itinerant evangelism maintain an almost complete silence on political matters. Even during the period of heightened political tension when war with France brought with it the threat of imminent invasion, this absence of political comment remained the rule. The omission can be attributed to several possible causes. By emphasising exclusion from the rights of full citizenship the abortive movement to abolish the Test and Corporation Acts may have reinforced the sense of detachment towards social and political affairs traditionally exhibited by the general body of English dissenters.[6] There was undoubtedly a desire by those who adopted the traditional position to demonstrate political reliability and thereby to preserve existing freedoms. Within such a viewpoint political quiescence appeared axiomatic. To these considerations must be added the more general pietist distaste for participation in secular affairs; the strong conviction that evangelical activity rather than politics was the proper sphere for the Christian.

Some evangelistic societies formulated an explicit 'no politics' rule;[7] others contented themselves with avowals of their nonpolitical character.[8] Even for individuals there was a widespread belief that politics were not a legitimate interest for those engaged in evangelism. In a typical ordination charge in 1807, William Steadman, before urging the duty of itinerancy as part of the local

---

[5] William Winterbotham, a Baptist minister from Plymouth, was found guilty of sedition by a jury at the Devon assizes in 1793 and was sentenced to four years imprisonment and a fine of £200. The basis of the charge consisted of statements made in two sermons preached in November 1792.

[6] See for example the article entitled 'The civil state of dissenters in England' in [*The Baptist Annual*] *Register* [ed J.] Rippon 4 vols (London 1793–1802) 1 p 524.

[7] The minute book of the Essex congregational union formed in 1798 records as an initial resolution the decision 'That at the meetings of this union no political conversation be introduced'. Essex County Record Office, D/NC 9/1.

[8] See for example the 1800 report issued by the ministers of the Staffordshire congregational association quoted by A. G. Matthews, *The Congregational Churches of Staffordshire* (London 1924) pp 197–8; also the 1812 circular letter of the Northamptonshire baptist association pp 3–4.

pastoral commitment issued a warning against the 'snare' of politics which had only a few years previously caused 'no small injury both to ministers and people, by employing too much of their time and thoughts'.[9]

Within the records of evangelical organisations political comment in the period prior to 1815 was normally confined to issues of direct concern to their own religious interests: the attempt to repeal the Test and Corporation Acts, the impact of the window tax on seminary buildings, proposals to restrict itinerancy by legislation, and the campaign waged in 1813 to allow missionaries into India. Most unrestricted and aggressive in its political aspect was the moral campaign against the slave trade in which dissenters sided with the Clapham sect.

This non-political stance did not imply a lack of awareness or insulation from the general climate of war fever. Dissenters suffered from the same taxes and shortages as other citizens, they faced the same threat of invasion, and in the majority of cases ran the same risk of compulsory service in the militia (although they did enjoy certain exemptions in this area and the majority of church members would have been unlikely to have enlisted in the armed forces voluntarily).

The expression of corporate attitudes towards the conflict with France where it did emerge showed some degree of variance. In December 1792 in the wake of loyalist activity by the citizens of Southampton, the town's dissenters chaired by the Independent minister of Above Bar chapel, William Kingsbury, himself to become a prominent apologist for village preaching, reinforced their membership of the local loyal association with a statement expressing sincere attachment to the existing constitution.[10] Over the following decades a succession of similar declarations of support for government and monarchy issued at the national level from the committee of the Deputies and from the General Body of Protestant Dissenting Ministers of the Three Denominations. At crucial moments in the war with France this loyalty was

[9] W. Steadman, *The Christian Minister's Duty and Reward. A sermon addressed as a charge to Mr Richard Pengilly, when ordained pastor of the baptist church at Newcastle upon Tyne, August 12, 1807* (Gateshead 1807) pp 21–22. Steadman advised Pengilly, 'I do not wish you to be wholly ignorant of the political state of your country ... but do not, I beseech you, let politics engross so much of your thoughts, or your conversation, as to cause the duties of the citizen to interfere with those of the preacher'.

[10] A. T. Patterson, *A History of Southampton* (Southampton 1966) pp 84–5.

English dissent and the European conflict

reiterated. John Rippon, the minister of Carter Lane Particular Baptist congregation in Southwark, preached in encouraging tones to the volunteers at Margate on 19 October 1803 and repeated the sermon in front of various congregations of dissenters and volunteers during the following weeks as England awaited Napoleon's invasion. Two years later, after the victory at Trafalgar, the London itinerant society joined many churches in taking up collections in aid of a patriotic fund.[11] Not only was there a considerable measure of positive support but any sign of disaffection was promptly condemned. In November 1793 the trustees of Cheshunt College[12] lost no time in investigating the truth of an allegation that 'all the students [were] disaffected to the present government, and wish[ed] success to the French Revolution'. At the quarterly meeting of the parent society held on 1 January 1794, the college president declared that the charge was groundless.[13]

Far more common, however, than these affirmations of support for the loyalist cause were remarks of an entirely neutral character conveying only a sense of the horror of war and a belief that in the midst of the contemporary state of political upheaval and crisis the Christian's duty was to pray for the return of peace and to do good wherever possible. In 1794 the report of three congregations in the Baptist western association noted that the churches 'are in peace themselves, but lament, as most of the sister churches do, a war, by which thousands in different counties [sic?] are reduced to penury and starving; and thousands on thousands have been unnecessarily hurried into the eternal state'.[14] The inaugural sermon for the Bedfordshire Union of Christians in October 1797 conveyed concisely the sense of crisis then prevailing: 'Never was there such an age as that in which we live. The nations are shaken. The desire of all nations approaches'. The sermon in its appeal for 'real Christians' to unite in the task of evangelising their society disclaimed any objects other than the purely religious and displayed a curious sense of detachment from the scene of international chaos.[15]

---

[11] Minutes 20 December 1805, Congregational Library, MS Ii 35.
[12] The successor of the Countess of Huntingdon's institution at Trevecca for the training of itinerant preachers.
[13] Apostolic society minutes, Cambridge, Westminster College, Cheshunt MS C1/2.
[14] Rippon, *Register* 2 p 184.
[15] S. Greatheed, *General Union Recommended to Real Christians in a Sermon preached at Bedford, October 31, 1797* (London 1798) pp viii–ix and xvi–xvii.

An absence of personal involvement in war there may have been, yet many felt the need to continue the earlier eighteenth-century tradition of observing days of fasting and prayer for the return of peace. At Olney John Sutcliff the Baptist pastor prayed daily for a cessation of hostilities between England and France,[16] and his personal concern merely reflected at the individual level the attitude of many county associations and local congregations throughout the years of war.[17] The combination of pacifist idealism and evangelistic endeavour is shown most clearly in some words addressed by David Bogue to the Hampshire association of Independent ministers in 1797:

> On the stable foundation of Christianity endeavour to the utmost of your power to promote the peace of the world, and to aid in giving the deadly blow to destruction and misery which have extended their triumphs so widely over the face of the earth. But to display the spirit of peace is not enough for a Christian. To be blameless and harmless forms but a small part of his character. To a pacific temper you must unite benevolence; and like Jesus of Nazareth go about doing good.[18]

Both the assessment of the international situation and the impulse to evangelise tended to be associated in evangelical pronouncements with those apocalyptic expectations which characterised the later 1790s.[19] The blows suffered by the papal *imperium* together with the more general political cataclysm brought even to the most cautious mind those eschatological passages of the bible connected with the downfall of Antichrist and the onset of the millennium. At least one contemporary writer, James Bicheno of Newbury, responded to the situation with a detailed hermeneutical interest which he sustained through six or more publications spanning the period from 1793 to 1817, trimming his interpretation of scripture to each new political circumstance. Most commenta-

---

[16] Anonymous unpublished typescript entitled 'Sutcliff: the meeting and the man', Bristol Baptist College, MSS G98 p 139.
[17] For example 1807 circular letter of the Oxfordshire and East Gloucestershire baptist association p 14; 1812 circular letter of the baptist midland association p 12; Blunham Bedfordshire Old Meeting House (baptist) minutes 24 January 1794.
[18] Hampshire association circular letter 1797 p 3.
[19] Late-eighteenth and early-nineteenth-century millennial views are discussed by S. C. Orchard, 'English Evangelical eschatology 1790-1850' (unpublished PhD thesis, Cambridge 1969); see also D. N. Hempton, 'Evangelicalism and eschatology' *JEH* 31 (1980) pp 179-194.

English dissent and the European conflict

tors, however, contented themselves like William Roby of Manchester with the more circumspect if somewhat imprecise conviction that Christ's reign was rapidly approaching.[20]

Despite this heightened millennial interest the immediate preoccupation of the later 1790s lay with evangelism. By comparison with the energy expended on that objective the war with France retreated to the periphery of dissenting consciousness. Even so its impact was felt as it created both limitations and opportunities for those involved in itinerant preaching. It was by no means uncommon during the early years for preachers to be interrupted or even physically assaulted, but it seems to have been largely a matter of chance that James Hinton's assailants during a service in the village of Woodstock near Oxford included a group of Irish recruits *en route* for their regiment.[21] More serious yet equally fortuitous was the threat posed by the Nore mutiny and by government counter-measures to the commencement of itinerancy in the Rayleigh area of Essex in June 1797.[22] Neither of these events held any sinister implications for dissenting evangelism. Opportunities even arose out of the very circumstance of war. Probably the most obvious example is seen in the visits paid by itinerants and by academy students to French prisoners of war interned in camps like those at Porchester and at Norman Cross in Huntingdonshire.[23] Few details of this enterprise are available but those that do exist indicate a desire to turn the events of war to direct missionary advantage.

In one specific aspect of the war dissenters were brought by the claims of conscience into regular conflict with the authorities. Under the provisions of the local militia legislation they were subject to the ballot for service in its ranks, only those described as 'Protestant Dissenting ministers' being exempt. The issue of exemption was one which in wartime and in the context of evangelistic expansion was almost bound to cause trouble. Recognised ministers were unquestionably exempt from service:

---

[20] W. Roby, *The Glory of the Latter Days* (2 ed London 1814) preface.
[21] *The Protestant Dissenter's Magazine* 6 vols (London 1794–99) 2 pp 252–256.
[22] Essex baptist association minute book 1805–1864, introductory historical notes, Baptist Union Library.
[23] J. Bennett, *Memoirs of the Life of the Rev. David Bogue, D.D.* (London 1827) p 214; J. Brown, *The History of the Bedfordshire Union of Christians. The Story of a Hundred Years* ed D. Prothero (London 1946) p 54.

but this was a period of less formal categories. How were academy students and the growing number of full-time itinerants to be treated? From the meeting-house viewpoint the issue was clear-cut: such men merited exemption in the same way as settled ministers. To the more determined supporters of the establishment like viscount Sidmouth qualifying as an undisciplined itinerant was clearly a device employed by the devious and disaffected to escape the obligations of loyal citizenship.[24] A loophole, therefore, needed to be closed.

Apart from the wider issue of countering the moral damage to society occasioned by the teaching of military skills to schoolchildren[25] or by the profanation of the sabbath with drilling and exercises,[26] a concerted attempt was made to keep theological students out of the militia either by paying the fines imposed on those who refused to serve or by insuring against the eventuality of selection in the periodic ballot. Thus it was that in 1808 Bristol Academy paid £5 10s. 'insuring five students from the militia' and a further £20 fine to excuse another man whose name had been drawn in the ballot.[27] The same academy had earlier appealed to the committee of the Deputies for advice as to whether or not the local magistrates were entitled to refuse permission for its students to qualify as dissenting teachers and if they would in consequence be liable for militia service or for finding a substitute. The reply had indicated that the most natural interpretation of the law did not give grounds for optimism.[28] One of Sidmouth's declared intentions in putting his bill to amend the Toleration Act before the House of Lords in May 1811, was to remove any ambiguity and allow only ministers of settled congregations to qualify for the privilege of exemption.[29] The unnecessarily provocative character of his proposed measure ensured its almost immediate demise, but

---

[24] *A Sketch of* [*the History and Proceedings of*] *the Deputies* [*appointed to Protect the Civil Rights of the Protestant Dissenters*] (London 1814) pp 105, 112, 117.

[25] As happened at the dissenting school in Leaf Square, Manchester, minutes 11 February 1812, Manchester Congregational College MSS.

[26] Apparent provision for Sunday training in militia bills of 1796 and 1806 stimulated dissenting fears and opposition. See minutes of the General Body of Protestant Dissenting Ministers for 3 November 1796–11 April 1797 and 15 April 1806, Dr. Williams's Library, MS 38.106–107.

[27] Bristol education society annual report 1808.

[28] Dissenting Deputies minutes for 29 November and 27 December 1799, Guildhall Library, MS 3083.

[29] *A Sketch of the Deputies* pp 115–7 and 120–1.

English dissent and the European conflict

in spite of a positive clarification concerning the situation of itinerant ministers, that of theological students remained the same, with exemption being denied to them.

The customary silence of the evangelical voice concerning matters political was broken only at one point in the course of the deepening international crisis, and even then by a small, though not insignificant, section of the leadership. In the months following the treaty of Amiens, while Britain moved rapidly from the brief experience of peace with her neighbour to the tense expectation of invasion, important sermons were preached by three prominent Baptist ministers: Joseph Hughes and John Rippon both with churches on the outskirts of the metropolis, and Robert Hall by contrast speaking in the provincial atmosphere of Cambridge and Bristol. Completely undenominational in tone the four sermons they produced on the subject of war reveal a good deal about the attitudes, preoccupations and differences prevailing among evangelical dissenters.[30] The views expressed take care to eschew political partisanship, confining their attention to the general implications of the war with France.

Central to each of the sermons is a view of history in which war is linked to the concept of divine sovereignty. As with any other human or natural event warfare for the evangelical Calvinist lies firmly within the sphere of providence. The writers, therefore, are able to regard it as a divine chastisement inflicted by God in response to national wickedness.[31] The corollary consists in the refutation of any idea of purely natural origins.[32] While Hall is prepared to recognise the importance of inquiry into the underlying causes of such calamities, they are at most secondary influences at the disposal of 'a Being placed above them, who can move and arrange them at pleasure.' The ultimate purpose of the

---

[30] In order of delivery the four sermons were: Robert Hall, *Reflections* [*on War A Sermon, preached at the Baptist Meeting, Cambridge, on Tuesday, June 1, 1802 being the day of thanksgiving for a general peace*]; Joseph Hughes, *Britain's Defence*. [*A Sermon, preached, August 21, 1803, in the Protestant Dissenting Meeting-House, Battersea*]; Robert Hall, [*The*] *Sentiments* [*Proper to the Present Crisis: A Sermon, preached at Bridge Street, Bristol, October 19, 1803; being the day appointed for a general fast*]; John Rippon, [*A*] *Discourse* [*delivered at the Drum Head, on the Fort, Margate, Oct. 19, 1803, the day of the general fast, before the Volunteers, commanded by the Right Hon. William Pitt; . . . and then addressed to the Volunteers of London and Southwark, Assembled with the Author's own Congregation in Carter Lane, near London Bridge, Nov. 13, 1803*].

[31] Rippon, *Discourse* (4 ed London nd) p 3.

[32] Hall, *Sentiments*, *Works* 1 ed O. Gregory (11ed London 1853) p 137.

visitation of such punishments is to induce men to acknowledge God's supremacy.[33]

With such a theory of causation introspection is inevitable, and it is scarcely surprising that each of the 1803 sermons is marked by a strong preoccupation with the moral state of the nation. A variety of evils prevalent in British national life is listed from sexual immorality and profaneness to the enormity of the slave trade, though underlying these more obvious manifestations of iniquity is seen to be the alarming scale of contemporary irreligion.[34] Britain finds herself faced with an invasion which can easily be interpreted as the legitimate outcome of her own moral behaviour. Yet the overall note sounded remains one of hope: a belief that the adverse characteristics are more than balanced by the evident signs of God's favour to the nation and by a noticeable revival of godliness both among the civilian population and within the ranks of the armed forces. Hughes succinctly expresses this optimism saying: 'I cannot persuade myself that on such a land the vengeance of the Almighty is about to pour down despair and ruin. We have too many righteous and devout men among us to permit the apprehension.'[35] This is a conviction upon which subsequent patriotic exhortations to personal virtue and to the courageous performance of military duty are able to build.

All the writers regard war as a scourge and as a lamentable calamity. In the course of such national conflicts many people are launched precipitately into an unexpected eternity, and civilian populations suffer the terrible experience of pillage, rape and murder at the hands of marauding armies; indeed Britain herself faces that prospect if Napoleon's invasion is successful. There is, moreover, the insidious moral influence of warfare: creating injustice, undermining the spirit of common humanity, inuring people to brutality and enervating vital religion. Within the sermons there is a strong and sustained polemic against the irreligious tendency of war, a strand of criticism which regards such aspects as the undue reliance placed upon material defences in preference to spiritual resources as being at least as harmful as the direct impact of violence.[36]

---

[33] *Ibid* p 138.
[34] Hughes, *Britain's Defence* (3ed London 1803) pp 20–21; Rippon *Discourse* pp 27–29; Hall, Sentiments, *Works* 1 pp 172–178.
[35] Hughes, *Britain's Defence* p 33.
[36] Rippon, *Discourse* pp 20–26; Hall, Sentiments, *Works* 1 pp 139–141.

English dissent and the European conflict

Despite this universal condemnation there is the admission that war may at times constitute the right course of action; but whereas Rippon and Hall appear to regard national conflict as the inevitable outcome in certain circumstances, Hughes' pacifist inclinations and his horror of the bloodshed involved take him much further than the others in arguing for its avoidance at any cost. Even when the defiance of the enemy is most insulting, the justice of Britain's cause universally acknowledged and a successful outcome most likely, he says, 'I would ask, "is there not some gentle expedient which we have overlooked?"'[37]

One of Robert Hall's concerns is to strip away the false glamour which attaches itself to military exploits.[38] Although neither he nor Rippon share Hughes' degree of pacifism, they are nevertheless giving their assent principally to the concept of defensive war. Assuming that the justification exists for engaging in such a venture there is the strong conviction that it should be entered upon in a spirit of prayer; that Christian servicemen as well as those remaining at home should pray for true repentance and forgiveness as well as for their king and country and a victorious outcome. At this point one is close to the idea of the just war and to the conduct appropriate to such a righteous undertaking. Indeed the very text of Rippon's sermon[39] with its emphasis upon the need for God's embattled people to guard themselves against every form of evil suggests this idea, especially when it is contrasted with Napoleon's tyrannical cruelty.[40]

To the very end Hughes stubbornly refuses to depict the cause of arms as something with which a Christian country ought to be associated. He prefers instead to approach the conflict from

---

[37] Hughes, *Britain's Defence* p 10. Hughes' irenic remarks appear restrained, however, when compared with the vigorous opposition to the war expressed by Thomas Wilson, the leading London Independent who was treasurer of Hoxton Academy. A letter soliciting support for the patriotic fund established in the wake of Nelson's victory of 1805 elicited a characteristically firm response: '... it is my sentiment that war is contrary to Christianity that it can only be justified upon the principle of defence—and it is my firm conviction that the American war and all the wars since with France—have neither been just or necessary—consequently my family shall never reflect on me for giving any thing voluntarily to support a system of murder abroad and corruption at home.' Thomas Wilson, Autobiographical notes and correspondence p 13, Congregational Library, MS.II.d.5.
[38] Hall, Reflections, *Works* 1 p 98.
[39] Deuteronomy 23:9.
[40] Rippon, *Discourse* pp 30–32.

another direction, suggesting that reformed living on the part of individual members of society would, through the presence of God with the country, accomplish a remarkable and presumably peaceful reconciliation with France.[41] By contrast Rippon ends his sermon on an explicitly patriotic note. Having exhorted the volunteers to fight bravely and to face death calmly as true Christian soldiers he envisages their triumphant return to a grateful nation and to proud relatives. The theme of patriotism is not completely absent from Hughes' work, but is transformed into the less martial language of dissenting enthusiasm for crown and constitution.[42] In October 1803, however, Robert Hall was prepared to declare his support for the impending armed struggle in even stronger terms than Rippon. The closing sentences of his fast day sermon assume an almost lyrical quality as they extol the coming efforts of the British forces in the field of battle on behalf of freedom and religion.

In spite of this emotional conclusion Hall's two sermons provide evidence of deeper reflection upon the conflict with France. He attributes the peculiar intractability and ferocity of the struggle to the involvement of principle. The war has derived its strength from an implacable hostility between the forces of change and those of conservatism: it reflects a fundamental schism between society's opinions and its structures.[43] In the intellectual sphere those who believe in the absolute character of virtue and religion now find themselves opposing the dangerous utilitarian tendency of the age with its supreme criterion of expediency. It is this contemporary philosophy with its disregard for ultimate values which has produced a breed of cruel men whose contempt for true religion and liberty is now, he believes, only too plain for all to see.[44] With these observations on the most pressing political issue of the day one has to be content, for, from November 1803 onwards, the three commentators appear to have been overtaken by their earlier reluctance to speak.

When peace at length returned to Europe in 1815 the reaction of the dissenting community was curiously muted. Even the charac-

---

[41] Hughes, *Britain's Defence* pp 41–42.
[42] *Ibid* p 27.
[43] Hall, Reflections, *Works* 1 pp 101, 104.
[44] Hall, Sentiments, *Works* 1 pp 161–9, 183–5.

teristically non-political tones of county association minutes and reports might be expected to have included a paragraph rejoicing in the divine providence experienced by the nation. Instead a universal silence broods over the considerable range of contemporary records. In 1802 they had submitted an address to the king expressing their loyalty, gratitude and satisfaction concerning the restoration of peace both in the British dominions and more generally throughout Europe.[45] Twelve years later the annual circular letter of the Baptist midland association mentioned that most of the member churches seemed 'peculiarly conscious of their obligations to the divine goodness in restoring peace and prosperity to the nations', and it expressed the wish that every congregation should 'set apart some time for the express purpose of thanksgiving for the merciful and astonishing interposition of Heaven'.[46]

Why then was there silence in 1815? In part it may be attributed to the normal reticence concerning political issues. There may also be a certain sense of doubt that following two earlier short-lived periods of truce peace would prove to be any more enduring. What seems equally likely, however, is that the return of peace, given the extremely difficult financial circumstances facing the country, was proving to be a mixed blessing. There seemed little to rejoice about when many people faced unemployment and starvation, and when congregations in consequence were experiencing serious difficulties and even the threat of dissolution. If the records maintained a strict silence concerning the cessation of hostilities the same was not true of the economic recession which followed. Having endured years of high prices and heavy taxation the disappearance of wartime economic buoyancy affected some areas particularly severely. Thus the midland association meeting at Bilston in Staffordshire in 1816 commented: 'Most of the letters from our different societies deplored the painful pressure of the times; but the affairs of the neighbourhood in which we assembled were peculiarly distressing. Pray, dear brethren, that in the midst of judgment God would remember mercy.'[47] Clearly the reality of victory and peace did not live up to some of the more sanguine expectations.

Beyond the political silence and non-involvement it does seem

[45] Rippon, *Register* 4 p 943.
[46] Circular letter for 1814 p [1].
[47] Circular letter for 1816 p 2.

possible to detect a certain progression of thought over the entire period of conflict. The heady optimism of 1790 with its emphasis upon the benefits of the political changes in France soon gave way to the terror and to the period of more general warfare in Europe. No longer was it possible to justify the upheaval in terms of beneficial social change: instead the interpretation developed along more traditional lines bearing out the orthodox Christian understanding of the plight of mankind and of the consequent need for evangelism. Although the emergence of new themes tended to be an indistinct process, this explanation of the inevitability of war had by the early years of the new century yielded in turn to a more pragmatic approach. By 1803, confronted with the threat of invasion, the full and terrible reality of war seems to have impressed itself even upon the preoccupied evangelical consciousness to the extent that it evoked a practical response; one in which some of the more notable preachers endeavoured to influence public morale through patriotic sermons. While identification with the national cause may for some have represented the end of the process, there is also evidence of a parallel stream of anti-war sentiment. This pacifist factor seems in the latter years of the war to have merged with the growing sense of weariness and disillusionment, and this may have contributed to the conspicuous absence of reaction to ultimate victory.

St Mary's College
University of St Andrews

CHRISTIAN RESPONSES TO THE INDIAN MUTINY OF 1857

by BRIAN STANLEY

IN AN article published over a decade ago, Olive Anderson demonstrated the major contribution made by the Indian mutiny to the growth of Christian militarism in Victorian Britain.[1] The Crimean war had accustomed the British public to the view that Britain's soldiery had spiritual needs which could and should be met by the exertions of voluntary subscription, but it was the mutiny which established the more ambitious claim that Christian soldiers were the best ones. The military exploits of Henry Havelock and others of similar piety in stemming the tide of the sepoy rebellion enshrined Christian faith of an evangelical stamp as an almost indispensable ingredient in the constitution of the Victorian hero.[2] The intention of this paper is to endorse and amplify Anderson's conclusions by examining the responses of Christian opinion in Britain to the mutiny at its most alarming stage in the later months of 1857. Specific attention will be given to the reactions of nonconformists, in the light of the generally accepted view that early Victorian nonconformist attitudes to foreign affairs were characterised by a firm commitment to pacific principles and a disinclination for imperial entanglements.[3]

India possessed unique significance for early Victorian Christians. Religious minds seized on the undoubted fact that British annexations in India were undertaken 'frequently in the absence of advices from home, and even counter to the deliberate commands of the chief authorities',[4] and could see no other explanation than that a singular providence had been at work—India had been entrusted to Britain in order that she might give it

[1] Olive Anderson, 'The growth of Christian militarism in mid-Victorian Britain' *EHR* 86 (1971) pp 46–72.
[2] See also C. I. Hamilton, 'Naval hagiography and the Victorian hero' *HJ* 23 (1980) pp 381–98.
[3] See [N. W.] Summerton, 'Dissenting attitudes [to foreign relations, peace and war, 1840–1890]' *JEH* 28 (1977) pp 151–78; [D. W.] Bebbington, *The nonconformist conscience: [chapel and politics, 1870–1914]* (London 1982) pp 106–7.
[4] [William] Clarkson, *India and the gospel; [or, an empire for the messiah]* (London 1850) p 296.

back to God through the work of Christian missions.[5] India received more British missionaries than any other field at this time, and correspondingly sent more missionaries home to enthuse the Victorian public than did any other field. Evidence from the records of the Church Missionary Society (CMS) and London Missionary Society (LMS) suggests that approximately one in every two missionary speakers at provincial anniversary meetings in the period 1838 to 1873 came from India.[6] This predominance of Indian missionaries in deputation work appears, incidentally, to have been particularly marked in the years immediately following the mutiny.[7] India was not only the most widely publicised of early Victorian mission fields; it was also generally regarded as the most difficult. There the scandal of 'heathen idolatry' was to be found in its most sophisticated form: 'India, as the sphere of human apostasy from God, is altogether unparalleled', pronounced the LMS missionary William Clarkson.[8] India, acknowledged a Wesleyan missionary candidate in 1853, was 'the very stronghold of Infidelity and Idol-worship'.[9] All missionaries were engaged in a spiritual conflict with idolatrous religious systems which challenged the sovereignty of God, and Indian missionaries were in the thickest of the fight. Even before 1857, therefore, British Christians were habituated to thinking of India as a battleground in which the soldiers of Christ were fighting for the honour of God against satanic forces of awesome magnitude. The source of the 'heathen rage' lately unleashed in India, commented one cleric in October 1857, 'must be sought in the deadly feud which has ever been going on between Christ and Christ's enemy'.[10]

The outbreak of the mutiny in May 1857 horrified all elements of British opinion. Britons were shocked at Indian 'ingratitude',[11]

[5] Clarkson, *India and the gospel* pp 291–302; Henry Rowley ed, *Speeches on missions: by the Right Reverend Samuel Wilberforce, D.D., late bishop of Winchester* (London 1874) p 97; George Smith, *Our national relations with China; being two speeches delivered in Exeter Hall and in the Free-Trade Hall, Manchester, by the bishop of Victoria* (London 1857) pp 5–7.

[6] See my unpublished PhD thesis, 'Home support for overseas missions in early Victorian England, c.1838–1873' (Cambridge 1979) p 226.

[7] *Ibid* p 226.

[8] Clarkson, *India and the gospel* p 110.

[9] S[chool of] O[riental and] A[frican] S[tudies], Methodist Missionary Society archives, home letters, box 15, S. Lord to G. Osborn, 11 March 1853. I am grateful to the Methodist Church overseas division (Methodist Missionary Society) for permission to cite material from this archive.

[10] The Rev. Mr Fitzgerald of Camden chapel, St Pancras, in *The Times* 8 Oct 1857 p 7 col 3.

[11] [Christine] Bolt, *Victorian attitudes [to race]* (London 1971) p 157.

Christian responses to the Indian mutiny

shocked to discover how tenuous was Britain's military hold on the sub-continent, and, above all, shocked beyond measure by the exaggerated reports of atrocities perpetrated on British subjects. The usual Victorian indignation at atrocities inflicted on defenceless civilians was heightened to hysteria when the victims of massacres and outrages were British women and children.[12] The violence with which British feeling demanded retribution is well known. Less well known is the pervasiveness of a more sombre and self-critical mood which gathered force during the autumn of 1857. The mood was in large measure created by the churches, and given its greatest fillip by the calling of a 'day of national humiliation' for 7 October 1857.[13] Services were held in all Anglican places of worship and in a considerable proportion of nonconformist chapels. It was a day of 'great outward solemnity', in which rain fell with providential appropriateness from noon till night, 'very unfavourable' weather, remarked *The Nonconformist* with grim satisfaction, 'for those who wished to turn the occasion into a recreative holiday'.[14] Over one hundred and thirty humiliation day sermons preached in London pulpits were reported at some length in *The Times* the following morning, and these reports constitute the most important single source of the analysis which follows.[15]

The great majority of humiliation day preachers accepted without reservation the notion implicit in the royal proclamation of the day of national humiliation that the mutiny was a divine judgement upon Britain for her sins as a nation.[16] The cataclysmic nature of the mutiny rendered this interpretation even more general than the understanding of the Crimean war in similarly

---

[12] For accounts of the atrocities, real and alleged, see Christopher Hibbert, *The great mutiny: India 1857* (London 1978) pp 206–15; S. B. Chaudhuri, *English historical writings on the Indian mutiny 1857–1859* (Calcutta 1979) pp 256–65.

[13] This was the last of a series of days of national fasting and humiliation called in the nineteenth century; see [Olive] Anderson, '[The] reactions of Church and Dissent [towards the Crimean War]' *JEH* 16 (1965) p 215n.

[14] *The Nonconformist* 14 Oct 1857 p 803.

[15] There is no reason to suppose that the views expressed from London pulpits were unrepresentative of views expressed in the nation at large: 'The discourses delivered in our large towns were similar in substance to those addressed to metropolitan hearers': *The Nonconformist* 14 Oct 1857 p 805.

[16] The Queen's proclamation stated that the object of the humiliation day was 'that so both we and our people may humble ourselves before Almighty God in order to obtain pardon of our sins, and in the most devout and solemn manner send up our prayers and supplications to the Divine Majesty for imploring His blessing and assistance on our arms for the restoration of tranquillity': *The Times* 28 Sept 1857 p 4 col 2.

providentialist terms in 1854–5.[17] As the High Churchman Robert Liddell explained, providence 'did not inflict a national chastisement except for national sins. Individuals were amenable for their conduct to a judgement hereafter, but not so with nations. They, as such, could only be punished or rewarded in this world'.[18] There was some variety in identifying the particular sins which had contributed to God's displeasure: at Westminster Abbey Dean Trench deplored Britain's involvement in the opium trade;[19] while at the Crystal Palace the twenty-three year old C. H. Spurgeon, addressing a congregation of 23,564, pointed to the toleration of prostitution on the streets and of indecent amusements on the stage.[20] But both Trench and Spurgeon also fastened on that sin within India itself which most Christian observers believed to be the chief cause of the rebellion: East India Company rule had done little to promote the gospel and had involved itself in the maintenance of Hindu idolatry. Decades of missionary agitation against Company involvement in the support of Hindu temples lay behind the widely drawn conclusion that at last 'the Lord had let loose upon us that idolatry'.[21] God's method of retribution had simply been to permit the 'horrid systems' of idolatry to 'overflow on ourselves'.[22] The atrocities of the mutineers were not to be wondered at, since they were committed by those long accustomed to the religious atrocities of *sati*, self-torture and the Juggernath festivals.[23] Confronted by such an intrinsically immoral creed, British rule in India would have been secure only if 'some counteracting influence' had been powerfully present 'to prevent such principles breaking out into action'.[24] 'The forbearance which Christianity inculcates would have prevented the collision', the Rev. W. C. Moore assured the 11th Hussars at Kneller-Hall and Hounslow barracks; 'but, as Christianity has not had the sway, the trumpet has sounded, and tens of thousands have fallen. There is, then, a necessary and most striking connexion

---

[17] See Anderson, 'Reactions of Church and Dissent' pp 214–16.
[18] *The Times* 8 Oct 1857 p 5 col 5. See also 'National sins the sources of national calamities' C[hurch] M[issionary] I[ntelligencer] 8 (1857) pp 241-51.
[19] *The Times* 8 Oct 1857 p 5 col 4.
[20] *Ibid* p 8 col 5.
[21] Rev. Or M'Caul in *ibid* p 6 col 2. See also Rev. John Forster on p 6 col 5.
[22] *CMI* 8 (1857) p 249.
[23] Rev. Richard Chaffer in *The Times* 8 Oct 1857 p 6 col 6.
[24] Rev. W. Goode in *ibid* p 6 col 3.

Christian responses to the Indian mutiny

between the diffusion of Christianity and the diminution of war'.[25] Christian opinion in 1857 was virtually unanimous in its contention that the mutiny could have been averted if Britain had done not less but more to evangelise India.

The humiliation day preachers found no difficulty in combining their acceptance of the retributive nature of the mutiny with a confidence that British fortunes in India would be restored if the nation united in earnest and repentant prayer. Previous national fast days during the cholera epidemic and the Crimean war had, it was claimed, brought almost immediate relief.[26] Although the new testament promised efficacy only to the 'effectual fervent prayer of a righteous man', the righteous, as the Rev. C. J. D'Oyly reminded his congregation at St Mark's Longacre, were in the bible not the blameless but the repentant.[27] The old testament 'abounded with instances of beneficial effects resulting from national prayer'.[28] On the Sunday before the humiliation day the Rev. J. H. Titcomb of Christ Church, Barnwell, Cambridge, impressed a juvenile congregation (which included the adult Joseph Romilly) with his narrative of the national fast days observed by Nineveh in the days of Jonah and by Jehoshaphat in 2 Chronicles 20, when 'all Judah stood before the Lord with their little ones'; Romilly found the parallel 'most deeply interesting and touching and could not keep the tears out of my eyes'.[29] The comparison with Israel or Judah seemed singularly appropriate: like Israel of old, Britain had failed to heed God's warnings against compromising with the idolatry of the Canaanites, and had tasted the bitter fruit of her disobedience.[30] Yet, as with Israel, Britain had not by her disobedience forfeited all claim upon God's assistance, for the honour of the divine name was at stake. It was an easy and logical step from the existing evangelical conception of India as a battleground between God and Satan to the identification in 1857 of British arms with the cause of God.[31] It is significant that of the

---

[25] *Ibid* p 8 col 4.
[26] *Ibid* p 5 col 6 (Dr Crely) and p 7 col 1 (Preb. James).
[27] *Ibid* p 6 col 5.
[28] *Ibid* p 5 col 6 (Dr Crely).
[29] Cambridge University Library, Add. MS 6834 p 279.
[30] Rev. A. B. Suter in *The Times*, 8 Oct 1857, p 6 col 4.
[31] See especially Rev. B. M. Cowie in *ibid* p 5 col 1 and Rev. Warwick R. Wroth on p 7 col 6.

137 sermons reported at any length in *The Times*, 117 were based on old testament texts.[32]

Although old testament accounts of war between the people of God and his enemies fashioned the language and attitudes of humiliation day preachers, the assumption implicit in most sermons and explicit in some was that the mutiny was not a war in the usual sense of the term. What had occurred was a lawless and murderous revolt, a collective crime which required punishment. 'The revolt . . . was not that of a nation', declared Spurgeon, 'as when patriots strived to free their country from the yoke of an oppressor, but it was the revolt of treasonous and seditious subjects'.[33] It followed that the suppression of the mutiny was a judicial act: 'As the arrest of murderers was not war, so the arrest of Indian Sepoys was not war', Spurgeon concluded. British troops were instruments for the execution of divine justice on the guilty. This conviction was capable of a variety of applications. In the hands of the more temperate, the principle was a limiting one: punishment was to be restricted to those proven guilty of atrocities, but the innocent must be spared, and justice always tempered with mercy, so that the superiority of Christian to heathen ethics might be demonstrated.[34] At least one courageous sermon was preached in London on the Christian's duty to love and forgive his enemies.[35] For others, however, the assumption that British forces were the appointed agents of divine retribution threatened to become a licence for indiscriminate revenge. One sermon reported fears from India that 'Exeter Hall' would now begin to 'wail' on behalf of the 'mild Hindoo sepoy', but insisted that, on the contrary, Christian voices were raised in lament solely for the butchered victims of Indian brutality, a lament that would not be hushed until 'this vast gang of murderers' had been 'put down'.[36] Nonetheless, it must be emphasised that only a few sermons were thus preoccupied with intemperate demands for vengeance;[37] the majority were more concerned to deplore the sins of a Christian nation than to condemn the enormities of a people

---

[32] The total of 137 omits the further sermons briefly reported in *ibid* p 8 col 6 and p 9 cols 1–2.
[33] *Ibid* p 8 col 5.
[34] *Ibid* p 5 col 6 (R. Liddell), p 8 col 1 (C. Brown), p 8 cols 3–4 (J. Kelly).
[35] Rev. Spencer Pearsall in *ibid* p 7 col 5.
[36] Rev John Baillie in *ibid* p 7 col 3.
[37] See the comment in *The Nonconformist*, 14 Oct 1857, p 803.

Christian responses to the Indian mutiny

who had so largely been denied the light of Christian morality.

Some sermons, mainly but not entirely from nonconformist pulpits, deplored the 'inordinate, secular, selfish ambition' which had marked the course of British rule in India.[38] At Carr's Lane chapel, Birmingham, the veteran peace advocate John Angell James claimed that patriotism was leading some Christians to minimise the culpability of Britain for the conduct of the opium trade, and attacked the tendency of some newspapers to fan the flames of British indignation.[39] Congregationalists and Baptists in Leeds heard G. W. Conder appeal to 'the Christian feeling of the nation to temper justice with mercy' and seek the first opportune moment to put the sword into its scabbard. Yet Conder was in no doubt that, for the present, military suppression of the mutiny was 'perfectly just and necessary'.[40] Other nonconformists accepted the need for military action in defence of British imperial commitments with even fewer qualms than Conder. Henry Christopherson told his humiliation day congregation at New College chapel, London, that 'we are not now fighting for a colony, we are fighting for our *prestige*, and therefore our security among the empires of the globe'.[41] Edward Baines, who led in prayer at the humiliation day service in East Parade chapel at which Conder preached, had the pleasure of interrupting the anniversary meeting of the Leeds auxiliary of the LMS on 26 October with the sensational news that the British had re-captured Delhi; loud cheers greeted Baines's announcement that at a cost of 640 British lives the centre of the rebellion had been crushed, thus removing, according to Baines, 'the great obstacle to the progress of Christianity in India' and giving 'us control over the whole of the north-western provinces of India'.[42]

For Baines as for the majority of nonconformists, any hesitations about the dangers of militarism were outweighed by the implications of the dominant concern common to all evangelicals

---

[38] The congregationalist James Spence in *The Times* 8 Oct 1857 p 6 col 3. Spence was, however, in no doubt about the intrinsic righteousness of Britain's position in India.
[39] *The Nonconformist*, 14 Oct 1857, pp 805–6. For James's peace principles see Summerton, 'Dissenting attitudes' p 169.
[40] *The Nonconformist* 14 Oct 1857 p 806.
[41] *The Times* 8 Oct 1857 p 7 col 1.
[42] *Leeds Mercury* 27 Oct 1857 p 4 col 1. For the limited nature of Baines's pacific commitment see Summerton, 'Dissenting attitudes' pp 163, 167; Derek Fraser, 'Edward Baines' in Patricia Hollis ed, *Pressure from without in early Victorian England* (London 1974) p 200.

to be faithful to the presumed purpose of Britain's God-given commission in India. The first dispatch on the mutiny to reach *The Nonconformist* from its correspondent in Calcutta pointed out that the interest of the crisis for the 'very large number' of the newspaper's readers who were supporters of Indian missions lay supremely in its bearings upon the future of missionary work. *The Nonconformist*'s correspondent was unequivocal in his assertions that God had entrusted India to Britain for his own purposes of salvation, that in future the 'Government must not disown its own professed Christianity and tamper with caste and with idolatry', and that the immediate remedy for the outbreak was a reduction in the sepoy army and twenty thousand more European troops for India.[43] The next issue of the paper did print a letter from an aggrieved Cobdenite deploring the sanction given to British military aggression in India by the presumption of divine purpose, yet the writer had to concede that the Calcutta correspondent was very probably correct in his judgement that many of *The Nonconformist's* readers accepted the providential legitimacy of Britain's role in India.[44] Moreover, Edward Miall as editor of *The Nonconformist* lent firm support to the evangelical view: East India Company rule had been too deferential to the immoral system of caste and to the 'cruelties and abominations of the devotees of Brahma'.[45] The difficulty for Miall and other radical liberationists was in combining the evangelical interpretation of the mutiny with voluntarist principles, but it was not an insuperable difficulty. *The Nonconformist* objected to the manner in which the humiliation day proclamation made the Queen to command 'what can only be acceptable to the Almighty as a reverential and exclusive recognition of *His* authority', but enthusiastically endorsed the humiliation day in principle.[46] By 14 October Miall was voicing the fear that public opinion, in steering away from the Scylla of an irreligious policy in India, was veering towards the Charybdis of a policy which sought to promote Christianity by government agency. Yet he went on to insist that British rule in India must be unashamedly Christian in character, and that it should be so

---

[43] *The Nonconformist* 15 July 1857 pp 553–6.
[44] *Ibid* 22 July 1857 pp 563–4.
[45] *Ibid* p 571. See also Arthur Miall, *Life of Edward Miall* (London 1884) pp 218–20.
[46] *The Nonconformist* 6 Oct 1857 p 781; cf Anderson, 'Reactions of Church and Dissent' pp 216–17.

Christian responses to the Indian mutiny

characterised by its fearless pursuit of justice. Justice implied toleration of all religions, but also a refusal to tolerate 'every species of tyranny, cruelty, rapacity, or immorality' which had previously flourished under the 'pretence' of religious sanction.[47]

Miall's views were accurately reflected in the special minute of the executive committee of the Liberation Society on the future government of India passed on 18 November 1857.[48] Far from being in any sense anti-missionary, as two recent historians imply,[49] the minute affirmed that British rule in India should discharge its responsibility to God by placing 'the Christian religion in as favourable a light in the eyes of the natives as its divine origin and intrinsic excellence deserve'. Government should abstain scrupulously from any official patronage of missionary work and maintain complete religious freedom for all. Yet the interests of justice must be paramount: 'no plea of conscience should be permitted to override the plain course of law and equity'. The organs of justice should no longer recognise the right, 'grounded on religious pretexts, to annoy, injure, despoil, or destroy others ...'; such a determination, the minute acknowledged, would inevitably 'come into conflict with the ancient and inveterate prejudices of a large part of the population'.[50] Spurgeon's humiliation day sermon went considerably further along the same path: 'Religious liberty was a principle dear to all, but when religion taught immorality he said at once, "Down with it".'[51]

With evangelical passion so dominant in moulding nonconformist as much as Anglican reactions to the mutiny, those who

---

[47] *The Nonconformist* 14 Oct 1857 pp 801–2.

[48] G[reater] L[ondon] R[ecord] O[ffice], Liberation Society executive committee minutes 1853–61 (A/Lib/2). The special minute was based on the report of a sub-committee comprising Miall, Dr C. J. Foster (chairman of the society's parliamentary committee) and the secretary, J. Carvell Williams (minute 758 dated 30 Oct 1857).

[49] W. H. Mackintosh, *Disestablishment and liberation: the movement for the separation of the anglican church from state control* (London 1972) pp 100–1, wrongly construes the fourth paragraph of the society's minute as designed to protect native interests (whereas in fact it warned that native 'prejudices' must yield to the interests of justice), and exaggerates the difference between liberationist and Anglican missionary responses to the mutiny. G. I. T. Machin, *Politics and the churches in Great Britain 1832 to 1868* (Oxford 1977) pp 294–5, fails to perceive that nonconformists were at least as concerned to promote a Christian policy in India as to ensure that government did not infringe voluntarist principles; see *Baptist Magazine* 49 (1857) pp 758–9.

[50] GLRO, Liberation Society executive committee minutes 1853–61, circular dated 18 Nov 1857.

[51] *The Times* 8 Oct 1857 p 8 col 5.

maintained an inflexible commitment to pacifist or anti-imperial principles found themselves increasingly isolated. Richard Cobden was compelled to concede by mid-October 1857 that it was 'quite useless' in the present public mood to give expression to his view that 'sending red coats as well as black to Christianize a people is not the most likely way to insure the blessing of God on our missionary efforts'.[52] It was the mutiny as much as any other foreign or domestic development in 1857 which signalled the final collapse of Cobden's role as spokesman for the significant sector of (mainly nonconformist) opinion which had carried the label of the 'Manchester school'.[53] The prevailing blend of missionary and militaristic zeal left Cobden in pitiful isolation: 'With such views as mine, what am I to do in public life in the midst of all this excitement and enthusiasm for reconquering and *Christianizing* India? . . . For a politician of my principles there is really no standing-ground.'[54] The committee of the Peace Society observed with alarm the growth amongst the European community in India of a 'settled feeling of hatred and scorn' towards the native population, and made representations to the missionary societies to remind their Indian missionaries of their Christian duty to promote moderation and mercy: 'It is not impossible', the Society warned the LMS, 'that their own minds may to some extent have been tainted by that violent and vindictive spirit which is breathed everywhere around them.'[55] Such fears were probably justified. Not only were missionary organs quick to exploit the mutiny to argue that optimistic secular evaluations of the Indian character had been refuted by the incontrovertible evidence of the sepoys' 'deeds of perfidy and blood',[56] but some Christian commentators on the military campaigns were prepared to resort to crudely racialistic explanations of British success. 'No fact', wrote William Brock in assessing Havelock's victory at Bithoor in August 1857,

---

[52] [John] Morley, [*The*] *life of* [*Richard*] *Cobden*, new edn 2 vols (London 1896) 2 p 206.
[53] Cf Summerton, 'Dissenting attitudes' pp 171–2.
[54] Morley, *Life of Cobden* 2 p 214; see also D. Read, *Cobden and Bright: a Victorian political partnership* (London 1967) pp 205–7.
[55] SOAS, Council for World Mission archives, LMS home office incoming letters, box 11, H. Richard on behalf of committee of Peace Society to LMS directors, nd [1859?]. I am grateful to the Council for World Mission for permission to cite material from this archive.
[56] *Annual report of the London Missionary Society,* 1858 p 1; see also *Wesleyan Methodist Magazine* 5th ser 3 (1857) p 1131.

has been more clearly established in the course of his insurrection than that Asiatics, whatever may be their strength, cannot resist the charge of the smallest number of Englishmen. There is something in the sight of Europeans advancing at a run, with stern visage, bayonets fixed, determination marked in every movement of the body, which appals them; they cannot stand it—they never have stood it yet.[57] The mutiny did not so much create a new evaluation of Indian capacity and character as greatly strengthen and popularise attitudes which had hitherto been largely confined to the missionary magazine or meeting.[58]

The implications of the mutiny for the Christianisation of the army and the militarisation of Christianity have been well outlined by Olive Anderson and need not concern us here. The further implication of the Christian response to the mutiny suggested by this paper relates rather to Christian attitudes to the moral and religious legitimacy of British military endeavour in defence of the empire. The impressive catalogue of unashamedly Christian officers who figured in the military successes of the Indian campaign was interpreted not merely as evidence that men of war could without incongruity be men of prayer, but also as confirmation of the justice of the British cause in India. God had honoured with military victory those who had honoured him through their open profession of Christian faith in public office, and had thus given the stamp of his approval to Britain's role in India, provided that its true objectives were adhered to.[59] 'We have seen', reflected the annual report of the Baptist Missionary Society for 1857-8,

> the tide of rebellion turned back by the wisdom and prowess of Christian men, by our Lawrences, Edwardes, Montgomerys, Freres, and Havelocks, fighting as one of the noblest of them said, for the glory of Almighty God and the cause of humanity and order; God, as it were, especially selecting them for this

---

[57] [W.] Brock, [*A biographical sketch of*] *Sir Henry Havelock* [, *K.C.B.*] 4 edn (London 1858) p 210; see also *ibid* p 188.

[58] This interpretation differs in some respects from that of Bolt, *Victorian attitudes* pp 165, 178–83.

[59] See Rev. Edward Auriol in *The Times* 8 Oct 1857 p 6 col 4, and Eugene Stock, *The history of the Church Missionary Society: its environment, its men and its work* 4 vols (London 1899–1916) 2 p 217.

purpose, thereby to rebuke the folly of those who professed to see in the progress of the gospel the sure ruin of our Eastern empire.[60]

To a generation of Christians whose theological system was founded upon the concept of providence the eventual British victories were ultimately explicable only in terms of divine blessing. Havelock publicly attributed his first victory of the mutiny, at Futtehpore in July 1857, to

> the fire of British artillery, exceeding in rapidity and precision all that the Brigadier has ever witnessed in his not short career; to the power of the Enfield rifle in British hands; to British pluck, that great quality which has survived the vicissitudes of the hour, and gained intensity from the crisis; and to the blessing of Almighty God on a most righteous cause, the cause of justice, humanity, truth, and good government in India.[61]

Baptist though he was, Henry Havelock entertained no doubts about the justice and morality of the British suppression of the mutiny. All the evidence suggests that the great majority of English nonconformists, as well as Anglicans, shared his confidence. Years of missionary rhetoric had accustomed them to viewing India as a theatre of spiritual warfare in which the honour of the divine name was pitted against the false idols of the heathen; they had also come increasingly to accept that Christian standards of morality and justice could never be safeguarded while the devotees of Hinduism retained control in India. The reports of atrocities during the mutiny appeared to confirm that view. The suppression of the mutiny thus became a moral imperative demanded by the interests both of the Christian gospel itself and of the high standards of morality and justice which it prescribed for all men. Nonconformist disinclination for imperial extension and military adventures was weighed in the balances against these fundamental evangelical concerns, and was found wanting. Most nonconformists continued to oppose needless imperial entanglements in other parts of the globe until the 1890s, but the mutiny years had laid the foundations for the growing endorsement by nonconformists of a Gladstonian foreign policy which was prepared to countenance

---

[60] *Baptist Magazine* 50 (1858) p 323.
[61] J. C. Marshman, *Memoirs of Major-General Sir Henry Havelock K.C.B.* new edn (London 1902) p 294. For the importance of the concept of providence to Havelock see Brock, *Sir Henry Havelock* p 143.

armed intervention when the interests of religion, justice and morality were at stake, and ultimately for the more full-blooded Christian imperialism of the Boer war era.[62] In the shorter term, the mutiny fuelled both Anglicans and nonconformists with a renewed zeal to wrest India from the grip of the evil one by means of the soldiers of the cross.[63] In the words of one of the humiliation day sermons, 'the gospel is the only medicine for India's deadly sickness. We must build our churches there as well as our factories, send out our missionaries as well as our collectors of revenue; not only our brave soldiers, but that valiant army whose only weapon is the sword of the spirit.'[64]

Spurgeon's College
London

---

[62] See Bebbington, *The nonconformist conscience* pp 106–26; Summerton, 'Dissenting attitudes' pp 167–78.
[63] See my article, "Commerce and Christianity": providence theory, the missionary movement, and the imperialism of free trade, 1842–1860' *HJ* 26 (1983) pp 71–94.
[64] Rev. W. Sparrow Simpson in *The Times* 8 Oct 1857 p 6 col 2.

THE INSTRUMENTS OF PROVIDENCE: SLAVERY, CIVIL WAR AND THE AMERICAN CHURCHES

by PETER J. PARISH

ON 13 September 1862, when Abraham Lincoln was awaiting an opportune moment to issue his Emancipation Proclamation, he received at the White House a delegation from a meeting of Chicago Christians of all denominations. In pressing hard the case for immediate emancipation of the slaves, they assured the president that such action would be in accordance with the will of God. In a characteristically wry, tongue-in-cheek reply, Lincoln observed that:

> I hope it will not be irreverent for me to say that if it is probable that God would reveal his will to others, on a point so connected with my duty, it might be supposed he would reveal it directly to me; for, unless I am more deceived in myself than I often am, it is my earnest desire to know the will of Providence in this matter. And if I can learn what it is I will do it! These are not, however, the days of miracles, and I suppose it will be granted that I am not to expect a direct revelation.[1]

Nine days later, he issued his proclamation of emancipation, strictly as a war measure. Its reception was mixed, and veteran abolitionist crusaders, who had long since lost patience with the evasions and prevarications of politicians in general, and Lincoln in particular, were less than generous in their praise. They disliked the limitations of the proclamation, and its dry, legal language, which studiously avoided the higher moral ground. Many of them remained unimpressed by its presidential author, and one of them, Lydia Maria Child, while piously accepting the mysterious ways of the Almighty, confessed that 'Providence sometimes uses men as instruments whom I would not touch with a ten-foot pole'.[2]

---

[1] [Abraham] Lincoln, [*Collected Works*] ed Roy P. Basler] 8 vols (New Brunswick, New Jersey 1953) 5, p 420.
[2] Quoted in Benjamin Quarles, *Lincoln and the Negro* (New York 1962) p 86.

These two quotations, from the president and his abolitionist critic, come close to the heart of the problem which faced the American churches as they sought to penetrate the meaning of the Civil War, in relation to the two great issues of the salvation of the Union and the emancipation of the slaves. What was the relationship of Providence, of the divine will, to the causes, course and ultimate significance of this huge internal upheaval, the greatest war anywhere in the century between 1815 and 1914? Virtually everyone, whatever his denomination, shared a providential view of the war. They were certain that it had a place—and a crucial place—in the divine scheme of things, but they were anything but united in their interpretation of what precisely that place was.

I

If Lincoln was modest and tentative in his attempts to probe the purposes of the Almighty,[3] many of the clergy were much more confident in their knowledge of the divine will and in their assumption that God was unreservedly on their side. Such attitudes can only be understood in the context of their closely-linked beliefs, first in an activist and interventionist deity who would certainly be no mere spectator as the drama of the Civil War unfolded, secondly in the special (and divinely-ordained) historic mission of the United States, and thirdly in the role of the protestant churches as pillars of American society and the American way of life, and as apostles of America's world mission.

The first of these beliefs—in a God who was an active participant in history—was shared, or at least expressed with greater or lesser conviction, by ministers of virtually every denomination. They believed that the Civil War had not happened by accident or simply through human fallibility, and that its outcome would not be determined by chance. The sermons of George Ide, a prominent New England Baptist, illustrate this belief both in an all-embracing divine plan, and in specific and selective interventions by God to help the Northern cause. He argued that the nineteenth-century American equivalent of the

---

[3] Lincoln 8 pp 332–3; 5 pp 403–4. For a wider discussion of Lincoln's religious beliefs, particularly in relation to the Civil War, see William J. Wolf, *The Almost Chosen People: a Study of the Religion of Abraham Lincoln* (Garden City, New York 1959) especially pp 145–8, 153–6.

The Instruments of Providence

moving pillar of cloud by day, and fire by night, which had guided the children of Israel was 'the Pillar of God's Providence [which] is the presiding Presence, arranging all, overruling all . . . In every unfolding of the world's history Divine Providence is the controlling power'. Ide applied this belief to the specific circumstances of the Civil War, and God's purposes in using the conflict to save the Union and free the slaves. In another sermon, he offered very specific instances of God's helping hand to the Northern cause. Marvelling at the prosperity of the North despite the economic burdens of war, he found the key in the signal interposition of Providence:

> At the very point of time when the wants of the Government required extraordinary revenues, and the sources were closed from which treasure had been wont to flow in from abroad, the almighty Disposer of events ordained short crops and scarcity for Europe, and ample harvests and overflowing plenty for ourselves; thus creating a demand for bread there, and a supply here, which have caused the tide of wealth to set strongly upon our shores.[4]

If Ide testifies to the skill of Providence in the field of international economics, some of the claims of other ministers that God willed that certain generals should be appointed to command, or certain plans of campaign executed, must cast some doubt upon the divine grasp of military strategy. The essential point, however, is that Ide is typical of many, in his faith both in an over-arching divine plan, and in the readiness of God to intervene directly in the Civil War. As the *Observer*, a New York Presbyterian paper put it, 'It is not superstitious to believe that God rules in the affairs of men. It is not cant, or puritanism to say so. If God is, he is a rewarder of the good and the terror of the wicked.'[5]

Ide and the *Observer*, and others like them, clearly subscribed also to the belief in America's special mission, and in the role of the churches in its implementation. There is no need here to labour the obvious point that most Americans had assumed from its birth that their country had a unique destiny and a unique role to play in the advancement of liberty and republican virtue, and the progress

---

[4] [George B.] Ide, [*Battle Echoes, or Lessons from the War*] (Boston 1866) pp 137–8, 41–2.
[5] 'The Government of Nations; or, When is God on our Side' *Observer* (New York) 2 October 1862.

of Christian civilisation. Between the Revolution and the Civil War, political democracy, social egalitarianism and evangelical protestantism advanced closely in step towards what Timothy Smith has called 'the manifest destiny of a Christianized America'.[6] The rhetoric of churchmen—and of others, too—moved easily and constantly to and fro between the progress of American society and the advancement of Christian civilization. The constitution was ordained by God, (although its human framers had inadvertently and unfortunately neglected to mention him in its preamble), and America's special destiny was also divinely-inspired. In the oft-quoted words of Bishop Matthew Simpson of the Methodist Episcopal church, confidant of Lincoln, and champion of the Union cause: 'if the world is to be raised to its proper place, I would say it with all reverence, God cannot do without America'.[7]

As Simpson was prepared to admit, his certainty about America's divinely-inspired destiny was not matched by precise knowledge of what that destiny was to be. In his fascinating book, *American Apocalypse*, published in 1978, James H. Moorhead has highlighted the millennial and apocalyptic message of many Northern churchmen in the era of the Civil War. They preached that the day of the Lord was at hand, and that 'the war was not merely one sacred battle among many but was the climactic test of the redeemer nation and its millennial role'.[8] All students of this subject are profoundly indebted to Moorhead and his book must be the starting-point of any further work in this field. However, in making the millennial theme the focal point of his work, he has almost inevitably tended to over-emphasise it in comparison with other, less dramatic, interpretations, of the religious meaning of the Civil War. It is not simply that emphasis on one interpretation may have a distorting effect—but also that there may well be a distinction between the message, and the language and the images used to convey it. Much of the religious press, and the sermon and pamphlet literature of the time, conveys the impression that

---

[6] Timothy L. Smith, *Revivalism and Social Reform: American Protestantism on the eve of the Civil War* (Baltimore, repr 1980) p 7.

[7] [George R.] Crooks, [*The Life of Bishop Matthew*] *Simpson* [*of the Methodist Episcopal Church*] (New York 1891) pp 381–5. See also James E. Kirby, 'Matthew Simpson and the Mission of America' *Church History* 36 (Chicago 1967) pp 299–307.

[8] James H. Moorhead, *American Apocalypse: Yankee Protestants and the Civil War, 1860–1869* (New Haven 1978) p x.

The Instruments of Providence

churchmen, thoroughly versed in the old testament as well as the new, resorted to apocalyptic and millennial images as a habitual and convenient form of expression—in some cases, almost as a kind of professional jargon. Some of them undoubtedly believed quite literally that the Civil War heralded the apocalypse. Others, one suspects, used language which was at once familiar and yet vivid, to dramatise a more prosaic message. A sampling of the religious press and literature of the day reveals how much of it was devoted to discussion of the military campaigns, or Lincoln's leadership, or the problem of emancipation, in practical, political, secular terms. Not infrequently, such a sober analysis in a religious newspaper or periodical, was "topped and tailed" with an introduction and conclusion, which placed the immediate issue in the providential scheme of things, sought to discern evidence of divine intervention, and foreshadowed the imminent coming of the day of the Lord. Such passages are more than ritual invocations, but surely often less than literal interpretations of what the Civil War portended. It will be suggested later that grand-scale millennial interpretations of the Civil War may be less characteristic than a more modest and prosaic understanding of the war as a process of purification, which would restore both republican and Christian virtue to their pristine American glory. Even some of those who wrote of God's direct intervention in the war—like the author of the article in the *Observer* cited above—adopted a defensive and semi-apologetic tone, as if they were somewhat nervous about the reception of such ideas.

Be that as it may, the Civil War clearly posed a set of serious challenges to the interlinked beliefs and assumptions of the American protestant churches. What could be the divine purpose in permitting such a bloody conflict to develop? What had gone so badly wrong with the ever onward and upward pursuit of America's destiny? How, in fact, was that destiny to be fulfilled? Hitherto, it had been generally accepted that America's world mission was to be achieved by the sheer moral force of the American example. Was moral force now to give way to physical force, and was the Civil War to be simply a bloody American campaign in the age-old and world-wide struggle between the armies of good and evil?

II

This study will concentrate upon the attitude to the war, and the war issues, of the Northern protestant churches during the four years of the conflict itself, from 1861 to 1865. Catholic opinion has been excluded because it was much less important at this time, and, on the whole, the instinct of the American Catholic bishops was to avoid controversy on issues related to the war. Evidence of Southern religious opinion is less prolific and less accessible than for the North, but it is clear that the great majority of churchmen gave their loyalty to the cause of their section. A description of the attitudes of the Southern churches would almost certainly produce something like a mirror image of their Northern counterparts.

The Northern protestant clergy of all denominations were overwhelmingly loyal to the Union, and almost equally supportive of the war to save it, though they differed much more in their attitude to slavery, and to the question of emancipation during the war. The churches had wrestled for decades with the problem of slavery. Some of the most ardent antislavery campaigners and some of their sternest critics were men of the cloth. Differences of opinion were at least as much within denominations as between them. However, because the tradition, history and geographical spread of the major denominations differed, the impact of the issues of slavery and war did vary significantly from one to another.

The two largest protestant churches in mid-nineteenth century America, the Methodists and the Baptists, enjoyed strong Southern support, and both had split, North and South, on the slavery issue back in the 1840s. The Baptists were less strong and influential in the North, but some of their prominent spokesmen, like George Ide, were vigorous champions of the Union cause, and bold interpreters of God's purposes in the conflict. The Northern Methodists gave solid, if not unanimous, support to the Union cause, but were generally rather conservative on the question of emancipation, with some very conspicuous exceptions like Gilbert Haven.[9] The Congregationalists had suffered no split in the pre-

---

[9] [D. G.] Jones, [*The Sectional Crisis and*] *Northern Methodism:* [*a Study in Piety, Political Ethics and Political Religion*] (Metuchen, New Jersey 1979) pp 80–96; [William] Gravely, [*Gilbert*] *Haven,* [*Methodist Abolitionist: a Study in Race, Religion and Reform, 1850–1880*] (Nashville, Tennessee 1973) pp 74–90, 94–102.

The Instruments of Providence

war period, mainly because they were almost entirely a Northern denomination, dominated by New England influence. They were staunch supporters of the war for the Union, and more inclined towards antislavery than any other major Northern denomination. In contrast, the Episcopal church had support in both North and South but had been able to avoid a split, largely because its structure enabled each diocese to go its own way on the slavery issue.

Undoubtedly, of all the five major protestant denominations, it was the Presbyterians who were most painfully stretched on the rack by the coming of the war, and the issues which it raised. Slavery had not split the Presbyterian church before the war, but other issues had—predictably perhaps because American Presbyterians shared the taste of their British counterparts for schisms, secessions and disruptions. The main division into Old School and New School Presbyterianism, which took place in 1837, resulted from disagreements over doctrine and organisation. The New School, largely confined to the North, and especially the Northwest, had been heavily influenced and infiltrated by Yankee Congregationalism, after the Plan of Union of 1801 with the Congregationalists. It was generally less conservative than the Old School, and moved cautiously towards an antislavery position before 1860, and rapidly into full support for the Union cause in 1861. The Old School, with a membership twice that of the New, felt the full brunt of the secession crisis and the coming of the war. It had a substantial membership in North and South, a conservative disposition which inclined it towards supporting the federal government, and years of practice in evading the really awkward questions about slavery. Evasion of the war issue was difficult in 1861, for as luck would have it, the Old School general assembly met in May, just a month after the opening shots had been fired. Much of the Southern membership was unrepresented, but there was still a fierce debate, before a resolution pledging 'to strengthen, uphold and encourage the Federal Government' was carried. During the Civil War, Southern Presbyterians went their own way—and were particularly vigorous in their defence of slavery. Northern Presbyterians generally supported the Union cause with increasing fervour, but many remained uneasy about their church's political commitment in 1861, and most insisted, at least through the first half of the war, that the struggle was exclusively to restore the Union and not to free the slaves.[10] Charles Hodge, editor of the *Biblical Repertory and Princeton Review*, and the most intellectually able and influential spokesman for conservative Presbyterianism, argued consistently, if tortuously, that, while the private convictions of individual church members could (and, he believed, should) lead them to support the war for the Union, the general assembly of the church should not seek to dictate the political allegiance of its members. In the second half of the war, he moved on to argue, with equal dialectical skill, that, while emancipation might be justifiable as a means of fighting to save the Union, it could not be justified as a war aim in its own right.[11]

III

Four central questions may be posed as a means of imposing some order on the debate over the religious issues raised by the war. Was war justifiable at all? Was this particular war justified? How did the slavery issue affect the arguments advanced for and against support for this particular war? In the broader historical context, how were the purpose and significance of the struggle interpreted and evaluated?

There is a certain chronological, as well as logical, order to these four questions. The first two predominated at the outbreak of the war and in immediate justifications of it. In this war, as in most conflicts, the arguments used to justify participation, at the moment of entry and during the early stages, were based upon sheer necessity, inevitability, force of circumstances. The struggle was depicted as one of survival, or at least for the defence of absolutely vital interests. However, as a war continues and its cost mounts, to fight simply for one's interests seems too little, if not indeed somewhat unworthy; higher purposes must be invoked—a moral crusade, a national rebirth, a spiritual revival, a new world order—to give the struggle a deeper, and a nobler, meaning. In the case of the Civil War, one crucial link between the earlier justifications of the war as a defence of national interests and the later interpretations of its profounder significance may be found in

---

[10] [Lewis G.] Vander Velde, [*The Presbyterian Churches and the Federal Union, 1861–1869*] (Harvard Historical Studies 33, Cambridge, Mass. 1932) pp 15–73.
[11] Charles Hodge, ['The General Assembly'] *Biblical Repertory [and Princeton Review]* 33 (Philadelphia 1861) pp 556–567; ['The War'] *ibid* 35 (1863) pp 150–5.

The Instruments of Providence

the third of the four questions listed above: the relationship between the war for the Union and the emancipation of the slaves.

The predominance in 1861 of the argument from sheer necessity is indicated by the answers given to the first of the four questions: was war, as such, justifiable at all? As the Union was sundered, and the guns began to roar, the pacifist argument went almost, if not quite completely, by default. In the 1830s and 1840s, a peace or non-resistance movement had been active, if less than flourishing, as part of the ferment of reform of those decades. However, its extreme no-government stance limited its support, and, as the North-South crisis over slavery deepened, many of its members put their antislavery loyalties first. The coming of war in 1861 led to a flight from the peace camp although a few of the old peace campaigners remained true to the cause. Others showed resourcefulness in seeking the best of both worlds. For example, Rev. A. P. Peabody, professor of Christian morals at Harvard, convinced himself that the fighting 'had none of the moral characteristics of a war. It was rather a vast police movement for the suppression and punishment of multitudinous crime.' Others again threw over their pacifist principles completely, and embraced war as the instrument of abolition. 'I abhor war', wrote Lydia Maria Child, '. . . yet I have become so desperate with hope-deferred, that a hurra goes up from my heart, when the army rises to carry out God's laws.'[12] Even William Lloyd Garrison, architect of the New England non-resistance movement in the 1830s, and most prominent of all the abolitionists, wrote in 1863 that:

> Ardently as my soul yearns for universal peace, and greatly shocking to it as are the horrors of war, I deem this a time when the friends of peace will best subserve their holy cause to wait until the whirlwind, the fire and the earthquake are past, and then 'the still small voice' may be understandingly and improvingly heard.[13]

The religious press welcomed the 'conversion' of many peace advocates to support of the war for the Union, but mixed mockery and irony with its praise. The *Independent*, probably the leading

---

[12] Peabody and Child are both quoted in Peter Brock, *Pacifism in the United States from the Colonial Era to the First World War* (Princeton, New Jersey 1968) pp 692, 696–7.

[13] W. L. Garrison, *The Letters of William Lloyd Garrison* ed W. M. Merrill 6 vols (Cambridge, Mass. 1971–81) 5 p 164.

non-denominational religious paper of the day, welcomed resolutions of the Peace Society in support of the government's efforts to suppress the rebellion, but took the opportunity to ridicule the argument that war was a sin *per se*. The *Christian Examiner* took the view that 'forcible resistance to evil is a duty we owe to the evil-doer, no less than to ourselves'. Law backed by force must be supported until the day dawned when love could rule unchallenged. Less than six months after the outbreak of war, in an article in the Congregational quarterly, the *New Englander*, James M. Sturtevant, president of Illinois College, expressed the hope that the fighting would cure America of a 'morbid philanthropy' which taught that even a defensive war was criminal. To seek to extinguish the evils of a war by a pledge not to take up arms was, he thought, about as effective as the attempt to banish the vice of drunkenness by persuading individuals to pledge themselves never to take an intoxicating drink. Americans should be, not shocked, but inspired by the belligerence of many of the great figures of the old testament. The age of true peace would not come

> till men shall have so learned in the school of hard and bloody national experience the relations of retributive justice and penalty to all order, to all freedom and to all government, that they can enjoy long peace and freedom without reproaching as bloodthirsty cut-throats, those ancestors by whose bravery and prowess on the field of battle these blessings were purchased.[14]

More sensitive, or perhaps more cautious, preachers and writers took care to preface their assurances that war could be justified in the eyes of God, with appropriate recognition of the miseries and horrors which it inevitably brought in its train. Frequently the sufferings of war were presented as a sacrifice. George L. Prentiss urged his audience to remember that 'we do not enjoy today a solitary civil or religious privilege which is not perfumed with the heroic and suffering virtues of former times; not one which did not cost blood, treasure and painful toil.'[15] Charles Hodge insisted that

[14] 'Per se, per saltum' *Independent* (New York) 6 June 1861; 'The War' *Christian Examiner* 71 (New York 1861) pp 98–9; [J. M.] Sturtevant, ['The Lessons of our National Conflict' *New Englander* 19] (New Haven 1861) pp 895–8.
[15] George L. Prentiss, *The Free Christian State and the Present Struggle: an Address Delivered before the Association of the Alumni of Bowdoin College* (New York 1861) p 35.

The Instruments of Providence

a just war must be fought not only for a moral end but by morally justifiable means, and he gave as examples the humane treatment of prisoners and respect for private property.[16]

Many other religious commentators were much less squeamish, and eagerly pledged their loyalty to the God of battles. Rev. A. L. Stone, of Park Street Congregational church in Boston, saw war as a Christian duty, 'as sacred as prayer—as solemn as sacraments'. He spoke of a minister of the Gospel, turned soldier, who, after despatching his enemies one after another with 'unerring bullets', addressed his victims from afar: '"My poor fellow, God have mercy on your soul." That is the way to fight . . . it is mercy to go strong and strike hard . . . This is the message of the Law of Love.'[17] Methodist Bishop Ames declared in 1861 that 'were it his duty to join the Union army and fight the rebels, he should shoot very fast, he would "fire into them most benevolently".'[18] Joseph P. Thompson, a leading New York Congregationalist, was one of many preachers who drew lessons from the old testament: 'The Scriptures teach us that the arbitrament of war is a method of referring to Almighty God the righteousness of a cause against the machinations of bloody and deceitful men.' For all the horrors of war, Christians had not merely a right but a duty to rejoice in military victories won in a righteous cause.[19]

There were of course more judicious and restrained analyses of the justification of war. A particularly thoughtful and illuminating discussion came, not from one of the mainstream protestant denominations, but in an article in the *Universalist Quarterly* in 1861. Until the war came, the author had thought war incompatible with the teachings of the sermon on the mount. He had not been active in the non-resistance movement but had lived with the potential conflict between his disapproval of war and his support for a government which rested ultimately on force, in the same way as he managed to live from day to day with the doctrines of free will and necessity. Now the war had swept metaphysical discussion to one side and demanded immediate practical answers. Unless the Christian faith was to fail him in his hour of need, there

---

[16] Hodge, *Biblical Repertory* 35 (1863) pp 155–7.
[17] Quoted in [Chester F.] Dunham, [*The Attitude of the Northern Clergy toward the South, 1860–1865*] (Toledo, Ohio 1942) p 111.
[18] Quoted in Charles B. Swaney, *Episcopal Methodism and Slavery* (Boston 1926) pp 300–301.
[19] [Joseph P.] Thompson, *Peace through Victory, [a Thanksgiving Sermon]* (New York 1864) p 4.

must be a way of combining loyalty to the government with loyalty to 'the captain of our salvation'. What did it mean to be opposed to war? Surely everyone opposed war for its own sake. When a nation's rights and existence were threatened, there were two fundamental questions: are there alternative means of protection apart from war? and, if not, is it the Christian duty of the nation to sacrifice itself? If the answer to both questions was no, the decision to fight was justified. Government was ordained by God, and all government rested on force. The real question, therefore, was not whether a government could wage war, but whether a people had a right to government. War could be reconciled with the overall spirit of the Gospel, if it was fought in the spirit of loving one's enemies. In the American crisis, a Christian soldier was a better soldier, and could pray to God that his 'fearful missiles' would find their mark. The justification of war depended upon the justice of the cause. Examples from history—the English martyrs, the revolutionary heroes, Calvary itself—showed that there were interests more precious than life, which justified the sacrifice of life. The example of Christ himself had also established one of the cardinal doctrines of Christianity— that the innocent must suffer for the guilty. Having established the negative point that war was not forbidden, the author concluded on a strong positive note. Permission to act became in certain circumstances the command to act, and killing one's enemies was not justified as a right or a privilege, but as a duty. America's free institutions were a legacy in trust from God, and the Christian had the duty to defend them on behalf of generations yet to come. 'In such a contingency, we cannot be Christians unless we fight.' In that sense, this was indeed God's war.[20]

IV

The same line of argument, proceeding from harsh practical necessity to obedience to divine command, was frequently, if not always so skilfully, deployed in answer to the second question: was this particular war justified? In view of the consensus that war was justified if it was undertaken in a good cause, the task of preachers and religious writers was simply to demonstrate that justice was on

---

[20] 'Christianity and the War', *Universalist Quarterly [and General Review]* 18 (Boston 1861) pp 373–95.

The Instruments of Providence

the Northern side. In this they received not a little help from the secession movement in the South. Until 1860, the Northern clergy entertained divergent views on the political issues between North and South, and on the proper reaction to the problem of slavery in the Southern states. In response to the threat of secession, some ministers had even approved the idea that the erring sisters be allowed to depart in peace. However, as the states of the deep South rushed headlong into secession, in the wake of Lincoln's election, and proceeded to establish their own confederacy, the overwhelming majority of the Northern clergy lined up in support of the integrity of the Union. When the South actually fired the first shots in the conflict, the move to solid support for a defensive war against the Southern aggressors was only a short step. There were hints that, if the South had sought separation by peaceful and constitutional means (which was perhaps a contradiction in terms) the proper Northern response would have been agreement to such a peaceful break-up of the Union.[21] However, once the Southern guns had fired on Fort Sumter, most Northern churchmen, like most other Northerners, saw no alternative to war.[22]

The first stage in justification of this particular struggle was therefore clearly the conviction that it was a defensive war. But a war in defence of what? The constant answer, from clergymen and politicians alike, was that war was necessary to save the Union. The struggle was one for survival—and on the survival of the Union, depended the future of America's free institutions, libertarian tradition, and mission to the world. What, if anything, was the distinctive contribution of the churches to the propagation of this basic message?

First of all, they played an active part in exciting patriotic fervour in the early stages of the war. Rev. W. W. Patton, minister of the First Congregational church in Chicago advised in April 1861 that 'the present struggle is one in which every Christian may rise from his knees and shoulder his rifle'. One Methodist minister in Illinois is alleged to have broken off in mid-sermon, and announced that, in his country's hour of danger, he must not preach but fight. 'Let every man who loves the Stars and

---

[21] See for example 'The War' *Christian Examiner* 71 (1861) pp 99–102.
[22] On the closing of Northern clerical ranks in support of the war in the spring of 1861, see Moorhead pp 47–51 and Dunahm pp 71–80 and 110.

Stripes follow me.'[23] As the war progressed, Bishop Matthew Simpson emerged as probably the leading evangelist of the Union cause. For his set-piece 'war speech' which he delivered in various towns and cities across the North, he could command a substantial fee. The performance included some actual, as well as a good deal of metaphorical, flag-waving, a discussion of the perils facing the Union, an assertion that twenty years of war and bloodshed were preferable to settling for an unsatisfactory compromise peace, and an assurance that the nation would emerge strengthened and purified to fulfil the great destiny assigned to it by Providence.[24]

As the war went on, the identification of the cause of the country and the cause of religion became increasingly close. George Ide who, from the outset, had stressed the harmony between Northern devotion to the Union and God's plans for America and for the world, was later ready to declare that 'the cause of our country and the cause of religion, the cause of humanity, the cause of eternal Right and Justice, are so intimately blended in this crisis, that you cannot separate them. The triumph of the Government will be . . . the triumph of a pure Gospel'.[25] Such an interweaving of secular and spiritual goals grew from an assumption that a war to defend the Union embraced loftier and broader aims as well, because of the high ideals and principles for which the Union stood. As a writer in the *Universalist Quarterly* puts it, the war was not to defend the Union per se: 'we are not idolators of the Union'. Rather, it was to defend the principles for which the Union stood—order, democratic liberty and popular institutions. The causes of Christianity and progress were the same, and both would be set back seriously, and perhaps fatally, if the great American experiment broke up. 'We carry the ark of the Lord and the blessings of the new covenant.' A fight in good faith was sure to succeed. 'To doubt this is atheism.'[26]

It was the more liberal Christian spokesmen and journals which tended most often to read wider goals into the struggle for the union. The *Independent* stressed from the outset in its editorials that this was a war to defend not only constitutional government but also principle and right. In June 1861, it condemned that 'rose-

[23] These examples are taken from Dunham pp 136, 139.
[24] Crooks, *Simpson* pp 381–5.
[25] Ide pp 125–6.
[26] 'Our Civil War' *Universalist Quarterly* 18 (1861) pp 264–9, 275–6.

The Instruments of Providence

water religion' which would not stand up for the right and condemn the Southern wrong. A year later, the *Independent* was still insisting that the struggle was to save not just the national life but the liberties and free institutions which went with it. Christianity was at the root of American liberty, and civil and religious liberty went together. 'The Altar and the Ballot Box, in America, will stand or fall together.'[27]

The presidential election year of 1864 provided the opportunity for a practical demonstration of the alliance of altar and ballot-box. A leaflet entitled *Religion Rebuking Sedition: Christianity versus Slavery and Treason* was obviously designed to aid the cause of Lincoln's re-election by detailing resolutions of support for the war from virtually all the Northern churches.[28] Two months before the election itself, Joseph P. Thompson helped the same cause with a slashing attack on the advocates of a compromise peace which would surrender basic principles. He urged his congregation to 'stand by the Government to the end: give it confidence; give it votes; give it prayer; give it money; give it men'.[29] Gilbert Haven, the leading abolitionist in the Methodist ranks, looked back over what the church had already done to advance the cause of liberty in America, and asked for one more effort:

> Let her once more march to the ballot box, an army of Christ, with the banners of the Cross, and deposit, as she can, a million votes for her true representative, and she will give the last blow to the reeling fiend.[30]

In contrast to the brave words of those who would hitch all kinds of great causes to the star of the Union, there were some more cautious voices which sought to circumscribe the purposes for which the North fought. In sharp contrast to the editorial policy of the *Independent*, for example, was the line consistently followed by the conservative Presbyterian paper, the *Observer*. During the secession crisis, it pleaded that North and South should live in peace, together if possible, separately if not: 'for the sake of the Prince of Peace, let us not dabble the banner of our common Christianity and our common country in fraternal blood.' When the conflict began, the *Observer* threw its support behind a war of

---

[27] *Independent* 25 April 1861, 2 May 1861, 27 June 1861, 13 September 1862.
[28] *Religion Rebuking Sedition: Christianity versus Slavery and Treason* (Philadelphia 1864).
[29] Thompson, *Peace through Victory* pp 9–13, 16.
[30] Quoted in Moorhead p 157.

patriotism and self-preservation, while insisting that it was a struggle purely over the form of government, and loyalty to it, and had nothing to do with slavery. Throughout 1861, 1862 and 1863, the *Observer* consistently argued that all government—and certainly the American government—was ordained of God, and that submission to it was submission to God. The Southern rebellion was therefore unjustifiable and must be resisted. 'Our national flag is sacred. Our national Constitution is holy. Our Executive Officers are anointed priests in the temple of law and liberty.' The goal of the war must be peace with union, and nothing more.[31]

The swelling chorus of ecclesiastical support for the war was interrupted by just a few discordant voices. Shortly after the firing on Fort Sumter in April 1861, the *Christian Advocate and Journal* still believed that 'we have too high a civilization and too much Christianity for a protracted war'.[32] Others continued to believe that war had been avoidable, and that it was quite impossible to restore the Union by coercion. The diehard opponents of the war were mainly men who saw no biblical objection to slavery, like Bishop James H. Hopkins of Vermont, and the Presbyterian Henry J. Van Dyke. They believed that the war had been caused, not by slavery itself, but by agitation of the slavery issue. In their eyes the abolitionists were the villains of the piece.[33] It is possible that there were more ministers who might have spoken out against the war on these or other grounds, but it took courage to resist the overwhelming pressure from public opinion—and one's own congregation—to bless the war for the Union. Dr. William Plumer of the Central Presbyterian Church, Allegheny City, Pennsylvania, and a professor at Western Theological Seminary, was forced to resign both his charge and his chair because he felt unable to pray for the success of Northern arms or to give thanks for Northern victories. Men could not be coerced to love, he argued, and swords and bayonets could not piece together a happy and enduring Union. Voices like his were very rare, and even

---

[31] *Observer* 7 February 1861, 16 May 1861, 22 August 1861, 7 November 1861, 2 October 1862, 19 February 1863, 2 July 1863, 31 December 1863.
[32] *Christian Advocate [and Journal]* (New York) 25 April 1861.
[33] John H. Hopkins, *A Scriptural, Ecclesiastical and Historical View of Slavery* (New York 1864) pp 16–17, 48–9, 53–4, 346–7; Henry J. Van Dyke, *The Character and Influence of Abolitionism* (New York 1860) pp 25–31.

The Instruments of Providence

more rarely heard, amid the clamour of the evangelists of God's war.[34]

V

Attitudes to slavery clearly had a crucial bearing upon attitudes to the war, but the relationship between the two was highly complex, and often shifting and unstable. A simple interpretation of the relationship was a luxury to be afforded only by those, whether churchmen or not, who took up extreme and unequivocal positions. The Van Dykes and their political counterparts defended Southern slavery, usually as an instrument for the civilization and conversion of an inferior race, and objected to any idea of making war against it. At the other extreme were abolitionists and radical Republicans (and their clerical allies) who saw the war from the outset as a struggle to destroy slavery. Between these two extremes were the great majority of churchmen and others who wrestled with the many-sided problem of slavery from day to day, and found no easy answers. At the outset, the declared purpose of the war, as stated by Lincoln and many others, was to save the Union; only in the minds of a small minority, consisting of abolitionists and antislavery campaigners, was emancipation a war aim, let alone the war aim. Yet in September 1862, Abraham Lincoln issued his first Emancipation Proclamation although he hedged it about with many qualifications and limitations and justified it purely as a war measure. Only in 1865 did the thirteenth amendment to the constitution complete the abolition of slavery. In the unfolding four-year debate on emancipation as the means and as the end of making war, the Northern churches made their own distinctive contribution.

The most illuminating way to analyse the attitudes of the churches to the issue may be to start from each of the two extremes in turn, and work towards the middle, where most of them found some common ground, through recourse to divine intervention and trust in the wonderful workings of Providence. It has already been shown that, on the extreme conservative side, there were those Northern apologists for slavery who believed that a sensible willingness to conciliate and compromise could have avoided war, and who blamed the abolitionists for precipitating

[34] Vander Velde pp 280–333, and especially pp 295–9.

the conflict. In his extraordinary book *Pictures of Slavery and Antislavery*, published in 1863, John Bell Robinson, argued that the only temporal salvation for the African race lay in servitude to white men. God had so guided the Philadelphia convention of 1787, which framed the American constitution, that it left slavery intact. Now antislavery agitation had led to war, and only an end to harassment of the South could restore peace. Robinson felt driven to despair when he saw the Christian church in the North, 'the anchor and safeguard to all free institutions, advocating the war on our Christian brethren', and claiming that God was on their side. On the contrary, he believed that God had allowed the war to come 'to teach us that we cannot trample upon the rights of our Christian brethren with impunity'.[35]

Much less extreme and eccentric was the solid weight of conservative opinion which adhered strictly to the view that the sole purpose of the war was to save the Union. This view has already been discussed, but it should be added here that 'the war for the Union' was often, though not always, a code-word for a conservative attitude towards slavery. One exponent of this point of view who was more explicit than most was Rev. William Barrows of Reading, Massachusetts. Sharing the same unwavering belief as Robinson and innumerable others in the innate inferiority of the Negro race, he pointed to the 'wonderful contentment' of their nature, and their acceptance of what, he confidently asserted, was a not unpleasant fate. They were not ready for freedom, and sudden emancipation through a violent upheaval would do them great harm, and would raise the acute problem of what to do with millions of freed slaves. Such a move would serve only to consolidate Southern white support for the war. The will of Providence was clearly that rebellion should be struck down and the Union saved, and an attack on slavery would only complicate matters and obstruct achievement of that primary goal.[36] Even after Lincoln's Emancipation Proclamations, a conservative paper like the *Observer* continued to press for a more moderate, gradualist and peaceful approach to the removal of slavery, attacked abolitionists as being just as disloyal as the 'Copperheads', or Peace

---

[35] John Bell Robinson, *Pictures of Slavery and Antislavery* (Philadelphia 1863) pp 261–75.
[36] William Barrows, *The War and Slavery, and their Relations to Each Other* (Boston 1863) pp 10–18.

The Instruments of Providence

Democrats, and insisted that defence of the government and the Union remained the basic consideration.[37]

A further conservative step towards the middle ground found expression in hints that the Union must be saved, even if slavery had to be destroyed in the process. Early in the war, in July 1861, the author of an article in the *Christian Examiner* acknowledged that 'we are bound to save the Union, even if in doing it we are forced to abolish slavery'.[38] In 1862, the Pittsburgh Methodist conference adopted a report which stated that 'this unholy rebellion . . . should be crushed out at all hazards, and at any cost. If this cannot be done without crushing out slavery, let slavery be crushed.'[39]

It was but one more short step along the road to acceptance of emancipation, if not as an aim, at least as a likely consequence, of the war, to indulge in speculation that slavery might be a casualty or an incidental victim of this long and bitter struggle. Interestingly enough, both the *Observer* and the *Christian Examiner* showed signs by 1863, of moving at least this far from their initial caution of two years earlier. 'Let slavery take its chance', said the *Observer*. 'If the war breaks it up root and branch, so be it.' A writer in the *Christian Examiner* in September 1863, looking back on the North's midsummer victories, rejoiced that oppressed men might be liberated through these successes. 'But the contest itself, we wage on other grounds. We do not consider philanthropy a fit matter for the arbitrament of war.' The task was to save the nation first and then consider the future.[40] But perhaps the most shameless use of this kind of argument came from Bishop Simpson in his popular war speech. His biographer reports him as saying that the war should be fought, not to destroy slavery but to restore the authority of the government. 'But if, while we are striking blows at the rebellion, Slavery will come and put its black head between us and the rebels, then let it perish along with them.'[41]

As the slavery issue, and public opinion, evolved in 1861 and 1862 some conservative opinion moved more clearly to the view that emancipation might be a necessary and proper means of

---

[37] See, for examples, *Observer* 2 October 1862, 21 May 1863, 4 June 1863, and 8 December 1864.
[38] 'The War' *Christian Examiner* 71 (1861) p 100.
[39] Jones, *Northern Methodism* p 82.
[40] *Observer* 4 June 1863; 'A Month of Victory and its Results' *Christian Examiner* 75 (1863) pp 277–8.
[41] Crooks, *Simpson* p 384.

waging the war for the Union, though not a legitimate war aim. The case of Charles Hodge, of Princeton, is particularly instructive, above all because of the quality of his mind and thought. He defined abolitionism as the doctrine that slave-holding is in itself sinful and that immediate emancipation was a moral duty. This he regarded as contrary to the word of God. However, he loyally supported the war for the Union, and, as early as 1862, admitted that if the North were to be faced with the stark choice between the preservation of slavery and the preservation of the Union, slavery would have to be eliminated. In the interests of all, including the slaves, he preferred a programme of gradual and voluntary emancipation, but feared that the intransigence of the South would compel a more drastic solution. In an 1863 article, he argued brilliantly the case that emancipation may in certain circumstances be the means, but must not be the end, of prosecuting the war. The existence of an evil—whether slavery or despotism or 'false religion'—was not sufficient to justify war against it. A legitimate object of war must be something which a nation has not only the right to attain, but the duty to secure—for example, its unity or its survival. The abolition of slavery was not one of the ends for which the federal government was instituted, and, therefore, to make abolition the end of the war was contrary to both the constitution and the law of God. 'The difference between its being a means and an end is as great as the difference between blowing up a man's house as a means of arresting a conflagration, and getting up a conflagration for the sake of blowing up his house.'[42] When, in 1864, the Presbyterian general assembly belatedly passed a resolution supporting abolition (eighteen months after Lincoln's first emancipation proclamation) Hodge bent his formidable skill in argument to the task of demonstrating the essential consistency of his church's attitude to slavery. Emancipation had evolved from a possible means of fighting the war to an inevitable consequence of it—and, in the final overthrow of slavery, Hodge discerned the hand of God.[43]

In this he was by no means alone. There was something relentless about the evolution of conservative opinion from support for the war for the Union, to the need to save the Union even if it

---

[42] Hodge, *Biblical Repertory* 35 (1863) p 152.
[43] For the evolution of Hodge's views, see *ibid* 34 (1862) pp 519–22; 35 (1863) pp 150–5; 36 (1864) pp 541–551; 37 (1865) pp 436–40.

The Instruments of Providence

meant bringing slavery to an end, to the notion that slavery might be the incidental victim of war, then on to approval of emancipation as a means of prosecuting the war and acceptance of the end of slavery as a consequence of the war. Those who looked back in 1863 or 1865 to the outbreak of the conflict pointed out quite rightly that no one in 1861 had foreseen slavery's imminent demise. They pointed also to the remarkable shift in popular attitudes in a few short years. Above all they were quick to discern the hand of God in this rapid transformation, and to glimpse the divine purpose in allowing the war to happen, to last so long, and to cost so much.

The truly remarkable aspect of this interpretation of events is that more liberal and radical antislavery churchmen, starting from opposite premises, arrived at much the same conclusions. Many antislavery campaigners in the churches naturally wanted to make emancipation a war aim from the outset. Henry Ward Beecher, the most renowned preacher of his day, believed that war must force respectable Northern churchmen to sweep aside years of cowardice, selfishness and evasion. Prudential questions had been put before moral ones far too long. Writing in the *New Englander*, N. H. Eggleston reminded his readers that 'wherever there is sin, God has made it possible to be free from it'. God was now bringing all Americans face to face with the question of slavery, and the practical question, 'what is to be done with slavery?' came up side by side with the question 'what is to be done with rebellion?'. Gilbert Haven debated the issue with a conservative opponent, in the Methodist press during the summer of 1861, and insisted that, in the Civil War, 'the object of God is to liberate these children of his who have cried day and night unto him for these many generations'. In what was virtually its first comment on the war, the *Independent* forecast that, by provoking war, the South would bring upon itself a form of emancipation which the Northern abolitionists could never have devised.[44]

A month later the *Independent* injected a slightly more cautious note, and commented on the tactical decision of some abolitionists, including, notably, William Lloyd Garrison, not to press the

[44] [Henry Ward] Beecher, 'The Church's Duty to Slavery' [*Freedom and War: Discourses on Topics suggested by the Times*] (Boston 1863) pp 211–20; N. H. Eggleston, 'Emancipation' *New Englander* 21 (1862) pp 785–6; Gravely, *Haven* pp 88–90; 'God's Hand in War' *Independent* 18 April 1861.

emancipation issue at once, but to wait for the pressures of the war to develop. The paper commended their discretion and their willingness to 'resign that question [of emancipation] to the logic of events, or rather to the developments of an all-wise and all-righteous Providence'. If the war had been made into an antislavery crusade from the beginning, the tide of volunteers for the army would have ebbed rapidly. At the same time, the instinctive feeling of all classes was that the war, if efficiently prosecuted, would be the doom of slavery. This was not the plan of the administration, or the army or even the abolitionists; 'it is the decree of Providence written upon the face of events, so that he that runneth may read'.[45]

This editorial offers much more than an insight into abolitionist tactics. It reveals the two main channels through which antislavery churchmen arrived at a position not too far from that reached by their conservative counterparts, travelling from the opposite direction: the inescapable logic of events and the inscrutable ways of Providence. If conservative churchmen increasingly accepted, however reluctantly, that emancipation might be, first a means of waging war, and then an inevitable consequence of it, liberals and radicals rejoiced at the same prospect, as the conflict grew to the point where re-establishment of the status quo ante bellum looked impossible. Many indeed took the view that, in his wisdom, God was allowing the war to be prolonged in order to ensure the demise of slavery. In the *Christian Examiner*, as elsewhere, the humiliating Northern defeat in the first major battle of the war, at Bull Run, was interpreted as a blessing. Victory at Bull Run might have been followed by a restoration of the Union as it was:

> But this was not to be, and it is well it was not. It was better that the old slavery-ridden Union should never be restored, that the day of cringing and compromise should be wiped out even from memory, if it could be. The flag, which had for so many years been dipped in African blood must be baptized in our own before it could become the symbol of a truly great and free nation . . . The old Union was forever lost at Bull Run. It is a nobler and a better one we have been laying the foundations of since.[46]

[45] 'The War and Slavery' *Independent* 9 May 1861.
[46] 'The War Policy and the Future of the South' *Christian Examiner* 73 (1862) pp 440–1. See also [Gilbert] Haven, [*National Sermons*] (Boston 1869) pp 266–8.

The Instruments of Providence

Gilbert Haven took the same view of Bull Run and others, including Horace Bushnell and Henry Ward Beecher, made the same distinction between restoration of the Union as it was, and establishment of the Union as it should be, without slavery. They discerned God's will in the shift of emphasis from one to the other.[47] The anonymous author of the pamphlet, *The Extinction of Slavery a National Necessity* warned that restoration of the Union with slavery would lead to the same consequences as before:

> We should but repeat our history, and, from a wrong beginning, not corrected, come to the same disastrous conclusions; for they are not accidents, but have come by a necessitating law of nature which the Creator has established in his righteous government of the world . . . Our only hope is . . . that the nation now at last, before it is too late, may be '*Born Again*'; the same and not another, yet the Union, 'new-created in righteousness'.[48]

By mid-war, most of the Northern clergy had bowed, whether reluctantly or enthusiastically, before the logic of events and the wondrous ways of the Almighty. As John Ware put it 'God is using us as instruments in bringing about a mighty change'. Perhaps, he speculated, the 'Great Disposer' had deliberately allowed the creation of a separate power, like the Confederacy, based on slavery, in order to demonstrate its horror and iniquity, and bring about its fall. Celebrating the second emancipation proclamation of 1 January 1863, the *Independent* saw in the history of recent decades, 'the Divine hand preparing a VICTIM for illustration of Eternal Justice'. Gilbert Haven declared that slavery had 'died BY THE VISITATION OF GOD'. Looking forward optimistically to a future of racial equality and harmony, he saw a good omen in the fact that 'the favorite nickname of the negro and the nation, "Sambo" and "Samuel" is of the same origin. Is not this prophetic of their future identity?'[49]

An examination of more conservative interpretations of the role of Providence in achieving emancipation through war suggests

---

[47] [Horace] Bushnell, ['The Doctrine of Loyalty' *New Englander* 22 (1863)] pp 579–80; Beecher pp 337–9; Haven pp 266–7. See also Ide pp 140–2.
[48] *The Extinction of Slavery a National Necessity before the Present Conflict can be Ended* (n.p., n.d.) p 6.
[49] John F. W. Ware, *Our Duty under Reverse* (Boston 1861) pp 9, 10; *Independent* 1 January 1863; Haven pp 435–6.

that, while the tone was more temperate and less triumphalist, the understanding of God's purposes was much the same. For example, the moderate conservative *Christian Advocate*, a Methodist weekly, discerned the hand of God in the evolution of events from the start of the war, but at first it counselled patience. Providence was never in haste, and, although the fate of slavery must be decided by the war, it was the part of wisdom to wait until events pointed the way. By January 1862, the *Advocate* confessed that its own views were changing, though it feared that they might be condemned as heretical. 'We did think that the rebellion could be subdued without emancipation; we doubt it now; we believe the United States is shut up, by God's providence, either to do justice or to be dissolved'. By the time of the emancipation proclamation, the *Advocate* was ready to see it as 'evidently a part of the programme of Providence in this war', and it gave more credit to the divine sense of timing than to the president's sense of the political realities. A week later, the paper reflected on the long years when church and state had tossed the problem of slavery back and forth to each other.

> Now however Providence has removed all delicacy from the subject, and brought it to men's business, and homes, and bosoms. It speaks to us in the drumbeat, the tramp of armed men, the lint, the bandages, the hospitals, the taxes; in the lame, the halt, the blind that crowd the streets from the battlefield, and in the state papers that issue from our capital. Slavery has long been sapping the foundations both of Church and State, and both are now compelled to resist it for their own salvation.[50]

For all the eloquence of the *Advocate*, the last word on God's intervention to guide the United States towards emancipation must surely go to the inimitable George Ide whose penchant for vivid and elaborate figures of speech was equal to the occasion. His description of Providence at work is perhaps stronger on drama than dogma:

> In the pride of our vain wisdom, we marked out for ourselves the way to political greatness. Across the shaking morasses of Expediency, over the bottomless bog of Compromise, we

---

[50] *Christian Advocate* 17 October 1861, 21 November 1861, 23 January 1862, 2 and 9 October 1862.

The Instruments of Providence

formed the track, and laid the rails, and put on the train, and got up the steam, and with rush and roar were sweeping onward in our self-confidence, heedless of the abyss which Slavery had dug in our path, and whose yawning depths lay just before us. But God put his hand on the brakes, and switched us off on a new track, which He laid, and not man. There was surprise, terror, outcry at first. There are doubts, apprehensions, tremblings still. But the road is firm and straight, the engine sound, the cars stanch, the Conductor all-wise and all-powerful, and the end of our journey—a vindicated Government, a restored Union, a Free Nation—already in sight.

By 'a Free Nation', Ide of course meant a nation without slavery. He had no doubt that the emancipation proclamation had 'allied us with Heaven'. Since the 'soft breath of Christian influence' had failed to melt away slavery 'God purposed to blow it out of the universe with Parrott guns'.[51]

There is no reason to doubt the sincerity of the widely-shared belief in the workings of Providence, which took the form of a faith not only in an overall divine plan, but in a God who intervened directly in history to manipulate people and events in a way which served his purposes. However, it is equally true, that, in the context of the Civil War, and particularly of the slavery issue, this was a very convenient doctrine. The war, particularly when identified as God's instrument, solved, at least for the time being, all manner of problems and dilemmas. It dealt with the problem of slavery which had for many years defied all human attempts to resolve it. It purged feelings of national, ecclesiastical and individual guilt over slavery, in the copious bloodshed of many a field of battle. It not only saved the Union, but re-furbished its image, and set it on the way to becoming a stronger, more tightly integrated, nation. For the moral crusaders against slavery, who had shunned conventional politics for fear of pollution by them, it brought with unexpected celerity the achievement of their goal. For conservatives, loyal to the Union, but opposed to agitation of the embarrassing issue of slavery, it contrived at one and the same time to reinforce their patriotism and eliminate the cause of their embarrassment. For those of more liberal persuasion too, it

---

[51] Ide pp 153–4, 155, 239–40.

brought a much closer alliance between their national loyalty and their moral purposes.

No one benefited more than the churches and churchmen from the Providential power of war to release them from difficult dilemmas. Gilbert Haven, Methodist and abolitionist, appreciated the way in which war was interlinking the passion for Union and the passion for liberty:

> Abolitionists, though sound on the rights of men, were, as a whole, unsound on the necessity of the Union to attain and maintain their rights. Different classes of the people were the depositary of different ideas. The one cried "Union at any cost. Down with the abolitionists who are disturbing it. Union is liberty. Union is democracy. Let it alone, even if it becomes the patron of slavery. Some way and some time it will emancipate the State from that iniquity." The other party, with equal and superior fervour, cried, "The Rights of every man at any cost. Down with the Union, if it stands in the way of liberty."
>
> As in the material world, the orbit pursued is the resultant of the forces employed upon the orb itself, so here. The centrifugal lovers of liberty, and the centripetal lovers of Union . . . were each at heart lovers of the democratic and federative ideas. Both sought their preservation. Both contended together because each felt his own principle was in danger of destruction through the purpose of his antagonist's idea. The shock of arms united them. The one saw that Union now meant universal liberty. The other that abolitionism meant Union, and only under its banner could the nation be preserved.[52]

Lest anyone should doubt who was the architect of this happy conjunction, Haven reminded his audience that 'the wisdom of God is wiser than men' and that 'He is pushing us forward to His, not our Millennium'.[53] Haven saw that millennium in terms of racial equality and fraternity, and the speedy crumbling of such hopes is a reminder that the apparent ability of God's war to resolve dilemmas expired with the conflict itself. The tangled history of postwar reconstruction, the persisting problem of race

[52] Haven p 383.
[53] *Ibid* p 384.

relations in America, the gross materialism of American society in the gilded age, and the mounting problems of industrialisation and urbanisation soon put into sombre relief the problem-solving powers of the Civil War.

VI

The main focus of this study has been on the responses of Northern protestants to the issues of war and slavery, as they unfolded during the conflict itself. As both postscript and conclusion, it may be appropriate to sketch very briefly some of the main themes of attempts during the war years to set the religious meaning of the struggle in the wider context of American history and American destiny. How could the war be related to God's broader and more enduring purposes for America?

Some of the main themes of the response to this question are too well-known or too predictable to need consideration here. There was a good deal of emphasis on the moral advantages and benefits of engaging in a righteous war, on war as an agent of moral regeneration, and on the encouragement of the manly virtues. There was equal emphasis on the role of the war in consolidating and reinvigorating American nationalism. Horace Bushnell, spokesman of Yale Congregationalism, saw the war as the crucible of national loyalty, and the creator of a new national spirit. The sacrifice and bloodshed of war would transform the United States from a compact or confederation into a nation—'God's own nation, providentially planted, established on moral foundations.'[54] Although Bushnell has received particular attention, many other preachers and authors were expressing similar views.

Beyond these well-worn themes, shared by the secular as well as the religious press, three more specifically religious emphases stand out very clearly. The first lays emphasis on the punishment of sins, and on the need for atonement and repentance. While chastisement for the sin of slavery received plenty of attention, it did not by any means dominate to the exclusion of others. The emphasis was on national sins and national guilt—but often, too, on individual sins which were alleged to be rife throughout American society. The catalogue of American sinfulness is

---

[54] Bushnell p 581. See also George M. Fredrickson, *The Inner Civil War: Northern Intellectuals and the Crisis of the Union* (New York 1965) pp 25–6, 137–44.

impressive enough—at the individual level, neglect of God, intemperance, adultery and Sabbath-breaking, (there was lively discussion whether victory won in a battle fought on a Sunday could carry with it God's blessing); at the national level, boastfulness, hypocrisy, prejudice and unfaithfulness to American principles. It was particularly stressed that, because nations would not be present at the last judgment, they must expect judgment in this world. Most frequently of all, the war and its suffering were seen as punishment for the sins encouraged by American prosperity—luxury, idleness, selfishness, corruption and materialism.[55]

The war offered the opportunity for atonement and repentance if God's punishment was accepted in the right spirit. Medical metaphors were much in vogue. Gilbert Haven talked of 'the wounds of the Great Surgeon and Physician' and the unpleasant medicine which Americans must take for their own good. Rev. S. W. S. Dutton wrote of the war healing by wounding, by 'using the caustic', or the surgeon's knife. A writer in the *Biblical Repertory* believed that blood-letting was needed, rather than mild sedatives, to purge the virus of rebellion. He was confident that the nation would emerge chastened and purified.[56]

This comment opens up a second, related but distinct theme: the war as ordeal, as sacrifice, above all as purification. There was a strong sense that Americans were living at a great historic moment, a crisis or turning-point for the United States and indeed for the world. Never given to under-statement, George Ide thought the Civil War one of the 'grand peaks in human history, overtopped only by Bethlehem and Calvary'.[57] Repeatedly, religious commentators depicted this crisis as a time of trial, an ordeal by fire, a testing of American character, institutions, liberties, and nationhood. The war was interpreted as a test, designed by Providence, of American civilisation, and specifically of its capacity to reconcile prosperity and virtue. The American character was to be tempered in the furnace of war. Out of that

---

[55] For statements of the punishment theme, and comprehensive lists of punishable sins, see Ezra S. Gannett, *Repentance amidst Deliverance* (Boston 1863) pp 7–15, and Sturtevant pp 895–6, 899–912.
[56] Haven pp 382, 423; S. W. S. Dutton, 'Home Duties during the War' *New Englander* 19 (1861) p 681; 'The History and Theory of Revolutions' *Biblical Repertory* 34 (1862) p 273.
[57] Ide p 228.

process would come a purified American society and way of life.[58]

The purification of war would prepare America to fulfil its God-given destiny in the world. This third theme in the religious interpretation of the conflict found frequent, but not often very explicit, expression. It often amounted to little more than a re-affirmation of the significance of the great American experiment not merely for Americans themselves but for the world. The Civil War did not inspire any major redefinition of America's world mission, but rather a belief that a purified and re-born America would be better able to fulfil its historic mission, to promote liberty and free institutions around the world—or, in spiritual terms, to further Christ's kingdom on earth.[59]

It is true that, as Moorhead has amply demonstrated, many American churchmen saw the war as the immediate prelude to the millennium, or at least cast their assessments of its significance in millennial terms. However, the direction in which many of them looked was backward at least as much as forward. The war was often seen as restorative rather than innovative, let alone revolutionary or apocalyptic. Its achievement would be to put America back on its true course, to purge it of the corruption and vices which long years of peace and prosperity had fostered, to wipe away the foul blot of slavery which had tarnished its image before the world, and to reinstate both the republican virtues of the Founding Fathers and the Christian virtues of the Pilgrim Fathers. The churches looked at least as much to the recovery of a golden age from the past as to the arrival of the millennium in the future. They were solidly in that American tradition, a blend of a taste for nostalgia and a belief in progress, which Richard Hofstadter described as a forward-looking return to the past.[60] The colourful rhetoric of the millennialists was never outshone, but possibly sometimes outweighed, by the more sober words of those

---

[58] For examples of the purification theme, see *Christian Examiner* 71 (1861) pp 109–115; *Independent* 27 November 1862, 1 January 1863; Jones, *Northern Methodism* pp 88–9; N. West, *Establishment in National Righteousness and Present Causes of Thanksgiving* (New York 1861) pp 36–7. West, incidentally, moves straight from this passage to a much more dramatic, millennial interpretation of the Civil War. *Ibid* pp 37–9.

[59] See for example Crooks, *Simpson* pp 381–2; Joseph P. Thompson, 'The Advancement of Christ's Kingdom by War' *New Englander* 24 (1865) pp 316–8; Hodge, *Biblical Repertory* 35 (1863) pp 167–8.

[60] Moorhead passim; Richard Hofstadter *The American Political Tradition and the Men who made it* (New York 1948) v-vii.

who talked of chastisement, purification and the restoration of true American and Christian values.

Let the last word go to that organ of cautious, conservative Presbyterianism, the New York *Observer*. As early as 16 May 1861, in an editorial headed 'Perfect through Suffering', it encapsulated the inter-related themes of punishment, trial, suffering, purification, restoration and rebirth. It came straight to the point:

> Trials are as good for nations as individuals. Great afflictions make great Saints, and why may it not be that a people need to go through the furnace to be purified, tempered and tried.

Since the revolution, the country had suffered no calamities, and luxury had made it selfish, effeminate and corrupt. 'And now the baptism of fire is the baptism with which she is to be baptized. She is to be saved and glorified.' In the temple of American liberty, those who held office must return to true standards of honesty and integrity.

> It will be blessing indeed if the chastisement of war, a calamity always to victors and vanquished, shall restore the country to the purity of her better days, and teach her sons that righteousness exalteth a nation and sin is a reproach to any people.[61]

University of Dundee

---

[61] *Observer* 16 May 1861.

'ULSTER WILL FIGHT AND ULSTER WILL BE RIGHT': THE PROTESTANT CHURCHES AND ULSTER'S RESISTANCE TO HOME RULE, 1912-14

by R. F. G. HOLMES

'ULSTER WILL fight and Ulster will be right'. Randolph Churchill may never have uttered these emotive words during his visit to Ulster in 1886—they appeared in a public letter to a Glasgow Liberal unionist[1]—but they undoubtedly expressed the belligerence and self-righteousness of the Ulster protestant resistance to the prospect of home rule for Ireland. Joseph Lee has observed correctly that 'Orangemen did not need to be told that they were right or that they would fight',[2] but after 1886 it was not only Orangemen who made such claims, nor even opportunist tory politicians like Churchill, but protestant churchmen and solid middle class citizens and farmers who would previously have distanced themselves fastidiously from Orangeism. In this paper we shall examine the encouragement and support given by protestant churches and churchmen—Presbyterians in particular—to the movement to resist home rule by force in the period 1912-14.

In the same public letter of May 1886 Churchill had declared that 'Ulster, at the proper moment, will resort to the supreme arbitrament of force', but that moment did not come in 1886 for Gladstone's home rule bill was defeated in the Commons, nor in 1893 when his second bill was rejected by the Lords. Arms dealers who sent catalogues of rifles for sale to the Ulster unionist leader, E. J. Saunderson, were acting prematurely in 1886.[3] The time of decision for the opponents of home rule came in the years 1912-14 after the parliament act of 1911 had removed the House of Lords' ultimate veto on decisions of the Commons and it became clear that Asquith's Liberal government, dependent for its majority upon

---
[1] W. S. Churchill, *Lord Randolph Churchill* 2 vols (London 1906) 2 pp 64-5.
[2] [J.] Lee, [*The Modernization of Irish Society, 1848-1918*] (Dublin 1973) p 133.
[3] R. V. Lucas, *Colonel Saunderson M.P. A Memoir* (London 1908) pp 98-101.

Irish nationalist votes, would introduce some measure of home rule for Ireland.

The crisis did not come upon the unionists 'as a thief in the night', as Churchill had suggested it might in 1886, nor did it find them unprepared. And, from the beginning, their defiance was articulated and encouraged by leading protestant churchmen.

On the eve of the general election of 1910 which brought the Liberals to power, eleven former moderators of the Irish Presbyterian general assembly took the unprecedented step of publishing a manifesto in which they contended that the best interests of *all* the people of Ireland were safeguarded by the union with Great Britain.[4] Acknowledging that 'the grave errors of British rule in Ireland were written on the page of history', they argued that 'the determination of the British people to provide just and equal legislation for this country' had been demonstrated 'beyond challenge'. An independent Irish parliament, however, would reverse this process and establish a Roman Catholic ascendancy with 'clerical control' even in matters that were 'purely civil and secular'.

This was and remained the nub of the Ulster protestant case against home rule, although the ex-moderators' manifesto also expressed anxiety about the effects of home rule upon industry and agriculture. They disclaimed any intention of coercing Roman Catholics but they refused to entrust their civil and religious liberties to Roman Catholic control. They were unimpressed by government promises of safeguards for the protestant minority in Ireland, guaranteed by the Imperial parliament, or by the assurances of Irish nationalists. The protestations of men like John Dillon that 'they would no more take their political guidance from the pope of Rome than from the sultan of Turkey'[5] or conduct their affairs 'at the bidding of any body of cardinals'[6], if they had ever been heard at all, were not believed. The moderator of the general assembly of 1912, Henry Montgomery, an earnest Evangelical and founder of the Shankill Road Mission, declared that 'such promises and pledges are not worth the breath used in speaking them or the ink required to write them'.[7]

[4] [*The*] *Witness* 14 January 1910.
[5] F. S. L. Lyons, *John Dillon: a biography* (London 1968) p 92.
[6] *Ibid* p 94.
[7] *Witness* 19 July 1912.

'Ulster will fight and Ulster will be right'

In particular Ulster protestants refused to believe that a subordinate parliament in Dublin would be a final settlement of the question of Anglo-Irish relations. 'We are convinced', declared the Irish Presbyterian weekly newspaper, *The Witness*, 'judging from the public expression of its sympathies and from its public acts, that the heart of Irish nationalism is set on complete separation'.[8] Had they not heard Parnell's ringing affirmation of the rights of nationhood?—'No man has the right to fix the boundary to the march of a nation'.[9]

Questions were being asked, however, by some Irish protestants about the wisdom and propriety of identifying the causes of protestantism and unionism, of aligning their churches with a political faction. *The Witnesses* which, from the beginning of the home rule crisis, assumed an uncompromisingly unionist stance, insisted that it was innocent of 'the blasphemy as well as the arrogance' of associating God with one party rather than another, and admitted that 'neither party is God's party'.[10] The church's supreme concern was to advance the kingdom of God but, *The Witness* contended, it was because home rule would hinder that advance in Ireland that it was being opposed.[11]

On 1 February 1912 a convention of Irish Presbyterians was held in the Assembly Hall in Belfast, with overflow meetings in some of the inner city churches, to give expression to their reaction to the political crisis. The convention was not an official court of the church and it was criticised both by those Presbyterians like the Rev J. B. Armour of Ballymoney who supported home rule, and by those who disapproved of their church taking a partisan stand on a political question.[12] It attracted considerable support from Presbyterians in general however, and *The Witness* rejoiced in its unequivocal reaffirmation of the opposition to home rule previously expressed in 1886 and 1893.[13]

Some of the speakers who addressed the convention did not shrink from the ultimate implications of their position. T. G. Houston, headmaster of a leading grammar school, insisted

---

[8] *Ibid.*
[9] P. Bew, *C. S. Parnell* (Dublin) p 70.
[10] *Witness* 28 January 1910.
[11] *Ibid.*
[12] [W. S.] Armour, [*Armour of Ballymoney*] (London 1934) pp 252–7.
[13] *Witness* 2 February 1912.

323

that no sacrifice was too great for their noble cause: 'in the last resort they should be prepared to sacrifice even life itself rather than yield to what would prove the ruin of themselves and their country'.[14] He warned the government that their threats were not 'empty vapour', they were made, not in a jingo, but in a martyr spirit. R. D. Megaw, a lawyer of Liberal background, was applauded when he argued that the Roman Catholic church had declared, in Pius IX's Syllabus of Errors, its opposition to free speech, a free press, liberty of conscience and the toleration of dissent in religion.[15] Much was heard, then and later, of the iniquities of the *ne temere* and *motu proprio* decrees, which were alleged to have demonstrated the claims of the Roman Catholic church to be above the ordinary law of the land. This was the ecclesiastical power which would be dominant in the future Irish state.

The Presbyterian convention received a message of sympathy and support from the Church of Ireland primate, Archbishop Crozier, assuring them that their action 'in the present terrible crisis' would be followed by a similar demonstration of Anglican feeling.[16] And, indeed, the synod of the Church of Ireland subsequently expressed its 'unswerving attachment to the legislative union now subsisting between Great Britain and Ireland', with only five members of synod voting against.[17] The vice-president of the Irish Baptist Union offered the convention his 'hearty sympathy'[18] and shortly afterwards Irish Methodists held a similar assembly to express opposition to home rule.[19]

The impression of protestant solidarity given by these demonstrations of opposition to home rule was weakened by the fact that articulate and influential churchmen like J. B. Armour, who was one of the lord lieutenant's chaplains, took a different view and even more by the support given to Asquith's government and its Irish policy by Scottish churchmen and English nonconformists. David Bebbington, in his recent study of the British nonconformist conscience, has shown how nonconformists were divided on the Irish home rule question between those whose

[14] *Ibid.*
[15] *Ibid.*
[16] *Ibid.*
[17] [R. B.] McDowell, [*The Church of Ireland, 1869–1969*] (London 1975) p 103.
[18] *Witness* 2 February 1912.
[19] *Ibid* 9 February 1912.

'Ulster will fight and Ulster will be right'

loyalty to Liberal, and, they believed, Christian principles, compelled them to support home rule as a measure of justice for the majority of the Irish people, and those whose protestantism and anti-catholicism led them to share the anxieties of the Irish protestants.[20] Their dilemma was reflected in the suggestion of the English congregationalist, R. F. Horton, that a solution to the problem might be found in an exchange of population—Irish in Britain returning to Ireland with Irish protestants moving to Britain, but this was ridiculed by *The Witness*.[21] Were Irish protestants to give up their farms and factories to returning exiles from the slums of British cities?—a tacit admission, it might seem, that, as their critics suggested, it was really their privileges and property that Irish protestants were worried about.

Undoubtedly many elements combined to make the Ulster protestant resistance to home rule the implacable force it became—religious conviction and prejudice, economic self-interest, national consciousness and culture, perhaps even, as Joseph Lee has suggested, racialism.[22] 'Racialism, articulated in religious idiom', he considers, 'dominated Scotch-Irish hostility to home rule'. The economic argument of the unionists, he believes, had racialist overtones, successful Ulster businessmen suspecting that the Celt was incapable of mastering the industrial virtues. But of course there was racialism on the other side of the Irish divide with hatred and contempt for the English playing an important part in Irish nationalist ideology from Tone to Pearse. Pearse claimed that O'Donovan Rossa, as a good Gael, looked upon the English as an inferior race, morally and intellectually.[23]

Whatever the roots of the Ulster protestants' antipathy to home rule, it is clear that they resented the fact that many of their co-religionists in Britain did not support them and they responded with accusations of betrayal and with attempts to win a better understanding for their position.[24] Deputations visited Britain to

---

[20] D. Bebbington, *The Nonconformist Conscience. Chapel and Politics 1870–1914* (London 1982) pp 84–105.
[21] *Witness* 16 February 1912.
[22] Lee p 130.
[23] P. Pearse, *O'Donovan Rossa: A Character Study* quoted in F. Shaw, 'The Canon of Irish History—A Challenge', *Studies*, 61 no 242 (Summer 1972) p 126.
[24] *Witness* 16 February 1912. Editorial articles in *The Witness* 1912–14 returned often to this problem.

address ecclesiastical gatherings and statements of their case were offered to religious journals.[25]

They themselves remained unmoved by the arguments of friend and foe. It was in vain that Winston Churchill, on a brief and turbulent visit to Ulster in 1912, following in his father's footsteps but moving in the opposite direction in the colours of a different party and cheered by different supporters, offered Ulster protestants a different challenge in a novel interpretation of his father's famous call to arms:

> Let Ulster fight for the dignity and honour of Ireland. Let her fight for the reconciliation of races and for the forgiveness of ancient wrongs. Let her fight for the spread of charity, tolerance and enlightenment among men. Then, indeed, gentlemen, Ulster will fight and Ulster will be right.[26]

But in 1912 Ulster unionists, with the blessing of protestant church leaders, were preparing to fight in the original sense of Winston's father's words. Winston's fine sentiments sounded to them like a call to humiliation and defeat. On Easter Tuesday, 1912, 100,000 men paraded at Balmoral on the outskirts of Belfast in an impressive show of strength which began with a religious service led by the church of Ireland primate and the moderator of the general assembly.[27] Bonar Law, leader of the opposition at Westminster and, remarkably, the son of an Irish Presbyterian minister, addressed them in the emotive idiom of Ulster protestantism's seventeenth-century conflict: 'Once more you hold the pass for the empire. You are a besieged city. The timid have left you; your Lundys have betrayed you; but you have closed your gates'.[28] A few months later, at a Conservative and Unionist demonstration at Blenheim palace he went even further along the road towards armed resistance. Describing the government as 'a revolutionary committee which has seized upon despotic power by fraud', he said: 'I can imagine no length of resistance to which Ulster can go in which I should not be prepared to support them'.[29] This was, of course, strange language in the mouth of a leader of the tory party, but it was the unionist contention that the Liberals,

---

[25] *M[inutes of the] G[eneral] A[ssembly]* 12 (1911–15) p 908.
[26] *Witness* 9 February 1912.
[27] *B[elfast] N[ews] L[etter]* 10 April 1912.
[28] *Ibid.*
[29] [A. T. Q.] Stewart, [*The Ulster Crisis*] (London 1967) pp 56–7.

'Ulster will fight and Ulster will be right'

by failing to put the home rule issue fairly before the electorate in 1910 and by destroying the powers of veto of the House of Lords, which could have been used to force a general election on the question, had behaved unconstitutionally. The fact that eminent constitutional lawyers like A. V. Dicey seemed to share this view must have encouraged many normally law-abiding citizens to believe that they were justified in the last resort in contemplating armed resistance.

Ulster protestants were primarily concerned, of course, by the threat which they claimed home rule posed to their civil and religious liberties and prosperity. But was it a threat which justified armed resistance? The Rev. J. B. Armour, who believed that the idea that their liberties and prosperity were in danger was an illusion fostered by tories and landlords in their own interests, thought not. He never wavered from his opinion that to resist home rule by force was wrong, that force would beget force and ill-will would engender ill-will throughout Ireland.[30]

Few seem to have shared his convictions, however, or been prepared to say so if they did. Of course in the siege atmosphere which was developing in Ulster dissent from the majority position could bring disapproval and unpopularity. Some Presbyterian ministers who opposed the campaign against home rule and the threat of armed resistance found themselves under considerable pressure in their congregations and some were glad to move to Britain or further afield.[31] A substantial minority, however, in spite of these pressures, continued to oppose the agitation of political questions in the courts of their church with the result that, in 1912, no debate on the home rule issue took place in the general assembly. After protracted negotiations behind the scenes, J. B. Armour seconded a resolution, proposed by Thomas Sinclair, the leading layman in Irish Presbyterianism and a prominent unionist, which stated that, as the views of the vast majority of Presbyterians on the home rule question had been expressed in the Presbyterian convention, no statement by the assembly was necessary.[32] It is scarcely surprising that, afterwards, both sides were dissatisfied with this compromise. Armour, acknowledging that a majority of Presbyterians had expressed their views on home

---

[30] Armour pp 248–9.
[31] See eg. H. C. Waddell, *John Waddell* (Belfast 1949) pp 42–47.
[32] *Witness* 7, 11 June 1912; Armour pp 257–60; *M.G.A.* 12 (1911–15) p 350.

rule, reminded the assembly that ten righteous men could save a city!³³

The Witness, however, continued to pour scorn on those who did not share the majority view that resistance to home rule, even in arms, was a sacred duty.³⁴ 'There are some who say that that is an unwise and unchristian attitude', declared an editorial article in July 1912,

> that the prudent and Christian attitude should be for the Ulster protestants to lick the rod and bite the dust and lie down and let their conquerors trample over them; better chains of slavery than resistance . . . That might be a counsel of perfection and of peace but it is a perfection which even the British nonconformists, who are its greatest preachers, did not and would not practise in their own case and it is peace at the price of freedom . . . a peace at too great a price. For weal or woe it will not be paid.³⁵

It was scarcely fair, perhaps, to compare the nonconformist campaign of 'passive resistance' to Balfour's Education Act of 1902, though it put some ministers into prison, with what Ulster protestants were proposing in opposition to home rule, although they might have retorted that the issue was much more fundamental in their case.

The Witness' Dublin correspondent, who, throughout the crisis, took his stand with his Ulster brethren, argued that they were not the aggressors; their fight was defensive:

> How can it be affirmed that we are transgessing the law of Christ? The New Testament does not teach nations the law of non-resistance any more than the Old. In 1690 our forefathers . . . successfully fought our great battle for civil and religious liberty. What sort of spurious Christianity is this which tells us that we must not lift up a voice in protest or a hand in our defence. God's witnesses in all generations cry shame on such a proposition.³⁶

And F. E. Smith, hitherto little known as an authority on Christian ethics, was quoted as asking an assembly of Orangemen on 12 July:

---

³³ Armour p 259.
³⁴ *Witness* 12 July 1912.
³⁵ *Ibid* 19 July 1912.
³⁶ *Ibid.*

'Ulster will fight and Ulster will be right'

'If we are not prepared to die for our faith, in the name of God and of men what is there we would die for?'[37]

The climax and supreme demonstration of the Ulster protestants' determination to resist home rule was the signing of the Covenant on 28 September 1912, known as Ulster Day. The text of the Covenant was largely the work of the Presbyterian ruling elder, Thomas Sinclair, and recalled the historic Scottish covenants which occupied a hallowed place in Presbyterian memories and imaginations. It was, Joseph Lee has suggested, 'the traditional Presbyterian technique of reminding God whose side He was on'.[38] It pledged its signatories, 'humbly relying on the God whom our fathers confidently trusted ... to stand by one another in defending for ourselves and our children our cherished position of equal citizenship in the United Kingdom, and in using all means which may be found necessary to defeat the present conspiracy to set up a home rule parliament in Ireland'.[39]

As the great day approached there were appeals from the moderator of the general assembly, the bishop of Down and the vice-president of the Irish Methodist conference for moderation and self-control, accompanied by calls to prayer. D'Arcy, the bishop of Down, claimed that their opposition to home rule was 'essentially religious':

> We contend for life, for civil liberty, for progress, for our rightful heritage of British citizenship. We contend for faith and the freedom of our souls. We are fighting not for ourselves alone but for the whole country for these are the things which alone can make Ireland great and happy.[40]

There was some opposition from churchmen in the south of Ireland to their Ulster co-religionists' decision to support the signing of the Covenant. The bishop of Cork claimed that many of their people in the south—the Church of Ireland was much more a 'national' church than was the Presbyterian, which was firmly based in Ulster—objected to being in any way identified with the Ulster resistance to home rule, but, in the end, all five northern bishops and two retired men, Stack of Clogher and Montgomery of Tasmania, the father of the future field-marshal, signed.[41]

---

[37] *Ibid.*
[38] Lee p 135.
[39] Stewart pp 61–2.
[40] *Witness* 30 August 1912.
[41] McDowell, p 104.

The moderator of the general assembly, Henry Montgomery, declared that it was not enough that religious services should accompany the signing of the Covenant, as had been arranged, and he appointed the previous Sunday, 22 September, as a day of humiliation before God and supplication for deliverance.[42] But prayer, he insisted, did not imply 'the discarding of the sword, it may only involve the strengthening of it', though he added:

> We sincerely hope no sword will be necessary and our chief hope and faith are founded on a solemn belief that God is still in his heaven and will turn the hearts of evil men from the iniquity and injustice they are contemplating and from the havoc they would create in this Ireland of ours.[43]

The Witness published lists of centres where religious services would be held and where the Covenant could be signed.[44] There were over 300 such centres. Services were usually to be held in the local parish or Presbyterian churches, occasionally in Methodist chapels and, in some places, services were to take place in the open air. In Tobermore in county Derry the service was to be held in the Baptist church in which the famous Alexander Carson had preached so influentially in the nineteenth century. The Covenant was to be signed in local halls—in the City Hall in Belfast and sometimes in town halls in provincial centres—occasionally in church halls or precincts but never, so far as official directions went, in a church building itself.

Significantly, at the ceremony in the City Hall in Belfast, the signatures of the moderator of the general assembly and the bishop of Down followed immediately after those of Sir Edward Carson and Lord Londonderry. Preacher after preacher at services throughout the province, fully reported in the columns of *The Witness*, insisted that it was a religious, rather than a political, occasion. They emphasised that they bore no enmity towards their Roman Catholic fellow-countrymen but they opposed any establishment of a Roman Catholic ascendancy in Ireland.[45] The moderator of the general assembly declared: 'There are two nations in Ireland, differing in race, in religion and in their sense of national and civic responsibilities; the fusion of the two is an absolute

---

[42] *Witness* 13 September 1912.
[43] *Ibid.*
[44] *Ibid* 20 and 27 September 1912.
[45] *Ibid* 4 October 1912.

impossibility',[46] and *The Witness* commented: 'If Ireland should be separated from Britain, Ulster should be separated from Ireland'.[47] The issue might be regarded as religious but its implications were clearly political. It was becoming clear, also, that if they could not stop home rule for Ireland, the Ulstermen would divide the country. 237,368 men signed the Covenant and 234,046 women a parallel document.[48]

The shadow of possible armed conflict hung over and gave solemnity to the occasion. In Belfast cathedral the bishop of Down spoke of the terrifying prospect of civil war:

> Oh! my friends, let us pray unceasingly for deliverance from such a horror. Nevertheless we must face the fact that there are things worse than war . . . Our trust is in God. Let there be no vaunting, no spirit of self-confidence. On the contrary let us feel our dependence on Him, and confessing our shortcomings, commit ourselves to Him that judgeth righteously and having so committed ourselves let us act in the way our consciences dictate.[49]

A few voices continued to be raised in protest against the majority Ulster protestant opinion. The Rev. R. W. Hamilton of Lisburn claimed that he could not recognise the will of God in the home rule question as clearly as some of his brethren but *The Witness* found his obscurity of vision incomprehensible.[50] Nor was *The Witness* impressed when a number of distinguished Irish literary figures, including W. B. Yeats, G. B. Shaw and Arthur Conan Doyle, took part in a public meeting in London under the auspices of the Protestant Home Rule Association to protest about the 'bigotry and intolerance' of Irish protestants in their opposition to home rule.[51] These men had never been associated with protestantism in Ireland, observed *The Witness*, they were associated rather with 'literature, art and humbug'.[52]

The fact that *The Witness* found it necessary to return again and again in editorial articles to the subjects of religion and politics, war and peace suggests that there were still those who had not

---

[46] *Ibid.*
[47] *Ibid.*
[48] Stewart p 66.
[49] *Witness* 4 October 1912.
[50] *Ibid* 25 October 1912.
[51] *Ibid* 6 December 1912.
[52] *Ibid.*

been convinced by their arguments.[53] The dread implications of home rule were reiterated *ad nauseam*. It would reverse the revolutionary settlement of the seventeenth century on which their liberties depended. They resented accusations of bigotry and intolerance against them when they were only opposing the bigotry and intolerance of Rome! They insisted that they had no animosity towards their Roman Catholic fellow-countrymen but they could not entrust their civil and religious liberties to them for, as good Catholics, they would be bound to obey their church upon which their hope of salvation depended. They continued to attack British nonconformists and all who, assuming their own superior spirituality, counselled non-resistance and they looked back wistfully to men like Spurgeon and Dale who had been unionists in politics and who were extolled as exemplars of the authentic English puritan spirit.

They accused the government of attempting to divide Ulster 'by bribes, by corrupt patronage, by rewarding sychophancy, by polluting the streams of justice, by all the thousand and one ways of overriding a people which are known to those who command the public purse and the public service'.[54] Only home rulers and Roman Catholics could hope for public recognition and reward. Nevertheless their determination to resist was undiminished. 'Unless the cabinet drops its mad policy there can be no escape except in a baptism of blood', declared *The Witness'* Dublin correspondent, though he added, 'As an Irishman I deplore the terrible situation. I hate all appeals to armed force'.[55]

A memorial from 131,351 members and adherents of the Irish Presbyterian church was addressed to its 1913 general assembly reaffirming their 'determined and unyielding' opposition to home rule and was approved by 921 votes to 43, though J. B. Armour argued that even 131,351 represented only a minority of the church's membership.[56] What was striking was the large number of abstentions—165. Perhaps they represented those who continued to disapprove of the agitation of such questions in the courts of the church.

The celebration in 1913 of the tercentenary of Irish Presby-

---

[53] eg *Ibid* 25 October 1912; 31 January, 31 March, 2 May 1913.
[54] *Ibid* 28 March 1913.
[55] *Ibid*.
[56] M.G.A. 12 p 636, and Armour p 273.

terianism inevitably stimulated Presbyterian pride in their heritage. When a professor of church history recalled the threat to their forefathers' lives and prosperity from ' the boar out of the wood and the wild beast of the field', he scarcely needed to add, though he did, 'you will have no difficulty in identifying these marauders'.[57] And few of his hearers can have failed to understand the message of his closing exhortation: 'A great cloud of witnesses . . . are looking down on us at this moment . . . Let us be true to the heritage they have left us and not surrender lightly what they have won for us at so great a cost'.[58]

Commenting on the annual Orange demonstrations in July 1913 *The Witness* confessed that it had seldom in the past regarded these manifestations of party feeling with much enthusiasm but now it applauded the Orangemen as soldiers preparing for battle:

> How could men die better than facing the forces of Rome for the faith and liberty of their fathers, for the life and liberty of their children. There may be some who think this wanton and wicked. We would say that anything else is weak, cowardly and traitorous, we hope that history will never have to level these charges at the people of this generation who represent such a noble ancestry.[59]

Already their preparations for armed resistance and their need to discipline their more belligerent followers had resulted in the formation of the Ulster Volunteer Force and the columns of *The Witness* began to carry reports of Volunteer parades, of sermons preached at parade services and of arrangements to provide hospitals and an indemnity fund to support the Volunteers if armed conflict became inescapable. The so-called Curragh 'mutiny' was hailed with delight—the apparent unwillingness of some Army officers to move against the Ulstermen confirmed their optimistic hopes that British soldiers would never act against those who only wanted to remain British citizens.[60] And when, in April 1914, thousands of rifles and millions of rounds of ammunition were smuggled into the province, *The Witness* hailed the achievement with the headline, 'Great Volunteer Coup'.[61] Major Fred

[57] *300 Years of Presbyterianism in Ireland 1613–1913* (Belfast 1913) p 20.
[58] *Ibid.*
[59] *Ibid* 11 and 18 July 1913.
[60] *Ibid* 17 April 1914.
[61] *Ibid* 1 May 1914.

Crawford, the principal 'gun-runner', could boast descent from some of the founding fathers of Irish Presbyterianism and in his own account of his gun-running adventures he recalled how, when it seemed as though he and his cargo would be apprehended:

> I went into my cabin and threw myself on my knees, and in simple language, told God all about it: what it meant to Ulster, that there was nothing sordid in what we desired, that we wanted nothing selfishly. I pointed out all this to God and thought of the old psalm(!), O God, our help in ages past. I rose comforted.[62]

Addressing the general assembly in June 1914 the moderator, James Bingham, described the Volunteers as:

> A great and noble army of men drawn from all ranks and organised on thoroughly democratic principles . . . preparing to defend themselves and us from the dangers that threaten our citizenship, liberties and religion. Ulster at present is an armed camp. We have not chosen this attitude, we have been driven to it. They had a right to resist and he was ready to share with them in their resistance.[63]

In the event, whether they were right or not, the Volunteers did not have to fight, though many of them were to die fighting for Britain in the war against Germany which prevented home rule for Ireland becoming a reality in 1914. Whether or not they would have fought against British troops if the troops had been ordered to take action against them, must remain a question of debate. What seems clear is that many protestant churchmen in Ulster considered that they would have been right to fight. They did not want to fight. At the height of the crisis in 1914 the general assembly's state of the country committee urged Presbyterians to continue to show 'calmness and self-restraint' at a time of 'unexampled provocation' and to use their influence with others 'to promote peace and good order in the community',[64] but there was no suggestion that they would be wrong to take up arms if that was forced upon them. The Rev. Robert Moore, later minister of agriculture at Stormont, told a parade of Volunteers at Ringsend near Coleraine in June 1914 that the battle which they

---

[62] F. H. Crawford, *Guns for Ulster* (Belfast 1947) p 39.
[63] *Witness* 2 June 1914.
[64] *Ibid* 10 April 1914; M.G.A. 12 (1911–15) p 908.

were being called upon to fight was the Lord's: 'We are fighting for our homes, for our liberties and for our prosperity . . . We are fighting for our religion, for its very existence in this land'.[65]

It is hardly surprising that Irish nationalists like Pearse, who saw war, not as a necessary evil, but as a means of national, if not personal, redemption, should have found an Orangeman with a rifle a much less ridiculous figure than a nationalist without one.[66] There is a way which seems right to a man, even a man of God, but the end of it is death.

Union Theological College and the Queen's University,
Belfast

---

[65] H. S. Morrison, *Modern Ulster* (London 1920) pp 95–6.
[66] Stewart p 106.

WAR, THE NATION, AND THE KINGDOM OF GOD: THE ORIGINS OF THE NATIONAL MISSION OF REPENTANCE AND HOPE, 1915–16

by DAVID M. THOMPSON

THE NATIONAL Mission of Repentance and Hope, launched by the archbishops of Canterbury and York and led by the bishop of London in the autumn of 1916, has not been regarded as one of the more successful episodes in the history of the Church of England. Hensley Henson, who can always be relied upon for a suitable comment, called it 'a grave, practical blunder', whilst a very different type of churchman, Conrad Noel, called it 'the Mission of Funk and Despair'.[1] Its treatment in the secondary sources is curious. Bell has a chapter on it in his life of Randall Davidson, but it says much about Davidson and little about the Mission. The same is true, *mutatis mutandis*, of Iremonger's treatment in the life of Temple. S. C. Carpenter chose to omit the chapter on the National Mission from his life of Winnington-Ingram. Lloyd depends heavily on Bell; Wilkinson is more rounded, but the fullest account by Mews remains unpublished.[2]

In the past attention has been concentrated on what seemed to flow from the National Mission—the life and liberty movement, perhaps, or the reports of the archbishops' committees of inquiry, especially the fifth report on 'Christianity and Industrial Problems'. Temple was much involved in both of these developments, and closer investigation suggests that Temple used the Mission as a lever to push forward these ideas. In other words, the

---

[1] [E. F.] Braley, *Letters [of Herbert Hensley Henson]* (London 1950) p 14; R. Groves, *Conrad Noel and the Thaxted Movement* (London 1967) p 176.
[2] [G. K. A.] Bell, [*Randall*] *Davidson* 3rd ed (London 1952) pp 767–74; [F. A.] Iremonger, [*William*] *Temple* (London 1948) pp 204–19; S. C. Carpenter, *Winnington-Ingram* (London 1949) p 4; [R.] Lloyd, [*The*] *Church of England [1900–1965]* (London 1966) pp 226–31; [A.] Wilkinson, [*The*] *Church of England and [the First World] War* (London 1978) pp 70–9; S. P. Mews, *Religion and Society in England in the First World War* (unpub. Cambridge Ph.D. dissertation 1974) pp 224–301.

Mission may more properly be regarded as the occasion, rather than the cause, of these initiatives. A study of the origins of the National Mission, however, illuminates the response of the Church of England to the first world war, particularly when it began to go badly. The changes between what was originally proposed and what eventually happened also indicate the differing appraisals of the contemporary situation that existed within the church.

There was no single source for the idea of a National Mission. When the archbishop of Canterbury first made his proposal public in November 1915, the *Record* claimed that the first suggestion of a national mission had been made in a letter from 'F' twelve months earlier, whilst the *Church Family Newspaper* recalled that it had urged the need for 'a great National Mission in all parishes of the land' in January 1915.[3] The concept of a simultaneous mission shared by these two evangelical newspapers, however, was precisely that which Davidson and his advisers did not intend. William Temple wrote that

> A group of laymen who met together two or three times in the late spring and early summer of 1915 became convinced that though there were few open signs, yet under the surface there was a very deep stirring, though they were puzzled and distressed that, on the whole, the nation seemed so little alive spiritually.[4]

This group wrote to Davidson, who showed little enthusiasm for their proposal of some special effort: but when they persisted, he promised to take some preliminary steps.[5] The group was probably that responsible for the Laymen's Christian Crusade, with whose secretary, A. P. Charles, Temple kept in touch throughout the summer of 1915. The concern of this group may well be represented by an article by Viscount Bryce in the *Layman's Bulletin* for June 1915, entitled 'The Immediate Duty of Christian Men', which concluded with these words:

> Must we not make another effort to bring the individual life and the social life and the business life and the national life

---

[3] *Record* 18 Nov 1915, referring to a letter in the issue for 8 Dec 1914; *Church Family Newspaper* 12 Nov 1915.
[4] [W.] Temple; *A Challenge [to the Church]* (London 1917) p 1.
[5] Iremonger, *Temple* pp 206–7. This is not mentioned by Bell and I have been unable to trace this correspondence in the Davidson papers so far.

nearer to those Christian ideals in following which, as we believe, the best hopes for the peace and welfare of humanity are to be found?[6]

Meanwhile in March 1915 Yeatman-Biggs, bishop of Worcester, wrote to Davidson expressing his concern that the spiritual opportunities of the war, which he had referred to in a letter to the *Times*, should be seized. Davidson replied in April saying that, after consulting Lang, archbishop of York, he would like to appoint a small group to think about it. In late May or June he began to discuss possible names with Dr A. W. Robinson, Warden of the College of Mission Clergy at All Hallows Barking by the Tower. On 24 July 1915 Davidson invited Robinson to gather the group together.[7] The group consisted of E. A. Burroughs, chaplain of Hertford College, Oxford; B. K. Cunningham, Warden of Bishop's Hostel, Farnham; W. H. Frere, of Mirfield; Peter Green, of Manchester; Archdeacon E. E. Holmes, of St Paul's Cathedral; Canon G. C. Joyce, of Hawarden; J. G. McCormick, of St Michael's Chester Square; A. W. Robinson, of All Hallows; Canon V. F. Storr, of Winchester; and William Temple, of St James, Piccadilly. To these were added J. O. F. Murray, Master of Selwyn College, Cambridge and W. B. Trevelyan, of Beaconsfield.[8] It is not known why Davidson chose Arthur Robinson for this task. His younger brother, Armitage Robinson, Dean of Wells, was well known to Davidson, who had worked with him on various liturgical matters and had asked him, among others, to prepare prayers at the outbreak of war.[9] Robinson's work as Warden of the College of Mission Clergy had involved him in leading numerous missions, retreats and quiet days; and as chaplain of the London Diocesan Lay Helpers' Association he was in touch with a large number of the

---

[6] Viscount Bryce, 'The Immediate Duty of Christian Men' *Layman's Bulletin* June 1915: in the A. W. Robinson papers.

[7] [Lambeth Palace Library], D[avidson] P[apers]: 'War' Box 14: bishop of Worcester to Davidson, 9 Mar 1915; Davidson to bishop of Worcester, 19 Apr 1915; A. W. Robinson to Davidson, 19 Jun 1915; Davidson to Robinson, 24 Jul 1915.

[8] Gore was not a member of the group, as stated by Wilkinson, *Church of England and War* p 72.

[9] Bell, *Davidson* p 736. Armitage married Mrs Davidson's secretary in Lambeth Palace chapel in Jan 1915. Lloyd, *Church of England* p 226, mistakenly says Armitage Robinson was asked to be chairman. H. E. Sheen, *Canon Peter Green* (London 1965) p 80 makes the same mistake.

laity involved in church work. In November 1914 Davidson had asked him to prepare a homily which could be used in connection with the Day of Intercession planned for Sunday 3 January 1915, the prayers for which were being prepared by his brother. His work was widely appreciated, particularly for his ability to cross the party divisions in the church.[10]

Robinson agreed to the archbishop's request, and on 29 July Davidson invited those nominated to take part in

> the consideration of ways in which we can effectively 'buy up the opportunity' which the War affords and by the help of God bring good out of its manifold evil. We want thought to be given to our sins and shortcomings and to the best mode of overcoming them; we want fresh modes of prayerfulness, both public and private: and there are many other things in which a little spiritual counsel on the part of capable men would be, we believe, abundantly fruitful of good.[11]

All those invited accepted, and Robinson suggested that they should each set aside the hour between noon and 1.00 pm on Mondays for special prayer, with a view to holding a conference of one or two days later on.[12] The initial emphasis on prayer and spiritual devotion is therefore clear.

The group met for conference at The Yews, Beaconsfield from 4 to 6 October 1915. Frere and Green were absent, but had sent letters. After a wide-ranging discussion Robinson drafted a report for the archbishop, which commented on the current situation and made various proposals for greater freedom in worship. The key sentence was as follows:

> We are unanimous in recommending that before the inevitable reaction sets in, which will follow the War, there should be a National Mission led by the Archbishops; that it should be on a scale such as we have never yet contemplated, and should extend throughout all the cities and towns and villages of the land.[13]

---

[10] A. W. Robinson, *The Way to Pray* (London 1931) pp 23–7.
[11] [A. W.] R[obinson] P[apers]: circular letter from Davidson, 29 Jul 1915. I am grateful to the Rt Revd Dr J. A. T. Robinson, Trinity College, Cambridge, for allowing me to consult his father's papers, which are in his possession.
[12] RP: circular letter of A. W. Robinson, Aug 1915.
[13] RP: *The Spiritual Call [to the Nation and the Church: What is being taught by the War and What should be done]* (privately printed) p 6.

War, the Nation, and the Kingdom of God

The report was considered by the bishops on 26 October, and Davidson made the first public mention of the idea in a letter to the *Times* published on 8 November, in which the second part of the sentence quoted above was included. Discussion of the idea in the church press then began.

On 24 November a meeting was held under the chairmanship of the bishop of London betwen members of the group and the bishops of Oxford, Salisbury, St Asaph and Chelmsford. Frere, Joyce and Storr were unable to attend. It was this meeting at which 'the determined pessimism' of Green and Gore became apparent.[14] Some thought the church should undertake 'a definite extensive movement . . . which might be described as a National Mission', whilst others thought that the church was not spiritually ready for such an appeal and needed a considerable time of preparation. Perhaps surprisingly the meeting agreed, with only Gore abstaining,

1. THAT the present emergency demands some special action on the part of the Church to bring home to the Nation the call of God in the War, viz:
    a. To realise its responsibility before God:
    b. To recognise the duty of preparing afresh to serve the Kingdom of Christ throughout the world; and to this end
    c. To put out of its own life the things that are contrary to righteousness and that make brotherhood impossible.

2. THAT as a preliminary to this action efforts should be made to rouse the Church
    a. To realise the greatness of its opportunity to proclaim Christ crucified, risen, and ascended as the present Lord of Life;
    b. To seek to be filled anew with the power of the Holy Spirit; and to this end
    c. To be forward in putting away from every department of its life all that can hinder fellowship, and make worship and witness unreal.[15]

---

[14] Bell, *Davidson* pp 767–8; Robinson to Davidson, 24 Nov 1915.
[15] RP: [Informal] report of a Conference [held at London House on] November 24, typescript, pp 2, 3 5–6.

The decision on the next step was left to the archbishop of Canterbury. Notwithstanding the hesitations expressed by many about the title, 'National Mission', he decided to proceed on that basis. In January 1916 he invited seventy people to form a central council for the mission, modelled on the organisation for the Pan-Anglican Congress of 1908. The bishops agreed to his plans on 27–28 January, and the first meeting of the Council took place on 14 February, when the Mission was arranged for October-November 1916. On 15 February Davidson announced the proposal at the Convocation of Canterbury, and Lang told the Convocation of York the following day.[16] Winnington-Ingram, bishop of London, became, in his own words, 'chief of the staff of the National Mission'—a post which the original group had conceived as 'analagous to that of the "Minister of Munitions"'.[17] Though he threw himself heart and soul into the task, his vision of the National Mission was different from the original one, and Temple may not have been too unkind when he commented acidly that 'Ebor, London, and a good lot more just want a few mass meetings in the Albert Hall.'[18] More calmly later he said that after the Council's retreat at Westfield College, London, 28–30 March 1916, 'there was on the Council a perfect unity of spirit', though differences of opinion still remained.[19]

Before turning in more detail to the ideas behind the Mission it is worth noting that the months during which it was planned saw a significant change in the public mood about the war. Attempts to break the military stalemate on the western front ended in mid-October, but the alternative to that front collapsed when troops were evacuated from the Dardanelles in December. On 5 October, during the meeting at Beaconsfield, Lord Derby was appointed to take charge of the last major voluntary recruitment drive with a six-weeks time limit. On 5 January 1916 the Military Conscription Bill was introduced in the House of Commons. For those who favoured conscription this was the climax of a campaign to assert that the nation had the right to demand the lives of its citizens in a national emergency. It marked a radical break with British tradition: it also posed problems for the church

[16] *The Chronicle of Convocation, 1916* pp 3–8; *The York Journal of Convocation, 1915–16* pp 95–98.
[17] *The Chronicle of Convocation, 1916* p 52; *The Spiritual Call* p 6.
[18] Iremonger, *Temple* p 208.
[19] Temple, *A Challenge* p 3.

because of the question of whether clergy should be exempt. This developing public emphasis on service and commitment may also have assisted the movement away from the more spiritual concerns of August-October 1915.

Much of the discussion at Beaconsfield was taken up with the failure of the clergy to provide for the spiritual needs of the nation. Frere was particularly critical: 'we have allowed ourselves to be paralysed by a prevailing spirit of Cathedral mattins which makes very little demand on anybody but the choir'.[20] In a later letter he wrote:

> Prayer for the dead is one of our greatest levers & our neglect of it one of our worst faults. Our neglect of the H. Euch. comes in the same category: we are starved & dumb, particularly in face of death. While of preaching we have already too much & for lack of the prayer it runs to waste.[21]

But Frere was not a lone voice: a very different kind of churchman, Francis Storr said that the clergy did not know how to visit or how far to lead in prayer, and that they had failed in 'memorial' services of all kinds.[22] The group wanted to see greater freedom in church services, more open prayer-meetings, eucharists arranged 'at an hour at which the largest number of communicants can be expected'. They also recommended that the clergy

> should call their people to prayer from the pulpit, giving them help in the offering of prayer, but not confining themselves to the reading of set collects. It might be ordered that the Churches should be opened for some hours every day for private prayer, and that in every Church there should be at least one special service of Intercession during the week.[23]

The suggestion was also made that churches in a deanery might arrange a rota of continuous intercession, by leagues of prayer and such like—though Davidson himself was dubious about this idea.[24] The emphasis in Robinson's correspondence about the need for

---

[20] RP: Frere to Robinson, 30 Sept 1915.
[21] RP: Frere to Robinson, 21 Oct 1915.
[22] RP: Robinson's ms notes of Beaconsfield meeting, October 1915. Except where otherwise indicated statements made at this meeting come from this source, which is unpaginated.
[23] *The Spiritual Call* pp 6, 8.
[24] DP: 'National Mission' Box 1: Davidson to Mrs Penrose, 23 Jun 1915; Davidson to Robinson, 6 Aug 1915.

appropriate biddings after the third collect or before the sermon suggests that it was widely felt that the clergy were liturgically unimaginative or unadventurous. Does this mean therefore that the first world war is the point from which a more spontaneous and less book-bound approach to worship in the Church of England is to be found? It is certainly a reminder that the forces behind prayer-book revision in the 1920s were not solely anglo-catholic. Perhaps the widespread custom of leaving Anglican parish churches open on weekdays dates from the war too.

But the group at Beaconsfield felt that the war had done more than expose the spiritual inadequacies of the Church of England. They interpreted the war as part of God's purpose in history and his purpose for the nation. In his opening remarks Temple asserted the divine character of the nation, appointed by God for a purpose, and said that 'our nation must be made a province in Christ's Kingdom'. The theme is more fully expounded in his Bishop Paddock lectures in New York given early in 1915 and subsequently published as *Church and Nation*. 'The nation as well as the Church is a divine creation', he wrote: 'the world is by divine appointment a world of nations, and it is such a world that is to become the Kingdom of God'.[25] Such an understanding drew on the critical study of the old testament, and the ideas of Maurice and Westcott. For this reason Storr said at Beaconsfield that the old testament ought to 'live' after this war. The old testament, however, also taught the need of repentance: in his account of the National Mission Temple wrote:

> In 1914 God called us, as a nation, and we heard and obeyed His call . . . But though we answered God's call, it cannot be said that we answered it as His. It was the call of right, but we did not find in it the claim of God upon our lives, for we had grown unaccustomed to relate our religion to the national life.[26]

Corporate repentance was therefore necessary. E. S. Talbot, bishop of Winchester, also drew an old testament analogy to explain the Mission at the meeting with nonconformist representatives at Lambeth in July 1916:

---

[25] W. Temple, 'Our Need of a Catholic Church' *Papers for War Time* 2nd series, no 19 (London 1915) p 14; *Church and Nation* (London 1916) pp 44–5.
[26] Temple, *A Challenge* p 12.

War, the Nation, and the Kingdom of God

When the Assyrians came in the land Isaiah called on the nation to think of their sins. It was in this prophetic spirit that the Mission gave its call to repentance.[27]

The group were prepared to go further in their appraisal of the positive benefits of the war. Despite the ambivalent evidence of the state of religion on the western front, they looked deeper. Presenting their report to the meeting at London House in November 1915, Robinson summed up their thinking as follows:

> Briefly these thoughts were that the chastisement of the War was a preparation of the nation by discipline to fulfil some great task, that the heroism and self sacrifice which had been revealed showed that the Nation had the latent spiritual power to accomplish that task, that the idea of the Nation as a corporate body which was uniting all men today made it seem that men would be more ready than ever before for the message of the Kingdom of God, and that the opportunity before the Church ought to be bought up before the inevitable reaction should set in after the War.[28]

Hence they believed there was 'an almost universal desire . . . for more peremptory leadership', what Temple called 'the almost passionate hunger for orders'.[29] McCormick was worried that the archbishop would not see how much they felt 'that something drastic & even dramatic is wanted in the way of leadership'.[30] Only Cunningham expressed some reservations about how widespread this desire was.[31] The group therefore looked for a call to service which would draw on the kind of heroism manifested in the war. Temple wrote:

> Men at present do think that the Church exists for the sake of its own members; consequently they are not attracted to it; when they feel that it exists, like the Army and Navy, for an end beyond its own members, and to which its members may have to be completely sacrificed, they will come in; and this is the original idea of the Church cf. Mark 8 v 34; Matthew 28 v 19.[32]

---

[27] DP: 'National Mission' Box 1: Notes of [Private] Conference [at Lambeth], 21 July 1916.
[28] RP: Report of a Conference, November 24, pp 1–2.
[29] *The Spiritual Call* p 4; RP: Temple to Robinson, 22 Oct 1915.
[30] RP: McCormick to Robinson, 20 Oct 1915.
[31] RP: Cunningham to Robinson, 20 Oct 1915.
[32] RP: Temple to Robinson, 22 Oct 1915.

This letter was written as the Derby scheme for voluntary enlistment was getting under way, and its general tone is illuminating.

For Temple this linked easily with his view that all national sins were rooted in one fundamental one—'the fact that we do not feel in any effective sense members one of another'. He pointed out that at the outbreak of war the country was on the brink of civil war in Ireland and the greatest labour war in history.[33] Members of the group were well aware of the fragile state of domestic politics. Murray wrote that

> The War found us with a mass of unsolved problems in an acute state & there are clear signs that the mere lapse of time is not reducing the tension. There can be no doubt that we are in for a period of serious domestic trouble as soon as the War is over, unless the whole of our social and political life can be raised to a higher plane.[34]

It is not difficult to understand therefore why members of the group like Temple felt it natural and right that the church should cooperate with other groups, like the labour movement, the women's movement, the temperance movement, the purity movement and so on, as part of this campaign. Involvement in social issues for them was not an extra added on to an evangelistic campaign: but it is doubtful whether Davidson ever fully understood this, and Winnington-Ingram certainly did not see it in the way Temple did, though he had his own interest in temperance and purity. These are important clues as to why the concept of the National Mission was vague, not helped by the fact that all agreed it was a misleading title but they could not think of a better one.

The different conceptions of the National Mission also affected the decision over its timing. The group which met at Beaconsfield were quite clear that the Mission should take place immediately after the war, before 'the inevitable reaction' set in. Davidson's immediate response was that they 'should avoid talking too glibly & easily about what we are going to do when the War is over'.[35] At the November meeting at London House, as has already been stated, opinion was divided between those who thought there should be a Mission and those who thought the church was not

---

[33] Temple, *A Challenge* p 15.
[34] RP: Murray to Robinson, 8 Oct 1915.
[35] RP: Davidson to Robinson, 8 Oct 1915.

War, the Nation, and the Kingdom of God

ready for it. It was also felt by many that those who ought to lead such a Mission were either away at the front or stretched to the limit at home. Lang felt strongly that the Mission ought to precede not follow the end of the war.[36] Eventually the bishops in January agreed to this policy. In effect they decided to use the name 'National Mission' for what many of the original group had regarded as the preparation for the Mission. This decision— perhaps a typical Davidson way of getting round a problem—was probably responsible for the fatal confusion over the Mission's purpose. Temple wrote to Davidson that 'on first hearing of the date I did not grasp how much it would affect the scheme of the Mission as I had myself contemplated it'.[37] Even Lang complained to Davidson after the first Council meeting that Winnington-Ingram seemed more concerned to get a decision on October-November as the dates for the Mission than on the right ways to prepare for it. As it was, of course, because the National Mission was held in 1916, the idea of an effort after the war was gradually forgotten, unless perhaps COPEC can be seen in this light.

Another way in which the view of the Mission changed, though here more quickly, was over the question of cooperation with nonconformists. At Beaconsfield Burroughs spoke of a revival of united religion, and noted that much was now being done that was complained of at Kikuyu, the controversial missionary conference of 1913. Gilbert Joyce's notes of proposals at the end of the meeting included this one:

> A religious War council to be summoned by the Archbishop & to consist of Roman Catholics & Nonconformists as well as Churchpeople. This would be purely an emergency organisation to meet an emergency.[38]

Robinson, however, envisaged the archbishop telling the nonconformists what the Church of England was going to do. Other members of the group were much more hesitant about cooperation: Trevelyan felt that they had not sufficiently emphasised their protest against the 'bugbear of undenominationalism'.[39] By the time of the London House meeting Robinson noted that 'it seemed to be the opinion of all that definite cooperation

---

[36] DP: 'War' Box 14: Lang to Davidson, 11 Dec 1915.
[37] DP: 'War' Box 14: Temple to Davidson, 7 Feb 1916.
[38] RP: Notes of Beaconsfield Meeting, additional memo.
[39] RP: Trevelyan to Robinson, 6 Oct 1915.

(with other religious bodies) would not be desirable or possible and practicable'.[40] Murray was prepared to justify this in terms of the conception of the Mission itself: he said at Beaconsfield that the national character of the Church of England was of the *esse* of the Church. Referring to Figgis and Maurice he spoke of the need to tell the nation of its corporate redemption in Christ: this was what distinguished the church's message from that of nonconformists, which centred on individual redemption. Evangelical Anglicans, however, saw the matter differently, and the announcement of the National Mission coincided with a decision by the London Evangelical Campaign to invite the American evangelistic team of Chapman and Alexander to London in the spring of 1916 (an invitation which they declined). Davidson had to write letters to Prebendary Webb-Peploe of the L.E.C. explaining that the National Mission would not be interdenominational, and he also had to reassure anxious anglo-catholics that it would not be like the London Evangelistic Campaign. Temple wrote to Davidson saying that it was vital that the Mission must be an effort of the Church of England:

> but only less vital does it seem that people generally should regard it as an advance by the different sections of the Church in concert. I see only one way to arrange this. It is that privately the Free Church leaders should be informed of what is contemplated and told that while we think any movements must be initiated by the different bodies themselves, cooperation between parallel movements will be welcomed from our side to the very utmost possible degree.[41]

This was the solution Davidson adopted in February 1916 when he wrote to Cardinal Bourne and the Free Church Council before the official announcement to Convocation. This course of action did not prevent evangelical disappointment, however, and J. H. Shakespeare, President of the Free Church Council, told Davidson in a private interview at Lambeth that the adjective 'national' in the title of the Mission 'had repeatedly been taken hold of . . . as implying claim on our side to be coextensive with the Nation'.[42] At a conference of nonconformist and Anglican leaders at Lambeth in July, Shakespeare and others expressed the prayerful support of

[40] RP: Report of a Conference, November 24, p 4.
[41] DP: 'National Mission' Box 2: Temple to Davidson, 17 Dec 1915.
[42] DP: 'War' Box 14: Memo of interview with Shakespeare, 23 Mar 1916.

the free churches for the Mission, and said they would make their own effort after the war.⁴³ It is ironic that they chose the time originally envisaged by the Church of England, though in the event nothing was done. Despite the official policy, however, the National Mission can be seen as the occasion of the beginning of friendlier relations between Anglican and nonconformist leaders, which made the Lambeth conversations after 1920 possible.

The object of the National Mission, said the bishop of London, in a statement in March 1916, is that all shall know the Lord from the least to the greatest. If achieved this would solve our national problems—'the inequalities in our social system, the want of brotherhood between man and man, the tyranny of drink and lust, the misunderstandings between men and women'.⁴⁴ Temple also believed that the message went to the individual—but 'to the individual first and foremost as a citizen . . . There is a real difference between a converted nation and a nation of converted individuals.'⁴⁵ The difference between these two positions, which at first sound so much alike, explains why Winnington-Ingram could not really lead the campaign proposed at Beaconsfield. In the same statement he quoted an Oxford undergraduate who had written to him from the trenches saying that war is a great purge.

There was also a third view:

> I profoundly disbelieve in the possibility of any good coming of war (wrote Peter Green), and I regard all talk about war in itself being a moral purge, and a wholesome discipline, and a school of character, and all the rest of it, as being either profoundly immoral and antiChristian, or mere moral platitudes.⁴⁶

This in turn indicates that Peter Green's scepticism about the National Mission went deeper than his belief that the influence of the clergy was nil and religious revival of the war had been exaggerated. Not only was he poles apart from Winnington-Ingram; he could not really share the view of war, the nation and the kingdom of God that characterised a man like Temple. In the same essay Green wrote

> Merely social and political work is not what is wanted of the

---

⁴³ DP: 'National Mission' Box 1: Notes of Conference, 21 July 1916.
⁴⁴ *Church Times* 3 Mar 1916, p 219.
⁴⁵ Temple, *A Challenge* p 7.
⁴⁶ Peter Green, 'The Humiliation of War' in G. K. A. Bell, ed *The War and the Kingdom of God* (London 1916) p 60.

Church, or of its officers the clergy, or even of its members *qua* Churchmen. The remodelling of our industrial system may or may not be desirable, and may or may not be practicable . . . But whether practicable and desirable or not, I am sure it is no part of the Church's duty to work for or to advocate such a change . . . it is the spirit of Brotherhood which the Church should labour to produce.[47]

But Green was not like Henson, who regarded the Mission as a blunder because it gave 'sudden, and wholly unmerited importance' to 'a number of foolish persons, ardent, bigotted, and ill-informed, who would not otherwise have gained a hearing'.[48] He was not even like Conrad Noel who thought that the Mission was a confidence trick to give the impression of a social concern that was not there. Noel was wrong: the concern of men like Temple and Kempthorne, bishop of Lichfield, who expressed his anxiety to Davidson that 'the *social* aspects of a National Mission were not adequately emphasised'[49], was genuine enough. Green's critique of the church in the first world war was more fundamental than most. He believed the root failure was a failure to put into practice the teaching of the sermon on the mount on non-resistance and evangelical poverty. The saying 'resist not evil' implied that no physical force can ever effect moral results, and that where material things were concerned, the Christian was called to suffer himself. Green was not a pacifist. He believed that England had been morally bound to declare war in 1914, but he believed that war was always morally wrong. England had lost the power to act rightly, and that was why repentance was necessary. He ran his great mission in Salford in 1926, ten years after the National Mission.[50] Perhaps he was the only one of the twelve who stuck to the original vision: careful preparation, rooted in prayer, and after the war. All that was lacking was the emphasis on the nation, but perhaps during the war more weight had been placed on that than it could ultimately bear.

Fitzwilliam College, Cambridge

[47] *Ibid* pp 91–2.
[48] Braley, *Letters* p 15.
[49] DP: 'National Mission' Box 2: bishop of Lichfield to Davidson, 11 Feb 1916.
[50] Sheen, *Peter Green* pp 98–108.

ET VIRTUTEM ET MUSAS:
MILL HILL SCHOOL AND THE GREAT WAR

by CLYDE BINFIELD

'IT IS the duty of every Christian man to regard his religion as the Expeditionary Force of his soul'.[1]

In the autumn of 1950 W. H. Balgarnie, a retired public school-master, was asked to reminisce about his early days in the profession. Balgarnie's boys certainly remembered him, 'very young-looking for his age, so much so that on one occasion we were rejoiced by a parent approaching him on the touch-line of the football field and saying: "Can you tell me where Mr. Balgarnie is, my boy?"'[2] Balgarnie replied from his house in Cambridge:

... I came in 1890, and stayed only 3½ years, and know nothing of the great Eltham days. 'S.S.M.' was our abbreviation for 'School for the Sons of Missionaries', wh. I suppose was held not terse enough for a slogan on the football field. The School was quite small in my time, and 50 was accounted a full house. The Rev. Edward Waite was Headmaster—a beautiful reader of the Psalms at morning prayers—and I was under Mr. Hayward for only a year: it was he who took the motto from the Apocrypha, *Filiorum gloria Patres.*

I came to The Leys in 1900, and left 3 or 4 times, but always had to return: now I've *finally* left (*memini tangere lignum*), and live opposite the School, like Mr. Chips, with whom I've been fancifully identified.[3]

The identification was not so fanciful, nor was Mr. Chips, even at one remove, Eltham College's only link with middle-brow novels and family cinema. From 1908 to 1919 Eric Liddell, rugby international, Olympic athlete, China missionary and a hero of 'Chariots of Fire' was at the school, two incidents of his sporting after life reclaimed for *The Glory of the Sons*. One of them, 'perhaps

---

[1] [*The*] M[*ill*] H[*ill*] M[*agazine*], June 1922 p 6.
[2] [*The*] Glory of the Sons [*A History of Eltham College School for the Sons of Missionaries*]ed. C. Witting (London 1952) p 164.
[3] *Ibid* p 39; W. H. Balgarnie to C. Witting, 6 Brookside, Cambridge, 26 August 1950.

unique in the history of rugger took place at Cardiff on 3rd February 1923, when, Scotland having beaten Wales by 11 to 8, the Scottish threes, Liddell and Gracie among them, were carried off the field by the Welsh as a compliment to their magnificent game'. The other occurred at the 1924 Paris Olympics when, running 'with an inspired and passionate intensity', Liddell first set a world record for the four hundred metres and then refused, on conscientious grounds, to run the hundred metres heats on a Sunday. 'That act, by which he brought an even greater honour to his old school, will perhaps be held in more enduring memory than the fact that he set up a world record.'[4]

No doubt much might be drawn from this introductory collage about sport, school spirit and public school religion, flies caught together in the brittle amber of a privileged little world. But two things should be noted. The first is that this public school collage is in fact of a Free Church school world. The Leys, opened in Cambridge in February 1875, was a Wesleyan school; Eltham College, opened in Walthamstow in January 1842 was for the sons of missionaries, chiefly Congregational and Baptist. When Balgarnie knew it, it was at Blackheath; since 1912 it has been at Mottingham, hence its present name, Eltham College. The second point is that Gracie and Liddell, those glories of public school boyhood, moved with their school from Blackheath to its new name, its new charter, and the experience of war. Gracie, who bowled W. G. Grace when he brought a team to Eltham in 1914, won every event in his last school sports. That was in 1915. Two years later came his military cross[5]. Liddell stayed at Eltham throughout the war. Like his father and younger brother he was destined for missionary work in China ('When he left for China, he had a tremendous send-off from the Edinburgh students at Waverley Station, singing the hymn, "Jesus shall reign where'er the sun"').[6] His war was to be the second world war, with death in Japanese internment.

To return to Mr. Chips, retired by 1950 at Brookside, a row, almost a terrace, of variably Victorian, invariably donnish Cambridge houses, which were none of them what they seemed,

---

[4] *Ibid* p 77.
[5] *Ibid* pp 270, 278.
[6] *Ibid* p 155.

Et Virtutem Et Musas

for they looked across Trumpington Road to the Methodist Leys School while packed behind them since its opening in October 1915 was Cheshunt, the dissenting theological college originally established at Trevecca by Lady Huntingdon. In 1944 Cheshunt's president, J. S. Whale, left to become headmaster of the best known of the Free Church schools, Mill Hill.

An interconnexion might easily be made of Free Church parents, preachers, teachers and fellows, an ivy league threaded among the Cambridge colleges. But would there be any distinctiveness about such an interconnexion? And would there be much significance in isolating such threads as happened to lie in times of war?

James Obelkevich, sensitively *parti pris* in his study of Lincolnshire religion, has savaged that contradiction in terms, the Christian gentleman[7]. More recently Dennis Smith, less sensitive, still suggestive, has considered the education, public school pioneered and grammar school undergirded, which prolonged the Christian gentleman's life and broadened its social range[8]. It was a liberal education in which gentlemen and professional men, Christians all and all-round chaps, might coincide, here a City businessman, there a Fabian socialist, a socially integrated old boy network of commercial and political pacesetters, fundamentally incompatible no doubt, but sharing a *lingua franca*, united in a distrust of technical specialisms, distanced from, indeed denying, the industrial civilisation which provided their wealth. So where stood the Methodist schools, the Quaker schools, the schools for sons of ministers and missionaries, the Tauntons and Tettenhalls, Bishop's Stortfords and Mill Hills in this integration of incompatibles? Where, especially, stood one of them, Mill Hill, when the Christian gentleman faced the ultimate test, fighting for king and country, and when its own purpose had been the selective assimilation to national standards of boys for whose families war had perhaps been a distant option but never a personal obligation?

On 18 June 1845 Algernon Wells, secretary of the Congregational Union, spoke at Mill Hill's Public Day. The man fitted the occasion. Wells was one of a group of leading Congregational-

---

[7] J. Obelkevich, *Religion and Rural Society: South Lindsey 1825–1875* (Oxford 1976) pp 44–6.
[8] [D. Smith], *Conflict and Compromise: [Class Formation in English Society 1830–1914: A Comparative Study of Birmingham and Sheffield]* (London 1982) pp 252–5.

ists—Robert Vaughan of Lancashire Independent College, Manchester, and Thomas Binney of the King's Weigh House Church, London, were others—convinced of their denomination's formative role in the new age of great cities. Theirs was the social pivot on which the national future balanced. The Protestant Dissenters' Grammar School, founded at Mill Hill in 1807, shared its architect, Sir William Tite, with the Scotch National Church in Regent Square, Binney's Weigh House chapel in Fish Street Hill, a string of railway stations, some banks and the Royal Exchange. Each was an earnest of the future, none was as suggestive as the school: the 'improved training of the sons of intelligent Dissenting families, with a view to their acting a worthy part, on high moral and religious principles, in the great intellectual struggle of our own and coming times, is an object the importance of which can be hardly overrated'.[9]

So Wells spoke at Public Day, his theme the school, his audience its whole constituency, 'scholars and parents, tutors, committee, former pupils, and governors', the occasion 'one of the bright days of life given to pleasure, affection, and hope', the content predictably measured.[10] He spoke of a school that was grammar, public and Christian. Wells spoke for a grammar school since the study of language is, 'next to reason itself, perhaps the noblest and most curious work of God in our world . . . he who has become a master of sentences is prepared for every department of study, he is disciplined for the intellectual life.'[11] He dwelt upon the perfection of the classics, ('Let the Bible be used to teach religion only, at least to youth'), and since 'Mill Hill is no scene of negligence, or indolence' he stressed that 'Mathematics are diligently taught. The usual requisites to a mercantile education receive due attention. Modern languages take their place. Occasional lectures on science are given.'[12] But Wells spoke too for a public school. 'It is public property, is under public care, is established for public objects . . . [is] instituted to promote an effective rudimental education in the higher walks of literature, by

---

[9] A. Wells, *An Address Delivered in the Chapel of the The Protestant Dissenters' Grammar School, Mill Hill, On Occasion of Public Day, June 18th, 1845* p 2.
[10] *Ibid* p 3.
[11] *Ibid* pp 4, 5: Sir James Murray, the lexicographer, was a master at Mill Hill from 1870 to 1885.
[12] *Ibid* p 6.

Et Virtutem Et Musas

public and combined efforts.'[13] His imagination played with his oratory upon the thought. A public school was a good sized school, a 'secluded, but real and active commonwealth',[14] providing what no family 'in that class of society from which the pupils of Mill Hill are gathered' could provide:

> There are rules, laws, and hours that must be kept. Needful discipline is maintained, Salutary fear is established. Boys feel that they are governed. . . . In such institutions boys can play. They find playfellows and playroom. They can obtain a resolute trial of strength and skill . . . nerves are braced, senses are exercised, limbs are strengthened, tone is gained for life amidst the strenuous games of free and gladsome boys breaking forth from school application into the open air and scenes of nature . . . But there is another great good in the plays of boys. In them equals meet equals. Courtesy and disguise are equally out of the question. Rights are maintained, and offences are punished with prompt decision. There is a code of laws and a standard of conduct, which are summarily enforced. The play field is indeed but mimic and miniature life, but still it is social life. It schools lads in the art of meeting and acting among their fellows in the real world they are soon to enter. Here conceit is humbled, mean tricks are scorned, unfair advantage-taking is repelled, arrogant assumptions are brought down, and a lad is made to feel that he must be frank and honourable among his fellows, and respect their rights, or be thrust out of their society.
>
> In other words he is disciplined for future life.[15]

Or, to put it another way, 'the good schoolboy, subject to his master, diligent in his class, spirited among his fellows, makes the true man, prompt in business, kind at home, pleasant in society, and firm in troubles'; and thus the good school's principal care must be to 'cherish a right tone of social feeling among the pupils as a community'.[16] Wells wanted more yet, for he spied a community in perpetuity. Mill Hill 'should be the school of successive generations', the son at work and play 'where his father studied and frolicked before him'.[17] And here, almost lost in the charm and

[13] *Ibid* p 10.
[14] *Ibid*.
[15] *Ibid* pp 8–9.
[16] *Ibid* p 10.
[17] *Ibid* pp 11–12.

interest of lengthened associations ('after all there may one day be a Dissenting institution covered with the hoar and the moss of antiquity'), Algernon Wells came up against the fact of dissenting dissidence and the need for schools where 'the fathers of our faith and liberty will never be mentioned but with reverence, and where simple worship, free thought, and personal responsibility in religion, shall make their constant appeals to opening reason and impressible conscience'.[18]

So of course he ended with soul welfare. 'Evangelical Dissenters have their unalterable convictions on the subject of religion . . . They labour for the conversion of their children'. Mill Hill, where gathered 'the hopes of numerous households', was to train 'the gentleman, the scholar, and the Christian' *as evangelical dissenters understood the concept.* 'Whose heart does not involuntarily appeal to the Father of lights for his blessed working in the intellects, affections, and consciences of these young heirs of immortality?'[19]

There is already here an Edwardian foretaste ('fathers of our faith and liberty') but the tone is surely Arnoldian, and Wells was speaking three years to the month after Thomas Arnold's death. It is also rhetoric for the age of Peel, a high flown but practical intensity, politically disturbed, socially excited, though not yet intellectually disoriented. There are tensions to be perceived in it.

It was decades before Mill Hill achieved the stability which Wells sought; indeed the school had to be reconstituted in 1869. Other Free Church schools suffered equally for the dissent which created them defined their constitution: since the great public and grammar schools were at once over protected and shackled by their endowments, dissenting schools should be proprietary schools, unendowed, relying on the success bred by success, reflecting the free trade spirit. Consequently they suffered. Even if Bishop's Stortford could get by with Felsted or Framlingham there could be no easy competition between Tettenhall and Rugby or Taunton and Clifton. They were affected in another way. They catered for families increasingly aware that they were in the social vanguard of the world's greatest and most civilised industrial nation. The inbuilt dissidence which created these schools kept them slim, but what kept them going was less social pioneering

[18] *Ibid* pp 12–13.
[19] *Ibid* pp 14–15.

Et Virtutem Et Musas

than social conformity. The social vanguard of the new England which men like Algernon Wells hailed was far more likely to be a social guard's van, going where the age of steam took it. Thus the opinion formers of England's alternative society were harnessed to England's main society and since, though it was often touch and go, the dissenting schools survived, all of them eventually looking far beyond their immediate constituency, they formed over the generations so keenly anticipated by Wells a powerful agent in assimilation, perhaps in reconciliation; or perhaps they were simply the Trojan Horse in the chapel Troy, for if Dennis Smith is right in his contention that England's 'aristocratic-cum-clerical wing of the old order had particular success in shaping the new industrial society through the medium of formal education' to its own satisfaction[20], the Free Church schools were willing partners in the process, with the Great War as its chief test.

The Great War was a test because through conscription, the nation's right to demand that its young men die for it, it brought the national emergency directly home to every adolescent boy. Inevitably it tested the accumulated assumptions of several generations of liberal education, carefully distanced from technical expertise but carefully geared to the tasks of competitive leadership. And after the War any distinctive Free Church peculiarities dissolved into an educational atmosphere. Increasingly most staff and certainly most boys in Free Church schools were off-comers.

In 1914 Mill Hill was at last where Algernon Wells would have wished, a dissenting Rugby, even a nonconformist Eton, if ever there had to be one, its boys working and frolicking in cousinly perpetuity. Since 1891 its headmaster had been J. D. McClure, big, cheerful and strenuous. 'I never met any Millhillian, even the rottenest, who had not an immense respect and love for him.'[21] McClure was Lancastrian Scotch, a Congregationalist, a barrister and musicologist, and doctor of both, from London and Cambridge. When he came to the school there were sixty one boys. At his death, thirty years on, there were three hundred and sixty one.[22] McClure was more than his school's greatest

---

[20] *Conflict and Compromise*, p xii.
[21] (Kathleen Ousey) *McClure of Mill Hill, A Memoir by his Daughter*, (London 1927) pp 9, 276.
[22] *Ibid* p 10.

headmaster; he belongs to that smallish band of nationally known public school headmasters (literally so, he was elected to the Head Masters' Conference in 1895 and to its committee in 1910) whose school became their creation, plant and curriculum alike transformed. At Mill Hill the transformation began with Basil Champneys's Chapel of 1898. Champneys was a wonderfully apt architect. If his Newnham College, Cambridge, were all Kate Greenaway and his Mansfield College, Oxford, all John Wyclif, Mill Hill's new chapel was seventeenth-century as if Laud or 1662 had never been:[23] stalls and organ case; barrel vault, strapwork plastered; a columned arcade to the apse and the right touch of baroquerie throughout. By 1914 McClure was an educational statesman, recently knighted, a leader in his denomination and in the world of music. And his school?

Schools are usually seen through official histories, which are success stories, or magisterial biography, which has a prejudice for its subject, or old boy memory, which cannot be neutral.

There is a fourth source: the school magazine. Naturally this cannot be wholly independent since, unless it is *samizdat*, it has been sanctioned by authority; but it has an immediacy denied to the other sources, and *The Mill Hill Magazine* claimed with some truth to be 'Conducted by the Mill Hill Boys'.[24]

The magazine had been running since June 1873[25]. Forty years on it reflected a sizeable school: two hundred and sixty one in November 1913, twenty seven of them day boys[26]. Its interests were predictable. 'Dear Sirs,—Don't you think it would be advisable to allow more people to change in the bath . . . ?'[27] And they were predictably chronicled: rugby football against The Leys and Eltham, Christ's Hospital and U.C.S., Haileybury and Merchant Taylors'; cricket against Whitgift and Highgate, Berkhamsted and Aldenham; and its own specialism, single-handed hockey. Predictably too it is in sporting vignettes that the boys flash naturally to life. Thus Maurice Basden of the first XV,

---

[23] As McClure put it at the school's centenary: 'I do not complain of the exclusion. Those to whom it was due knew what they wanted, and took the direct course to the realisation of their desires, and I know from my own experience how prone I am to be ruthless when I have my own way'. *Ibid* p 138.
[24] Thus the title page of each issue.
[25] *MHM*, June 1923 p 2.
[26] *Ibid* November 1913 pp 91, 93.
[27] *Ibid* p 117.

Et Virtutem Et Musas

'A very tall forward who is most useful in the line-outs where he makes the most of his reach. Rather clumsy and has a poor wind. 12 st.'[28] Basden was killed in France three years later.

On most fronts the image projected is one of the professional and commercial and still Liberal middle classes in embryo, a junior bourgeoisie, boys of conscience, arguably of responsibility, carefully fostered. Their headmaster told the Old Boys that he was 'more than ever impressed with the importance of the Public Schools of England, if only they would rise to their opportunity and produce men who, in no spirit of superiority, but of sympathy and love, would endeavour to overcome the prejudices and malice of uncharitableness existing between class and class;' and he deplored 'the self-conceit and snobbishness with which the healthy spirit of *esprit de corps* too often degenerated amongst those who enjoyed great advantages'.[29] The Hon. Lionel Johnston came in to tell Old Boys-to-be of the Cavendish Club, designed to arouse 'especially in 'Varsity and Public School men, a deeper sense of their obligations as regards social service' and he mentioned 'that on that evening . . . the Prime Minister and the Archbishop of Canterbury were dealing with the same question at a great meeting in the Queen's Hall'.[30] Millhillians were very much 'Varsity men, perhaps a dozen of them at Oxford and thirty at Cambridge in July 1914, their magazine letters full of the summer (Smith's 'white blazer and imperturbable calm brought him spotless through the wild "squashes" of punts, which follow the six o'clock race each evening . . .') and the welcome promised to their successors—four on the line already for Oxford—in their

> City of friends and echoes, ribbons and music and colour,
> Lilac and blossoming chestnut, willows and whispering limes.[31]

Beyond this communal 'varsity face lay the Old Millhillians, for whom the magazine was no doubt chiefly composed, two hundred and sixty of them annually dining in October 1913, their marriages, births, and honours, sometimes their deaths, duly noted, a network of nonconformist success, generations thick, not yet wholly engulfed by suburbia or the home counties. In 1907, the

---

[28] *Ibid* March 1914 p 149.
[29] *Ibid* November 1913 pp 98–9; December 1913 p 132.
[30] *Ibid.*
[31] *Ibid* July 1914 pp 52, 45, 47.

school's centenary, there had been seven Old Millhillian M.P.s, all Liberals. This was a heritage whose motive power illumines the correspondent who felt that the new school houses, as yet A, B or C, might 'imagine themselves to be the supporters of that stalwart Parliamentarian who resisted the encroachments of Charles I' or might be Brownists or Independents: 'for our part we are inclined to favour the chances of the Brownists.'[32] Perhaps this ancestral piety lies behind the ponderous fascination with socialism in essays, 'A man of original tastes, who shows a disinclination to submit to the conventions arbitrarily imposed by society, is usually labelled a Socialist, and hence anathema';[33] in correspondence, 'The Conservative and Liberal sections of the School each have their representative papers in the Scriptorium, why should not the Socialists also have theirs? I feel sure that there is a sufficient number of boys with advanced tendencies to make it worth while to introduce the *Daily Citizen* into the Scriptorium';[34] or verse:

> Are the men of the age yet awake to the fact
> That they're born in the world to their share,
> ....
> Why should they that are men in this world full of health
> Toil for those puppets which all of them hate,
> Those accursed and fattening nurslings of wealth?[35]

This poem was severely taken to task by a boy ('I myself am a socialist in the purer interpretation of the word') who urged cooperation and dependency rather than revolution or equality, certain that 'sooner or later, the power will come into the hands of the labourers', fearful lest mere agitation would explode into civil war and so bypass the true misery of poverty, 'the impossibility of saving any money and the consequent ease of the descent into absolute beggary, the awful monotony of the work, and the horrible despair of unemployment, the depressing gloom and filth of the surroundings, the soul-destroying coarseness and vulgarity which pervades the whole atmosphere. These are the true horrors of poverty'.[36]

[32] *Ibid* December 1913 p 136.
[33] 'On Labels' *ibid* November 1913 p 106.
[34] *Ibid* March 1914 p 172. The editor replied 'The newspaper of the Socialists is the *Daily Herald*, which used to appear in the Scriptorium but was stopped by the authorities. The *Daily Citizen* represents the Labour Party'.
[35] 'Awaken' *ibid* April 1914 p 176.
[36] 'Awaken' *ibid* June 1914 pp 13, 15–16.

Et Virtutem Et Musas

Here was progressive Liberalism, perhaps social democracy, happily comprehending votes for women, finding schoolboy parallels for the reasonableness of militancy and the hunger strike and debating (winning by twenty two votes to thirteen) that 'the State ought to take care of those who are incapable of taking care of themselves'.[37]

Here too was an enlarging of views, as in the review of an Old Millhillian architect's monograph on *Baroque Architecture*. Baroque was Romish, materialistic and artificial, but it also 'taught us many things about the broader aspects of architecture in an age when life was easy and spacious—how to plan and design on a monumental scale, how to make our surroundings less austere, how to glorify the gifts of Nature in garden and fountain, how to appreciate the grace of the human form, and lastly, how to beautify our cities'.[38] Shades alike of Central Hall, Westminster, and Hampstead Garden Suburb; and of Mill Hill School Chapel too.

War is prefigured only in retrospect. The school had had an O.T.C. since 1911. It reached 'record numbers' in 1913 but its summer camp in 1914 would have to be cancelled because of german measles. 'As the prospects of a large number attending camp were very bright, this is particularly unfortunate'.[39] Bisley's 'splendid sporting fortnight' was a fixed point of the school year.[40] In March 1914 library accessions recorded *With the Victorious Bulgarians* and a volume on aviation.[41] The same number contained an account, natural in a school proud of its German, of eleven weeks in Germany, factual rather than friendly.[42] There was one instance only of 'invasion' literature: a grim little story of guttural voiced invaders and fifth columnists (waiters and second-hand clothes dealers) and sudden death.[43] That was in June 1914, an issue whose frontispiece showed 'Clark finishing the Half Mile in

---

[37] thus 'Votes for Women' *ibid* March 1914 pp 150–4. This, like the essay 'Awaken' was by G. B. B[arber], 'A strong forward who is hard to stop. Should be good next year with a better knowledge of the game.' *Ibid* p 150. Also pp 164–5.

[38] Norman Brett James' (master and commandant of OTC) review of M. S. Briggs, *Baroque Architecture*, 'Baroque Architecture' *ibid* December 1913 pp 132–5.

[39] *Ibid* November 1913 p 92; July 1914 p 73.

[40] *Ibid* June 1914 p 38.

[41] *Ibid* March 1914 p 170.

[42] 'A Short Visit to Frankfurt-On-Main', *ibid* pp 160–3: 'German police require to be armed with a sword at their waist—a London policeman by raising one hand stops an endless stream of traffic'. (p 161).

[43] N. M. G[oodman], 'War: An Incident' *ibid* June 1922 pp 33–4.

Record Time', head flung back, arms out wide, while straw boatered prefects stood in nonchalant appreciation by the finishing post.[44]

In one respect Mill Hill had a good war. Its numbers rose from two hundred and seventy nine in 1914 to three hundred and eighteen in 1918 and perhaps it suffered less than some from the inevitable importation of superannuated temporary staff.[45] Indeed there were positive advantages in the arrival of so old a Radical hand as C. A. V. Conybeare in 1916 or Prebendary Ross of Wells in 1917.[46] Nonetheless the cumulative impact of war, unrelenting, its reality extending into 1919 and beyond, may be charted in five distinct ways. There is the sense in which the school became unassailably part of the national public school community, nature's officers all. There are the editorials and letters to the editor. There are the essays and poems, notes on occasional lectures and debates, lists of library accessions. There is the most obvious impact of all, that on the Old Boys. And there is religion, which ought most naturally to be obvious but is in fact the most elusive to identify, perhaps because it was assumed to be as much part of the warp and woof of Mill Hill life as of all public school life.

The sense of public school fraternity is conveyed by the magazine's contemporaries. In 1917, for example, these included the *Cheltonian, Epsomian, Marlburian, Malvernian, Sedberghian* and *Felstedian,* but also the *Boys' Brigade Gazette* and *College Echoes* from Anglo-Chinese College, Tientsin.[47] Sometimes their contents were reproduced. Thus, again from 1917, the *Shirburnian's* ode, 'Pro Tot Tantisque Beneficiis', ending:

> For the lessons taught to the ageing by eager striving of youth,
> By the firm unswerving devotion of all man's being to Truth,
> For making the most of the throw of the dice, be it even or odd,
> And, beyond and above the rest, for the long-sought vision of God,

---

[44] The record time was two minutes, twelve and four fifths seconds, *ibid* p 17.
[45] *Ibid* November 1914 p 89; November 1918 p 40.
[46] C. A. V. Conybeare (1853–1919) was a barrister who had been M.P. for Camborne from 1885 to 1895, and briefly imprisoned under the Coercion Act in 1889.
[47] *MHM* November 1917 p 89.

Et Virtutem Et Musas

Sherborne, I thank thee!
Or a last stanza from *The Leys Fortnightly:*
> O England, guard thine ancient faith and freedom!
> Oh, hear us who have died!
> What if thy heart, when now the world most needs it,
> Should fail through lust or pride?
> Our bodies we have broken: shall our spirits
> Also be crucified?[48]

At Mill Hill there was no cricifixion of spirit and there was a level headed sense of proper freedom. '[T]his is primarily a School Magazine and intended for School news', the first wartime editorial announced before turning to the half dozen 'who have sacrificed their school careers in order to join the colours,' and to the Old Boys, over three hundred of them already serving their country, filling the school 'with pride, aye, and with something not very far removed from envy'; and to the O.T.C. which 'Practically the whole School has joined'; and to football:

> Some people even go so far as to say that all games should be stopped during the war . . . we would like to suggest that Football is an essential part of school training . . . If any one intends to try for a commission . . . it is Football that can train his mind and body and fit him for the service of his country. The boy who can go down to a forward rush, or go 'all out' for a try, will yield good enough material even for an officer. Waterloo was won on the playing-fields of Eton. Then, before Heaven, let this struggle be won on the Rugger fields of Mill Hill and her compeers.[49]

The message was consistent. In December 1914 'every day finds us even more impatient to be up and doing something for our country'.[50] By March 1915, although 'by the time you read this, Germany may have given in and the war have been finished or London may have been destroyed by Zeppelins' it was more likely that 'the war may still be going on next year, and possibly—who knows?—the year after that. We begin to count the days to that time when we, too, shall be free, and to wonder whether there may not after all, be a chance even for us . . .—So each, at his

---
[48] *Ibid* pp 87, 89.
[49] *Ibid* November 1914 pp 77–9.
[50] *Ibid* December 1914 pp 115–6.

appointed time, breaks from the ordered life of School, and goes out to do his bit whatever that may be . . .'[51]

That year's Christmas number was to go to each serving Old Millhillian. 'In all parts of the world, wherever British troops are stationed, Old Boys are inevitably thinking of home just now, and then their thoughts turn back to their old School . . . the rags they took part in, the masters they were under . . . whatever may have been their position in school . . . they are part of the School'.[52]

By 1916 the war was routine fact ('Economy envelops us successfully') though still to be welcomed bravely. 'Some of us are treading the speedy way of school-life for the last time, but the usual melancholy sentimental feeling of farewell does not come to us as it came to those who left in a former day—we are actually pleased to . . . step into the sterner discipline which we meet forthwith'.[53]

That discipline was now no longer voluntarily embraced, hence the shadow behind November 1916's knightly editorial: 'Militarism seems to envelop us on every side'.[54] The sense of compulsion, however willingly accepted, deepened. 'The Government has required each of us this term to spend a specified time . . . on agricultural work; this is necessarily taken out of school hours. In addition to this compulsory work an appeal has been made for voluntary work on half-holidays . . ., the response has been in every way worthy of the School.'[55] So to 1918: 'the belated summons has reached us; we are bidden to exchange the pen for the sword'.[56] 'Us' was W. E. Bater, a delayed classical exhibitioner at Christ Church, Oxford. His school career precisely spanned the war. There were three more war editorials. That for June 1918, reflected that all 'who have edited this Magazine during the last four years, and, for aught we know, for years before that, have served their country in active warfare. Now, . . . we wonder whether we may ever have the fortune to serve with them.'[57] That for July began baldly, 'It is an unfortunate fact that there is a war on . . .' and went on: 'Shooting and farming

[51] *Ibid* March 1915 pp 139–140.
[52] *Ibid* December 1915 pp 85–6.
[53] *Ibid* April 1916 pp 147–8.
[54] *Ibid* November 1916 p 61.
[55] *Ibid* June 1917 pp 2–3.
[56] *Ibid* April 1918 p 150.
[57] *Ibid* June 1918 p 1.

Et Virtutem Et Musas

have claimed their weekly and daily devotees'.[58] That for November was the first to make no reference to war.[59]

An editorial needs the balance of correspondence. Much of the magazine's was predictable and pseudonymous. The five correspondents of July 1915 ranged from 'Decorum', on leaving chapel after service, to 'Balls', who asked why so many cricket balls were lost.[60] In spring 1917 a Bournemouth Old Boy wrote in. He was what 'an American would describe as "mad"' at 'No Glutton's' defence of the school tuck shop:

> Nobody enjoys seeing a schoolboy have a good 'tuck in' more than I do, but in the present circumstances it's not 'good form'. Boys, as well as 'grown-ups', can help in this war, and I would like to see Mill Hill boys take the lead by closing the Tuck Shop till Lord Devonport says our food and our sugar supply is all O.K.

It took 'Magister' to calm the gallant captain with chapter and verse as to the school's war consciousness.[61] It was a different sort of letter, most poignant in the war's first year, which underlines its impact. In April 1915 'Virtutem et Musas' suggested that 'a photo of the Head Master be put in, as I feel sure that the Old Boys, especially those at the front, would be pleased to have it; and secondly . . . photos of our Old Boys who have been killed in action'.[62] Previous issues had printed extracts of letters from the Front, all cheery ('We went to a ripping concert last night . . . It was an awful rag . . .'), a few uncomfortably factual beneath the cheer and the clean-limbed slang, some recreating the school community ('Another section in our platoon consists almost entirely of Old Leysians, and nearly every other School is represented in the regiment').[63] One of them, covering a Sunday and a Monday in France, may stand for the rest:

> . . . It was gorgeously fine, bright blue sky. At 10 am in the morning we had service . . . 300 to 400 there I should think. Well, anyhow, it was a splendid service, but it was one of the

---

[58] *Ibid* July 1918 p 19.
[59] *Ibid* November 1918 p 39.
[60] The others were 'Lance-Corporal', on the role of NCOs in the OTC; 'One who tends to always split his infinitives', and 'Seven Vols of Tennyson's Works' who 'would jolly well like to know why we have completely vanished from the Library'. *Ibid* July 1915 pp 53–5.
[61] *Ibid* April 1917 pp 175–7.
[62] *Ibid* April 1915 pp 199–200.
[63] *Ibid* March 1915, p 153, 152.

most extraordinary I've ever been to, for the day was perfect for aeroplanes, and right in the middle of the service would come the bang, bang, bang of the aeroplane guns, and the chatter of the maxims. I've seldom heard better singing, and then in the last hymn the climax was reached in a splendidly sung 'Stand up, stand up for Jesus', just as our big guns roared out; it made one rather smile—

'This day the noise of battle',

Well, we hope the line goes on . . .

Next, some comrades' graves, beautifully turfed, nicely fenced, prelude to a Monday morning march

Splendid for aeroplanes, and a beast of a German spotted us . . . It was a topping march, I can honestly say I thoroughly enjoyed it, though it lasted five hours and more . . . Moreoever, I spent quite a cheery time meeting friends—Day, of Mill Hill . . . young Russell-Smith, sometime of Johns, and Mr. Gemmell, late my Form Master at Mill Hill; meeting him was rather humorous, as he now is my junior, being a second Lieutenant . . . I am in splendid condition, as hard as a bell.[64]

German beastliness was seldom obtrusive even in the magazine's slender literary content, its essays, stories, poems, occasional reviews. Some of these were thoughtful although few sustained the level of 'Civilisation' with its conviction that war and civilisation are incompatible, its suspicion that 'even when war and extreme poverty are eliminated, civilizations may not be tending in the right direction', its determination that this should be the last war and 'that the evils which war does help to cure, must be cured speedily by other means'?[65]

If 'Civilisation' was in a spirit of Liberal internationalism, 'Great Britain and the War' was in the spirit of Liberal imperialism and Kipling's *Recessional*.[66] It was a résumé of J. A. Cramb's *England and Germany* (1913) with its thesis that history's underlying motive is the desire for empire, 'a national creed almost religious in its intensity . . . the restless craving for a better state . . .' Thus Germany, 'the youngest, most vitally alive nation in Europe, imprisoned on every side . . .' is, beneath and despite

[64] *Ibid* April 1915 p 179.
[65] 'Civilization' *Ibid* November 1914 pp 79-83.
[66] first published in *The Times* in 1897.

Et Virtutem Et Musas

the tawdry disguise of Prussian bombast and Nietzschean philosophy, 'secure, indomitable, serene, richer in mind and spirit, richer in energy and vitality than any other foe that England has had to face'. These were no 'sausage-fed, beerswilling myrmidons' and this was to be a long conflict, and a crucial one, for it was Goth against Rome, and the question must be, was England, 'at that stage of a nation's career where expansion has ceased and stagnation begins to appear,' to follow Rome? 'Can we show the world that Britain, at any rate, is not like other Empires, that her spirit is immortal, indomitable, her glory, based on the true foundation of Christianity, is permanent, enduring to the end?'[67]

G.S. could not agree. To 'Great Britain and the War' he replied with 'Mankind and the War', a return from imperialism to internationalism, distrustful of the secret diplomacy of great powers. For G.S. the pre-war 'restless craving for a better state' was not fuelled by the ideals of empire, anachronistic and hardly Christian, but by 'a body of thought which is growing out of science and the changed social condition,—a philosophy which is of man, not of nation or class; international, great as the world'. And the path of duty was clear.

> We must smash German militarism; but we must also make sure that the people, of whom we are a part, have some control over those forces which, working in the dark, can without a word of warning plunge the whole labouring world into a hellish struggle such as this, which has neither rhyme nor reason.[68]

Here perhaps was the authentic Mill Hill. It showed itself in March 1916 on 'Heroism', clumsily recognising the heroic element in Quakerism.[69] It was there again in December 1917 on 'Peace and War' with the development of an Asquithian text: 'We must banish once and for all the time-honoured fallacy that if you wish for peace you must prepare for war'.

> Strange to say, there are even some to whom the chief lesson of the present war is that we must never again allow ourselves to be caught unprepared . . . Has any nation ever gained for

---

[67] 'Great Britain and the War' *MHM* March 1915 pp 141–5.
[68] 'Mankind and the War' *ibid* April 1915 pp 182–4.
[69] 'A new order should be instituted by the King for men who stand up for their views against all comers', and it quoted Emerson 'Heroism' *Ibid* March 1916 pp 120–2.

itself a reasonable period of true peace by means of preparation for war?

This essayist was an optimist: human nature must change, we must effect the change, for that is our duty, and at last we have the agent for this change in the 'magnificent cosmopolitanism' of a great idealist statesman, Woodrow Wilson.[70] Then the tone changed. Heavy humour came to the fore; or travel ('Wild Elephants in Burma'); or a past master's 'Eight Months on the Land', a pastoral of 'pure air and sweet odours, sunsets and rising mists—God's earth, man's purest joy!'; or the Boy's Own conquest of the air, that ultimate fascination ('A Daylight Patrol'; 'The Raiders'); or a word from the O.T.C.'s old sergeant on musketry: 'rub in all you know to your own men . . . Get them keen and interested, and make it your duty to press each man until he reaches the highest standard in this very important branch of his training'.[71]

This reinforced the sentimental element, never absent, that was more naturally expressed in stories or verse . . . 'Le Drapeau' was a tale of the spirit of Alsace; 'The Iron Cross' told how pompous little Carl von Essenheim really won promotion.[72] These were stories. The poems were more numerous: 'To the Special Constables who Guard the Armoury'; the grumbling Cockney of 'Unto Them Be the Glory' who 'charged the enemy's trenches to the lilt of a music-hall song';[73] the grumbling lady tea-gossiping over 'Those Belgians', until told:

> Now is not the time for scandal,
>   Think what Belgium's done for you.
> Try to picture their position;
>   Try to take a broader view.[74]

Or, simply, 'Tomorrow':

> They'll call us next, boys,
>   To battle the stern tomorrow,
>
> . . . .
>
> It won't be, perhaps on the battlefield,
>   Playing our country's game;

---

[70] 'Peace and War' *ibid* December 1917 pp 104–8.
[71] *Ibid* November 1918 pp 49, 53–5; March 1918 pp 131–4; July 1918 pp 20–2, 28–9.
[72] *Ibid* April 1915 pp 187–9; July 1915 pp 35–7.
[73] *Ibid* November 1914 pp 83, 108.
[74] *Ibid* March 1915 pp 158–9.

Et Virtutem Et Musas

    May be in the office or workshop,
        But it's fighting just the same.[75]
That call persisted throughout 1915, a moral conscription for boys whose school was now all about the officer class and empire's duty, though their families had never fought.
    Have you forgotten the deeds of your sires,
        Britain made great and her Empire free?
    Rally again, lads, the nation requires,
        Service from you, lads, and service from me.[76]
Changes were frequently rung. In 1917 there were sombre sonnets
    And mothers weeping with a rueful joy
        At Death's serene, unsearchable abyss.[77]
'Instability' was naturally about British steadfastness, 'the seed
    Of an immense, an unconquerable breed
    Which, being free, is yet at God's command.[78]
In 1916 it had been personalities, Joffre, 'heaven-sent leader of our ancient Gaul' or Kitchener:
    O rocks of the Orkneys, relentless and ruthless.
        What did you see of our Kitchener's end?[79]
In 1915 it was epic outrage, the three parts and forty stanzas of 'Louvain' (to rhyme with 'chain') contrasting with the swift schoolboy vogue for the Hymn of Hate.[80] In March 1916 the magazine reprinted Christ's Hospital's 'The Persevering Hun'. This concerned Von Humperstein's airship crew who
    Sang the Hymn of Hate
    From half-past six to half-past eight,
        As Teuton warriors of late
            Habitually do.
A month later Mill Hill produced its own Von Gumboilbosch, 'a really true-bred Hun',
    (Did I describe Von G. to you?
        A florid, horrid man)
    He sang with glee the Hymn of Hate,
        As only a German can.[81]

---

[75] *Ibid* p 163.
[76] *Ibid* July 1915 p 35.
[77] *Ibid* July 1917 p 52.
[78] *Ibid* December 1917 p 96.
[79] *Ibid* June 1916 p 6; July 1916 pp 27–8.
[80] *Ibid* June 1915 pp 6–10.
[81] *Ibid* March 1916 pp 145–6; April 1916 pp 150–1 Christopher Isherwood, in April 1916, at

School magazines are not places for subtlety. Everything—humour, sentiment, morality—is heavy. Toleration is tolerable only as a plea for fair play. There can be little doubt as to the general mood in the school. In March 1916 the magazine congratulated three award winners, two to Cambridge, one to Oxford. One of these was B. K. Martin, the impossible parson's son, who had entered Mill Hill as a day boy in 1914. 'Success sometimes finds the right people'.[82] As Kingsley Martin of *The New Statesman,* B. K. Martin had mixed recollections of his last school. He respected, indeed liked, McClure, 'wonderfully tolerant of my eccentric attitude to the war'.[83] He respected the classics master, John Hampden Haydon (the forenames tell all), who coached him for his scholarship, more in retrospect than in actuality. He disliked school sport; and as a consequence of facing a tribunal as a conscientious objector while at school (the commanding officer of the OTC, Norman Brett-James, the school's historian, spoke up for his sincerity) he found himself turned out of his study, boys hitting him on one cheek to see if he turned the other one. He wrote a defence of his views for the magazine 'which was refused because it was thought to reflect badly on the school's reputation'.[84]

Yet it is hard not to feel that Martin's unpopularity (and he was, even so, a prefect) was a matter more of personality than of views, of manner rather than content. Indeed he recalled that he won a measure of respect for his stand, his rejected essay passed round and read by some of the older boys. As has been seen, the magazine had printed varying, even moderately dissenting views on the war, and in June 1916 it printed a *jeu d'esprit* by Martin, 'The Caprices of Clio', redeemed by his aside on 'the Christian Sergeant O'Leary who killed nine Germans single handed (This, we are told, does not constitute a record. Some years before, one Samson killed forty Philistines with the jaw bone of an ass)'.[85]

Saint Edmund's Hindhead wrote a 'Lay of Modern Germany:
Then out spoke fat Von Winklepop
Who composed the 'Hymn of Hate'
B. Finney, *Christopher Isherwood: A Critical Biography* (London 1979) p 32.
[82] *MHM* March 1916 p 119. *Impossible Parson* is the title of his father's autobiography: D. B. Martin, *An Impossible Parson* (London 1935).
[83] K. Martin, *Father Figures: a first volume of autobiography 1897–1931* (London 1966) p 58.
[84] *Ibid* p 66.
[85] BKM 'The Caprices of Clio' *MHM* June 1916 pp 8–10 especially p 9.

Et Virtutem Et Musas

That year the magazine's 'Valete' listed twenty boys. Eighteen of those were in the cadet corps. Of the remaining two, one joined up and the other, Kingsley Martin, went into the Friends' Ambulance Unit.[86]

In the previous year the magazine had listed the seven hundred Millhillians already in the forces.[87] It calculated that nearly eighty per cent of Old Boys between the ages of nineteen and forty served in some capacity; twenty-nine had died on service and forty-seven had been wounded; there were two DSOs, an MC, a Croix de Guerre, a Russian order, and six mentions in despatches. Sixty-one served in a medical capacity, chiefly in the RAMC, but there were five with the Red Cross, and two in the Friends' Ambulance Unit. And there was one 'Chaplain to Forces at Cambridge',[88] an interesting, indeed mystifying, inclusion because he was H. C. Carter, minister at Emmanuel Congregational Church, Cambridge, and a notable pacifist. Five hundred of the seven hundred Old Millhillians held commissions, but only nine were of colonel's rank. Such figures are tributes, striking yet unsurprising, to the pressures of volunteering, to the extent to which a dissenters' grammar school was assumed to produce officer material,[89] and to the novelty of what was now an almost universal experience. Mill Hill, its OTC notwithstanding, had no service tradition, for the armed services were not a natural career for Mill Hill families. Overnight, or at least over-year, the army, with the navy some way behind and with the airforce still the most captivating of dreams, had become a fact of life. Conscription merely dotted the i's.

The speed of it needs stressing. The first wartime magazine listed three hundred and forty nine serving Old Millhillians, their years ranging from 1873 to 1912, among them, although it was a while before the news reached the school, a French foreign legionary, and one of the school's first peers, Lt. Col. Lord Rochdale, 6th Batt. Lancs. Fusiliers, in Egypt. Two Old Boys had died in action, one in East Africa and one at Antwerp; the OTC's sergeant major had been killed in a local motor accident; and each

---

[86] *Ibid* July 1916 pp 54–6.
[87] *Ibid* December 1915 pp i–xviii.
[88] Thus *ibid* p iv.
[89] None of the eleven school servants listed in addition to the seven hundred Old Boys held a commission; an unsurprising fact which should nonetheless be noted.

of the three November school leavers had been in the OTC, and two of them were now attached to regiments.[90]

The OTC came inevitably to the fore. In November 1914 it had two hundred and twenty three members (with twenty probationers), it paraded twice a week, was lectured to twice a week, had a Saturday route march and dug lots of trenches.[91] By the following summer 'all but seven of the School are being trained' and next November its band 'gave a creditable performance in the village' escorting fifty recruits enlisted under Lord Derby's scheme.[92]

The bands and the field days were the gloss on a reality in which sports days had become attenuated, prizeless affairs, monies raised from them sent from the 'Public Schools of England' to a hospital 'somewhere in France', and in which physical activity had become a statutory matter of ten hours' military service a week for all eighteen year olds, seventeen year olds as well by 1917, with two of the ten hours taken from prep.[93] A grimmer reality lay in each issue's lengthening 'legio Millhilliensis', seven of them killed near Ypres in late spring 1915 and three in the Dardanelles by June; twenty-seven killed on the Somme in 1916, among them the foreign legionary.[94] No wonder a contribution dwelt on the envelope 'On His Majesty's Service' with its yellow slip of paper: '"You are required to present yourself for service with the colours . . ." The shock has come. He is a man'.[95] And the Oxford and Cambridge Letters of pre-war years were replaced by a Sandhurst Letter, for now there were five Old Millhillians at Sandhurst, with four to come, one of them from a Congregational manse. 'My mind was sore troubled . . . at Waterloo; would a third-class ticket suffice or should one consider oneself already an officer and therefore in bounden duty be forced to take a first-class ticket?'[96]

[90] *MHM* November 1914 pp 92–102, 88; for foreign legionary Rieu see *ibid* March 1915 p 147.
[91] Between 1911 and 1914 the OTC had already produced one hundred and forty Old Millhillians of whom ninety were in the forces, one hundred and twenty by June 1915, with eighty holding commissions. *Ibid* November 1914 pp 101–2; June 1915 p 20.
[92] *Ibid* December 1915 p 106.
[93] *Ibid* March 1915 p 161; November 1916 p 79.
[94] *Ibid* June 1915 p 3; July 1915 p 31; November 1916 pp 62–64. And an elderly Old Millhillian was drowned in the sinking of the *Lusitania, ibid* July 1915 p 43.
[95] *Ibid* March 1917 p 150.
[96] So he purchased a first class ticket, only to discover that third class smokers had been reserved for 'gentlemen cadets proceeding to Camberley'. *Ibid* July 1916 pp 33–35 especially p 34.

Et Virtutem Et Musas

It was some time before the listed deaths were illuminated by any suggestive detail. W. H. Andrews, whose starting of the rifle range had 'made the way easy for the O.T.C.', was the French master, 'chary of showing any emotion other than laughter', who compiled the lists of the legio Millhilliensis.[97] E. L. Milner-Barry, of Naval Intelligence, who had come with McClure and gone on to a chair in Bangor, was the German master. 'Years before the crash came, the gathering cloud . . . was visible to him, and the thought of its inevitableness filled him with foreboding . . . for there was much in Germany that Milner-Barry loved as well as much that he hated, and he knew how terribly strong she was.'[98] As to those killed, the myth (perhaps the essence?) is captured by the reproduction of Frank Salisbury's 'very speaking portrait' in airman's uniform, exhibited at the current Royal Academy, of his nephew F. T. E. Stafford, shot over the German lines, who died on St. George's day, 1917;[99] or by the recollection of Owen Lapthorn, killed in France a month later, who had 'a wonderfully clear idea of the meaning of the war, and . . . had felt a moral compulsion to fight';[100] or in Alec Boardman's letter home, just before his death on Salisbury Plain:

> There have been a good many accidents here because the weather has been so bad, but please don't let mother know, else she will only worry. Anyway, I am not frightened because my life is in greater hands than any stunt pilot's.[101]

From 1916 all school boy life ended in the war. Was there a reciprocal relationship? There was certainly a literary relationship. In November 1914 'Entente Cordiale' pleaded the cause of French books ('Let German "culture" plead its own cause—I will not') for the library whose six thousand volumes lacked any Molière, La Fontaine, Hugo, Daudet, de Musset; indeed 'Entente Cordiale' claimed that barely six works of French literature were to be found in it.[102] Perhaps so, and the advice was acted upon. More obviously the war encouraged the regular presentation of *Germany's Swelled Head, How Germany Makes War,*

---

[97] *Ibid* June 1917 pp 11–13.
[98] *Ibid* pp 13–14.
[99] *Ibid* p 7 with a reproduction of the painting.
[100] *Ibid* July 1917 p 28.
[101] *Ibid* June 1918 p 4.
[102] *Ibid* November 1914 pp 113–14.

Britain's Case Against Germany, The Prussian Hath Said in His Heart, To Ruhleben and Back, Sixteen Months in Four German Prisons, as well as Rupert Brooke's *Poems* and *War Letters of a Public School Boy.*[103] Another literary element is found in an Old Millhillian review, Basil Matthews' *The Secret of the Raj*, published by the United Council for Missionary Education and 'splendidly designed' to interest schoolboys. Matthews was made to harness the imperial dimension, necessarily also a missionary one in such a school as Mill Hill, to the war: 'One of the most remarkable features of the present war is the absolute ignorance of our enemies as to the real nature of the British Empire'. It was Matthews' thesis, so the reviewer felt, that there was 'a kind of Fate driving Englishmen to devote their lives to the task of government ... The English rule stands out as the one possible central government, pure, altruistic, and reliable, and having in the eyes of the native something of a supernatural sanction.' Altogether, 'in view of the tremendous problems in India needing solution in the near future, this is emphatically a book to read'.[104]

There was a mounting awareness of problems beyond the bounds of war lying nearer home. New Foundation Day (Public Day's replacement), 1915, was addressed by H. A. L. Fisher, then vice-chancellor of the university of Sheffield. He spoke breezily of 'the cleverest nation upon the face of the earth.'[105] But educational reform was in the air. Indeed, that was the opening sentence of a paper on the matter in November 1916 by one of the masters, J. P. Howard. It proved to be a plea for the traditional values of a humane education by a man 'lamentably ignorant of even elementary science,' horrified at the prospect of a school comprising boys (all those Spicers and Willses) 'whose industry in the class-room was regulated entirely by motives of pecuniary gain and worldly position,' designers of a world in which 'Chemistry is to be the chief end of life since chemistry is *useful* for farming!' Howard was comforted by what a London professor of engineering had said to him last Easter holidays: 'I would rather have boys coming to me quite ignorant of engineering and with a sound general education, than boys who have specialized too soon

---

[103] *Ibid* April 1915 p 193–4; December 1916 p 123; June 1917 p 24; June 1918 p 16.
[104] *Ibid* July 1915 pp 41–2.
[105] *Ibid* November 1915 p 68.

at the subject and whose general culture has been neglected.'[106] Therein lay right thinking in the matter of educational reform.

But it meant nonetheless that the public schoolboy's world was never again to be unquestioned. 'How many people . . . have noticed . . . the disappearance of the top-hat as the Sunday headgear of our Monitors?' or the stiff collar, or, who knew, the tail-coat? 'Considering that the most liberal estimate would limit the days on which it is worn to a score per term, and that on leaving school the wearers almost immediately don His Majesty's uniform, the tail-coat would seem to be a foolish extravagance.'[107] That was in July 1917. In November the magazine went beyond appearances to quote approvingly from a new Repton periodical, with pieces on Democracy (urging 'an open road for talent, an aristocracy of intellect, will and determination . . . from the Elementary School to the Universities') and Revolution ('something has been changed, an angel has passed through the air . . . A new set of ideas, of standards, of ideals has been liberated') and Public Schools after the War. This piece urged government scholarships at public schools for elementary school boys, and it stressed that any public school reform must start from within the schools themselves. The establishment must defuse its own revolution.[108] That was the message when W. E. Bater and two friends reviewed Alec Waugh's Shirburnian *succès de scandale*, *The Loom of Youth*, (*pro tot tantisque beneficiis?*) for despite its kernel of 'very real truth', most of its abuses 'can be reformed (without the necessity of rooting out the whole system) by the Public School boy himself, and by him alone'.[109] At a more exalted level that was what Balliol's A. L. Smith told a cloudless Foundation Day in July 1917: come peace, there would be no new English civil war between capital and labour, for education would prove a chief preservative of social well-being.[110]

The underside of this was the Literary and Debating Society, asleep since October 1914 but revived in March 1916 by Captain Brett-James of the OTC as a light-hearted inconsequential thing which nonetheless stumbled through reform of the public school

---

[106] J. P. H(oward) 'Reform in Education' *Ibid* November 1916 pp 84–8.
[107] AHM 'The Old Order Changeth' *ibid* July 1917 pp 34–5.
[108] 'A Public School Looks at the World' *ibid* November 1917 pp 75–6.
[109] *Ibid* March 1918 pp 138–40.
[110] *Ibid* July 1917 p 32.

system and class proving the ruin of England in the near future and pacificists being a menace to the state who should be deprived of their civil rights. That debate was marked by talk of the Kaiser in Westminster Abbey and conchie guards helping German prisoners to escape; but its result was a foregone conclusion. The motion was defeated by six votes to thirty four. Deprivation of civil rights was unBritish, indeed as W. E. Bater reminded his audience (to their applause), it was unMillhillian. Why else had their school been founded?[111]

Perhaps this was McClure winning through. Martin Briggs, the Old Millhillian architect, apparently captivated his audience with 'Michael Angelo' in October 1914: 'a lecture on art delivered to a boys' school at a time like this. . . ?'[112] From December 1915 there was a campaign, perhaps mounted by McClure and therefore successful, for a musical society.[113] In 1916, thanks to the tercentenary, 'we . . . have been inoculated with Shakespeare. We think Shakespeare, we talk Shakespeare, we act Shakespeare.'[114] In 1917, amid patriotic British and American songs, it was Benjamin Franklin's turn. A hundred and fifty years earlier he had stayed in Mill Hill. Now in a set surrounded by trees planted by Franklin's Quaker friend Collinson, a play by Captain Brett-James discussed electricity, daylight saving, and the perils of German influence.[115]

One dog has yet to bark: religion. Mill Hill's Christianity was still recognisably Free Church Christianity, probably more Congregationalist than anything else. Old Millhillian weddings tended to be chapel weddings rather than church; and school chapel was Chapel, not Church. But it was also a public school Christianity: 'Surely the aim of a religion is to keep men straight, and the religion which does that best is the most successful, whether it be ours or not.'[116] Neville Goodman's poem 'Revelation', phrased this with more sophistication:

> Fiercely rebelling, I cursed Him and straightway expected to die,

---

[111] *Ibid* April 1916 pp 163–5; March 1917 p 154; November 1917 pp 83–4.
[112] *Ibid* November 1914 p 112.
[113] *Ibid* December 1915 p 116 (was McClure himself the correspondent, disguised as 'Out of the Mouths of Babes and Sucklings'?); April 1916 p 170.
[114] *Ibid* July 1916 p 26, with review, and photographs, pp 45–9.
[115] *Ibid* July 1917 pp 44–5.
[116] 'Heroism' *ibid* March 1916 p 122.

Et Virtutem Et Musas

When God in His mercy pitied and I heard a voice from on high—
'To true seekers of Light, God ever reveals,
God the true God is the God of Ideals.'[117]

In the school its focus was of course the chapel, which chiefly appears in the magazine as a blackout problem and already too small and the source of schoolboy nightmares.[118] Even so, in December 1915 'Custos' wanted to know 'why we hear so little of the war in Chapel?' The war litany has ceased, the national anthem is never sung, sermons make no reference, indeed 'Mr. Pearson's sermon of a few weeks ago on David and the well at Bethlehem, and the searching question, 'Are we worthy of the sacrifice?' were the first reminder that many of us have had for some while of the war and its meaning for us all.'[119]

Yet such reminders appeared with increasing frequency in the magazine. 'Well Dad, we are going up the line soon. You know what the student told his men: "If wounded, Blighty: if killed, the Resurrection". If the great possibility happens, think of me only as part of a great stepping-stone on which the world will rise to better things.'[120] Thus a letter home; thus too an encounter between the Merchant Taylors' padre, 'a short, square-shouldered humorist, who owned to damaged knee joints collected on the football field,' and who was about to read the burial service and so commit some of our lads, 'to the care of the great G.O.C. of us all', and the weary Millhillian liaison officer, who recalled a famous victory against Merchant Taylors' ('Footer turns boys into men at Mill Hill') and reflected that 'the Padre was a better padre because he led the school pack, and I hope that I am a better officer because I, too, once wore the chocolate and white.'[121]

This is a flavour best distilled in 'Sentences from a Charming Book' a magazine selection by an Old Millhillian Congregational minister. Ernest Hampden-Cook, from a Canadian Old Millhillian's (and manse son's) letters home:

I am setting out on a crusade . . . I have a growing trust that

---

[117] *Ibid* December 1914 pp 133–4.
[118] 'For the Choir Secretary to find that the Head Master's list of hymns does not agree with the organist's, and the boards both tell a different tale'. *Ibid* March 1916 p 136.
[119] *Ibid* December 1915 p 113.
[120] *Ibid* July 1918 p 23.
[121] 'Reminiscences' *ibid* November 1918 p 46.

whatever God decides for me will be best and kindest . . . We've been carried up to the Calvary of the world, where it is expedient that a few men should suffer that all the generations to come should be better . . . Life has become so stern and scarlet—and so brave! Today I am genuinely happy, for I feel that I am doing something which has no element of self in it. The men are splendid . . . and when the governess, Death, summons them to bed they obey her with unsurprised quietness . . . I am quite disillusioned about the splendour of war. The splendour is all in the souls of the men who creep through the squalor like vermin. Poor lonely people, so brave and so anonymous in their death! . . . When you see how cheap men's bodies are, you cannot help but know that the body is the least part of personality . . . Dimly one thinks he sees what is right, and leaves father and mother and home as though it were for the Kingdom of Heaven's sake. Perhaps it is. One can't explain.[122]

Mill Hill's war could not end with the Armistice, although that was delight enough, with a verse competition, the national anthem in the Large, a service of thanksgiving in the chapel, processions with flags and tea-trays round the top-field and into the village, and, culminating joy, a guard of honour for the king and queen, with tea from Sir Albert Spicer, shared with The Leys, at the Free Church Thanksgiving in the Albert Hall.[123]

The prime practical issue was an appropriate memorial for the hundred and ninety-two killed on service out of the eleven hundred who had served.[124] This had been in train since the

[122] *Ibid* November 1917 pp 64–6.
[123] *Ibid* December 1918 pp 72–7.
[124] A comparison with some other Free Church schools is instructive: at Taunton of a thousand and four serving at least one hunded and sixty-five were killed; at Bishop's Stortford of nearly six hundred serving fifty-five died; at Tettenhall of over two hundred serving, twenty-four died; at Eltham College (for missionaries' sons) of one hundred and twenty serving, twenty-nine were killed; at Silcoates (for Congregational ministers' sons) two hundred were fighting by February 1917, and by 1919 forty-one had died; at Caterham (for Congregational ministers' sons) sixty-nine died. The respective sizes of the schools is not easy to determine. Of the three comparable schools Mill Hill topped three hundred by 1917; Taunton was larger; Bishop's Stortford smaller. Tettenhall had one hundred and thirty four boys by 1919; Eltham one hundred and sixty by 1919; Caterham had over two hundred by 1919; Silcoates was the smallest, varying between seventy-three and eighty-nine boys between 1914 and 1919. See S. P. Record, *Proud Century: The First Hundred Years of Taunton School* (Taunton 1948) p 175; J. Morley and N. Monk-Jones, *Bishop's Stortford College, 1868–1968. A Centenary Chronicle* (London

Et Virtutem Et Musas

proposal of June 1916 to found scholarships for the sons of Old Millhillians killed in the war.[125] By late 1918 there was a triple thrust to the memorial: the scholarship scheme; a memorial 'of artistic beauty'; and, since 'Science, whose developments have counted for so much in the War, should have greater facilities at Mill Hill for developments appropriate to the time of peace', laboratories and lecture rooms. The need was for £25,000.[126] The memorial of artistic beauty, in the shape of a classical gate of honour, was opened by Lord Horne in October 1920.[127] A memorial lectern designed by Basil Champneys followed in July 1921 and a *Book of Remembrance and War Record,* 'a model of all that such a book should be', in 1922.[128] It was only in February 1924 that the reticently neo-Georgian science block could be opened, for it was only then that the prince of Wales, 'after two postponements made inevitable through accidents', could provide the school's first royal visit, a well briefed affair, with the tactful royal recollection that he and the headmaster were undergraduates at Oxford together (cheers).[129]

This headmaster was not McClure but Maurice Jacks, an Oxford newcomer, for McClure, who was a Cambridge man, had died suddenly two years before, the magazine's insertion sufficient memorial: 'I have written no books and I shall write none; you are my books'.[130]

The school's return to normalcy with first peace and then a new headmaster to be learned was not always smooth. Numbers slipped.[131] The political background was not to be disregarded. The first peace time editorial focused on the drawbacks of the public school system with a quotation 'from the pen of Labour'. Its conclusion misfired: 'Let us start a movement for the Redecoration of the Public Schools on simple yet artistic lines'.[132] In March 1919

1969) p 55; *The Tettenhallian. College Centenary* Vol xxxiv June 1963 No 3 p 126; *The Glory of the Sons* p 74; H. H. Oakley, *The First Century of Silcoates* (Cheltenham 1920) p 56; H. Stafford, *A History of Caterham* (Shrewsbury 1945) p 100.

[125] *MHM* June 1916 pp 5-6.
[126] *Ibid* December 1918 pp 88-9.
[127] *Ibid* December 1920 pp 108-9.
[128] *Ibid* July 1921 pp 22-3; June 1922 p 23.
[129] *Ibid* April 1924 pp 242-5.
[130] *Ibid* March 1922 facing p 89.
[131] to 283 in June 1922; *ibid* June 1922 p 23.
[132] *Ibid* December 1918 pp 65-6.

it was the turn of George Lansbury, pleading for tolerance, 'the mental quality of suffering with and respecting the opinions . . . of others'. This time the conclusion was the duchess's remark to Alice that '''tis love, that makes the world go round'. And Lansbury himself came that month to lecture on 'Reconstruction' in the music schools, a 'unique opportunity', as the headmaster observed, to put 'ourselves in the position of the working-class man . . .'[133] In July it was 'The League of Nations and the School', which meant religious training as the international keynote, and the importance of teaching modern (that is to say, 1815 to 1915) history.[134] And in that month W. L. Hichens spoke on industry and morality. Again McClure chaired, and the magazine's commentator wrote critically of one of Hichens's answers to questioning that 'to provide a thorough education for the working classes is a burden which the country in its present financial exhaustion cannot possibly bear.'[135] In November the debating society decided that Lloyd George was incapable of governing the country and in early 1920 it contemplated a programme of debates which justified Sinn Fein, argued that Labour (like Lloyd George) was unfit to govern, that governmental inefficiency was directly due to public school education and that Drinkwater's *Abraham Lincoln* was the greatest play since Shakespeare.[136]

But the casualties of war continued. There was news from an Old Boy whose war had been spent in Vienna ('It is a terrible experience to be on the losing side'); of another killed in Russia; of Herbert Ward, Old Boy *par excellence,* miner, sail-maker, seaman, stockrider, circus gymnast turned explorer, fashionable sculptor, expatriate Frenchman, friend of Lord Northcliffe, advocate of allied friendship, author of *Mr. Poilu.*[137] War stories still featured, with 'An Incident of '15' about German murderousness in a prisoner of war camp, as the most savage of them all.[138] War books were still given to the library. But it was jazz that was now conquering:

[133] *Ibid* March 1919 pp 99–100; April 1919 pp 153–5.
[134] *Ibid* July 1919 pp 37–9.
[135] *Ibid* pp 58–60.
[136] *Ibid* December 1919 pp 155–6; March 1920 pp 205–6: Sinn Fein was justified by twenty five votes to ten, 'the most exciting debate of the session'.
[137] 'Tidings from Vienna' *ibid* June 1919 pp 17–18; November 1919 p 110–12, and N. G. B. J(ames) 'Mr. Poilu' *ibid* March 1917 pp 134–6.
[138] *Ibid* April 1919 pp 155–8.

Et Virtutem Et Musas

'Will you walk a little faster', said the prefect to the lad;
'There's a monitor behind me and he's jazzing it like mad;'
....
'You can really have no notion how delightful it will be
When they take us up and whirl us, with the fellows, after tea.'[139]

This was on a par with 'Enthusiasm and House Spirit,' the most philistinely sporting editorial for years: '. . . Before you is peace. The traditions that you set now will be the ruin or salvation of schoolboys (and through them of your country) for the next fifty years'.[140] The Oxford and Cambridge Letters returned, joined by one from Glasgow; and soldiers' tales from afar gave way, in the new, Smuts-coined consciousness of Commonwealth, to pieces on Australia and tea-planting in Assam and wireless. The wireless club, whose activities later reached the prince of Wales, by June 1921 had heard concerts 'from the Hague, from Berlin, and from Croydon; and voices from the cross channel aeroplane.'[141]

Did any room remain for protestant dissent among such enlarged horizons? Certainly the early post war issues printed more overtly 'churchy' pieces than had been the magazine's normal custom. When P.C.H. contributed 'Ad Saecula Saeculorum' as an understanding of Roman Catholicism (In claiming the liberty of Christ, we too often forget the fear of God. That is what we may learn from the Church of St. Peter'), an Old Millhillian responded fiercely from Spain with 'For Ever and Ever', a condemnation of Spanish Catholicism.[142] The exchange embarrassed the editor. The Free Church schools were now at the point, already foreshadowed in this paper, where Free Churchmanship must be a minority commitment in class and staff room alike, reflected only in the flavour of chapel, the composition of governing bodies, the scattered presence of manse sons. At the very point at which they had tested their membership of the public school community and then of the national community, they were slipping both from their own immediate hinterland and from what was to be the mainstream of the

---

[139] *Ibid* March 1919 p 121.
[140] *Ibid* June 1919 pp 1–3.
[141] 'Australian Types' *ibid* pp 9–11; 'Australia and Peace' July 1919 pp 54-5; 'Tea-Planting in Assam' November 1920 pp 81–6; December 1920 pp 111–3; June 1921 pp 15–16.
[142] *Ibid* November 1919 pp 112–4; March 1922 pp 181–3.

educational future, although it would take the second world war, whose aftermath saw them at their most prosperous, to make that clear.

Yet in 1919 they were still intimately connected with the Free Church leadership. In that year, for example, the chairman of the Congregational union was Mill Hill's headmaster, Sir John McClure; the president of the Baptist union was one of its best known Old Boys, Herbert Marnham; and the moderator of the Presbyterian church of England, Alexander Ramsay, was the father of another.[143] Three years later, 14 May 1922, McClure's successor, the twenty eight year old Maurice Jacks, preached his first sermon in Mill Hill school chapel. The magazine printed it in full:

> religion does more than face the crises which are already there—it creates new crises; it does more than help us in our old perplexities—it gives birth to new perplexities; it does more than show us which way to choose in embarrassing positions—it makes more positions embarrassing.[144]

That was in all respects a sermon for the 1920s, its persuasively non-evangelical rhetoric inconceivable without the shared experience of total war, even at schoolboy remove. 'It is the duty of every Christian man to regard his religion as the Expeditionary Force of his soul'.[145]

University of Sheffield

---

[143] *Ibid* June 1919 p 5.
[144] 'Sunday, May 14th, 1922' *ibid* June 1922 pp 4–9 especially p 7.
[145] *Ibid* p 6.

THE COWLEY FATHERS AND THE FIRST WORLD WAR

by BRIAN TAYLOR

THREE SUNDAYS after the outbreak of war, Fr Congreve, aged nearly 79, preached in the society's church in Oxford, and gave a summary of professor J. B. Mozley's sermon on war, delivered during the Franco-Prussian War in 1871, 'for the sake' he said, 'of those of us who do not know it'.[1] Fr Benson, the founder of the society, lived until 14 January 1915. At the age of 90 he kept abreast of the news, and was angered by the German bombardment of West Hartlepool and Bridlington; 'he spoke with scorn of this effort of the enemy, and again and again spoke of its uselessness from a military point of view.'[2]

The Superior General of the Society of St John the Evangelist, Fr Maxwell, realised that the war would cause a reduction in subscriptions. While no new work would be undertaken, he urged 'we are really anxious to impress upon our friends that by far the greater part of our work is not such as can be retrenched without causing much suffering, and without crippling our effort in the future'. For example, they had the care of young children in the missions, who could not wait for 'their next meal until after the war is over'.[3]

After this the *Cowley Evangelist* had few references to the war, apart from limited news of members of the community who were serving with the forces—news which became much more informative after Fr Bull became Superior General in 1916; even lay brothers were mentioned sometimes then. In March 1916 there was a sombre article on Lent by Fr Congreve. He referred to the crosses borne by the French, Belgians and Serbians, 'whose fields and cities are ravaged'. At home 'the war has roused a manly and serious temper among us, has chastened us by sacred suffering, quickened us to unselfish efforts. . . . Everyone is ready for self-

---

[1] C[owley] E[vangelist] September 1914 p 195.
[2] *Ibid* February 1915 pp 25–6.
[3] *Ibid* October 1914 p 224.

denial today.' So, he concluded, a good Lent should be kept.⁴ Most of the pages continued to be filled with devotional articles, and news from Africa and India.

Fr Maxwell addressed the general chapter of the society a year after the declaration of war, sharing the views of most thoughtful patriots. 'The war dominates our thoughts. . . . The sacredness of the cause for which we are fighting; the conviction that if we are to fail in our duty the cause of freedom, and of right as against might, would be seriously imperilled; the fact that as the war develops it becomes more and more clear that we are fighting for our very existence as a free country and Empire; all this makes it less likely that the absorbing interest we take in the progress of the war will really hinder our life or destroy our Prayer. . . . It seemed to me right not only to increase the number of newspapers but to put them into the various common rooms earlier in the day. I have no doubt that at the end of the war it will be quite easy to return to our usual custom and rule in that matter.'⁵

But some members of the society were away with the troops. Fr P. N. Waggett was working in Cambridge when war was declared. Fr Congreve's nephew, General W. N. Congreve VC, was commanding the 18 Brigade, which soon arrived in Cambridge to camp on Midsomer Common. Fr Waggett discussed possible service with general Congreve, and early in September he was taken to France as an unofficial chaplain. He was soon serving under fire, and was mentioned in despatches for his bravery at the battle of Ypres, probably for help with evacuating the wounded. Waggett officially joined the RAChD on 17 December 1914. He was a vigorous and active man, well known in church and academic circles, and his service as a chaplain was busy, and he travelled much, and met influential people. After being mentioned twice more in despatches, he was brought back to England, and was senior chaplain at Tidworth from early in 1917 until May 1918, when he began two years as a political officer in Palestine.⁶

Even before Fr Waggett went to France, another member of the community had been gazetted as an army chaplain, on 20

---

⁴ *Ibid* March 1916 p 53.
⁵ SSJE Chapter Minutes, 3 August 1915, pp 192–4. I am grateful to the Superior General for making the minute book available to me.
⁶ An account of Waggett's war service is in John Nias, *Falme from an Oxford Cloister* (London 1961) pp 127–140.

August. Fr M. W. T. Conran was a very different kind of man. On his death in 1945 he was described as 'a man of simple faith, passionately desirous for the conversion of souls',[7] and his letters told of his efforts to bring men to a deep devotion and a reasonable understanding of the Christian faith. He issued a simplified version of his *Two Chaplets of Prayer*, and distributed it to 'those who would undertake to [say the prayers] twice a week—and so grow in devotion and religious habit, not just formal adhesion to the Church'.[8] Bishop A. F. Winnington-Ingram commended this way of prayer: 'Soldiers can learn it by heart, and repeat it (as has been found by experience) even in the heat and excitement of a great charge.'[9] Conran served with the 25 Field Ambulance in France. He was mentioned in despatches in January 1916, and was awarded the MC in the same month, but the *London Gazette* gave no citation.[10] Conran then appears to have fallen sick, or to have been wounded, and he resigned his commission in June 1916.[11]

In April 1917, Fr Bull, the Superior General, wrote, 'Several of our Lay Brothers volunteered early in the war for military service, before it was compulsory, and are faithfully at work on the Western Front at the moment.'[12] In that same month the society suffered its only death by enemy action, when novice brother Walter Frederick was killed in France. In 1915 he had wanted to enlist in the RAMC, but was not successful, so he joined up for active service. After six months in France, and with the rank of lance-sergeant in the Royal Fusiliers, he was taking part in the attack on the Arras-Cambrai road on 23 April 1917. His arm was shattered by a piece of a shell, and no-one had time to dress it and save his life. The brother is commemorated in the society's former church in Oxford, where the second of the E.A. Fellowes Prynne stations of the cross is his memorial.[13] Two other brothers, William John and Maxwell John, served with the RAMC until the end of the war.[14]

---

[7] *CE* December 1945 p 99.
[8] *Ibid* February 1915 pp 33–4.
[9] Preface to M. W. T. Conran, *The National Mission* (London 1916) p 5.
[10] 14 January 1916. Information about Fr Conran, and also Frs Peacey, Strong and Wigram has been kindly supplied by Major R. Gresty, Defence Services.
[11] *CE* July 1916 p 167.
[12] *Ibid* April 1917 p 77.
[13] *Ibid* April 1917 p 77; July 1917 p 149; October 1917 p 224; July 1918 171. D. M. Hope to the author, 6 January 1982.
[14] SSJE Chapter Minutes, 2 August 1916 p 259; August 1918 p 334.

The Congress of USA declared war on Germany on 6 April 1917—Good Friday, and SSJE in America permitted several novices to volunteer for service. In November 1918 it was reported that 'several of the American Novitiate are in France in the American army, and Mr Ballard we hope by this time is in Mesopotamia'.[15] Arthur Lee Ballard was an Englishman, ordained in Canada, who became a novice in America in 1917. He travelled to England in 1918 hoping to obtain an army chaplaincy. He was unsuccessful, but was accepted as a YMCA secretary, 'but for the purpose of doing priestly work with the British troops [in Mesopotamia]. He is to assist an Army Chaplain, a good Catholic priest, who reserves the Blessed Sacrament in his tent.'[16] Ballard was fit when he set out on the long journey to Mesopotamia, through Calcutta, and was 'able practically to do chaplain's work . . . till the close of the war'. His health failed, and 'several of his teeth dropped out from lack of proper food'. He returned to America a sick man, and died on 8 February 1920 'of influenza pneumonia . . . caught while nursing others in the community.'[17]

The other six American novices who went to the war were laymen. Only two of them were subsequently professed in the society, and both were ordained, brother Walter James, as Fr Morse, and brother Raymond as Fr McDonald. Brother Walter James 'seems to have spent the greater part of his time in the army at the Artillery unit at Camp Jackson, South Carolina, and was released as a sergeant major'.[18] Brother Raymond was also at Camp Jackson, but then went to Camp Merritt, New Jersey, for embarkation for France in July 1918. Brother Edwin was in France by May 1918, and enjoyed attending mass and other devotions in the village church, as well as the Corpus Christi procession, for which an American regimental band played. No record has been found of the others—brothers Leonard, Richard and Francis. The brief reports are given in a style of moral earnestness, illustrated by a quotation from Henry Suso. An angel 'drew near to the Servitor, and clothed him in a coat of mail, and said to him, "O!

---

[15] *CE* November 1918 p 239.
[16] *The Messenger* (the magazine of St John the Evangelist Bowdoin Street, Boston, in which SSJE American news also appeared) August 1918. Cuttings from *The Messenger* were supplied by Fr David Allen SSJE.
[17] *CE* July 1918 p 160.
[18] D. Allen to the author, 5 February 1982.

Cowley Fathers and War

Knight! hitherto thou hast been but a Squire; but now it is God's will that thou be raised to knighthood." And the Servitor gazed at the spurs and said with much amazement in his heart, "Alas, what has befallen me? Must I indeed become a Knight? I had rather remain in peace." '[19]

In the meanwhile, as the war entered its fourth winter, the supply of military chaplains was insufficient, and archbishop Davidson called for more volunteers.[20] There was a generous response from the society in England. 'In view of the new call on the nation's manhood, . . . the Home Chapter of the Society has decided to give all whom it can spare, and who are fitted for it, to work in the Army. Father Strong, Father Wigram, and of our Novices Mr. Peacey, Mr. Balcomb, and Mr. Ballard will volunteer for work as Chaplains, or in the R.A.M.C.'[21] Of these novices, only Fr Peacey was subsequently professed in the community. He had been a regular soldier as a young man, and had served as a trooper in the South African War. He volunteered as a chaplain, and was gazetted on 9 September 1914. In 1915, however, it was discovered that he was teaching the soldiers how to go to confession, and he was cashiered by Bishop Taylor Smith. Now he joined the YMCA, and was sent first to France and then to Belgium, and returned to Cowley in 1919.[22]

Ballard's service has already been mentioned. A. J. Balcomb was only briefly in the novitiate. He was accepted by the YMCA in 1918 and, like Ballard, set off for Mesopotamia by way of India. From Calcutta he was sent to Simla. He quickly formed a conviction that he should work in India, and for a while was a probationer with the Oxford Mission to Calcutta. Later he served with SPG in the villages south of the city.[23]

L. T. Strong joined the RAChD on 17 May 1918. His obituary notice described him as 'a vigorous and forceful missioner, with a special gift for uncultured people. He was of an ardent and impulsive nature, and had a great love of souls'.[24] He was sent straight away to Salonica where he was stationed at the 43 General

---

[19] *The Messenger* August, September and November 1918.
[20] G. K. A. Bell, *Randall Davidson* (3 ed London 1952) pp 848–50.
[21] *CE* May 1918 p 118.
[22] *Ibid* June 1918 p 139; November 1952 pp 133–4.
[23] *Ibid* November 1918 p 239; *A Hundred Years in Bengal* (Delhi 1979) p 151.
[24] *CE* October 1959 p 145.

Hospital. There had not been a chaplain there before, and at first he had very small numbers of communicants. He reserved the sacrament in the church tent. He was astonished at the ignorance of the Christian faith among the soldiers, but persevered in befriending them. His speciality was long walks on Mondays, which helped the men to get to know him better. When the war ended, the Roman Catholic chaplain had exposition of the sacrament all day, so Strong said that he would keep watch before the reserved sacrament all night, and a few soldiers joined him for part of it. In the morning there were two well attended celebrations of the eucharist, at which he 'used the Collect for Victory at Sea adapted'. He reported a good Christmas, with one hundred and sixty-four communicants at seven celebrations of the eucharist. He carried on as a chaplain into 1919, with responsibility for a wider area. He wrote that many lads 'come here and make themselves coffee and find smokes, and a real work of evangelization is going on'. He had some men for confession on Good Friday, and communicants were increasing. In the middle of the year he was transferred to Constantinople, and while there he was asked by a naval chaplain to conduct a mission on HMS *India* during exercises in the Black Sea. Strong arrived back in Cowley on Christmas Day 1919.[25]

Fr Wigram became an army chaplain on 28 May 1918, and served with the 1/9 Batallion Highland Light Infantry Territorial Force in France. He reported that he was not getting much response, but after a few months he had heard one soldier's confession, and eight were being prepared for confirmation. He encountered brother Maxwell John, and so was able to celebrate the eucharist daily. On 12 October he was wounded in the face during an engagement near le Cateau while helping to bring back wounded soldiers. He was awarded the MC, and the citation read, 'His fine example of coolness and absolute disregard of danger was a great encouragement to the stretcher-bearers and helped to save many lives.' After a short time for recovery in England, Wigram was back in France in time for Christmas, when he was disappointed at having only four communicants, even though the second mass was a parade service. An officer said of the men, 'It

[25] *Ibid* June 1918 p 139; August 1918 pp 175–6; September 1918 p 192; October 1918 p 212; November 1918 p 235; January 1919 pp 12–13; March 1919 p 53; July 1919 p 134; September 1919 p 173; December 1919 p 231; January 1920 p 19.

Cowley Fathers and War

isn't that they don't want to, but they have to be terribly strong-minded.'[26]

War work of a completely different kind was undertaken by brother Michael, who had been at St Edward's House, Westminster since 1908. Soon after the outbreak of war two soldiers asked him for crucifixes. He gave them, and very soon there were further requests. By the end of the war about six thousand service-men had received crucifixes, and had been enrolled in the 'Knights of the Crucifix', described by archbishop Davidson as a 'simple association . . . for banding together a great company, prepared to testify quietly & simply to their loyalty to Our Lord'.[27] There were no rules—only the promises made at baptism. Many soldiers and sailors called at St Edward's House, and links with as many of the 'knights' as possible were kept up with letters and booklets which the brother wrote. He met many more soldiers while helping the military chaplains in the 5 London (City of London) General Hospital, which was established at St Thomas' from 1915 to 1919.[28]

When the war ended, in November 1918, Fr Congreve had been dead for seven months, so his observations were not available. The main article in the December *Cowley Evangelist* had no reference to the armistice, but in January the Superior General wrote on 'The achievement of peace', and discussed the demands of the future. The society's experience of war had been parallel to that of many families and streets. As far as possible normal work and responsibilities were maintained. Some enlisted, either as chaplains or as combatants, at the first opportunity, while others responded later to the archbishop's urgent call for volunteers. Honours were won. There was experience of wounds and sickness, and one death in battle. When we have information about the wartime service of members of the society, it is consistent with what we know of them from other sources, or remember of them. Fr Waggett moved in high circles, as always, and was given work that his gifts enabled him to do. Fr Conran and Fr Peacey continued the

---

[26] *Ibid* June 1918 p 139; September 1918 pp 193–5; November 1918 p 239; February 1919 p 33; *London Gazette* 30 July 1919.
[27] R. T. Davidson to brother Michael, 19 March 1920.
[28] B. Taylor, *Brother Michael* (Gloucester 1965) pp 12–17; E. M. McInnes, *St Thomas's Hospital* (London 1963) pp 160–1. Some wards had been in use for wounded service-men since September 1914.

personal pastoral ministry in which they excelled. Fr Strong's direct manner and methods found an evangelistic opportunity for which he was well suited. For some, like Balcomb, the war provided a suggestion for other work in the future. On the other hand, the wartime freedom from the normal discipline of community life was a factor in unsettling both Fr Strong and brother Michael, who soon were separated from the society, and perhaps it partly explains why most of the American novices did not return when they were demobilised.

There was a great confidence in the rightness of the allied cause, and president Woodrow Wilson was quoted with approval when he spoke of 'force, force to the utmost, force without stint or limit, the righteous force which shall make right the law of the world and cast every selfish dominion down in the dust'.[29]

Guildford

---

[29] *The Messenger* November 1918.

CHRISTIAN PACIFISM IN THE ERA OF TWO WORLD WARS

by MARTIN CEADEL

'WHENEVER THE actual historical situation sharpens the issue, the debate whether the Christian Church is, or ought to be, pacifist, is carried on with fresh vigour both inside and outside the Christian community.'[1] Thus wrote Reinhold Niebuhr, the American commentator on Christian ethics, in 1940, having himself been converted first to pacifism and then back again in the course of the interwar period. Final agreement in this debate is, of course, improbable. But this paper will argue that the Christian cases for pacifism and non-pacifism alike were clarified, at least in Britain and for several decades, by the extraordinary 'sharpening' of the issue afforded by the 'actual historical situation' in the era of the two world wars. The shock of the first world war produced unprecedented support for Christian pacifism; and the aggressions of the 1930s, culminating in the crisis of 1940–1 when Britain faced the possibility of invasion and defeat, provided a series of tests which only the most rigorously thought-out version of that faith could survive—but, having survived them, it could survive anything.

This clarification was not confined to pacifism of Christian inspiration, so it is helpful to begin with a consideration of the characteristics of pacifism in general. For all its apparent simplicity as a belief, it raises three difficulties which must each be discussed: difficulties over its definition, over its orientation towards practical politics, and over its inspiration or justification.[2] The definition of pacifism here adopted is that in normal usage since the mid-1930s: the personal conviction that, war being the greatest evil, it is wrong to take part in it or to support or condone it in any way. Defining it in this way has the effect of excluding two categories

---

[1] Reinhold Niebuhr, [*Why the Christian church is not pacifist* (London 1940)] p 7.
[2] This framework was first developed in Martin Ceadel, *Pacifism in Britain 1914–1945: the defining of a faith* (Oxford 1980), to which the reader is referred for a justification of the generalisations advanced here. The present paper reiterates some of the arguments of the book, but also uses some new illustrative material.

of anti-war belief often wrongly claimed to be pacifist. The first encompasses objections to fighting which fall short of being principled objections to war as such. For instance, some objectors do not regard war as wrong, merely their personal participation in it (on the grounds that, as the elite or the elect, they should be exempted). Certain members of the Bloomsbury group and certain millenarian sects fell into this category during the first world war. They are here described as 'quasi-pacifist'. The second category of beliefs excluded by the present definition is that to which the word 'pacifist' was understood to refer for the first three decades after it was coined soon after 1900. 'Pacifism' then implied, not its more precise modern meaning, but no more than the belief that war was a poor way to resolve disputes—a rejection of militarism, in other words. Since this position would now be described as merely 'pacific' rather than pacifist, the word used to describe it will be— in accordance with a developing convention—*pacificist*.[3] Most members of the British (and other countries') peace movement have been *pacificists*, of course, since they have mainly pinned their hopes for war-prevention on to political causes such as the establishment of international institutions, or of socialism, or the abolition of nuclear weapons, rather than on to personal renunciation of war. Unlike pacifists, they would be willing to resort to military force if it were essential in order to achieve or protect such reforms. Yet, although the ablest members of the peace movement have usually understood the differences between pacifism on the one hand and *pacificism* or quasi-pacifism on the other, clarity concerning the definition of pacifism has understandably not always been achieved.

Clear-minded *pacificists* have, however, commonly condemned pacifists for being concerned more to salve their consciences rather than to prevent war. This relationship (if any) of pacifist belief to practical politics has been its second difficulty. In effect pacifists have adopted one of three orientations towards politics. Some have insisted that pacifism *is* practical politics—that nonviolence would be the most successful national defence policy. The difficulty of

---

[3] The term *pacificist* (here italicised both in recognition of its etymological artificiality and to avoid visual confusion with pacifist) was first used in this sense by A. J. P. Taylor, *The Trouble Makers* (London 1957) p 51n. Reviewing my book, Mr Taylor noted that the word was 'borrowed from me and which I gladly lend him' (*London Review of Books* 2 Oct. 1980 p 4).

this approach has been meeting both the practical objection that it would not work against an adversary like Hitler or the imperial Japanese and the theoretical objection for some Christian pacifists that, if it worked, it would do so as a sophisticated tactic for 'winning' a conflict whereas pacifism should aspire to effect reconciliation and thereby abolish conflict.[4] A larger second group has argued that pacifists should support, as interim improvements, *pacificist* remedies for war such as the curbing of aggression by sanctions applied by the League of Nations or United Nations. But this raises the question: can a pacifist support the use of, say, an international army in which he would feel personally unable to serve? The third orientation towards politics has been to admit that pacifism is a faith rather than a political recipe—that pacifists cannot expect to prevent war by following their consciences and may indeed even hasten it; their duty is to witness to the values of peace while waiting for the rest of humanity to be converted to the same way of thinking. As will be seen, this sectarian orientation (as it may be called) has come to be accepted by the most thoughtful pacifists; but it can have little mass appeal because it is not 'a stop-the-war trick'.[5]

In addition to these difficulties of defining pacifism and determining its orientation towards the political world, all pacifists have faced problems in justifying why they are pacifists in the first place. Three types of inspiration for pacifism are found. The first is political, claiming that, for example, a socialist or anarchist must also be a pacifist. The second deduces pacifism from humanitarian beliefs of various sorts, such as humanism, rationalism and utilitarianism. The third inspiration is religious: most commonly the claim that Christianity is a pacifist religion. Disagreements between pacifists moved by different inspiration have presented surprisingly few problems for the pacifist movement (although each inspiration has tended to respond differently to political circumstances). More difficult has been the task of justifying to their fellow socialists, humanists, Christians, or whatever, why the

---

[4] For this reason several Christian pacifists were disappointed with Gandhi when they met him in the autumn of 1931. See the *Friend* 18 Dec. 1931 p 1150; London, British Library of Political and Economic Science, Fellowship of Reconciliation, minutes of executive committee 18 Nov. 1931; London, Friends' House Library, minutes of Friends Peace Committee 5 June 1930.

[5] A phrase used by the sectarian pacifist journal *Reconciliation* Aug. 1935 pp 145–7.

pacifist interpretation of their common inspiration is in fact the correct one.

Each of these difficulties—over definition, orientation, and inspiration—was confronted in the era of the two world wars, as an examination of the evolution of Christian pacifist thought can now reveal. Prior to the first world war, despite being able to trace its ancestry back almost two millennia to the early church, it was surprisingly inchoate. The problems of definition were wholly unresolved. For one thing, much of what passed for Christian pacifism was quasi-pacifist. One interpretation of the pacifism (whether complete or partial) of the early church takes this view, attributing refusal to bear arms to a dislike of pagan ritual, notably the idolatrous military oaths required by the Roman army, rather than to a rejection of war itself. But, whatever the truth about the early church, it was clear that Christian pacifism was wholly sustained for fifteen centuries after Constantine's conversion by a series of unorthodox sects, most of which were quasi-pacifist. The major exception was the Society of Friends, held in high esteem by mainstream Christianity, which itself, partly under Quaker influence began in the nineteenth century to acquire a tiny pacifist minority of its own. But when the first world war broke out quasi-pacifists still outnumbered pacifists. The largest single category of conscientious objectors was the Christadelphians, who were prepared, unlike true pacifists, to work in munitions factories;[6] so, in the words of one objector: 'It was assumed that every pacifist . . . was a narrow-minded religionist, basing his creed upon the literal reading of Biblical texts . . . . And indeed there *were* many conscientious objectors of this type . . . .'[7]

As well as confusion with quasi-pacifism, there was confusion with *pacificism*. Before 1916 there was no conscription in Britain to sort pacifists out from mere war-haters: it is noteworthy that one of the most active Christian pacifists in the first world war, the Revd. Leyton Richards, had already been able to clarify his views as a result of seeing the military training provisions of the 1910 Australian defence act in operation while spending three years as a congregationalist minister in Melbourne. Another pre-war

---

[6] Their objection was to coming under military authority. See John Rae, *Conscience and Politics* (London 1970) pp 88–9.

[7] Gilbert Thomas, *Autobiography 1891–1946* (London 1946) p 128.

Christian Pacifism

experience which had alerted certain pacifists, including Stephen Hobhouse and the Revd. Cecil Cadoux, to the full implications of their faith was reading Tolstoy. But the majority of Christians believing themselves to be 'pacifists' were lulled by the length of time which had elapsed since Britain's last major involvement in European war into believing that war was unlikely and British participation in it even more so, which meant that it was not important for them to decide whether they were pacifists or *pacificists*. The major pacifist society, the Peace Society (which had been established by Quakers in 1816 as the Society for the Promotion of Permanent and Universal Peace) had become penetrated by *pacificism*, so much so that its chairman in 1914 supported the war.[8] The major study of Christian pacifism to appear at this time was, significantly, preoccupied to a considerable extent with showing that Christian pacifism had not been superseded by, and was not incompatible with, the *pacificist* analysis of writers such as Norman Angell.[9]

It was thus in the crisis of August 1914 that many anti-militarists, such as bishop Hicks of Lincoln, an advocate of arbitration and former pro-Boer, had to make up their minds somewhat hastily whether they were pacifists or *pacificists*. Reeling from the shock of Germany's violation of Belgian neutrality, most—including Hicks—decided they were in the latter category and that the war had to be fought in order to end war. Some of these later believed that they had thereby taken the wrong decision: for example, William Robinson, who served in the war and afterwards became principal of Overdale college, Selly Oak, and a pacifist who was convinced that in 1914 people like himself 'were caught napping. They had been in a sense unconscious pacifists, but with no thought-out convictions. Then the challenge came . . . . It was necessary to act quickly. How were they to act? . . . There was no definite code to which they could appeal . . . .'[10]

This confusion of pacifism with quasi-pacifism or with *pacificism* before 1914 was related to its problems concerning orientation and inspiration. Because so much hope was vested in *pacificist* measures

[8] Oxford, Bodleian Library Gainford Papers, J. A. Pease to J. B. Hodgkin, 4 Aug. 1914.
[9] By the Quaker William E. Wilson: *Christ and War: the reasonableness of disarmament on Christian, humanitarian and economic grounds* (London 1913 and revised edn. 1914).
[10] For Hicks, see Alan Wilkinson, *The Church of England and the First World War* (London 1978) p 27; for Robinson, see his *Christianity is Pacifism* (London 1933) p 9.

such as free trade, arbitration and disarmament, it was simply assumed that pacifists should collaborate with them. Any special obligations incurred by being pacifist rather than *pacificist* were largely ignored. And the prevalence of quasi-pacifism illustrated how poorly the Christian inspiration for pacifism had been expounded: with too much sterile text-swapping and too little theological inquiry.

The subsequent refinement of Christian pacifist thinking took place in three stages: under the impact of the first world war; while the League of Nations was being challenged from 1931 to 1935; and under the shadow of Hitler from 1936 to 1940. The contribution of the first world war was thus important but far from decisive. On the question of definition, the minority which stood out against the tide of jingoism and crusading *pacificism* in August 1914 made clearer the distinctiveness of pacifism as an anti-war belief. So, *a fortiori*, did the introduction of conscription in 1916, which elicited from heroic absolutists such as Hobhouse a principled objection to compulsory service of any kind which contrasted with the willingness of most quasi-pacifists to do anything which exempted them from combatant service. Yet it was possible to oppose the war or be a conscientious objector for non-pacifist reasons (some socialists, for instance, rejected the war because it was 'imperialist' and not a people's war, and con-scription could be objected to on purely voluntarist grounds) and quasi-pacifists were numerous, so that some confusion could and did persist.

This partial clarification of the meaning of pacifism was reflected in the setting up of a new society that was explicitly Christian and pacifist: the Fellowship of Reconciliation (F.o.R.), a discreetly named body founded at a necessarily unobtrusive gathering at Cambridge in the last days of 1914 (and still in existence). The F.o.R. formulated a five-point 'Basis', which argued that 'Love, as revealed and interpreted in the life and death of Jesus Christ, involves us in more than we have yet seen, that it is the only power by which evil can be overcome, and the only sufficient basis of human society.' Those accepting this had to do so 'fully, both for themselves and in their relation to others, and to take the risks involved in doing so in a world which does not as yet accept it.' F.o.R. members of whom there were 8,000 by 1918 were called 'to a life of service for the enthronement of Love in

Christian Pacifism

personal, social, commercial and national life.' This established that Christian pacifism had to be justified in terms of the essential spirit of Christianity which applied to all aspects of political life, rather than a selective treatment of ambiguous texts about force. Yet, in seeking to apply its Basis the F.o.R. was, as a Congregationalist founder-member, the Revd. W. E. Orchard, noted, too 'heterogeneous', encompassing as it did a handful of Anglicans and Christian socialists as well as Quakers and all varieties of nonconformist. Even at the end of the war, Orchard admitted, 'a really Christian pacifist philosophy was still in need of formulation'.[11]

Progress in expounding the inspiration for Christian pacifism was matched by a similar awareness that, if pacifism was theologically correct, its political consequences were secondary. This view was accepted during the war by a majority of members of the F.o.R., which remained a quietist organisation, and by the leading Christian conscientious objectors, who accepted that, since pacifism was justified with reference to the sanctity of the individual conscience, it could not be made the subject of a mass propaganda campaign (which could at best produce superficial, rather than truly conscientious, conversions). Nevertheless some F.o.R. members and conscientious objectors wished to see their stand as a politically-effective campaign against the military machine. The difficulty in taking this view is always that, once political effectiveness is defined as the objective, then pacifism is reduced to being a mere means to that end—and a means, moreover, which may well have to be discarded in favour of a more obviously practical one. This happened to many of the socialist pacifists who in 1916 had seen resistance to conscription as the best available form of protest against militarism, but who by 1917–18 were coming to see that an increasingly war-weary labour movement offered a far more potent weapon against war than a few thousand conscientious objectors ever could. In other words, pacifism itself could do little; it would be a broader *pacificist* campaign that would end the war if anything did. Socialist pacifists were thus faced with a choice. Some opted to remain pacifists, while abandoning their belief that pacifism itself could have an independent political impact, and accepting that if they wished to work to end the war they had to collaborate with

---

[11] W. E. Orchard, *From Faith to Faith* (London 1933) p 122.

pacificist measures. But this merely prompted the question: why remain a pacifist? In response to this, others switched from pacifism to *pacificism*. Christian pacifists were less excited by the prospect of revolutionary activity against war by the labour movement; but when in 1920 the League of Nations was set up, stimulating hopes that it could prevent war by applying moral, economic, or, in the last resort, military sanctions, they were among its most enthusiastic supporters. Although compared with the years before 1914 the difference between pacifism and *pacificism* was more generally understood, many pacifists resumed their pre-war habit of assuming that *pacificist* schemes would prevent war, without, however, facing up to the question of how it was possible for a pacifist to endorse League of Nations sanctions. Characteristic of the state of Christian peace thinking after the first world war was the way pacifists collaborated with *pacificists* in the 'Christ and peace' campaign, a series of meetings started in the autumn of 1929, the main achievement of which was the declaration by the Church of England's 1930 Lambeth conference: 'War as a method of settling international disputes is incompatible with the teaching of our Lord Jesus Christ'—an ambiguous statement, which was interpreted as anodynely *pacificist*.

It was not suprising, therefore, that those newly converted to Christian pacifism in the 1920s were not attracted by its potential for war-prevention. In several cases they were Anglicans (whose importance in the formerly Quaker- and nonconformist-dominated pacifist movement dates from this time), who viewed pacifism as an ecclesiastical purgative—an issue of principle on which the Church of England could redeem itself for its wartime worldliness. Thus the Revd. H.R.L. ('Dick') Sheppard declared himself a pacifist in 1927 while going through a phase of acute 'impatience' with the church; and canon Charles Raven did the same three years later because he regarded pacifism as the best issue with which to follow up the COPEC movement (so called after the much vaunted but ultimately disappointing conference on politics, economics and citizenship he had co-organised at Birmingham in April 1924). When pressed, by socialists in particular, to explain why pacifism was chosen as the key issue instead of the other forms of exploitation condoned by modern society, pacifists began to evolve a domino-theory of reform. Thus Leyton Richards argued in 1929 that it was

Christian Pacifism

not irrational to isolate the problem of war from those other problems and practical difficulties which call for the exercise of coercive force in human relationships. The history of moral achievement suggests that organised evil is eliminated from the common life of man by a succession of attacks in detail rather than a mass attack all along the line.[12]

At any stage in history, Richards and others argued, there was a key issue which could become the thin end of a reforming wedge. The abolition of slavery had started off a series of humanitarian reforms in the nineteenth century. The renunciation of war would, they claimed, be the equivalent issue for the twentieth century; thus as Raven later put it, it would be 'in the campaign against war' that the first blow against 'the evils of competitive capitalism' could be struck.[13] The problem with this argument was, of course, that it was far harder for a nation to opt unilaterally out of war than out of the slave trade. The argument saw pacifism primarily as a domestic political issue—a test of the idealism of the church or a strategy for moralising society. The international context was ignored, mainly because *pacificism* seemed to be in the ascendant.

It was thus only when the international situation began to deteriorate and *pacificism* began to falter in the 1930s that pacifism could make further progress. Before the Japanese attack on Manchuria in September 1931, it had been assumed that in practice moral pressure brought to bear by the League of Nations would be enough to prevent aggression. When the Japanese flouted world public opinion, this view had to be revised. One immediate Christian pacifist response (devised by Maude Royden, the Christian socialist preacher at the Guildhouse in Pimlico, and backed by Dick Sheppard, the Revd. Herbert Gray and the Revd. Donald Soper, among others) was to step up the moral pressure by despatching an unarmed Peace Army to interpose itself between the Japanese and Chinese troops. The idea proved impractical, however; and after Hitler's accession to power in January 1933, most pacifists remained convinced that the League of Nations still offered the most practical means of war-prevention, even though it was clear after the Manchurian crisis that economic sanctions at

---

[12] Leyton Richards, *The Christian's Alternative to War: An Examination of Christian Pacifism* (London 1929) p 58.
[13] Charles Raven, *Is War Obsolete?* [*A study of the conflicting claims of religion and citizenship* (London 1935)] p 52.

least, if not military measures, would be necessary. Could pacifists collaborate with such measures? On the question of economic sanctions, an increasing number of pacifists became aware that a blockade, which would involve starving the civilian population, was objectionable. Yet it continued to be widely hoped that a trade boycott would be both Christian and effective;[14] not until the Abyssinian war of 1935-6 was it realised that an effective sanction, however humane, would provoke a military retaliation. More helpful for clarifying pacifist thinking in the meantime was the proposal made by a number of League supporters as a result of the Manchurian setback, that the League should be equipped with an international police force. Some Christian pacifists such as Leyton Richards came to admit in 1934 that 'an International Police Force equipped for military operations. . . would be a striking and significant step towards the realisation of a Christian world order.' But Richards also argued that a pacifist 'cannot himself enlist in an International Police Force'. He admitted he was thereby applying a double standard, but found it hard to produce a coherent justification for it.[15] Others found difficulty too. A humanitarian pacifist, C. E. M. Joad, put forward what amounted to a quasi-pacifist argument for exemption from a socially necessary duty because his refined sensibility would find the experience less congenial than would an ordinary citizen; and a writer in the F.o.R.'s journal recommended that pacifists simply evade the issue.[16] But a clear answer was obtained from Charles Raven, a former dean of Emmanuel College, Cambridge, who had in 1932 returned to that university as regius professor of divinity. He admitted that pacifists seemed to be saying: 'Eighty per cent of you are unchristian, and of course may fight: I am a Christian and I won't.' But what they were really doing was accepting different vocations and admitting the limits of revelation. 'Absolute truth is and must remain beyond us. . .', he insisted. 'Hence it by no means follows that a judgment valid for me is necessarily valid for another.'[17] He further insisted that pacifism had its own practical contribution to offer to peacemaking, because a declaration of pacifism by the

---

[14] See the Revd. E. N. Porter Goff, *The Christian and the Next War* (London 1933) pp 76–82.
[15] Leyton Richards, *The Christian's Contribution to Peace: a constructive approach to international relationships* (London 1935) pp 137–8, 142–3.
[16] *New Statesman* 25 Nov. 1933 p 653; *Reconciliation* May 1934 pp 118–9.
[17] *Reconciliation* March 1934 p 66; Charles Raven, *Is War Obsolete?* p 86.

Christian Pacifism

British churches would have a major (but unspecified) impact on the international situation. Thus, as explained by Raven, a pacifist endorsing as a second-best the establishment of an international police force in which he was not prepared to serve, was humbly doing his own thing for peace while being careful to give support to those whose vocations differed from his.

In addition to this discussion of pacifism's orientation, more thought was being given at this time to its Christian inspiration. For example, in 1933 William Robinson's *Christianity is Pacifism* made clear that pacifists regarded the new testament as a higher source of revelation than the old; and in 1934 Canon Stuart Morris began stressing the importance for pacifism of the idea of redemption (interpreting the pacifist role as that of a redemptive minority).

This intellectual activity was matched by organisational advance in the years 1933–5. Pacifist groups were established within most Christian denominations: in May 1933 Leyton Richards reactivated the Christian Pacifist Crusade within the Congregational church which had first been set up in 1926; and in November 1933 the Revd. Henry Carter, himself converted from *pacificism* to pacifism earlier in the year, launched the Methodist Peace Fellowship. These, plus a newly established Unitarian Peace Fellowship, were represented along with the F.o.R., the Society of Friends, and the Church of Scotland Peace Society on a Council of Christian Pacifist Groups set up late in 1933 and reinforced the following year by a Presbyterian Pacifist Group, a Baptist Pacifist Fellowship, and a Church of England Peace Fellowship. This last was largely the initiative of Stuart Morris, who helped to persuade Dick Sheppard to send his famous letter to the press on 16 October 1934, asking for postcard pacifist pledges, which led finally in May 1936 to the establishment of the world's largest pacifist society, the Peace Pledge Union (P.P.U.). Though catering for pacifists of all inspirations (and having a predominant humanitarian pacifist element), the P.P.U. owed its origins and its most important leaders to Christian pacifism.

1936 proved to be a major watershed in British thinking about the international situation. Mussolini's conquest of Abyssinia, Hitler's remilitarisation of the Rhineland, and Franco's rebellion in Spain all demonstrated that economic sanctions could not guarantee peace and that, to be effective, collective security requires a readiness to go to war. Only a minority of former League enthusiasts were then prepared to accept this, for, as the *Church Times* put it: 'The League . . . was founded to promote peace and not as an instrument of war.'[18] The drift of support away from the League which had begun slowly in the early 1930s increased markedly after 1936. The greatest beneficiary was the appeasement movement, which called for fairer treatment of the 'have not' nations (Germany and Italy) by the 'haves' (Britain and France). But a significant minority went all the way to pacifism: the P.P.U., set up in May 1936 to cater for this, grew rapidly in 1936–7, attracting a hundred-thousand pledges of total pacifism. The problem of definition was thus solved: after 1936 pacifism could no longer be confused with *pacificism*, and attention could more easily be given to the problems of orientation and inspiration.

Most of those who signed the pacifist pledge did so because they believed pacifism alone could prevent war, their reasoning being: all other means of war-prevention have been tried and found wanting; pacifism is thus the only remaining option. But by 1938 it had become clear that, although organised pacifism was unprecedentedly influential, it would never have enough clout to influence government policy in Britain, let alone elsewhere. And many pacifists had by then come to doubt whether a nonviolent defence policy would work, even if the government suddenly espoused it. Bishop Barnes of Birmingham, for instance (the sole pacifist on the ecclesiastical bench), was admitting privately by the spring of 1938 that 'pacifism in England would be taken as a sign of weakness by the dictators and lead them to make increasingly extravagant demands.' Though remaining a pacifist, he looked increasingly to appeasement to prevent war, supporting Neville Chamberlain and going out of his way to be generous towards Germany in the interests of good relations.[19] Most Christian pacifists who were motivated largely by the desire to avoid war did the same. Leyton Richards' response to the Munich settlement was to claim that 'the parallel between the action of the Czechs and the events of Calvary is not too remote for us to see the

---

[18] Editorial, *Church Times* 15 May 1936.
[19] John Barnes, *Ahead of His Age: Bishop Barnes of Birmingham* (London 1979) p 350. For his willingness to say that 'German legislation on "race hygiene" was on the right lines as it provided for voluntary sterilisation' see p 351.

Christian Pacifism

redemptive principle at work';[20] while the Marquess of Tavistock (later Duke of Bedford), chairman of the Anglican Pacifist Fellowship established (as will shortly be noted) in 1937, became overtly pro-German and anti-semitic.[21] Tempering all such support for appeasement must have been awareness of the ill-treatment of German churchmen by the Nazis (although it was not much discussed in Christian literature on pacifism). After the Prague crisis of March 1939, when Hitler took control of the non-German rump of Czechoslovakia and thereby revealed himself to be an imperialist aggressor rather than a nationalist restorer of Germany's lost territories, it was hard to believe that appeasement could work anyway. As this reality dawned, many pacifist-appeasers recanted: such as the Revd. Leslie Weatherhead of the City Temple, who had been converted to both causes in the Abyssinian crisis. A few, including Maude Royden, delayed their recantation until the outbreak of war in September 1939. And the Dunkirk crisis and fall of France in the summer of 1940 weeded out from the pacifist ranks a rather larger remainder of those whose 'pacifism' had really been based on an isolationist feeling that Britain could and should avoid war (by appeasing Germany or, once war started, by negotiating peace in accordance with Hitler's offers). By mid-1940 the political implications of pacifism had been made starkly clear: a pacifist had to believe it was a greater wrong to resist Hitler than to submit to him.

Those whose pacifism survived these successive tests of the years 1936 to 1940 were those prepared to accept the sectarian orientation that pacifism had no necessary political relevance and might indeed be disadvantageous in worldly terms. It was, in other words, a faith—the personal conviction that war was the greatest evil—rather than a political strategy for reforming the international or domestic order. Some pacifists whose inspirations were political and humanitarian came to accept this fact; but it was easier for Christians to accept that the correctness of their belief did not depend on political circumstances. (In the case of one leading pacifist intellectual, John Middleton Murry, the realisation that pacifism was sectarian led to his conversion from political pacifism to Christianity.) As Donald Soper, who had once

---

[20] Leyton Richards, *The Crisis and World Peace* (S.C.M. Press Crisis Booklet No. 4 London, Dec. 1938) p 50.
[21] See his article in *Peace News* 30 Oct. 1942. He launched the British People's Party in 1939.

expected pacifism to prevent the second world war, expressed it during that war: 'The utilitarian argument for nonviolence breaks down under the overwhelming pressure of brute fact. I am alone sustained by the Christian faith which assures me that what is morally right carries with it the ultimate resources of the universe.'[22] Thus whereas in the mid-1930s it had been somewhat overshadowed by the mainly humanitarian pacifism of the P.P.U., the explicitly Christian pacifist movement enjoyed a revival immediately before and during the second world war. The F.o.R., which had lost support since 1918, trebled its membership between 1936 and the start of the war (when it stood at 9,813 members), and although suffering two-hundred resignations in the summer of 1940 managed further expansion during the war. In 1937, moreover, an Anglican Pacifist Fellowship was set up to fill a gap (the Church of England Peace Fellowship of 1934 having apparently collapsed when Morris and Sheppard turned their attention to the P.P.U.): it had fifteen hundred members by September 1939, gaining a further thousand by May 1940, and a further hundred by 1945.[23] This can be compared with the P.P.U., which, though gaining recruits until April 1940 (when it claimed 136,000 members), suffered significant net losses thereafter and ended the war with only 98,414 pledges in its files. It can be compared also with the rate of conscientious objection among successive batches of conscripts, which fell steadily throughout the war (from 2.2 per cent to 0.2 cent).

But Christian pacifism had no cause for complacency. Its enrolled numbers were few, perhaps fifteen thousand at most,[24] and constituted a tiny minority even of the small pacifist movement. Although since 1914 it had expanded from the historic sects into first the nonconformist churches and then into the Church of England, it had captured no church and made no inroads at all into Roman Catholicism.[25]

[22] *Peace News* 15 Dec. 1944. Soper remained pacifist throughout the war.
[23] These figures are taken from the newsletters of the Anglican Pacifist Fellowship, consulted through the courtesy of its present secretary, the Revd. Sidney Hinkes, at St Mary's Church House, Headington, Oxford. In July 1982 its membership stood at 1131 and was on the increase.
[24] To arrive at this figure one has to assume negligible overlap of members between the F.o.R. and the various church pacifist fellowships—a very unlikely assumption.
[25] The only Roman Catholic pacifists I have discovered in this era are Francis Meynell (who abandoned pacifism in 1935) and Eric Gill, both of whom can be classified as political as much as Christian pacifists. For a book which came close to explicit pacifism, however,

Christian Pacifism

Moreover, as Christian pacifism had begun, particularly in the latter half of the 1930s, to expound its theological principles more clearly, it had found itself driven unexpectedly onto the defensive. The first blow came from the Church of England leadership. During the Abyssinian crisis, William Temple, archbishop of York, condemned pacifism as heretical. He subsequently admitted he should have written '"heretical in tendency" for I do not know any formal condemnation by the Church of pacifism as such', but made clear that in his view pacifism committed the marcionite, manichean and pelagian heresies.[26] This did not overly dismay pacifists, however: Raven argued that such criticism 'is compelling us to that deeper examination of our principles which is essential to the growth and unifying of our movement';[27] and Sheppard still felt it worthwhile in September 1936 to try to arrange a deputation to the archbishops 'both to hear our reasoned statement on this issue and to tell us in what way we seem to be lacking in loyalty to the mind of Christ and the Catholic Church'.[28] Worse than the hostility of ecclesiastical leaders was the second blow, a new current of criticism from theologians and writers on Christian ethics. In September 1936 G. H. C. Macgregor, professor of divinity and biblical criticism at Glasgow and president of the Church of Scotland Peace Society, had completed a major study, *The New Testament Basis of Pacifism*. This admitted that Christian pacifists had formerly been 'too apt to assume without a sufficient proof that Jesus' ethic is incontestably "pacifist" and that, even if so proved, he intended the pacifist ethic to be applied to the wider sphere of social and national politics.' Rather than base pacifism on selected texts (although he discussed these fully), Macgregor explicitly defined the 'positive imperative of the Christian ethic' as he saw it, which comprised three basic principles: 'love towards one's neighbour'; 'belief in a Father God who loves all men impartially'; and the principle that all Christ's teaching 'must be interpreted in the light of his way of life, and above all of the Cross'. These basic principles—with which most Christian pacifists would have agreed[29]—led him to pacifism, not merely in its

while staying discreetly within the just-war orthodoxy favoured by Roman Catholicism, see Gerald Vann, O.P. *Morality and War* (London 1939) esp pp 72–3.
[26] *Church of England Newspaper* 1 Nov. 1935.
[27] *Reconciliation* Dec. 1935 p 320.
[28] *Church Times* 18 Sept. 1936.
[29] See e.g. A. Herbert Gray, *Love: the one solution* (London 1938).

negative aspect of refusal to fight but also its more important positive commitment to love and sacrifice.

Yet, just as pacifists were making clear that they took an immanent interpretation of the Christian faith, that view was coming under attack. At the rarified level of theological scholarship, the works of the Swiss-born theologian Karl Barth were being translated into English, 'reaffirming the transcendentalism and otherness of God' (to quote Raven)[30] as against the pacifist stress on the 'divinity' of man and the 'humanity' of God. At a more popular and therefore more influential level, the writings of the American lapsed-pacifist Reinhold Niebuhr—which had 'broad affinities'[31] with those of Barth—attacked pacifism for having 'reinterpreted the Christian Gospels in terms of the Renaissance faith in man', thereby ignoring 'the contradiction between the law of love and the sinfulness of man'. It is rarely noted that Niebuhr did not object to sectarian pacifism, which was 'not a heresy. It is rather a valuable asset for the Christian faith. It is a reminder to the Christian community.' His scorn was reserved for the view that nonviolence would work, that (as he put it in 1940) 'if Britain had been fortunate enough to have produced 30 per cent instead of 2 per cent of conscientious objectors to military service, Hitler's heart would have been softened and he would not have dared to attack Poland'.[32] But for pacifism of any kind to be dismissed as humanist or utopian by a radical like Niebuhr came as a considerable shock to those accustomecd to regard themselves as the true idealists and strictest adherents to Christian principles who had constantly to battle against ecclesiastical hierarchies prepared to compromise the faith in the interests of political acceptability. G. H. C. Macgregor was forced to issue a second book in 1941 as a reply to Niebuhr, which paid a grudging tribute to his influence: 'To the non-pacifist in the churches, his arguments have come as a veritable godsend, and no one has been so successful in weaning the pacifist from the pure milk of his faith.'[33] Thus, as a result of

---

[30] Charles Raven, *Is War Obsolete?* p 96.
[31] Ronald H. Stone, *Reinhold Niebuhr: prophet to politicians* (Nashville 1972) p 120. For discussion of the differences, which on domestic politics were considerable, between Niebuhr and Barth, see pp 122-32.
[32] Reinhold Niebuhr pp 11, 18, 30, 32.
[33] G. H. C. Macgregor, *The Relevance of the Impossible: a reply to Reinhold Niebuhr* (London 1941) p 11.

Christian Pacifism

the growing criticism from the Anglican leadership and the most influential thinkers of the decade, Christian pacifists had to come to terms with the fact that they were the liberal deviationists of their faith rather than its incorruptible fundamentalists.

The humbling effect of this realisation was reinforced by the predicament in which Christian pacifists found themselves in the second world war. The harsh treatment conscientious objectors received in the first war had, paradoxically, kept their morale high: they felt themselves to be martyrs at the hand of a repressive state. Their more generous treatment in the second war, and the fact that the war was, moreover, as close to a just war as any modern war could be, made them feel guilty rather than defiant. Whereas the finest conscientious objectors of 1916–19 had rejected alternative service and gone to gaol, their counterparts of 1939–45 were eager to undertake Quaker-type humanitarian work and drew comfort from the respect they could win from non-pacifists for such service. The mellowing of Christian pacifist attitudes to society that resulted can be illustrated by two pacifist documents issued during the worst phase of the war, in 1940. The first was the 'agreed report on a deputation of pacifist clergy to the archbishops of Canterbury and York, Lambeth Palace, Tuesday, June 11th, 1940', in which the pacifist deputation expressed 'its deep sense of gratitude to the archbishops for their unfailing courtesy and understanding in their treatment of *a rather obscure minority.*'[34] The second was a circular letter written by the Revd. C. Paul Gliddon on 25 October 1940 from a heavily blitzed part of London to members of the Anglican Pacifist Fellowship, of which he was honorary secretary. Gliddon was unsentimental about the fellowship's achievements: 'We have attraced a small section of the people who go to Church, we have interested a further section of the type who go to meetings and take interest in movements; but the rest we have left in unruffled indifference.' And he pointed out that this was partly the fault of Christian pacifists: 'We shall never win men's conversion until we have won their confidence; we shall never win their confidence until we have won something like their affection.' Successful enterprises like the Pacifist Service Units (which undertook community service and relief work) showed, however, that attitudes were changing for the better:

---

[34] Anglican Pacifist Fellowship leaflet, July 1940, shown to my by the Revd. Sidney Hinkes; italics added.

There has been a tendency to appreciate more fully the courage and sincerity of those who do not take up the pacifist position, a softening of a criticism which was often carping and sometimes cruel, and an eagerness to travel in company with those from whom we differ in conviction just as far as our loyalty to our own principles would permit. A pacifism which was sometimes precious and often factious is giving place to an attitude which is practical, good humoured, humble and understanding.[35]

To sum up this paper: under the cumulative impact of the first world war, the crisis of the League in the years 1931–5, and the threat from Hitler from 1936 to 1940, the meaning of pacifism became clearly defined in Britain for the first time; the difficulties presented by its orientation towards politics were appreciated, also for the first time, and it was realised by its leading exponents that lasting pacifism was a faith rather than a political strategy; and the liberal theological assumptions that were required in order to interpret Christianity in a pacifist way came to be more generally recognised as such. Of course some confusions remained, as the operations of the tribunals to determine conscientious objection in the second world war and after were to show.[36] But in general, like other forms of pacifism, Christian pacifism was refined into a rigorous faith, thereby ensuring it was hardy enough to survive, but reducing its appeal to the casual war-hater. Indeed, so exacting was the Christian pacifist faith shown to be that few have embraced it since the second world war, despite the extraordinary difficulty of fitting thermonuclear war into the just-war tradition of orthodox Christianity.

New College, Oxford

[35] Circular letter, in the collection of Anglican Pacifist Fellowship newsletters.
[36] See especially the complaints (mostly about what is here called quasi-pacifism) by a member of the south-western tribunal 1940–4: G. C. Field, *Pacifism and Conscientious Objection* (London 1945) esp pp 3–7.

THE SWORD OF THE SPIRIT:
A CATHOLIC CULTURAL CRUSADE OF 1940

by STUART MEWS

IN THE anxious second half of 1940 certain developments took place which cardinal Heenan, the late archbishop of Westminster, was to describe, somewhat grandly, as 'the opening chapter of the modern history of religion in Great Britain'.[1] He was referring to an unprecedented series of events which led up to and flowed from a letter to the *Times* in December extolling the five peace points of pope Pius XII. The letter was signed not only by the Roman Catholic archbishop of Westminster, cardinal Hinsley, but also by the two Anglican primates and the moderator of the Free Church council. Such a public manifestation of religious harmony reflected the national unity of the hour and was further reinforced a few months later by two joint meetings which were each addressed by both catholic and protestant leaders. But the pressures for national and religious cohesion which were at their height in 1940–41 were to decline with the passing of the immediate threat and to be effectively countered by the resurgence of older and more powerful denominational suspicions and susceptibilities. What might have been an 'opening chapter' turned instead into little more than an isolated essay in inter-church relations. As such it would hardly justify closer scrutiny but the episode is more significant because it throws light on several problems which arise when religion has to function in a modern society at a time of crisis. More particularly it draws attention to the pressures and constraints involved in the mobilization of religious commitments in the national interest and to the strategic considerations which impelled church leaders to opt for a particular course of action when confronted by a complex web of national needs, institutional inhibitions and popular sentiment. This paper does not attempt a comprehensive analysis of the various facets of the situation but concentrates on those aspects which relate to the Roman Catholic church in England.

[1] [John C.] Heenan, [*Cardinal Hinsley*] (London 1944) p 181.

The final three years of the life of cardinal Hinsley, the leader of England's catholics, were the most glorious period of his career. At his death in 1943 the British press unusually eager to turn national leaders into heroes, eulogized him as 'the greatest English Cardinal since Wolsey', 'probably the best loved Cardinal England has ever had', and 'a leader in a world at war against unrighteousness'.[2] In 1939 newspaper assessments would probably have dismissed him as a genial, impulsive and slightly inept stop-gap whose public reputation rested chiefly on his whole-hearted support of nationalist Spain and total opposition to communism in any shape or form; his most famous utterance was his unfortunate description of the pope at the time of Abyssinia as 'a helpless old man'.[3] The next three years, with the additional perils of a world war, could have been disastrous but Hinsley's recognition of the need for new religious initiatives and ready response, even though he did not always seem to anticipate entirely the logical consequences of his actions, crowned his career and preserved the reputation and integrity of his church.

Several factors contributed to this extraordinary outcome. Some were peculiar to this particular war, and others were a legacy of previous wars. The total nature of twentieth-century war requires the mobilization of every aspect of national life. The need to justify war to a civilian population and a conscript army, to sustain their morale and weld them into unity, necessitates the conduct of war at an ideological and cultural level in addition to the conventional clash of rival military machines. On such occasions the state usually expects religious leaders to legitimise the national cause, and, as we have seen in the Falklands conflict, is all too rarely disappointed. The most effective appeals usually come from those who already have an established public reputation, and especially those who possess that streak of individuality which marks them out as 'personalities'. No member of the Roman Catholic hierarchy came into that class in 1939, though there were a few, like Downey of Liverpool, who had built up a considerable reputation as leaders of provincial opinion. The somewhat surprising emergence of cardinal Hinsley as a national religious warleader was the result of an unusual combination of personal,

---

[2] *Ibid* 8–11; *Daily Mail, Yorkshire Post* 18 March 1943.
[3] In his Golders Green sermon of 1935: Heenan pp 51–62.

historical and strategic considerations. It was a role which would more naturally have fallen to a member of the established church (as it had in the first world war in the person of the bishop of London, A. F. Winnington Ingram) but which on this occasion Anglicans either could not or would not take. The reasons which prevented them from accepting it were precisely those which prompted cardinal Hinsley to fill the vacuum.

The public behaviour of many religious leaders in 1939 was conditioned by their memories of the first world war and its consequences. In 1914 protestant and catholic alike had given religious sanction to the conflict. At first religious rhetoric had concentrated on Britain's moral obligation to Belgium and condemned Germany for failing to acknowledge international treaties. But as the war situation deteriorated and the casualty lists lengthened, a more dramatic interpretation, which relied heavily on Lord Bryce's report of alleged German 'atrocities', gained ground. 'We are up against the devil incarnate', proclaimed one Anglican bishop; 'Germany has made a devil's war and if she wins it will be a devil's world', stated the leading Free Church journal.[4] In 1914 Germany had been attacked for not behaving as a gentleman, but in 1915 the charge was one of not even being human. It was asserted that dark subterranean forces had broken through the thin crust of civilization and captured Germany's mind and soul. From this point on, as the bishop of London insisted, it was a holy war;[5] Britain was on the side of the angels and the angels were on the side of Britain. From pulpit and platform the clergy breathed belligerance with every breath. 'It is nothing but a crusade or culture-war against Germany', exclaimed a troubled Ernst Troeltsch, 'which exploits all existing differences to create a universal, unconquerable antipathy'.[6] A small minority feared future repercussions. 'We wonder how the Christian pulpit is going to answer the charges that will be made after the war, when these things are collected and served up, as they will be, for purposes of infidel propaganda', wrote W. E. Orchard in 1917.

It will be recalled that Christianity has blessed and discovered sanctions to every war that Christians have ever waged, and

---

[4] *Church Times*, 24 June 1915; B[ritish] W[eekly] 20 May 1915.
[5] *Guardian* 10 June 1915.
[6] *Der Geist Deutschen Kultur*, quoted in T. F. A. Smith, 'German War Literature' *Contemporary Review* CIX (1916) p 633.

it will be recognized that this war was fundamentally no different from the rest. Christianity will therefore stand forth as a system of thought which blinds the mind, intensifies hate, pours oil on a conflagration, provides beautiful ideals to lure whole peoples to destruction.[7]

Orchard's gloomy prophecy was soon to be fulfilled. In 1921 dean Inge was lamenting that the wartime fury of the clergy 'may have been good for the Allies, but (was) not favourable to religion'.[8] And in 1934 when the pacifist reaction was in full flood, the National Secular Society published *Arms and the Clergy (1914–1918)*, a collection of extracts from the sermons and writings of over 200 clergy, the first name to be mentioned being that of the bishop of London whose belligerent appeals were described as 'indistinguishable from the language and sentiments of a cannibal chief'.[9] In the very different atmosphere of the 1930s, that kind of anthology provided a serious embarrassment to the professional ministers of the Prince of Peace, and led many to resolve that never again would they allow themselves to give way to the heated emotions of war.

In 1939 protestant leaders were understandably reluctant to go beyond the cautious admission that they could see no alternative to a 'just' war against Hitler. Old Winnington Ingram, now 82, who had providentially retired from the see of London a matter of weeks before the outbreak of war, was nevertheless anxious to demonstrate that he had learned nothing and forgotten nothing by publishing in 1940 *A Second Day of God*—a book which was almost as objectionably jingoist as his earlier *A Day of God* published in 1914.[10] But the general level of protestant rhetoric was decidedly more temperate than in the previous world war.

In the summer of 1940, however, when the situation had become really desperate, there were demands, as in 1915, for a more effective harnessing of the nation's spiritual resources. 'Consideration has to be given to the part that religion can play in the

---

[7] *The Outlook for Religion* (London 1917) pp 80, 40.
[8] *Lay Thoughts of a Dean* (London 1917) p 308.
[9] *Arms and the Clergy (1914–18)* (London 1934) p v.
[10] See also the double-edged comment in the *Church Quarterly Review* April–June 1941: 'We need only say that one could hardly imagine any pages more completely characteristic of their much loved author.'

The Sword of the Spirit

crisis', noted the B.B.C.'s controller of programmes.[11] But where to find an established religious leader with sufficient character and conviction to impress a public more sceptical than in 1915? It was no use looking to the Church of England. The archbishop of Canterbury, C. G. Lang, was too weary, too unctuous, too much associated with All Souls and appeasement, Baldwin and Chamberlain, the old gang who had brought the country to the very edge of the precipice. 'How wearisome is the constant and petulant cry for "strong leadership",' he recorded on 26 August 1940 '. . . But I dare say I lack the strident tones which some people think "leadership". And in truth I am conscious of a certain lack of pushful ardour, which no doubt is a sign of growing old'.[12] Nor was his colleague at York likely to help. William Temple had made very clear through his 'Lansdowne' letter to the *Daily Telegraph* in December 1939 that he preferred the role of keeper of the Christian conscience to that of religious leader of a national crusade.

As for Dr Orchard, the Free Church pacifist minister, whose prophecy had been so tragically fulfilled, the first world war had been but one stage in his progressive disenchantment with both the national and nonconformist churches of Britain. Deeply impressed by Benedict XV's peace note of 1917 'however little some of his subjects followed him',[13] Orchard had come to the conclusion that the only supranational organization with sufficient spiritual power to prevent war was the Roman Catholic church. He submitted in 1932. It was ironic that the man who had taken such a brave and lonely stand in the first world war should have thrown in his lot with a church which in its English branch had learned a different lesson and drawn different conclusions. The very factors which inhibited protestant leaders in their endorsement of the second world war led cardinal Hinsley to take the place which would more naturally have fallen to them.

The Roman Catholic hierarchy in Britain had been more unanimous in its zealous patriotism in the first world war and less critical of the government's conduct of the war than any other

---

[11] Programme Directive by Basil Nicolls, 4 June 1940, quoted [Asa] Briggs, [*The History of Broadcasting in the United Kingdom* vol iii *The War of Words* (London 1970)] p 216.
[12] J. G. Lockhart, *Cosmo Gordon Lang* (London 1949) p 430.
[13] W. E. Orchard, *From Faith to Faith* (London 1933) pp 289, 127.
[14] C. C. Martindale, *Bernard Vaughan, S.J.* (London 1923) p 196.

group of religious leaders. Even pro-war enthusiasts had been shocked by the brutal and candid utterances of Father Bernard Vaughan, then the leading Catholic orator.[14] Willing cooperation was extended to government agencies which sought to influence Catholic opinion in neutral countries, especially Portugal and the United States,[15] while in Rome itself cardinal Gasquet 'John Bull's other cardinal' exercised every skill at his command to offset the influence of pro-German and Austrian factions in the Curia.[16] Yet despite their exemplary patriotism those deep engrained English suspicions that Catholics were men of divided loyalties were never quite quelled. Throughout the war, the English press periodically railed against the 'pro-German' Vatican, especially after the Papal peace note of 1917.[17] And when the Irish bishops refused to sanction conscription in 1918 the *Times* was all set to raise once again the hoary banner of 'No Popery'.[18] It was all too evident that there was danger in any deviation from the path of super-patriotism.

It was during the first world war that Arthur Hinsley had received his first major promotion which was to lead eventually to the Westminster archbishopric. In 1917 he was appointed rector of the English college at Rome, a post which at such a time would only have gone to a man of unquestioned national loyalty. Hinsley's patriotism was never called into question and though his attitude throughout the second world war showed that he had learned the lessons of history and correctly interpreted the contemporary situation, it was a case of prudence coinciding with personal inclination.

British Catholics were vulnerable not only because of the charge of double allegiance but also because of suspicions that catholic beliefs encouraged anti-democratic sympathies. 'We know the suggestion is being made all over the country that the Catholic church is backing Fascism', Hinsley was told in February 1939.

---

[15] Shane Leslie, *Long Shadows* (London 1966) ch 14; *From English Catholics to their Portuguese Fellow-Catholics* n.d.
[16] Shane Leslie, *Cardinal Gasquet* (London 1953) chs XI–XIII; William A. Renzi, 'The Entente and the Vatican during the Period of Italian Neutrality, August 1914—May 1915' *The Historical Journal* XIII 3 (1970) pp 491–508.
[17] *Tablet* 17 April 1915; *Pope Benedict XV and the Belligerent Nations* (London 1917).
[18] *Times* 24–25 April, 7 May 1918; *Tablet* 4 May 1918. For a comprehensive treatment of both catholic and protestant reactions see Stuart Mews, 'Religion and English Society in the First World War' (Unpub University of Cambridge Ph.D thesis 1973).

The Sword of the Spirit

'This is doing untold harm; it is alienating the sympathies of our fellow-countrymen'.[19] Catholics were apparently thought to favour the Italian and Spanish brands of Fascism. 'People here think the Vatican is tied to him', lamented Dr Orchard, of Mussolini, 'whereas the Vatican does not like him.' But if the British public was mistaken in its beliefs about a Catholic-Fascist rapprochement in Italy, even Orchard could not deny the truth of the allegations about Spain. 'Our catholic papers are tying their hopes far too much to Franco and to the sword generally. See if it does not put our convert numbers down again this year.'[20]

When war broke out Hinsley's task was to mobilize the Catholic community and to demonstrate Catholic loyalty to both the general public and the British government (which would no doubt bear in mind any lukewarmness when negotiating the next education bill). Unfortunately these three goals were not complementary. Sometimes it was possible to fulfil all three at once—as on most occasions did the cardinal's radio broadcasts where 'that grating masculine voice' became 'a national asset'.[21] An early example of how the satisfactory fulfilment of one of these goals could jeopardize the success of another arose in the case of Spain.

In August 1939 Hinsley through an intermediary passed on to the Foreign Office a suggestion from Father C. C. Martindale that British Catholics should appeal for funds to send a 'spiritual but concrete' gift to help refurbish the damaged churches of Spain.[22] It was an idea that strongly appealed to a British government which was keenly interested in neutralizing Spain in any forthcoming clash with the Axis powers,[23] but felt unable to risk the political storm which would inevitably follow any conciliatory gesture at government level.[24] The Catholic hierarchy was the one formally organized section of British society which could help them out. It

---

[19] [Archives of the Archdiocese of Westminster] B[ourne] P[apers] (many of Hinsley's papers have been wrongly filed amongst the papers of his predecessor, cardinal Bourne) 1/76 S. J. Gosling—A. Hinsley 3 February 1939.
[20] Bodleian Ms Eng. lett. c 301/127 W. E. Orchard—J. Marchant 26 January 1938.
[21] [David] Mathew, [*Catholicism in England*, 3 ed (London 1955)] p 269 [W. F.] Brown, [*Through Windows of Memory* (London 1946)] p 99.
[22] BP 1/124 C. C. Martindale—V. Elwes 8 August 1939. A similar offer of assistance was also made by German Catholics.
[23] Dante A. Puzzo, *Spain and the Great Powers 1936–1941* (New York and London 1962) ch IX.
[24] BP 1/124 L. M. Feery—V. Elwes 16 August 1939.

had long-standing connections with influential figures in rebel Spain, and could claim some expertise in Spanish affairs. Moreover it was the only body which because of its past and present support for the Franco cause (even at the height of the war Hinsley is said to have kept a photograph of the Caudillo on his writing table[25]) could lay some claim to Spanish sympathy and consideration. These reasons alone were sufficient to justify the government's support but there was another reason for a display of goodwill to the Spanish hierarchy. An emissary from the Foreign Office expressed the conviction that Catholicism alone could save Spain 'if it can exercise a moderating influence on Falanges'. Not surprisingly the diplomat was himself a Catholic and had spent three years at the Madrid embassy. He asserted that 'Franco and Suñer are excellent Catholics' and that only a minority of the rank and file favoured more extreme Fascist doctrines.[26] This assumption that being an excellent Catholic implied opposition to Fascism was to prove dangerously complacent in the case of Serrano Suñer, Franco's fanatically Fascist brother-in-law, sometimes described as 'the Spanish Laval'.[27]

Following negotiations with the archbishop of Toledo and Lord Perth, chief adviser on foreign publicity to the Ministry of Information (and a convert to Catholicism), who arranged for a ministry contribution of £500, an appeal was launched in the Catholic press.[28] It was arranged that archbishop Amigo of Southwark and major-general Sir Walter Maxwell Scott (a descendant of Sir Walter Scott) should travel to Spain in the summer of 1940 to present the gifts on behalf of the Roman Catholic Bishops' Committee for Spanish Relief. As Hinsley told Lord Phillimore in declining the proferred assistance of the Friends of Nationalist Spain committee, 'It was all important that the Mission should not have the character or implication of British propaganda'.[29]

Hinsley's wartime activities make it apparent that he was deeply

[25] Robert Speight, *The Life of Eric Gill* (London 1966) p 274.
[26] BP 1/124 L. M. Feery—V. Elwes 16 August 1939.
[27] [Viscount] Templewood, [*Ambassador on Special Mission* (London 1946)] pp 56f, 167f; Thomas J. Hamilton, *Appeasement's Child* (New York 1943) p 109.
[28] [Archdiocese of Westminster] H[insley] P[apers] 2/217 D. Mathew—A. Hinsley 10 February 1940; BP 1/124 Lord Perth—A. Hinsley 11 August 1939; A. Hinsley—Lord Perth 14 August 1939; A. Hinsley—Goma Y Tomas 18 August 1939.
[29] HP 2/217 A. Hinsley—Lord Phillimore 1 June 1940.

interested in the subtleties of propaganda. It was at his suggestion that a distinguished Irish (but loyal British) Catholic was appointed director of the British Institute in Madrid. Hinsley hoped that he would 'constitute a spearhead against Nazism and Facism'.[30] In October 1940 Hinsley wrote to Churchill complaining about the feeble efforts of British propaganda in Spain and enclosing a memorandum on the subject from the Maquis del Moral.[31] It contained nothing that had not already been reported by Sir Samuel Hoare, the new ambassador,[32] but was particularly scathing about the ineffectiveness of Hoare's predecessor especially for his failure to invest in the Spanish press.

German manipulation of the Spanish press aided and abetted by Suñer was most apparent in August 1940[33], as Hinsley had good reason to know. According to the *Times* certain Spanish newspapers were carrying reports that he had stated in his broadcasts that Britain was *not* fighting in the war for Christianity. But this was exactly what Hinsley did claim, and he demanded a retraction from the Spanish ambassador. The Duke of Alba soothed the cardinal by recalling the 'deep gratitude' felt by the whole of Spain for the 'sympathy and support received from your Eminence and the Catholics of the British Commonwealth during our war of liberation and our struggle in defence of Christianity'.[34] In a letter to the *Times* Hinsley published the correspondence and put the record straight, but this reminder of English Catholic support for nationalist Spain touched a raw nerve in the *British Weekly*, the leading Free Church paper. After a hostile recitation of the relations between Catholicism and the Franco regime, it shifted the argument to new ground by asking, 'I wonder what cardinal Hinsley thinks of the Pétain government?' The writer believed that 'the Pétain government would like to appear as a Franco regime for France, Fascist, Roman Catholic and opposed to all the 'liberals' and the 'Reds' and that some not inconsiderable section of the Roman Church outside is prepared to regard them with sympathy in this light?'[35]

[30] HP 2/217 W. Starkie—A. Hinsley 11 June 1940; A. Hinsley—W. Starkie 15 June 1940.
[31] HP 2/217 A. Hinsley—W. S. Churchill 21 October 1940; Maquis del Moral—V. Elwes 25 October 1940; Notes on Propaganda in Spain by the Maquis del Moral (typescript).
[32] Templewood p 32.
[33] *Ibid* p 55.
[34] *Times* 12 August 1940; HP 2/13 A. Hinsley—Editor, *Times* 21 August 1940; A. Hinsley—Duke of Alba 13 August 1940, Duke of Alba—A. Hinsley, 21 August 1940.
[35] *BW* 5 September 1940.

Hinsley was not to be drawn by the *British Weekly*, but he was painfully aware of the difficulties caused for English Catholics by the changes in France. When France was tottering the archbishop had sent, at Churchill's request, a heartening message to cardinal Suhard.[36] But the French collapse and the Italian declaration of war created a new and more dangerous situation. Now England stood alone and her people knew that they were next on the list for a German invasion. Younger Catholic intellectuals who thought they knew Hitler's methods, and how their fellow countrymen would react, now became thoroughly alarmed. Barbara Ward, foreign editor of the *Economist*, submitted to Hinsley on behalf of the Plater dining group a recommendation on 'Catholic Propaganda and the War', and her views were reinforced in a long letter from Christopher Dawson, the distinguished historian of culture. Both were convinced that England was about to be subjected to one of the most subtle and sinister of propaganda exercises. In a careful study of what she called 'the new propaganda', Miss Ward warned Catholics that elsewhere such techniques had brought about 'a complete disintegration of social cohesion by means of accentuating every difference of opinion, widening every clash of interest and separating men more and more in distrust and suspicion from their fellow men.'[37] According to Dawson, 'the favourite method of causing division and strife is the exploitation of the 'ideological' conflict between Left and Right, which may be extended to cover almost every shade of opinion.' The Spanish civil war was an illustration of the most extreme form of ideological cleavage. 'The enemy would no doubt, like to see the same sort of situation arising here: and to that end they wish to see English Catholics identified with the "Right" and all anti-Catholic or anti-Christian forces fused together as the "Left".' Fortunately the traditional political divisions of English Catholicism would counteract the promotion of such a dichotomy, but one unsettling factor was the situation in France and the talk of the 'formation of a "Latin Catholic bloc" unfriendly to Britain'. 'I think there must be many catholics at the present time who are rather bewildered by the

---

[36] BP 1/141 A. Bevin—Lord Fitzalan, 1 June 1940, A. Hinsley—C. Suhard, 4 June 1940.
[37] HP 2/219 D. Retchford—A. Hinsley, n.d.; Barbara Ward, 'The New Propaganda' *The Month* 917 (November 1940) p 285.

recent trend of events in France and who feel very much in the dark and in need of leadership'.[38]

But Hinsley was already alert to this aspect of the situation. On 13 July 1940 he wrote a private letter to the editor of the *Tablet*:

> This is a serious warning that a clever propaganda campaign is starting to make Catholics appear to have adopted an anti-British attitude. I do counsel you not to publish statements or comments, even if they purport to come from Vatican sources, tending to give support to the present government of France. Recent quotations from *Osservatore Romano* and the Vatican radio have given a wrong impression to many of our fellow countrymen—Catholic and Protestant—and to some loyal Frenchmen.

On the same day he sent another letter to the manager of the Press Association and the editor of the *Times* pointing out that any suggestion from Vatican sources that the Pope supported the Pétain government were purely private speculations and not official pronouncements.[39]

Hinsley and his correspondents had reason for concern as they watched the mounting public hysteria which manifested itself in the search for spies and Quislings and labelled as 'Fifth Columnists' anyone who was not unambiguously behind the nation's war leaders.[40] Too many of the organs of sophisticated Catholic opinion came into that latter category, though there was never the slightest hint of national disloyalty. The *Tablet* was edited by Douglas Woodruff whose Bellocian triumphalism had a certain affinity with the thought of Charles Maurras[41] and predisposed him, despite Hinsley's warnings, to favour the Pétain government in 1940. Nor could the archbishop have been pleased by an editorial in the *Month* of July 1940 with its carping quibbles about a passage in Churchill's 'finest hour' speech. The prime minister's reference to the 'brave men of Barcelona' could only have been included, it was contended, 'to raise an ignorant cheer from the extreme left'. The editorial went on to deplore the tendency in the

---

[38] HP 2/219 C. Dawson—A. Hinsley 17 July 1940; the greater part of this letter was reproduced in *Sword of the Spirit Bulletin* 2, 23 August 1940.
[39] BP 1/141 A. Hinsley—D. Woodruff—Editor, *Times*—manager, Press Association 13 July 1940.
[40] Angus Calder, *The People's War: Britain 1939–45* (London 1969) pp 133f.
[41] Bernard Wall, *Headlong into Change. An Autobiography and a Memoir of Ideas Since the Thirties* (London 1969) p 24.

popular press to suppose that the fifth column of Nazi sympathizers was 'recruited principally from the so-called extreme Right.'[42]

It was evident that some Catholic publicists were playing with fire, and Hinsley was inevitably pushed into more emphatic demonstrations of national orthodoxy. A suggestion, approved by the pope, that the archbishop should urge the British government to give serious consideration to German peace proposals was sent to the apostolic delegate in London on 26 July 1940 by the cardinal secretary of state. According to Professor Chadwick, Hinsley sent 'a surprisingly, and to an Englishman gratifyingly, fierce reply.'[43] But in the circumstances it would have been even more surprising if Hinsley had reacted with restraint, and it was inconceivable that he could have favoured the proposal.

The most dramatic public demonstration of Catholic loyalty occurred on 1 August 1940 when Hinsley launched an ambitious enterprise under the title the 'Sword of the Spirit'. At the inaugural meeting he described it to an audience of leading Catholic laity as 'a movement for a more united and more intensive Catholic effort in support of the struggle which our country has been forced to enter.' On 7 August he explained to the other bishops that 'after the collapse of France, it seemed urgently necessary to show that we in this country were loyal . . . I had reason to fear propaganda against British Catholics if steps were not taken to forestall it.' But the archbishop insisted in his inaugural address that 'we are not inspired by a narrow patriotism' for not only England but 'the whole of Christian civilization is at stake.' An extract from one of Dawson's editorials in *The Dublin Review* had been sent out with the invitations to the meeting. It declared that Christians had a special responsibility for the maintenance and strengthening of the 'unity of Western culture which had its roots in Christendom'. It went on to argue that 'the Christian cause at the present moment is also the common cause of all who are defending our civilization . . . A first necessity is to make public opinion alive to the issues that are at stake and to

---

[42] *The Month* 176 (July 1940) p 5.
[43] Owen Chadwick, 'The Papacy and World War II' *JEH* 18 (1967) p 76. Maglione's telegram and Godfrey's reply are to be found in Pierre Blet *et al.* eds, *Le Saint Siege et la guerre en Europe, mars 1939–août 1940* (Vatican 1965).

The Sword of the Spirit

develop the consciousness of Western culture and the spirit of loyalty to the Western tradition.'[44]

Hinsley's initiative was given extensive coverage in the Catholic press on 9 August though the *Catholic Herald* included a letter from Professor Thomas Bodkin of Birmingham which urged the new organization 'without delay to wield its nebulous aspirations into a definite, detailed programme, to tell us how, when, where and behind what recognized leaders we are to rally' so that 'the cloudy effect of its first meeting will soon evaporate'. But the clouds were never completely dispersed. The name of the movement was taken from the title of a broadcast given by the archbishop on 10 December 1939. 'You know the Cardinal's original word for his first broadcast was the Sword and the Spirit', confided W. E. Orchard to a friend in May 1941. 'He altered it, at my humble suggestion, to something more scriptural: 'The Sword of the Spirit' and, dear man, never saw that it made a lot of difference: and consequently it has remained an ambiguity ever since.'[45] But if there was ambiguity about what the movement stood for there was no ambiguity about what it was against. Hinsley would have been gratified to learn that the German ambassador to the Vatican promptly lodged a protest, while archbishop and organization were both publicly attacked in the name of Dutch Catholicism in a radio broadcast from a German-occupied Holland.[46]

Meanwhile another sour note had come from Birmingham in August 1940 from archbishop Thomas Williams. He was convinced that world revolution was every bit as dangerous as the Nazi way of life and ought to secure equal condemnation in the campaign literature. Moreover he was unimpressed by the quality and obscurity of the executive committee who were mainly young lay intellectuals. He complained that prominent laymen 'such as Douglas Jerrold' were neither on the committee nor even invited to the meeting. 'This causes a suspicion in my mind that Catholics who stood up for Franco and tried hard to explain the meaning of the civil war in Spain to English audiences will not be very welcome. Yet such Catholics faced unpopularity then in a good cause, and they not only spoke well but know how to organize

---

[44] HP 2/219; 'The Sword of the Spirit: What the Movement Stands For' (leaflet).
[45] Bodleian Ms Eng. let. c301/152 W. E. Orchard—J. Marchant 14 May 1941.
[46] Notes de Mgr Montini 17 août 1940, Pierre Blet *et al* eds *Le Saint Siege et la guerre en Europe, Juin 1940–Juin 1941* (Vatican 1967) p 113; Heenan p 188.

such a work.'⁴⁷ Organization, particularly in the early months, turned out to be one of the weaker points in the campaign, but then the bulk of the committee were 'ideas men' rather than 'organization men', and that not only in the sense of being relatively inexperienced in the mechanics of social movements but also to the extent that they gave priority to Catholic values rather than Catholic norms.⁴⁸ The omission of men such as Douglas Jerrold who had taken an active role in promoting the Spanish rebellion was no accident.⁴⁹ 'There should be no extremists among us.', Hinsley had warned. 'Eyes neither right nor left: eyes front'.⁵⁰ After taking precautions to exclude those publicly identified with the extremities of political opinion, the archbishop was furious when one of the chosen few on the executive contributed what he judged to be an injudicious letter to the *Tablet*. It seems that Dr Letitia Fairfield had been incensed by the behaviour of a priest at a 'Sword' meeting for French sympathizers. The priest had not only 'defended the Pétain (anti-Semitic) decrees in their most extreme interpretation' but also objected to the preparation of Sword of the Spirit leaflets for de Gaulle's army because 'the soldiers were not intelligent enough to understand the general principles'.⁵¹ Dr Fairfield countered by calling attention in the *Tablet* to the 'far too much tenderness for the Government of Vichy among Catholics . . . it has been far too rashly assumed that the social order marshal Pétain is trying to create is distinctively Catholic.' 'The Sword of the Spirit', she concluded, 'has need of its cutting edge'. Not surprisingly Woodruff, the editor, thought her letter unfair to Vichy, and in its equation of Catholicism with democracy a serious distortion of the faith; he let fly in the editorial columns.⁵²

Hinsley was bitterly disappointed, and found little consolation in Barbara Ward's attempts to smooth matters over. She had to admit that it was no easy task to fuse Catholics of right and left,

---

⁴⁷ HP 2/219 T. L. Williams—A. Hinsley, nd; copy in Coverdale Deposit, Archives of the Archdiocese of Westminster.

⁴⁸ For the distinction between norm-oriented movements and value-oriented movements see Neil J. Smelser, *Theory of Collective Behaviour* (London 1962). Archbishop Williams is remembered as a supporter of the movement by Mrs Freda Beales whose help and hospitality I gratefully acknowledge.

⁴⁹ Douglas Jerrold, *Georgian Adventure* (London 1937).

⁵⁰ Heenan p 186.

⁵¹ HP 2/219 L. Fairfield—A. Hinsley 12 January 1941.

⁵² *Tablet* 28 December 1940.

The Sword of the Spirit

supporters of Christian monarchy and Christian democracy, into a common cause: 'and one of the difficulties that the "Sword of the Spirit" is up against is the extraordinary lack of charity on both sides'.[53] Dr Fairfield for one was quite unrepentant:

> I do indeed appreciate the need for unity. But can we do anything practical to assist the rebuilding of Europe unless we clarify some of the issues.'[54]

The archbishop was not convinced: 'she accentuated the difference of view amongst us. The attitude of the bishops was not conciliated by her hot-air effusion.'[55]

Hinsley had good reason for looking over his shoulder to his fellow bishops, many of whom were deeply suspicious of the Sword movement from the moment of its foundation. He had tried to reassure his flock in his next broadcast on 8 September 1940, the national day of prayer, much to the annoyance of the B.B.C. who had not expected a sudden reversion to type and were quite unprepared for the shoal of complaints 'about Roman Catholic propaganda and the preaching of Mariolatry'. But Catholics were delighted.[56] Having made this bow to traditional Catholic sentiment, the archbishop felt free to make a major ecumenical gesture by signing with the heads of the other English religious bodies the famous letter to the *Times* of 21 December calling for any future peace settlement to include the five points proposed by the pope.[57] It was regarded by the Catholic press as something of a coup for the cardinal, and he was encouraged to take a further step.

Even before the inception of the Sword, one of those who was to become a member of its executive, Richard Hope, a ministry of Information official, had attempted to get Catholic participation in a proposed series of civic gatherings of churches as an expression of united Christian witness. Hinsley had rejected the idea.[58] But if Catholic participation in civic meetings on equal terms with other bodies was out of the question, non-catholic participation in

[53] HP 2/219 B. Ward—A. Hinsley 7 January 1941.
[54] HP 2/219 L. Fairfield—A. Hinsley 12 January 1941.
[55] HP 2/219 Note by Hinsley on letter from B. Ward 7 January 1941.
[56] HP 2/13 J. W. Welch—V. Elwes 12 September 1940; HP 2/219. Lady Winifrede Elwes—V. Elwes 9 September 1940.
[57] The text of the letter was drawn up by Miss Ellis and archbishop Godfrey: HP 2/141 W. Temple—A. Hinsley 30 November 1940. A. Hinsley—W. Temple 2 December 1940.
[58] HP 2/141 R. Hope—D. Mathew 26 June 1940; A. Hinsley—R. Hope 27 June 1940.

Catholic meetings to follow-up the *Times* letter was another matter. On 10 and 11 May 1941 two public meetings under the auspices of the 'Sword' were held at the Stoll theatre, London, presided over respectively by the archbishops of Westminster and Canterbury. The meetings were an immense success, aroused considerable enthusiasm and were followed by similar united demonstrations in other parts of the country. 'Let us have a regular system of consultation and collaboration', Hinsley had said at the first meeting, '. . . such as his Lordship the Bishop of Chichester has suggested, to agree on a plan of action which shall win the peace when the din of battle is ended.'[59] It looked as if a new era had dawned, and a united Christian front had come into existence. But as cardinal Heenan has remarked 'all this time the demon of dogmatic difference was restlessly active'.[60] And in addition to traditional suspicions and institutional inhibitions, it was not certain that the sword itself, when taken from its scabbard, was strong enough for its task.

'The two meetings at the Stoll Theatre have been so successful that they are likely to involve a major crisis for the Sword of the Spirit', reported its secretary A. F. C. Beales. Press reports now took the movement for granted as an established institution. 'But this can only cause concern to those who know how far the Sword falls short of what the public imagines it to be.' The reputation which had been acquired for clear and active leadership, efficient organization and sound team-work bore no relation to reality. 'In actual fact it has hardly any leadership at all . . . It is still true, as critics have remarked from outside, that the Sword "has no policy" . . . the organization has been in fact three persons: myself, my wife, and Miss Webb acting as voluntary assistant in the Office . . . Elsewhere, there has been drift and delay and lack of co-ordination, and many a local crisis because the Office was not informed of steps taken by individual members of the Committee'. It was all very disconcerting, especially when 'the leaders of Protestant societies tell me they envy the "hierarchical organization" of Catholic bodies, as enabling one to "get things done".'[61]

[59] Heenan p 193; for Bell's speech: G. K. A. Bell, *The Church and Humanity (1939–46)* (London 1946) pp 48–57.
[60] Heenan p 193.
[61] HP 2/219 A. F. C. Beales—V. Elwes 16 May 1941.

The Sword of the Spirit

Even Catholic support could not be relied upon. 'It was the non-catholic co-operation that saw me through' wrote Beales after the Stoll meetings. Only one ordinary and two auxiliaries out of the 25 Catholic bishops had attended; five had sent good wishes but 14 had not even replied to the invitation. Nor was a single bishop present in time to welcome the archbishop of Canterbury. All this was only too characteristic of the "casual", off-hand indifferentism that has at times been the bane of Catholic public life.'[62]

But even if the majority of Catholic bishops were either hostile or indifferent to the movement, a noisy minority of Free Church men were actively antagonistic. The council of the Protestant Truth Society felt that evangelical protestantism was in danger while the World's Evangelical Alliance began lobbying traditionalist members of the executive of the Free Church Federal Council. According to the Alliance's general secretary:

> It is not the Sword of the Spirit, it is the sword of hypocrisy and deceit . . . Cardinal Hinsley and the Roman Catholics in this movement, and in other clever moves at the present time, are out for two ends: (a) kudos for the Pope, and (b) the shelving of the question of religious freedom.

Once more Spain was the decisive *skandalon*. 'There is scarcely a vestige of religious freedom in Spain today, and while I am writing active steps are being taken, in consultation with Vatican representatives in Rome, in Spain and other countries, to make effective rules or regulations, and even law, which shall establish the Roman Catholic Church as "the only religion in Spain".'[63]

Prodded by its Baptist treasurer, Wilson Black, the Free Church council's general purposes committee produced a skilful face-saving formula. It was asserted that the moderator's signature to the *Times* letter only implied agreement with the Pope's five proposals so far as they went. They were not a full expression of Free Church convictions especially since there was no reference to the rights of religious minorities. Hence the Sword of the Spirit was mistaken in commending the letter as a full and sufficient basis for a Christian peace, especially since it was now maintained that 'the only admissible interpretation of the Pope's points is that of their author'. A further resolution was sent to the Foreign

---

[62] *Ibid.*
[63] H. M. Gooch—S. M. Berry June 1941 quoted in [Henry] Townsend, [*Robert Wilson Black* (London 1954)] pp 132–3.

Secretary urging the British government to accept President Roosevelt's demand that liberty of conscience and worship should be an essential element in any peace settlement.[64]

Such a resolution was hardly likely to reassure a suspicious Catholic hierarchy, which had in any case been shaken by Hinsley's twin concessions at the Stoll meeting: the promise of collaboration and the recitation of the Lord's Prayer.[65] The Sword of the Spirit had always been open to non-catholics but after the Stoll meetings and the involvement of the determined bishop Bell, there was the possibility of a large influx of new non-catholic members. Christopher Dawson, aware of the dearth of active Catholic leadership suggested the co-option of Nathaniel Micklem and J. H. Oldham to the executive.[66] But would non-catholics be content to work under Catholic leadership? Or would they eclipse the existing leadership (as bishop Bell had done at the first Stoll meeting) and wrest control of the organization from Catholic hands? Catholic fears that they might be at most submerged and at least embarrassed were only credible to those who knew the true state of the movement. For non-catholics impressed by its apparent strength and vitality, the fear as expressed by archbishop Lang to Bell, was that their participation might be used astutely for Catholic propaganda.[67]

Various solutions were proposed. One scheme envisaged the division of the movement along denominational lines with separate organizations working under the same name in the same building with a co-ordinating committee. But Father John Murray thought that Catholic bishops would strongly disapprove and might withdraw such support as had been pledged. He feared that the Catholic sword might become insignificant compared with the non-catholic branch. But his proposal that the non-catholic sympathizers should band themselves together under another name was opposed because 'what becomes of His Eminence's leadership of the movement?'[68]

In the end caution prevailed. At the first annual meeting on 9

[64] Townsend p 134.
[65] BP 1/174 R. Hope—V. Elwes 5 May 1941; B. Ward—A. Hinsley, 20 May 1941.
[66] BP 1/174 C. Dawson—A. Hinsley 13 June 1941.
[67] R. C. D. Jasper, *George Bell, Bishop of Chichester* (London 1967) p 252.
[68] BP 1/174 Minutes of the executive meeting of the sword of the spirit 16 July 1941; T. Bodkin—B. Ward, 10 September 1941.

The Sword of the Spirit

August 1941 Hinsley with great regret and some embarrassment announced that non-catholics were only eligible for associate membership of the Sword of the Spirit and had no voting rights. A parallel non-catholic movement was set up under the title 'Religion and Life', and it was agreed that both bodies should launch simultaneous but separate campaigns with joint literature and study and one joint meeting on social and international topics. But there were to be no more united acts of worship or prayer.[69]

Such a result was probably inevitable. In the twelve months since the summer of 1940 the situation had changed. A successful German landing now became a remote possibility instead of a high probability and the political panic which forced Hinsley's hand had evaporated. With the disappearance of the situation which had called it into existence, the Sword of the Spirit now developed in a direction which had not been envisaged. Hinsley had been surprised by the enthusiasm which it had evoked, but much of the enthusiasm seemed to be inspired more by the prospect of breaking down religious barriers than by the ostensible aims of the movement. Such a development, whilst not unwelcome to the cardinal imposed new strains which counteracted his original motives in bringing the movement into existence. One of Hinsley's main aims had been to provide a focus for Catholic unity. But the shift of emphasis after the Stoll meetings had exerted new tensions within his own community. According to bishop David Mathew, who was intimately involved in the various negotiations, ecumenical co-operation was welcomed by Catholic laity in the south of England but 'it found no support among the northern catholics', which meant, of course, the majority of English Catholics. Nor did it make any appeal to the clergy.[70] As bishop Brown remarked 'how could our clergy be working with the local vicar, and at the same time trying to persuade members of his congregation to believe he had no valid orders, and to leave his church?' Consequently 'the movement failed to take root in the parishes, except in comparatively few places . . . although there

---

[69] For a detailed discussion of these developments see Michael J. Walsh, 'Ecumenism in Wartime Britain. The Sword of the Spirit and Religion and Life, 1940–1945 (1)' *Heythrop Journal*, July 1982 pp 243–58. For the subsequent development of the Sword into the Catholic Institute for International Relations, a name adopted in 1965, see M. J. Walsh, *From Sword to Ploughshare* (London 1980).

[70] Mathew p 263.

was much activity and Press publicity.[71] Nor was the hierarchy any more helpful. They were not all as forthright as the archbishop of Cardiff who asserted that 'the movement, carried on as it has been in England so far, would prove a catastrophe to the Church in Wales'[72] but they left little room for the cardinal to manoeuvre. Indeed it was becoming increasingly difficult for Hinsley to integrate the different roles of national religious leader, Catholic archbishop and leader of a semi-autonomous ecumenical campaign for cultural renewal.[73]

From the Catholic point of view a further dysfunctional factor was the priority given by the lay intellectuals associated with the direction of the Sword movement to cultural forces: ideas, beliefs, values. Culture was more important to them than structure. The battle for the mind came before holding the ecclesiastical fort. This was a view which came naturally to professional academics, journalists and preachers: those who have words and ideas as their stock-in-trade. The relegation of social structure and institutions to a secondary level inevitably made it easier to embark on ecumenical dialogue, and quickly established a common bond with protestants who shared that cultural pessimism which was manifest both in the writings of Christopher Dawson and in bishop Bell's book of 1940 on *Christianity and World Order*.[74]

But religion, as a leading sociologist has reminded us, 'is never only cultural.[75] Culture lives in and through social structures and institutions, which include churches. It might be argued that the officers of the Sword were mistaken in attaching too much importance to culture, to mental processes, psychological factors, and the 'new propaganda'. Perhaps Dr Goebbels' most effective piece of brainwashing was to instil the notion that propaganda was a really decisive factor. It was here that their neglect of structure let Dawson and his friends down. If they had taken structure as well as culture seriously they would not have been able to draw those analogies with Spain and France, nor posit the pseudo-

---

[71] Brown p 100.
[72] BP 1/174 M. McGrath—A. Hinsley 15 November 1941.
[73] For a discussion of the problems of role conflict, especially in a situation of ideological dialogue see Alasdair MacIntyre 'The Christian-Communist Rapprochement: Some Sociological Notes and Questions', D. Martin ed, *A Sociological Yearbook of Religion in Britain* 2 (London 1969) pp 173–186.
[74] On this aspect see the comment by Hensley Henson: Jasper p 248.
[75] Talcott Parsons, 'Theory in the Humanities and Sociology' *Daedalus* (Spring 1970) p 499.

The Sword of the Spirit

sociological 'laws' which prompted Hinsley to create the Sword.[76] If they had looked more carefully at Holland they would have seen that it was not propaganda which had opened the door to Germany but overwhelming superior force. Winston Churchill took no interest in propaganda and once told Hinsley that if Spain stayed neutral it would be commercial considerations which carried weight.[77]

Finally it is important to note the shadow of the Spanish civil war 'the last great cause', which overhung the ecclesiastical politics of the period. For some, that catastrophic series of events brought about a total revolution in their religious outlook.[78] The editor of the *Church Times* Sidney Dark had loyally supported Lord Halifax's attempts to reunite the Church of England with Rome. 'But the Spanish Civil War changed my opinion':

> The people who acclaim Franco as a Christian hero have a conception of Christianity so fundamentally different from mine that the alliance of my church with theirs now seems to be as undesirable as happily it is improbable.[79]

Dark was consequently not impressed by the Sword of the Spirit. And for William Temple, Spain was a reminder of the ambiguity of Roman Catholic attitudes:

> I have joined with others in pressing upon some leading Roman Catholics in this country the desirability of their using their influence to check the persecution in Spain. The reply is always that in all matters other than those of the faith itself, the Church acts independently in every nation . . . I need not say that I regard all this as profoundly unsatisfactory, but it affords a kind of defence behind which Roman Catholics in this country take up their position of co-operation with us. . . . I sympathize with those who hold that if all this be true we should refuse any form of co-operation; but I cannot agree partly because I think the best hope of instilling a new attitude into Roman Catholics is through taking every opportunity of effective intercourse. But I think we ought

---

[76] For a useful discussion which does take structure and culture with equal seriousness, G. A. Almond, 'Comparative Political Systems' *Journal of Politics* 18 (1956).

[77] This topic has been discussed in detail in Briggs pp 5f, 221f. In retrospect Duff Cooper, the first wartime minister of Information, came to accept Churchill's view *Old Men Forget* (London 1955) p 278.

[78] D. R. Davies, *In Search of Myself* (London 1961) pp 179f.

[79] Sidney Dark, *The Church Impotent or Triumphant* (London 1941) p 77.

also to take opportunities of making quite clear our condemnation of the kind of thing that has been going on in Spain.[80]

Unfortunately when that letter was written, 20 November 1942, there was little opportunity of effective intercourse. Within four months Hinsley was dead, and Catholic-protestant relations went into that deep freeze from which they have only just recently emerged.

University of Lancaster

[80] William Temple, *Some Lambeth Letters 1942–44* ed F. S. Temple (London 1963) pp 39f.

THE FALL OF FRANCE

by GAVIN WHITE

'AS FOR the good things of this life and its ills, God has willed that these should be common to both' the righteous and the unrighteous.[1] So wrote a well-known north African theologian of the fall of Rome in AD 410, an event which many observers attributed to the abandonment of ancient religious practices and beliefs in favour of Christianity. That they should do so was perhaps natural; it is always easier to claim betrayal than to admit defeat in the field of battle. Even Gibbon, who was judicious enough in assessing the causes of the fall of Rome, held that the main cause was 'the domestic hostilities of the Romans themselves',[2] and implied that the city might not have fallen had it not been that, 'At the hour of midnight, the Salarian gate was silently opened . . .'.[3] And what was said of the fall of Rome was also said of the fall of France.

'It has been said with some truth that a disintegration as complete as that of France could not be the result of military defeat alone. The roots of disaster must have gone deeper', wrote Barbara Ward in 1940,[4] and it was common to assert that some gate must have been silently opened to let the German armies pass. In fact historians see the failure as largely military; it has been pinpointed, perhaps unfairly, on the Cadennes battalion of the 39th Infantry during a single day of May.[5] Admittedly France was unprepared for war, but at that stage so was Britain. The army was defeated in the field but, 'Since in 1940 no military leader would admit that the army had failed the nation, the fault must lie elsewhere.'[6] Defeat was therefore blamed on secular schools, lack of religion, and above all on the teachers who had taught neither

---

[1] Whitney J. Oates, *Basic Writings of Saint Augustine* (New York 1948) vol 2 p 11 (book 1 chap 8).
[2] Edward Gibbon, *The History of the Decline and Fall of the Roman Empire* (London 1900) vol 8 p 313.
[3] *Ibid* p 321.
[4] Barbara Ward, 'The Fall of France' *Dublin Review* October 1940 p 213.
[5] [Henri] Amouroux, [*La Grande Histoire des Français sous l'Occupation*] (Paris 1976–81) vol 1 p 309.
[6] W. D. Halls, *The Youth of Vichy France* (Oxford 1981) p 9.

patriotism nor God.⁷ There was a great outcry against such evidence of slackness as the paid holiday, against a low birth-rate, and against adulterating the French race by the easy naturalisation of foreigners, especially Jews.⁸ And leading this outcry, though not on the whole against the Jews, was the Church which, for the first time in living memory, provided an explanation of events which the French people were anxious to accept.

France had been punished for good living and bad thinking, her sin had made her lose the war. 'France has sinned, France must atone', it was claimed, and there was a new theology of purification through suffering.⁹ Of course there were churchmen who protested against a theology which implied that God was awarding the nazis, but popular fervour swept them aside.¹⁰ In the immediate aftermath of defeat there was a religious revival as sincere as it was shortlived.¹¹ In prison camps the daily communicants were numbered in the hundreds, in one camp alone over two thousand officers went on retreat, and in the unoccupied zone which was the traditional centre of anti-clericalism the churches were filled Sunday by Sunday. Ten million consecrated themselves to Notre-Dame-de-Boulogne and in the *grand retour* the figure of the Madonna in the boat, actually four figures in four boats, moved throughout France.¹² And as is well known the French workers in Germany responded to the priest workers with such zeal and devotion that this seemed the natural answer to the disillusionment of the post-war proletariat of France.¹³

So much for France; this has been well-documented. But the aim of this paper is to consider the British response to the fall of France, and especially the British Christian response as seen in the press. And that response was not dissimilar. If the French said, 'We have sinned, we must atone', the British said, 'They have sinned, they must atone', and gave the French a few knocks to help the process along. For the British were tempted in their turn. As they faced the German military machine they could attribute its

---

⁷ *Ibid* pp 108, 309.
⁸ *Ibid* p 11; Amouroux vol 5 p 149.
⁹ [Jacques] Duquesne, [*Les Catholiques français sous l'Occupation*] (Paris 1966) pp 25–29; Amouroux vol 2 pp 268–269.
¹⁰ Duquesne p 31.
¹¹ Amouroux vol 2 pp 273–274.
¹² Duquesne pp 25–26.
¹³ *Ibid* p 312; Pierre Andreu, *Les Grandeurs et Erreurs des Prêtres–Ouvriers* (Paris 1955) p 67.

The fall of France

victories either to its superiority, which meant they themselves had little chance, or to moral failings amongst the French, which made those victories irrelevent in the battle for Britain. And as they hailed the moral weaknesses of the French they also hailed the moral strength of the British, though it was recognised that these only applied if Britain stood alone. Air Marshal Dowding may have had special reason to fall on his knees and thank God when France fell,[14] but others shared his reaction.

It was not initial policy to admit that Britain stood alone; after the fall of France the newspapers were full of assertions that Britain was not alone. On 18 June 1940 when Petain sued for peace *The Times* took the official line of Britain having 'what we did not enjoy in 1806, not only the strong co-operation of an empire grown to manhood, but the promise of full assistance from the boundless resources of the United States.' But a correspondent lower down the same page quoted a Wordsworth sonnet from 1806, 'And we are left, or shall be left, alone',[15] of which the full text exulted in a lack of allies and held that 'in ourselves our safety must be sought.'[16] That day's *Manchester Guardian* quoted the same sonnet in its leader but then denied the parallel, since 'To-day Britain is a great federation of independent peoples', but somewhat spoiled the effect of the argument by re-printing a cartoon from the *Evening Standard* over the caption, 'Very well, alone.'[17] The *Birmingham Post* of that day made the usual reference to Napoleon in its leader appearing under the title 'Alone', but then referred to the dominions to show Britain was not alone.[18] In the following weeks all things French were regarded with suspicion. Of all countries occupied by Hitler, only France was described with the word 'fall', while everything was done to dissociate France from the continuing war effort. When French ships were seized in British ports personal effects were looted,[19] the massacre of French seamen at Mers-el-Kebir horrified the royal navy officers who had to give the orders but not their seamen,[20] and in later years there

---

[14] Eleanor M. Gates, *The End of the Affair: The Collapse of the Anglo-French Alliance 1939–40* (Berkeley 1981) p 566.
[15] *The Times* 18 June 1940 p 7.
[16] William Wordsworth, *Poetical Works* (London 1837) vol 3 p 200 (sonnet 26).
[17] *Manchester Guardian* 18 June 1940 pp 4, 6.
[18] *Birmingham Post* 18 June 1940 p 4.
[19] Amouroux vol 3 p 33.
[20] Arthur J. Marder, *From the Dardenelles to Oran* (London 1974) p 268.

was continued distrust seen in disregard for potential allies in north Africa at the time of the invasion,[21] disregard for the resistance,[22] and a tendency to treat liberated France as a nation needing Anglo-Saxon government in every particular.[23] 'As we have dealt with the French navy, so we shall deal with the French nation', threatened the *Birmingham Post* in mid-July,[24] and if others were not so forthright their thoughts were not dissimilar.

But it must be admitted that suspicion was not directed only at the French. 'Since the French capitulation, workaday England has become more insular than it has ever been before', observed one journalist with regret, 'it has little sympathy with the interned refugees, even though they are anti-nazi. It has a certain suspicion of the Poles and Czechs and the other foreign contingents now in this country. "We can look after ourselves, can't we?", said a bus conductor to me last week, "And you can't trust them foreigners."'[25] Refugees were not only interned but sometimes beaten and robbed in the presence of police,[26] and when many drowned when their ship was torpedoed on the way to Canada there were gloating stories of their panic.[27] Some reparation was made when the country regained its sense of proportion and was horrified at its own actions, but the very horror indicated how untypical the times had been. And the times had been untypical not just through suspicion of foreigners in general, but through a real fear that these particular foreigners might undermine resistance to Hitler through their 'weakness of moral fibre'.[28]

In all this the churches shared, though not to the same extent that the church in France shared in the national agony. The fall of France could hardly mesmerise Britain for long, succeeded as it was by falling bombs. But for one short month the churches tried to explain the fall of France as they saw it.

Not, however, the churches of Scotland. The Scots treated faith in a national character which was largely English with a degree of

---

[21] Jacques Robichon, *jour J en Afrique* (Paris 1964) pp 69, 76, 83, 85.
[22] Amouroux vol 4 p 447.
[23] Robert Aron, *De Gaulle before Paris* (London 1962) pp 28, 47.
[24] *Birmingham Post* 15 July 1940 p 2.
[25] *Church Times* 26 July 1940 p 513.
[26] Peter and Leni Gilman, *'Collar the Lot': How Britain Interned and Expelled its Wartime Refugees* (London 1980) p 216.
[27] *Glasgow Herald* 29 June 1940 p 2; *Birmingham Post* 5 July 1940 p 2.
[28] *Ibid* 23 August 1940 p 2.

The fall of France

reserve, and though Scottish newspapers gave some coverage to the theme of Britain being alone,[29] they were more casual about it than their English counterparts. Some heat was generated by a letter to the press from the very jingoistic moderator of the general assembly of the Church of Scotland, joined by fourteen ex-moderators. Asserting that, 'We are entirely guiltless' of causing the war, and that 'we can reverently claim to have with us the greatest of all allies',[30] this letter brought down upon its authors' heads the wrath of twenty-four Scottish church notables who complained of the 'sin of self-righteousness', adding that 'the hope of the world is not the British empire',[31] while a young layman named Patrick Rodger could not agree that 'it is the function of the church to be a sort of elevated branch of the ministry of information.'[32] Meanwhile the United Free Church had taken a typically liberal stand against all war, standing out for conscientious objectors while allowing grudging respect for those of its members who fought.[33] This in its turn led to opposition.[34] But there is no evidence of a concern for the fall of France in the available literature.

Turning to the Church of England it is convenient to begin with the *Church Times* even though that journal may not have been representative of the Church of England; some would prefer to treat it as a quite separate denomination. What distinguished *Church Times* coverage of this issue was its usual distaste for Rome and its usual lack of proportion. In the same issue the fall of France was first blamed on generals and politicians and then on 'bourgeois atheism' which had sapped France's allegiance to the Catholic faith.[35] But the fall was also blamed upon Roman Catholics being inclined to fascism, and since German protestants were erastian and all Romans inclined to totalitarianism, only Anglicans were left.[36] But the key position of Anglicanism was also deduced from national history, since 'it has been ordained by divine providence

---

[29] *Scotsman* 18 June 1940 p 4.
[30] *Glasgow Herald* 29 June 1940 p 2.
[31] *Ibid* 19 July 1940 p 3.
[32] *Ibid* 3 July 1940 p 5.
[33] *Minutes of the Proceedings of the United Free Church of Scotland General Assembly* (June 1940) p 98.
[34] *Scotsman* 19 June 1940 p 5.
[35] *Church Times* 28 June 1940 pp 459, 462.
[36] *Ibid* 5 July 1940 p 476.

that the British people should be chosen with their brethren from across the seas to stand alone against the embattled (sic) forces of evil.'[37] Furthermore, 'If England were to die, all those practical things which our Lord in the sermon on the mount told us to cherish would undergo eclipse.'[38] Yet again, 'Faith in the British cause is at bottom faith in God . . . the faith of the creeds in God is the staff of the national cause to-day.'[39] Finally and most revealingly, 'As, therefore, Great Britain is now facing the hordes of tyranny and cruelty alone, so the English church has alone to strive for the permeation of secular society with the principles of the catholic faith.'[40] For the survival of Britain depended on spiritual assets, and 'the greatest asset of all is the spirit of a freedom-loving people, learning through adversity that trust in God engenders courage, confidence, and persistence.'[41]

If the *Church Times* managed to apply the concept of Britain standing alone to the Church of England standing alone, it not only ruled out other churches but other peoples, quoting Churchill out of context to show that all who fell to Hitler were 'rotted from within'.[42] Nor did it favour refugees in Britain. Though archbishop Temple had spoken in their favour, the *Church Times* claimed they had better allowances than soldiers' wives and should be 'interned and given the chance to grow their own food',[43] that while some might be released the campaign against their original internment was 'hysterical nonsense',[44] and in August when some actually were released described them 'returning to London bronzed and well, and full of appreciation of the way in which they have been treated.'[45] But the paper did oppose the 'hooligan attacks on Italian shops' which were a characteristic of the period.[46]

Of course there were other Church of England journals. None of them showed much interest in the fall of France, but none of them showed much interest in anything else in public life. But they

[37] *Ibid* 28 June 1940 p 462.
[38] *Ibid*.
[39] *Ibid* 12 July 1940 p 490.
[40] *Ibid* p 487.
[41] *Ibid* 21 June 1940 p 943.
[42] *Ibid* 19 July 1940 p 499.
[43] *Ibid* 7 June 1940 p 411.
[44] *Ibid* 26 July 1940 p 511.
[45] *Ibid* 9 August 1940 p 535.
[46] *Ibid* 14 June 1940 p 427.

The fall of France

did reflect something of the national pride at being chosen to stand alone. 'It may well be that God has allowed all this to come upon us to teach us to turn to him',[47] suggested the *Church of England Newspaper*, with an insular disregard for what God had done to the French. The *Record*, an evangelical organ, noted that 'we fight alone – – – yet not alone, for our brethren in the Colonies are in this conflict with us to the end.'[48] Elsewhere the *Record* was surprisingly sympathetic to the French, but by August had begun worrying that foreign troops in Britain might lose the war for Britain by playing soccer on Sunday which, 'when we expect so much from God', was 'definitely against the national interest.'[49]

From individual churchmen came opinions less precise than those of the *Church Times* but in line with the national trend. Cuthbert Bardsley was unusual in saying that many of the reasons for the fall of France also applied to Britain, but he said it showed that 'the results of personal compromise with sin are national collapse.'[50] The bishop of Chelmsford admitted there were some military reasons for the fall of France, but said that 'the real strength of a nation lies in its character', and 'our spirit will not break.'[51] The bishop of Ripon said Britons should be 'humbly proud that God should have entrusted to us, in this small island, that most supreme task in history . . . that we alone should stand against the foe.'[52] The bishop of Exeter said that 'the future of the world depends on Britain',[53] while Lord Halifax said this was a struggle between 'the forces of Christ and anti-Christ.'[54] As for the archbishop of Canterbury, his correspondence only shows an acceptance of the common belief that the fall of France came from 'a betrayal of spirit'.[55] Of course there were more thoughtful reactions as well. The Oxford theologian Oliver Quick thought Britain and France were partly responsible for the war, so 'we can hardly claim before God that we deserve to win it', while he believed others such as Alec Vidler were even more sceptical

---

[47] *Church of England Newspaper* 28 June 1940 p 6.
[48] *Record* 21 June 1940 p 292.
[49] *Ibid* 16 August 1940 p 365.
[50] *Church of England Newspaper* 5 July 1940 p 6.
[51] *Record* 26 July 1940 p 388.
[52] *Ibid* 28 June 1940 p 300.
[53] *Church Times* 12 July 1940 p 493.
[54] *Ibid* 26 July 1940 p 511.
[55] Lambeth Palace Library, Lang Papers, Lang to Osusky 24 October 1940.

about the allied claim to righteousness.[56]

On the Roman Catholic side only one journal, the *Tablet*, adumbrated a sectarian theory of the fall comparable to that of the *Church Times*. Like the secular press, the *Tablet* made much of a recent book on French history by D. W. Brogan and went on to stress the differences between Catholic France and secular France rather than those between France and Britain. The *Tablet* was not entirely consistent. In June it attributed the weakness of France to 'a creed of non-cooperating individualism',[57] but by July was arguing that only the Catholic church in France stood for individual liberties in the face of an impious state.[58] There was much about 'the bigotry of the secularists',[59] and denunciation of French 'secular hedonism'.[60] There was some hope for a future France in which thinkers might revive catholic ideals, 'making amends for the false trails which the French philosophers blazed two hundred years ago.'[61] This was repeated by Philip Hughes in language that would have made a Breton blush. He stated that 'the soul of France is the catholic faith', that 'the third republic was a compromise, almost an accident, that just happened', that after 1899 'the extreme of Masonry-inspired hatred of religion came to full power', and that the Dreyfus case was in some vague way unfair to Catholicism, as was the condemnation of *action française*.[62] By August the *Tablet* had even discovered 'a direct connection in the history of ideas between the French revolution of 1789 and the German revolution of 1933.'[63] If the *Tablet* did once admit that the fall of France had military origins, it was only so that they could blame the French and also the British authorities for not having followed the advice of that great military expert, Hilaire Belloc.[64] But if the pages of the *Tablet* trumpeted general hostility to the third republic, they also quoted cardinal Hinsley who had addressed the French by radio and was much more understanding. If he spoke of serving false gods and of the evils of birth

[56] *Ibid* Quick to Chaplain, Letter 413 15 July 1940 and Letter 417 undated.
[57] *Tablet* 8 June 1940 p 586.
[58] *Ibid* 20 July 1940 p 45.
[59] *Ibid* 8 June 1940 p 586.
[60] *Ibid* 22 June 1940 p 604.
[61] *Ibid* 29 June 1940 p 622.
[62] *Ibid* 13 July 1940 p 25.
[63] *Ibid* 3 August 1940 p 87.
[64] *Ibid* 22 June 1940 p 601.

The fall of France

prevention, he only did so when referring to British Catholics and not when referring to French.[65] At this time he was much engaged in the creation of the Sword of the Spirit for Catholic social action, and while that movement may have been aided by reflections on French experience it really owed little to the events of 1940.

Other journals were more vague and disordered in looking at France. The *Universe* claimed that France fell because 'The moral fibre of her people had been weakened by unrestrained pursuit of pleasure', the type of pleasure being indicated by the following comment that higher birth-rates would have meant larger armies.[66] Later in July the *Universe* admitted that Britain had decayed almost as much as France, but, 'We have been given time . . .'.[67] The *Catholic Herald* expressed the democratic wrath of Michael de la Bedoyere against the 'appalling amount of sheer and unadulterated infidelity' amongst Catholics in Germany, Italy and Spain, to explain how Britain could be ranged against such Catholic or partly-Catholic lands.[68] A leader on France came down heavily against Gallicanism and nationalism and also against the 'pagan internationalism of the renaissance.'[69] In the *Dublin Review* Christopher Dawson told Catholics that they had a special responsibility in 1940 since, 'They are the heirs and successors of the makers of Europe.'[70] Meanwhile Christopher Hollis in the *Clergy Review* showed cool sanity in supporting the war, 'not because we are exceptionally good but because our enemies are exceptionally bad.'[71] The *Month*, generally similar to other journals in its outlook, noted that Churchill had referred uncharacteristically to Britons resisting like 'the brave men of Barcelona', and complained in view of that city's record being 'so foul with arson, murder, and sacrilege.'[72]

One thing was absent from all this. In the preceding decades English Roman Catholic journals had an obsession about the Church of England, and were constantly taking its pulse to see

---

[65] *Ibid* 6 July 1940 p 8.
[66] *Universe* 5 July 1940 p 6.
[67] *Ibid* 19 July 1940 p 6.
[68] *Catholic Herald* 21 June 1940 p 4.
[69] *Ibid* 28 June 1940 p 4.
[70] *Dublin Review* July 1940 p 1.
[71] *Clergy Review* June 1940 p 473.
[72] *Month* July 1940 p 5.

when they might inherit its estate. Yet this theme was forgotten when dealing with the fall of France and with British resistance, though it still made itself mildly felt on pages not related to those matters.

Free Church journals said less of France. This may have been because their constituents were of a social class not much concerned with the continent, or because their editorial policies were too rigid to be altered by current events. Yet there was something. The *British Weekly* quoted the Wordsworth sonnet and said, 'At last we are alone, and, explain it how you will, we feel better.'[73] As for France, it was 'for the time being a mere geographical term: dust and a shade.'[74] The collapse of France was 'the last straw, but the balance has tilted the right way', since it made the British 'dedicated'.[75] The *Methodist Recorder* and *Christian World* both emphasised the military nature of the collapse, contrary to the general trend, and the Methodist president of confernece made the usual remarks about 'the years following Austerlitz' and the world's hopes depending on England.[76] Throughout the summer the tone of these journals was one of mild congratulation at Britain being more virtuous than France.

But if the fall of France was usually interpreted by the religious press in vaguely religious ways, almost all journals joined in the frenzy against alien refugees without giving that any religious context at all. Only two journals, the *Catholic Herald* and the Church of Scotland's *Life and Work*,[77] had editorials sympathetic to the refugees, though in most other journals some correspondent wrote on their behalf.

That the interest in the fall of France and its cause was very much a British phenomenon may be seen by comparing British with Canadian and American church papers which scarcely dwell on it at all. In fact, the leading American church paper paid the question of why France fell the ultimate insult of saying it could safely be left to the historians.[78]

In conclusion, the reaction to the fall in Britain may seem to be

[73] *British Weekly* 27 June 1940 p 151; 4 July 1940 p 157.
[74] *Ibid* 18 July 1940 p 177.
[75] *Ibid* 20 June 1940 p 135.
[76] *Methodist Recorder* 18 June 1940 p 4.
[77] *Catholic Herald* 28 June 1940 p 4; *Life and Work* August 1940 p 232.
[78] *Christian Century* 26 June 1940 p 815.

a mirror image of the reaction in France, but there were significant differences. There was no religious revival in England. The churches were talking to themselves, and no-one else heard them or felt they needed to hear them. The legend of how Britain stood alone lives on to-day in popular mythology, but the churches are not part of that legend. Most Britons felt they could face Hitler as they were without having to change; the French had to find an alternative set of ideals after the defeat, and the Catholic set was the one most readily available and convincing. This was not so in Britain. And if we consider the fate of the church in France once the popular outlook to which the church had become committed had itself collapsed, that was just as well.

University of Glasgow

HOLY MEN AND RURAL COMMUNITIES IN ZIMBABWE, 1970-1980

by TERENCE RANGER

Introduction

A GOOD deal has been written about the response of the mission churches to the guerilla war in Zimbabwe. Much less has been written about their *experience* of it. Yet it has been persuasively argued that the real significance of the war for the churches lay not at the level of institutional pronouncements upon it but at the level of the participation of churchmen in the sufferings of local rural communities. The war was an embarassment to institutional spokesmen. In the early colonial past the leaders of the catholic and protestant churches in Southern Rhodesia had legitimated war, providing chaplains for the white columns that defeated the Ndebele in 1893 and suppressed the risings in 1896 and preaching the duty of the representatives of Christian civilisation to overthrow barbarism. By the 1960s some churchmen had come to condemn violence—both the institutional violence of the Rhodesian state and the revolutionary violence of the nationalist and liberation movements. As guerila war spread in the 1970s, hardly any church spokesmen could move beyond this position. It became clearer and clearer that the majority of their African rural flocks supported the guerillas and even clearer that African rural Christians were suffering terribly in the violence of civil war. But no-one was able to articulate a theology appropriate to such a crisis.[1]

Critics of this inadequacy on the part of the ecclesiastical establishments pinned their hopes on those who were experiencing the war and thereby producing a theology of action and endurance. As Ian Linden wrote in 1980:

> The difference between Church life in the towns and in the Tribal Trust Lands could not have been greater. Missionaries tended their gardens in the Salisbury suburbs, charismatic

[1] Shelagh Ranger, 'Theological Responses to Political Conflict in Rhodesia since U.D.I.' (Manchester Theology B.A. thesis May 1978).

groups of white Catholics met together, and the conventional routine of parish life went on as usual. Only the exhausted figures of the rural missionaries, haggard and ill, coming into convalesce from their stations in the TTLS . . . reminded the visitor of the war outside . . . . While all the structures of authority in the Church remained intact . . . a terrible emptiness seemed to fill the ecclesiastical superstructure. Authority lay elsewhere, in the suffering of the rural church . . . . More than ever the ecclesiastical world of the institutional Church appeared like a hard shell containing new and different sources of power and growth.[2]

Father J. Kerkhofs, looking back on the war in January 1982, adopted a very similar position. He distinguished between 'the "old" Church of the theological reflections, corresponding mainly to the "urban" Church of the institutional character' and the new rural church, committed 'to listen to the heart beat of the African faithful and translate it into viable norms within its theological reflection and pastoral practice'. This new church:

> revealed itself in various ways: the individual African priest taking publicly a different stand on Church policy over the prevailing opinion of his European associates; villagers expressing their confidence in trekking to Salisbury to tell the Justice and Peace Commission of their plight; . . . the open and solid support given by African clergy, religious and lay people to the liberation movement; the well-balanced and expressive views of young clergymen on communism, stressing pointedly other aspects than those usually advanced by church leaders.

Kerkhofs wrote of the war:

> Missionary activity in the rural areas along structural ecclesiastical lines was almost totally strangled during the difficult years of war and destruction. Yet the number of faithful has continued to increase. The people of Zimbabwe, therefore, have lived their faith. Some were willing to die for it, whereas others committedly supported their missionaries by guaranteeing their safety . . . local lay leaders stepped forward and took it upon themselves to keep the community's faith alive. They led the people in prayer and Scripture

---

[2] Ian Linden, *The Catholic Church and the Struggle for Zimbabwe* (London 1980) pp 234–268.

Holy Men and the Zimbabwe War

reading and kept the lines of communication with other church sections open.

And he concluded:

> The local communities, which kept the faith alive in so many places and which structured the Church over so long a period, can be used as active cells of spiritual life, by which an ever progressive bond of communion may be forged. Their members are not likely going to be reduced again to a state of passivity.[3]

It is the purpose of this paper to test and illustrate these interesting but general assertions. What *did* happen to priests and people in Zimbabwe's rural areas during the war and what *are* the consequences for the Church of those happenings? I shall seek to answer by focussing on one Zimbabwean district, Makoni district in Manicaland where in 1980 and 1981 I carried out fieldwork and talked to many Christians about the war. Three mission churches have been important in the religious history of Makoni—Catholicism, Anglicanism and American Methodism. The position of American Methodism during the war was complicated by the fact that Abel Muzorewa was AME Bishop and that he had been brought up and served his first ministry in Makoni. Many American Methodists therefore continued to support Muzorewa even when the guerillas became hostile to him, and found themselves in a predicament which deserves a paper to itself but which does not fit precisely here. I shall write, therefore, first about the experience of Catholicism in Makoni during the war and then about the experience of Anglicanism.

Catholic Holy Men and the war in Makoni

Three particular centres of Catholic influence had developed in Makoni. The oldest was the huge mission farm at Triashill and St Barbara's, on the north-east border of the district. The others were the stations of St Theresa's, in the large Chiduku TTL in the south-west of the district, and St Benedict's bordering Weya TTL in the north-west. The European clergy at all three centres lived right among the African peasantry. During the 1950s and 1960s these Irish priests had tried to keep their flocks away from

[3] J. Kerkhofs, *The Church in Zimbabwe. The Trauma of Cutting Apron Strings* (Pro Mundi Vite Dossiers, January 1982) pp 16–25.

nationalism, stressing the evils of godless communism in their lectures to the local Catholic Associations. By the 1970s, however, the repressive nature of Rhodesia Front rule and the overwhelming hostility of African Christians towards it had made a deep impression on the white clergy. Government agents began to watch them closely.

Thus in December 1974 the Rhodesian Special Branch reported to the Secretary for Internal Affairs that Father Paul Hughes at St Theresa's 'is known to have suggested that the policies of the Government would bring about an internal revolution, as the minority rules over the majority'.[4] In April 1976 a Government spy reported that he had paid a visit to St Theresa's:

> The father there, P. Hughes, began talking on the present situation in Rhodesia. He is 'very pessimistic' about the state of affairs in this country. He blames it mainly on our present Government and leaders. He thinks there can be no solutions through talks and he says that it can and will only end in bloodshed . . ... He said that everything started getting worse after the Pearce Commission in 1971, the results of which were a true reflection of all Africans.[5]

The bloodshed predicted by Hughes began in Makoni in 1976 when guerilla operations commenced in the district and were met by ferocious Government repression. When Father Peter Turner arrived at St Theresa's in 1977 he found the war in full swing and found his flock in full support of the guerillas. He himself made contact with the guerillas and negotiated with them to keep the station open so as to ensure continued services to the people. But, as he told me, 'I was given a very tough time by the Security Forces and was arrested by them on false information. There must have been an informer at the mission but in general people were extremely loyal'. Turner remained at St Theresa's until early in 1979; after his departure there was no priest for the remainder of the war.[6]

At St Benedict's, too, the Irish priest in charge, Father O'Loan, found himself close to the people and sharing their predicament. At St Benedict's there was intensive contact between the guerillas

---

[4] Officer Commanding, Special Branch, to Secretary, Internal Affairs, 7 December 1974, file 'Schools. St Theresa's', District Commissioner's office, Rusape, Makoni.

[5] *Ibid*, 'Report for week, Tuesday 20/4/76'.

[6] Interview with Father Peter Turner, Umtali, 14 March 1981.

Holy Men and the Zimbabwe War

and the mission school boys during 1976. 'The students would go down to the fields in the evenings and sing songs with the guerillas'. This activity attracted the attention of the Security Forces and placed the mission and school at risk from army attack. So in January 1977 O'Loan 'initiated a meeting with the guerillas because he wanted to decide whether to re-open the school or not. The guerillas gave him assurances that they would allow the school to run without interfering'. O'Loan and the guerilla commander came to a ten point agreement which was noted down in full by the guerilla recorder.

What happened next illustrates to the full the missionary predicament during the war. In June 1977 the guerila recorder and three comrades were visiting Father O'Sharkey at St Michael's out-station when an army patrol arrived. The guerillas fled, embarassingly leaving behind them 'several boxes of medicine labelled St Michael's'. Even more embarassingly, the guerilla recorder was killed and his diary taken by the Security Forces. In it they found the ten point agreement. On 20 June O'Loan was taken to Rusape for questioning by Inspector Cutting of Joint Operational Command who confronted him with the full details. Cutting told O'Loan that 'they were prepared to forget the past if he was willing to cooperate. The Inspector said that if he would give them information in future the forces would protect the pupils and staff'. If O'Loan refused, on the other hand, the army would treat St Benedict's as hostile territory. O'Loan was in a dreadful dilemma. On the one hand he believed 'that the pupils would not be able to withstand the interrogations which are done by the Security Forces. The students are stripped naked, laid on the ground with a towel over their faces and sprayed with a hose until they feel as if they are drowning or suffocating. This kind of torture leaves no tell-tale marks'. On the other hand, all his African staff rejected the idea of informing, which 'would be much more dangerous for all concerned, and they were willing to accept the consequences of his refusal'.

O'Loan therefore refused. Almost immediately three African teachers were arrested for interrogation. On this occasion O'Loan was able to protest 'to the Provincial Eduation Officer that the army was interrupting African education more than the "boys" (guerillas) and that he would have to close his school if his teachers weren't released'. They were released and the school briefly continued. But the pressures on St Benedict's were too great and before long the school was closed, O'Loan and the other clergy were withdrawn, and the mission buildings, looted by white farmers and black peasants alike, lay roofless and desolate.[7]

These two examples show the solidarity which priests came to develop with their people. On the other hand, they *don't* show the survival and expansion of active 'cells of spiritual life'. After the stations at St Theresa's and St Benedict's closed down and the clergy withdrew it was difficult to keep local Catholicism together. St Benedict's was on the border of Weya TTL, scene of some of the most savage fighting and atrocities of the war; the embittered people made no call for its re-opening once the war was over and it lay abandoned and crumbling when I visited it in March 1981. As for St Theresa's, priests and sisters *did* return there to re-open the school and station at the invitation of the ZANU/PF District Committee, but they were received with some hostility. Threats were made against their lives; they had to be once again withdrawn; and in early 1981 the National Army of Zimbabwe was sent in to garrison the mission station and to deal with 'dissidents'. In an ironic inversion of the war itself, planes were sent by the new Zimbabwe Government to shower leaflets over the area saying 'Go to Church; there is nothing wrong with Church'.[8] The solidarity of priests and people in 1976 and 1977 was not enough in itself to found a united local church community.

Father Peter Turner explained this to me in terms of the inadequate foundations of local Catholicism in the pre-war period:

> At St Theresa's the community itself is a divided community. There are many different and competing churches—Anglicans, Methodists, Seventh Day Adventists, Roman Catholics and the Black Moses Church. There used to be five churches in a single village. The only exceptions to this were the African prophetic *Vapostori* villages, which were very solid, keeping themselves to themselves and not intermingling at schools or clinics. Moreover, there were many very disgruntled people moved in off farms. I was told that there were thousands of Catholics but I couldn't find them when I went there in 1977. By no means everyone in the ten villages

---

[7] Report on St Benedict's, Weya, 1977, Catholic Commission of Justice and Peace file 'St Benedict's', CCJP Archives, Salisbury.

[8] Interview with Comrade Believe (Miss Needmore Ndhlovu), Old Umtali, 9 March 1981.

Holy Men and the Zimbabwe War

of St Theresa's were Catholic. After all, St Theresa's did not open as a station until 1956 and it has never got over the out-school mentality. There had been a very great decrease in church going when the schools closed. At Triashill and St Barbara's people say 'Here the Church was built first and the schools came later'. At places like St Theresa's the school came first.[9]

It is not surprising, then, that the experience of Triashill and St Barbara's, together with their off-shoot station of St Killian's in Makoni TTL, was a different one. Here we come close to the 'local communities which kept the faith alive'. Triashill was the original Catholic foundation in Makoni district—established by the Trappists in the 1890s, taken over by the Jesuits in the 1930s and then by the Irish Carmelites in the 1950s. In its early days there had been an aggressive policy of Catholicisation on the huge mission farm—polygamists, pagans and protestants were all alike threatened with expulsion. There had been a good deal of tension over the years between priests and people, with vigorous protests against the coming of the Jesuits. By the 1970s all this was in the past. The mission farm had become a stronghold of a relaxed folk Catholicism no longer policed by the clergy; priests and people joined in elaborating and celebrating a peasant eco-religion. During the 1970s themselves the Church even managed to rid itself of the invidious managerial responsibility for the farm land and the villages became part of the neighbouring TTL: all rental obligation to the Church came to an end and in the upheaved conditions of the 1970s the Rhodesian Government had abandoned attempts to enforce the hated conservation rules. Here, then, was the ideal Catholic rural community. Moreover, great granite hills ran all the way from St Barbara's to St Killians; these formed a series of strong bases for the guerillas. After fierce fighting in 1977 the Rhodesian Government more or less abandoned any attempt to maintain a regular presence in the area, limiting itself to incursions by air-lifted troops. It became the nearest thing to a 'liberated' zone, in which guerillas could be seen helping with the ploughing, rifles slung over their backs.

In this context church attendance *did* increase during the war; popular Catholicism *did* combine with guerilla ideology in much

---

[9] Interview with Father Peter Turner, Umtali, 14 March 1981.

the way postulated by Linden and Kerkhofs. But remarkably, in the middle of all this African 'liberated' Catholicism, two Irish priests remained at their stations throughout the whole war— Father Kenny at St Barbara's and Father Vernon at St Killian's. Their stories, told to me in 1981, illustrate the role of the Holy Man in the midst of popular religious community growth. The two priests combined the classic qualities of the Holy Man—a local mediating and peace-making authority—together with the capacity to link the local community advantageously to the institutions at the centre.

It was a role played by Irish priests in the ghettos of English industrial towns in the nineteenth century—as we were reminded by a conference paper last year. And the fact of Father Kenny's and Father Vernon's Irishness *was* a significant factor in their ability to remain in place. Father Vernon had first brought himself to the critical attention of Government by asking awkward questions to the Pearce Commissioners in 1972. 'I told them the whole thing was typical of the British approach in Northern Ireland. They should have solved it once for all long ago but they kept on pushing it away'.[10] Father Kenny told me that his 'worst moment of the war' came at the very end of it when the British monitoring force set up a base at St Barbara's. 'You can imagine an Irishman's blood when I saw the Union Jack hanging from my church?'[11]

An Irish sense of solidarity with a peasant people was rewarded with a peasant sense of solidarity with the priest. Father Vernon recalls:

> The comrades (guerillas) were often very young, inexperienced and suspicious. Band after band came into and through our area and I had to come to terms all over again with each one. The agreement was that the comrades would never come on to the mission station armed. If they had done so it would at once have been known at Rugoyi Fort, with its garrison of soldiers, which was so close to us. The comrades became on the whole well-disposed to us, despite the bad reputation of the Catholic Church in Mozambique. This was

---

[10] Interview with Father Vernon, St Killian's, 15 February 1981. All other citations of Father Vernon are from this interview.

[11] Interview with Father Kenny, St Barbara's, 26 February 1981. All other citations of Father Kenny are from this interview.

Holy Men and the Zimbabwe War

because St Killian's had good relations with the people. The people couldn't tell lies about us.
Father Vernon's African catechists were 'the bravest comrades in Zimbabwe, and travelled everywhere among the people thoughout the war. One was killed—apparently by the comrades—and buried hastily somewhere unknown. But in the end we discovered that he had in fact not been killed by guerillas at all but by a private grudge gang. Then I negotiated with the comrades to have the body exhumed and given full Christian burial'. And the bravery of the catechists extended to lay Christians. After the closure of the school at St Killian's Father Vernon was left there with four girls who cooked for him and cared for the station. 'They were arrested by the Security Forces and taken and tortured at the Fort to make them reveal secrets but they would not. I used to tell them that if they were threatened by violence they should say whatever their interrogators wanted to hear—tell them that I used to sleep with them, or anything else that would please their questioners. If such things were said under torture they could not be made to stick. But the girls would not say anything'. At St Barbara's, too, girls from the mission station were taken away to the Rugoyi Fort and given electric torture to make them incriminate Father Kenny: again they would not do so.

For their part the guerillas—some of whom came into the area with war-time nicknames like 'Black Jesus', or spoke to the peasants about 'Jesus Christ as colonialist'—mostly came to respect the strength of local folk Catholicism and to appreciate the Africanity of its rituals. Father Kenny tells how one All Souls Day he was in the graveyard praying for the dead and for rain. A guerila, Comrade Salisbury, was watching. 'Then he said, "Father, I'd like to have a word." He said to the people: "Whose graves are these? Father's ancestors are not buried here yet he cares for the dead. Your ancestors *are* buried here. But look at the mess! Next time I come I want to see this graveyard tidied up". And it was!'

Local solidarities were very important, then. But the white priests were in two ways part of wider networks, with broader horizons than their peasant parishioners. For one thing, they had taught at other missions in Rhodesia and by so doing had built up contacts with hundreds of young men, many of whom were now guerillas. Father Vernon describes how:

I was summoned to meet the comrades as early as 1974 or 1975, two years before the war began in this area. I was told to park my car in a certain spot and walk along a certain path. Suddenly I was surrounded. The first man I saw was a boy I expelled from school! I was led in silence along the paths until I came to the leader. He asked me: 'Do you know that man?' I answered: 'Yes, I do, and I expelled him'. The leader said: 'Yes, and you were quite right too!' I said: 'Yes, I was and I'd do it again!' . . . From this meeting and other intimations I knew what was coming. That was one reason why I built up good facilities so that the church could face up to the coming challenge. But the people of the area were too narrowly focussed and did not think out what their response to the guerillas should be so that the boys were among them before they knew.

Father Kenny described how:

Quite a few of the fellows knew me from previous areas I had worked in, the Hondi Valley, etc. One chap I used to know as a small child in the Hondi came to St Barbara's as a comrade. One man called 'Black Jesus' stopped me at Triashill and told me that I had given him house-room with his little sister when I was in Maranke. I felt at ease with them.

These contacts, together with the prestige that the priests enjoyed among local peasant Catholics, enabled them to act as local law-givers or peace makers. Father Vernon made it clear to the guerillas that any help he gave them must not be at the expense of the people. He would give them clothes and food, because enough came in from Relief organisations to meet the people's needs as well as those of the guerillas. But he would not give them cigarettes or liquor because that would cost money which should be spent on amenities for the people. Nor would he give them money for the same reason:

The comrades made me produce four or five years' worth of accounts before they were satisfied I did not have a big cash surplus . . . The comrades wanted me to keep the place open. They knew that if this mission was closed the people had absolutely nothing. . ... I used to drive three or four times a week to Rusape for supplies, bringing in masses of food and clothes, sometimes coming back in at night with my headlights off. The comrades told me whenever the road was mined or an ambush was planned but I told them that if they blocked the road permanently I could not bring in supplies and the people would suffer.

Father Kenny was able similarly to influence guerilla action. He describes how in January 1977:

I saw a light down at the church. When I got there I found Mandeya's Bus and all the passengers surrounded by comrades. They were threatening the conductor for having driven into a war zone. He said he did not know it was a war zone and I told them that I had not myself been notified that no buses were allowed. I persuaded them to let the conductor off. Then the comrades ordered all the passengers off the bus and said they would burn it in front of the church. I said that this would get me into trouble with the Security Forces so they let the bus go, though they took the money collected for fares and gave the conductor a bullet wrapped in a letter to the bus owner.

The other network of wider contacts also enabled the priests to help the people. This they could do because they were in touch with central agencies of the church. Through such agencies they brought in food and clothes. And through such agencies they could seek to stop torture or to secure the release of arrested people.

Father Kenny describes one incident:

Early in 1977 a 'contact' was made up in the mountains. I heard the shooting and then I saw the helicopters coming from the mountains with black plastic wrapped bodies hanging from them. They dropped the bodies in front of the church. It was a terrible sight, the corpses naked and mangled as if a madman had been let loose in a butcher's shop. I went into the church to fetch oil to anoint the bodies. Security force men arrived with 16 or 17 girl *mujibas* (assistants of the guerillas); the soldiers tried to stop me anointing the bodies but I insisted. Then the soldiers ordered the girls to load the bodies on to trucks but I managed to prevent them from having to do so. As the girls were driven away on the trucks I gave them a little salute with my hand. At once I sent into the villages to check the names of all girls who were missing. I then sent the names to Legal Aid in Salisbury. Within a week all the girls were released and came straight here to thank me. That meant an awful lot to the people.

Once again Kenny recalls:

> Girls from St Barbara's were taken to Rugoyi Fort to be given electric torture. I did nothing the first time this happened but when it happened again I phoned Bishop Lamont's representative in Umtali suggesting that he write to Ian Smith, saying 'one of my priests has informed me, etc'. This was done, but since Rugoyi was mentioned it was fairly clear that the priest concerned was me. I believe that the Security Forces from then on were determined to get me and that a dirty tricks group was sent to the mission to shoot me and blame it on the guerillas. But when they arrived I was away from home.

Actions such as these are warmly remembered in the area. Agnes Manhide who worked in the kitchen at Triashill describes how:

> In 1977 the war intensified and the comrades used to send people to call us to Changunda village where we attended all night meetings . . . In 1979 I suffered most. One day the soldiers came and when I heard they were coming to the mission I began to run away but they saw and captured me . . . When I got caught I was beaten and they tied my neck with boot-laces half throttling me and then releasing me. They did this several times and they also poured water into my nose in an attempt to make me tell them where the boys were but I didn't. Fortunately Father Kenny stopped by the mission and when he saw this torture going on he intervened successfully, managing to drive the soldiers away.

So the peasants and their Holy Man experienced the war together. Both changed their attitudes. The people began to add more and more 'traditional' elements to their popular Catholicism: Father Vernon used to go to funerals and tell the people that when he had finished the orthodox prayers 'you can do what you like'. On the other hand, there was an increase in marriages in church because the people refused to go to the District Commissioner to have their marriages registered and the bishop approved of them being celebrated as church marriages without any civil recognition. As for the two Irish priests, they came to see the Rhodesia Front Government rather than the Marxist guerillas as the true enemy of the Church.

Holy Men and the Zimbabwe War

'The Government *hated* the Church', says Father Vernon, and tried everything they could to stop its work. On one occasion African Auxiliaries came on a Sunday morning to St Killian's and demanded to address the congregation. Vernon refused, saying that the people had not come for politics. The Auxiliaries were angry and abusive. The guerillas then sent a note telling him that for the safety of the people the church should be closed. 'But I thought, No, what am I here for? and I decided to go on. However, the next Sunday the Security Forces showed up in strength and I sent out my Church committee members to tell the people not to come. For five weeks no-one came. Then I called them back to church and the numbers coming increased from then on'. At St Barbara's soldiers came in Holy Week in 1977 and entered the church to strip the shirts of all the male worshippers in order to detect marks on their back made by carrying guns and other loads into the hills for the guerillas. One white soldier grabbed the Mass Server and began to disrobe him. Kenny 'saw red. I was saved by my Irish temper. I was in such a rage I could hardly talk'. He caught hold of the white soldier and ejected him from the church; demanding and receiving an apology for such disrespect.

One final story illustrates the government's concern to deal with the priests. In 1977 Kenny saw:

> a helicopter land behind the mountain. I assumed that it was carrying troops but word came from the people that it had landed a band of mock guerillas . . . The band came to St Barbara's that night and I looked out of my window to see 12 or so all standing pointing their rifles at the house. They knocked at last and I answered. They said they were fighting for their native land and asked for food. I refused. They threatened to burn down the mission. I still refused and they went off. I knew that I had to make an official report otherwise they would tell the authorities I had not reported the presence of guerillas. But I did not want to be thought by anyone to be reporting guerillas, even bogus ones. So I phoned Lamont's man in Umtali and told him the situation, speaking Gaelic, asking *him* to report. In the morning planes came and bombed all round. I was totally useless. I didn't know what was happening; I thought 'My God, maybe they really *were* comrades'. But the people told me afterwards that they had seen the bogus guerillas signal to the helicopters to

pick them up and they had then directed the bombing. It was an expensive way to frighten us—but it worked!

Priests and people survived the war, changed in these various ways. Some guerilla bands were threatening despite everything; one particular band was said in 1978 to have 'demanded large supplies of strong drink and drugs'; to have forced African Sisters and candidates to attend night meetings and told them 'that they should not be Sisters and that they must bear children'.[12] But the church grew. At St Barbara's 'church attendance was very very good through the war'; at St Killian's 'the church grew during the war. The boys used to send their *mujibas* to Mass'.

At these stations, then, the war really did forge a closer community which 'kept the faith alive' and which might be 'used as active cells of spiritual life'. 'Today when I go to Umtali for mass hosts', says Father Vernon, 'other priests are astonished at the 300 regular Sunday communicants at St Killian's and tell me stories of abandoned churches'. In March 1981 a newly elected Chairman of a village ZANU/PF committee wrote to the party headquarters in Salisbury to complain that Vernon was still at St Killian's, denouncing him as a 'fascist'. Bishop Lamont, a junior minister, a ZANU/PF member of parliament, the ZANU/PF district committee and others called the people around St Killian's together and read the letter to them. They replied that Father Vernon had lived through the war with them and that they wanted him to stay with them until he died. The committee chairman was dismissed.

Stephen Matewa and grass-roots Anglicanism

There were no white Anglican priests in Makoni likely to emulate Vernon and Kenny. The most prominent white Anglicans, indeed, were notoriously outspoken supporters of the Rhodesia Front. The Anglican bishop denounced the guerillas. African Anglicans were disillusioned with their church and almost everywhere in Makoni a church which had once enjoyed mass support and been seen as a defender of the peasantry came out of the war in a discredited and feeble state. However, even Anglicanism could throw up a Holy Man.

---

[12] 'Report on Christe Mambo School and Convent', May 1978, CCJP file 'Guerilla Reports', CCJP Archives, Salisbury.

Holy Men and the Zimbabwe War

Stephen Matewa, headmaster of Toriro school in Chiduku TTL became an auxiliary Anglican priest during the war. Matewa had been associated in the past with the co-operative farming ventures at St Faith's and Nyafaru and had been a member of ZANU since 1963. When the war came to Makoni, he was looking after large numbers of refugee children at Toriro, as well as local school children and his congregation. The mountains behind the school soon became a key guerilla base and Matewa found himself in the firing line:

> At the time of writing [he wrote in December 1976] the war has been on—firing, real fighting, people dying violently just 2 kilometres away ... in Ruwombere Mt ... Children are running away from their homes to relatives ... The children running from the spot saw soldiers rolling off stones they were standing (on) presumed dead .... The war here is terrible and fierce ... We have never seen suffering before. We are all filled with fear, daily fear.[13]

Nevertheless, Matewa overcame his fear. Soon he emerged as the indispensable mediator between the local population and the guerillas. The Anglican authorities in Salisbury were persuaded, however reluctantly, that he must be allowed to work with the guerillas and to provide them with food and clothes so that he could influence them. The Anglican authorities hoped that this might mean the guerillas surrendering; Matewa himself wanted rather to achieve recognition of some local ground rules which would mitigate the sufferings of the war. This he achieved.

> We have a big pressure from my friends [he wrote to church authorities on 4 November 1978]. They want clothes. I have bought some twice with the help from the Dean, now we need more ... The boys are behaving reasonably well. There are no killings in the area and their conduct with the people is very good. They now talk and get questioned by the people freely. The understanding that we are cultivating in the area is very encouraging. I feel it is important that this be encouraged. We are able to keep the war sensible. The boys now have respect of the tribesmen and talk with them as with their parents. The killings in this area has ceased and people

---

[13] Stephen Matewa to Guy Clutton Brock, 28 December 1976, Matewa Correspondence, Toriro.

are a little happier than before . . . We need to keep these boys well fed and clothed.¹⁴

Matewa managed for some time to have Toriro declared an open zone, immune from military action; this was achieved by means of the influence of the Anglican hierarchy. The authorities hoped that by this means the guerillas would be induced to lay down their arms: instead the open zone of Toriro was used by the guerillas for recuperation and supply. Matewa's wife, a trained nurse, gave medical treatment to wounded guerillas: Matewa himself managed to get one wounded guerilla into hospital in Salisbury disguised as his own son: he even applied to the Government Pensions Officer to try to get a pension for the wounded man!¹⁵ This was virtuoso manipulation of his wider networks. At the same time he was reporting violence against the people by the Security Forces to Christian Care¹⁶ and appealing for aid to the International Committee of the Red Cross:

> The need for help in this area is abnormally great. The people here have suffered and are suffering particularly those around the big mountain Ruwombe. Their crops were destroyed by cattle and baboons when there was fighting and what was in their granaries was burnt by the Security Forces blaming the people for feeding the freedom fighters. People here need help not because they are lazy but because they have been unfortunate in being in the battle field.¹⁷

Matewa sustained his mediating role to the end of the war. In November 1979 he was still explaining to the Anglican hierarchy the need for material aid to the guerillas; still explaining why it was that in return for this the guerillas could not come over to the Government side; still emphasising the interests of his people:

> The boys in our area are a bit under our little influence. The boys around our school have stopped killing or beating people. The boys and the people talk and seem to get on well together . . . We have converted some hard core boys into very reasonable human beings, who are teaching others to do the same. Most are keen to see the war come to an end but

---

[14] *Ibid*, Stephen Matewa to Bishop of Mashonaland, 4 November 1978.
[15] *Ibid*, Stephen Matewa to Pensions Officer, Salisbury, 24 July 1979.
[16] *Ibid*, Stephen Matewa to Ci-ordinator, Christian Care, 3 and 29 August 1979.
[17] *Ibid*, Stephen Matewa to Medical Co-ordinator, International Red Cross, 8 November 1979.

do not want to come home in case more brutal boys come and begin to harm the masses unnecessarily . . . Most of them do not want any to cross to the other side but to ask those who can get on well with the community to move and talk with the people as freely as possible and get the people's feelings to the boys without fear of being punished . . . The boys must feel loved. The number of boys wanting help is increasing daily. Food is becoming scarce . . . We need food to help the boys and some families in these areas which are near the mountains.[18]

Matewa was much more than a shrewd manipulator of his ecclesiastical supervisors. He was himself arrested and beaten to insensibility by the Security Forces while he was out on the mountain searching for missing girls—'You are pretending to die', the soldiers accused him.[19] Teachers at Toriro told me that Matewa refused to punish alleged 'sell-outs'—a woman whose husband was a Muzorewa supporter, for example. The headman told me that 'this man Matewa saved the people in the war'. Certainly today Toriro stands as an island of Anglican health in a sea of Anglican troubles.

Conclusion

Among Matewa's papers is an address given to the Anglican Synod in July 1980 by Reverend N. P. Mudzvovera:

In the previous successive governments, leaders of the Anglican church used to speak often and very loudly on the current issues but now it is all silence. In what direction is the Anglican Church going? . . . If leaders shape the life and spiritual destiny of their followers . . . in what direction are the followers going now that the Anglican leaders are all silent? . . . Since the 4th April 1966 when the first guns were fired at Sinoia, Christians in Tribal Trust Lands became open to war propaganda. This propaganda has shaped the thinking and life of these Christians to such an extent that some of these Christians are now different Christians from the Christians they were before the war started. Their thinking has been very much coloured by the events of the war . . .

[18] *Ibid*, Stephen Matewa to Dean of Salisbury, 2 November 1979.
[19] Interview with Stephen Matewa, Toriro, 23 March 1981.

They need to hear what role they should play in an independent Zimbabwe. They need to hear what sympathies and encouragements the leaders have for them, but it's all silence. In what direction is the Anglican church in Zimbabwe going?[20]

I began this paper by quoting Kerkhofs' answer to the question of where the Church might go. I think it appropriate to end it by showing that such an answer is being given very widely by Zimbabwean Christians themselves. In September 1981 a meeting of Christians was held in Salisbury which was attended by delegates from Makoni and three other rural districts. They heard an address by a protestant minister, Victor Kwenda, entitled 'From Analytical Theology to a Theology of the People', which contrasted the two worlds, 'the one of religious abstractions and the other of daily concrete experiences'. 'The Church must recognise', said Kwenda, 'that reflexive theology is already being done by Zimbabweans at the grass roots level, and is finding expression in song, in wisdom, in prayer'.[21]

In the first months of 1982 a travelling liason officer for the Buriro/Esizeni Reflection Centre set up at the 1981 meeting, travelled to visit 14 rural communities, two of them in Makoni district. This month, July 1982, a report on these visits has been published. I can fittingly end this paper with an extract from it:

> Methods and ideas which were effective in previous years no longer had the same impact since the liberation war had changed congregations from unquestioning, passive recipients of the word coming from authority into challenging, analytical thinkers who recognise that degree of authority which is within themselves . . . . A Protestant pastor shared his unique approach to guiding his people's thinking to see the validity of the Gospel for todays' liberated Zimbabwe. Newly appointed to a church that had been the brunt of much resentment and physical abuse during the war, he spent some time visiting the people and helping them out with reconstruction work at their homes. Eventually he summoned people to 'morare' (morale-building through dancing and

---

[20] 'Hopes and Aspirations of the Black Anglican Christians in the Independent Zimbabwe', 9 July 1980, Matewa Papers, Toriro.
[21] Buriro/Esizeni Reflection Centre seminar, September 26/27 1981.

Holy Men and the Zimbabwe War

singing songs of liberation and encouragement) in the ruined church building. By the second week, the people wanted to dialogue with him, in the manner developed during the war between freedom fighters and the community members. They dialogued on the presence of God in their field work, reconstruction, illnesses and achievements. After some weeks of this, the people had worked out their own form of worship in which the pastor now took a more 'coaching' role, but in which the pattern of singing liberation songs and dialogue/discussion continues.[22]

This is plainly not a case in which a resident Holy Man endured the war. It will be fascinating to see what happens where such Holy Men are still resident in the communities which they served during the war; whether their authority will allow such input from their people; whether they will be able now that the war is over to carry out a mediating role between such local initiatives and the receiving institutional apparatus of the national churches.

University of Manchester

[22] Buriro/Esizeni Reflection Centre, Projects Investigation Report, July 1982.

ABBREVIATIONS

AASRP	*Associated Archaeological Societies Reports and Papers*
AAWG	*Abhandlungen der Akademie* [*Gesellschaft* to 1942] *der Wissenschaften zu Göttingen*, (Göttingen 1843–)
AAWL	*Abhandlungen der Akademie der Wissenschaften und der Literatur* (Mainz 1950–)
ABAW	*Abhandlungen der Bayerischen Akademie der Wissenschaften* (Munich 1835–)
Abh	Abhundlung
Abt	Abteilung
ACO	*Acta Conciliorum Oecumenicorum*, ed E. Schwartz (Berlin/Leipzig 1914–40)
ACW	*Ancient Christian Writers*, ed J. Quasten and J. C. Plumpe (Westminster, Maryland/London 1946–)
ADAW	*Abhandlungen der Deutschen* [till 1944 *Preussischen*] *Akademie der Wissenschaften zu Berlin* (Berlin 1815–)
AF	*Analecta Franciscana*, 10 vols (Quaracchi 1885–1941)
AFH	*Archivum Franciscanum Historicum* (Quaracchi/Rome 1908–)
AFP	*Archivum Fratrum Praedicatorum* (Rome 1931–)
AHP	*Archivum historiae pontificae* (Rome 1963–)
AHR	*American Historical Review* (New York 1895–)
AKG	*Archiv für Kulturgeschichte* (Leipzig/Münster/Cologne 1903–)
AKZ	*Arbeiten zur kirchlichen Zeitgeschichte*
ALKG	H. Denifle and F. Ehrle, *Archiv für Literatur- und Kirchengeschichte des Mittelalters*, 7 vols (Berlin/Freiburg 1885–1900)
Altaner	B. Altaner, *Patrologie: Leben, Schriften und Lehre der Kirchenväter* (5 ed Freiburg 1958)
AM	L. Wadding, *Annales Minorum* 8 vols (Rome 1625–54); 2 ed, 25 vols (Rome 1731–1886); 3 ed, vol 1–, (Quaracchi 1931–)
An Bol	*Analecta Bollandiana* (Brussels 1882–)
Annales	*Annales: Economies, Sociétés, Civilisations* (Paris 1946–)
Ant	*Antonianum* (Rome 1926–)
APC	*Proceedings and Ordinances of the Privy Council 1386–1542*, ed Sir Harris Nicolas, 7 vols (London 1834–7)
—	*Acts of the Privy Council of England 1542–1629*, 44 vols (London 1890–1958)
—	*Acts of the Privy Council of England, Colonial Series (1613–1783)* 5 vols (London 1908–12)
AR	*Archivum Romanicum* (Geneva/Florence 1971–41)
ARG	*Archiv für Reformationsgeschichte* (Berlin/Leipzig/Gütersloh 1903–)
ASAW	*Abhandungen der Sächsischen Akademie* [*Gesellschaft* to 1920] *der Wissenschaften zu Leipzig* (Leipzig 1850–)
ASB	*Acta Sanctorum Bollandiana* (Brussels etc 1643–)
ASC	*Anglo Saxon Chronicle*
ASI	*Archivio storico Italiano* (Florence 1842–)
ASL	*Archivio storico Lombardo*, 1–62 (Milan 1874–1935); ns 1–10 (Milan 1936–47)
ASOC	*Analecta Sacri Ordinis Cisterciensis* [*Analecta Cisterciensia* since 1965] (Rome 1945–)
ASOSB	*Acta Sanctorum Ordinis Sancti Benedicti*, ed. L'D'Achery and J. Mabillon (Paris 1668–1701)
ASP	*Archivio della Società* [*Deputazione* from 1935] *Romana di Storia Patria* (Rome 1878–1934, 1935–)
ASR	*Archives de Sociologie des Religions* (Paris 1956–)

ABBREVIATIONS

AV	Authorised Version
AV	*Archivio Veneto* (Venice 1871–): [1891–1921, *Nuovo Archivio Veneto*; 1922–6, *Archivio Veneto-Tridentino*]
B	*Byzantion* (Paris/Boston/Brussels 1924–)
Bale, *Catalogus*	John Bale, *Scriptorum Illustrium Maioris Brytanniae Catalogus*, 2 parts (Basel 1557, 1559)
Bale, *Index*	John Bale, *Index Britanniae Scriptorum*, ed R. L. Poole and M. Bateson (Oxford 1902) *Anecdota Oxoniensia*, medieval and modern series 9
Bale, *Summarium*	John Bale, *Illustrium Maioris Britanniae Scriptorum Summarium* (Ipswich 1548, reissued Wesel 1549)
BEC	*Bibliothèque de l'Ecole des Chartres* (Paris 1839–)
Beck	H-G Beck, *Kirche und theologische Literatur im byzantinischen Reich* (Munich 1959)
BEFAR	*Bibliothèque des écoles francaises d'Athènes et Rome* (Paris 1876–)
BEHE	*Bibliothèque de l'Ecole des Hautes Etudes: Sciences Philologiques et Historiques* (Paris 1869–)
Bernard	E. Bernard, *Catalogi Librorum Manuscriptorum Angliae et Hiberniae* (Oxford 1697)
BF	*Byzantinische Forschungen* (Amsterdam 1966–)
BHG	*Bibliotheca Hagiographica Graeca*, ed F. Halkin, 3 vols + 1 (3 ed Brussels 1957, 1969)
BHI	*Bibliotheca historica Italica*, ed A. Ceruti, 4 vols (Milan 1876–85), 2 series, 3 vols (Milan 1901–33)
BHL	*Bibliotheca Hagiographica Latina*, 2 vols + 1 (Brussels 1898–1901, 1911)
BHR	*Bibliothèque d'Humanisme et Renaissance* (Paris/Geneva 1941–)
Bibl Ref	*Bibliography of the Reform 1450–1648, relating to the United Kingdom and Ireland*, ed Derek Baker for 1955–70 (Oxford 1975)
BIHR	*Bulletin of the Institute of Historical Research* (London 1923–)
BISIMEAM	*Bullettino dell'istituto storico italiano per il medio evo e archivio muratoriano* (Rome 1886–)
BJRL	*Bulletin of the John Rylands Library* (Manchester 1903–)
BL	British Library, London
BM	British Museum, London
BN	Bibliothèque Nationale, Paris
Bouquet	M. Bouquet, *Recueil des historiens des Gaules et de la France, Rerum gallicarum et francicarum scriptores*, 24 vols (Paris 1738–1904); new ed L. Delisle, 1–19 (Paris 1868–80)
BQR	*British Quarterly Review* (London 1845–86)
Broadmead Records	*The Records of a Church of Christ, meeting in Broadmead, Bristol 1640–87*, HKS (London 1848)
BS	*Byzantinoslavica* (Prague 1929–)
Bucer, *Deutsche Schriften*	*Martin Bucers Deutsche Schriften*, ed R. Stupperich and others (Gütersloh/Paris 1960–)
Bucer, *Opera Latina*	*Martini Buceri Opera Latina*, ed F. Wendel and others (Paris/Gütersloh 1955–)
Bull Franc	*Bullarium Franciscanum*, vols 1–4 ed J. H. Sbaralea (Rome 1759–68) vols 5–7 ed C. Eubel (Rome 1898–1904), new series vols 1–3 ed U. Höntemann and J. M. Pou y Marti (Quaracchi 1929–49)
BZ	*Byzantinische Zeitschrift* (Leipzig 1892–)
CA	*Cahiers Archéologiques. Fin de L'Antiquité et Moyen-âge* (Paris 1945–)
CaF	*Cahiers de Fanjeaux* (Toulouse 1966–)
CAH	*Cambridge Ancient History* (Cambridge 1923–39)
CalRev	*Calamy Revised*, ed A. G. Mathews (Oxford 1934)

ABBREVIATIONS

CalLP	*Calendar of the Letters and Papers (Foreign and Domestic) of the Reign of Henry VIII*, 21 vols in 35 parts (London 1864–1932)
CalSPD	*Calendar of State Papers: Domestic* (London 1856–)
CalSPF	*Calendar of State Papers: Foreign*, 28 vols (London 1861–1950)
Calvin, *Opera*	*Ioannis Calvini Opera Quae Supersunt Omnia*, ed G. Baum and others *Corpus Reformatorum*, 59 vols (Brunswick/Berlin 1863–1900)
Canivez	J. M. Canîvez, *Statuta capitulorum generalium ordinis cisterciensis ab anno 1116 ad annum 1786*, 8 vols (Louvain 1933–41)
Cardwell, *Documentary Annals*	*Documentary Annals of the Reformed Church of England*, ed E. Cardwell, 2 vols (Oxford 1839)
Cardwell, *Synodalia*	*Synodalia*, ed E. Cardwell, 2 vols (Oxford 1842)
CC	*Corpus Christianorum* (Turnholt 1952–)
CF	*Classical Folia*, [*Folia 1946–59*] (New York 1960–)
CGOH	*Cartulaire Générale de l'Ordre des Hospitaliers de St.-Jean de Jerusalem (1100–1310)*, ed. J. Delaville Le Roulx, 4 vols (Paris 1894–1906)
CH	*Church History* (New York/Chicago 1932–)
CHB	*Cambridge History of the Bible*
CHistS	*Church History Society* (London 1886–92)
CHJ	*Cambridge Historical Journal* (Cambridge 1925–57)
CIG	*Corpus Inscriptionum Graecarum*, ed A. Boeckh, J. Franz, E. Curtius, A. Kirchhoff, 4 vols (Berlin 1825–77)
CIL	*Corpus Inscriptionum Latinarum* (Berlin 1863–)
Cîteaux	*Cîteaux: Commentarii Cisterciensis* (Westmalle 1950–)
CMH	*Cambridge Medieval History*
CModH	*Cambridge Modern History*
COCR	*Collectanea Ordinis Cisterciensium Reformatorum* (Rome/Westmalle 1934–)
COD	*Conciliorum oecumenicorum decreta* (3 ed Bologna 1973)
Coll Franc	*Collectanea Franciscana* (Assisi/Rome 1931–)
CR	*Corpus Reformatorum*, ed C. G. Bretschneider and others (Halle, etc. 1834–)
CS	*Cartularium Saxonicum*, ed W. de G. Birch, 3 vols (London 1885–93)
CSCO	*Corpus Scriptorum Christianorum Orientalium* (Paris 1903–)
CSEL	*Corpus Scriptorum Ecclesiasticorum Latinorum* (Vienna 1866–)
CSer	*Camden Series* (London 1838–)
CSHByz	*Corpus Scriptorum Historiae Byzantinae* (Bonn 1828–97)
CYS	*Canterbury and York Society* (London 1907–)
DA	*Deutsches Archiv für* [*Geschichte, -Weimar 1937–43*] *die Erforschung des Mittelalters* (Cologne/Graz 1950–)
DACL	*Dictionnaire d'Archéologie chrétienne et de Liturgie*, ed F. Cabrol and H. Leclercq (Paris 1924–)
DDC	*Dictionnaire de Droit Canonique*, ed R. Naz (Paris 1935–)
DHGE	*Dictionnaire d'Histoire et de Géographie ecclésiastiques*, ed A. Baudrillart and others (Paris 1912–)
DNB	*Dictionary of National Biography* (London 1885–)
DOP	*Dumbarton Oaks Papers* (Cambridge, Mass., 1941–)
DR	F. Dölger, *Regesten der Kaiserurkunden des oströmischen Reiches* (*Corpus der griechischen Urkunden des Mittelalters und der neuern Zeit*, Reihe A, Abt I), 5 vols: 1 (565–1025); 2 (1025–1204); 3 (1204–1282); 4 (1282–1341); 5 (1341–1543) (Munich/Berlin 1924–65)
DRev	*Downside Review* (London 1880–)

ABBREVIATIONS

DSAM	*Dictionnaire de Spiritualité, Ascétique et Mystique*, ed M. Viller (Paris 1932–)
DTC	*Dictionnaire de Théologie Catholique*, ed A. Vacant, E. Mangenot, E. Amann, 15 vols (Paris 1903–50)
EcHR	*Economic History Review* (London 1927–)
EEBS	Ἐπετηρὶς Ἑταιρείας Βυζαντινῶν Σπουδῶν (Athens 1924–)
EETS	Early English Text Society
EF	*Etudes Franciscaines* (Paris 1899–1938, ns 1950–)
EHD	*English Historical Documents* (London 1953–)
EHR	*English Historical Review* (London 1886–)
Ehrhard	A. Ehrhard, *Uberlieferung und Bestand der hagiographischen und homiletischen Literatur der griechischen Kirche von den Anfängen bis zum Ende des 16. Jh*, 3 vols in 4, *TU* 50–2 (= 4 series 5–7) 11 parts (Leipzig 1936–52)
Emden (O)	A. B. Emden, *A Biographical Register of the University of Oxford to 1500*, 3 vols (London 1957–9); *1500–40* (1974)
Emden (C)	A. B. Emden, *A Biographical Register of the University of Cambridge to 1500* (London 1963)
EO	*Echos d'Orient* (Constantinople/Paris 1897–1942)
ET	English translation
EYC	*Early Yorkshire Charters*, ed W. Farrer and C. T. Clay, 12 vols (Edinburgh/Wakefield 1914–65)
FGH	*Die Fragmente der griechischen Historiker*, ed F. Jacoby (Berlin 1926–30)
FM	*Histoire de l'église depuis les origines jusqu'à nos jours*, ed A. Fliche and V. Martin (Paris 1935–)
Foedera	*Foedera, conventiones, litterae et cuiuscunmque generis acta publica inter reges Angliae et alios quosvis imperatores, reges, pontifices, principes vel communitates*, ed T. Rymer and R. Sanderson, 20 vols (London 1704–35),3 ed G. Holmes, 10 vols (The Hague 1739–45), re-ed 7 vols (London 1816–69)
Franc Stud	*Franciscan Studies* (St Bonaventure, New York 1924–, ns 1941–)
Fredericq	P. Fredericq, *Corpus documentorum inquisitionis haereticae pravitatis Neerlandicae*, 3 vols (Thent 1889–93)
FStn	*Franzikanische Studien* (Münster/Werl 1914–)
GalC	*Callia Christiana*, 16 vols (Paris 1715–1865)
Gangraena	T. Edwards, *Gangraena*, 3 parts (London 1646)
GCS	*Die griechischen christlichen Schriftsteller der erste drei Jahrhunderte* (Leipzig 1897–)
Gee and Hardy	*Documents illustrative of English Church History* ed H. Gee and W. J. Hardy (London 1896)
GEEB CEM	R. Janin, *La géographie ecclésiastique de l'empire byzantin*; 1, *Le siège de Constantinople et le patriarcat oecumenique*, pt 3 *Les églises et les monastères* (Paris 1953);
EMGCB	2, *Les églises et les monastéres des grands centres byzantins* (Paris 1975) (series discontinued)
Golubovich	Girolamo Golubovich, *Biblioteca bio-bibliografica della Terra Santa e dell' oriente francescano*: series 1, *Annali*, 5 vols (Quaracchi 1906–23) series 2, *Documenti* 14 vols (Quaracchi 1921–33) series 3, *Documenti*, (Quaracchi 1928–) series 4, *Studi*, ed M. Roncaglia (Cairo 1954–)
Grumel Regestes	V. Grumel, *Les Regestes des Actes du Patriarcat de Constantinople*, 1: *Les Actes des Patriarches*, I: 381–715; II: 715–1043; III: 1043–1206 (Socii Assumptionistae Chalcedonenses, 1931, 1936, 1947)

ABBREVIATIONS

Grundmann	H. Grundmann, *Religiöse Bewegungen im Mittelalter* (Berlin 1935, 2 ed Darmstadt 1970)
Guignard	P. Guignard, *Les monuments primitifs de la règle cistercienne* (Dijon 1878)
HBS	*Henry Bradshaw Society* (London/Canterbury 1891–)
HE	*Historia Ecclesiastica*
HistSt	*Historical Studies* (Melbourne 1940–)
HJ	*Historical Journal* (Cambridge 1958–)
HJch	*Historisches Jarhbuch der Görres Gesellschaft* (Cologne 1880–, Munich 1950–)
HKS	Hanserd Knollys Society (London 1847–)
HL	C. J. Hefele and H. Leclercq, *Histore des Conciles*, 10 vols (Paris 1907–35)
HMC	Historical Manuscripts Commission
Holzapfel Handbuch	H. Holzapfel, *Handbuch der Geschichte des Franziskanerordens* (Freiburg 1908)
Hooker, *Works*	*The Works of . . . Mr. Richard Hooker*, ed J. Keble, 7 ed rev R. W. Church and F. Paget, 3 vols (Oxford 1888)
Houedene	*Chronica Magistri Rogeri de Houedene*, ed W. Stubbs, 4 vols, *RS* 51 (London 1868–71)
HRH	*The Heads of Religious Houses, England and Wales, 940–1216*, ed D. Knowles, C. N. L. Brooke, V. C. M. London (Cambridge 1972)
HS	*Hispania sacra* (Madrid 1948–)
HTR	*Harvard Theological Review* (New York/Cambridge, Mass., 1908–)
HZ	*Historische Zeitschrift* (Munich 1859–)
IER	*Irish Ecclesiastical Record* (Dublin 1864–)
IGLS	*Inscriptions greques et latines de la Syrie*, ed L. Jalabert, R. Mouterde and others, 7 vols (Paris 1929–70) in progress
IR	*Innes Review* (Glasgow 1950––)
JAC	*Jahrbuch für Antike und Christentum* (Münster-im-Westfalen 1958–)
Jaffé	*Regesta Pontificum Romanorum ab condita ecclesia ad a. 1198*, 2 ed S. Lowenfeld, F. Kaltenbrunner, P. Ewald, 2 vols (Berlin 1885–8, repr Graz 1958)
JBS	*Journal of British Studies* (Hartford, Conn., 1961–)
JEH	*Journal of Ecclesiastical History* (London 1950–)
JFHS	*Journal of the Friends Historical Society* (London/Philadelphia 1903–)
JHI	*Journal of the History of Ideas* (London 1940–)
JHSChW	*Journal of the Historical Society of the Church in Wales* (Cardiff 1947–)
JIntH	*Journal of Interdisciplinary History* (Cambridge, Mass., 1970–)
JLW	*Jahrbuch für Liturgiewissenschaft* (Münster-im-Westfalen 1921–41)
JMH	*Journal of Modern History* (Chicago 1929–)
JMedH	*Journal of Medieval History* (Amsterdam 1975–)
JRA	*Journal of Religion in Africa* (Leiden 1967–)
JRH	*Journal of Religious History* (Sydney 1960–)
JRS	*Journal of Roman Studies* (London 1910–)
JRSAI	*Journal of the Royal Society of Antiquaries of Ireland* (Dublin 1871–)
JSArch	*Journal of the Society of Archivists* (London 1955–)
JTS	*Journal of Theological Studies* (London 1899–)
Kemble	*Codex Diplomaticus Aevi Saxonici*, ed J. M. Kemble (London 1839–48)
Knowles, *MO*	David Knowles, *The Monastic Order in England, 943–1216* (2 ed Cambridge 1963)
Knowles, *RO*	———, *The Religious Orders in England*, 3 vols (Cambridge 1948–59)

ABBREVIATIONS

Knox, *Works*	*The Works of John Knox*, ed D. Laing, Bannatyne Club/Wodrow Society, 6 vols (Edinburgh 1846–64)
Laurent, *Regestes*	V. Laurent, *Les Regestes des Actes du Patriarcat de Constantinople*, 1: *Les Actes des Patriarches*, IV: *Les Regestes de 1208 à 1309* (Paris 1971)
Le Neve	John Le Neve, *Fasti Ecclesiae Anglicanae 1066–1300*, rev and exp Diana E. Greenway, 1, St Pauls (London 1968); 2, Monastic Cathedrals (1971)
	Fasti Ecclesiae Anglicanae 1300–1541 rev and exp H. P. F. King, J. M. Horn, B. Jones, 12 vols (London 1962–7)
	Fasti Ecclesiae Anglicanae 1541–1857 rev and exp J. M. Horn, D. M. Smith, 1, St Pauls (1969); 2, Chichester (1971); 3, Canterbury, Rochester, Winchester (1974); 4, York (1975)
Lloyd, *Formularies of faith*	*Formularies of Faith Put Forth by Authority during the Reign of Henry VIII*, ed C. Lloyd (Oxford 1825)
LRS	Lincoln Record Society
LQR	*Law Quarterly Review* (London 1885–)
LThK	*Lexicon für Theologie und Kirche*, ed J. Höfer and K. Rahnes (2 ed Freiburg-im-Breisgau 1957–)
LW	*Luther's Works*, ed J. Pelikan and H. T. Lehman, American edition (St Louis/Philadelphia, 1955–)
MA	*Monasticon Anglicanum*, ed R. Dodsworth and W. Dugdale, 3 vols (London 1655–73); new ed J. Caley, H. Ellis, B. Bandinel, 6 vols in 8 (London 1817–30)
Mansi	J. D. Mansi, *Sacrorum conciliorum nova et amplissima collectio*, 31 vols (Florence/Venice 1757–98); new impression and continuation, ed L. Petit and J. B. Martin, 60 vols (Paris 1899–1927)
Martène and Durand	E. Martène and U. Durand, *Veterum Scriptorum et Monumentorum Historicorum, Dogmaticorum, Moralium Amplissima Collectio*,
Collectio	9 vols (Paris 1729)
Thesaurus	*Thesaurus Novus Anedotorum*, 5 vols (Paris 1717)
Voyage	*Voyage Litteraire de Deux Religieux Benedictins de la Congregation de Saint Maur*, 2 vols (Paris 1717, 1724)
MedA	*Medium Aevum* (Oxford 1932–)
Mendola	*Atti della Settimana di Studio*, 1959– (Milan 1962–)
MF	*Miscellanea Francescana* (Foligno/Rome 1886–)
MGH	*Monumenta Germaniae Historica inde ab a.c. 500 usque ad a. 1500*, ed G. H. Pertz and others (Berlin, Hanover 1826–)
AA	*Auctores Antiquissimi*
Ant	*Antiquitates*
Briefe	*Epistolae 2: Die Briefe der Deutschen Kaiserzeit*
Cap	*Leges 2: Leges in Quart 2: Capitularia regum Francorum*
CM	*Chronica Minora* 1–3 (= *AA* 9, 11, 13) ed Th. Mommsen (1892, 1894, 1898 repr 1961)
Conc	*Leges 2: Leges in Quart 3: Concilia*
	4: *Constitutiones et acta publica imperatorum et regum*
DC	*Deutsche Chroniken*
Dip	*Diplomata in folio*
Epp	*Epistolae 1 in Quart*
Epp Sel	4: *Epistolae Selectae*
FIG	*Leges 3: Fontes Iuris Germanici Antique*, new series
FIGUS	4: , *in usum scholarum*
Form	2: *Leges in Quart 5: Formulae Merovingici et Karolini Aevi*
GPR	*Gesta Pontificum Romanorum*

ABBREVIATIONS

Leges	*Leges in folio*
Lib	*Libelli de lite*
LM	Ant 3: *Libri Memoriales*
LNG	Leges 2: *Leges in Quart* 1: *Leges nationum Germanicarum*
Necr	Ant 2: *Necrologia Germaniae*
Poet	1: *Poetae Latini Medii Aevi*
Quellen	*Quellen zur Geistesgeschichte des Mittelalters*
Schriften	*Schriften der Monumenta Germaniae Historica*
SRG	*Scriptores rerum germanicarum in usum scholarum*
SRG ns	, new series
SRL	*Scriptores rerum langobardicarum et italicarum*
SRM	*Scriptores rerum merovingicarum*
SS	*Scriptores*
SSM	*Staatsschriften des späteren Mittelalters*
MIOG	*Mitteilungen des Instituts für österreichische Geschichtsforschung* (Graz/Cologne 1880–)
MM	F. Miklosich and J. Müller, *Acta et Diplomata Graeca medii aevi sacra et profana*, 6 vols (Vienna 1860–90)
Moorman, History	J. R. H. Moorman, *A History of the Franciscan Order from its origins to the year 1517* (Oxford 1968)
More, *Works*	*The Complete Works of St Thomas More*, ed R. S. Sylvester and others Yale edition (New Haven/London 1963–)
Moyen Age	*Le moyen âge. Revue d'histoire et de philologie* (Paris 1888–)
MRHEW	David Knowles and R. N. Hadcock, *Medieval Religious Houses, England and Wales* (2 ed London 1971)
MRHI	A. Gwynn and R. N. Hadcock, *Medieval Religious Houses, Ireland* (London 1970)
MRHS	Ian B. Cowan and David E. Easson, *Medieval Religious Houses, Scotland* (2 ed London 1976)
MS	Manuscript
MStn	*Mittelalterliche Studien* (Stuttgart 1966–)
Muratori	L. A. Muratori, *Rerum italicarum scriptores*, 25 vols (Milan 1723–51); new ed G. Carducci and V. Fiorini, 34 vols in 109 fasc (Città di Castello/Bologna 1900–)
NCE	*New Catholic Encyclopedia*, 15 vols (New York 1967)
NCModH	*New Cambridge Modern History*, 14 vols (Cambridge 1957–70)
nd	no date
NEB	*New English Bible*
NF	Neue Folge
NH	*Northern History* (Leeds 1966–)
ns	new series
NS	New Style
Numen	*Numen: International Review for the History of Religions* (Leiden 1954–)
OCP	*Orientalia Christiana Periodica* (Rome 1935–)
ODCC	*Oxford Dictionary of the Christian Church*, ed F. L. Cross (Oxford 1957), 2 ed with E. A. Livingstone (1974)
OED	*Oxford English Dictionary*
OMT	*Oxford Medieval Texts*
OS	Old Style
OHS	*Oxford Historical Society*
PBA	*Proceedings of the British Academy*
PG	*Patrologia Graeca*, ed J. P. Migne, 161 vols (Paris 1857–66)
PhK	Philosophisch-historische Klasse

ABBREVIATIONS

PL	*Patrologia Latina*, ed J. P. Migne, 217 + 4 index vols (Paris 1841–64)
Plummer, *Bede*	*Venerabilis Baedae Opera Historica*, ed C. Plummer (Oxford 1896)
PO	*Patrologia Orientalis*, ed J. Graffin and F. Nau (Paris 1903–)
Potthast	*Regesta Pontificum Romanorum inde ab a. post Christum natum 1198 ad a. 1304*, ed A. Potthast, 2 vols (1874–5 repr Graz 1957)
PP	*Past and Present* (London 1952–)
PPTS	*Palestine Pilgrims' Text Society*, 13 vols and index (London 1896–1907)
PRIA	*Proceedings of the Royal Irish Academy* (Dublin 1836–)
PRO	Public Record Office
PS	Parker Society (Cambridge 1841–55)
PW	*Paulys Realencyklopädie der klassischen Altertumswissenschaft*, new ed G. Wissowa and W. Kroll (Stuttgart 1893–)
QFIAB	*Quellen und Forschungen aus italienischen Archiven und Bibliotheken* (Rome 1897–)
RAC	*Reallexikon für Antike und Christentum*, ed T. Klauser (Stuttgart 1941)
RB	*Revue Bénédictine* (Maredsous 1884–)
RE	*Realencyclopädie für protestantische Theologie*, ed A. Hauck, 24 vols (3 ed Leipzig, 1896–1913)
REB	*Revue des Etudes Byzantines* (Bucharest/Paris 1946–)
RecS	Record Series
RGG	*Die Religion in Geschichte und Gegenwart*, 6 vols (Tübingen 1927–32)
RH	*Revue historique* (Paris 1876–)
RHC,	*Recueil des Historiens de Croisades*, ed Académie des Inscriptions et Belles-Lettres (Paris 1841–1906)
Arm	*Historiens Arméniens*, 2 vols (1869–1906)
Grecs	*Historiens Grecs*, 2 vols (1875–81)
Lois	*Lois. Les Assises de Jérusalem*, 2 vols (1841–3)
Occ	*Historiens Occidentaux*, 5 vols (1844–95)
Or	*HistoriensOrientaux*, 5 vols (1872–1906)
RHD	*Revue d'histoire du droit* (Haarlem, Gronigen 1923–)
RHDFE	*Revue historique du droit français et étranger* (Paris 1922–)
RHE	*Revue d'Histoire Ecclésiastique* (Louvain 1900–)
RHEF	*Revue d'Histoire de l'Eglise de France* (Paris 1910–)
RHR	*Revue de l'Histoire des Religions* (Paris 1880–)
RR	*Regesta Regum Anglo-Normannorum*, ed H. W. C. Davis, H. A. Cronne, Charles Johnson, R. H. C. Davis, 4 vols (Oxford 1913–69)
RS	*Rerum Brittanicarum Medii Aevi Scriptores*, 99 vols (London 1858–1911). Rolls Series
RSCI	*Rivista di storia della chiesa in Italia* (Rome 1947–)
RSR	*Revue des sciences religieuses* (Strasbourg 1921–)
RStI	*Rivista storica italiana* (Naples 1884–)
RTAM	*Recherches de théologie ancienne et médiévale* (Louvain 1929–)
RV	Revised Version
Sitz	*Sitzungsberichte*
SA	*Studia Anselmiana* (Roma 1933–)
sa	sub anno
SBAW	*Sitzungsberichte der bayerischen Akademie der Wissenschaften*, PhK (Munich 1871–)
SCH	*Studies in Church History* (London 1964–)
ScHR	*Scottish Historical Review* (Edinburgh/Glasgow 1904–)
SCR	*Sources chrétiennes*, ed H. de Lubac and J. Daniélou (Paris 1941)
SF	*Studi Francescani* (Florence 1914–)

ABBREVIATIONS

SGra	*Studia Gratiana*, ed J. Forchielli and A. M. Stickler (Bologna 1953–)
SGre	*Studi Gregoriani*, ed G. Borino, 7 vols (Rome 1947–61)
SMon	*Studia Monastica* (Montserrat, Barcelona 1959–)
Speculum	*Speculum, A Journal of Medieval Studies* (Cambridge, Mass., 1926–)
SpicFr	*Spicilegium Friburgense* (Freiburg 1957–)
SS	*Surtees Society* (Durham 1835–)
SSSpoleto	*Settimane di Studio sull'alto medioevo*, 1952– , Centro Italiano di studi sull'alto medioevo, Spoleto 1954–)
STC	*A Short-Title Catalogue of Books Printed in England, Scotland and Ireland and of English Books Printed Abroad 1475–1640*, ed A. W. Pollard and G. R. Redgrave (London 1926, repr 1946, 1950)
Strype, *Annals*	John Strype, *Annals of the Reformation and Establishment of Religion . . . during Queen Elizabeth's Happy Reign*, 4 vols in 7 (Oxford 1840)
Strype, *Cranmer*	John Strype, *Memorials of . . . Thomas Cranmer*, 2 vols (Oxford 1824)
Strype, *Grindal*	John Strype, *The History of the Life and Acts of . . . Edmund Grindal* (Oxford 1821)
Strype, *Memorials*	John Strype, *Ecclesiastical Memorials, Relating Chiefly to Religion, and the Reformation of it . . . under King Henry VIII, King Edward VI and Queen Mary I*, 3 vols in 6 (Oxford 1822)
Strype, *Parker*	John Strype, *The Life and Acts of Matthew Parker*, 3 vols (Oxford 1821)
Strype, *Whitgift*	John Strype, *The Life and Acts of John Whitgift*, 3 vols (Oxford 1822)
sub hag	subsidia hagiographica
sv	sub voce
SVRG	*Schriften des Vereins für Reformationsgeschichte* (Halle/Leipzig/Gütersloh 1883–)
TCBiblS	*Transactions of the Cambridge Bibliographical Society* (Cambridge 1949–)
Tchalenko	G. Tchalenko, *Villages antiques de la Syrie du Nord*, 3 vols (Paris 1953–8)
THSCym	*Transactions of the Historical Society of Cymmrodorion* (London 1822–)
TRHS	*Transactions of the Royal Historical Society* (London 1871–)
TU	*Texte und Untersuchungen zur Geschichte der altchristlichen Literatur* (Leipzig/Berlin 1882–)
VCH	*Victoria County History* (London 1900–)
VHM	G. Tiraboschi, *Vetera Humiliatorum Monumenta*, 3 vols (Milan 1766–8)
Vivarium	*Vivarium: An International Journal for the Philosophy and Intellectual Life of the Middle Ages and Renaissance* (Assen 1963–)
VV	*Vizantijskij Vremennick* 1–25 (St Petersburg 1894–1927), ns 1 (26) (Leningrad 1947–)
WA	*D. Martin Luthers Werke*, ed J. C. F. Knaake (Weimar 1883–) [*Weimarer Ausgabe*]
WA Br	Briefwechsel
WA DB	Deutsche Bibel
WA TR	Tischreden
WelHR	*Welsh History Review* (Cardiff 1960–)
Wharton	H. Wharton, *Anglia Sacra*, 2 parts (London 1691)
Whitelock, *Wills*	*Anglo-Saxon wills*, ed D. Whitelock (Cambridge 1930)
Wilkins	*Concilia Magnae Britanniae et Hiberniae A.D. 446–1717*, 4 vols, ed D. Wilkins (London 1737)
YAJ	*Yorkshire Archaeological Journal* (London/Leeds 1870–)
Zanoni	L. Zanoni, *Gli Umiliati nei loro rapporti con l'eresia, l'industria della lana ed i communi nei secoli xii e xiii*, Biblioteca Historica Italica, 2 series, 2 (Milan 1911)

ABBREVIATIONS

ZKG	*Zeitschrift für Kirchengeschichte* (Gotha/Stuttgart 1878–)
ZOG	*Zeitschrift für osteuropäische Geschichte* (Berlin 1911–35) = *Kyrios* (Berlin 1936–)
ZRG	*Zeitschrift der Savigny-Stiftung für Rechtsgeschichte* (Weimar)
GAbt	*Germanistische Abteilung* (1863–)
KAbt	*Kanonistische Abteilung* (1911–)
RAbt	*Romanstische Abteilung* (1880–)
ZRGG	*Zeitschrift Religions- und Geistesgeschichte* (Marburg 1948–)
Zwingli, Werke	*Huldreich Zwinglis Sämmtliche Werke*, ed E. Egli and others, CR (Berlin/Leipzig/Zurich 1905–)

GENERAL THEOLOGICAL SEMINARY
NEW YORK